The
ELT Grammar
Book

The ELT* Grammar Book

*ELT: English Language Teaching

A Teacher-Friendly Reference Guide

Richard Firsten

with Patricia Killian

Alta Book Center Publishers
14 Adrian Court Burlingame California 94010 USA

Acquisitions Editor: Aaron Berman
Content Editor: Jean Zukowski-Faust
Production Editor: Jamie Ann Cross
Cover Art and Interior Art: Andrew Lange Illustration
Interior Design and Composition: Leigh McLellan

Printed in the United States of America

© 2002 by Alta Book Center Publishers—San Francisco
14 Adrian Court
Burlingame, California 94010 USA
Phone: 800 ALTA/ESL or 650.692.1285—*Int'l*
Fax: 800 ALTA/FAX or 650.692.4654—*Int'l*
Email: info@altaesl.com • Website: www.altaesl.com

ISBN 1-882483-90-1
ISBN 978-188-2483-90-7
Library of Congress Control Number: 2001095445

Preface

The ELT Grammar Book is a reference for teachers of English to speakers of other languages and it's a grammar book with many differences. Right from the start, you'll notice the relaxed, informal style of the book; books like this one don't have to be written in stuffy "academese."

The purpose of The ELT Grammar Book is to make difficult, but basic areas of English grammar more comprehensible to a wide range of people: undergraduate and graduate TESOL students, ESOL and VESOL teachers, junior high and high school teachers, advanced ESOL students, and anyone who just wants to brush up on his/her skills in English. If you're a teacher and already have a clear understanding of how English works, the explanations in this book will prepare you to communicate the grammar better and give more effective examples to your students. If you're an advanced student or if you simply want to understand more clearly how English grammar works, this book will go a long way toward helping you master the grammar.

No attempt has been made to cover every aspect of the language; only the high frequency areas that traditionally seem most troublesome are dealt with on these pages. Nor have we attempted to give every single analytical detail of each grammar point covered; if you master the material we've provided, you'll be very well prepared to teach grammar effectively, directly or indirectly, or to use the language more effectively.

The ELT Grammar Book contains the following unique features:

The Socratic Approach: You'll be encouraged to observe, think about, and make conclusions about each grammar point covered. This technique, also referred to as the "inductive method," will allow you to explore the grammar in a way that will make the material much more meaningful to you in the long run. Instead of being spoon-fed the information, you'll work through it yourself to discover exactly what's going on.

And here's a tip to help you get the most out of this approach: Whenever you're asked to think of a reason or interpretation, take the time to do just that and write down your own thoughts on the lines provided. This exercise will be a lot more meaningful than taking the easy way out by jumping ahead to find the answers.

Troubleshooters: These comments are "asides," helpful insights that pop up in most chapters, focusing on those points which you can anticipate will bring problems to the teaching and learning of English because of language interference or other causes.

Teaching Tips: To help you create an atmosphere of fun and enjoyment in your class-room, whether you're a new or experienced teacher, these suggestions found at the end of each chapter offer an array of time-honored classroom activities, exercises, and games to enhance the teaching of specific grammar points.

Finally, to give you more suggestions to develop your teaching skills, you'll find appendices at the end of this book which deal in greater detail with certain topics covered in the chapters.

We hope that you find *The ELT Grammar Book* an inviting text, reference, and source book, and that you'll always find it a friend to help you out at tough moments when your mind goes blank and you're trying to remember exactly what native speakers of English say or why they say this or why they don't say that.

Richard Firsten
Patricia Killian

Acknowledgements

To my parents, who always instilled a love of learning in me and gave me the gift of a multilingual/multicultural environment to grow up in. And to Bruce Carl Fontaine, whose constant support of me and faith in me contributed greatly to this text becoming a reality. He is the wind beneath my wings.

To Jamie Ann Cross, an author's dream of an editor, whose total dedication to this book has made it a much better work than it would have been.

—Richard Firsten

To my special students, in particular Naushad Vadsaria, who with fire and electricity, reminded me daily why it is I do what I do.

—Patricia Killian

To all of the students we've had in TESOL courses over the years who kept asking us the question, "So when are you going to write the book?"

The Phonetic Alphabet

Here is a simplified version of the International Phonetic Alphabet (the IPA). We've simplified it for the purposes of this book and have replaced some complex symbols with ones easier for English speakers to recognize.

a	(f<u>a</u>ther)	ɔɪ	(b<u>oy</u>)	r		
æ	(h<u>a</u>t)	b		s		
e	(s<u>ay</u>)	č	(<u>ch</u>ip)	š	(fi<u>sh</u>)	
ɛ	(b<u>e</u>d)	d		t		
i	(s<u>ee</u>)	f		D	(butter) flapped "d"
ɪ	(s<u>i</u>t)	g		t̥	unreleased "t"
o	(n<u>o</u>)	h		θ	(wi<u>th</u>)
ɔ	(s<u>aw</u>)	ǰ		ð	(<u>th</u>e)
u	(t<u>oo</u>)	k		v		
ʊ	(b<u>oo</u>k)	l		w		
ə	(<u>a</u>bout)	m		y		
ər	(fi<u>r</u>st)	n		z		
aɪ	(eye)	ŋ	(si<u>ng</u>)	ž	(plea<u>s</u>ure)
aʊ	(n<u>ow</u>)	p				

: This symbol is used to show a lengthened sound.
- A hyphen will be used to separate syllables.

Contents

Preface	v	
Acknowledgments	vii	
Modified International Phonetic		
Alphabet (IPA)	viii	

1 Word Order   1
   *"Throw Mama from the train
   a kiss."*

The Basics   1
Adverbs of Frequency
   (How often?)   5
Adverbs of Frequency and
   Other Words in Initial Position   6
Other Peculiarities of Word
   Inversion   7
Teaching Tips General Information   8
Teaching Tips   9

2 The Articles   11
   *"It wasn't just a party,
   but the party to end all parties."*

The Indefinite Article   11
The Definite Article   17
Teaching Tips   24

3 The Presents   26
   *"These are the times
   that try men's souls."*

The Present Progressive   26
The Simple Present   30
The Present Perfect   37
The Present Perfect Progressive   41
Teaching Tips   45

4 The Pasts   50
   "What's done is done."

The Simple Past   50
The Past Progressive   53
The Past Perfect   60
The Past Perfect Progressive   63
The Expressions *Used To*
   and *Would*   64

5 The Futures   71
   "Qué será, será . . ."

The Present Progressive   72
The Simple Present   72
The Future with *Be Going To*   73
The Simple Future *(Will)*   74
The Future with *Be About To*   77
The Future Perfect   77
The Future Progressive   78
Two Marginal Future Expressions   82
Teaching Tips   86

6 Adjectives   90
   "It was an itsy-bitsy, teeny-weeny,
   yellow polka dot bikini."

Verbal Adjectives   90
The Ordering of Adjectives   96
When Nouns are Adjectives   104
Punctuating Adjectives   106
Teaching Tips   107

7 Some and Any   111
   "Come up and see me some time"
   . . . or any time.

Compound Pronouns   119
Teaching Tips   126

**8 Modal Auxilaries in
   the Present or Future**   128
   "I would if I could, but I can't,
   so I won't."

Can/Could   130
Will/Would   139
May/Might   143
Should/Ought To   147
Must   150
Semi-Auxiliaries (Periphrastic
   Modals)   153
Teaching Tips   155

9 Prepositions   158
   "There's a frog on a log in a hole
   at the bottom of the sea."

Literal (Physical) Meanings   159
Figurative/Idiomatic Meanings   169
The Prepositional Bane of
   Banes: *At*   171
Some Teaching Strategies   178
Post–posed Prepositions   180
Teaching Tips   184

10 Genitives   189
   "Mice's and men's best-laid
   plans / The best-laid plans
   of mice and men"

The -*S* Genitive   189
Group Genitives   196
The *Of*-Genitive   198
Partitive Genitives   200
Appositives   202
The Double Genitive   204
-'*S*/-*S*' vs. *Of*: Gray Areas   206
Teaching Tips   208

**11 Compound Nouns
   and Adjectives**   211
   "It was a one-eyed, one-horned,
   flying purple people eater."

Compound Nouns   212
Compound Adjectives   217
Teaching Tips   221

12 Modal Auxiliaries in the Past 224
   "There's no point thinking about
   what might have been."

Can/Could/Could Have   224
May Have/Might Have   230
Should Have/Ought to Have   233
Must Have/Had To   236
A Word about *Would*   239
Would Rather Have/
   Would Sooner Have   240
Teaching Tips   241

13 Passives and Causatives   243
   "What's done is done
   'cause I got it done."

The Passive Voice   243
Causatives   267
Teaching Tips   272

14 Direct Object Companions 278
"The Queen of Hearts' men
painted all the white roses red."

Noun Phrases 280
Adjective Phrases 283
Infinitive Verb Phrase DOCs 290
-ing Verb and Base Verb Phrases 293
Past Participle Phrases 307
Causatives and Direct Object
    Companions 309
Teaching Tips 313

**15 Autosegmental
    Features, Part 1** 316
"His name's Castro, but he's
not one of theee Castros."

Stress and Single Words 318
LEGATVM PERPLEXVM
ROMANVM—or, A Con-
fusing Legacy from Rome 320
More Examples of Stress
Changes and Parts of Speech 321
Stress and Noun Phrases 323
Stress and Verb Phrases 331
Teaching Tips 335

16 Indirect Speech 339
"He said that she said that
I said that . . . "

Lexical Transformations 340
A Note about Say 342
A Note about Tell 342
Backshifting 343
Time and Space 352
Infinitives 354
Direct to Indirect Questions 357
Exclamations 360
Teaching Tips 363

17 Two- and Three-Word Verbs 369
"Read it over, think about it,
and get back to me."

Two-Word Verbs 369
Three-Word Verbs 384
A Bounty of Nouns and
    Adjectives 386
Teaching Tips 387

**18 Autosegmental
    Features, Part 2** 391
"It's not always what you say,
but how you say it."

Stress and Whole Sentences 391
Some and Any Revisited 399
Intonation 404
Teaching Tips 413

**19 Subjunctives,
    Hopes, and Wishes** 416
"When you wish upon a star . . . "

The Indicative and Subjunctive
    Moods 416
Phrases Which Force the Present
    and Timeless Subjunctives 427
The Mandative Subjunctive 432
A Modern Language Oddity:
    The Formulaic Subjunctive 435
Teaching Tips 437

20 Conditional Sentences 438
"If music be the food of love,
play on."

Real Conditional Sentences:
    Timeless, Present, and Future
    Forms 439
Real Conditional Sentences and
    the Imperative 452

Unreal Conditional Sentences:
Timeless, Present, and Future
Forms   460

Because Of Goes Subjunctive   466

Unreal Conditional Sentences:
The Past   468

Mixing and Matching Unreal
Conditional Clauses   470

Phrases that Create Hypothetical
Situations   473

Teaching Tips   474

21 ELT "Waifs"   477
  *"We're poor little lambs
  who have lost our way . . ."*

Ellipsis   477

Relaxed Pronunciation   481

Intensifiers   483

More ELT Waifs   489

Negative Questions   498

22 Where English Is Going   501
  *"A journey of a thousand miles
  begins with one step."*

Nouns   502

Other Vocabulary Changes   502

-ly Adverbs   504

Verbs   504

Other Predictions   505

Appendix 1 Picture Files   509

**Appendix 2 More Strategies and
  Activities That Work**   512

Slot Substitutions   514

Cloze Procedures   516

Incomplete Dialogues   522

Appendix 3 Games   526

Tic Tac Toe (British "Naughts &
  Crosses"   526

Concentration   527

The Clothesline   528

Oral Matching   530

Scamblers   531

**Appendix 4 A Deeper Look at
  Reporting Verbs**   534

**Appendix 5 Troubleshooting
  Pronunciation**   543

The Letter "O"   543

The "D" in *Dry*; the "T" in *Try*   544

The "Flapped D"   545

Juncture   546

The Most Common Vowel
  Sound in English   547

That Final *-ate*!   548

Teaching Tips   548

**Appendix 6 It All Adds Up:
  1 + 1 = 2**   552

**Appendix 7 More Fun with
  Autosegmental Features:
  A Stress-Caused
  Metamorphosis**   554

**Appendix 8 Rejoinders,
  Exclamations, Etc.**   556

Index   559

1

Word Order

"Throw Mama from the train a kiss."

 The Basics

A: We're to next the beach week going.

B: What did you say?

A: I told you just next week to the are going we beach.

B: That's what I thought you said!

In the dialogue you've just read, it's obvious that Person B is quite uncomfortable with what Person A is saying and also that she's probably not alone. We're sure you, too, feel uncomfortable trying to understand what Person A has to say. That's because he's using a word order, or syntax, that might be fine in some other language, but certainly doesn't work in English. The question is, why doesn't it work? What rules are there that you can tell students when correcting their word order that will stick so that they don't continue to make the same mistakes over and over again?

From the outset, we want to make it perfectly clear that the aim of this chapter is not to cover every aspect of English word order. Most details aren't very troublesome and are covered at length in other grammar books. What we intend to show you are fresh approaches to looking at and teaching certain aspects of word order that are likely to be troublesome for English language learners. We'll demonstrate ways of perceiving word order that may make things easier for you and for your students.

For starters, let's discover the underlying basic rules for English word order by doing the exercise that follows:

Rearrange the following sentences to put them in the word order that you consider *basic* to English.

1. the paper / this morning / at home / he / read.

   _____

2. in the oven / I'm roasting / tonight / a chicken.

   _____

3. send / to Delhi / right now / this fax.

   _____

4. Marc / earlier / outside / took / the garbage.

   _____

5. a movie / last night / we / saw / on campus.

   _____

6. north / drove / today / Yoko / to Kyoto / the van.

   _____

The sentences should have this basic order:

1. **He read the paper at home this morning.**
2. **I'm roasting a chicken in the oven tonight.**
3. **Send this fax to Delhi right now.**
4. **Marc took the garbage outside earlier.**
5. **We saw a movie on campus last night.**
6. **Yoko drove the van north to Kyoto today.**

Now let's take a good look at how these sentences are set up. There's definitely a pattern we can discern. To begin with, they all start with a subject except for Sentence 3 (which we'll discuss further on). We've got these elements to work with as **subjects** or doers of the action:

he/I/Marc/we/Yoko

These subjects are all followed by **verbs**:

read/'m roasting/send/took/saw/drove

Next we have **direct objects**:

> the paper/a chicken/this telegram/the garbage/a movie/the van

To continue, we find **directions** or **places**:

> at home/in the oven/to Delhi/outside/on campus/north to Kyoto

Finally, there are **time phrases**:

> this morning/tonight/right now/earlier/last night/today

English tends to follow the word order that reflects the sentences that we've just looked at. For now, let's state the general rule of basic word order based on this information:

> **Subject + verb + object + direction/place + time.**

This order "translates" very nicely into a certain group of *wh-* words that many English speakers learn in a set order when they're children: **who–what–where–when**. These four *wh-* words correspond very neatly to the order of the basic English sentence. Take a good look and see for yourself.

In the basic pattern above, five separate segments are listed, but there are only four *wh-* words, so you might think that something got left out. Not so! In fact, it's amazing how this works. Follow along and everything should become clear:

> **Who** represents the subject—whoever/whatever it is;
> **What** stands for two segments: the verb and object(s);
> **Where**, of course, is the direction and/or place;
> **When** is the time.

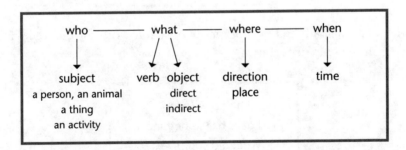

You can see that the five basic segments have been accounted for. The beauty of *what* representing both the verb and the objects is that keeping this pair of words together as a single concept reinforces one of the cardinal rules of English word order, one that many students have trouble with: **you normally don't separate a verb and its object(s) and place a word or words in between them.** In this case, since one *wh-* word stands for both segments, there's no way to separate them. As soon as your students are able to form the most elementary English sentences, start requiring them to learn the phrase *who–what–where–when* until they've memorized the words and their order. Make sure they consciously use this pattern whenever they speak or write English. As the students progress, they can start using variations on this basic pattern, but first get them to internalize the basic word order.

Even though we've given you a nice, tidy formula for this most basic example of English word order, be aware that there are variations that do occur. For example, we can have **what** as the subject ("The fire burned out of control"), and **who** as the object ("The smoke almost asphyxiated the O'Learys"). We can also have any combination of these two: **who/who** ("The firefighters rescued the whole family") and **what/what** ("The fire destroyed everything").

Here's another important point about the objects. There are direct objects and indirect objects. For example, in the sentence *Shah Jehan built the Taj Mahal for his wife*, *the Taj Mahal* is the direct object and *his wife* is the indirect object. Even when we change the order of the words (as we can sometimes do in English by dropping the preposition) and say "Shah Jehan built his wife the Taj Mahal," the segments that have been called direct and indirect object are still just that. What's interesting to note is that whether **the direct object is before the indirect object, or vice versa, the two objects are still kept side by side,** and that's another aspect of word order that never varies. In fact, we can take this analysis a step further and see that these three elements (the verb, direct object, and indirect object) all stay together in this basic English word order pattern.

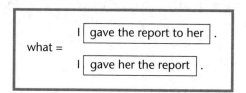

Notice that *what* will be the appropriate question word for the following questions based on the sentences above:

A: What did you do?
B: I gave her something.
A: What did you give her?
B: The report.

Let's get back to Sentence 3 for a moment: "Send this fax to Delhi right now." When we utter an imperative form, a command, we're really including the subject *you* before the verb even though we don't normally say it. (*You send* sounds forceful, emphatic.) Therefore, there really is a subject in Sentence 3 as well, an understood you: "(You) send this fax to Delhi right now." This point can be easily demonstrated by listening to any English-speaking parent who's momentarily upset with his/her child and says something like, "You stop that whining this instant!" There it is! The subject *you* has surfaced. So Sentence 3 is just fine. It has a subject, albeit hidden, a verb *(send)*, a direct object *(this fax)*, direction *(to New Delhi)*, and time *(right now)*.

In the segment we call **where**, we noted that a direction or a place might fill that place. In Sentence 6 we can see this "where" in action: "Yoko drove the van <u>north to Kyoto</u> today." Here we have an example containing both the direction *(north)* and place *(to Kyoto)*. Remember that when both elements are used in one phrase, **the direction word comes first**. Other direction words are the rest of the compass points and words like *home* and *away*:

Drive <u>east on 42nd Street</u> and make <u>a right at Broadway</u>.
Kenji is going <u>home to Kobe</u> for the summer.
Silvia went <u>away to the mountains</u> for the weekend.

Now let's discuss the placement of time phrases. Notice where they appear in those first six example sentences. This is one segment (and there are others!) that can be pushed to the front of a sentence if deemed appropriate to do so. It's more or less up to the individual to determine if it's appropriate to place it there. The rule of thumb tends to be that **the time phrase can precede all other segments of the sentence if the speaker wishes to emphasize or linger on it**:

<u>For the past six years</u>, our company has made steady profits.

✈ Adverbs of Frequency (How often?)

These adverbs are words such as *always/usually/often/sometimes/seldom/rarely/never*. Figure out the rules that govern their placement by looking over this dialogue.

A: Misha's a terrific employee!

B: I know. He's **rarely** late for work and he's **never** sick.

A: Besides that, he's **always** had his work done on time.

B: And he **seldom** makes any big errors.

A: He has **never** fought with the boss.

B: And he's **always** trying to help his co-workers.

A: We could **never** have sold so much this year without him.

1. If the verb *be* is used, the adverbs of frequency are placed _____

    _____.

2. If simple verbs are used, the frequency words are placed _____

    _____.

3. If complex verbs are used, these adverbs are placed _____

    _____.

Let's check out your ideas. **These adverbs are always placed in these specific places:**

1. **after the verb *be*:**
   He's <u>always</u> on time.

2. **before other verbs in their simple forms:**
   He <u>never</u> gets to work late.

3. **after the first auxiliary in the complex verb:**
   He'll <u>rarely</u> get angry. / He's <u>never</u> been fired from a job.

Adverbs of Frequency and Other Words in Initial Position

All languages have their peculiarities, and English is certainly no exception. One case in point is the strange phenomenon that occurs if we place the following adverbs of frequency at the start of a sentence for emphasis:

<u>Seldom</u> does it snow in Vancouver.
<u>Rarely</u> will he complain about anything.
<u>Never</u> have I seen such a beautiful sunset!

What do you see happening in the sentences above? Write a statement or two to explain this phenomenon.

If these adverbs of frequency are placed in initial position, _____

_____.

In case you haven't hit upon this particular way of looking at what's happening, think about the phenomenon this way: **If those adverbs of frequency are**

placed as the first word of a sentence, a pattern like a yes/no question follows (... does it snow ... / ... will he complain ... / ... have I seen ...), which, by the way, creates a more formal air. And, by the way, there's a good general rule of thumb that works for this particular point and many others, and that is, **when you change any element of the typical English sentence, the change is likely to set off other changes**.

There's another interesting observation we can make about those frequency adverbs: Keep in mind that **only those adverbs that have a negative connotation, i.e., those which mean "less than 50% of the time," are normally fronted**.

We've dealt with negative adverbs of frequency which create this change in word order when they appear in initial position, but this phenomenon of English isn't limited to them alone. Notice how the same change, creating a yes/no question pattern, occurs when the following words are fronted:

barely:	<u>Barely</u> *had they left* the building when the fire started.
hardly:	<u>Hardly</u> *had she finished* cleaning the house when company arrived.
neither:	He can't cook a decent meal. <u>Neither</u> *can he bake* well.
nor:	They have no children, <u>nor</u> *do they want* any.
scarcely:	<u>Scarcely</u> *had he completed* the test when the bell rang.

Other Peculiarities of Word Inversion

Before we leave our observations on the phenomenon we've been discussing, there are six more we can mention. Consider these sentences:

> The cake was so delicious that we didn't leave a crumb.
> He was such a good boy that everyone loved him.

Here's an alternative form for these sentences, although again taking on a much more formal air:

> So delicious <u>was the cake</u> that we didn't leave a crumb.
> Such a good boy <u>was he</u> that everyone loved him.

Note again how the inverted forms contain the inverted word order that is commonly used for a question ("... was the cake ..." / "... was he ..."). This yes/no question-like pattern is the common thread found in all of these unusual forms.

Next we have a sentence that contains a correlative conjunction (a pair of words that work together):

> He <u>not only</u> wrote the music, <u>but</u> he <u>also</u> wrote the lyrics.

With this sentence construction, you can opt for an inverted word order:

> Not only <u>did he write</u> the music, but he also wrote the lyrics.

Moving right along, we come to a sentence like the following:

They've considered our proposal only recently.

In this case, you can front the adverbial part (beginning with the word *only*) and end up with this sentence order:

Only recently <u>have they considered</u> our proposal.

Here are some other examples of this occurrence:

Only now <u>does he admit</u> his errors.
Only by sheer luck <u>was his life spared</u>.

Then we have sentences which invert the word order when their prepositional phrases are fronted. Look what happens with these two examples:

The bicycle I wanted was behind the house. →
Behind the house <u>was the bicycle I wanted</u>.

The town where I live lies beyond those mountains. →
Beyond those mountains <u>lies the town where I live</u>.

Finally, there's the matter of some specific exclamations. Once again, we'll use the word order common in yes/no questions to create these statements:

Boy, <u>was it</u> hot this afternoon!
<u>Can I make</u> a wonderful spaghetti sauce!
Wow! <u>Did they mess up</u>!

Teaching Tips General Information

Before we begin the *Teaching Tips*, a regular feature of each chapter, we'd like to make several suggestions about them. First, you'll find that the *Teaching Tips* suggest dividing the class into pairs or small groups. The main purpose for this division is that students are much more likely to get a chance to speak when they're in small groups. It would be ideal if all teachers had small classes, but we realize that a class of eight students is a dream. Small group work is a way to increase each student's chance to speak and be heard.

Second, we'd like to suggest how to divide the class into these groups. Separate students from the same language background if you can. We realize that many teachers have homogeneous classes as far as language background goes, but if you have students with several different home languages, you can mix the members in each group so that they all don't speak the same language, thereby decreasing the likelihood of students using their native languages with classmates and keeping more of the communication in English.

Third, as your students are doing the task you've set up, wander around the room and help out when you're called on or needed. Try to do so with a minimum of interference and only interrupt for a good reason. Your students need to talk more than you do! In most cases it's best to be an observer and a helper, not a participant.

Fourth, you'll notice that we often suggest putting the assignment on a handout. If that's not possible for you to do, there's always the chalkboard.

Finally, we've deliberately omitted references to proficiency levels in all the *Teaching Tips*. It's true, for example, that articles are taught early on in an English course and the past perfect is taught much later, but by not mentioning any particular proficiency level, we hope that each activity can be adapted for any class you may have. An activity may be too advanced for your particular needs today, but it may be appropriate for your students later on. This feature can help you to recycle teaching points: what was taught in September can be reviewed in December; what was taught in Level One can be reviewed in Level Three. And now, on to the *Teaching Tips*.

Teaching Tips

1.1 Making Stories

Before class, collect or write interesting phrases (choose phrases that cover different positions in a sentence: a variety of noun phrases, verbs, adverbials, prepositional phrases, etc.). They need not be on a specific topic; in fact, the activity will be more interesting if they're not all related. Distribute a set of these phrases (five to seven) to pairs or small groups of students. Have them write a coherent story using several of the phrases they've received. When the stories have been written, let the students read them aloud to the class.

1.2 Scrambled Paragraphs

Before class, completely scramble a paragraph, but be sure to leave the punctuation intact (scramble the words within each sentence and rearrange the sentences within the paragraph). Dictate the scrambled sentences to your students sentence by sentence. Have the students unscramble the dictation at the sentence level first and then arrange the sentences into the correct order for the paragraph to make sense. This exercise can be done individually or by pairs or small groups.

1.3 Writing Fast Emails

Create a scenario in which a very hastily written email might be sent: You're on vacation and are supposed to be back on Monday. Unfortunately, the air traffic controllers are on strike and the airport is closed down. You're in a hurry to notify your boss about the problem on your laptop, which communicates via satellite. / You're on a business trip and accidentally left an important document in your office. You have very little time before your next business meeting, so you email your assistant to send it to you. Make sure you describe the document carefully and where it's located. Pair the students up or have them form small groups. The students' task is to write the emails.

1. They must organize the information carefully and eliminate unnecessary function words since they're writing emails so hastily!

2. When they have written their emails, they should exchange them with the other groups and decide if any further information should be included.

3. Have the students exchange the emails again and tell them to rewrite the complete text of the emails. Note that if your students find this activity difficult, you can prepare them by giving them emails and asking them to add the words that must have been deleted.

1.4 Acronyms

Before class, think up some well-known acronyms or invent some of your own (TESOL, PDQ, ASAP, AFL–CIO). Explain what an acronym is to your students and show them how one works. Then give them the list of acronyms you've prepared and have them write phrases or sentences of their own invention by using each letter of an acronym to start each word (e.g., The Elephant Sat On Louie; Please Don't Quit; A Sweet Afghan Puppy; Anthony Finds Love and Cleo Is Obliging). Make sure students use correct English word order in their phrases/sentences.

Variation: North American license plates are frequently combinations of letters and numbers. Have your students create license plates for famous people. Here are some examples: LWB 123 (Lawrence Welk's Beat, a–1, a–2, a–3); WTC 1066 (William the Conqueror, 1066); B5S (Beethoven's 5th Symphony). Have them create license plates for themselves, too.

1.5 Making Questions

Before class, prepare several questions that use adverbs of frequency (How often do you read a newspaper? / Do you usually do your homework in the library? / Haven't you ever been uncooperative?) and present them to the students. Now have them brainstorm similar questions and then use the questions to interview one another (they can even interview you) and give reports to the class on what they've just found out.

2

Articles

"It wasn't just a party, but the party to end all parties."

The Indefinite Article

It's odd how this chapter wouldn't even appear in, let's say, a Russian or Chinese or Latin grammar book, and only the second part of this chapter, which deals with the definite article, might appear in an Arabic or Hebrew grammar book. Very curious indeed! The reason is that the articles (indefinite = *a/an*; definite = *the*) are features that simply don't exist in many languages, and the speakers of those languages get on perfectly well without them. (Other languages have other ways of indicating definite and indefinite.) This little bit of information may help you anticipate certain problems when you teach students whose native languages have no articles or at least no indefinite article.

Pronunciation

Before we go on with the standard usage of the indefinite article, let's discuss its pronunciation for a moment. The usual pronunciation is like the unstressed syllable (first syllable) in the words *about* or *agree*. The symbol *schwa* /ə/ in the phonetic alphabet represents this sound.

We do have an alternate pronunciation, however. It's the same sound as the name of the letter, *a* /e/ and is used more for emphasis or in slowed-down speech. Make sure your students understand that it's *not* the standard sound in normally flowing speech.

"A" vs. "An"

The word *a* has a variant form, *an*. How can we know when to use *a* and when to use *an*? Here's a hint: it has to do with sound. Look at the following examples and see if you can figure out the two phonological rules that govern *a* and *an*:

a plum	an apple
a melon	an orange
a nice apple	an old banana
a ripe pear	an overripe peach

First Rule:

_____

Second Rule:

_____

_____

As it happens, the rules seem quite clear cut: **If the noun or adjective begins with a consonant, use the word *a*. If the noun or adjective begins with a vowel, use the word *an*.** Simple, right? Well, almost.

a harp	an hour
a happy child	an honorable man
a united faculty	an uncle
a eulogy	an ugly wart

Above are some exceptions to the rules—or are they? Figure out what's going on with the indefinite article in front of these words and write your conclusions below:

_____

_____

_____

Come to think of it, we really haven't come across any exceptions to the rules after all; in fact, the examples above make our case even stronger. We use *a* before *harp* and *happy child* because the words after the article begin with a consonant, or rather, a consonant *sound*. We use *an* before *hour* and *honorable man* because, even though the words after the article begin with a consonant letter, they don't begin with a consonant sound but with a *vowel* sound because the initial *h* is silent in both words.

One possible exception that bears mentioning is certain multi-syllabic words (*historical, historian, hysterical, heroic,* etc.) Even though the traditional rule dictates that we say "<u>a</u> historical novel" and "<u>a</u> heroic deed," more and more native speakers tend to say "<u>an</u> 'istorical novel" and "<u>an</u> 'eroic deed." It seems that there's a tendency to drop the *h* in these words and this triggers people into using *an* instead of *a*. The explanation has to do with the fact that **the primary stress in these words is not on the first syllable**. Nobody says "an HIStory book," but more and more people say "an 'isTORical novel."

Taken to its farthest limits, this phenomenon can be observed regularly in Cockney English, a dialect spoken in a certain section of London. It's a standard rule in Cockney phonology to drop all initial *h*'s and, by so doing, use the article *an* instead of *a*: *an 'ammer* (a hammer); *an 'and* (a hand).

Getting back to our last list, we say *a* before *united faculty* and *eulogy* because the initial sound isn't a vowel (as in <u>o</u>nion or <u>oo</u>ze), but a *glide* like the sound of "y" in *youth*. After all, no native speaker would ever say "an yellow submarine." We say *an* before *uncle* and *ugly wart* because the words after the article in these two cases do begin with vowel sounds.

So, our rules should be amended a bit: **Use *a* before words that begin with consonant <u>sounds</u>; use *an* before words that begin with vowel <u>sounds</u>.**

"A" vs. "One"

What does the word *a* mean? It represents one way that we communicate that **something is singular and countable** (*a* book, *a* flower, *a* whale). **It's also the article we use in general statements** (*An* apple is *a* fruit) and **the first time we mention something as long as it isn't something exclusive or unique** (While I was walking home, I saw *a* pretty house for sale. *The* house was in my favorite architectural style.).

But the number *one* does the same thing, doesn't it? In some cases, it does, and we'll discuss them later, but right now let's look at some comparisons and see if we can find a distinction between *a* and *one*:

I bought <u>a</u> book.	I bought <u>one</u> book.
He gave her <u>a</u> flower.	He gave her <u>one</u> flower.
They have <u>a</u> parakeet.	They have <u>one</u> parakeet.

Do you sense a difference? If you do, write down the difference you find between *a* and *one* on the lines that follow:

_____

_____

For students whose native languages have only one word for the indefinite article and the number one, such as Spanish with *un[o]* (masculine) or *una* (feminine), there's usually some confusion as to when to use the article and when to use the number in English. As it happens, **the indefinite article means that the noun is singular, countable, and** just **<u>one of many</u>**; the number *one*, on the other hand, tends to be used when we respond to the question "How many . . . ?" or "How much . . . ?" or when we're stressing the singularity of something. In other words, **we normally use *one* when counting**.

Are there times when *a* and *one* can be used the same way? Let's find out. Here are some examples for you to look at. If you can substitute *one* for *a/an*, check the box after each sentence.

1. Would you like to hear <u>an</u> interesting story?　　　　　　　☐
2. I found close to <u>a</u> hundred old coins in my basement!　　　☐
3. I told my brother, and he said it was probably <u>a</u> treasure somebody had hidden there.　　　　　　　　　　　　　　　　　☐
4. In fact, what I had found was only <u>a</u> third of the total treasure hidden in my basement!　　　　　　　　　　　　　　　　　　☐
5. I looked closely at some of the coins. There was <u>a</u> dollar, <u>a</u> dubloon, <u>a</u> kroner, and <u>a</u> ruble.　　　　　　　　　　　　　　☐
6. I put some of the coins in <u>a</u> little leather pouch.　　　　　☐
7. That tiny pouch must have weighed at least <u>a</u> kilo!　　　　☐

Do you see any rules at work? In a moment we'll look into what rules there may be. The boxes we'd check go with **Sentences 2**, **4**, **5**, and **7**. In all of those sentences, the word *a* can be substituted perfectly well with *one*. So why is that? Why can't we do the same for the other sentences? Think about how you'd categorize the words following *a* in the sentences you've checked and list the categories below:

a/one hundred　　　_____

a/one third　　　　_____

a/one dollar, etc.　_____

a/one kilo　　　　_____

The categories we hope you've come up with are **numbers**, **fractions**, **money**, and **weights** or **measurements**. With words in these categories, *a* and *one* can be used interchangeably.

One last point we should discuss is in answer to the question "What is the plural of the indefinite article?" The answer is simply *nothing*. When a noun that has *a* before it is pluralized, it drops the article:

a pin	pins
an anchor	anchors
a grape	grapes
an unpaid bill	unpaid bills

Among many linguists, this lack of an article actually has a name of its own; it's called the "zero article."

The Zero Article

As we've just mentioned, the zero article is used when a countable noun that takes *a* in the singular is made plural. It's also used when we deal with uncountable nouns *(butter/water/snow)* in general terms.

There are some peculiarities in its usage, though, that we should also mention. Compare the words in bold in the following mini-dialogues and see if you can make any conclusions about when the definite or indefinite article is used as opposed to the zero article.

> A: You just bought **a car**, didn't you?
> B: Well, it's really **a used car**.
>
> A: Do you go everywhere **by car** or do you use the bus?
> B: Now I hardly ever go anywhere **by bus**.

Before you become totally perplexed, we'll make it easy for you. The simple fact is that **there's often a zero article in certain "pat phrases"** (preposition + noun). **These phrases usually deal with abstract uses of concrete nouns.** In other words, **they don't refer to one specific item, but rather to an item in a general activity.**

For example, *a car* is a concrete item; *by car* is an abstraction that indicates a means of transportation. *Going to church* refers to an activity rather than one specific building; *the church* does that. *Staying in bed* is another example of a general activity, while *the bed* refers to a concrete item.

Other examples of pat phrases made up of prepositions and the zero article are in the following list:

> in or to + class/college/court/hospital (British)/jail/school/town
> at + school/sea/home/work
> on + call/consignment/holiday (British)/land/leave/top/vacation

Another interesting example of the zero article is with some verbs of movement such as these:

> leave + home/school/town/work
> go, fly, or drive + home/uptown/downtown

You should understand why the zero article is used in this way—your students don't have to. They should simply learn these kinds of pat phrases just as they are and not bother analyzing them. As you'll read later on in this chapter, part of good language learning is to be accepting of the idiosyncrasies of the target language.

A Word About Change

In just about every prescriptive English grammar we've come across (the ones that tell you what you *should* say), the lesson dealing with countable and uncountable nouns is quite straightforward: here are the nouns that you can count (in which case, you can use the indefinite article or a number accompanied by a plural marker on the noun), and here are the nouns you cannot count (in which case, you can't use the indefinite article or a number and a plural marker on the noun).

In the list of uncountable nouns, we find words such as *beer, coffee, tea, water, bread,* and *lettuce.* The lesson goes on to tell us that we must use such words as *a glass of, two cups of, a loaf of,* and *two heads of* in order to count the uncountable items we've just mentioned. Then we go out into "the real world" and listen to what people really say. Go into any restaurant and you just may hear statements like these:

> "Let's see, that'll be a vodka on the rocks and two beers, right?"
> "Hey, Antoine, the chef's gotta make a little more salad, so go get a lettuce,
>   an endive, and a can of anchovies, okay?"

So what should English teachers do? Are we to "go by the book," remain staunch defenders of prescriptive grammar, and be blind to the changes that are taking place in the language? After all, if enough native speakers decide to contradict what the grammar books say, what should we do?

Our advice, for the time being, is to say that you should teach the prescribed grammar, but that it's perfectly acceptable to mention the current alternatives that your students will surely hear once they're exposed to enough native speakers. We'll call these alternatives when dealing with countable and uncountable nouns "fast food English." It could have developed out of the desire for restaurant people to abbreviate their messages whenever possible in order to keep up a certain pace on the job. After enough time passed and enough customers kept hearing these fast food phrases, they caught on with the general public and have now become fairly acceptable alternatives.

You may choose not to have your students use these alternative forms actively, but your students can at least be made aware that they do exist. Sometimes it can be dangerous to judge what's right and what's wrong in language.

☙ The Definite Article

Pronunciation

We've already mentioned that the definite article is the word *the;* the first thing we should consider is its pronunciation. Just as when choosing to use *a* or *an,* there are pronunciation concerns that must be taken into account. Read the following examples out loud and see if you find yourself using two different pronunciations for "t-h-e."

the angel	the plant
the onion	the fruit
the elm	the birch
the ink	the pen

There are some people who would pronounce "t-h-e" the same way with all these nouns, but that's considered non-standard. Note any observations you can make about how you pronounced "t-h-e" in the column on the left, and how you pronounced it in the column on the right.

In the left-hand column,

_____

_____

In the right-hand column,

_____

_____

If you look back at the rules we figured out for *a* and *an,* you recall that it all depended on whether the first sound in the following word was a vowel or consonant sound. That holds true for these pronunciation rules as well. **If the following word begins with a vowel sound, pronounce the vowel in "t–h–e" as the name of the letter, "e" /i/. If the following word begins with a consonant sound, pronounce the vowel in "t–h–e" the same way you pronounce the *a* in *about* /ə/.** This pronunciation rule also holds true for those deceptive words that begin with silent *h (honor)* or the glide *y* /y/ *(union)*. When the *h* is silent, we treat those words as if they begin with vowel sounds; the *y* is a glide, so we treat those words as if they begin with consonant sounds.

One other pronunciation to keep in mind is that we often pronounce the *e* in "t–h–e" as the name of the letter when we emphasize or stress the noun it precedes:

A: Did you say that his name's Jason Rockefeller?

B: Yes, I did.

A: Is he one of **theeee** Rockefellers?

B: No such luck.

Meaning and Usage

We've already said that *a* is the article to use in general statements; the same can be said about *the* (The orange is a fruit of Asian origin). Is there a significant difference if we substitute *an* for *the* in the example in parentheses? Not really, at least, not for the purposes of this book. In fact, there are three ways that we can talk in generalities about subjects: using the indefinite article *(a)*, using the definite article *(the)*, or using no article (the zero article) and making the noun plural. Here's an example of the three ways we can discuss the same topic in a general statement:

1. A <u>rabbit</u> is an animal loved by children.
2. The <u>rabbit</u> is an animal loved by children.
3. <u>Rabbits</u> are animals loved by children.

Keep in mind that the use of *the* in Sentence 2 is restricted and doesn't reflect the usual meaning of this article. To discover the most typical use of *the*, let's examine another group of sentences. If the sentences sound right to you, write the word *okay* on the lines after them; if they don't sound right, put the word *odd* on the lines.

1. Where's <u>a</u> newspaper I was reading?   _____

2. A: Look at that peeling paint!
   B: Where?
   A: On <u>a</u> front door!   _____

3. Want to see some card tricks? Good!
   Take <u>the</u> card out of <u>a</u> deck.   _____ — _____

4. Hey, Pete, we ate at <u>the</u> great restaurant!   _____

In case you were wondering about your better judgment, don't be alarmed. **You should have written** *odd* **on all of the lines above.** But why are they all odd? Let's examine each one and find the reason.

The question in the first example refers to a specific newspaper that the person was reading earlier, and *the* **is the article we choose when referring to a specific thing that both speaker and listener are aware of.** Example 1 should be, "Where's **the** newspaper I was reading?"

In **Example 2**, Person A is talking about a specific door, the one and only front door that the house would have. The door being referred to is specific; therefore, we again need to use *the* and the corrected version should be, "On **the** front door!"

Example 3 has two misuses. The corrected sentence should read, "Take **a** card out of **the** deck." The speaker needs to say *a* card because it's one of the fifty-two and refers to a general or vague thing (this card, that card—any card); the speaker has to say *the* deck because our amateur magician is referring to the specific deck which the participant sees, not any deck of cards in general.

If left alone, **Sentence 4** would probably force Pete into wondering whether he'd previously recommended some outstanding restaurant to the speaker. He'd be uncomfortable because the speaker is making no reference to a previous conversation that he can pinpoint. The sentence should be, "Hey, Pete, we ate at **a** great restaurant!"

By now, we realize that **the all–important use of *the* is to refer to something or someone specific or known, <u>not</u> general**.

How about the following sentences? All four of them are right, but information about the direct object in each one is different. What assumptions can we make? Explain the differences between the paired direct objects (depending on which article is used with them) on the accompanying blank lines.

1a. Please pass me <u>a</u> salt shaker.   _____

1b. Please pass me <u>the</u> salt shaker.   _____

2a. Did you see <u>a</u> film last night?   _____

2b. Did you see <u>the</u> film last night?   _____

In **1a**, we can assume that **there are at least two salt shakers** on the table. The speaker is saying he doesn't care which one the other person passes to him. In **1b**, however, there can **only be one salt shaker** on the table, and the speaker needs to use *the* because it's the one and only specific item he's asking for.

In **2a**, the speaker is asking the other person if he saw just **any movie last night**; it doesn't matter which one. In **2b**, the speaker is asking if the person saw the movie that they'd previously discussed, probably at some recent point in the past. In other words, **both speaker and listener know exactly which movie** is being referred to.

To sum up everything we've touched on so far, all we need to do is remember this basic difference between *a* and *the*: *A* **is for generalities about people, animals, places, things, or ideas.** The <u>zero article</u> **works this way, too.** *The,* **on the other hand, is for specific people, animals, places, things, or ideas.**

🎐 *Troubleshooter* 🎐

 In many languages, e.g. Spanish and French, the definite article is more commonly used than in English. In fact, contrary to English usage, the definite article is typically used when making statements about things in general, not just specific things as in English.

Some cases in point:

☞ In French, it's   *C'est* | *la* | *vie,* but in English it's

        That's | × | *life.*

☞ In Spanish, it's | *El* | *agua es un tesoro,* which is

        | × | *Water is a treasure.*

So be prepared to deal with this if your students add *the* where we wouldn't normally use it in English.

 As we mentioned at the beginning of this chapter, there are many languages which have no articles at all—definite or indefinite. If you have students whose native languages fit into this group (Russian and Japanese are two good examples), plan accordingly for the double challenge of getting your students to understand the concepts involved and getting them to use the articles appropriately.

An interesting way to look into other uses and misuses of the definite article is to put ourselves right in the classroom and deal with situations as they arise. Here are examples of typical questions that students ask their teachers. What would you say to these students? Let's start out with just a couple of questions:

1. Is it all right to call her "<u>the Roxanne</u>"?

2. Why can't I say "<u>It's the Roxanne's book</u>"?

_____

_____

   Things get quite interesting right away with our **first question**. Can we ever say *the* before a person's name? Absolutely! Just check out the following examples:

1. <u>The Roxanne</u> you're talking about isn't my sister; she's my cousin.
2. I've just bought a new sailboat. I'm calling it <u>the *Roxanne*</u>.
3. A: Isn't Roxanne's last name Bergerac?
   B: Yes, it is. In fact, <u>the Bergeracs</u> live next door to me.

   In our first example, the rule is that **we can use *the* before a person's name if we're speaking about one of the two or more people with that same name**. In this situation, there are two Roxannes.

   In Sentence 2, the rule is that **we can use *the* before names when referring to things like ships or boats, buildings, aircraft, paintings, and any other things that we've given names to**.

   Example 3 is a little different. **When we refer to a couple, a whole family, or any group of people with a collective name, it's customary to put *the* before the name and then add the plural marker (*-s* or *-es*) onto the name**.

   While we're on the subject, is it ever possible to put *a* or *an* before a name? Again, the answer is *yes*, although it's more common to do so before a last name. **When speaking of one member of a group or family, it's quite proper to use the indefinite article before the name, signifying this person is just one member of the group** (which the indefinite article represents under any other circumstances, too).

> You've disgraced the whole family! <u>A Lynch</u> never gives up!

   Let's go back to the students' questions. As for **Question 2**, the reasoning that students often have for coming up with a phrase like "the Roxanne's book" is really intriguing. They know it's <u>the</u> book, and they know it's <u>Roxanne's</u>, so their sense of efficiency dictates that they should combine the two phrases to produce "the Roxanne's book." Quite clever actually, but the reason it can't be done is that **we cannot put the definite article before a possessive form of a name**. In the chapter on adjectives, you'll see that the definite article and the possessive pronoun or noun both fit into the same blank or spot before the noun; therefore, using both of them is impossible in English.

Now let's look at two more typical questions that students have been known to challenge their teachers with.

1. I'm confused. I don't understand why you changed my words. When you asked me what I'd done over the weekend, I said, "Last Sunday I went to see <u>the</u> tennis match. The match was very exciting." You corrected me and said, "Last Sunday you went to see <u>a</u> tennis match." Why?

_____

_____

_____

2. English is very crazy! You tell me I can't say that I come from <u>the</u> Iran, that I should say only "Iran." But when Pol said that he comes from <u>the</u> Netherlands, you didn't correct him. Why not?

_____

_____

_____

For some people, the question posed in **Example 1** is a real "head scratcher." What we have here is a simple rule that even most native speakers aren't aware of: **When you mention something countable for the first time, you normally say *a*; if you happen to mention it again, you change *a* to *the*.** Here's a longer example of this rule at work:

When I got home yesterday, I saw <u>a</u> cat up <u>a</u> tree in front of my house. <u>The</u> tree was very tall and <u>the</u> cat was very scared. I asked <u>a</u> passerby if he'd help, but <u>the</u> man wasn't interested. Anyway, I finally managed to coax <u>the</u> cat down from <u>the</u> tree with <u>a</u> can of tuna.

The answer to **Example 2** isn't very hard to explain. **Countries that are collectives** (unions, republics, island groups, etc.) **use *the*.** Others don't. In addition, we use *the* for regions or areas (the Caucasus, the Crimea, the Yukon, etc.).

While we're on the subject of geographical designations, let's discuss an area that can be perplexing. Fill in the blanks with the word *the* before the following names of these natural or man-made features or places if you think you should.

1. _____ Nile   4. _____ Stockholm   7. _____ Lake Como

2. _____ Himalayas   5. _____ Hague   8. _____ Vatican

3. _____ Mt. Ararat   6. _____ Puget Sound   9. _____ Vatican City

10. _____ Niagara Falls   12. _____ Steppes   15. _____ Deep South

11. _____ Panama Canal   13. _____ Tokyo Bay   16. _____ Silicon Valley

14. _____ Glen Garriff

You should have had no trouble with **Numbers 8, 12**, and **15**; they're regions or areas, and as we've just mentioned, **regions use *the***.

Cities (**Numbers 4, 5**, and **9**) are like countries in that **they don't use *the*.** *The Hague* is a well-known exception, its name being directly translated from Dutch. One other exception not in our list is *the Bronx*, a borough of New York City. It's believed that *the* is used because the name originally referred to the first Dutch family who settled in the area. In addition, **we don't use *the*** with the names of places like valleys or glens, so that's why you shouldn't put *the* in **Numbers 14** and **16**.

Now let's talk about mountains (**Numbers 2** and **3**). **We use *the* with mountain chains, but we don't use *the* for individual mountains.** An exception to this general rule is *the Matterhorn*, again because the name was translated verbatim, this time from German.

Confusing, isn't it? Now let's deal with *water*. We've noticed some very strong tendencies that we'd like to pass along to you. We think you'll find that for the most part, it'll be hard to find exceptions to this line of thinking. See what you think.

We find there are two basic categories we can sort water into: *open water* and *closed water*. **Open water refers to bodies of water that are not perceived to have borders or limits because of their impressive size.** Water in this category uses *the*. *Open water* is all the oceans, seas, rivers, and canals (the Indian Ocean, the Sargasso Sea, the Yellow River, the Suez Canal). By the way, the Caspian and the Black are called "seas" rather than "lakes" because of their impressive size even though technically they are lakes. So, **Numbers 1** and **11** use *the* because they're *open water*.

Closed water is perceived to have borders or limits and bodies of water in this category don't use *the*. Bays, lakes, sounds, and waterfalls are examples (Hudson Bay, Lake Victoria, Long Island Sound, Angel Falls). That's why **Numbers 6, 7, 10**, and **13** don't use *the*.

One last area to discuss deals with **place names that contain the preposition *of*** (see *Appositives*, page 202). **In all of these cases, *the* must be included in the name.** Examples are the Gulf of Tonkin, the Straits of Gibraltar, the Mount of Olives, the Vale of Kashmir, the Valley of the Kings, the University of Illinois, the Arc de Triomphe, and the Leaning Tower of Pisa.

Should you teach your students all these rules? Maybe yes, maybe no, but at least if you understand how articles interact with these categories, you can teach these items in meaningful groupings. In this way, your students can learn to use or not to use the article inductively rather than deductively.

Teaching Tips

2.1 Realia

A collection of realia is very useful for teachers to have; realia can be used in many different ways (role plays, for example). In this case, bring in realia that represents occupations, sports, or actors and their roles. Examples might be a pilot's cap, stethoscope, wig, book bag, swimming goggles, mortar board, Mickey Mouse ears, etc. If you don't have any of these items, you can often get them at toy stores, second-hand shops, and yard sales. Your students may even have some they'll bring in to class. Hand out the props, or let the students choose them, and say as you point to a student: "She's a rock star." / "He's a doctor." / "She's a professor." If you have duplicate props, you say: "They're pilots." / "They're Mouseketeers." Have the students repeat after you individually or as a group. Continue with questions ("Who's the doctor?" / "Is Jenna a chemist?") or by pointing to a student and saying: "Clerk." Student responses may be the following: "Who's a dentist?" / "Is Genghis a teacher?" / "I'm a swimmer." / "She's not an actor; she's a ballerina." When the students are comfortable with the articles, let them take over the questioning.

2.2 Picture Files

Before class, select several pictures from your Picture File (see *Appendix 1*). Be sure that the pictures you choose have plenty of items in them. (It's also possible for you to let your students select a picture themselves.) Ask the students to describe the various items in the pictures using articles where necessary.

2.3 I Can Remember . . .

Bring in twenty to twenty-five items that represent a variety of countable and uncountable nouns (a book, some sand, a newspaper, some paper, etc.). Spread them out on your desk before class and cover them up. When the students come in, have them gather around your desk and uncover the items. Give the students a few minutes to remember as many items as they can before you cover them up again. Have the students return to their desks and ask them to list the items, making sure they use articles in their list.

2.4 Plans

Divide your class into pairs or small groups and have them plan a party, barbecue, picnic, or trip. Ask them to write up a list of the equipment and items that they'll need for the event. Again, make sure that they include appropriate articles on their list. When each group has made up its list, bring the class back together and compare the lists.

2.5 *I Want / I'll Change*

Have your students write down (1) ten to fifteen items that they'd like to have, given unlimited money or (2) ten to fifteen things that they'd like to change about themselves, their lives, or their world. Make sure they use articles with their items. Collect the lists and redistribute them. Students need to interview one another to find out whose list they have. Students must use appropriate questions in order to discover who the lists belong to.

2.6 *Menus*

Before class, collect or prepare various menus. Divide the class into small groups; one student will be the "server" and the others, the "customers." Have the students role play ordering food. The server should write down the order as it's being given so that he/she can repeat the order at the end to see if it's correct. Make sure that the servers and customers use appropriate "restaurant English."

2.7 *Headlines*

Before class write up or collect various newspaper headlines. Have enough headlines so that each group of students has three or four to work with. Divide the class into pairs or small groups and have them reconstruct complete headlines by adding articles, helping verbs, etc.

Variations:

1. Have the students reconstruct abbreviated emails instead of newspaper headlines.
2. Ask the students to write newspaper headlines or emails using the shortened "telegraphic" style.

2.8 *The Alphabet Game*

This activity is commonly called *The Alphabet Game* because it uses the order of the alphabet in selecting items. Students build up vocabulary lists based on a pre-determined category (a supermarket, drugstore, nouns, adjectives, etc.). One student begins the game by saying: "I went to the supermarket and bought an avocado." The first word must begin with an *a*. The next student repeats what the first student said and adds an item of his/her own, this time a "b" item. "I went to the supermarket and bought an avocado and some butter." The third student repeats what's been said by the other two, adding a "c" item, and so on through the alphabet.

Variation: Have the students write an *Alphabet Poem*: A is for Austria, the country of the waltz. B is for bananas, the fruit I love the most. C is for chocolate, my passion, yum, yum. D is for . . . , etc.

3

The Presents

"These are the times that try men's souls."

The Present Progressive

> Auxiliary BE + Verb + ING
>
> I **am** work**ing**   we **are** work**ing**
>
> you **are** work**ing**   they **are** work**ing**
>
> he, she, it **is** work**ing**

Let's get started by asking you a question. After looking at the "brain teasers" given below, can you determine the time or meaning of the present progressive in these sentences? There's a blank line after each example on which you can write your descriptions. We've done the first one for you to get you started.

1. He's starring in *Macbeth* on Broadway. _____ real present _____

2. Tommy's being good for a change. _____

3. What are you doing? _____

There's one basic use of the present progressive in these examples. They show the real present, that is, that the action is *at this time*, and that there's no other major focus. If you wrote something like **the real present** or **the present** on the blank lines after these examples, you're doing fine.

Present Progressive as the Real Present

Some of you may know the present progressive as the "present continuous." Whatever its name, among the important points to remember about it is that **its primary function is to communicate the <u>real</u> present**. We find that the name "progressive" is more appropriate than "continuous" because it implies that the action is "in progress," and that's a fairly accurate description.

One of the most difficult things for teachers to get across to their students is that, except for a relatively small number of verbs, English normally uses the present progressive to communicate that the action is in the true present. (We'll deal with that small number of verbs at length under the heading *The Simple Present: Stative Verbs*.) Here are a couple of sample dialogues to demonstrate this focus:

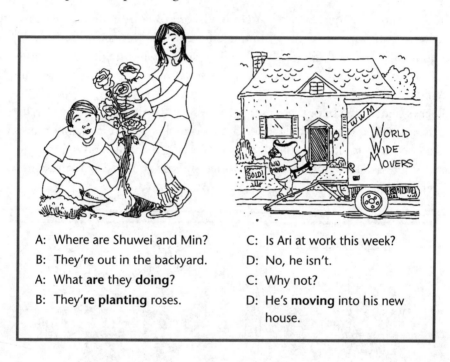

A: Where are Shuwei and Min?
B: They're out in the backyard.
A: What **are** they **doing**?
B: They**'re planting** roses.

C: Is Ari at work this week?
D: No, he isn't.
C: Why not?
D: He's **moving** into his new house.

Notice how both dialogues deal with the concept of *now*, but *now* doesn't represent the same idea in both. In the first dialogue, *now* literally means "at this very moment"; in the second, *now* refers to "this week." Make it a point to explain to your students that the concept of *now* can mean this moment, this week, this month, this year, etc.

Present Progressive as a Temporary Situation

When we use a verb that can either focus on a temporary situation or a long-term (or permanent) situation, **we use the present progressive to communicate that the situation is temporary**. Look at this sample dialogue:

A: Scientists say that the earth **is getting** warmer.

B: I didn't know that. How come?

A: People **are putting** too much CO_2 into the atmosphere.

B: That sounds serious!

In the dialogue above, Speaker A could choose to communicate that this situation is long term or permanent by using a different form for the verbs (i.e., the simple present, which we'll get to shortly). The speaker has deliberately chosen the present progressive to show not only that this situation is in the present, but also that it may not be long term.

There's one more use of the present progressive that we should consider. It's a use which is not typically covered in classes, but it's one that we can certainly hear on any day in any conversation. Take a look at the following dialogue and identify how the present progressive is being used. Also notice the use of the simple present, which we'll get to next:

A: Happy birthday!

B: Oh, you knew! Well, thanks very much.

A: So, any big plans for after work?

B: You know, it's funny. When I got home last night, I couldn't find the kids anywhere. I look around . . . my husband **isn't puttering** in the garden as usual and the kids **are**n't **watching** TV. Noises **are coming** from the basement, so I go downstairs and there they are. They**'re making** decorations for a surprise birthday party for me. They don't see me, so I go back upstairs and say nothing the rest of the evening.

A: So they**'re throwing** you a surprise birthday party, eh?

B: It looks that way!

A: See you this evening!

Doesn't it seem odd that Speaker B is talking about something that happened in the past but uses two forms of the present to do so? For the moment, let's concentrate on the present progressive in this dialogue. Can you think of a way to categorize it for this use? If you can, write down your idea on the following line:

The use of the present progressive in this dialogue is very common in conversational English, especially in what we call *colloquial speech*. We call it the **narrative style** because it's used to help narrate a story. Many people opt to use this form when they want to bring the listener into more of a sense of temporal involvement with the action of the story. Using the present progressive in this way (and the simple present, too, as we'll see shortly) tends to make the story *come closer* to the listener in time. In other words, the narrator is deliberately trying to make the listener a party to the event.

☙ *Troubleshooter* ☙

Students tend to drop or simply forget the auxiliary *be* when making the present progressive. Be prepared for this eventuality!

Stress the use of the auxiliary and drill it as much as possible so that your students will remember it!

 The Present Progressive in a Nutshell

the <u>real</u> present (for most verbs):
She's cooking.

temporary actions:
We're spending this summer at the beach.

past ——————— right now ——————— future

the narrative form:

"She's waiting for the bus, so I ask her if I can drop her off anywhere in my car and she says . . ."

The Simple Present

> I, you, we, they **work**
> he, she, it **works**

Here we have the one verb form in English that has the most inappropriate name. Why? Because the form is neither "simple" nor "present" in its broader usage. Here are some more brain teasers for you to consider. When you think you know how the simple present is being used, describe its time or meaning on each accompanying blank line:

1. Birds fly and fish swim. _____generalization_____

2. She gets up at 6:30 on weekdays. _____

3. I work in my uncle's drugstore. _____

4. I don't like soup. _____

5. "He takes aim. He shoots. He misses!" _____

Most of the uses of the simple present in the examples above share a common thread, but there are fine points that change the focus of the meaning. **Sentence 1** doesn't really deal with time at all; it's a **timeless** use that communicates a fact about birds and fish. It can be considered **a generalization**, **fact**, or **truth**. **Sentence 2** indicates that the activity is **a habit or routine**. **Sentence 3** communicates that this activity is **long term** or **permanent**. **Sentence 4** is just like **1**, a simple fact. Does **Sentence 5** remind you of something seen earlier in this chapter? If you said this example is another instance of the **narrative style**, you're right. In this case, it's the form commonly used by someone witnessing an event such as a sportscaster talking to the audience.

Let's take a look at another way we hear the narrative style used in everyday conversation by examining the following dialogue. As we've seen with the present progressive, it can also be used in this way:

A: I saw in the paper that Sludgeco's been fined again for polluting Silver Bay.

B: That's right, and I witnessed the pollution first hand.

A: What do you mean?

B: I **go** down to the bay to take some photos at sunset and I **smell** something awful. I **realize** that I**'m** right near Sludgeco's drain pipes. So I **walk** over to the pipes and tons of foul-smelling waste are pouring out of the pipes into the bay. I **take** some pictures—lucky I have my camera with me—and **send** them to the nearest Environmental Protection Agency office.

A: You mean you proved Sludgeco was polluting again?

B: Just me and my little old camera!

One curious point that we should clear up about using the simple present and present progressive in this narrative style is to determine when the speaker opts for the simple form and when he/she decides to use the progressive form. Can you think of any reason to choose one and then the other? Write your thoughts on the following lines:

_____

_____

There's a very interesting rule that's being put into use in the dialogue: **When the verb can be used in the past progressive, the speaker opts for the present progressive; when the verb can be used in the simple past, the speaker opts for the simple present.** In other words, there's a mirror image, so to speak, of one form with the other in the narrative style.

So now you know why we say that the so-called "simple present" is not at all simple or the true present. The examples presented show the most common uses of this verb form. Take a look at the following dialogue which shows some of the uses of the simple present mentioned above:

A: Look at that big shark in the tank over there!

B: Wow! Is it big!

A: Did you know it **loses** a row of teeth every time it **eats**?

B: How **do** you **know** that?

A: I **read** lots of nature magazines.

Two great mistakes are committed in most grammar books that lay the foundation for student confusion that is very hard to straighten out later on. The first great mistake is teaching the simple present before teaching the present progressive. There are probably two reasons for this. First, old-style grammarians felt that the simple present was easier for students to deal with because it's just the base form of the verb with only the addition of an *-s* or *-es* on the end for third person singular. "No conjugations to speak of plus no auxiliaries to deal with in the statement form equal an easy verb form to teach." They're wrong because of the immediate challenge of introducing the auxiliary *do/does* in the negative and question forms.

Second, those same grammarians realized that a number of high frequency verbs are among those which almost exclusively use the simple present and not the present progressive. Because they're such high frequency verbs, these grammarians figured they should be taught early on, and therefore the need to teach the simple present right off. This arbitrary decision has proven to be more of a hindrance than a help. Because it's the first verb form students are typically exposed to, and since it's called the simple *present,* students naturally assume that it's indeed the present—the real present—in English. This is where the confusion begins. Another reason to reverse the order in which these forms are taught is that it's much easier to get across the idea of the real present to students than it is to communicate the abstract, vague concept of habitual, general, or timeless situations. To sum up, **we recommend that you teach the present progressive** (affirmative and negative statements, question forms, and short answers) **before teaching the simple present**.

Stative Verbs

Note that with some special verbs, if you change their form, you change their meaning. We've twice alluded to a relatively small group of verbs that uses the simple present almost exclusively. They're called **stative verbs**, which means that they deal with states of being rather than actions. To make these verbs more manageable for your students, you might want to teach them that these verbs can be subdivided into five basic groups: verbs of **liking, the senses, possession, mental processes,** and **states of being**. Here are the ones of higher frequency. (The asterisks preceding some verbs are there to indicate that these are the special verbs that go through a change of meaning peculiar to English if the present progressive is used instead of the simple present. These changes will be discussed in more detail later on.)

STATIVE VERBS				
Liking	Senses	Possession	Mental Processes	States of Being
adore	*hear	belong	believe	astonish
desire	perceive	*have	doubt	be
detest	resemble	lack	feel	concern
dislike	see	own	forgive	cost
hate	*seem	possess	guess	depend
like	*smell		imagine	deserve
love	sound		intend	equal
mind	*taste		know	*fit
prefer			realize	matter
want			recall	mean
*wish			recognize	need
			regard	owe
			remember	tend
			suppose	
			*think	
			understand	

Here's an overview of the special stative verbs from the box above.
(SP = simple present; PP = present progressive)

feel: SP = the involuntary sense of touch anywhere on the body
Most people shiver when they <u>feel</u> cold breezes.

SP = believe
The jury <u>feels</u> that the defendant is innocent.

SP or PP = physical or mental states
I <u>feel</u> ashamed that I lied to her. / I<u>'m feeling</u> ashamed.
Jim <u>feels</u> a little ill today. / Jim<u>'s feeling</u> a little ill.

hear: SP = the involuntary use of the ears; to be told
Oh, no! I <u>hear</u> the baby crying again.
We <u>hear</u> that you've quit your job.

PP = witness what others are saying; imagine sounds
What we<u>'re hearing</u> from the government is talk of war.
She needs psychiatric help. She<u>'s hearing</u> voices.

see: SP = the involuntary use of the eyes; understand
Joe <u>doesn't see</u> well without his glasses.
I <u>see</u> what you mean, but I don't agree with you.

PP = witness what others are doing; have a
romantic involvement with; hallucinate
What we<u>'re seeing</u> is a slowdown in population growth.
Did you know that Boris <u>is seeing</u> Natasha?
I <u>don't see</u> anything in that field. You<u>'re seeing</u> things!

smell: SP = the involuntary use of the nose; how the odor of something
is perceived; have a bad odor
I think I <u>smell</u> something burning in the kitchen.
These flowers <u>smell</u> so good!
Throw out those old boots. They <u>smell</u>!

PP = the voluntary use of the nose
Mom<u>'s smelling</u> the milk because she thinks it's spoiled.

taste: SP = how food or drink is perceived
This soup <u>tastes</u> wonderful!

PP = the voluntary use of the taste buds; test or check for taste
The chef<u>'s tasting</u> the soup for seasoning.

Remember that most sensory verbs have a difference in meaning and usage depending on whether they're voluntary or involuntary actions. **Make it a point to stress to your students that the form used depends on whether these verbs are voluntary or involuntary actions.**

fit: SP = harmonize; conform
Her current project <u>fits</u> the company's immediate goals.
Your qualifications <u>fit</u> what we're looking for.

SP = able to be put into or on a certain area without difficulty
<u>Does</u> that carry-on bag <u>fit</u> in the overhead compartment?
I love this new shirt. Look how well it <u>fits</u>.

PP = put something into a certain area without difficulty
I won't need two boxes. I<u>'m fitting</u> it all into this one.

have: SP = possess, own
The Kims <u>have</u> a lovely house.

SP = be sick
Carla <u>has</u> the flu.

PP = a situation that the subject is involved in
Peter<u>'s having</u> trouble with his car again.
We<u>'re having</u> a party. Come over right now!

involving food or drink
Hello, Helen? We're at Robb's Grill. We're <u>having</u> lunch.
I<u>'m having</u> tea. Would you like some?

think: SP = believe
Let's postpone the picnic. I <u>think</u> it's going to rain.

PP = (sometimes with prepositions *of* or *about*) = use the mind;
imagine; consider
Be quiet for a moment. I<u>'m thinking</u>.
<u>Are</u> you <u>thinking</u> of what to serve at the party?
Gus <u>is thinking</u> of moving to Canada.
What's he <u>thinking</u> about?

wish: SP = communicate unhappiness with a situation;
tell people what you would like for them
Philip <u>wishes</u> he earned more money.
We <u>wish</u> you long life and happiness!

PP = (with preposition "for") express a hope for something
Now that I've blown out the candles on my birthday cake, I<u>'m</u>
<u>wishing</u> for another great year like the one I just had!

At this point, let's see if you can distinguish the differences in meaning between the following pairs of sentences:

1a. Did you know that Ken's grandparents are living with him?
1b. Did you know that Ken's grandparents live with him?

2a. Harriet's writing an article for the *New York Times*.
2b. Harriet writes articles for the *New York Times*.

3a. Faisal's being a brat.
3b. Faisal's a brat.

Here's how it goes: in **Sentence 1a**, the idea is that Ken's grandparents are with him **temporarily** and that the situation is taking place now. Perhaps they had a fire in their home or their own home is being remodeled. Whatever the case may be, it's a temporary situation. In **Sentence 1b**, however, Ken's house is their **permanent** residence because no specific time is mentioned.

The next two sentences work along similar lines. In **Sentence 2a**, Harriet is probably a freelance writer who's just writing this one article for the newspaper at the present time, and it's safe to assume it's a **temporary** assignment. In **Sentence 2b**, Harriet seems to be a **regular** contributor to the paper.

The last two sentences follow suit. Some people might consider the use of *be* in **Sentence 3a** idiomatic. That doesn't change the basic meaning, which is a **temporary** situation. The speaker is communicating that Faisal isn't always a brat; he's acting this way just today or just right now. In **Sentence 3b**, however, it's clear that Faisal is a brat **all the time**; this is his personality. And that insight leads us to a rule that we can remember about the verb *be*: **we can use the verb *be* in the present progressive to describe temporary states of personality as opposed to how someone behaves all the time.** Two more examples follow:

> Don't mind him. He's being petty.
> Why are you being so stubborn?

A Special Note About the Word "Always"

In traditional grammar books, *always* always appears with the simple present. That, of course, is reasonable since one of the key meanings of simple present is "all the time." Language, however, isn't always reasonable or logical.

A case in point is the very common use of joining up *always* with the present progressive: "She's always making fun of my dog, Butch!" The best explanation for this phenomenon is that **we use *always* with the present progressive to emphasize the habitual, unrelenting nature of an action.** The person who adds *always* to a progressive form is usually expressing a feeling of annoyance or irritation. This usage has become so widespread that it must be considered an acceptable alternative to using the simple present. By the way, *forever* and *constantly* can work the same way here as *always*:

> They're forever repairing the house.
> He's constantly doodling during our meetings.

 ### The Simple Present in a Nutshell

- **the real present (only for a select group of verbs):**
  I hear you.
- **general, timeless facts:**
  She cooks very well.
- **habitual, routine actions:**
  We spend every summer at the beach.
- **narrative style:**
  " . . . and runner number 3 wins the marathon!"
  "So when I tell her she's won the contest, she kisses me on the cheek and jumps up and down for joy!"

✍ The Present Perfect

auxiliary HAVE + Past Participle of verb

I, you, we, they **have** work**ed**

he, she, it **has** work**ed**

Many an English language teacher has wished that the present perfect would just disappear overnight from the language, probably because it contains many subtleties and nuances. If you take each use one by one, you can manage to do a good, clear, concise job of teaching this complex form.

Present Perfect as a Bridge from Past to General Present

Read these sentences and answer the questions.

1. Rolf lived in Budapest for many years.
   Does Rolf live in Budapest now?   yes ☐   no ☐

2. Rolf has lived in Budapest for many years.
   Does Rolf live in Budapest now?   yes ☐   no ☐

The answer to **Sentence 1** is **no**. We're clearly given to believe that Rolf either moved away from Budapest some time ago or he's now deceased. The answer to **Sentence 2** is **yes**. We know for a fact (from the grammatical form) that Rolf still lives in Budapest. He moved there many years ago and he's still there.

There's one other point to mention here. The present perfect can be used for an action that's been uninterrupted since it began in the past: "Rolf has lived in Budapest for many years" is an example of an uninterrupted action. Compare it to this sentence: "Maria has visited Budapest many times." Maria has made many visits to the city and each one of them was completed in the past. You'll learn why we use present perfect in this case as you read further.

We know the answers to these two questions because we understand the use of the simple past versus the present perfect: with the simple past, the action is completely finished in the past; with the present perfect, **the action began in the past and comes to an indefinite time in the general present**. Here's a dialogue that will demonstrate this use more fully:

A: I **haven't had** a hot meal in a
    long time.

B: That's because you**'ve been** too
    busy to cook one.

A: And nobody**'s invited** me to
    dinner either.

B: You poor thing! Come over to
    my house tonight.

Present Perfect as a Foot
in the Door to the Future

Read each of the following sentences and answer the questions.

1. My grandfather traveled from Europe to Africa many times.

    Is Grandfather alive or dead?   alive ☐   dead ☐   don't know ☐

    Do you think he'll take the trip again?   yes ☐   no ☐   maybe ☐

2. My grandfather has traveled from Europe to Africa many times.

    Is Grandfather alive or dead?   alive ☐   dead ☐   don't know ☐

    Do you think he'll take the trip again?   yes ☐   no ☐   maybe ☐

It's really amazing how the change in a verb form can create such subtle but important differences. Let's see how you did with the questions. In **Sentence 1**, which uses "traveled," most people would guess that Grandfather's **dead**, although others would be justified in saying that they don't honestly know. As for whether or not Grandfather will take the trip again, most people would check **no** because the simple past means that the action is completely finished in the past and cannot recur.

In **Sentence 2**, which uses the present perfect, most people would guess that Grandfather's still **alive**, and as for whether or not he'll take the trip again, they would check **yes** or **maybe**. Quite a difference from the answers to the first two questions! Coming up is the explanation that will make it all clear.

Why should the sets of answers be so different? The reason lies in this second important meaning of the present perfect, that the action happened in the past **and may happen again at some point in the future.** In other words, we're leaving the door open a little in case the event should happen again; we're not shutting the door forever on Grandfather's taking another trip to Africa. The simple past communicates the idea that an action is completely finished in the past and has no real connection to the present, much less the future. This is where the simple past and the present perfect differ so greatly. Let's look at another sample dialogue to see this in action.

> A: **Did** you **watch** TV last night?
> B: No, I **didn't**.
> A: Then you **haven't seen** that new show.
> B: No, I **haven't**, darn it!
> A: Don't worry. It'll be on every week.

✳ *Troubleshooter* ✳

You may have students who speak French. If that's the case, they will probably confuse the English present perfect with a form of the simple past in French known as the "passé composé," which also uses the auxiliary *have* + the past participle of the verb. They will invariably think that the present perfect means the simple past and end up using it in sentences with words like *ago*. Anticipating this problem may save you a lot of grief!

Present Perfect as a Recent Event or an Event from the Past that Affects the Present

Once again, read these sentences and answer the questions.

1. Brendan and Maureen got engaged.
   When did Maureen accept Brendan's proposal?

   some time ago ☐   recently ☐   don't know ☐

2. Brendan and Maureen have gotten engaged.
   When did Maureen accept Brendan's proposal?

   some time ago ☐   recently ☐   don't know ☐

The answer to **Sentence 1** is **some time ago** or **don't know**. We know it took place in the past, but it could have been a hundred years ago or two days ago for all we know. It's vague and leaves us guessing about the time in the past unless we have additional information. The answer to **Sentence 2**, however, is **recently**. We know because the present perfect was used. We still don't know the exact time in the past, but we certainly understand that the event happened so recently that friends and family are probably still excited about the news.

This is what we mean when we say that another important use of the present perfect is **it communicates that an event happened recently and still touches on, or affects, the present**. That's why Brendan's and Maureen's relatives are probably still excited.

> A: **Have** you **heard** the news?
> B: What news?
> A: Brendan's just **proposed** to Maureen!
> B: Well, **has** she **accepted**?
> A: Yes! And they**'ve** even **set** the date.

It should be mentioned that an acceptable variation in American English for this use of the present perfect is to use the simple past in situations related to the word *just*:

> A: Did you hear the news?
> B: What news?
> A: Brendan just **proposed** to Maureen!
> B: Well, **did** she **accept**?
> A: Yes! And they even **set** the date.

 The Present Perfect in a Nutshell

uninterrupted actions from the past to an indefinite time in the general present; these actions may continue into the future:
They've raised horses ever since they bought that farm.

```
past ——————————— general present ——————————— future
```

separate actions completed in the past that may occur again:
She's received several promotions since she started working there.

```
past ——————————— general present ——————————— future
```

recently completed actions that still affect the present:
Thanks for offering me part of your sandwich, but I've just eaten.

past ——————— ⊟ present ——————— future

The Present Perfect Progressive

> auxiliary HAVE BEEN + Verb + -ING
> I , you, we, they **have been** work**ing**
> he, she, it **has been** work**ing**

This form of the present perfect can be troublesome for students until they learn two facts. To begin with, there's a simple but effective rule that can be made about the present perfect and present perfect progressive: **Any verb that can be used in the simple present can be used in the present perfect, and any verb that can be used in the present progressive can be used in the present perfect progressive.** If we can say "Fiona lives," we can say "Fiona's lived"; if we can say "Fiona's living," we can say "Fiona's been living."

Don't forget about those stative verbs; some of them can't take the present progressive form, so that goes for the present perfect progressive as well. Since you can't say "Sean's knowing you," you can't say "Sean's been knowing you" either. It's as simple as that!

Now take a look at the following sets of sentences and see if you perceive a difference in meaning between them:

> 1a. Pat's worked here for three years.
> 1b. Pat's been working here for three years.
>   ☐ a difference   ☐ no difference

> 2a. We've traveled in Southeast Asia.
> 2b. We've been traveling in Southeast Asia.
>   ☐ a difference   ☐ no difference

There's really no important difference in meaning between 1a and 1b. Native speakers will use them interchangeably. **There is a difference in meaning, however, between 2a and 2b.**

These examples bring us to the second fact. In 1a and 1b, because of the nature of an action like "work," we can change the focus of our time frame and think about Pat as a permanent employee by saying "Pat works here," but we can also think about her present employment by saying "Pat's working here." Both focuses work, so we can do the same thing with the perfect forms ("Pat's worked here" / "Pat's been working here") and there's no big difference noted.

In 2a and 2b, we perceive that there's a big difference because of the kind of activity involved. In 2a, there was either one or more completed trips, so we're using present perfect to communicate that they're trips in the past and there may be a future trip as well. In 2b, we're talking about one uninterrupted trip that began at some point in the past and is still going on at this moment. In this case, the present perfect progressive is used **for an action that began in the past and is continuing up to this moment**, and not for an action that was completed in the past but may occur again.

 ### The Present Perfect Progressive in a Nutshell

uninterrupted actions from the past to an indefinite time in the general present; these actions may continue into the future:
They've been raising horses ever since they bought that farm.

past —————————————— general present —————————————— future

A Note About the Words "Since," "For," and "In"

When the perfect forms of the verbs are taught, the first words that always seem to accompany them are *since* and *for,* but few people ever consider *in*. First, let's look at some sentences containing *since* and *for*. Study these examples and determine what common elements can be found in each group of sentences and, therefore, what rules are in play to govern using *since* or *for*.

1. He's been a teacher for a long time.
   He's been a teacher for twenty-six years.
   He's been a teacher at this school for three terms.
   He's been a teacher here for just a couple of months.
   He's been a teacher here for only a little while.

2. He's been a teacher since he graduated from college.
   He's been a teacher since 1962.
   He's been a teacher since he moved to this city.
   He's been a teacher since the early '70's.

Have you figured it all out? Here's what's happening: phrases like *a long time, twenty-six years,* and *a little while* all deal with a **quantity of time**. The rule is **use *for* after the perfect forms of the verbs if you're going to talk about a quantity of time; use *since* to tell when an activity began**. (Note: "1962" is considered the name of a year, not a quantity.)

So what about *in*? Let's look at some sentences. Use both *in* and *for* in the blanks wherever possible.

1. I haven't heard from them ——————— weeks.

2. She hasn't been to work ——————— three days.

3. They've worked on the project ——————— hours and hours.

4. He hasn't seen us ——————— a long time.

5. We've been here ——————— what seems like an eternity.

Have you figured out what's going on? In **Sentences 1, 2,** and **4,** you should have written **both *for* and *in***. In **Sentences 3** and **5,** you should only have written *for*. The reason is that **if the present perfect or present perfect progressive are affirmative, you can only use *for*. If they're negative, both *for* and *in* are interchangeable**.

But what about this sentence? "Emily's gotten three promotions in the past five years." Here's a sentence that's affirmative, but we can use *in*. In fact, it would be ungrammatical to use *for*! What's going on now? We obviously have to revise our rule. How would you revise it?

———————————————————————————

———————————————————————————

The reason we use *in* in this last example is that we're dealing with separate actions completed in the past that may occur again. In our sentence, *in* really means "at some time during" or "within this time frame." In other words, Emily has gotten three promotions at some time during the past five-year period, and *in* can never mean "from five years ago to now." So our revised rule must be **if the present perfect or present perfect progressive are affirmative and uninterrupted actions, you can only use *for*. If they're negative or separate, completed actions, both *for* and** *in* **are interchangeable.** Here are a few more examples for you to look at just to make this clearer:

1. He's lived here for seven months.
   (affirmative, uninterrupted action; can only use *for*)

2. He hasn't lived here for/in seven months.
   (negative, uninterrupted action; can use *for* or *in*)

3. They've tried to quit smoking three times in two years.
   (affirmative, separate, completed actions; can only use *in*)

Note that the progressive form can't be used with *in*. Just take a look at these examples:

They've been buying a new car twice in the past five months.
The bank has been opening five new branches in six months.

Why do you think it is that *in* doesn't work? Write down your thoughts on the following lines:

_____

_____

The reason these two sentences are ungrammatical is that **the meaning of the verb form is contradicting the meaning of the sentences.** The progressive form means that the action or event is continuous, i.e., without stopping, and that goes against when we can use *in,* which can only be used in affirmative sentences with completed events.

Before we move on, there's something curious we'd like you to look at. Let's go back to one of the versions of Sentence 2 above: "He hasn't lived here for seven months." Whereas Sentences 1 and 3 only have one interpretation each, Sentence 2, using the preposition *for,* has two interpretations, depending on the context that the sentence would normally be found in in a conversation. Can you figure out the two interpretations? Write them down on the following lines:

_____

_____

We hope you smiled a little when you realized what the two interpretations are. On one hand, the sentence can mean simply that **he moved out seven months ago**

and hasn't lived here since; on the other hand, the sentence can be a rebuttal of sorts, correcting what somebody else has just said about how long he hasn't lived here:

> **A: He's lived here for seven months, I think.**
> **B: He hasn't lived here for seven months.**

Some Other Companion Words with the Present Perfect

Traditionally, the present perfect has been the verb form to use when the following words or phrases are employed: *already, yet, lately, so far,* and *up to now.* Here are some examples:

> We've already seen that movie. / We've seen that movie already.
> We haven't seen that movie yet.
> We've seen some very good movies lately.
> We've seen two movies so far this month.
> Videos haven't put movie theaters out of business up to now.

It just seems to be the case that when these words or phrases are employed, the present perfect is the verb form to use. Notice, however, that we said "traditionally" the present perfect is used with all of these words. In modern, colloquial speech, it's very common to hear the simple past used with several of these expressions:

> We already saw that movie. / We saw that movie already.
> We didn't see that movie yet.
> We saw two movies so far this month.

True, most educated speakers of English tend to feel that using the present perfect with all of these words is "better English." This use, nonetheless, is a matter of style nowadays, not hard and fast grammar.

Teaching Tips

3.1 Miming the Progressives

Write up brief situations that use the present progressive on slips of paper (e.g., you're a dentist checking the teeth of one of your patients; you're frying an egg; you're waiting for a bus to come; you're trying to cross a busy road, etc.). You need at least one slip for each student in your class. The students mime their activities individually while their classmates guess what's happening.

Variation: Provide activities that are much more complicated (tying your shoes while answering the phone; feeding a baby while trying to type a term paper; putting on make-up while eating breakfast, etc.). Again, students mime the actions while their classmates figure out what's happening. Make sure your students are aware that they must prepare their pantomimes precisely in order for their classmates to be able to understand them.

3.2 The Fashion Show

For more advanced students and those who know the vocabulary of clothing, colors, and patterns, this is an ideal activity for practicing the present progressive. Present a fashion show, complete with walking across a mock stage, pirouetting, indicating the important features of the garments, etc., just as a real model might do. Before the show begins, divide the class into small groups. Each group will prepare commentaries that will be used to describe the clothes of the various models in their groups. The commentaries need to focus on the actual items the students are wearing and the colors and patterns of the various garments. The show begins! Students model their clothes and their group members give a running commentary on the clothes that the models are wearing.

3.3 Narrating Skits

An excellent way to practice the simple present is by having students narrate skits. An added benefit of the activity is that you can recycle other grammar points. This skit recycles imperatives (commands) and possessive forms.

1. Before class, write up two or three skits using commands that, when acted out and narrated, tell a story. For this example, you have a narrator and two actors. One actor leaves the room with these commands: a) Open the door. b) Look around the room. c) Spot a friend. d) Smile at him/her. e) Enter the room. f) Take your seat.

2. Give the second actor these directions: g) Return your friend's smile. h) Wave at him/her.

3. Give the narrator all the commands in proper order and some concluding remarks: "It's 10:00 a.m. What happens then?"

4. The skit begins! While the actors are acting out their commands, the narrator describes what's going on using the simple present. "Kenji opens the classroom door and looks around. He spots his friend and smiles at her. She returns his smile and waves at him. He enters the room and takes his seat. It's 10:00 a.m. The bell rings and class begins."

5. Have the students produce their own skits in small groups.

Variations:

1. Tape bits of TV programs with the sound turned down; select programs that have action suitable for narration. But be careful; if there's too much action, students can't narrate the story fast enough. If there's too little, then there's

nothing much to tell. Have them prepare the narration to be presented along with the taped TV bits.

2. Tape a series of sound effects that have potential story lines (knocking on doors, machines running, footsteps, screams, etc.). Have students write up narratives that describe the action as it's happening to go along with the sound effects.

3. If you have a video camera, this is the perfect opportunity to use it. Let your students prepare skits with accompanying narration and then record them for presentation to the entire class. Quiz the class orally about the skits after viewing them.

3.4 Likes and Dislikes

Put a grid on the board similar to the one that follows. Use items that your students may either like or dislike. Have students go up and check the choices that are true for them and then discuss what they've checked off. Be sure that the students use the simple present.

	ice cream	poetry	movies	flowers	tennis	ballet
Rubina	✔		✔		✔	
Shaheen	✔	✔		✔		✔
Farideh	✔		✔	✔		

Variation: Students copy a blank grid on a piece of paper and go around the room filling in the information about their classmates. They then give a report about what they've found out.

3.5 Travel Guides

Give students pages from travel guides that use international symbols. Have the students write up a description of the information they've got using the simple present.

Here's a sample hotel description. We've put the symbols in parentheses to show you how they might be interpreted. Hotel Brickell is a 4-star hotel (★★★★) in downtown (🏢🏬🏛🏨) Washington, D.C. The hotel has 500 beds (🛏) and a telephone (☎) and TV (📺) in each room. The hotel has a concierge (🍸) and medical personnel (✚) available 24 hours a day . . .

3.6 *What Is It?*

Before class, write up a list of animals, professions, or things for students to describe using the simple present. If your students have research skills, give them topics that they don't know much about or that they don't know at all (planets, famous people, etc.). Example: *Horse:* it runs fast; it has a mane; it loves apples; it often lives in a barn. *Farmer:* he grows crops; he plants seeds; he milks cows.

3.7 *Proverbs*

If you choose to recycle this grammar with an intermediate or advanced group, bring in some examples of proverbs: A stitch in time saves nine; Familiarity breeds contempt; Absence makes the heart grow fonder, etc. Discuss the meaning of those that the students aren't familiar with and then have them provide examples from their own languages. Stress the fact that you want only those proverbs that contain the simple present.

3.8 *Body Spelling*

The present perfect provides an additional problem for students—the past participles, especially those for the irregular verbs. It's fun to practice these forms by doing "Body Spelling." Prepare a list of irregular verbs before class begins. Divide the class into groups of seven to eight. You may need to make the groups larger if the verbs that you're using have more than eight letters (such as *forgotten, understood*). And if you have verbs that have fewer letters than the groups have members, two or more students can "become" one letter. Distribute several verbs to each group. The students then have to spell the past participles using their bodies as the letters and their classmates have to figure out what they're spelling. *Body Spelling* is an enjoyable way to practice present participles, too.

3.9 *Ouch!*

Pass out various short exclamations to students. Students will read their exclamations out loud, using appropriate intonation, and add explanatory statements to clarify the reason for their exclamations. Here are some exclamations to distribute to the students:

Oh my gosh!	Ouch!	Stop it!	So?	Rats!	Do it again!
No, thanks.	Oh, no!	No way!	Why?	Ahhh!	Why not?
Good luck!	Yes!	Bye-bye!	Yes?	Damn!	Congratulations!
Fantastic!	Sorry!	Please?	What?	Wow!	Please!

These are the kinds of responses that you might expect students to produce: "Oh, my gosh! I've just swallowed something strange!" / "Ouch! I've just stuck myself with this pin." / "Congratulations! You've just passed your driving test." / "Ahhh! I've never tasted anything so good!"

3.10 Analyzing the News

Because the present perfect is a difficult verb form for most students, it may be helpful for them to be able to analyze how native English speakers use the various forms in actual speech. This activity gets them thinking about these difficulties. Record bits of TV or radio news reports before class. Or, if you prefer, collect items from newspapers or magazines. Note instances of the present perfect. Present the tape or clippings to the students and have them write down some examples of the present perfect forms that they hear or find. Have them analyze why present perfect was used.

Variation: After the students have done their initial analyses, have them write their own news stories, record them, and then play them for the entire class. Even if a tape recorder or video recorder isn't available, the students can still present their stories to the class.

4

The Pasts

"What's done is done."

The Simple Past

A: I call**ed** you on the phone, like a hundred times last night!

B: Really? Well, I **was**n't home.

A: I figur**ed** that out by myself.

B: So, why all the calls?

A: I **made** those calls to try out my brand new cell phone. My wife **bought** it for me.

B: You tri**ed** somebody else then, **did**n't you?

A: No. The battery **went** dead after all those calls to you.

First Meaning

The parts in bold in this dialogue show us that the time is in the past, the simple past. It's called the "simple" past because we have a verb form that's relatively uncomplicated to make and use.

There are three meanings implied by using the simple past. The first one is shown above with examples of regular verbs *(called / figured / tried)* and irregular verbs *(was / made / bought / did / went)*. What simple description for this meaning can you come up with? Think about the verbs in the dialogue and then write down how you'd define the simple past on the line below:

_____

What we see in the dialogue are examples of **actions that happened before now** and **a state of being that existed before now, and both are finished**; this is our first meaning of the simple past. Keep in mind that the verbs in the simple past in the dialogue have no connection with the present and are like a closed door. Compare this concept to the discussion we had in Chapter 3 about how verbs in the present perfect can keep that door open.

〰 *Troubleshooter* 〰

Students always have a hard time dealing with the pronunciation of the regular verbs in the simple past form with the suffix *-ed* or *-d*. Here are the three phonological rules that you can teach them:

☞ If the verb ends in a voiced consonant *sound** except for /d/ (b, g, j, l, m, n, ŋ, r, v, z, ð) or in a vowel sound, the *-ed* suffix is simply pronounced /d/:

/rab/ → /rabd/,   /pil/ → /pild/,   /sno/ → /snod/

☞ If the verb ends in a voiceless consonant *sound* except for /t/ (f, k, p, š, č, s) the *-ed* suffix is simply pronounced /t/:

/pik/ → /pikt/,   /hæč/ → /hæčt/

☞ If the verb ends in /d/ or /t/, the *-ed* suffix is pronounced /ɪd/ or /ɛd/:

/bred/ → /bred-ɪd/,   /ri-spɛkt/ → /ri-spɛkt-ɪd/

*Note: We're talking about sounds, not letters. Be careful that your students don't look at the final letter of the verb; they have to think about the final sound.

Second Meaning

There's another meaning for the simple past in the opening dialogue that isn't so apparent. Maybe you can figure it out by looking at this next example. Compare the alternative responses that Person B could say at the end of the dialogue and see if you perceive a difference.

> A: I hear you **had** some excitement outside your house last night.
> B: I'll say! I **got** into a fight with my neighbor.
> A: Why? What **happened**?
> B: He **hit** his dog. / He **was hitting** his dog. I really hate that.

Ask yourself which one of Person B's options would make it clearer as to why he got into that fight. When you've answered that question, you'll probably have figured out what the difference between the two verb forms is. Write your conclusions on the following lines:

_____

_____

It turns out that Person B's saying "He was hitting his dog" seems to explain more clearly why the fight took place; with the response "He hit his dog," it just doesn't seem as much of a justification for a fight between neighbors. Why is this so? It's because Person B's response in the simple past *(hit)* leaves us with the impression that he only hit the dog *once* if no further information is supplied; the verb form *was hitting* makes us think that he did this many times—but more about that later on in this chapter.

So here we have the second meaning for the simple past that isn't so apparent: **the simple past can mean that the action happened only one time**.

Don't think we've forgotten about that third meaning for the simple past. We're going to put it on hold for a little while.

The Simple Past in a Nutshell

actions finished in the past (without further context, implying one time only):

I called you like a hundred times last night!

I sent the letter.

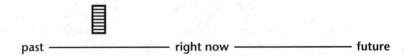

past —————————— right now —————————— future

The Past Progressive

> auxiliary BE + VERB + ING
> I, he, she, it **was** work**ing**
> we, you, they **were** work**ing**

First Meaning

We're going to talk about three meanings that the past progressive connotes, but to start off our investigation into this form, let's look at the following dialogue.

A: What **were** you do**ing**?

B: Doing? When?

A: Last night around 11.

B: Oh! I **was rummaging** through the trash cans outside my house.

A: I know that! But why?

B: I **was looking** for my watch. My little boy thought the trash can was a big jewelry box!

All the verbs in bold are in the past progressive. There's something very subtle, but very useful, that this form is imparting to the verbs, and there's a good reason that the speakers have chosen this form over any other.

All the actions in bold have really been caught at the moment they were happening. Let's see how you perceive this form as it appears in the dialogue. Read the following statements about the verbs from this dialogue and check the boxes in front of the statements that you agree with.

- ☐ 1. The verbs in bold tell us when they began.
- ☐ 2. The verbs don't tell us when they began.
- ☐ 3. The verbs tell us when they ended.
- ☐ 4. They don't tell us when they ended.
- ☐ 5. These actions are finished.
- ☐ 6. These actions were in progress.

Because of the way these verbs appear in the context of the dialogue, the boxes to check are **2**, **4**, and **6**, and this conclusion leads us to our first observation about this verb form: **We use the past progressive when the actions were in progress and**

there's no focus on any definite beginning or end. It's the activity in progress that counts, nothing else.

⚡ Troubleshooter ⚡

Students often think that we transfer a verb from the present to the past in the following way:

simple present ⟶ simple past

he writes ⟶ *he wrote*

present progressive ⟶ past progressive

he's writing ⟶ *he was writing*

Anticipate this confusion and be prepared to show them that it isn't as simple as that. Don't let yourself or your students fall into this linguistic trap!

Second Meaning

Now let's look at a conversation between a police officer and a motorist.

A: I **wasn't doing** anything, Officer!

B: You **were speeding**.

A: It's just that I **was hurrying** to City Hall.

B: And why **were** you **rushing** there?

A: To pay some overdue speeding tickets.

The easiest way to begin examining this verb form as it appears in this conversation is to ask the question: If we change the verbs in bold to the simple past, will the conversation work?

"I <u>didn't do</u> anything, Officer!"

"You <u>sped</u>."

"It's just that I <u>hurried</u> to City Hall."

"And why <u>did</u> you <u>rush</u> there?"

"To pay some overdue speeding tickets!"

It doesn't completely work, you say? You're right, it doesn't. But why not? What difference is there between using the past progressive in the dialogue and using the simple past? Take a few moments to compare each verb as it appears in both versions of the dialogue. Decide whether they're grammatical in this context and then write down any thoughts you may have about why one form works and the other doesn't, if you've found that to be the case.

(wasn't doing) _____

(didn't do) _____

(were speeding) _____

(sped) _____

(was hurrying) _____

(hurried) _____

The most important reason that the **past progressive** seems to work better for most of these verbs is that there are **implied, but unspoken, ideas** in each utterance. For example, when the motorist says "I wasn't doing anything," the unspoken idea might be " . . . when you pulled me over." Can you supply other implied ideas for the following lines from the dialogue?

1. "You were speeding _____."

2. "I was hurrying to City Hall _____."

Here are some possibilities for filling in the implied idea for **Sentence 1: . . . when I stopped you / . . . when I spotted you / . . . when I pulled you over.**

Some options for **Sentence 2** are these: . . . **when you made me stop / . . . when you caught me / . . . when you pulled me over.**

Let's digress just for a moment and talk about the meaning of a couple of the sentences in this dialogue when the simple past is used. How about the lines "You sped" and " . . . I hurried to City Hall?" Why do you think we're uncomfortable with the simple past in these sentences in the context of this dialogue? Can you figure out the reason?

If you recall what we said earlier about the first meaning of the simple past, it was that *the action is completely finished.* Let's test out the two lines we've cited and add implied ideas to see if they work.

"You <u>sped</u> *when I spotted you.*"
"It's just that I <u>hurried</u> to City Hall *when you saw me.*"

What do these sentences really say now? Check the box that precedes the description you agree with.

Both sentences mean that

☐ one action was in progress when the other happened.

☐ the first actions were the results of the second actions.

The truth is that if both verbs in each sentence are in the simple past, we get the feeling that we're dealing with cause and effect. In other words, the motorist only began to speed when the police officer spotted him, and he hurried to City Hall only when the officer saw him, so we should check the **second box**. These verbs in the simple past might work in a different context, but they're not the ideas we're trying to convey in this instance.

To compound the confusion, if the motorist says that he . . . *hurried to City Hall,* it gives us the impression that he'd already reached City Hall before he spoke to the police officer, so how could he be sitting out there on the side of the road talking to him? There's no logic in this situation.

The all-important reason for using the past progressive with these verbs is to show that the actions were *not* finished **and that they were interrupted by some other actions**. That's why these two sentences won't work in the simple past. You may have heard this verb form referred to as the "past continuous," but we prefer to call it "past progressive" to reinforce the idea that the action was still *in progress.*

Let's go over some basic points about the past progressive before we go on to anything else. Look at the following sentences and focus on the underlined verb forms. Write **G** in the space provided if the verb is grammatical or **U** if it's ungrammatical.

1. A: What <u>were</u> you <u>doing</u> when I called you last night?   _____

   B: I <u>slept</u>.   _____

2. A: What <u>did</u> you <u>do</u> when the fire alarm went off?   _____

   B: I <u>was leading</u> my frightened students out of the building.   _____

3. A: I <u>was hearing</u> that you were sick last week.   _____

   B: I <u>was having</u> a terrible cold.   _____

4. A: That boy's a brat. He <u>yanked</u> that little girl's hair.   _____

   B: It's awful that he <u>was yanking</u> her hair!   _____

Let's check your perceptions of these verb forms in the context we've put them: **1A** is **G** but **1B** is **U**; **2A** is **G** but **2B** is **U**; **3A** and **3B** are both **U**; **4A** is **G**, but **4B** is **U**.

Sentence 1B is **ungrammatical**. Remember that the past progressive is used to show that the action was in progress and was interrupted. The simple past doesn't communicate that the speaker was already in the midst of sleeping at the moment that the phone rang. The sentence should read "I <u>was sleeping</u>."

Sentence 2B is **ungrammatical** for exactly the opposite reason: it communicates that the speaker was in the midst of leading his frightened students out of the building, but he wouldn't have been doing so before the alarm went off. The sentence should be "I <u>led</u> my frightened students out of the building." Using the simple past here shows cause and effect, which is logical in this case, and it also shows that the action was completed.

Sentence 3A is **ungrammatical** because *hear* is one of those sensory, stative verbs we talked about in Chapter 3 that normally doesn't take the progressive form. The sentence should read "I <u>heard</u> that you were sick last week."

Sentence 3B is **ungrammatical** for a similar reason; the verb *have* is only used in the simple form when referring to illness, so the sentence should be "I <u>had</u> a terrible cold."

Sentence 4B is **ungrammatical** in the context of this dialogue. "He <u>yanked</u> that girl's hair" suggests that he did it one time. "He <u>was yanking</u> that girl's hair" suggests many times and, if the second speaker is reiterating what the first speaker said, he'll be doing so inaccurately if he uses the past progressive.

Third Meaning

What's the third meaning of the past progressive, and what third meaning can we find for the simple past (remember we put off talking about this matter earlier in the chapter)?

To find the answers, let's take another look at Sentence 1A:

> What <u>were</u> you <u>doing</u> when I <u>called</u> you last night?

We have two actions, both in the past, but there's an important difference between them. As we've previously seen, *do* (the first verb, which is in the past progressive) deals with an activity that was already happening when the other action occurred. The action *call* (the second verb, which is in the simple past) interrupts or cuts into the first action and takes but a few seconds. So, with this comparison in mind, what can we say about the *length of time* for the simple past and the past progressive? Check the box for the statement which best describes the verbs in our example:

☐ Both verbs lasted the same amount of time.

☐ The first verb *(do)* was of longer duration than the second verb *(call)*.

☐ The first verb *(do)* was of shorter duration than the second verb *(call)*.

This is the basic rule to show you if you've checked off the right box: **When two actions occur at the same time in the past, but one action is longer than the other, the longer action is put in the past progressive and the shorter action (which seems to cut into the other) is put in the simple past**. So, you should have checked off the **second** box.

Here are a few more examples to demonstrate this point:

1. We <u>were playing</u> soccer when it <u>started</u> to pour.
      (longer action)   (shorter action)

2. I <u>dozed off</u> while my aunt was <u>singing</u> some folk songs.
     (shorter action)   (longer action)

Here's an interesting question: Of the two actions in the past, what if one weren't significantly longer than the other? Look at the following examples and see for yourself. (Only one of these four sentences is ungrammatical. Can you find which one it is and then explain why it doesn't work?)

1. While I <u>was preparing</u> the salad, my son <u>was setting</u> the table.
2. While I <u>prepared</u> the salad, my son <u>set</u> the table.
3. When the car <u>backfired</u>, I <u>jumped</u> out of my seat.
4. When the car <u>was backfiring</u>, I <u>was jumping</u> out of my seat.

Sentence _____ is ungrammatical because _____

_____ .

Sentences 1 and 2 are really quite interesting. They use different verb forms and yet both seem grammatical. The reason is that **when the two actions are relatively long and of more or less the same duration, they can both be placed in the same verb form,** and in the case of these two sentences, it doesn't much matter if they're both in the past progressive or simple past; they still communicate that the two people began their tasks more or less at the same time and completed those tasks also at about the same time.

Well, if those two sentences are grammatical, that only leaves us with Sentence 3 or 4 to be the ungrammatical one. The answer is that **Sentence 4 is ungrammatical**. Reason? It goes back to the concept we mentioned before about the simple past representing short actions. How long does it take for a car to backfire? How long does it take to jump out of one's seat? The answer to both questions is "no time at all," or shall we say, only a second at most. If we try to use the **past progressive** for this kind of action, it **seems odd because we're using a form that normally represents long duration for two actions having almost no duration at all.** So the correct sentence should be "When the car backfired, I jumped out of my seat."

The Past Progressive in a Nutshell

actions that are unfinished, in progress in the past, which don't focus on any beginning or end:
Pardon me, but I wasn't talking to you.

when two actions are at the same time in the past, but one action is longer than the other:
She caught up on her correspondence while she was recuperating.

```
              caught up
                        was recuperating


past ————————————————— right now ———————————— future
```

A Special Note About the Words "When" and "While"

In most standard grammar books, the following sort of statement is made about how to use *when* and *while*:

> Use *when* with the clause in the simple past.
> Use *while* with the clause in the past progressive.

So according to this rule, we should always say:

"When he lived in London . . ." and "While he was driving to work . . ."

That's all well and good, but it really doesn't completely reflect the way native speakers use these words. It should be mentioned here that there seems to be a great deal of overlap between the two words, and you could very likely hear people say

"While I lived in London . . ." or "When I was driving to work . . ."

What, then, accounts for this switch-over? Look at the following and check off the boxes for those sentences which you feel are *ungrammatical*. Leave the verbs alone; they're fine just the way they are. Focus on *when* and *while* and consider whether they both work in the sentences. Then see if you can figure out why some of these sentences don't work, but the others do.

☐ 1a. While he fell, he hurt his knee.

☐ 1b. When he fell, he hurt his knee.

☐ 2a. When I was watching TV, I fell asleep.

☐ 2b. While I was watching TV, I fell asleep.

☐ 3a. While she left the house, she forgot to lock the door.

☐ 3b. When she left the house, she forgot to lock the door.

☐ 4a. While the dog was napping, the cat stole his bone.

☐ 4b. When the dog was napping, the cat stole his bone.

First, let's see which boxes are ungrammatical. You should only have checked off **1a** and **3a**. Now take a moment to think about why only those two sentences don't work (considering the use of *while* and *when*) and write your conclusion on the line that follows:

_____

The reason those two sentences don't work with *while* is that the verbs following are not of long enough duration to warrant the use of this word. Remember that **while is normally used with verbs of relatively long duration**, and we're fairly consistent about when it is or isn't appropriate to use.

So now we have to find a reason that explains why *when* works in the rest of those sentences. It's simply that *when* is more loosely rule-governed than *while*. In prescriptive grammar books, the student is led to believe that *when* should be as strictly regulated as *while*, but that's misleading. The truth is that **native English speakers don't consider it a cardinal sin to use *when* in place of *while***.

The Past Perfect

> I, you, he, she, it, we, they **had worked**

Here are some sentences for you to examine. If they're grammatical, write **G** on the line following each one; if they're ungrammatical, write **U** on the line after each one.

1. When I met Carlos, he lived next door for only a short time. _____

2. The company went bankrupt because they didn't show a profit for over two years. _____

3. Mintsu admitted that she didn't like cooking very much. _____

4. As I reached the corner, the light turned red. _____

5. Tom couldn't write because he broke his thumb. _____

The sentences are as follows: **1** is **U**; **2** is **U**; **3** is **G**; **4** is **G**; **5** is **U**. If we correct the three ungrammatical sentences, this is how they should look:

1. When I met Carlos, he <u>had lived</u> next door for only a short time.
2. The company went bankrupt because they <u>hadn't shown</u> a profit for over two years.
5. Tom couldn't write because he <u>had broken</u> his thumb.

Why should we use the past perfect in these three sentences and not the other two? What difference in time do you perceive between the two verbs used in Sentences 1, 2, and 5 and in Sentences 3 and 4? Take a moment and write down your impressions on the following lines:

In Sentences 1, 2, and 5 _____

_____ .

However, in Sentences 3 and 4 _____

_____ .

Notice that **Sentences 3 and 4** have both verbs in the simple past *(admitted/didn't like; reached/turned)*. That's because the two verbs in each sentence take place during the same period in the past. In Sentence 3, when Mintsu made the admission, her feelings about cooking were concurrent. In Sentence 4, both verbs happened at approximately the same moment. It makes sense grammatically that **both verbs in each sentence should be placed in the same form to show that they were basically concurrent.**

On the other hand, **Sentences 1, 2, and 5** have verbs that didn't take place at the same time in the past, and that's the reason we should use the past perfect. **If two or more verbs in the past didn't happen at more or less the same time, you need the past perfect for one of them.**

But now the question arises, which verb should be in the past perfect? What would you say? Look back at those sentences and write down your answer to the question.

We should use the past perfect _____

_____ .

In Sentence 1, Carlos moved in next door first and the speaker met him some time later. In Sentence 2, profits didn't exist for the company for two years prior to their declaring bankruptcy. In Sentence 5, Tom first did the damage to his thumb and, as a result of the mishap, he couldn't write. We can clearly see that the two verbs in each of these sentences can't be put into the same period of time. Now we can answer the question about which verb should be in the past perfect: **When two or more verbs are in the past, but they didn't happen at the same time, the verb that happened <u>first</u> is put in the past perfect**.

But does this sequence always indicate the case? Do we have a hard-and-fast rule to go by? Not necessarily. There are many cases in which the past perfect is avoidable, especially in informal or conversational speech. One example occurs when we use time words that clearly set up the chronology for us so that there's no confusion over the sequence of events. Look at the following sentences which demonstrate this concept:

1. <u>Before</u> he got home, he stopped at a grocery store to buy some bread.
2. I lay down on the couch to take a nap <u>after</u> I had lunch.
3. <u>As soon as</u> they reached the beach, they dived into the water.

As you can see, there's no confusion about the chronological order of the actions in these three sentences. Conservative speakers would say that the past perfect should still be used in these sentences, but in informal or conversational English, it really isn't necessary. Impress upon your students, however, that in formal usage (especially like that found on tests such as the TOEFL and the Cambridge University Test of English), they should always use the past perfect where appropriate.

 ## *The Past Perfect in a Nutshell*

two or more actions happening at different times in the past, this form for the verb that happened first (further back in the past):
I hadn't known her age until she told me.

The Past Perfect Progressive

I, you, he, she, it, we, they **had been** working

You'll recall that one of the distinctions we made in Chapter 3 between the present perfect and the present perfect progressive was that the present perfect starts in the past and continues to the *general* present rather than to one specific moment (or right now). The progressive form is more *pinpointed* since it comes up to the primary sense of "now."

This same basic principle holds true with the past perfect progressive. Let's see how this works by having you look at some pairs of sentences. Decide whether using the past perfect or past perfect progressive makes any noticeable difference.

1a. He'd worked here for twenty-five years when he retired.
1b. He'd been working here for twenty-five years when he retired.

☐ a difference   ☐ no difference

2a. She told me she'd written some letters.
2b. She told me she'd been writing some letters.

☐ a difference   ☐ no difference

There's really no perceived difference between Sentences 1a and 1b, but there certainly **is a difference between 2a and 2b**. Sentence 2a communicates that her letter-writing activities were completed by the time she talked to me. In 2b, we understand that she began the letter writing sometime before she talked to me or that she wasn't finished. It could also mean that my talking to her interrupted her letter writing.

What rule, then, can we come up with to explain the use of the past perfect progressive? Simply put, **with certain types of activities, the past perfect progressive does what its name implies: it shows that the activity was still in progress from some earlier time in the past when another past action happened.**

 The Past Perfect Progressive in a Nutshell

showing that one action began earlier in the past than other actions, but instead of being completely finished before the other actions happened, it overlapped onto them

They said they had been waiting for over an hour (when the train finally arrived).

✍️ The Expressions *Used To* and *Would*

Used To

Read this sentence and interpret what it means to you without any further context offered. Check off the descriptions of this sentence that you agree with.

I got up at 6:00 a.m.

- ☐ 1. The action is in the past and finished.
- ☐ 2. The action is in the past, but not finished.
- ☐ 3. This action happened repeatedly.
- ☐ 4. This action happened one time only.
- ☐ 5. I'm not sure how many times the action happened.

What information is given to us in this sentence and how should we go about interpreting it? We know that the simple past has been used, meaning that the action is completely finished, so we should check the **first box**.

What we're uncomfortable with, lacking more context, is whether or not this happened one time or repeatedly. We might assume that it happened only once, but we just don't have enough information to be certain, so we should check off the **fifth box**.

Suppose we want to embellish our idea. How can we get more information into our sentence? The answer is that we can do so very efficiently by adding *used to*, which is often considered a semi-auxiliary or periphrastic modal, after the subject:

I <u>used to</u> get up at 6:00 a.m.

This little phrase adds important extra information to our basic idea. What further information can you interpret from this addition which has two extra pieces of information added to our basic idea? List whatever comes to mind on the following lines:

1. _____

2. _____

The first additional piece of information is that the action we're discussing **occurred repeatedly over a rather long span of time**. The second extra detail is that **we assume this action isn't so today**. We've now included an implied meaning, just as we did with the past progressive. Here's how the sentence might look if we include the implied idea:

I used to get up at 6:00 a.m., <u>but I don't anymore</u>.

The negative form of *used to* is quite interesting. We can form the standard negative and say *didn't use to*, but many native speakers tend to use the adverb of frequency *never* and create the negative by saying *never used to*. Remember that we can often assume that the contrary is true for the present, just as it is in the affirmative:

She never used to like spinach, <u>but now she does</u>.

We should mention that the British have another negative form, *used not to (usedn't to)*, but it's not very commonly heard these days:

She <u>used not to</u> like spinach, but now she does.

☀ *Troubleshooter* ☀

Students almost invariably confuse *used to* with the expression *be used to*. Be aware that this problem will surely arise. Whenever it's appropriate to do so, point out that the grammar involved with these two expressions is quite different:

☞ *be used to* needs the verb *be*, and any verb that follows the expression has *-ing* attached to it:
> They*'re* used to hav*ing* dinner by 7:00 p.m.
> (It's their custom, their habit.)

☞ *used to* never has *be*, and the verb after this expression is always in the base form:
> They used to have dinner by 7:00 p.m.
> (They don't anymore.)

 "Used To" in a Nutshell

🥜 **state of being existed or action happened repeatedly over a relatively long span of time in the past with implied idea that the situation isn't so any longer:**
The Sahara Desert used to be a fertile, lush area.

🥜 **something didn't exist or happen before, but now it does:**
There never used to be any holes in the ozone layer.

Would

There's a fine point of distinction between *used to* and *would* in discussing events of the past. Remember that one of the meanings of *used to* is that the activity or state of being took place over a relatively long period of time. Now let's see if you discern any difference between the following sentences. Check the boxes for the statements you agree with.

1. I <u>used to</u> play chess with my roommate.
2. I <u>would</u> play chess with my roommate.
   - ☐ Both sentences can stand alone.
   - ☐ Sentence 1 offers more information than Sentence 2.
   - ☐ Sentence 2 offers more information than Sentence 1.

Most native speakers would only check off the **second box**. The reason is that only Sentence 1 can stand alone; it doesn't need anything added to be a complete idea because we have enough information in the expression *used to* to feel comfortable with it.

Sentence 2 doesn't supply us with enough information and creates some sort of gap in our understanding of the idea. What if we add some more information? Let's try it:

<u>When I was in college</u>, I would play chess with my roommate.

Suddenly it works! That extra information about when this chess-playing happened has now made the sentence a more complete idea. What if we were to substitute *would* with *used to*? The sentence would now read:

<u>When I was in college</u>, I used to play chess with my roommate.

Is there any major difference between the two sentences now? No, not really. The commonality between *used to* and *would* is that we understand they both took place over a rather long period of time in the past, but the sentence that contains *would* seems to suggest that this was traditional, something done routinely, and there's a tie-in with another activity, namely, being in college. We should keep in mind that the addition of the word *would* is really superfluous—even redundant—because most everyone can arrive at the same interpretation with just the use of the simple past; the clause "When I was in college . . . " prepares us for this meaning. So it is in general with the word *would*. There's really no need for it; we use it simply for reinforcement. The big difference between *used to* and *would* that we should keep in mind is that **used to doesn't necessarily need extra information about the time period in order to stand alone; would must have this extra information, that is, a time phrase**.

One other way we use *would* is to communicate that certain activities were in a sequence as well as parts of a routine. Look at the following passage which demonstrates this use:

During my high school years, I would get up at 6:00 a.m. I'd take a shower and wake up my little brother. After that, I'd get dressed and go to the kitchen to make my own breakfast. I wouldn't eat much, just some toast and cheese, and I'd have some coffee, too.

It's clear that the word *would* serves to reinforce the routine nature of these activities and gives us to understand that they were more or less a set pattern in this person's daily life. Would the passage convey the same feeling if the word *would* were eliminated and replaced with just the simple past? Let's take a look and see.

> During my high school years, I got up at 6:00 a.m. I took a shower and woke up my little brother. After that, I got dressed and went to the kitchen to make my own breakfast. I didn't eat much, just some toast and cheese, and I had some coffee, too.

What difference, if any, is there now that the simple past has replaced the word *would*? Most people agree that there's no real difference, but we tend to lose something by eliminating the word *would* which helps us remember that we're listening to or reading about someone's past *routine* activities. This isn't to say that we should use *would* before every single verb. On the contrary, the best plan is to use a combination of *would* and the simple past to enrich the communication.

What about *used to*? Can we apply this expression in place of *would*? Yes, we can, even though there's that slight change in focus since *used to* includes the idea that this description might not be true nowadays.

"Would" in a Nutshell

- **can be used the same way as *used to*, but doesn't necessarily imply that the contrary is true now:**
  Even as a child, I would have coffee in the morning.

- **tends to communicate that the past activities mentioned were parts of a routine and must be used with a clause that supplies additional information to place it accurately in a time frame:**
  During those long winters when I lived up north, I'd start a fire in the fireplace after waking up, and then I'd boil some water for tea.

Teaching Tips

4.1 *Family Photos*

Have the students bring photos of themselves or any pictures that mean something to them to class. Bring one yourself. You can start the activity by showing your picture and explaining why the picture is important, why the picture was taken, and what other pertinent information there is about it. Urge the students to ask questions about the pictures, being sure to focus questions, answers, and discussions in the past. Then students can take turns explaining their photos and their stories. For homework, the students can write up short passages of their photos in the past.

4.2 Who Am I?

Write the following topic and phrases on the board: Five Years Ago/My Family/My Friends/School/Holidays/My Appearance/My Hobbies and so on. Pair up the students and have them interview one another, writing down the information that they learn about their partners. Brief statements are acceptable (*Family:* lived in Canberra; bought their first home; got a new dog. *Hobbies:* sang with a choir; went swimming almost every weekend; etc.). After the pairs have collected their information, have them give oral reports (or write up reports) based on their classmates' life experiences, using the appropriate past tense forms and *used to/would*.

4.3 10,000 BC and 1500 AD

Have the students brainstorm things that they or others use, have, or do in their daily lives (electrical appliances, transportation, entertainment, clothes). Then tell the students that they're going to consider how their ancestors lived their lives in the years 10,000 BC and 1500 AD. Have the students compare their lives today with those of their ancestors. ("I use a hair dryer to dry my hair, but in 10,000 BC, my ancestors didn't even wash their hair!" / "I wash my clothes in an automatic washing machine, but my ancestors in 1500 used to wash all of theirs by hand." / "In the year 1500, my relatives wouldn't travel more than a few miles away from home because traveling was too dangerous.")

4.4 Family Trees

Provide a model of a family tree (it can be an imaginary one, one for a famous person, or even your own). Tell each student to write a letter to an artist asking him/her to draw a family tree for the student's photo album. The letter should include brief details about each family member in order for the artist to draw the tree properly. ("My grandfather was born in 1908. He married my grandmother in 1931. They had six children.") Have the students exchange letters and become the artists. When the artists finish their commissions, tell them to return their work to their clients, who will check the work for accuracy.

4.5 Intriguing Sounds

Note: This is a variation of the second variation in 3.3. Record a variety of sounds—cars beeping, a train going by, doors slamming, interesting noises (swoosh, creak, pop, etc.). Make sure you have enough sounds; eight to ten will work well. Divide the students into small groups and have them construct a story about the events that occurred, for example, "on their way home from class," incorporating a variety of the pasts and the sounds into the story line. The students then tell their stories adding in the sound effects at the appropriate moments.

Variation: Have the students record their own sound tracks to accompany a story or skit they'll write and/or act out.

4.6 Daily Schedules

Prepare a daily schedule sheet similar to the one that follows. Have the students go around the room and interview several of their classmates about what they did the previous day. After they've gotten enough information, have them give a report about what they've discovered. Make sure they use the various pasts and time words. (While Nur was taking a shower, Hassan was getting up. Carla ate breakfast at 7:00 yesterday, *etc.*).

Time	Nur	Hassan	Carla	?	?
6:00					
6:30	shower	got up			
7:00			ate		
7:30					
8:00					
8:30					
etc.					

4.7 Once Upon a Time

Start out a story "Once upon a time there lived a little girl named Suzanne and her little brother, Kevin. They were very funny children, always telling jokes and doing silly things. One day while they were walking home from school, Suzanne . . . " Have the students add on bits to the story, letting their imaginations go where they will, but making sure they keep to the story line that's being created. Every once in a while, have a student go back and retell what's gone on up to that point. That reminds the students about what's happened and helps to keep the story line from wandering.

Variation: At the end of each student's contribution, the student suggests a verb that he/she wants incorporated into the next student's bit of story.

4.8 The Scene of the Crime

Invent a crime with specific details (time, place, witnesses, etc.). Call on two students to play the suspects. Have them leave the room, inventing an alibi while outside. Tell the suspects that their alibis must be as detailed and specific as possible. While the suspects are planning their alibis, have the rest of the class prepare questions to ask the suspects. Bring the suspects back into the room *one at a time;* this way neither suspect will hear what the other one has said. After the interrogations, poll the students to decide which suspect is guilty.

4.9 I Never Did That Before!

Ask the students to write down several things that they had never done before they came to North America or before they entered high school or began learning English. The students should begin their sentences with "Before I ..., I had ..." Collect the answers and have the class arrange their seats in a circle, or in any fashion so that they can all see one another's faces. Tell the students that you're going to read some of their responses and that they should guess who wrote them. Have them write down their guesses and be sure to tell them to keep straight faces when the responses are being read, otherwise they may give themselves away. When you've read all the statements that you've chosen and the students have made their guesses, reread them and ask each person to identify him-/herself. To find out who the best detective in the class is, see who guessed right the most times.

4.10 How My Life Has Changed

Have the students write down examples of how their lives have changed in the past ten or twenty years (brief descriptions are okay). Then have them give reports on those changes, using *used to* where appropriate.

5

The Futures

"Qué será, será ..."

A: **Are** you **taking** Jacques to the airport tomorrow?

B: Yes, I **am**. His flight **leaves** at 6:15.

A: **Will** you **have** enough time to get there after work?

B: I**'m taking** off early so I **won't have to** rush.

A: **Are** you **going to** call him so he knows what time to be ready?

B: Yes. In fact, I**'m about to** call him now.

A: The traffic's awful at that time of day.

B: Don't worry. By the time I meet you for dinner tomorrow evening, I**'ll have dropped** Jacques off at the airport and he**'ll be flying** somewhere over the Atlantic!

How many ways are there to express the future in English? There are lots of them! Actually, you've just gone over most of them in the dialogue above. Let's see what kind of sleuth you are by having you identify as many of them as you can. Try to explain why they're being used in their particular sentences. (Here's a hint: There are seven different forms of the future that you need to come up with.)

1. _____

2. _____

3. _____

4. _____

5. _____

6. _____

7. _____

No doubt you recognized certain verb forms that we've already discussed at length in previous chapters, but there are some forms that appear here for the first time. Let's get into the forms that we've already dealt with in other contexts and then proceed to the new ones.

Ä̸ The Present Progressive

"<u>Are</u> you <u>taking</u> Jacques to the airport tomorrow?"

This sentence has one of the most commonly used forms to express the future in current spoken English, yet it's rarely introduced early on in most ELT grammar books as a way to express the future ... and it should be!

The reason that the speaker's asking this question in the present progressive is because he's referring to **a planned event in the near future**. We can also think of it as **something in the future that is being anticipated in the present**.

While we're on the subject of planned events in the near future, we should mention an alternative form that can mean the same thing, and it's the expression *be going to,* which we'll discuss shortly.

Ä̸ The Simple Present

"His flight <u>leaves</u> at 6:15."

It may seem strange, when you stop to think about it, that the verb form which normally represents routines should also be used to represent the future.

The question is why the speaker would choose this verb form for something in the future. What nuance is communicated this way that isn't made if other future forms are used? The answer is that **we use the simple present to represent <u>formalized, scheduled</u> future events**. In this case, it's not that Jacques' flight will leave tomorrow at 6:15 and never do so again. The airlines schedule certain flights to leave at predetermined times, and even though we're referring to Jacques' flight, which is still in the future, we're also communicating that it's a scheduled flight, not just a unique event that will happen one time only in the future and never be repeated. This is the reason the speaker has chosen the simple present. Notice the neat connection to that basic concept of the simple present: routines. Note also that without the time expression (*at 6:15*), the present tense cannot have a future meaning.

The Future with *Be Going To*

"<u>Are</u> you <u>going to</u> call him . . . ?"

The expression *be going to* has two basic uses. Our dialogue features one use, namely, **future plans** or **intentions**. In this case, instead of asking "Are you taking Jacques to the airport tomorrow?" the speaker could just as easily have asked, "<u>Are</u> you <u>going to</u> take Jacques to the airport tomorrow?" Both the present progressive and *be going to* mean the same thing here, but in other situations they're not interchangeable. We'll get back to this point and discuss *be going to* more in depth a little later.

What, then, is the other use of this expression? Look at this sentence and see if you can figure it out:

A worldwide oil shortage <u>is going to</u> be
a very big problem for future generations.

Be going to is used for _____.

If you've written **a prediction**, you've got it right.

We've now covered the two basic uses of *be going to*, but we should really discuss another category which falls into the realm of both an intention and a prediction, namely, a **threat**. Just look at these lines:

If you don't stop acting like that, you're going to be sorry!
You'd better not come in late anymore. You're going to get fired.

A Note on Pronunciation

Many teachers fail to teach the typical pronunciation of *be going to* and inadvertently have their students practice sentences with this expression in its utterly pristine state without taking into account how native speakers normally say it. Although formal speech still dictates that we pronounce each word in the expression separately and clearly, "I'm going to" /aɪm go-ɪŋ tu/, the acceptable variation in conversational English is /aɪm/ or /am gənə/ or /gɔnə/, that is, the words *going to* are pronounced as if they were written "gunnuh" or "gawnuh"—and there's nothing wrong with it!

> ### ❦ *Troubleshooter* ❦
>
> Keep in mind that there's a distinct difference in the pronunciation of *going to* in the future expression *be going to* and in the case of the common verb *go* in its progressive form.
>
> ☞ Most native speakers of American English tend to say / gənə / ("gunnuh") or / gɔnə / ("gaw-nuh") in the expression *be going to* in such sentences as *She's going to quit her job.*
>
> ☞ Most native speakers tend to say / gó-ɪn-tə / or a variation of this pronunciation when they say such sentences as *He's going to the grocery store.*

❦ The Simple Future *(Will)*

"<u>Will</u> you have enough time to get there after work?"

Why has the speaker chosen to use *will* in this question rather than some alternative form? In this case, *will* represents what is referred to as the **pure future** or **simple future**. This doesn't mean that you couldn't hear someone say, "<u>Are</u> you <u>going to</u> have enough time to get there after work?" That's a possible form, too. We could be thinking of a planned future event or even a prediction in either case.

The "pure future" concept of *will* can also deal with future **predictions**. In our introductory dialogue, one of the speakers says, "I'<u>m taking off</u> (from work) early so I <u>won't</u> have to rush." Why do you think he switches from the present progressive in the first verb to *will* with the second?

He's using the present progressive in the first verb because _____

_____.

He's using *will* with the second verb because _____.

The speaker has chosen the present progressive for the first verb because it communicates that this is his plan of action for the future. He's used *will* with the second verb to show that he's making a prediction.

Another example of using *will* to make a prediction can be found in a sentence like this one:

My car isn't working. When I turn the ignition key, it <u>won't</u> start.

Are we finished with *will*? Not by a long shot! There are more cases in which *will* has various nuances. Take a look at the following examples and see if you can categorize the way that *will* is used in each situation.

1. I'll call you tonight.   _____

2. Will you give me a hand?   _____

3. You'll be sorry you did that!   _____

4. He'll often forget the time.   _____

In the first three examples, it's clear that we're referring to things in the future even though there are differences in usage. In **Sentence 1**, the person is making **a promise**; in **Sentence 2**, someone's making **a request**; in **Sentence 3**, someone's making **a threat**.

In **Sentence 4**, however, something very different is happening. In this case, *will* doesn't carry future meaning at all; it's used here to mean what is **apt to happen** or to show **a tendency** for something to happen on a regular basis. Another example of this unusual use is in the saying "Boys will be boys," which parents might say after their sons have gotten into some sort of mischief, played too roughly, or gotten too dirty.

There's no doubt that *will* can be a very tricky word. In many ways, it's unfortunate that the word is taught exclusively as a form of the future in most ELT grammar books. What happens is that the students latch on to this word and think it can be applied to every situation in the future—and how wrong that assumption is! In fact, it's just possible that *will* is used less frequently than other forms to express the future.

Moreover, the simple fact is that forms like the present progressive, *be going to*, and *will* are sometimes interchangeable, but at other times, they aren't. Look at the following sets of sentences. Compare the sentences in each set and check off if you're comfortable that *all three are interchangeable* or if you're not so comfortable with that prospect.

1. They're meeting us at 3 o'clock.
   They're going to meet us at 3 o'clock.
   They'll meet us at 3 o'clock.
   ☐ comfortable   ☐ not comfortable

2. A: Any plans for today?
   B: I'm going to the beach.
   I'm going to go to the beach.
   I will go to the beach.
   ☐ comfortable   ☐ not comfortable

3. It's raining later tonight.
   It's going to rain later tonight.
   It will rain later tonight.

   ☐ comfortable   ☐ not comfortable

In the first set of sentences, we're comfortable that all three versions are interchangeable. The reason is that all three communicate variations of the same common futurity without many nuances getting in the way. The present progressive tells us that we're anticipating a near future event; *be going to* predicts that future event; *will* can also predict a future event. So all three variations share common features and seem all right to us.

With the two remaining sets, we're <u>not</u> comfortable with the prospect of interchanging all the variations in these three sentences. Let's look each set over and discover why we're not comfortable with it.

All three sentences in the second set are grammatical, so that's not our problem. *I'm going* and *I'm going to go* are both acceptable because they overlap in meaning: they can both represent plans for the future. *I will go*, on the other hand, is more commonly used for predictions or the pure future, so *will* just doesn't work. The sentence seems to be missing something without the idea that this is my intention or plan. Therefore, even though all three are grammatical, most native speakers would tend to use either of the first two forms, but not *will*.

✺ Troubleshooter ✺

💡 A word about *shall*: There's a certain degree of controversy over this modal auxiliary, and that probably won't end with this book.

Except in certain circumstances, *shall* is not the word of choice in American English for the pure or simple future; we let the word *will* do that job for us.

☞ In formal language, *shall* can be used to make suggestions:

> Shall we leave now?

☞ Again, in formal speech, *shall* can be used to introduce an offer:

> Shall I do that for you?

💡 Even when *shall* is used as a pure future form, it's restricted in its use with the pronouns *I* and *we*, and is rarely used with the combined phrase *you and I*.

💡 It's interesting to note that *will* is the preferred modal auxiliary in every English-speaking country and that *shall* is losing ground even in the British Isles.

In the third set, the present progressive is our culprit. We're comfortable with interchanging *It's going to rain* and *It will rain* because both have something in common: they can both be used for predictions. **The present progressive isn't used for predictions; it's used for certainties,** like the real present or future planned events.

If you remember, we said a few pages back that we weren't done with *will* by a long shot—and we're still not! Because there's so much to say about this word and its counterpart, *would*, we're going to get back to it in Chapter 8.

⚕ The Future with *Be About To*

"I'm about to call him now."

For a change, we've got something with no ambiguity and no nuances. The semi-auxiliary *be about to* has just one meaning: **the subject is on the verge of doing something**. In other words, it's the nearest that the future can be to the present.

⚕ The Future Perfect

"By the time I meet you . . . I'll have dropped Jacques off at the airport . . ."

Once again we've hit upon a verb form that leaves no ambiguity for us to wonder about. Why does the speaker use this form in our dialogue? Think about the sentence from the dialogue which we've quoted above and come up with a description of what the underlined portion means in this time frame. Write your idea on the following line:

_____

The future perfect is an odd way for us to look at the past by way of the future. **We project ourselves to some point in the future, stop, turn around, and look back at what's already in the past for us at <u>that</u> moment.** In a way, it's a form of hindsight. There are two uses of this verb form, but in short, the future perfect tells us what will already be finished by the time we arrive at a certain point in the future.

In the sentence quoted from our dialogue, the speaker is saying that at the point in the future when he meets the other person, the action of his dropping Jacques off at the airport will already be completed. This meaning represents the first use of the future perfect.

The second use has to do with something that's happening currently. When the speaker in our dialogue says he'll drop Jacques off at the airport before the two people meet that evening, he's referring to a short-term action that has its whole beginning and end in the future. But the future perfect can also refer to another time frame.

Look at the following example and see if you can come up with an explanation of what the future perfect represents in this case. Write down your thoughts on the following line:

Midori <u>will have been</u> a nurse for twenty years by the year 2015.

We can view an action or state of being at some point in the future even though it's already happening now. Midori is a nurse now; in fact, she's been a nurse since 1995. If we want to project Midori's career status into the future from the time she first became a nurse and see what her total years in the profession will be in 2015, the future perfect is our vehicle for doing so. What we're really doing is jumping from the past into the future and bypassing the present.

We do have another aspect of this verb form, **the future perfect progressive**. Let's go back to our subject, Midori, and project something else about her professional life. Let's say that Midori began working as an operating room nurse in 1998 and she has no intention of changing her specialization. If we want to project what she'll be doing in the year 2015, we can say it like this:

By 2015, Midori <u>will have been working</u> as an
operating room nurse for seventeen years.

Of course, we can also say that Midori *will have worked* as an operating room nurse for seventeen years; in other words, we can use the simple form or the progressive form of the future perfect in this idea. Remember the discussion about these two versions for the present perfect in Chapter 3? The same basic rule we applied then holds true now, too: **If a verb can be used only in the simple present, use only the simple form of the future perfect; if the verb can be used in the present progressive form, you can opt to use the progressive form in the future perfect.**

A̅ỳ̈ The Future Progressive

" . . . he<u>'ll be flying</u> somewhere over the Atlantic!"

For awhile now, we've had the good fortune to deal with a future expression *(be about to)* and a verb form (future perfect) that offered us simplicity of meaning and a respite from some of the more complicated topics that we've braved so far in this book. Well, the respite is over and we're back into the thick of grammar rules and exceptions!

First of all, we'll deal with the most common use of the future progressive, which reflects the basic concept of the present and past progressive forms. Let's go back to our original dialogue and take another look at the sentence we've quoted under the subtitle and compare it to the same sentence with the simple future form instead of the progressive form:

1. By the time I meet you for dinner tomorrow evening, Jacques <u>will be flying</u> somewhere over the Atlantic!

2. By the time I meet you for dinner tomorrow evening, Jacques <u>will fly</u> somewhere over the Atlantic!

One of these sentences is ungrammatical—any fluent speaker would sense it immediately. Explaining why one just doesn't work is another matter. What's your guess? Draw a circle around the number of the sentence you think is ungrammatical.

We're sure that you didn't hesitate at all in deciding that the ungrammatical sentence is the **second one**. But why? Think of the whole idea that the sentence conveys, especially the information supplied in the first part. Then think about the basic concept of the progressive forms which we discussed in previous chapters. Now come up with a reason that makes the future progressive work in this sentence and write your conclusion on this line:

_____

Just as its name implies, and just as is the case with the past and present progressive forms, the future progressive deals with an action that's in progress at a specific moment which we're pinpointing, this time an action in the future. The opening part of the sentence says "By the time I meet you for dinner," which means *during that period in the future when I meet you and we are having dinner.* The opening part of the sentence sets up the idea. It means that **something else will be in progress in that same time period, so we use the future progressive to show which action will be in progress at that time.**

Here's another example which clearly shows how this verb form communicates that the underlined action will be in progress at that future time we're pinpointing:

I know that Jacques <u>will be working</u> on that import/export deal we discussed when I get to see him in Paris next week.

Let's return to the sentence "By the time I meet you for dinner tomorrow evening, Jacques will be flying somewhere over the Atlantic." Now we need to discover why using the simple future form doesn't work in the context of this sentence. Think about what type of verb *fly* is. Then think about what meaning you get from this action in the isolated phrase "he will fly over the Atlantic." Now come up with an explanation to show why the simple future form is ungrammatical with this verb and in this context. Write your conclusion on these following lines:

Because *fly* is an action, or dynamic, verb, not a stative one, it conjures up a definite beginning and end. When we say "He will fly over the Atlantic," we get the impression that it's a completed future event. Perhaps in your mind's eye, you can picture him leaving New York and arriving in Paris. In other words, the idea is too complete and sabotages the very essence of what our original thought was. **We don't want to focus on a completed act; quite the contrary, we want to focus on an act *in progress*,** and that's why "By the time I meet you for dinner tomorrow evening, Jacques will fly over the Atlantic" doesn't work.

Here's a sentence that does work with the simple future form because we're using a stative verb instead of a dynamic one:

By the time I meet you for dinner tomorrow evening,
Jacques <u>will be</u> home in Paris.

⚡ *Troubleshooter* ⚡

In the example in the sentence above, note the part of the sentence that says *By the time I meet you . . .* In some other languages, it would be grammatical to use the equivalent of the future form of *meet*. After all, we are referring to a future form, aren't we? Many of your students will more than likely put a verb after *by the time* in the future if that's the time of the sentence. Be prepared to explain the following:

☞ If we're referring to some point in the future, we don't use a future form after the following words or phrases, which are in dependent clauses:

when/while/as soon as/just as/before/after/until/by the time

Here are some more examples:

• As soon as he *wakes* up, I'll make him breakfast.
• Before I *leave* work, she'll have the report ready.
• They won't offer more scholarships until the proper funds *are* allocated.

☞ Another thing to note and point out to your students is that it's the *other* part of the sentence which contains the future verb form, not the one with one of the above expressions!

There are certain situations in which using the simple future form or the future progressive form can make quite a difference. Look at the following pairs of sentences.

Decide if you feel there's no big difference in meaning between the sentences in each pair or if their meanings are definitely different:

1. Will you see Mr. Chang before you leave work today?
   Will you be seeing Mr. Chang before you leave work today?
   ☐ no big difference   ☐ big difference

2. The Grants won't sue their neighbors.
   The Grants won't be suing their neighbors.
   ☐ no big difference   ☐ big difference

3. Will you come to our party on Sunday?
   Will you be coming to our party on Sunday?
   ☐ no big difference   ☐ big difference

4. I'll spend next summer in the mountains.
   I'll be spending next summer in the mountains.
   ☐ no big difference   ☐ big difference

It's hard to predict whether your students will ever develop the language sensitivity needed to get a "feel" for the differences that can be found in Pairs 2 and 3, but not in Pairs 1 and 4. However, it certainly would be nice if a student asks you one day to explain the differences and you can! Let's go over each pair of sentences and find out why there are or aren't big differences in meaning.

To *see someone* can mean two basic ideas in English. It can mean to have someone in your view or it can mean to have an appointment or date with someone. In the first pair of sentences, it can even mean just to check in with someone before leaving work for the day. In this context, it seems obvious that we're talking about either meeting Mr. Chang for an appointment or checking in with him before leaving work. For this reason, **we don't perceive any real difference in meaning between the two forms "Will you see" and "Will you be seeing."**

In the fourth pair of sentences, the same principle applies. There are really no shifts in meaning which are carried in one form or the other, so there's really no difference perceived between saying "I'll spend" and "I'll be spending" in this context.

The second pair, however, is a different matter. The first sentence tells us that the Grants refuse to sue their neighbors. It's an idea we can even apply to a hypothetical situation that might come up in a discussion about suing. The second sentence makes us believe that a real situation has arisen in which the Grants could be considering a law suit. The sentence tells us that, at least on this occasion, the Grants aren't going to sue their neighbors, but it doesn't imply that they would never consider doing so.

The sentences in the third pair are also very different. The first sentence is an invitation in the form of a question. The second sentence is not an invitation but a way of asking for a confirmation from a person who has already been invited.

ATS Two Marginal Future Expressions

There are two more expressions that show futurity although their main focus isn't necessarily on time so much as it is on other ideas. Let's take a look at the following dialogue which includes these two expressions.

> A: When is Mr. Aziz arriving in town?
> B: His flight **is due** in at noon, I believe.
> A: Fine. He**'s to see** Mr. Craig as soon as he gets here.
> B: All right. I'll make a note of it.

"Be Due" (+ infinitive verb/adverbial phrase)

Can you think of other ways to express the phrase "His flight <u>is due in</u> . . . " as it appears in our dialogue? See if you can come up with at least two phrases that mean the same idea and write them on the lines below:

_____

_____

Chances are you've come up with phrases such as these:

- His flight is expected in / is expected to arrive
- We anticipate that his flight will get in / arrive
- His flight should be in / should arrive

All of these synonymous phrases clearly show that their focus is on expectations about Mr. Aziz's flight; the secondary consideration is that we're dealing with a future event.

We can use *be due* with an infinitive verb ("He's due <u>to arrive</u> at any moment") or with an adverbial phrase ("He's due <u>in town</u>" / "He's due <u>here</u> by 3 o'clock").

So when do we tend to use this expression? Think about the situation we've presented in the dialogue and any other situations you can imagine when *be due* is appropriate. What would you say is its main use? Write your conclusion on the following line:

_____

To sum up, **we tend to use *be due* for events that are scheduled in the future**. Actually, *be due* accomplishes the same thing that the simple present accomplishes in this use, but the difference is that ***be due* carries the extra nuance that tells us what is expected**. Compare these two sentences:

They appear in court tomorrow at 3 p.m.
(They're scheduled to appear in court tomorrow at 3 p.m.)

They're due to appear in court tomorrow at 3 p.m.
(We expect them to appear in court tomorrow at 3 p.m.)

"Be To" (+ base verb)

Let's approach this expression the same way we looked at *be due*. Can you think of at least two ways to express the same idea as in our dialogue? Remember, the sentence is "He's to see Mr. Craig as soon as he gets here." Write your phrases down on the following lines:

_____

_____

Here are some possible synonymous phrases:

- **He's supposed to see Mr. Craig . . .**
- **He should see Mr. Craig . . .**
- **He has to see Mr. Craig . . .**

What would you say is the focus or the main intent of this expression? Just as you did for *be due*, think about the situation in our dialogue and come up with other situations in which *be to* would be appropriate. When you've formed a conclusion, write it down on the following line:

_____

The overriding focus of this expression deals with **instructions**, **orders**, **arrangements**, or **planned events**. There's also something very formal sounding about this expression. And then, of course, there's the idea of futurity, too.

If we expand the dialogue we've already presented to you, something interesting happens to the expression *be to*. Take a look at this example and figure out what's happened:

> A: Be sure to make a note of it. Oh, and by the way, he **isn't to speak** to anyone until he's seen Mr. Craig. Have you got that?
>
> B: Don't worry. I'll make sure he doesn't.

An interesting development, right? What other phrases would you think of that could substitute for "he <u>isn't to speak</u> to anyone"? Think of at least two and write them down on these lines:

_____

_____

Once again, here are some of the possibilities you could have chosen as synonymous phrases:

- **Don't let him speak to anyone . . .**
- **He mustn't speak to anyone . . .**
- **He isn't allowed to speak to anyone . . .**

Even though we can still make a case for the element of futurity in this expression, when it's used in the negative, it only represents an order, a prohibition. It's interesting how making this expression negative takes away its other possible uses.

But we aren't quite finished with this little dialogue you've just been thinking about. There's something else going on that's unusual, grammatically speaking. Read the dialogue again and see if you can spot the unusual feature. Here's a hint: It occurs twice in the dialogue. When you think you've zeroed in on what we're thinking of, write the two examples of it on the following line:

_____

The two sentences that we're thinking of are "Be sure you make a note of it" and "I'll make sure he doesn't." What's so unusual about the grammar in these two sentences is that by some quirk of the language, **the verb in the dependent clause after the phrase** *be sure* **or** *make sure* **normally takes the simple present even though it represents a future action**.

The Futures in a Nutshell

Present Progressive

- **a planned event in the near future:** I'm going to a ball game tonight.
- **present anticipation of a future event:** They're moving sometime next spring.

Simple Present

- **scheduled future events:** The next semester begins on May 28th.

Simple Future (Will)

- **a basic future idea with no nuances:** We'll see you later.
- **making predictions:** I think they'll be successful.
- **making promises:** I'll do it before I leave the office.
- **making requests:** Will you help me move this furniture?
- **making threats:** You'll regret the day you were born!
- **tendencies:** It will usually rain here every day between June and November.

Be Going To

- **showing future plans or intentions:** We're going to have a party next weekend.
- **making threats:** If you don't clean your room today, you're going to be punished!
- **making predictions:** I hear she's going to have twins!

Be About To

- **on the verge of doing something:** Quiet, please! The guest speaker's about to begin.

Future Perfect

- **project ourselves to some point in the future, stop, turn around, and look back at what is already in the past for us at that moment:** The next time you see me, I'll have finished the last chapter of my manuscript.

Future Perfect Progressive

- **works the same way as the present perfect progressive does in relation to the present perfect, and shows something in progress:** I'll have been working on that manuscript for over six months by the time I see you again.

Future Progressive

🥜 **can be used at times as an alternative to the simple future:**
I'll be giving you this report by the end of the week.

🥜 **can show an action in progress at some future point:** When we
arrive at my folks' house, they'll be getting dinner ready.

Be Due

🥜 **scheduled future events with the nuance of expectation:** The baby's
due in the middle of October.

Be To

🥜 **in the affirmative, used for future instructions, orders, arrangements, planned events:** You're to fill out this application form and then
set up an appointment for an interview.

🥜 **in the negative, used for (future) prohibitions:** You aren't to take this
medicine on an empty stomach.

Be Sure . . . / Make Sure . . .

🥜 **verb in the dependent clause following either of these expressions
uses simple present to represent future:**
Be sure you leave before 7 p.m. tomorrow night.
Make sure the report is on my desk by Tuesday morning.

Teaching Tips

5.1 Making Schedules

Before class, prepare two detailed schedules that show activities and times that are
similar, but not identical. Make as many copies of the schedules as you have students.
Pair up the students and give each student *one half* of a schedule. Tell the students that
they need to find a time that will suit both of them to study for a big test, for example. The students must explain when they can and cannot meet by asking questions and giving responses using the present progressive form.

Note: Students aren't permitted to see one another's schedules—they have to *ask*
for the information. Your two schedules might look something like these, though yours
will likely have many more details:

Student A	Monday	Tuesday	Wednesday	Thursday	Friday	Saturday	Sunday
8:00 a.m.	get up		go to class	post office		shopping	rest
noon	lunch	work	lunch	work	airport		

Student B	Monday	Tuesday	Wednesday	Thursday	Friday	Saturday	Sunday
8:00 a.m.	breakfast		go to class	get up	library	breakfast	church
noon	dentist	lunch	lunch	study	lunch		party

Responses may be similar to the following: "What are you doing at 8:00 Tuesday morning?" "I'm not doing anything." / "When are you having lunch on Thursday?" "I'm not eating lunch on Thursday; I'm going to the dentist instead."

5.2 *Travel Plans*

This activity focuses on the use of simple present in scheduled future events. Feel free to prepare this activity initially as a reading exercise because it's rather involved and the students will have to refer to it to accomplish the activity. Pairs of students will set up travel plans for the president of an import/export company. They'll base the travel plans on the following information. The president, Mr. Watson, is going to Asia for his annual twelve-day buying trip and will visit the factories that he imports from in Tokyo, Singapore, Hong Kong, and Seoul. He always begins his trip in Tokyo and ends up in Singapore. As "administrative assistant" and "personal secretary" to Mr. Watson, the pairs of students must arrange the trip (arrival and departure times, meetings with factory managers, side trips) and any other details that seem appropriate for a business traveler.

Mr. Qing is the factory manager in Singapore, as is Mr. Wong in Hong Kong, Mr. Pak in Seoul, and Mr. Matsuo in Tokyo.

While in Tokyo, Mr. Watson wants to take a side trip to Mt. Fuji; in Seoul, he wants to visit the Temple of Heaven; in Hong Kong, he wants to eat at Jumbo's floating restaurant; and in Singapore, he wants to have high tea at Raffles Hotel.

1. The pairs of students are to work together to plan out the details of Mr. Watson's itinerary, and both students should write them down.
2. Once they have prepared his itinerary, rearrange the pairs of students.
3. Have one member of each new pair be the administrative assistant and the other, Mr. Watson's personal secretary. The administrative assistant needs to tell the secretary the exact details of the trip that he/she planned out with the *original* partner.
4. After the administrative assistant has done so and the secretary has copied it all down, the students should reverse roles and repeat this procedure.
5. When they finish, they are to read out what they wrote down while playing the role of secretary to check for accuracy.

5.3 Rewriting Paragraphs

Find or create paragraphs that use *will* to indicate the future. Have your students rewrite the paragraphs using *be going to*. This technique is one that can be adapted for almost any grammar point and is similar to those activities found in *10 Steps* and *26 Steps* by Longman.

5.4 The Trip of a Lifetime!

Divide the class into pairs or small groups. Have the students plan the trip of a lifetime ("The Perfect Honeymoon," a "Family Getaway," or "The Anniversary Trip"). Have the pairs/groups report their *detailed* itineraries to the class, making sure that they use *will* where appropriate. "The trip will begin at the airport where Romeo and I will board a private jet for Paris. We'll arrive there a short time later and take a limousine to the Georges V Hotel. We'll have a suite reserved for us for the three weeks we'll be there …"

5.5 What Happens Next?

Select several pictures from your Picture File, or even have your students bring pictures that they like to class. They can be actual photos or pictures from magazines or books. Have the students brainstorm as many predictions about what "will occur" next in the various photos as they can.

Variation: After the class has brainstormed what comes next, have students develop a complete story line for their pictures. They can tell their stories as groups or individually, in writing or orally.

5.6 A Perfect World

Divide the class into small groups. Give the students a small, blank city map, one that has only the streets and blocks indicated on it. Ask them to design their ideal city or a city of the future by indicating where the following kinds of places or buildings will be: government offices, water treatment plant, shopping centers, hospital, zoo, etc. Then have the students give a report on what they have come up with. Make sure that they use various future indicators in their reports.

5.7 TV/Radio Predictions

Before class, record a TV or radio program that has lots of action and a strong story line. Note points in the program where you can stop the tape and get the students to predict what's about to happen, what's apt to happen, what will happen next. Present the program to the class, stopping at each point you've noted and ask the students to use various futures to interpret the drama. Don't play them the end of the program. Have the students brainstorm various endings in small groups and then act them out for the entire class to enjoy.

5.8 *Predicting My Future*

Have your students imagine themselves ten, twenty, or thirty years from now. Ask them to predict what they think their lives will be like then. Typical answers are predictions like these: By the year 2010, I'll have learned English well enough to get a good job. By the same year, I'll have been working for this company for fifteen years. By then, all my children will have grown up and left home.

Variation: Give your students the name of a famous person and have them do some research on that person's life. Then have the students give reports on their subject. Start off the reports with the following to encourage the future perfect and future perfect progressive: "It's _____ (date) and _____ (person) has just been born. By _____, he/she will have _____."

5.9 *Predicting Events*

Find a picture of a wedding or other event which permits speculation about it. Have the students brainstorm vocabulary and questions that they want answered about the event. (Who are the people? How old are they? What are they wearing? What will they promise in their vows? What's he about to do? Where will they be spending their honeymoon? Where do people in your culture go on a honeymoon? Where will they live after the wedding? How many children are they going to have?) Write any vocabulary or information on the board that will help students with the rest of the assignment. Divide the class into small groups and have them write various versions of the picture: a newspaper report, a letter from the bride-to-be to someone who can't come to the ceremony, an invited guest, describing the event to someone over the phone, etc. Have the class share the various versions of the event with their classmates.

5.10 *Orders*

Before class, think up as many situations as you can where orders are issued (what you say to a child; what a sergeant says to recruits; what a chef says to the kitchen personnel; what a father says to his teenage son or daughter; what new home owners say to their furniture movers, and the like). Have students brainstorm as many different instructions, orders, arrangements, etc. as they can using *be to* in the affirmative and negative.

6

Adjectives

"It was an itsy-bitsy, teeny-weeny, yellow polka dot bikini."

Some readers may wonder why we've included a chapter devoted to adjectives; after all, are they really a troublesome part of English? The answer is *yes*, but we hope they won't be by the time you've finished this chapter! What we have to say about adjectives won't deal so much with problems as it will with helpful insights and ways of understanding and teaching some interesting phenomena that occur with these descriptive words.

Verbal Adjectives

We call two kinds of adjectives "verbal" because they grow out of verbs, the action words. Look at the following dialogue to see both kinds (verbs and adjectives made from them) in action:

> A: I know you like anthropology very much. What part of the subject **interests** you the most?
>
> B. I'd say that paleoanthropology, the study of human origins, is the most **interesting** part for me.
>
> A: Really? Why is that?
>
> B: I guess it's simply that I'm very **interested** in answering that primal question: Where do we come from?

As you can see in the dialogue, the verb *interest* has two kinds of adjective forms that grow out of it, *interesting* and *interested*. The question we know that you know we'll ask is what the difference between these two adjective forms is. What does the *-ing* adjective (the present participle of the verb) describe and how is that different from what's described by the *-ed* adjective (which is really the past participle of the verb)? Think about what you know about the *-ing* form of any verb (for example, which tenses does it occur in?). Consider what you know about the verb forms that end with *-ed*, for example, which tenses it occurs in and how it works in the passive voice. Think about these two points for a moment and write down any thoughts you have on the following lines:

_____

_____

Let's look at a basic idea that Person B supplied in the dialogue:

Paleoanthropology interests me.

Paleoanthropology is the subject, of course, but more importantly, it's responsible for creating or causing the interest in Person B. This insight gives us the answer to one part of our question: **The *-ing* adjective describes the person, thing, or situation that's the <u>cause</u> of the feeling or reaction in the direct object.**

Conversely, the direct object (Person B in this case) is receiving the reaction or feeling. **We use the past participle adjective to describe the person or thing that receives the feeling or reaction;** it describes the state or condition of the recipient. So, paleoanthropology is interest*ing* and Person B is interest*ed* (in it, by it). Remember that we said the *-ed* adjective is really the past participle, or third form of the verb; if the verb is irregular, there won't be an actual *-ed* on the end (as in the verb *to freeze: freeze, froze, <u>frozen</u>),* but *frozen* is still a past participle, even without the *-ed!*

At this point, we'd like to offer you a list we've compiled of one hundred verbs from which the most common verbal adjectives are made (note that there are others). You will see that some verbs are preceded by a star; we'll get to the reason for that in a little while.

★ absorb	addict	aggravate	alarm	amaze	amuse
annoy	appall	astonish	astound	baffle	bewilder
blind	bore	calm	challenge	charm	★ chill
civilize	clean	comfort	★ compromise	confuse	connect
convince	corrupt	★ crush	damage	dazzle	deafen
deceive	defeat	demoralize	depress	devastate	disappoint
discourage	disgust	dishearten	disquiet	★ distinguish	disturb
embarrass	encourage	engross	enlighten	entertain	entice

exasperate	excite	exhaust	exhilarate	fascinate	★freeze
frighten	frustrate	gratify	hearten	horrify	humiliate
incriminate	infuriate	inspire	interest	★intoxicate	intrigue
invigorate	★invite	jangle	love	minimize	mislead
mortify	★move	mystify	nauseate	overwhelm	perplex
★pierce	please	★punish	puzzle	refresh	relax
satisfy	shock	soothe	stabilize	stimulate	★strike
★stun	surprise	tempt	terrify	thrill	tire
★touch	trust	upset	vex		

And now to the verbs that have stars. The most important reason that they've been singled out is to show that the adjectives made from these verbs have figurative meanings besides the literal ones. Below is a list of the figurative uses.

absorb: mentally occupy completely
It was an <u>absorbing</u> account of life in Antarctica.
He was fully <u>absorbed</u> in his work.

chill: frightening, scary
I read a <u>chilling</u> report on the increase in AIDS cases.
(**chilled:** literal meaning only, as in *chilled water*)

compromise: expose to danger, suspicion, or dishonor
By asking me to disregard the corruption I've seen, you're putting me in a <u>compromising</u> situation.
When the judge realized that he knew the defendant personally, his <u>compromised</u> position forced him to recuse himself.

crush: devastate emotionally
The <u>crushing</u> realization that her brother had betrayed her sent her into the depths of depression.
When she realized what her brother had done, she was <u>crushed</u>.

distinguish: dignified
He looked very <u>distinguished</u> in his new navy blue suit.
(**distinguishing:** literal meaning only, as in *a distinguishing mark*)

freeze: extremely cold (rather than water becoming solid)
It's <u>freezing</u> in here! Turn on the heat.
I'm <u>frozen</u> stiff. I don't think the furnace is working.

intoxicate: stimulate; excite; arouse
That's a very <u>intoxicating</u> perfume you're wearing.
The steady rhythm of the drums made the dancers feel <u>intoxicated</u>.

invite: alluring; enticing; tempting
I must admit that that's a very <u>inviting</u> offer you've made me.
(**invited:** literal meaning only, as in *an invited guest*)

move: affect deeply (emotionally)
We found her patriotic speech very <u>moving</u>.
The audience was so <u>moved</u> that a total hush fell over the room.

pierce: a high-pitched, sharp sound; penetrating
I can't stand the <u>piercing</u> noise of jet planes flying overhead.
Her <u>piercing</u> stare unnerved me.
(**pierced:** literal meaning only, as in *earrings for pierced ears*)

❧ *Troubleshooter* ❧

Three -*ed* adjectives have derived from verbs, but they're paired with typical participial adjectives. These three are very common but very unusual because they're pronounced in two syllables, not one:

- *aged* /e-j̆ɪd/ as in *an aged person*, somebody who's old
  Compare with /ej̆d/ as in *aged cheese* that has undergone a process called "aging."

- *blessed* /blɛ-sɪd/ as in *a blessed event*, meaning an event that has good fortune attached to it
  Compare with /blɛst/ as in *a blessed church*, that is, a church that's been given a blessing.

- *learned* /lər-nɪd/ as in *a learned person*, somebody who's wise and well educated
  Compare with /lərnd/ as in *a learned behavior*, which is a behavior that didn't come naturally but was developed.

There are some adjectives that look like they're derived from the past participles of verbs, but they aren't—at least not in the same way. Here are some typical ones:

bowlegged	*peaked	wicked
jagged	ragged	wretched
naked	rugged	

Each of these words is pronounced with a separate syllable on the -*ed*. However, you'll note that there are no such related verbs as *to bowleg*, *to crook*, *to jag*, *to nake*, *to rag*, *to rug*, *to wick*, or *to wretch*. Therefore, they're only "look-alike" participial adjectives.

*Peaked is interesting for a different reason. When pronounced as two syllables, / pi-kɪd /, it means "tired," but when it's one syllable, /pikt/, it's the simple past of the verb *to peak*, which means *to bring to a high point.*

punish: physically painful; injurious
We made that <u>punishing</u> ride through the mountainous region of the country in a Land Rover.
(**punished:** literal meaning only, as in *a punished child*)

strike: immediately or vividly impressive (*-ing* adjective)
I love that gown you have on. It's really <u>striking</u>.
This sonata is a <u>striking</u> example of his musical genius.

afflicted with emotion or disease (*-ed* adjective)
People <u>stricken</u> with Parkinson's disease suffer from uncontrollable shaking of the hands and head.
The doctor gave the report of their child's surgery to the <u>stricken</u> parents.

stun: astonishing; excellent (*-ing* adjective)
Her <u>stunning</u> performance in the opera brought the people in the audience to their feet for a standing ovation.

stupefied; shocked (*-ed* adjective)
We felt <u>stunned</u> when we heard about his sudden death.

touch: move emotionally; elicit a tender reaction
It was <u>touching</u> to watch the little boy help an injured bird.
I sincerely appreciate this gift. I'm very <u>touched</u>.

Other Uses of -ing Adjectives

There are two other important uses of this verbal adjective form that we should take a look at. See if you can figure out one use by looking over this dialogue and write your guess on the lines that follow.

A: Gustav, have you seen the **watering** can? I've got to water the potted flowers in front of the house.

B: Look in the tool shed out back.

A: Are the **pruning** shears there, too?

B: Probably. By the way, we need some more **potting** soil so I can transplant the mums into larger pots.

In these phrases, the *-ing* adjectives serve to tell us what purposes their nouns have:

- The can is used for <u>watering</u> the flowers, so it's a *watering* can.
- Those shears are used for <u>pruning</u> plants, so they're *pruning* shears.
- The soil that Gustav needs is used for <u>potting</u> plants, so it's *potting* soil.

We'll discuss this use of the *-ing* adjective more in Chapter 11, which is on compounding.

By the way, in the dialogue did you notice the use of *potted* in the phrase *potted flowers*? Why must we use the past participle form of the adjective to describe the flowers?

The past participle adjective is used here because, as our rule said, **it describes the state or condition of the flowers which received the action of being put into pots!** That is, someone *potted* the plants.

Now look at these sentences, which exemplify one use or more of the *-ing* adjective and figure out what they tell us in these cases. Write down your thoughts on the lines that follow.

- She's a <u>nursing</u> mother.
- Professor Fouad is <u>Acting</u> Dean this semester.
- When you scuba dive, never go near <u>feeding</u> sharks.

In this other use, the **-ing adjectives explain the activities that are being carried out by the nouns they describe**. For example, a **nursing** mother is a mother who's <u>nursing</u> her baby; an **acting** dean is a school administrator who's temporarily <u>acting</u> as dean until a permanent person can be found for the position; **feeding** sharks are sharks that are <u>feeding</u> on some sort of prey.

A The Ordering of Adjectives

Incredible as it may seem, there are eighteen categories into which adjectives can be placed. And even more incredible is the fact that we're going to deal with them!

It's as if there were 18 empty blanks in front of every noun into which different kinds of adjectives could fit. In other words, there are 18 kinds of adjectives and a similar number of positions in which adjectives can be put before the head noun, that is, the noun that's being described. Luckily, we've never heard anyone utter a phrase that included even close to that many adjectives, and we're sure you haven't either!

Here's one note before we get under way. In many cases, words that are actually nouns will be referred to as adjectival forms in this chapter. These nouns are actually going to be used as adjectives because they describe the nouns we're going to focus on. We'll get into all the details about these specially used nouns in Chapter 11. For right now, though, we'll just concentrate on the order of real adjectives and the nouns that can function as adjectives.

Let's begin our investigation of adjective order by looking at three mixed-up phrases and seeing if we can rearrange the adjectival forms to make the phrases grammatical. (The words that are boxed in are the head nouns, the ones that get all the description.)

1. coffee electric pot _____

2. water gas heater _____

3. alarm battery-operated clock _____

Without much trouble, we can see that the things being described are:

1. an electric coffee pot

2. a gas water heater

3. a battery-operated alarm clock

So what rule for ordering the descriptive words can we come up with? We see that the words *coffee, water,* and *alarm* tell us what the pot, the heater, and the clock are used for or how they're used, or what purpose they serve. These three words are examples of the nouns, not adjectives, that we've mentioned you'll be coming across in this chapter.

The other three words, *electric, gas*, and *battery-operated*, all have their own common feature: they're the power sources. Now we've discovered the order of these two categories of adjectives:

power   purpose | head noun |

Let's describe these items in more detail, but before we do, we'd like to explain that we intend to work with phrases that are longer than what people normally utter just for the sake of demonstration.

We want to describe what materials our items are made of. The pot is *stainless steel*, the heater is *aluminum*, and the clock is *plastic*. So where should we place these descriptive words? Take a moment, think about where you'd put them, and jot the phrases down on the following lines:

1. a/an _____ coffee pot

2. a/an _____ water heater

3. a/an _____ alarm clock

The answer is that they should be placed before the power source words:

1. a stainless steel electric coffee pot

2. an aluminum gas water-heater

3. a plastic battery-operated alarm clock

Now we have another category, material, and we can expand our ordering rule:

material   power   purpose | head noun |

Let's get back to our coffee pot for a moment. Suppose we want to describe it even more. We could talk about whether we think it's an attractive or ugly piece, we could mention whether we thought it was reasonably priced or expensive when we bought it, and we could tell where it came from. So let's opt for the adjectives *expensive*, *Brazilian*, and *elegant*. Now the question is, in what order should we put these words or where in our phrase should we place them? Try writing a sequence out yourself and then we'll see if your solution fits in with ours.

a/an _____ coffee pot

It turns out that these three words should be placed before all the others we've already used to describe the pot, and this is how your newly-expanded phrase should look:

an **elegant, expensive, Brazilian stainless steel electric coffee pot**

But perhaps you had *expensive, elegant* instead of *elegant, expensive*. The truth of the matter is that both of these versions are correct; the question is, why?

We need to check which categories are being used this time. Words like *expensive* and *elegant* are really opinions. Maybe you think the price for that coffee pot was high, but I might think it was reasonable. The same holds true for *elegant*; I might think it's very attractive, but you might think it's nothing special. As for *Brazilian*, this word is obviously a word describing origin. So now we have two more categories, opinion and origin. Here's our new version of the rule for ordering adjectival words:

| opinion | origin | material | power | purpose | head noun |

Why is it, though, that we can say *expensive, elegant* or *elegant, expensive,* and the ordering works both ways? It's because both adjectives are in the same category, and within the opinion category, the adjectives are interchangeable.

One thing we'll throw in for free at this point is where you place the articles (*a, an/the*) or demonstratives (*this, that/these, those*); in short, they go before everything else. For the sake of efficiency, we'll refer to these words as "determiners." There are more determiners than articles and demonstratives, however. (*My* and *your* are also determiners . . . possessive determiners, for example.)

Now, how about going back to our heater and our clock? If you recall, we said it was an aluminum gas water heater and a plastic battery-operated alarm clock. Here are some words for you to play with:

stylish/Swiss/energy-efficient/Cosmos (brand name)

Place two of the above words in the phrase describing the heater and the other two in the phrase describing the clock and write both complete phrases.

1. (heater)

_____

2. (clock)

_____

Your expanded phrases should now look something like these:

1. an **energy-efficient Cosmos gas water heater**

2. a **stylish Swiss plastic battery-operated alarm clock**

What about color? We'll make the coffee pot white, the water heater black, and the alarm clock pink. Where should the colors be placed? Write in each color under the appropriate caret.

1. an ⇡ elegant ⇡ Brazilian ⇡ stainless steel ⇡ electric ⇡ coffee pot

2. an ⇡ energy-efficient ⇡ Cosmos ⇡ aluminum ⇡ gas ⇡ water heater

3. a ⇡ stylish ⇡ Swiss ⇡ plastic ⇡ battery-operated ⇡ alarm clock

This is how it goes: **white** should be between **elegant** and **Brazilian**; **black** should be between **energy-efficient** and **Cosmos**; **pink** should go between **stylish** and **Swiss**. Do you think you've solved another piece of the puzzle? You have!

determiner   opinion   color   origin   material   power   purpose | head noun |

We know when you've had enough of coffee pots, water heaters, and alarm clocks! Let's move on to something else to continue our exploration into adjective order.

Let's talk about clothes for a change; in fact, let's specifically talk about a dress and a coat. First of all, let's go back to color for a moment. We've already determined where color should be placed in our ordering of adjectives, but we need to break color down into two subcategories, namely, true color and pattern. Let's say our dress has a floral pattern and it's yellow, and let's say that our coat is tan and has a plaid pattern. Write these descriptions on the two lines that follow:

a _____ dress

a _____ coat

What you should have come up with is **a yellow, floral dress** and **a tan, plaid coat.** So the order for the broad category of color is **true color + pattern**.

Next we can describe these items by mentioning the **seasons** they were made for. Let's say that the dress was made for the summer, so it's a *summer dress*. The coat was made for the winter, so it's a *winter coat*.

Now choose two of the following words to add to the description of the dress and the other two for the coat: brand new/heavy/old/light

a _____ summer dress

a _____ winter coat

What you've probably come up with is either **a light, brand new summer dress** and **a heavy, old winter coat**, or **a light, old summer dress** and a **heavy, brand new winter coat**. The important thing to keep in mind is whether you placed the descriptive words in the same order as we did. What name can we give to the category of words like *light* and *heavy*? One way is to consider them **conditions**. As for *old* and *brand new*, these are obviously words concerning **age**. Now we have two more categories to add to the whole picture:

determiner   condition   age   season | head noun |

Where can we stick the words *long* and *short* which, of course, fall into the category of **measurement**? Give it a try and copy the two complete phrases on the lines that follow:

a _____ summer dress

a _____ winter coat

Most native English speakers would opt for putting *short* and *long* before the words describing condition, so two of the four possible phrases could now be expanded to **a short, light, brand new summer dress** and **a long, heavy, old winter coat**.

determiner   measurement   condition   age   season | head noun |

The dress and coat that we've been talking about probably belong to somebody, but we haven't accounted for ownership yet. If we want to mention who the owners of these clothes are, we've got to figure out where to place the possessive forms. Let's use *her* and *Vladimir's* and see what happens. Think about where you'd place these possessives into our phrases about the dress and coat and fill in the next two lines:

a _____ summer dress

a _____ winter coat

What happens is very interesting. For the first time, we have to come up with a different kind of strategy in order to use the possessive words; it's not merely a matter of sticking these words in some place. Instead of finding a spot where they can be inserted, we have to take out the determiners we've been using and replace them with the possessives. In other words, the possessive forms share that spot (the determiner's spot) in our ordering rules when they're needed:

her short, light, brand new summer dress
Vladimir's long, heavy, old winter coat

Why do we remove the article *a*? It's simply because a possessive form is a kind of determiner and needs to take the same spot that the article *a* would take! In this slot, there can be only one word (not like the opinion category), and the most specific word takes the spot. (*Vladimir* is more specific than either *a* or *the*.)

Before moving on to some other subjects, let's discuss one more way we can define a different dress and a different coat. The dress is one that many people would think is a style *not suitable for daytime hours*; it's something fancier or more elegant. The coat is one that a European gentleman would have worn *in the early part of the day* at the beginning of the twentieth century. Can you think of the two adjectival words that would identify these articles of apparel?

her _____ dress

Vladimir's _____ coat

So, how good are you at answering such riddles? We were thinking of an **evening dress** and a **morning coat**. We'll let you know right off where this category, which we simply call **time**, is placed relative to all the other categories we've been working with. **Time normally appears in the same slot as season**, and it would be quite rare, if ever, that you'd find a phrase containing both season and time. If you did, the longer period of time would come first: *a winter evening dress.* (It's warmer than a *summer evening dress.*)

How about switching to another subject now? Let's talk about cars. Imagine that there's a long line of cars just coming out of the factory. There are all kinds of cars in the line, but we're looking to pick out specific ones. Here's what we're looking for:

1. Three of them should be large. They should be the first ones we see in the line.
2. Two of them should be small. They should be the last ones we see in the line.

Using the information supplied by the descriptive words underlined, produce the two phrases we need to describe the specific cars we're looking to pick out.

1. the _____ cars

2. the _____ cars

The order in which you probably put these words is **the first three large cars** and **the last two small cars**. How did we come by this particular order? First, we need to examine what kinds of words we're using now and decide what categories they fall into.

Words like *first*, *next*, and *last* are called **ordinal numbers** as they indicate the order in which items appear, or **position words**; words like *one*, *two*, and *three* are called **cardinal numbers**, or **counting words**. So what order do we see these words falling into?

determiner   ordinal   cardinal | head noun |

And notice where we put the words *large* and *small*: they were placed after the ordinals and cardinals (*the first three large cars* and *the last two small cars*). We can call this category **size**.

determiner   ordinal   cardinal   size | head noun |

Now we're getting near the end of all the categories that adjectives can be sorted into. We just have two more to go. Let's talk about two heavenly bodies, the sun and a comet. Here are adjectives we can use to describe them: *round, oval, hot, cold*. First, let's determine what categories we can place these adjectives in. *Round* and *oval* are **shapes**; *hot* and *cold* are **temperatures**. At this point, write a phrase to describe each one by using these adjectives.

The sun is a _____, _____ heavenly body.

A comet is a _____, _____ heavenly body.

You most likely came up with **The sun is a hot, round heavenly body**, and **A comet is a cold, oval heavenly body**. What further rule for ordering adjectives can we discern? It appears that temperature comes before shape:

determiner　temperature　shape　│ head noun │

Believe it or not, we just have one more category to go, and that happens to be **location**. Let's say we have more than one telephone in our house. There's one in the kitchen and one in the bedroom. How can we refer to them for easy identification? Well, we can use color if they have different colors, so let's say one's beige and the other's blue. But how do we add the information about where the phones are located? Think a moment and see what order you come up with.

a _____ phone

a _____ phone

The answer is that we should place location closer to the head noun because it's more important for our needs of identification: **a beige kitchen phone** and **a blue bedroom phone**.

The one last question we'd like to pose is about how we would place two adjectives describing location. Let's say one of our phones is hung on a wall in the kitchen and the other one is on a little desk in the corner of the bedroom. Fill in the following lines with a full description of each phone including location and color.

One's a _____.

The other's a _____.

This is what we've come up with: **a beige kitchen wall phone** and **a blue bedroom desk phone**. We can see that **the general location comes before the specific location**. Like the season and time slot, the larger element precedes the smaller one. So we've come to the last ordering rule for adjectives that we need to deal with in this chapter:

determiner　color/pattern　location (general)　location (specific)　│ head noun │

At long last, we've covered them all! We've accounted for eighteen categories (seventeen positions) that adjectival words fall into, and we've worked on various combination phrases to show how they're positioned with one another. The last step we should consider is how all of them look in theory if we could devise a hypothetical phrase that would include every single one of them. In that way, we can always pick and choose among the categories to describe anything we want and keep the basic order that we've seen emerge from all of this work. Generally speaking, English adjectives precede head nouns in the following order:

Determiners/ Possessives	Ordinals	Cardinals	Opinion	Size	Measurement
18	17	16	15	14	13

Condition	Age	Temperature	Shape	Color/ Pattern	Origin
12	11	10	9	8	7

Season/ Time	Material	Power	Location	Purpose	head noun
6	5	4	3/2	1	

What we'd like to reiterate is that you can pick and choose among all these categories to place adjectives in their usual positions before the head noun. Think of any two or three head nouns, and then come up with two or three adjectives belonging to different categories for each head noun you've thought up. Place your adjectives by category before your head nouns in the order appearing above. It'll work out every time!

By the way, an interesting viewpoint that some people hold about why the adjective order developed in this way is that **we tend to place the more crucial descriptions closer to the head noun**. In other words, purpose is more crucial for describing a heater than is power, but power, in turn, is more crucial for our description than is opinion or determiner—and that's how we end up with **an energy-efficient gas water heater**.

Yet another way of looking at this ordering of adjectives is to think of the adjectives as being either more specific features for identification or less specific features. **The more specific the adjective, the closer it is to its head noun**. In our minds, at least, both of these viewpoints seem to hold up quite well.

Just to have some fun before we end this chapter, we're going to talk to you about a hamper. There are all kinds of hampers, but according to our rules for ordering adjectives, telling you its purpose would be the most important item of identification we can give you—and it is.

It's a laundry | hamper | .
1

That eliminates any other kind of hamper. Laundry hampers can be kept in all sorts of places, but this one is kept in the *bathroom*.

It's a bathroom laundry ⟨hamper⟩ .
          2   1

Laundry hampers don't have power sources, but they're made of some sort of material. In this case, we're thinking of *wicker*.

It's a wicker bathroom laundry ⟨hamper⟩ .
        5   2   1

Not only have we eliminated all hampers not used for laundry from our discussion, but we've also eliminated any hampers not kept in the bathroom or made of wicker. We've already narrowed down the identification tremendously. (Have you noticed that our numbered categories seem to be fitting in just right?) Our hamper could be lost among thousands of other hampers made anywhere, but ours was *made in China*.

It's a Chinese wicker bathroom laundry ⟨hamper⟩ .
        7   5   2   1

We've narrowed the identification a lot more now. Our hamper is that gorgeous shade of *red* that China is famous for, and telling you the color at this point will eliminate thousands of other Chinese wicker laundry hampers.

It's a red Chinese wicker bathroom laundry ⟨hamper⟩ .
        8   7   5   2   1

What about its shape, age, condition, and size? It's *cylindrical*. It's also *large*. It's old, too. Besides all that, it's *brittle* because it's so old, and it's *mine*. So, it's . . .

my large, brittle, old, cylindrical, red Chinese wicker bathroom laundry ⟨hamper⟩ !
18   14   12   11   9   8   7   5   2   1

⚘ When Nouns are Adjectives

Every language there is has practical means of generating new vocabulary. One used commonly in English is known as *compounding*, and we have a whole chapter devoted to this phenomenon. It's appropriate, though, that we discuss one compound form in this chapter. Technically speaking, **compound forms are created by using two unrelated elements stuck together in order to create a new word**. For the purposes of this chapter, we're going to talk only about **noun + noun**. Examples of these are *ranch house* and *bank vault*. Consider the fact that the word *ranch* and the word *house* are two words that don't have any natural connection, but when stuck together, they create a third word. The same holds true for *bank* and *vault*.

Why are we talking about nouns when this is a chapter on adjectives? The reason is that **the first element in this compound form acts exactly as an adjective does; namely, it describes the second element**. Let's go back to the word *house*. Of course there are all kinds of houses used for all kinds of purposes, and a very efficient way of describing them is by placing a compound element in front of *house*. In this way, we end up with such items as *schoolhouse, bathhouse, gatehouse, courthouse,* and *jailhouse.* Notice how the first element describes the following word—just as an adjective does.

Attorneys General?

If you think about it, the title for this section is really strange. It seems to contradict a basic rule of English, that adjectives come before nouns.

So how do we explain this noun + adjective? To find the answer, we need to look at how other languages operate. In quite a few of them, the adjective normally comes after the noun (French and Arabic are examples of such languages). And that's where our answer lies. Over the centuries, English has borrowed many words and phrases from other languages, and in so doing, has sometimes anglicized the borrowed bits and pieces. There are times, however, when it's retained the original placement of the elements as they appeared in the foreign languages. Here's a case in point:

We've borrowed the French job title *notaire publique* without changing much at all. True, *notaire* has evolved into *notary,* and the spelling of *publique* has changed to the English word *public,* but we've kept the French word order in this noun phrase and call the job a *notary public* instead of a "public notary"—even though the adjective should normally be placed before the noun in English. Another phrase that has evolved like this is *proof positive.*

But what should we do about making the title *notary public* plural? Is it okay to say *notary publics*? What would be your guess? Write down your opinion and your reason for saying so. By the way, if you don't think it's okay, what should the plural form be?

In short, the answer is that it's *not* okay to say *notary publics* even though it probably doesn't hurt your ears to say it. So what should the correct plural form be? It should be **notaries public**. The reason goes back to that rule about adjectives: **in English, we can't put a plural marker on an adjective that accompanies its noun**. That means our only choice is to put the plural marker where it belongs, on the noun, and the noun in this case is *notary,* not *public.* Here are some other examples of this phenomenon:

Finally, even though the following examples really don't belong here since they don't contain adjectives, we're going to throw them in for free. They're not words that have been borrowed from other languages, but they do fit the same pattern for making plurals, and here they are:

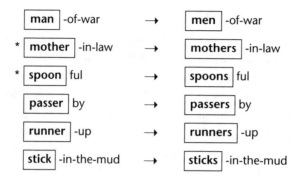

man -of-war	→ **men** -of-war
* **mother** -in-law	→ **mothers** -in-law
* **spoon** ful	→ **spoons** ful
passer by	→ **passers** by
runner -up	→ **runners** -up
stick -in-the-mud	→ **sticks** -in-the-mud

Note that, in these expressions, the plural suffix is added to the noun. Here's a special note about a number of these terms. Because so many native speakers have consistently used the more standard pluralization pattern by sticking the plural marker at the end, we now accept *attorney generals, court martials, mother-in-laws,* and *spoonfuls* as alternative plurals in *informal* speech. Two exceptions are that we always put the plural marker on the end of *ne'er-do-wells* and the flowers called *forget-me-nots,* even in formal speech. The reason may be that the first element of each of theses two compound nouns isn't a noun and therefore cannot take a plural marker.

◢ᐟ Punctuating Adjectives

Let's take a look at the following phrases for a moment. See if you can determine three categories for the adjectival forms you find:

> those big, old, rusty metal garden tools
> a young, energetic Australian sheep dog
> our gorgeous, expensive, large backyard swimming pool

What we've come up with is **determiners** (demonstratives like *those* and possessives like *our*), **"real" adjectives** (big, old, rusty, young, energetic, Australian), and **nouns used as adjectives** (metal, garden, sheep, backyard). After looking over all of this information, can you make an observation about where it's necessary to punctuate with commas in phrases like the ones we've just seen?

The interesting point to make here is that **we only place commas between "real" adjectives**, those words listed in any English dictionary as being adjectives, the words we traditionally consider to be adjectives. **We never place a comma between a determiner and a real adjective** *(those, big ones)* **or between a "real" adjective and a noun used as an adjective** *(rusty, metal things)*. This rule is neat and tidy, so you can give it to your students to help them learn where it's necessary to punctuate a phrase or sentence that contains more than one real adjective.

Teaching Tips

6.1 "What Do You Call . . . ?"

An effective way to practice the *-ed* and *-ing* adjectives is to prepare situations in which you can use the phrase "What do you call _____ ?" The blanks are filled in with phrases that provide the noun to be described and an appropriate verb. Here are some examples. "What do you call a fluid that cleans? / lies that convince people? / information which misleads you? / events that puzzle the police? / people who exasperate you?" and the like. Note that all the answers to these questions use the *-ing* adjective *(cleaning fluid, convincing lies, misleading information, puzzling events,* and *exasperating people).*

The same question can be asked to elicit the *-ed* adjective: "What do you call a friend you trust? / an enemy that you've demoralized? / customers that you have satisfied? / sleep that was disturbed by phone calls? / pipes that the plumber disconnected?" (They are *a trusted friend, a demoralized enemy, satisfied customers, disturbed sleep,* and *disconnected pipes.*)

You can make this activity more challenging by setting up pairs of "What do you call" questions that use both verbal adjectives. "What do you call fluids that clean and carpets cleaned by the fluid? ("cleaning fluid and cleaned carpets") and service that satisfies and customers that you satisfy?" ("satisfying service and satisfied customers").

6.2 "A Mixed Bag"

Before class, think up four or five nouns for each student you have and write each noun on a slip of paper. Then think up two adjectives for each of the nouns and write them in any order on a separate slip of paper. Put all the slips in a bag to mix them up and then have each student pull out eight to ten slips. The students should then go around the room to their classmates and find slips that will appropriately match the slips they have. Many different combinations are possible, not just the ones you originally thought up. Have them report their combinations to the class, making sure that they've ordered the adjectives correctly.

6.3 Personal Preferences

Before class prepare several grids similar to the one that follows. (You can draw them on the board if it's easier.) Fill in the boxes in the grids with appropriate vocabulary or have the students brainstorm their own vocabulary and then fill them in. Once the grids have been filled in, have students write down their preferences and collect their sheets of paper. Redistribute the responses and have the students circulate around the room to find the person whose paper they have. Ask the students to give a report on their classmates' answers.

I prefer . . .

cool	stormy
hot	sunny
bright	brisk

. . . weather

I prefer . . .

Alpine	backpacking
Canadian	ski
European	seaside

. . . vacations

I prefer . . .

quiet	romantic
noisy	secluded
peaceful	crowded

. . . places

6.4 Another Memory Game

(This activity is a variation of 2.3.) Bring in a group of fifteen to twenty common and not-so-common items to class (dictionary, tennis ball, safety pin, hair dryer, butterfly net, can opener, table tennis paddle, etc.). Spread them out on your desk. Pick each one up and ask what it does or what it's used for. Then cover them up. Gather the students around your desk and uncover the items. Tell the students that they'll have a couple of minutes to study the items *in detail*. Cover the items back up and have the students return to their desks. Tell them they have five minutes to list and describe as many of the items as they can remember. After they've written down the items and their descriptions, check their responses. Give the students one point for each correctly remembered item and one point for each descriptive adjective they've used properly. Give the winning students extra points for telling what each thing does or is used for.

6.5 *Writing Ads*

Select colorful pictures of products or things from your Picture File (see *Appendix 1*). Divide the class into pairs or small groups. Let the groups choose one of the pictures and have them write advertising copy for the product or item they've chosen. Note that if your students aren't familiar with advertising English, it will help them if you prepare a mini-lesson on the language of advertising before they begin the project. Bring in some ads for them to examine and have them practice talking about items for sale.

6.6 *Travel Brochures*

Let the students select travel pictures from the Picture File or have them bring in pictures of places that they've been to or are interested in. Have them work in small groups to prepare a travel brochure for the tourist industry about the place they've chosen. Be sure the students use ample adjectives to entice prospective customers among their classmates to travel to these places.

6.7 *The Lost Luggage*

Help! You've lost your luggage and everything in it. Go to the Lost and Found Office of the nearest bus station/train station/airport and make a report. First divide the class into two groups: the "Lost and Found agents" and the "unfortunate travelers." The agents will brainstorm questions that they need to ask the travelers and the travelers will make up the items in their suitcases. Remind the agents that they need to ask very specific questions about the lost luggage and that the travelers must have detailed descriptions of the suitcases and their contents. When the questions and details have been worked out, pair up an agent and a traveler and have them role-play the encounter.

6.8 *"Good Lookers"*

Divide the class into small groups. Have the groups study one another carefully; they're going to need to remember as many precise details about the members of the other groups as they can. After a couple of minutes of studying the other groups, send the groups to different parts of the classroom and let them discuss what they've just observed . . . and . . . have them change something about themselves. One student may take off his glasses. Another may comb her hair in a different way. Two students may exchange sweaters. After a few minutes, have the groups face one another again and try to reconstruct the "original look" of the groups. Award points for correct reconstructions; the team with the most points is declared the "Best Lookers."

6.9 *The Signs of the Zodiac*

This activity gives your students a chance to discuss astrology and prepare horoscopes for themselves and their classmates. First, find out if they know their own signs of the zodiac. List them on the board; you should even include your own. Prepare a handout like the one that follows which lists the signs, dates, students' names, etc. (You can also draw one on the board.) If possible, get a copy of the actual constellations and their places in the sky and samples of real horoscopes to show the class. Have the students fill in the charts for one another and then write up horoscopes based on what they've learned.

Constellation	Sign	Dates	Traits	Student	Student's Own Traits
	Virgo	Aug. 23 to Sept. 22	sensitive artistic in control	Patricia	
	Libra	Sept. 23 to Oct. 22	fair creative outgoing	Ricardo	

6.10 The Crime

Before class think of an imaginary crime (you only need to provide the most general details). Divide the class into two large groups, police investigators and witnesses. Have the police investigators prepare as many questions to ask the witnesses as they can think of. At the same time, have the witnesses prepare a story of what actually happened (location of the crime, victims, sequence of events, weather conditions). When all the stories and questions have been prepared, divide the class into small groups and have them role-play the investigation of the crime.

7

A Look at Some *and* Any

"Come up and see me some time" . . . *or any time.*

While you were looking over the Table of Contents in this book, you may have been a bit surprised to see a chapter reserved for *some* and *any,* the two most commonly used quantifiers in English. The thing is, these two words invariably end up being difficult and even vexing points for teachers and their students. In fact, the more advanced the students are, the more troublesome *some* and *any* become. This trouble all stems from the amazing variations in meaning and usage that both words have; furthermore, as students become more and more aware of the nuances in meaning that English words can have, these sometimes subtle and sometimes not-so-subtle differences become increasingly more noticeable.

Let's begin exploring *some* and *any* by observing the most typical uses taught in lower-level classes. Here's a dialogue to start things off:

A: So how's life way out in the country?

B: It isn't really out in the country. It's just ten miles from town. By the way, have I told you what happened last weekend? Believe it or not, I saw **a** Florida panther in my back yard. I could hardly believe my eyes because they're so rare.

A: That's great! I've seen **some** panthers over the years, but usually in really remote areas.

B: Well, I was really happy to see it. I didn't think there were **any** panthers left in Florida. They're on the endangered species list, you know.

Did you notice that we have the article *a* in bold along with *some* and *any*? That's because there's a connection between the indefinite article and these quantifiers that most ELT grammar books don't touch on. Can you figure out what the connection is? If you come up with an idea, write it down on the following line:

_____

In Chapter 2, while discussing the uses of the indefinite article, we mentioned that we can use the zero article—in other words, nothing—when the singular noun that goes with the indefinite article is changed to the plural: **a book → books**. There is, however, another way to deal with an indefinite singular becoming an indefinite plural, and that's by changing *a/an* to *some/any*: **a book → some/any books**. Keep in mind that **in a statement, *some/any* can be the plural of *a/an* and that it represents an unspecified number or amount**.

By analogy, we can take *some* one step further in this use as an unspecified amount and put it into the context you'll find in the following mini-dialogue. On the line below the dialogue, write down how you would interpret *some* as it appears here:

> A: So how many people finally showed up for the rally?
> B: The media figured there were <u>some</u> 1,500 people there.

_____

This idiomatic use of *some* is an example of a meaning rarely taught, but it's a meaning we shouldn't overlook. ***Some* can be used with numbers or amounts to mean *more or less*, *about*, or *approximately*.**

In the same way as with numbers or amounts, ***some* can stand for an unspecified person, place, or thing** even when numbers or amounts aren't involved:

> We always like to go to <u>some</u> exotic place on our vacation.

Now let's examine the quantifier *any*. Our opening dialogue shows its most typical use, the one that students learn early on. How would you explain *any* juxtaposed with *some* when Speaker B says "I didn't think there were <u>any</u> panthers left in Florida"?

_____

Person A says that she's seen *some* panthers over the years, but Person B says that he didn't think there were *any* panthers left in Florida. Person A's idea is affirmative, and **we use *some* after affirmative verbs in statements**; Person B's idea is negative, and we use *any* **after negative verbs in statements to mean** *not even one*. These last two rules are the most typical ones that students are given for *some* and *any*. If only it were that simple! The rest of this chapter will deal with showing you how it's not necessarily so simple.

Look at the way *any* is used in the next dialogue without the aid of negative verbs and explain why it's still being used:

> A: Honey, could you go to the grocery store for me? We have hardly **any** butter left, and we'll need some for dinner.
>
> B: What? Now?
>
> A: Now's a good time. You never see **any** long lines at the check-out at this hour.
>
> B: Exactly my point!
>
> A: Come on. Don't be so lazy. You'll be able to get in and get out without **any** trouble or standing in line.

So what's your guess? Why has Person A used *any* in these sentences when there are no negative verbs?

The answer lies in the words *hardly, never,* and *without.* These three words really stand for negative ideas (*hardly* = almost not; *never* = no time/not ever; *without* = not present/not having). **Because these words carry negative connotations, we use** *any* **for the same reason that our previous rule told us to.** A bit sneaky, but it still follows the basic rule.

We'll move on now to other uses for *some* and *any* by looking at another dialogue:

A: Wei Li, **some** of the figures in these accounts just don't seem to add up. Do you have **any** time to look them over for me?

B: Sure, Jien Guo, but it'll have to wait until this afternoon, okay?

A: Fine. Oh, but the way, do you have **some** extra file folders? I'm out.

B: I thought I had **some** in this drawer, but I guess I've used them all. Gee, I guess I don't have **any** after all.

A: That's okay. I have to go by Mei Lan's desk on my way to Marketing, and I know she's always got tons of file folders on hand.

B: Why the visit to the Marketing Department?

A: I want to get **some** information from them on how our ad campaign for "Liu Hong's Tiger Salve" has been going.

Let's see how good you're getting at explaining the uses of *some* and *any*. We'll repeat the phrases or sentences that the words appear in, and you can write down your interpretations on the lines we've provided as you would give them to your students:

... *some* of the figures ... _____

_____

Do you have *any* time ... ? _____

_____

... do you have *some* extra file folders? _____

_____

I thought I had *some* ... / I don't have *any* ... _____

_____

... *some* information ... _____

_____

Here are our interpretations, so check how close your ideas are to ours:

. . . *some* of the figures . . . When we use *some of* (and occasionally *some* on its own), we're really saying a certain portion, part, or percentage of the whole. *Some of the figures* means a certain portion of the figures, but not all of them.

. . . do you have *any* time? In yes/no questions, it's typical for the speaker to use *any* when he doesn't know what the answer will be or when he anticipates that the answer will be *no*.

. . . do you have *some* extra file folders? Contrary to both the use of *any* just discussed and to rules found in various ELT grammar books, it's perfectly acceptable to use *some* in yes/no questions when the speaker has a reason to expect that the answer will be *yes*, or he hopes it will be *yes*.

Before going on to the remaining phrases we're examining, let's take a breather and test out the explanations we've just given you for the two questions in our dialogue. Take a look at the following sentences. Decide if the underlined words sound okay or not and check the appropriate box, or if you can't make up your mind, check that box:

1. I'd like to use this vending machine. Do you have <u>some</u> change?
   ☐ sounds okay   ☐ doesn't sound okay   ☐ can't decide

2. I didn't know you were married! Do you have <u>any</u> kids?
   ☐ sounds okay   ☐ doesn't sound okay   ☐ can't decide

3. Did you hear <u>any</u> odd sounds? Like a bird's wings flapping?
   ☐ sounds okay   ☐ doesn't sound okay   ☐ can't decide

4. I know I heard a weird noise! Didn't you hear <u>some</u> strange sounds?
   ☐ sounds okay   ☐ doesn't sound okay   ☐ can't decide

We wonder if this last exercise left you feeling a little confused or even irritated. It very well may have because what at first seem to be clear-cut rules that we can give our students aren't really so clear cut after all.

We have a confession to make: we've just played a little trick on you! It really doesn't matter whether you checked "sounds okay," "doesn't sound okay," or "can't decide" because, in the long run, **the use of *some* or *any* is acceptable <u>depending on the viewpoint of the speaker</u>**. Even though this statement is true, we'd still like to offer you a few interpretations of why many native speakers might gravitate to one of the quantifiers instead of the other in the sentences you've just gone over.

In Sentence 1 the typical question would probably contain the word *any*, but if the speaker expects that the other person has change for the vending machine, he can opt to use *some*.

In Sentence 2 using *any* sounds okay probably because the speaker really has no idea of what the answer will be. After all, she's just found out that the other person's married and has no idea whether he has children or not.

In Sentence 3 many people would opt for *any* because the speaker doesn't know whether the other person heard weird noises or not. Opting for *some* is a viable alternative, though, if the speaker expects the other person to say *yes*.

In Sentence 4 many people would choose to say *some* because, even though the question is in the negative, once again the speaker is hoping for a *yes*, or at least a *maybe*. As in Sentence 3, however, the speaker can opt to use *any*.

Remember that these are our interpretations. The point of this activity has simply been to reinforce that **perhaps we shouldn't teach that *some* is always affirmative and *any* is always negative**. We might also want to be more careful about having our students use *any* exclusively in yes/no questions and negatives. *Some* and *any* are both acceptable in questions depending on the expectation of the speaker. At least we're offering you food for thought.

And now to the rest of those items from our dialogue:

I thought I had *some* . . . / . . . I don't have *any* . . . In both cases, *some* and *any* are being used as pronouns (substitutions for noun phrases). Because the listener knows what's being discussed, it isn't necessary for the speaker to repeat the noun phrase, *extra file folders.*

. . . *some* information . . . Even though a noun like *information* can't be counted and doesn't have a plural form in English, we can still think of information existing in relative amounts. (Note that *some* is used with both countable and uncountable nouns: *some children* and *some information*.) Besides *some*, which stands for a moderate amount, we have phrases like *a little* and *a lot of* that can be used with this kind of noun. Other examples of such nouns are *advice, furniture,* and *trouble.*

Up to this point, we've dealt with *any* in questions and in negatives when it means *not even one*, but that isn't the only way we use this word. How would you interpret *any* in our next dialogue?

> A: Didn't you go to the movies last night?
>
> B: Uh-huh. We saw the new Mel Gibson movie.
>
> A: Was it **any** good?
>
> B: I liked it a lot, but Nadia wasn't feeling well, so I don't think she enjoyed it very much—and that's unusual because if she can have her choice of **any** kind of film, it'll always be one with Mel Gibson in it!
>
> A: I'm sorry to hear she didn't feel well. Is she **any** better today?
>
> B: Yeah, lots. She even went to work.

Obviously, *any* isn't being used in negative contexts here, although we're using it once again in questions. So what does it mean in the context of the questions in this dialogue? Try to think of a new meaning or meanings for *any*. Then write your ideas down on the following lines:

_____

_____

In these instances, *any* has two distinct uses. In our first and third encounter with the word ("Was it <u>any</u> good?" / "Is she <u>any</u> better today?"), **we use *any* with adjectives in questions to mean "just a little" or "even a little."** This use occurs when *any* is combined with various adjectives either in their basic form (*any good*) or in their comparative form (*any better*). Of course, in these cases we find the word once again in the context of yes/no questions, and the meaning isn't different from when the word is used with nouns ("Do you have <u>any</u> children?"). **We can use *any* to mean "just a little" or "even a little" with all adjectives that can take intensifiers (words like *very*)**. This special use of *any* also works with the comparative form of adverbs:

Can he read in his language <u>any more quickly</u> than in English?

Any plus a noun can also mean "even a little" or "even a few" when the context shows that the subject isn't sure about a situation (such as when there's a negative connotation) or we find the words *if* or *whether*:

I doubt that they've received <u>any word</u> from Paolo yet.
We'd be surprised if she's written <u>any poems</u> lately.
It's unlikely that they've made <u>any progress</u>.
It's unclear whether that drug has helped <u>anybody</u>.

You've now seen how *any* can have this special meaning with adjectives, adverbs, and nouns, and since we've been going back and forth between *some* and *any* in this chapter, it's only reasonable for us to ask you if there's a counterpart for *any* in this usage. Is it *some*, or is it another word?

Coming up is another mini-dialogue for you to look at. We've deliberately left a blank where our mystery word should go. Read it through, think it over, and write down your choice for the blank on the line that follows. And by the way, think of something other than *a little* for your answer!

> A: I hear your wife's been quite ill.
> B: Yes, she's been pretty sick.
> A: Well, is she feeling **any** better now?
> B: She's feeling —————— better, but I'm afraid she's still got a long way to go.

It so happens that we do have a counterpart for *any* when it means *even a little.* The word we're thinking of for this meaning is the compound form **somewhat,** but it's normally used with adjectives and adverbs, and even with nouns, though commonly followed by *of:*

A: Is her health <u>any</u> better?
B: It's <u>somewhat</u> improved.

A: Is he typing <u>any</u> better than before?
B: Yes, he's typing <u>somewhat</u> more accurately.

It was <u>somewhat</u> of a shock to see them together again.

Now what about that second encounter we had with *any* in the dialogue (" . . . if she can have her choice of <u>any</u> kind of film . . . ")? In that case, **any means *no matter what, whichever, it doesn't matter which,*** or ***this, that, or the other.*** The field's wide open when we use *any* in this way.

But there's something very interesting, very unusual—and very tricky—with this new use of *any.* This phenomenon not only affects the meaning of *any,* but the meaning of *some* as well. The occurrence we're thinking of has to do with which word or words should receive the primary stress in the spoken language. **When *any* means *it doesn't matter which,* it receives the primary stress.** To see our point, just check it out in the third phrase that follows compared to the other two phrases from the dialogue that we've already gone over. (The capitalized words are the ones that get the primary stress):

Was it any GOOD?
Is she any BETTER?
. . . ANY kind of film . . .

You can clearly see that in normal speech, *any* only receives the primary stress in the third phrase where it means "it doesn't matter which." (Remember that in the first two phrases, *any* means "even a little.")

This stress change for *any* comes about because of an often overlooked component of English language teaching called autosegmental features, also known as prosodics. This fascinating area of the language is covered in Chapters 15 and 18. By the way, you'll be revisiting *some* and *any* in Chapter 18, which will show you more ways that autosegmental features influence these two words.

✍ **Compound Pronouns**

To complete our investigation of these two most commonly used quantifiers, we should mention the compound pronouns that we make from them. Because they contain the words *some* and *any,* these compound forms also tend to be troublesome for teachers and students, especially at the higher levels. Let's see how many of these words you can think of, all of which begin with *some* or *any.* Even though we know it isn't fair to ask you to come up with them without help, we ask you to try it for the fun of it! We've filled in the first compound pronoun in each column to get you started. And use every blank!

Compounds with *Some*

somebody

_____

_____

_____

_____

_____

_____

_____

_____

_____

Compounds with *Any*

anybody

_____

_____

_____

_____

_____

_____

_____

Here are the rest of those useful pronouns we get from our two quantifiers:

someday	anyhow
somehow	anymore
someone	anyone
something	anyplace
sometime	anything
sometimes	anytime
someway	anyway
somewhere	anywhere
somewhat	

It's interesting to note that *anymore, anyplace,* and *anyway,* when written as compound words, have different meanings from *any more, any place,* and *any way* written as separate words. How would you explain the differences?

Anymore means _____

_____.

Any more means _____

_____.

Anyplace means _____

_____.

Any place means _____

_____.

Anyway means _____

_____.

Any way means _____

_____.

It can be so hard to explain what appear to be simple words or expressions! Here are the meanings we've come up with, so compare them to yours:

Anymore means ***no longer, no more time***: "I can't help you anymore. I have given you as much help as I can."

Any more in a statement means ***no more of something***—whether it be cake or pencils or space or money: "There aren't any more patients in the waiting room. There were quite a few, but they aren't there now." Both *anymore* and *any more* can be used both in negative statements or questions.

Anyplace is synonymous with *nowhere* and ***follows a negative verb*** in a statement: "I don't know anyplace more beautiful than this." It is ***also used in questions***: "Do you know anyplace more beautiful than this?"

Note that the stress is on the first syllable for this meaning. (The stressed part is capitalized and underlined): <u>A</u>nyplace

Any place can mean ***whichever place, it doesn't matter where***: "I'll follow you to any place on earth!"

Note how the stress shifts for this meaning: any PLACE.

Anyway means *in any case, just the same, nevertheless, at any rate*, or even *anyhow*: "They broke an old vase of mine, but that's okay. I didn't like it anyway."
Note that the stress is on the first syllable: <u>A</u>nyway.

Any way means *in whatever manner, means, or method* in an affirmative sentence: "Do it any way you see fit." It can be used after a negative verb to mean *no way, no means*, or *no method*: "I don't know any way other than the one I'm using." Note that the stress has shifted for this meaning: any <u>WAY</u>. As with *anyplace/any place* and *anymore/ any more*, *anyway/any way* can be used in questions: "Wouldn't you like to go there anyway?"

Does anyone still think that *some* and *any* aren't challenging? Well, there's one more point we'd like to bring to your attention to prove to you one more time just how multi-faceted these words can be. How would you explain the completely grammatical use of *some* with a noun phrase and in a compound pronoun in the following examples?

A: How about hiring my nephew to work in the store?
B: I don't want to hire <u>some</u> teenager for that sort of job.

A: Want to try a little of this hot sauce on your food?
B: No, thanks! I'd never eat <u>something</u> that would make
   my mouth feel like it's on fire.

On the surface, it seems as if these two examples go completely against the rule given in ELT grammar books that says when the accompanying verb is negative or the idea is negative, use *any*. Using *some* in this way occurs when **one person is rebuffing or rebuking what another person has just said**. In fact, the use of *some* with a noun phrase (*some teenager*) is really quite derisive. Here are two more examples:

A: Feel like using my uncle's cabin on the lake?

B: I don't feel like going <u>someplace</u> that's got no
   central heating. It gets cold in those woods.

Sorry, but that's not <u>something</u> I enjoy talking about.

Compounds with "Any-" vs. Compounds with "No-"

Our final dialogue is a conversation between a teacher and one of his students. Let's see if you can help the teacher clarify things:

S: Hello, Mr. Firsten. I'm really excited about the class party you're having at your house. It's very nice of you to do that.

T: Thank you, Enikö. I'm happy to do it.

S: Can I bring somebody to the party?

T: Anybody. That's fine with me.

S: You mean I can't?

T: No, I said you could.

S: Oh, okay. Would you like to join me for lunch?

T: Haven't you already had something to eat?

S: Anything. I was too busy earlier.

T: You mean nothing, not anything.

S: But I didn't have anything. Isn't that good English?

T: Well, that sentence is, but...

S: You said "anybody" to answer my question, so why can't I say "anything" to answer yours?

T: All right, Enikö. Let me explain why you have to say *nothing* and not *anything*.

Who can blame poor Enikö for being befuddled! You'll notice the confusion she had when the teacher said she could bring "anybody" to the party. Why do you think Enikö felt that the teacher was saying *no*?

It seems that Enikö was confused over the meaning of *any* in the compound form *anybody*. She was so accustomed to hearing *any* used in negative contexts that she was under the misconception that the word always has a negative meaning and is therefore equal to *nobody*. This is a typical error that students make, so we're glad that we can help you prepare for the inevitability of hearing it. **Students forget that *any* is negative only if it follows a negative verb.**

What explanation can you offer Enikő and your students as well to clear up when we say the negative *any* on its own (any lunch) or in a compound form (anything) and when we say "no" on its own (no lunch) or in a compound form (nothing)? Before getting into your answer, you might find it useful to list all the counterparts for *any* that begin with *no-*. We've repeated the list you saw earlier in the chapter and filled in the first one to get you started:

Any	**No**
anybody	nobody
anymore	_____
anyone	_____
anything	_____
anywhere	_____
any (quantifier)	_____
any (on its own)	_____

Here's how we'd fill in the rest of those blanks: ***no more, no one, nothing, nowhere, no,*** and ***none***. And now to your explanations!

1. *Any* as a separate entity or as the first element in a compound form has a negative meaning if the verb that accompanies it is ————————.

2. *Any* as a separate entity or as the first element in a compound form means a certain amount of something if the verb that accompanies it is —————.

3. *No* is used as a separate entity or as the first element in a compound form if the verb that accompanies it is ——————————.

4. *No* as a separate entity or as the first element in a compound form means a zero amount of something if the verb that accompanies it is —————.

Does it seem a bit hard to put into simple words? Here's how we'd complete these four sentences. Compare our thoughts to yours and see how closely they match:

1. *Any* as a separate entity or as the first element in a compound form has a negative meaning if the verb that accompanies it is **negative:** "I <u>don't</u> have any change for the vending machine."

2. *Any* as a separate entity or as the first element in a compound form means a certain amount of something if the verb that accompanies it is **part of a question**: "Do they have anything to tell me?"

3. *No* is used as a separate entity or as the first element in a compound form if the verb that accompanies it is **affirmative**. This idea goes along with that basic rule of English grammar which says you can't have two negatives in one idea: "I <u>have</u> no change for the vending machine."

4. *No* as a separate entity or as the first element in a compound form means a zero amount or number of something if the verb that accompanies it is **affirmative**: "I saw no one while I was walking the dog."

It follows that if we use *no* or a compound form beginning with *no-* when there isn't a negative verb present, we can use it to begin a sentence or to answer somebody's question in one word:

> A: We just don't see your point.
> B: <u>Nobody</u> understands me!
>
> A: Any interesting programs on TV tonight?
> B: <u>Nothing</u>.

So what do we tell poor befuddled Enikö about Mr. Firsten's reply that she could bring *anybody* she wanted to the party? How would you explain what he meant?

If you recall what we said earlier about the meaning of *any way* in an affirmative sentence, you can basically bring into play the same interpretation for *anybody*. It means **this person, that person, another person—it doesn't matter which person**. In addition, the teacher should give Enikö examples to show her how *any* will work the same way in affirmative statements whether on its own or as the first element of a compound form:

> Okay, Billy, if you have <u>any</u> money left after you buy
> those groceries for me, you can get some candy with it.
>
> A: Can I ask you to do me a favor?
> B: Sure, <u>any</u>thing you want. What is it?

 ### *"Some" in a Nutshell*

 indefinite plural of *a/an* in affirmative sentences representing an unspecified number or amount:
A: I need an empty folder to put these reports in.
B: You'll find some folders on top of that cabinet. And you'll find some labels there, too.

- **equals** *more or less, about, approximately*:
  There are some two thousand students in my school.

- **representing an unspecified person, place, or thing:**
  I can't believe how lucky I've been. Somebody up there likes me.
  Something will be done to correct that problem.

- **substitutes for noun phrases:**
  A: I don't see those folders on top of the cabinet.
  B: You don't? I know there were some up there awhile ago.

- **equals** *a portion, a percentage, a part of*:
  Some of my friends/Some friends of mine think that we should have more nuclear power plants.

- **equals an unspecified amount of a normally uncountable noun:**
  Can I offer you some advice?

- **expecting or hoping for a** *yes* **after yes/no questions:**
  Would you like some help with those heavy packages, ma'am?

- **used when rebuffing or rebuking what has just been said (even though the accompanying verb is negative):**
  How old is she? Sorry! I don't want some seventy-five-year-old person to take care of my kid. Can't we find somebody younger?

"Any" in a Nutshell

- **negative counterpart of** *some* **which represents the idea of** *zero* **after a negative verb in statements:**
  A: I need an empty folder to put these reports in.
  B: Sorry, I don't have any empty folders left.

- **substitutes for noun phrases:**
  A: I don't see those folders on top of the cabinet.
  B: Are you sure there aren't any there?

- **used together with** *hardly, never,* **and** *without*:
  I'm so busy, I hardly have any time to relax these days.
  She never returns any phone calls.
  He went through the surgery without any complications.

- **not knowing what the answer will be or expecting a** *no* **after yes/no questions:**
  I'm out of stamps. Do you have any stamps you can lend me?

- **equals** *even a little* **or** *even a few* **with basic or comparative adjectives, comparative adverbs, or nouns:**
  Is that route any shorter than the one I used to take?
  Will this new filing system help us work any more efficiently?
  Is there any chance at all that you'll be able to help us?

---

 used when the speaker is in doubt:

I wonder whether she has any idea how rude she was.

 equals *it doesn't matter which, whichever*:

Let me try out this card trick. Pick a card. Any card will do.

If there's anything you need, just let me know.

Teaching Tips

7.1 A Modified Cloze

Create a modified cloze activity (see pages 519–521) that contains a good variety of the various uses of *some* and *any* in it. Have the students complete the cloze on their own or in small groups. Collect the completed cloze examples, correct them, and return them to the students. If your students are able to, let them correct their classmates' clozes.

Variation: Use that modified cloze as a dictation activity. Put the cloze on a handout making sure that the blanks aren't too close together. It's too hard for the students to complete if the blanks are too close; they can't write the word fast enough before another blank comes up. Tell the students to put their pencils and pens down as you read the *entire* cloze to them. Read it again, this time letting your students fill in as many of the blanks as they can. Tell them that you'll be reading it a third time so they can check what they've written and fill in any blanks that they've missed.

7.2 Limericks

Students enjoy poetry, and limericks are especially fun as examples of poems. Limericks are five-lined poems whose first, second, and fifth lines rhyme and whose third and fourth lines rhyme. They often begin with "There once was/were . . ." and contain a rhythmic pattern similar to the one in the following example: lines 1, 2, and 5 have eight to nine beats; lines 3 and 4 have six beats. Don't be a slave, however, to this rhythmic pattern, or to the rhyme for that matter!

> There once was some cheese in our house
> Not being saved for any old mouse.
> When some mice did it see,
> They were all full of glee.
> There wasn't any cat that might pounce!

Go over the limerick with your students enough times so that they can eventually repeat it by heart. Divide them into small groups and let them create limericks of their own using *some* and *any.*

Variation: Create a tongue twister that contains *some, any,* and *no* or their compound forms. ("Any apples Amy's aunt ate were all Amy's." / "Some of Sally's shoes smell somewhat sweet, so sometimes Sally has some sweet feet.")

7.3 Sentence Combining

This Tip can be used with almost any language point. It's a sentence combining activity that has the students put back together short dialogues that contain examples of *some* and *any* (see *Appendix 3,* for complete details of this activity). Before class, create or copy short dialogues with *some* and *any.* Give each dialogue a name or number. Separate the dialogues into two parts, putting each part of the dialogue on a separate slip of paper. Write "1" on the first half of the dialogue slip and "2" on the second half. Mix up the slips and distribute them to your students. Have any student who has a "1" slip read it aloud. The student who has the matching "2" slip completes the dialogue. Continue until all the dialogue slips have been rematched.

7.4 Remembering Details

This tip can also be used with any language point that your class is working on; in this case, however, you'll be focusing on *some* and *any.* Before class begins, prepare a story containing numerous examples of *some* and *any* in it. The text needs to be sufficiently rich in details so that your students are challenged to retain the details you'll ask them to remember after they've heard the text. If you can, record the text; if not, you can read it aloud to your class. Prepare a list of details, some correct and some incorrect, about the text and put them on the board or on a handout. If you've written these facts on the board, cover them up until after you've read the text two or three times. Have the students divide a piece of paper into two columns, writing *correct* at the top of one column and *incorrect* at the top of the other. Divide the class into small groups and have them list the details under the proper column. When all the information has been put into the proper columns, read the story to them again and have them correct the facts that are wrong.

Variation: Create a dialogue with several people talking about what they have or don't have, need or don't need, etc. (Make sure the dialogue contains several examples of *some* and *any.*) Provide a handout with a list of the items discussed and some which weren't discussed in the dialogue. You can also put the items on the board. Have the students check off what they've heard and then have them divide up into groups and reconstruct the dialogue they've just worked on.

8

Modal Auxiliaries in the Present or Future

"I would if I could, but I can't, so I won't."

One of the biggest challenges to an instructor is successfully teaching the uses of the surprisingly complex little words and phrases that we call **modal auxiliaries**. Modals are a real challenge because

- they have several meanings,
- they can vary in usage from one part of the English-speaking world to another,
- they have many "gray areas" where they overlap in meaning, and
- they may exhibit differences in meaning and usage from one speaker to another even in the same region.

Because of all these complexities, we'd like to give you some advice for the information you're about to discover in this chapter: Pick and choose among what we have to offer; there will be points that you feel can be useful to you in your teaching, but there will be other points that you may decide aren't appropriate or necessary for your English grammar lesson or should be reserved for more advanced students. That, of course, doesn't mean *you* shouldn't become sensitized to those points—you never know when an astute person in one of your classes may throw a question at you on one of those points, and it would be nice if you could answer the student with confidence . . . or at least understand the question and recognize what the student is asking without surprise!

Just exactly which words are we talking about? Here's a list of them: *can, could, will, would, shall, should, ought to, may, might,* and *must.* Some grammarians also include *used to, would rather, had better,* and *had best,* but we'll be dealing with these four and some others under the heading "semi-auxiliaries" (also known as "periphrastic modals").

We can explain what modals are by comparing them to ordinary verbs. (Note the stars [*] before most of the following examples; we're using stars to mean that the phrase is ungrammatical):

- Modals never take the infinitive *to* (*to can/*to may).
- They never add the *-s* to 3rd person singular in the present or general time (*he mays/*it shoulds).
- They never require the *-ed* ending for the past (*we shoulded).
- They never have *-ing* attached to them (*by oughting).
- They never use forms of *do* or *be* to make negatives, yes/no questions, or tag questions (*you don't can/*he isn't mighting); instead, they use the word *not* after them for the negative (you cannot/he might not).
- Their forms don't necessarily indicate the tense of the sentence (Sure, I could do it tomorrow.).

We call them "auxiliaries" because their main function is to *help* a true verb by altering its meaning, that is, adding some extra meaning or nuance that the verb itself doesn't have alone.

There are some other general points we should mention about modals:
- In *standard* English, two modals can never be used together:

    *I think Pancho <u>might could</u> be at the office.

- All modals can refer to the present or the future using the same form—even *will* can accomplish this goal in a certain context as you'll see later on:

    We <u>can</u> take samples of the lake water *now.*
    We <u>can</u> take samples of the lake water *tomorrow.*

- What many people commonly call the past form of modals (like *could, would,* and *might*) isn't really the past at all the way we normally use these words:

    <u>Could</u> you give me a ride downtown tomorrow?

These forms are only truly the past when they're clarified with additional information or through context:

    He <u>couldn't</u> come *(yesterday).*

Because most grammar books created for students only give a superficial presentation of modals and usually don't mention semi-auxiliaries such as *would rather,* we're going to fill in the gaps and give you a more complete picture in this chapter.

Before we get under way, we should mention that this chapter will only deal with the modals in their present/future use. You'll find a detailed exploration of the modals in the past in Chapter 12.

A3 Can/Could

We're going to begin our exploration of the modal auxiliaries by taking a good look at the words *can* and *could*. Read this first dialogue and figure out what the exact uses of *can* are. You'll notice a number attached to the modal for each use that's being demonstrated in the dialogue. This system will help us discuss the various uses of modals in all of the dialogues that follow, too.

When you think you've figured out what each use of *can* is in this dialogue, write your idea on the following lines that numerically match them:

A: Did you know that different species of whales **can**[1] create different kinds of "songs" to communicate with one another?

B: Yes, I knew that. And I've met a famous marine biologist who **can**[1] tell one species of whale from another just by listening to their "songs."

A: You **can't**[2] be serious!

B: I am!

A: **Can**[3] people really do that?

B: Trust me. They can.

---

1. _____

2. _____

3. _____

Let's see how we interpret *can* in this dialogue. ***Can¹*** means **ability**. There's a slight difference, though, between the first modal labeled *1* and the second. In the first use, the modal means *innate* ability, but in the second it means *acquired* ability. Just as we don't distinguish between the two very much in real life, we don't bother differentiating these fine lines with the modal either.

Can't² has a different use. Here the modal in the negative expresses **disbelief** or **impossibility**. Person A is saying that he's having a hard time believing that Person B is serious (not joking) about a marine biologist having that special skill. At this point, take a look at the following two sentences in which *can't* and *couldn't* represent disbelief or impossibility. See if you can perceive a difference between the two and write your idea on the following lines:

1. You've been married how many years? You <u>can't</u> be!
2. You've been married how many years? You <u>couldn't</u> be.

_____

_____

What many native speakers will perceive as the difference between these two sentences is that ***can't* is a stronger form of disbelief or impossibility than** *couldn't*. In fact, using *couldn't* may actually soften the meaning enough so that it's used in a more tactful way communicating that something is "hard to believe" rather than "impossible." By the way, we'll be seeing another instance further on in this section when changing *can* to *could* softens its meaning.

We have yet another meaning of *can* in our dialogue. ***Can³*** expresses **hypothetical possibility**—that something is possible in theory. It doesn't mean, however, that this is a possibility likely to occur at any time soon; there's no reference to the near future as there can be with other modals as we'll soon see. In fact, we'll get back to this meaning of possibility shortly.

We should make it clear, moreover, that *can* is limited in its use as a modal of possibility. This is probably because it's easy to confuse it with the idea of *ability* in many sentences, and we try to avoid confusion whenever we can. Just look at the following little sentence, deliberately given to you here out of context and see what we mean:

He can be rich.

Most native speakers are likely to consider this sentence strange. They'll probably feel uncomfortable with it because they'll have trouble interpreting what *can* means. According to our definitions of *can*, however, you really have the option to interpret the idea to mean "It's possible that he's rich," or "He has the ability to get rich." You can see why we normally avoid using *can* for possibility in such ideas; it's much easier to use another modal that unambiguously conveys the idea of possibility.

Now let's look at two more uses of *can* and *can't*:

> A: Excuse me. Can I park my car here?
> B: Sorry, you can't park here. These spaces are for tenants only.

So how would you interpret *can* and *can't* in this mini-dialogue?

Can is used here to mean _____.

Can't is used here to mean _____.

⚡ *Troubleshooter* ⚡

There's a point concerning pronunciation that we'd like to bring to your attention. It may not seem like a major concern at first, but because it may interfere with accurate communication, we think it's important enough to mention.

💡 All the modal auxiliaries are unstressed in the context of a sentence when they're affirmative:

> He can GO with us on the trip.
> She can SPEAK three languages.

When the modals are negative, however, they're stressed along with their verbs:

> He CAN'T GO with us on the trip.
> She CAN'T SPEAK three languages.

💡 With the modal *can*, we have an important change in pronunciation between the affirmative and the negative which truly affects communication:

☞ Unstressed *can* is really pronounced /kɪn/. In fact, there's practically no vowel sound at all.

☞ Stressed *can't* on the other hand, has a strongly pronounced vowel which is /a/ in British English and /æ/ in most forms of American English.
   Moreover, the final /t/ in *can't* is an unreleased /t̥/ in many dialects when it comes before a verb, so for all intents and purposes, it's inaudible. These two phenomena, the added stress and the unreleased /t̥/, result in a modal that sounds negative simply because it has the stress on it and the strongly pronounced vowel: /kænt̥/.

Sensitizing your students to this change in communication brought on by these phonological changes will go a long way to stop any misunderstandings that could very well arise.

These two uses of the modal are quite clear. *Can* is used here to mean **permission**. Person A wants to know if he has permission to park in that space. *Can't* is being used to mean **prohibition**. Person B is telling Person A that he doesn't have permission to park in that space.

Now let's look at another dialogue and investigate these uses of *can* and *could*:

A: So tell me, how was your year in Rio de Janeiro?

B: Just wonderful! But you know, it **can**[1] get quite chilly in the hills outside of Rio in July.

A: I don't care about the weather! Tell me more about that good-looking Brazilian colleague of yours.

B: Well, he **can**[1] be very charming. And guess what! He **could** be here in the next couple of weeks on business.

A: Really? If he's as cute as you've said he is, I'd love to meet him.

B: Well, that **can**[2] be arranged.

A: Who knows. This **could** turn out to be a very interesting experience!

Can

1. _____

2. _____

Could

1. _____

Here we have completely different uses of *can* and we come upon *could* for the first time in a dialogue. *Can*[1] represents the idea of **capability**. First we have the idea that the temperature is capable of getting quite chilly in that area outside of Rio proper, and then we have the idea that this man is capable of being charming. Note that there's a big difference between the sentences in these pairs:

> It can get quite chilly in the hills.
> It gets quite chilly in the hills.
>
> He is very charming.
> He can be very charming.

The question is, how can you explain that important difference to your students if the subject comes up? Write your thoughts on the following lines:

_____

_____

The important difference is that when we use *can* in this way, we're communicating that **there's a potential for something to happen, but we're not claiming that it's always the case.** In our first example, Speaker B is saying that there's a potential for the temperature to get quite chilly in that area in July, but it doesn't necessarily mean that this weather condition is always true. In our second example, Speaker B is saying that her former colleague is the kind of person who has the potential to be quite charming, but that he isn't always like that. Actually, she might be implying that he can turn the charm on and off at will, and some listeners might even pick up a negative sub-text in this case! You can see how important using or not using *can* may be to the communication.

Can^2 and *could* represent the idea of possibility, but there's a difference: **Can** once again expresses **hypothetical possibility**. Person B says it's possible that a meeting between her friend and the Brazilian will be arranged, implying *if things work out*. **Could**, on the other hand, expresses what we call **real possibility**, that is, something that may actually come to pass in the future. Person B uses *could* when talking about the future trip her Brazilian colleague is planning to take because it falls within the categories we've just mentioned: "It's possible that he'll be here in a couple of weeks." Likewise, Person A ends the dialogue by saying that there's a good chance the experience of meeting the Brazilian will be interesting, and by communicating this idea as a real future possibility as opposed to some idea in theory only, she uses *could*.

Here are two sentences that demonstrate why *can* and *could* aren't always interchangeable because the focus they have on the kind of possibility being expressed is different:

1. With all the rain an El Niõ brings, dams c<u>an</u> burst.
2. With all the rain we've been having, the dam <u>could</u> burst.

Think about the difference in meaning between these two sentences and write down your ideas on the following lines:

_____

_____

In **Sentence 1**, *can* represents a **hypothetical possibility**. The focus isn't so much on a possible disaster that we think is about to happen as it is on the idea that we know dams are able to hold just so much water before they burst. In **Sentence 2**, *could* represents a **real possibility**; we're saying in this case that there's a real chance the dam is going to burst. It's more appropriate for our speaker to use *could* in this context since weather conditions have created that real possibility.

Another reason that *can* isn't used too commonly to mean possibility is that we deal with real possibilities most of the time, not hypothetical ones. This difference also explains why *can* isn't usually interchangeable with *could* for this meaning.

☀ *Troubleshooter* ☀

Be prepared for another inevitable occurrence: Many of your students will end up using *can* to mean *possibility* in every English sentence they create containing this idea. They'll produce all sorts of sentences like *The weatherman says it can snow tonight.*

This is most likely because the equivalent of the English modal *can* is used in many languages to mean *possibility* even when it's real and not just hypothetical, unlike English, which usually uses *could* for this idea.

Just keep reminding them that *could* is more common for possibility than *can*.

But we're not done with *can* and *could* yet. What uses do you find for them in our next dialogue?

A: Here the weekend's coming and I've got absolutely no plans. I have no idea what to do.

B: Well, you **can** get together with your friend Nancy. You haven't seen her in awhile.

A: That's true.

B: Or you **could** clean out your closet or finish that term paper that's due soon for your social studies class.

A: Thanks, Mom. You're just full of neat ideas. Mmmm. Maybe I'll give Nancy a call.

The first question we need to ask is, how are *can* and *could* being used in this dialogue? What ideas do you have?

Can and *could* are being used _____

It seems that *can* and *could* are being used in this instance as a way of giving **advice** or **suggestions**, but it's important to mention that these two modals leave room for other options. You'll see why this warning is important later on when we explore *should* and *ought to*.

The next question we need to ask is why Speaker B chose to use *can* in her first utterance, but switched to *could* in her next sentence. Any ideas on the subject?

_____

An interesting difference can be seen in the way Speaker B is thinking. When she gives her first suggestion, she's fairly confident that her daughter will react favorably to the idea of seeing her friend, Nancy. However, when she gives her next two suggestions, she knows perfectly well that there's only a slim chance her daughter will take these ideas seriously. It turns out, then, that **we tend to use *can* when we give advice that we believe has a good chance of being accepted, but we use *could* when we're not so sure our suggestions will be heeded**.

Now let's examine another two uses for *could*. Write your interpretation on the lines that follow the dialogue.

A: Hello, Mrs. Todd. Happy birthday!

B: Why, thank you, Jim. And thank you, everybody, for this lovely cake! **Could**[1] you help me blow out the candles, Jim?

A: I'm sure you can manage the two of them just fine!

B: Well, I don't know...a woman my age. It's a good thing they didn't put one candle on the cake for each year!

A: **Could**[2] I ask how old you are today?

B: I don't mind telling you. I'm seventy-two today.

A: No way! You can't be seventy-two!

B: Well, bless your heart. However, I'm afraid I am.

---

1. _____

2. _____

This use of *could*[1] is what most people refer to as **a polite form for making a request**. There are other ways to make requests with modals, most notably by using *can* or *would*. Most native speakers, however, perceive *could* as being more polite and more formal than *can*. In the sentence with our first example, Mrs. Todd is making a little joke by politely requesting that Jim give her some help blowing out the two candles on her cake.

The use of *could*[2] is a different matter; it represents **asking for permission**. In this case, Jim is **politely** and **deferentially** asking Mrs. Todd for permission to inquire about her age. Asking a person's age isn't something you normally do in many cultures, so Jim feels the need to ask for permission to pose this question and he softens it by using the polite use of *could*.

Before we leave *could*, let's read the following two mini-dialogues and decide if the lines in bold are acceptable or unacceptable:

Dialogue 1

A. Could I become a doctor?
B. Sure you could.

☐ acceptable   ☐ unacceptable

Dialogue 2

A. Could I borrow your pen?
B. Sure you could.

☐ acceptable   ☐ unacceptable

Native English speakers would say that Person B's reply in **Dialogue 1** is **acceptable**, but Person B's reply in **Dialogue 2** is probably **unacceptable**, yet they're exactly the same sentence. What's the difference, and why is it that the exact same sentence doesn't work in both cases? Here's some space for you to write down any solutions you have to solve this puzzle:

_____

_____

The explanations for this strange occurrence are as follows. The word *could* in Dialogue 1 expresses the idea of **possibility** and is being used by Person A as he wonders about the possibility of becoming a doctor. If we continue to develop the idea in that question, we can come up with phrases like "Could I become a doctor . . . if I wanted to/. . . if medical school weren't so hard to get into/. . . if tuition weren't so high and

I weren't so poor?" In any case, ***could* represents possibility both in the question and reply**: "Of course you could [become a doctor if . . .]" which equals "Of course you'd have the possibility [of becoming a doctor if . . .]."

The word *could* in Dialogue 2 is completely different. Here Person A is using it as a polite way to ask for **permission** to use Person B's pen. Remember that *could* represents this polite form of *asking for* permission, but it doesn't represent the way we *give* permission; for that, we use *can* (among other modals). So *could* is unacceptable in the reply to Person B's question in Dialogue 2 because *could* never means "I give you permission." We say "Sure you can [borrow my pen]."

 ## *"Can" in a Nutshell*

ability:
My friend Roger can speak three languages.

hypothetical possibility:
Successful surgeries can mean the start of new lives for patients.

permission:
You can park here without putting money in the meter after 6:00 p.m.

prohibition (when in the negative):
You can't smoke in a hospital.

capability:
He can be really cranky when he hasn't had enough sleep.

advice or suggestions (which are likely to be heeded):
If you're passed over for another promotion, you can always look for another job.

informally making a request:
Can you help me out for a moment?

informally asking for permission:
Can I take the car tonight, Dad?

disbelief/impossibility (when in the negative):
The ozone layer can't be disintegrating! Do you realize what that means? (disbelief)
He can't be there already. He only left ten minutes ago and it's a good twenty-minute ride to get there. (impossibility)

 ## *"Could" in a Nutshell*

real possibility:
Yes, I see your point. You could be right.

advice or suggestions (which aren't likely to be heeded):
Well, if you have nothing much to do tonight, you could take me out to dinner.

🥜 **politely making a request:**
Could you help me with these suitcases, please?

🥜 **politely or deferentially asking for permission:**
Could I take your picture?

🥜 **"softened" form of disbelief (when in the negative);
not very probable:**
He couldn't be your brother. He looks nothing like you.

Will/Would

The next two modals that we'll investigate are probably just as troublesome as *can* and *could* tend to be, but before we look at the next dialogue, we want to make mention of the fact that this is a continuation of the material covered in Chapter 5. There's so much to say about *will* that it *would* be overwhelming to do so in one chapter!

Let's look at the following dialogue to see *will* in some uses not covered in Chapter 5 and some uses for its counterpart, *would*:

A: Isn't Ahmed here yet?
B: No, not yet.
A: **Would**[1] you call his house to make sure he's on his way?
B: You ***would***[2] ask me to do that now that I'm sitting down and comfortable. He'll be here soon enough. Just take it easy!
A: I *will* take it easy, but I still think you should call him.
B: **Will**[1] you kindly stop nagging me?
A: You know me. I ***will***[2] go on and on when I worry. I can't help it. Please find out if he's on his way.
B: All right! All right!

Let's examine the uses of *will* and *would* the same way we covered *can* and *could*. On the following lines that are numbered to correspond to the modal uses in the dialogue, write down your interpretation of what these modals mean in their contexts:

Would	Will
1. _____	1. _____
2. _____	2. _____

Would[1] and *will*[1] express **polite requests**. Many native speakers, however, perceive a slight difference between the two words. They see *will* as being somewhat more direct or forceful than *would*, which sounds a little more polite, deferential, or formal.

Would[2] and *will*[2] are quite unusual. They represent **actions or behaviors characteristic of the person or thing you're talking about**. First, Person B says it's typical for Person A to insist on asking him to do something right after he's just sat down and gotten all comfortable; similarly, Person A says she knows she has the habit of going on and on about something to the point of obsessing on it, offering this thought almost as an apology. The difference between the two modals when used in this way is that *will* **expresses this idea about a general observation** just as the simple present can do when referring to habits, universal truths, etc. (refer to Chapter 3). *Would* **refers to the same characteristic behavior as *will* does, but is used by someone responding immediately to something that's just happened rather than just making a general observation.**

One more unusual point about this use of the two modals is that stress can play an important role in determining meaning. When the modals are unstressed, the usual intent is simply that this is, or was, typical behavior. When the modals are stressed, however, there's a negative implication that can be interpreted as criticism. Compare these two sentences as more examples of this usage:

> Whenever anyone's in trouble, she'll be the first one to help.
> (unstressed *'ll* carries no negative implication)

> A: Why is Fred always so tired in the morning?
> B: Well, he WILL stay up to watch the late night movie
> on TV every night. What can you expect?
> (stressed *will* carries a criticizing tone)

Go back to the dialogue for a moment and re-read the third sentence that Person A says. (The *italics* indicate stress on those words as it would be used in the spoken language by the two people.) Even though *will* appears stressed in two instances, it only changes meaning, resulting in that reproachful tone, in one instance: I *will* go on and on when I worry." In the other sentence where this stressed *will* occurs, its meaning isn't altered at all ("I *will* take it easy ... "). The word is stressed in this case simply to give it an emphatic quality as a retort to what Person B has just said. Words or phrases that have their meaning changed depending on whether or not they're stressed are part of a group called "autosegmentals," which we'll take up in Chapters 15 and 18. Here's something else to note about modals and stress: **You never contract modals when you want to stress them.** That's easy to understand when you consider how impossible it would be to try to stress the *'ll* when added to a pronoun ("They'll do it," for example).

Before we leave the subject of the stressed *will* that can indicate a pejorative or critical view of someone's behavior—depending on the context it's used in—we need to mention an alternative for *will* that is very typically heard in English. **Most speakers tend to use the word *do* the same way we've demonstrated *will* in this**

section to indicate that reproachful tone. In other words, instead of saying "I <u>will</u> go on and on when I worry," Person A could just as easily say "I <u>do</u> go on and on when I worry."

There are four final uses for *will* that we're going to investigate now, so take a look at the following dialogue and see what you can make of the modal in these cases:

A: Let me go answer the door. Someone's knocking.

B: Oh, that'**ll**[1] be Ms. Borgia. I invited her over for dinner.

A: Borgia? Oh, no! You know I can't stand her.

B: Look, she's my supervisor, and I think she's considering me for a promotion.

A: Oh that's nice: buttering up the boss!

B: Call it what you **will**[2], I think it's just good politics and I *won't*[3] discuss it anymore. You'**ll**[4] be nice to her and you **won't**[4] do anything to sabotage my chances of getting a promotion, right? Right!

1. _____

2. _____

3. _____

4. _____

The interpretation for ***will*[1]** is that it represents **a deduction** or **conclusion** based on some sort of information previously known. Actually, it's just about the strongest way you can express **probability** without really knowing the facts. Person B says in this case that she's 95% sure the person knocking at the door is her supervisor.

Will*[2]** is a bit tricky—and it's also a linguistic throwback to many centuries ago when our modal *will* was the Old English verb *willan* meaning *to want*. That historical information gives the answer away: in this instance, ***will* means *want, so Person A is saying "Call it whatever you want . . ." You can often hear this use of the modal in the currently popular parenthetical expression *if you will*, a phrase that is thrown into practically any kind of sentence and seems to mean "if you want to interpret **XZ** as I'm explaining it." Here's an example of how the expression is used:

> A: The steady destruction of the natural world, or the end of life as we know it, **if you will**, isn't just some bad dream anymore. It's real, and we've got to stop it.
>
> B: I just hope people all over the world wake up and realize how big the disaster will be if they don't take a stand.

Won't[3] represents **refusal** and, coincidentally, it can get stressed equally with its verb for emphasis in the spoken language.

Will[4] (both in the affirmative and negative) expresses **a command**, **an order**. Person B is saying in no uncertain terms that she expects Person A to be on his best behavior and expresses this idea with a strong, firm imperative form. Some native speakers take this use of *will* as the strongest imperative form we can muster up in English as it has the hidden meaning that the person saying it will accept nothing less than what's being demanded. We mentioned earlier that *will* can be used as a more forceful, polite request than *would* when used in a question ("Will you kindly stop nagging me?"). When we use *will* this way in a statement ("You will be nice to her . . ."), it's even *more* forceful.

"Will" in a Nutshell

 used for polite requests (more forceful than would):
Will you buckle your seat belt so I can start driving?

 used for an action characteristic of the person or thing being discussed (general time observation):
- Jack knows how to relax. He'll nap for hours under that tree.
  (unstressed *'ll* = no negative connotation)
- Antoinette is such a stubborn woman. She <u>will</u> have to have her way.
  (stressed *will* = criticism)
- Antoinette is such a stubborn woman. She <u>does</u> have to have her way.
  (stressed *do* as alternative for *will* = criticism)

 used for deductions or conclusions (probability):
Can you get the phone? That'll be Jim. Tell him I'm leaving now.

 will **used to mean** *want* **in some formulaic expressions:**
Do what you will with this ugly, old chair; just get it out of the living room.

 refusal (when in the negative):
You can complain about my salary all you want. I won't look for a different job!

used for a command/order:
You will eat everything on your plate and you will like it!

 "Would" in a Nutshell

 used for polite requests (softer than *will*):
Would you answer the phone, please? My hands are wet.

 used for an action characteristic of the person or thing being discussed (immediate reaction to something that has just occurred):
I should know you by now. You <u>would</u> embarrass me like that!
(stressed *would* = criticism)

May/Might

We'll continue our investigation into modals the same way we've discovered so many facts about those already covered. Let's look at this next dialogue to see how *may* and *might* can function:

A: Good morning, Mr. Snodgrass.

B: Good morning, Ms. Ketchum. **Might**[1] I have a word?

A: Certainly. What is it?

B: You **may**[2] not realize it, but your dog has been going through my garbage can again and tossing the garbage all over my front lawn.

A: My Muffie? I don't believe it. I'm sure it's the work of another dog.

B: Well, it **might**[2] be, but I very much doubt it.

A: Well, Mr. Snodgrass, if I **may**[1] say so, you **might**[3] consider using a garbage can with a tighter lid!

B: And if I may say so, Ms. Ketchum, **may**[3] you never find garbage strewn all over your front lawn as I have!

Now that you've looked over the uses of these two modals in the dialogue, write down your interpretation of what they mean in the different contexts on the following lines that are numbered to correspond:

Might		May	
1. _____		1. _____	
2. _____		2. _____	
3. _____		3. _____ **X**	
4. _____ **X**		4. _____	

Even though not the most common use of the word, *might[1]* is **the most polite, deferential, and formal way to ask for permission—it's also the least forceful.** Some native speakers even consider this use of *might* almost too much in this somewhat overly solicitous way of asking for permission. *May[1]* is the more common way we politely ask for permission to do something.

May[2] expresses the idea of **possibility**. "It's possible that you don't realize it . . ." is what Mr. Snodgrass is saying to Ms. Ketchum. When we see *might[2]*, it expresses **possibility** just as *may* does. The question is, do you discern any difference between *may* and *might* when they both express possibility?

Many prescriptive grammar books define *might* as being a weaker version of *may* when the meaning is possibility. The way these two modals have been used for possibility in this dialogue tends to uphold that perception of *may* and *might*. Mr. Snodgrass is less certain that a dog other than Muffie is the culprit than he is about Ms. Ketchum not realizing what her dog's been up to. In other words, he's using *may* for stronger possibility and *might* for weaker possibility. We want to make it clear, though, that not all native speakers sense this difference; that's probably why so many ELT grammar books teach these two modals together to mean possibility and don't bother to clarify any subtle differences between the two.

One further point we should make about *may* and *might* when they express possibility is that they both signify **real possibility** just as *could* does (as opposed to *can*). In fact, all three modals are usually interchangeable:

He may be late. / He might be late. / He could be late.

There's one occasion, at least, when the three modals aren't interchangeable, and that's when a rhetorical phrase is used to preface some sort of critical remark. Notice that *may* and *might* are the traditional choices for this use, but that *could* isn't:

> A: My English teacher says it's okay to say "I might could do it."
> B: Well, she **may (might)** be an English teacher, but she speaks a different dialect. Or maybe she doesn't know the difference between standard and nonstandard English!

As for *might³* in our dialogue, the modal expresses **an indirect way of making a suggestion**. Ms. Ketchum is gingerly suggesting to Mr. Snodgrass that he get himself a "dog-proof" garbage can. There are other ways to make suggestions with modals, and here's one we should take a look at immediately:

A: I know you're very upset about that broken leg of yours, but you **might as well accept** it and relax.

B: Relax? How can I relax? I'm so restless just sitting here day in and day out. Here it is, the middle of summer, and it **may as well be** the middle of winter since I can't go out anyway!

As you can see, we're dealing with the expression "*may/might as well* +base form verb" in this dialogue. The problem is that the expression doesn't mean the same thing in both cases. Can you paraphrase the meaning in each of these instances? Write your thoughts on the following lines:

_____

_____

Sometimes, finding just the right paraphrases isn't so easy, but here's what we've come up with. Compare our ideas with yours. In the first case, when Speaker A says "... you might as well accept it ..." she's making a **mild suggestion** (and we'll be discussing more about suggestions a little later on in this chapter). As for the next appearance of this expression in the dialogue, "... it may as well be the middle of winter ..." isn't a suggestion at all. It means **it doesn't make any difference ...**, so Speaker B is saying "It doesn't make any difference if it's the middle of summer or the middle of winter since I can't go out anyway!"

Now, getting back to the dialogue on page 143, we come to *may³*, which signifies a very formal way of hoping that something will happen. Mr. Snodgrass is saying in his very formal tone that he hopes Ms. Ketchum will never experience the mess he's found on his front lawn. Another thing to notice is that **this use of *may* requires a word order inversion so that *may* appears before the subject. In fact, *may* always appears as the first word in this kind of sentence.** We'll be discussing more about this use of *may* in Chapter 19.

Now that we've discussed *may* and *might,* look at the following mini-dialogues. Check which of Person B's responses is acceptable and which is not, and then explain the reasons for your decisions:

Dialogue 1	Dialogue 2
A. Might I ask you a favor? **B. Of course you might.** ☐ acceptable ☐ unacceptable	A. Might I ask you a favor? **B. Of course you may.** ☐ acceptable ☐ unacceptable

_____

_____

Person B's response in **Dialogue 1** is **unacceptable**. The reason will sound quite familiar to you if you recall the discussion we had about *can* and *could* for asking and giving permission. We can use *might* in a super-polite request when we *ask for* permission, but we don't use it when we *give* permission since it wouldn't be appropriate to be so overly polite in this case. Person B's response in **Dialogue 2** is **acceptable** because *may* is the correct way of giving permission in the formal style.

 ## *"May" in a Nutshell*

real possibility:
You may not believe what I'm about to tell you, but it's true.

permission (in polite or formal context):
Ladies and gentlemen, you may now take your seats.

hope that something will happen (in very formal style):
May you be blessed all the days of your life.

 ## *"Might" in a Nutshell*

possibility:
You might not believe what I'm about to tell you, but it's true.

an overly formal way of requesting permission:
Might I sit here?

an indirect way of making a suggestion:
If the regular doctors can't help, he might try a chiropractor.

a mild way of making a suggestion:
We may/might as well leave now. What do you say?

⚡ Should/Ought To

It's time for another dialogue! Let's see how *should* and *ought to* function in the following context. We'll work with these two modals the same way we've worked with the others, so think of explanations for how they're being used and write them down on the lines whose numbers correspond to the numbered modals:

A: I hate commuting to work every day.

B: Yeah, so do I.

A: Where's the 7:20 train? It's 7:20 now, and there's no train in sight.

B: Yeah, I know. It **should**[1] be here already.

A: Maybe I **ought to**[2] take my car to work.

B: Well, I know how you feel, but the hassles of taking your car, fighting rush hour traffic, and parking in the city **ought to**[1] stop you! Just calm down, and don't let it bother you so much.

A: You're right. I **shouldn't**[2] let train delays and all this nonsense get to me so much.

Should

1. _____

2. _____

Ought to

1. _____

2. _____

Should[1] and *ought to[1]* express **expectation**. Person B is saying that he expects the 7:20 train to be there already because the time is indeed 7:20. He then says that he expects all of those hassles to stop Person A from driving to work every day instead of taking the train.

Should[2] and *ought to[2]* have to do with **advisability**, **opinions**, or what's considered **a good idea**. Person A says that it might be a good idea for her to take her car to work. Then she says that she realizes it's not advisable for her to get so upset about such things as train delays. Both of these modals are what we call **benign advice** or **benign suggestions**; that is, when people use them to offer opinions or suggestions, they don't force their thoughts upon the listener or the person under discussion; in other words, it's up to the listener to accept or reject the advice. We'll talk about a modal that can force itself upon you when we get to *must*.

While we're on the subject of negatives like the one we've just used in the preceding paragraph ("I shouldn't let train delays . . . get to me."), there's a feature unique to *ought to* which doesn't happen to any other modal. Most native speakers, especially Americans, prefer to use *should* in the negative *(shouldn't)* rather than *ought to (ought not to)*; that's probably because *ought not to* and *oughtn't to* seem unwieldy to many people. The unique feature we're talking about is that when people do use *ought to* in the negative, they sometimes drop the *to* probably to make the phrase less unwieldy ("He oughtn't say such things!").

Going back to whether we prefer to use *should* or *ought to,* do you perceive any difference between these two modals when they both express expectation or advisability? According to prescriptive grammar books, *ought to* is perceived as being less forceful than *should* when expressing advisability, but not when expressing expectation:

>You ought to get a job. (not forceful)
>You should get a job. (somewhat more forceful)

>The bus ought to be here already.
>The bus should be here already. (no difference)

The difference between sentences in these pairs, however, is really quite slight, and that's why most ELT grammar books teach both of these modals at the same time when they deal with either advisability or expectation.

There are even some native speakers who claim that *should* deals with straightforward advice while *ought to* carries a moral obligation with it. Look at these two sentences and see what you think:

>You should call your poor mother more often.
>You ought to call your poor mother more often.

It's safe to say that the choice of whether to use *should* or *ought to* in the previous examples is really up to the individual. Always remember that each native speaker of a language has his/her own style for using the language (what linguists refer to as an *idiolect*) and that there aren't always hard-and-fast rules that we can give.

If you recall, when we were exploring *can* and *could*, we said that we were going to get back to these two modals when we got to *should* and *ought to*—and here we are. Let's bring back the suggestions that the mother gave her daughter in that dialogue that showed *can* and *could* as ways of giving advice:

>You <u>can</u> get together with your friend, Nancy.
>You <u>could</u> clean out your closet or finish that term paper.

What if we were to substitute *can* and *could* with *should* or *ought to* in these sentences? After all, they're all ways to give advice or suggestions, right? Well, let's see what happens:

You <u>should</u> get together with your friend, Nancy.

You <u>ought to</u> clean out your closet or finish that term paper.

Even though all four modals can be used to give advice or make suggestions, there's definitely a difference between the first two and the second two. What do you perceive the difference to be?

_____

_____

What it comes down to is that **when we use** *can* **and** *could* **for suggestions, there's an implied idea that there are other options; when we use** *should* **and** *ought to,* **however, we're clearly focusing in on just the one suggestion at hand with no implication that other options exist**. Quite an important difference indeed!

☙ *Troubleshooter* ☙

Even though we haven't come to the modal *must* yet, this is a good time to mention a problem that you may very well encounter.

Some of your students will end up inappropriately using the modal *must* instead of using *should* or *ought to*. This is probably because in many languages the same word is used to express these quite different ideas in English.

Should and *ought to* are modals that express soft advice as opposed to *must*, which expresses a command, order, or regulation of some sort. People who have some kind of authority over others can use *must* when talking to them, e.g. parents to children, bosses to employees, teachers to students. It's not appropriate, though, for the employee to use *must* when talking to the boss or the student when talking to the teacher.

This can be interpreted as a linguistic problem, but it can also be a cultural problem—and we know that language should never be taught out of cultural context. Make sure you're prepared to explain why *must* is or is not appropriate to use in certain situations, and why *should* and *ought to* often work better.

There's one last observation we'd like to make about *should*, and this is one time when *ought to* can't be interchanged with it. *Should* can substitute for *if* in a more formal style conditional sentence:

> If he arrives before three, tell him to wait. →
> Should he arrive before three, tell him to wait.

And it can even be used together with *if* as you'll see when we get to Chapter 20:

If he should arrive before three, tell him to wait.

"Should"/"Ought To" in a Nutshell

expectation:
If her work continues to be this good, she should get a raise soon.
He ought to feel much better once the medicine starts working.

advisability/opinions/a good idea (not considering other options):
You shouldn't eat so fast. You'll get indigestion. You ought to slow down when you eat.

should = if (in a conditional sentence):
If the two companies merge, our stock will go up. →
Should the two companies merge, our stock will go up.

A: Must

We've now come to the only modal that we haven't dealt with yet. Let's do it just as we have the others, so get ready to write down your interpretations of *must* as you find it in this dialogue:

A: You **must**[1] be Ms. Carroll, our new teacher.

B: Yes, that's right.

A: Well, I'm Hilda Pardo, your assistant principal.

B: How do you do.

A: There are just a few points I wanted to mention before classes start this morning. To begin with, you **must**[2] be in your room by 8:15. And while I think of it, you **mustn't**[2] allow students to eat or drink in the classrooms. We've had quite a problem with that.

B: Understood.

1. _____

2. _____

Must[1] expresses **a conclusion or deduction made from information already known**. (Recall how unstressed *will* can be used in the same way.) Ms. Pardo spots someone new at her school, knows that a new teacher is to begin working that day, and concludes that she's that new teacher, Ms. Carroll. We can paraphrase this sentence by saying "*I'm sure* you're Ms. Carroll, our new teacher." Of course, when we use *must* in this way, we wait for confirmation from the other person to be certain our conclusion is right.

Must[2] expresses **a requirement or necessity**, meaning that Ms. Carroll has no choice in the matter; she's obligated to comply or face the consequences. Even the negative of *must* in this use represents a requirement although it can also be interpreted as a prohibition *(**mustn't[2]**)*.

In the last "Troubleshooter" that you came upon, the discussion dealt with the cultural difference between using the modal *must* when *should* or *ought to* might be more appropriate. When you teach *should* and *ought to,* explain to your students that these are used when you give someone your advice or opinion about what to do, but that it doesn't mean the listener is obligated to take that advice. That's why we consider *should* and *ought to* as *benign* advice.

On the other hand, *must* leaves no options; when you use *must,* meaning that someone is to do something, it's a *forceful* idea—sometimes too forceful if said to a person who's in a higher social or authoritative position than the speaker is. Remember that when hearing *should* or *ought to,* the listener or subject being discussed can take the advice or not; when hearing *must,* the listener or subject of the idea supposedly has no choice in the matter. True, you'll hear native speakers at times say something like "Oh, you simply *must* see that movie! It was wonderful!" Of course, in this context, *must* isn't taken authoritatively; it simply expresses a strong suggestion that the speaker is making to a friend, for example.

Let's see how *must* can be used in other ways by looking at this next dialogue.

A: Hello, Ravi? This is Selim.

B: Hi, Selim. What's up?

A: You know, I hear the surf's really great today and we can find some big waves for our surfboards. You interested?

B: But we've got school today.

A: So what? We **don't have to** go to school every day!

B: I **mustn't** be absent today or my teacher will kill me. I've got a big test today and she hates when someone's out and she has to give a make-up.

A: That's dumb!

> B: It's not dumb. What **must** the teachers think of you, Selim, with your being absent so often?
>
> A: I never really give it any thought—nor should you!

Write your interpretations of the words in bold on the following lines:

don't have to = _____

mustn't = _____

must = _____

Don't have to is a phrase that means **it isn't necessary**. This concept is totally different from the idea of **must not** (***mustn't***), which means **prohibited** or **not to be done**. And along with this use of *mustn't,* we also find a negative imperative (command) form if it is put together with *you*:

> You mustn't blame yourself. = Don't blame yourself.

Remember to stress to your students that when we say something isn't required, we use *don't/doesn't have to*, but when we say something is not to be done or prohibited, we say *must not* (*mustn't*).

Here are some more examples to demonstrate these points:

deductions:	He must be very happy over that news. (We're sure he's very happy over that news.)
	She mustn't be very happy over that news. (We're sure she isn't very happy over that news.)
requirements/ necessities:	You must be here by nine o'clock. (You're required to be here by nine o'clock.)
	You mustn't take this medicine without food. (Don't take this medicine without food.)
lack of requirement/ necessity:	You don't have to take this medicine with food. (You aren't required to take this medicine with food.)
	She doesn't have to see the doctor. (It isn't necessary for her to see the doctor.)

As for **must**, the word is being used in our dialogue in quite an unusual way. In this context, the question "What must the teachers think of you . . . ?" really means "I wonder what the teachers think of you."

 "Must" in a Nutshell

used for a conclusion or deduction:
Marry Arnold? You must be kidding!

used for requirements/necessities:
•You must submit a note from your doctor if you're not at work for more than three consecutive days. (requirement)
•You must eat and drink in order to stay alive. (necessity)

used for prohibition/that something <u>not</u> be done:
An orthodox Jew or Muslim mustn't eat pork.

used in a question to mean *I wonder* . . . :
What must it be like on Mars?

✍ Semi-Auxiliaries (Periphrastic Modals)

The first thing we should do is list some of the semi-auxiliaries. Although there's disagreement among some linguists as to whether certain of these are semi-auxiliaries or not, we're going to include the following: *be able to, be unable to, have to, have got to, had better, had best, need, dare, used to, would rather,* and *would sooner.*

The next thing to do is explain the difference between modals and semi-auxiliaries. Semi-auxiliaries work the same way as modals do as far as altering the meanings of verbs. Unlike true modals, however, semi-auxiliaries don't always function grammatically in the same way:

• Some semi-auxiliaries don't have the same form for the present and future as true modals do (*I had to/I have to; I'm going to have to/I'll have to*).

• For questions, some semi-auxiliaries use *do/does/did* as the typical introductory question marker (*Do I have to?/Did they use to?*). Others use the inverted construction typical of modals and the verb *be* (*Is he able to?/Have I got to?/ Need we?/Dare she?/Would they rather?/Would you sooner?*). One little note: We don't normally use *had better* or *had best* in questions, preferring to use *should/must/have to/have got to* instead.

• For negatives, some semi-auxiliaries use *don't/doesn't/didn't* before them (*don't have to/didn't use to*), while others use *not* (*haven't got to/had better not/had best not/need not/would rather not/would sooner not*). One semi-auxiliary, *dare*, uses *not* in the present/future form (*dare not*), but *didn't* in the past (*didn't dare*).

We're not going to deal with every semi-auxiliary in this chapter because most of them aren't particularly troublesome; what we will do, though, is make some passing observations about those that aren't troublesome.

Be Able To (Be Unable To)

Why is it that English has this expression which is synonymous with *can/could* as long as the meaning is ability? Here are a couple of *ungrammatical* sentences for you to correct. Let's see how you correct the underlined parts:

1. For that job at the United Nations, he needs to <u>can</u> speak at least three languages fluently.

   _____

2. <u>Cann</u>ing speak four languages, he had no trouble getting that job at the UN.

   _____

Yes, we know that these are two really bizarre sentences! And that's just the point. The corrections should be "he needs to **be able to** speak ..." for **Sentence 1** and "**Being able to** speak ..." for **Sentence 2**. What observations can you make about why *be (un)able to* is so convenient at times?

_____

_____

In order for us to avoid such bizarre problems, **we use *be able to* instead of *can* after prepositions and when an *-ing* form is required**.

Along similar lines, there's a clever way we get around the problem of not being able to use two modal auxiliaries together, which was one of the general points about modals that we discussed at the start of this chapter. The way we do this in certain cases is to combine a modal with a semi-auxiliary. Look at the following examples of how this works:

We ⟨ must ⟩ ⟨ be able to ⟩ produce more food.

Nobody ⟨ should ⟩ ⟨ have to ⟩ go hungry.

Need

The meaning of *need*, when it's used as a semi-auxiliary, is the same as *must*, *have to*, and *have got to*, that is, **something is required or necessary**. Typically, in the affirmative and most questions, we use *need* as a regular verb with *to* after it ("I needed <u>to</u> see you." / "Does she need <u>to</u> apply right away?") Compare this question with the much more formal or even antiquated "Need she apply right away?" It's in the example just cited and in the negative that *need* can sometimes be seen as a semi-auxiliary. Look at these examples:

> She needn't let us know before Friday.
> He needn't ever know the awful truth./
> He need never know the awful truth.

In both of these examples, *needn't* means *doesn't have to* or *hasn't got to*; in other words, something is not required. We should mention, though, that many native speakers, particularly Americans, will probably find the sentences somewhat atypical because *need* isn't commonly used in many dialects of American English as a semi-auxiliary, especially in everyday speech.

Would Rather/Would Sooner

These two expressions are used to indicate **a preference**. Most native speakers consider *would rather* more formal than *would sooner*, but we think that's once again a matter of personal choice.

The grammar used with these semi-auxiliaries is a bit unusual. If only the subject is discussed, any verb that follows will be in its basic form ("*I'd* rather <u>have</u> a beach house than a house in town." / "*They'd* sooner <u>eat</u> chicken or fish than beef.").

However, if the subject is discussing a preference for somebody, (even him-/herself) or something else, the grammar changes radically ("I'd sooner *he* <u>were</u> here than at home." / "We'd rather *you* <u>didn't say</u> that word again.") The words we've underlined represent a grammatical form called the *present subjunctive,* a form that we'll deal with in detail in Chapter 19.

Teaching Tips

8.1 Telling Fortunes/Reading Palms

Ask the students what they know about fortune telling, crystal balls, and palmistry. Copy the hand you see here on the board, explaining that the lines on the palms of your hands are thought to predict your future. Also explain what the different lines are and what they're supposed to predict. Then ask the students to read three or four other students' palms being sure they use the various modals. Here are some typical answers: "You'll live a long life." / "You might work for the government when you graduate." / "You should be more careful of what you eat." Let your students read your palm, too. Students can also write up their predictions in a short composition.

8.2 *Creating Situations for Modals*

Before class, create various situations about your students, other people, places, or things (a student's absence, glass on the street, a dent in your car, a bad grade, etc.). Let the students brainstorm responses to the situations using modals: "Paco might be sick." / "Someone will get a flat tire if he or she runs over that glass." / "Jan should drive more carefully." / "Marjorie must study very hard; she always gets good grades."

8.3 *Real-life Problems*

Before class, create problems that contain a real-life conflict (e.g., You've just received a four-year scholarship to a very prestigious university, but you can't bring your spouse. / The person you're engaged to is pressuring you to get married soon, but you want to wait. / Your father is seriously ill and can no longer work. / You want to study sociology, but your family wants you to be a doctor, etc.). Put the problems on the board or on a handout. Divide the class into small groups and tell the students to discuss the problems. Have them come up with solutions to the situations. Tell your students to use at least three different modals and have all the members of each group write down their group's suggestions. While the groups are discussing their responses, walk around the room and "visit" each group. When the problems have been thoroughly discussed, have each person in the group give at least one of his/her responses to the whole class. While the groups are sharing their ideas with the entire class, if you hear contradictory statements made between two groups, note them down and go back to them after this activity is over. You can get lots of meaty material in this way for lively conversation practice.

8.4 *Television Guides*

Divide the class into pairs or small groups. Give them copies of a television guide and tell them that they're going to recommend programs appropriate for various groups (children, teens, adults). After they've looked through the listings carefully, have them come up with their program schedule using modals whenever possible:

> "Kids shouldn't watch X but they might enjoy Y."
> "An adult may enjoy Z but I might not."

8.5 *Giving Advice*

Prepare a list of people that might need advice. Divide the class into pairs or small groups and have them decide what advice they'd give a newlywed, a teenager on his/her first date, a person entering college for the first time, the new owner of a large company, their English teacher, a student learning English for the first time, etc. Encourage your students to use modals.

8.6 Inventing a New Sport

Divide the class into pairs or small groups and tell them they're going to invent a new game or sport. Have the groups write up the rules of their game/sport using modals whenever possible:

> "You must face each other."
> "You shouldn't move until the referee blows the whistle."
> "You must stay out of the game for two minutes after a foul."

Have the different groups share their games/sports with the entire class.

8.7 Questionnaires

Create a questionnaire (teacher- or student-generated) about a relevant or timely topic (up-coming elections, environmental issues, exams, etc.). Have the students interview two or three of their classmates, students in other classes, their teachers, or people outside school, etc. and prepare a report on their findings. Questions should have modals in them ("Should students _____ ?" / "Would you rather _____ ?" / "Could the President _____ ?" / "What might the government _____ ?" / "Should we _____ exams?").

8.8 Planning a City

Prepare a map of a city without details. Only the streets and any relevant natural landmarks like rivers, lakes, valleys, etc. should be shown. Provide a list of buildings and institutions that the city will have.

zoo	theater	fish market	secondary school
hotel	airport	train station	municipal offices
houses	museum	supermarket	elementary school
bakery	night club	swimming pool	jail/police station
library	post office	hardware store	highrise apartments
hospital	gas station	electricity plant	water treatment plant

Students will plan out the town suggesting where the various buildings *should/ would/mustn't/ can't* go. Let the students draw the buildings on their outline and then put them up on the board. Have various spokespersons from each group discuss their choices.

8.9 Dear Abby: Advice Columns

Advice columns appear in many newspapers and magazines. The typical advice column has two elements: a) a reader who has a problem and writes a letter asking for advice and b) a columnist who responds to the letter and suggests solutions. Clip out several examples or write up several of your own. Divide the class into pairs or small groups and distribute the columns to your students. Have them write responses to the person who wrote the letter suggesting solutions to the problem. If students have trouble coming up with acceptable solutions, for homework, let them ask teachers, native English speakers, students in other classes, or friends for ideas about what they might do. Encourage them to use modals in their responses.

9

Prepositions

"There's a frog on a log in a hole at the bottom of the sea."

hat are prepositions? In general, they're **words that show some sort of relationship or connection between two things**. In addition, **prepositions can help to answer such questions as** *where?, when?, why?,* **and** *how?* They can be **simple** (one word: *behind)* or **complex** (two or more words: *ahead of, in front of).*

In this chapter, we're going to deal mostly with simple prepositions and focus on the challenging aspects of teaching them. By the way, if you want complete lists of prepositions, you'll be able to find them easily in just about all student grammar books.

So what are prepositions? What they really are is the bane of all teachers!

Why is it that students always have so much trouble with prepositions? After all, don't they have them in their languages, too? Of course they do, although in some languages (like Turkish) they are *post*positions, words or word particles that show the same kind of relationship of one noun to another but come *after* the nouns they connect. In other words, learning to use prepositions isn't just a simple matter of translating a preposition from one language to another. To add to the difficulty, some languages (like English) have more prepositions than others. At any rate, English prepositions do cause a great deal of frustration and annoyance to students and their teachers.

There are three basic sections to this chapter. First, we'll deal with the meanings of some of the most commonly used prepositions. Along with this useful list, we'll give you ideas on how to demonstrate them in vivid ways so your students start developing a "feel" for them. We'll also deal with their idiomatic uses and how choosing one preposition over another can change meaning in very important ways. In addition, we'll offer insights on how to handle the teaching of prepositions in the classroom and how to present them more meaningfully and interestingly to your students.

A look at the chapters on prepositions in most scholarly grammar books can be quite unnerving; the array of uses and meanings the reader is presented with can be intimidating, even overwhelming. We don't intend to cover every single preposition, but we'll break some of them down into their basic meanings. Our main goal is to help you clarify some prepositions for yourself so that you'll be better prepared to deal with them in your classes. You can continue where we leave off and delve into the basic meanings of those we don't cover.

In many ways, the choice of which preposition to use depends on the viewpoint of the speaker or writer, especially when dealing with spatial relationships. Teaching the spatial, or literal, uses of prepositions comes early on in any curriculum, and visualizing them both on the board and with a little physical reinforcement has always proven to be an effective teaching technique.

✍️ Literal (Physical) Meanings

Let's see how astute you are at graphically visualizing the spatial meanings of some commonly used prepositions. Below, you'll find an assortment of them, each one followed by a box. Draw **an arrow** (for **movement**) or **a dot** (for **stationary location**) wherever you think it will best demonstrate the literal meaning of the preposition in relation to its accompanying box. For the sake of this exercise, let's say that the orientation of the boxes is just like this page you're reading; in other words, *the top of each box is in the same location as the top of this page.* Also, let's have all movements going *from left to right.* You'll find that it's easier to represent some prepositions graphically than others. We've done the first one to get you started. (By the way, we know you're going to cover up the section that follows with all the answers until you've finished, aren't you?)

onto/on ⬜   on ⬜   off (of) ⬜   into ⬜   in ⬜   out of ⬜

over ⬜   above ⬜   under ⬜   below ⬜

towards ⬜   to ⬜   from/away from ⬜

before ☐ after ☐ near ☐ next to/by ☐

past/by ☐ through ☐ (a)round ☐

It's interesting to visualize just what each of these prepositions looks like on paper, isn't it? Well, here are the answers we've come up with. Compare yours to ours. You may be surprised to find some answers that you didn't think of. You may also be surprised to see that it's not always very clear-cut when it comes to showing a visual representation of some of these prepositions. Remember: the arrow represents movement; the dot represents stationary location.

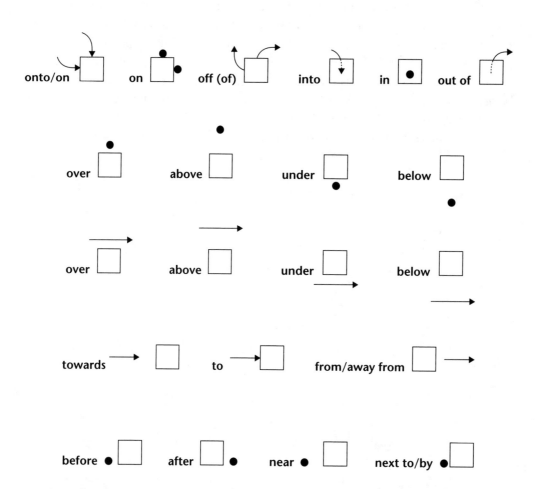

past/by ▭→   through ▭┄→   (a)round (▭↺)

Now that you've had a chance to compare your artwork to ours, let's see if you can come up with *literal* definitions for these prepositions. If their meanings are clear in your mind, it'll be much easier to communicate them to your students. Use the visualizations we've created and the example sentences we've provided to help you. Among other things, state whether they're prepositions of <u>location</u> or <u>movement</u> or <u>both</u>.

onto/on: He placed the star <u>onto/on</u> the top of the Christmas tree.

_____

_____

on: His family loved all the ornaments <u>on</u> the Christmas tree.

_____

_____

off (of)★: During the holidays, some of the ornaments fell <u>off (of)</u> the tree.

_____

_____

into/in: As the guests arrived, they came <u>into/in</u> the house.

_____

_____

in: When the guests were seated <u>in</u> the living room, their host served them some refreshments.

_____

_____

out of: The hostess came <u>out of</u> the kitchen carrying a basket of bread and rolls.

_____

_____

★We'll explain why we've put the secondary preposition in parentheses later on in the chapter.

out: The little dog almost fell <u>out</u> the window.

over: A: My legs are cold.
B: Here. Put this afghan <u>over</u> them.

While out in the woods on a fall day, we noticed a flock of geese flying <u>over</u> us on their way south for the winter.

above: The helicopter hovered <u>above</u> the field for a few minutes before flying off.

During the storm, the dark clouds passed <u>above</u> us at incredible speed.

under: Our dog likes to sleep <u>under</u> the dining room table.

Did you feel all that vibration and hear the rumbling? It was the subway passing <u>under</u> this building.

below: In this part of the country, the water table is many meters <u>below</u> the surface of the land.

_____

_____

There are places on this planet where water travels <u>below</u> the surface in subterranean rivers.

_____

_____

toward(s): The explorers continued traveling west <u>towards</u> the mountains.

_____

_____

to: I'm sending this postcard <u>to</u> my relatives in the States.

_____

_____

She gave some candy <u>to</u> her assistant as a sign of her appreciation for all his hard work.

_____

_____

from: He comes <u>from</u> Cairo, Egypt. I just got a letter <u>from</u> him.

_____

_____

away from: He went <u>away from</u> home at the age of eighteen.

_____

_____

before: When it was time for him to be sentenced for his crime, the convicted man was made to stand <u>before</u> the judge.

_____

_____

If you want the all-night coffee shop, it's the red brick building <u>before</u> the movie theater down this street.

_____

_____

after: Looking for the bank? It's the building <u>after</u> that gas station.

_____

_____

near/by: Don't you know that our house is <u>near/by</u> the stadium?

_____

_____

Don't go <u>near</u> the fireplace, Billy. It's very hot.

_____

_____

next to/by: You'll recognize our house when you see it. It's the yellow one <u>next to/by</u> the florist's shop.

_____

_____

past/by: We drove <u>past/by</u> your house last night, but we couldn't stop to say hello.

_____

_____

through: Last summer, we took a car trip <u>through</u> the Canadian province of British Columbia.

_____

_____

(a)round: Before the tunnel was built, our trip was a lot longer because we had to drive (a)round the mountain.

_____

_____

I like that arrangement of daffodils all (a)round the wedding cake.

_____

_____

On Sundays they used to like driving around in the country and taking in the beautiful scenery.

_____

_____

Without any ado, let's get right to our interpretations of the literal meanings of these prepositions.

onto/on: a preposition of movement which means something lands on or is placed on something else so that it touches that object's surface. In the case of a three-dimensional object, this meaning could include the top or sides:

> He placed the star onto/on the top of the Christmas tree.

Note that *onto* clearly relates to movement, whereas its short form, *on*, can be ambiguous: "He jumped onto the desk." vs. "He jumped on the desk." (Did he jump from the chair and land on top of the desk, or did he jump up and down while standing on the desk?)

on: a preposition that shows that something has contact with the surface of something else. If it's a three-dimensional object, it could be the top or sides:

> His family loved all the ornaments on the Christmas tree.
> That dress looks just beautiful on you!

off (of): The opposite of *onto*, this preposition shows the movement of one object leaving a surface of another:

> During the holidays, some of the ornaments fell off (of) the tree.

into/in: Another preposition of movement which refers to something entering the interior of an object:

> As the guests arrived, they came <u>into/in</u> the house.

in: A preposition showing stationary location. It means that something is encompassed or enclosed by something else:

> When the guests were seated <u>in</u> the living room,
> their host served them some refreshments.

out (of):   The opposite of *into* or *in,* this preposition also involves movement. It can mean one thing leaving the object that has encompassed or enclosed it. It can also mean *from*:

> The hostess came <u>out of</u> her kitchen carrying a basket of bread and rolls.

out: Without *of*, it means *through*:

> The little dog almost fell <u>out</u> the window.

over: In this first use, it's a preposition of stationary location. To many native speakers, *over* may mean that something is at a *slightly* higher elevation than the top of some other thing:

> During the final judging of the contestants, the master of ceremonies
> held his hand <u>over</u> the head of each finalist for the voting.

Over can include the idea of one thing being in proximity to or even touching or covering the other:

> A: My legs are cold.
> B: Here. Put this afghan <u>over</u> them.

In another use, *over* is a preposition of movement. In this use it means one thing moving horizontally at a higher elevation than the top of another thing. In the case of movement, how much distance there is between the two objects is not an issue:

> While out in the woods on a fall day, we noticed a flock of geese
> flying <u>over</u> us on their way south for the winter.

above: As with our first definition for *over*, this preposition means that one thing is at a higher elevation than the top of another thing. The difference between *above* and *over* is that, for many native speakers, *above* implies there's a greater distance between the two objects than *over.* In the example we've cited, the preposition is used with stationary location:

> The helicopter hovered <u>above</u> the field for a few minutes before flying off.

Above can also be used for movement:

> During the storm, the dark clouds passed <u>above</u> us at incredible speed.

under: This preposition is the opposite of *over* and is used for stationary location. It carries the same meaning as *over* in reverse:

> Our dog likes to sleep <u>under</u> the dining room table.

Likewise, *under* is the opposite of *over* for movement and carries the same meaning as that preposition in reverse:

> Feel that vibration and hear that rumbling?
> It was the subway passing <u>under</u> this building.

below: Here we have the opposite meaning of *above*. It has the same definition as *above,* but in reverse, and can be used for stationary location:

> In this part of the country, the water table is
> many meters <u>below</u> the surface of the land.

Below can also be used for movement:

> There are places on this planet where water travels
> <u>below</u> the surface in subterranean rivers.

toward(s):   A preposition of movement meaning that an object is going in the direction of another, but it doesn't imply that the moving object reaches any destination:

> The explorers continued traveling west <u>towards</u> the mountains.

to: This preposition of movement, whose opposite is *from,* means one thing going in the direction of and reaching or arriving at a destination of one kind or another:

> I'm sending this postcard <u>to</u> my relatives in the States.
> She gave some candy <u>to</u> her assistant as a sign of her
> appreciation for all his hard work.

from: This preposition, the opposite of *to,* refers to the starting point or source of something:

> He comes <u>from</u> Cairo, Egypt. I just got a letter <u>from</u> him.

away from: Here we have another preposition whose opposite meaning is *to* or *toward(s)*. Instead of reaching a destination or other object, or going in its direction, this preposition of movement means leaving a destination or other object:

> He went <u>away from</u> his home at the age of eighteen.

before: This stationary preposition is a synonym for *in front of* (which is an example of the complex prepositions we mentioned earlier in this chapter):

> When it was time for him to be sentenced for his crime,
> the convicted man was made to stand <u>before</u> the judge.

Before can also mean something you'll come upon immediately *preceding* another thing mentioned as a reference point:

> If you want the all-night cafeteria, it's the red brick building
> <u>before</u> the movie theater down this street.

after: This stationary preposition means that the object you're looking for is the place you'll come upon once you've passed another object mentioned as a reference point:

> You're looking for the bank? It's the building <u>after</u> that gas station.

near/by: The meaning of these prepositions has to do with proximity. They mean one thing is in the general area of another thing with a relatively short distance between them. The opposite preposition is *far from*. These prepositions can both be stationary:

> Don't you know that our house is <u>near/by</u> the stadium?

Only *near* can also be used for movement:

> Don't go <u>near</u> the fireplace, Billy. It's very hot.

next to/by: A synonym for these stationary prepositions is *beside*. They carry the idea of very close proximity, that is, with very little or no distance between two objects and, as their synonyms say, the reference points are the sides of two objects:

> You'll recognize our house when you see it.
> It's the yellow one <u>next to/by</u> the florist's shop.

past/by: These prepositions carry the idea of one thing moving in front of another thing and not stopping as it approaches. In other words, it passes the object:

> We drove <u>past/by</u> your house last night, but we couldn't stop to say hello.

through: The meaning of this preposition of movement carries with it the idea that one thing enters one end or side of another thing, traverses its interior, and comes out or reaches the opposite end or side:

> It was pitch black in our compartment as the train
> went <u>through</u> the tunnel.
> Last summer, we took a car trip <u>through</u> the Canadian province
> of British Columbia.

(a)round: This preposition can show movement meaning one thing partially or completely encircling another:

> Before the tunnel was built, our trip was a lot longer
> because we had to drive <u>(a)round</u> the mountain.

(A)round can also be a preposition of stationary location:

> I like that arrangement of daffodils all <u>(a)round </u>the wedding cake.

In its idiomatic use, in which case only *around* is used, it has the idea of movement with no specific destination:

> On Sundays they used to like driving <u>around</u> the country
> and taking in the beautiful scenery.

Of course, the definitions we've given you for these prepositions are ones that you might like to have for clarification, but it's probably inadvisable to give them to your students in this way. However, as we mentioned earlier, if their meanings are clear in <u>your</u> mind, it will be a much simpler job for you to demonstrate them for your classes. One further note: Remember that not all English speakers use every preposition in the same way; there's room for debate on some of these.

◢ ͣ Figurative/Idiomatic Meanings

Notice that we've concentrated on the literal meanings of these prepositions; that is, we've focused on their physical nature. Many of them also have figurative and/or idiomatic meanings. Remember that they can appear in the following patterns:

> **preposition +** *(pro)noun (above it all/above reproach)*
> **verb + preposition** *(think over)*
> **adjective + preposition** *(mad at)*

Here are examples of figurative uses and idiomatic expressions. (Fig. = figurative use; Id. = idiomatic expression):

onto*:   (Id.)   be onto somebody (not be fooled by someone; understand a
                          person's motives)

on: (Fig.)   about; concerning
               (Id.)   be on (performing, as if on stage or on duty);
                         be on something (medication or other drugs)

---

*You may have come up with something like the idiom "*Go on to* the next topic for discussion." If you did, you've confused the preposition *onto* with the preposition *on* which is allied with the verb *go.* In other words, it's really *go on,* and there's a secondary preposition needed before you can state the object, in this case, "the next topic for discussion." We'll deal with this kind of form in more detail later on in the chapter.

off:	(Id.)	be off (leaving/spoiled, as with food); go/be off one's rocker (crazy); be off the record (not for public knowledge)
into:	(Fig.) (Id.)	into the night; get into trouble/mischief be into something (interested)
in:	(Fig.) (Id.)	be in trouble/love/jeopardy/business be "in" (stylish/accepted); be in hock/debt
out (of):	(Fig.) (Id.)	be out of trouble/danger/touch be out of one's mind; run/be out of (have no more of something)
over:	(Fig.) (Id.)	more than; by means of (a telephone, the Internet, an intercom, etc.); over the holidays/the weekend be over the hill (too old); be/get over an illness/bad news, etc. (recovered)
above:	(Fig.) (Id.)	be above the law (not following the laws meant for everyone) be above someone (in social status or at work) be above it all (not bothered by mundane concerns)
under:	(Fig.) (Id.)	less than/fewer than under the circumstances; be under arrest/the weather (feeling poorly)
below:	(Fig.) (Id.)	be below one's dignity/wholesale (prices) to hit below the belt (make an unfair statement)
toward(s):	(Fig.)	toward a better tomorrow; be hostile/antagonistic toward(s) someone
to:	(Id.)	look to someone (for help, advice); do something to someone (a bad act, nasty deed)
from:	(Fig.) (Id.)	from the start/very first from nowhere (appeared suddenly); from now on
away from	(Fig.)	turn away from someone (abandon, reject)
before:	(Fig.)	before leaving; before two o'clock/the public/it gets dark

after:	(Fig.)	after dinner/six o'clock/the fact
	(Id.)	take after (resemble);
		look after (take care of)

| **near:** | (Fig.) | be near someone's age/the truth/the end (of a story) |
| | (Id.) | be near the end (dying) |

| **next to:** | (Fig.) | besides (Next to me, he's your best choice for the job.); |
| | | next to nothing (very little) |

| **past:** | (Fig.) | be past one's prime (getting older); |
| | | be past caring (apathetic) |

by:	(Fig.)	by midnight (before or at midnight);
		by all means
	(Id.)	By Jove/gosh/golly! [exclamation]
		by hook or by crook (whatever it takes);
		stand by (support);
		by the way (incidentally)

through:	(Fig.)	through the years (spanning time)
	(Id.)	get through (survive/recuperate/recover; finish);
		be through (be finished)

around:	(Fig.)	approximately
	(Id.)	beat around the bush (not coming to the main point of one's thought or idea);
		get around someone (arrange it so that a certain person doesn't interfere)

round:	(Fig.)	round about (approximately)
	(Id.)	go round the bend (go crazy);
		go round and round (not reaching a conclusion or solution)

✐ The Prepositional Bane of Banes: *At*

There's one more preposition—a troublesome one—that we should look at in the same way we've looked at the others. It's troublesome because many people have a hard time putting their finger on just what it means. The preposition we're thinking of is *at*. We're giving you four boxes, so you'll have four chances to place a dot or an arrow at whatever spot you think will graphically visualize the meaning of *at*:

☐ ☐ ☐ ☐

The truth is that you can place the dot practically anywhere outside each box (relatively close to each one, that is) and be quite accurate about how to visualize this preposition graphically. In its literal sense, **at usually means in the general area of something and, because it does refer to a general area, the dimensions of this something are really unimportant and the location isn't pinpointed**. The one notable exception to this interpretation of *at* is when it's used synonymously with *by* in such phrases as *at/by my side; at/by the door*.

Keep these ideas concerning the interpretation of *at* in mind as we go on exploring this troublesome preposition. As for the arrow, that can only be placed on either side of the box and pointing towards it to show direction and/or movement.

These ideas are especially useful for English speakers when they get into differences concerning location or direction that have a literal or idiomatic meaning. Using the vague word *at* or the more specific words *in* or *on* can sometimes make a great difference in meaning, but quite often that difference depends on more than just the choice of preposition. Below you'll find some sentences with this interesting twist. Check the box after each pair of sentences that you agree with:

1. They're waiting at the ship.   2. Meet us at the bookstore.
   They're waiting on the ship.   Meet us in the bookstore.

     ☐ a difference ☐ no difference   ☐ a difference ☐ no difference

Most native speakers would agree that there's a definite difference in meaning between the sentences in each pair above, so if you've checked **a difference** for both pairs, you're in the majority.

In the first pair of sentences, if you expect to find those people standing somewhere in the general area of the ship (<u>at</u> the ship), you're right; if you hear "They're waiting <u>on</u> the ship," you imagine them actually aboard the vessel.

As for the other two examples we've given you, "Meet us <u>at</u> the bookstore" probably makes you think you should be outside (perhaps in front of) the store or in the general area and wait for us there if you show up first, while "Meet us <u>in</u> the bookstore" tells you that you should be waiting inside if you get there first.

We can clearly see that there are important differences between *at* or *in/on* in the previous sentences. Now let's look at some more sentences and play the same game:

1. I work at a bank.   2. We met them at the corner.
   I work in a bank.   We met them on the corner.

     ☐ a difference ☐ no difference   ☐ a difference ☐ no difference

That last statement we made, that there clearly are differences between *at* and the other two prepositions, isn't always the case as the sentences you've just looked over show us. If you checked **no difference** for these two pairs this time, you're once again going along with the majority opinion. Most people would say that they don't discern any real difference in these sentences between *at a bank* or *in a bank* or *at* or *on the corner*.

So now the question arises: Why do we easily perceive a difference in meaning between the two sentences in the first two pairs, but not in the second two pairs? Give it some thought and write your ideas on the following lines:

_____

_____

What we have here is an amazing quirk in the language. Of course it's true that *at* and *in* and *on* can have very different meanings, but since we've now seen occasions when they really don't have such different ideas, we know that something else is at work—and that something else involves the verb and the object of the preposition in the context of each sentence.

So what's the bottom line? It's simply that **the meaning comes from the context**. It also sends us teachers a very good message: We can't expect our students to learn how to use prepositions based solely upon simple rules which they can memorize and activate like mathematical formulas, or that they can learn prepositions in a vacuum. Language just isn't that clear-cut!

And speaking of not being clear-cut, we have an idiomatic use of prepositions that we need to touch on. Let's look at three pairs of sentences, one in each pair with a literal meaning, the other, idiomatic. Meanings will depend on the combination of verb and preposition used. Note that we're dealing here with *to* vs. *at* and *in* vs. *at*:

> 1a. Fatima is in the hospital.
> 1b. Fatima is at the hospital.
>
> 2a. The little girl threw the ball to the boy.
> 2b. The little girl threw the ball at the boy.
>
> 3a. The little boy shouted to the girl.
> 3b. The little boy shouted at the girl.

How would you interpret the two sentences in each pair, and how would you explain them to your students? Try it out on the following lines:

_____

_____

_____

_____

_____

Sentence 1a tells us that **Fatima is a patient there,** and the sentence has an **idiomatic** meaning. **Sentence 1b** tells us **where Fatima is at the moment** and is **literal** in meaning.

Sentence 2a has a **literal** meaning. It simply tells us that **the girl tossed the ball to the boy**, intending for him to catch it. **Sentence 2b** is **idiomatic** and means that **she didn't intend for him to catch the ball**. It could even communicate that she was angry with the boy and meant to hit him with the ball.

Sentence 3a is **literal** and simply tells us **the direction that his shouting was going in. Sentence 3b** is **idiomatic** and could mean that **he was angry with the girl** or meant to **send her a warning**. The difference in communication is amazing!

Here are two more sentences. One of them makes sense, but the other doesn't. After you've decided which is which, write an explanation showing why you think Sentence 1 or Sentence 2 is nonsensical:

> 1. She was so angry that she hurled a vase to the wall.
>   ☐ makes sense   ☐ doesn't make sense
> 2. She was so angry that she hurled a vase at the wall.
>   ☐ makes sense   ☐ doesn't make sense

_____

_____

It turns out that **Sentence 1 doesn't make sense**, and in order to understand the reason, we need to remember what the difference is between *to* and *at* in the sentences about the girl throwing that ball. With verbs like *throw* and *hurl* the preposition *to* means that the doer intends for the object of the preposition to catch something. This idea works fine if the object of the preposition happens to be a person or perhaps a chimpanzee or dog, but it won't work at all if the object of the preposition is a non-living thing—in this case, a wall! Therefore, when the object is a thing, we use the preposition *at*.

Let's turn our attention to another difference between *at* and some other preposition. How would you explain the following corrections that invariably have to be made by probably all teachers from time to time?

> A: You look tired today, Ali.
>
> B: I am tired, Mrs. Klein. I was in a party almost all night. What a party!
>
> A: You mean, you were *at* a party, Ali.
>
> B: *At*? Why *at*?
>
> A: Uh, well, uh . . . Where was the party?
>
> B: In my friend's house.
>
> A: That should be *at* your friend's house, Ali.
>
> B: Again *at*? Why *at*?
>
> A: Well, you see, uh . . .

How would you rescue poor Mrs. Klein who's obviously stalling because she doesn't have an answer ready for Ali? What would *you* say to Ali? Write your explanations on the following lines:

_____

_____

_____

If we keep in mind that *in* usually deals with one thing being *encompassed* or *enclosed* by another thing, and that *at* refers to *general location*, we should be able to deal with Ali's questions. As for why native speakers would say <u>at</u> *my friend's house*, it's because **we don't want to limit ourselves in this context to one specific, enclosed area or room**; we're keeping it *open* to take in the whole, general area.

For similar reasons, we say <u>at</u> *a party* because a party isn't any specific area that can encompass or enclose us; the kind of party that takes place at a friend's house is **an event** that takes place in one room or several rooms and even perhaps outside of the house, such as in the backyard or patio. Because of this general nature of location, *at* works much better because it simply places us in the general area of the event. Compare it with the use of *in* in this little dialogue:

A: Where's Jack? I thought he was out here weeding the flower beds as I'd asked him to.

B: Nope. He's **in** the house watching *Batman*.

Note that there is another kind of *party*, a group of people going somewhere together, acting as a group. A person who is one person *in a party* of six that is reserving a table at a restaurant is *included* in the group.

Back to the idea of choosing *in* or *at*. Here are a couple of examples that will bring the point about a specific, enclosed area versus a general area in even sharper focus. Fill in these blanks with *in* or *at*:

He works _____ the security office _____ the annex _____ the airport.

Most people would say that this person works ***in*** the security office ***in*** the annex ***at*** the airport. Why do we use *in* for the office and the annex? And why do we use *at* for the airport? Write your thoughts on these lines:

_____

_____

The person works **inside the office** (he's <u>en</u>closed by it) and the office is a room **inside the annex** (the building encompasses the office), so he works *in* them. On the other hand, the building is located **in the general area that we call the airport**; that's why we say *at* the airport.

But we're not through with *at*. Let's get back to some other idiomatic uses for this little demon of a preposition. Keep your mind in its "interpreting mode." Here are some prepositional phrases dealing with both literal and idiomatic aspects of *at* which we'd like you to explain as you would to your students. Be brief, but clear!

1. *at* five o'clock

_____

2. *by* five o'clock

_____

3. *on* Maple Street

_____

4. *at* 223 Maple Street

_____

5. *on* Christmas

_____

6. *at* Christmas

_____

These are the kinds of phrases that drive students mad—and who could blame them? Native English speakers can appreciate the exactness of these prepositions, but our students just cringe when confronted with such exactness of meaning. Let's go over them now and see how closely your interpretations match ours.

At five o'clock means exactly when that hour arrives; *by* five o'clock means that something can occur before that hour or at that hour, but not after that hour.

On Maple Street gives us only a general idea of location; something is somewhere along that street. **We use** *at*, however, **when we have the actual house/ building number** to help us pinpoint the location. Does this use of *at* strike you as a contradiction of one of the first meanings we gave *at*, that it means in the general area and not a specific point? Initially, you might think so, but we have to look deeper. True, mentioning the number of the place does pinpoint the location for us, but *at* simply tells us that it's somewhere on those premises. For example, the real location of the person we're looking for could be *in* Apartment 12 *at* 223 Maple Street or *in* Suite 100 *at* 223 Maple. And even though it might border on the silly, we can take this explanation a step further and say that, if this is a private house, the person we're looking for could be *in* the kitchen *at* 223 Maple Street! So, all in all, there really isn't a big contradiction when *at* is used this way.

As for the last two phrases, **we think of *on* Christmas as meaning during that one specific day,** whereas **we tend to think of *at* Christmas as something taking place during the general time of that holiday**, not just on that one day.

Before leaving the prepositional bane of banes, let's explore other uses we have for *at* besides the ones we've covered so far. Since we've done it for the other prepositions cited in the chapter, it's only fair that we do it for this one, too. This time, though, we're going to carry out our investigation in a different way. You'll notice that we've set up this activity as a matching exercise. Match up the examples we've given you with the uses they represent by filling in the appropriate corresponding number in front of each example.

Use 1: conditions/states
Use 2: rates/scales/ages
Use 3: in the direction of
Use 4: reactions
Use 5: abilities

_____ Is he going to retire at sixty-five?   _____ We seem to be at odds.

_____ They were at a turning point.   _____ I didn't shoot at the birds.

_____ She cried at the bad news.   _____ Are you good at math?

_____ She's a genius at bridge.   _____ We laughed at her joke.

_____ He aimed at the target.   _____ Water boils at 212° F.

Of course you understand now that the different uses we've found for *at* depend on the context that the preposition is in. Here are the answers to this matching exercise for you to check your choices against: on the **left**—**2, 1, 4, 5, 3**; on the **right**—**1, 3, 5, 4, 2**.

Here are other examples that fit into the different uses for *at*:

Use 1: be at ease/an end/play/loggerheads/rest
Use 2: at 29,000,000 shares (stock market)/a fair price/age 70
Use 3: yell at/look at/glance at/grab at/lunge at/wave at
Use 4: balk at/cringe at/frown at/weep at/recoil at/sneer at
Use 5: be smart at/a whiz at/bad at/poor at/slow at

✍ Some Teaching Strategies

Before we go on to another topic, let's discuss some basic advice we can offer you for teaching prepositions. To begin, one technique we've always found useful and efficient is to teach pairs of prepositions that are opposite in meaning. For example, don't let your students learn *up* without learning *down*; don't let them learn *over* without learning *under* at the same time. When we've asked high intermediate students to give us the opposites of certain prepositions, many of them couldn't think of the right ones— in fact, many times they came up with bizarre answers. One reason that it's important to teach prepositions in this way whenever possible is that it will come in handy as the students get into two-word and three-word verbs (what some people refer to as *phrasal verbs*). By learning at an early stage of their English that *off* is the opposite of *on*, your students will find it easier to learn converse phrasal verbs such as *put on* and *take off* or *turn on* and *turn off*.

Another bit of advice we can offer is a grammar rule that many teachers avoid until the higher levels of ELT. It's really unnecessary to put it off, as we've proven in practice, because this rule is very straightforward and has *no* exceptions: **When a verb follows a preposition, add *-ing* to it** (before leav*ing*, after eat*ing*, for mak*ing*, by heat*ing*).

Some people might want to take exception to this rule and say that it doesn't hold up if you consider examples like *used to* or *be able to*. After all, they'd say, verbs don't have the *-ing* stuck on the end if they come after these expressions that end in a preposition ("I used to <u>like</u> spinach." / "They aren't able to <u>fly</u>"). The reason we don't consider these examples exceptions to the rule is that they belong to that category called **semi-auxiliaries** or **periphrastic modals**. Since they can substitute for modal auxiliaries, as we saw in Chapter 8, the verb that follows remains untouched just as it does after a modal:

He <u>can</u> go   =   He **[is able to]**   go
                         He **[is allowed to]**   go

She <u>will</u> go   =   She **[is going to]**   go
                         She **[is about to]**   go

We <u>would</u> go   =   We **[used to]**   go

Other expressions that fall into this category of semi-auxiliaries or periphrastic modals are *have to*, *have got to*, *be to*, *be about to*, and *be supposed to*. In short, the preposition *to* is an integral part of each of these semi-auxiliaries, not just a preposition on its own. Compare these expressions to something like *be used to*, which is an expression with an allied preposition that doesn't substitute for a modal auxiliary. Because this expression isn't a modal substitute, the verb that follows the preposition will have the *-ing* stuck onto it ("He's used to eat*ing* at 7 p.m.") just as any other verb would.

We're sure you'll see that the rule for putting *-ing* on a verb that follows a preposition isn't difficult for students to master once they understand what prepositions are.

An additional idea we'd like to give you is that nothing works better for teaching prepositions than physical demonstrations. If you've decided, let's say, to teach *in/out* and *on/off*, actually showing the class many different examples of these prepositions at work and then letting them go through the physical paces themselves will be your best bet for getting them to develop a feel for the concepts being taught. You should demonstrate many different examples for each preposition; if you're going to teach *on/off* in their literal uses, show them examples with a box, a desk, a chalkboard, a wall, a bulletin board, an article of clothing, etc. In order for the students to develop a feel for these words, they must be exposed to enough varied examples for the message to hit home and become real.

One last bit of advice we'd like to pass along at this point is that you're bound to come across times when your students overuse the second element in the complex forms, such as *out of* and *away from*. There are times when you may hear students say such oddities as "The dog is out of" instead of "The dog is out" or "The dog is outside." Another example is if you hear a student say "I put it into" instead of "I put it in." Why do you suppose the student sentences we've just cited are ungrammatical? Can you figure this out of—we mean, out?

_____

_____

The reason is that **we only require the second element when the complex form is followed _by an object_**. It's perfectly all right to say "The dog is out of <u>the house</u>" and "I put it into <u>the drawer</u>," but when we omit the objects, we omit the secondary element as well ("The dog is out." / "I put it in.") Note that _into_, although written as one word, is really a combination of two elements. If there's no object with the preposition _into_, the _to_ gets dropped just as our rule says.

While we're on the subject of prepositions and their objects, we should mention a mistake made by many native English speakers. Unfortunately, it's quite common to hear people say such phrases as "You can go to the show _with Charlie and I_" or "Just _between you and I_, he's really not such a nice guy." Why should we say "with Charlie and <u>me</u>" and "between you and <u>me</u>?" Come up with an answer and write it on the line that follows:

_____

_____

The answer is that **you can't have a pronoun in the subject form** _(I, he, she, we, they)_ **when it follows a preposition**. You must use the object form _(me, him, her, us, them)_ even when there are two pronouns separated by the word _and_. Note that this mistake occurs most commonly in a phrase with the first person singular pronoun _(*with so-and-so and I)_.

A̅j̅ Post-posed Prepositions

One very typical feature of English that has gone from being considered not so acceptable to acceptable is the final topic of this chapter. Its fancy name is the post-posed preposition, and many a native English speaker will remember being corrected in primary or secondary school for this infraction of old-style, traditional grammar. What was that infraction? It was ending a clause or a sentence with a preposition! Most traditional English teachers of days gone by didn't consider it "proper" to say sentences like these:

> The play (which/that) I was speaking <u>about</u> had a great plot.
> Which play were you speaking about?

Those teachers used to insist that we say these sentences this way:

The play <u>about which</u> I was speaking . . .
<u>About which play</u> were you speaking?

Most native speakers consider it very formal language to place the preposition at the beginning of the clause—but they themselves would rarely speak that way. It must be said, though, that things have changed considerably in the last few decades, especially in regard to the spoken idiom. As modern teachers, we should understand our responsibility to teach the language as it's *really* spoken and written and not hold on to some idealized, traditional form that no one would normally use in everyday language. Not only would it sound odd for a native speaker to say the last two example sentences we gave and which the old-fashioned English teachers preferred, but, in some situations, it would also sound affected and out of place. On the other hand, English is an international language and therefore, we have to hold with some kind of standard. Mostly, we try to strike a happy medium.

Before we go into detail about post-posed prepositions, we'd like to mention our viewpoint about this term. If you know some basic Latin root words, you know that *post-posed* literally means "put or place after," and we have to disagree with that term. To be "put after" gives you the idea that something is deliberately being moved and placed after something else—and that's not the case at all with this phenomenon so peculiar to English. To understand what post-posed prepositions are all about, you have to realize that the preposition isn't being moved and placed after anything; it's simply staying right where it is in the original idea/sentence. Take a look at the following diagram, which demonstrates how the preposition isn't moving anywhere—although other things are:

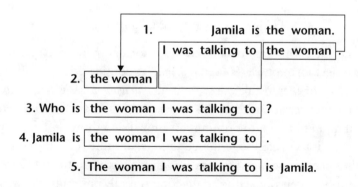

So what's happened? (**1**) We're looking at two basic ideas at our starting point: "Jamila is the woman." / "I was talking to the woman." (**2**) What we've moved to another position is *the woman* (the object of the preposition) and *not* the preposition! Note that we've moved *the woman* to the front of the sentence. Now we have the clause "the woman I was talking to," and this newly formed clause is going to serve many purposes as we can see. (**3**) We can add a question phrase before our new clause, or (**4**) some information, or (**5**) we can reverse the whole thing. Now we think you can see how the preposition hasn't been moved and placed anywhere new; it's actually right where it's been all along. Let's look at one more example of these changes at work:

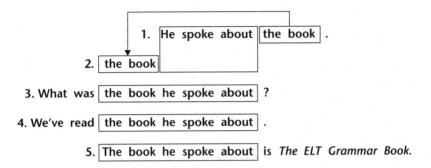

(**1**) Here we have our basic idea. (**2**) We've moved the object of the preposition (the book) to the front of the sentence so that we now have "the book he spoke about." (**3**) We've chosen to add a question phrase to the front so that we have a complete question. (**4**) Instead, we can choose to add some information to the front of the clause so that we now have a declarative sentence. And finally, (**5**) we've added some information after the clause to form another declarative sentence. It's a very slick operation!

There's one more thing we need to mention when these changes are made with our basic idea: we can add the words **who/whom** or **that** after the initial noun phrase if the noun is a person:

> The woman <u>who</u> I was talking to . . .
> The woman <u>whom</u> I was talking to . . .
> The woman <u>that</u> I was talking to . . .

These three variations are considered more formal by most native speakers, especially if the object form of *who* is used (*whom*). It's considered a more conversational style to omit *whom* or *that* in this construction: *The woman I was talking to . . .*

As for our sentences about the book, we can choose to use either **which** or **that** after the initial noun phrase if the noun is an animal or a thing. For some people, the effect of using *that* is to make the sentence somewhat more formal, and *which* sounds friendlier. Other people use *that* if the meaning is necessary to the sentence and *which* if the clause can be taken out without affecting the meaning much—with or without commas.

> The book <u>which</u> he spoke about . . .
> The book, which he spoke about so highly, is really excellent reading.
> The book which he spoke about so highly is really excellent reading.
>
> The book <u>that</u> he spoke about . . .
> The book that he spoke about is the one I'm reading.

Lets' take a look at one more diagram that shows how we get another so-called post-posed preposition:

In this diagram, you can see that the operations in this case are just about the same as in our other diagrams. Here, however, there are two slight differences. The first one has to do with the fact that we have an unknown as the object of the preposition, so we use the word *what* to signify that unknown object and we move it to the front of the clause. The other difference is that in order to form the question, we need to invert *she* and *was*, which is the normal way to make a *wh-* question with the verb *be* anyway. (To refresh your memory about making *wh-* questions, see Chapter 1.) Again, notice that the preposition hasn't moved at all!

As we come towards the end of this chapter, there's a peculiar—though traditional—teaching tactic that we'd like to discuss. In many traditionally conceived English grammar books, you'll find the following order given when post-posed prepositions are dealt with:

1. The woman is my neighbor. I was talking <u>to the woman</u>.
2. The woman <u>to whom</u> I was talking is my neighbor.
3. The woman <u>who(m)/that</u> I was talking <u>to</u> is my neighbor.
4. The woman I was talking <u>to</u> is my neighbor.

We think this a very odd way indeed to demonstrate the changes that take place in order to arrive at a so-called post-posed preposition. Notice how the preposition in Step 1 is in its *rightful* place together with its object (to the woman). Suddenly, in Step 2, it's been thrust in front of the clause and in Step 3, it's been moved down the line again back to its original spot after the clause! Isn't this peculiar? All that these traditional grammar books need to do is leave well enough alone. The only reason the preposition has been finally **post-posed** is because it was **pre-posed** in Step 2!

For one very strange reason, these traditional grammarians felt that the pre-posed preposition was somehow a more basic construction and should therefore be Step 2. This tradition came about in the mid-17th century when the English were trying their best to fit English grammar into the way Latin grammar worked. It really doesn't work because they were trying to fit a Germanic language onto the structure of an Italic language. We feel, on the contrary, that the pre-posed construction is not so basic as it is affected and doesn't seem to go along with the way English constructs this kind of sentence. By the way, an interesting note about this pre-posed arrangement is that you can't use the word ***that*** any longer in place of *who* or *which*:

    1a. The woman to whom I was talking . . .

    1b. ★The woman to <u>that</u> I was talking . . . (ungrammatical)

    2a. The book about which he spoke . . .

    2b. ★The book about <u>that</u> he spoke . . . (ungrammatical)

Before we close this chapter, we'd like to offer you a list of the clauses and sentences that you'll find post-posed prepositions in, or if you prefer, in which you'll find post-posed prepositions:

Statements:	I'd like you to look this <u>over</u>.
Wh- questions:	What are you thinking <u>about</u>?
Wh- clauses:	(Who I associate <u>with</u>) is none of your business.
Indirect speech:	He didn't tell me who he'd gotten the gift <u>from</u>.
Infinitive forms:	I can't find the right pot to cook this spaghetti <u>in</u>.
Relative clauses:	Here's another nice mess you've gotten me <u>into</u>!
Exclamations:	Sit <u>down</u>!

Teaching Tips

9.1 *Drawing Prepositions*

Because so many prepositions are spatial, a good way for students to practice them is to draw pictures to show the meanings of these prepositions. The pictures need not be detailed or elaborate; they only need to be clear enough to represent the meanings. This activity can be done individually, in pairs, or in small groups. Once the pictures are drawn, have the class compare and contrast the ways that they chose to depict the prepositions. Then have the class choose the drawings that best visualize the prepositions or draw a class composite that synthesizes the best representations. Put these pictures on a wall chart and leave the chart up for students to look at and refer to later.

over/under
above/below   out of   through   around

9.2 *Prepositional Visualizations*

Before class, find a text that has a variety of spatial prepositions in it. Copy the text leaving blanks where the prepositions should be. Have the students fill in the blanks with pictures to represent the prepositions. Exchange papers and have students read their classmates' papers aloud, interpreting the visualizations with words. You can also do this activity in the reverse. Have the students write stories (individually, in pairs, or in small groups) with the prepositions in them. Have them exchange their papers and let the new partners/pairs/groups visualize the prepositions. (Sami goes → _____ school _____ 8 every morning. He walks _____ the freeway and _____ a long tunnel.)

Variation: Use the same text as you used in *Teaching Tip 9.2*, only this time, leave the prepositions in. Put blanks after each preposition and have the students draw what the prepositions represent in the blanks. When all the students are finished drawing their prepositions, let them compare and contrast their visualizations.

9.3 *Back-to-Back*

Before class, find a picture that has prepositions represented in the various things and activities. Make copies for half of your students. Prepare a second handout for the other half of the class. This handout should have one or two features from the original picture on it, which will serve as starting points or points of perspective for drawing the rest of the picture. For example, if the complete picture has one particular landmark in it, draw just that on the handout. If the picture has a building in the middle, draw that.

You decide how much needs to be put on this handout. Pair off the students and seat them back to back. Then give each student in the pair a different picture. The students who have the complete picture will describe what's in it so that their partners can draw a faithful copy of the original. Encourage the "describers" to be as accurate as possible, but the "artists" are permitted to ask as many questions as is necessary to get the drawing right, to fill in the gaps in the information.

Variation:

1. If providing photocopies is a problem, you can draw a picture or put one up on the board and have all the "describers" face the board and all the "artists" face the other way.

2. For students with very limited vocabularies, provide a handout that's ready to fill in or just a blank piece of paper for them to draw and/or color in. Give directions yourself about how you want your students to complete the pictures. For example, tell your students to draw a [brown] easy chair in the upper left corner. Put an oriental rug in front of it. Hang [blue and white] curtains in the window. Place a table next to the [brown] chair and put a table lamp on top of it, and so on.

3. Divide a sheet of paper into boxes. The boxes can be as large as half a sheet or as small as a square inch (2½ cm.). Have the students fill in the different boxes according to directions given by you or another student. To make the exercise more interesting, don't have the students fill in the box in the upper left corner and then the one next to it and then the one next to that. Jump from corner to corner, from top to bottom, from center to side.

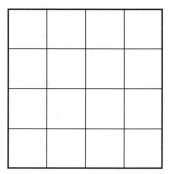

9.4 *Drawing Idioms*

In general, idioms are difficult for students; idioms that contain prepositions are especially difficult. This *Teaching Tip* has two levels to it, a serious one and one with tongue in cheek. When it's possible to represent these idioms as drawings, do so. Before class, select a group of idioms that can be "translated" into drawings. Pair the students up or have them work in small groups. Show them how to "draw an idiom" and then let them do the artwork for several of the idioms you prepared before class. Put the finished products up around the room and compare and contrast the various ways the students chose to represent their idioms.

on top of the world   under the weather   in hot water   over the hill   in a tight spot

Variation: **Pictograms:** Before class, prepare a list of idioms with prepositions. Make absolutely sure that these idioms can be visually represented. Show the students what a "pictogram" is—a way to represent idioms verbatim; they show exactly what the idiom is. Once the students understand how pictograms work, let them make their own versions of the idioms that you've given them to work on in pairs or small groups. Here are some examples to show you how pictograms work.

1. **ALL   AFTER**   ("after all")

2. **I N B E T O**   ("be into")

3. **the bl**^{outof}**ue**   ("out of the blue")

4. **above**
   all else   ("above all else")

5. **D ^{R}O   D ^{R}O**
   N U   N U   ("round and round")

6. **thought   th^{on}ought**   ("on second thought")

9.5 Obstacle Course

Before class, create an obstacle course with things that you have in your classroom. The obstacles can be as large as a desk or as small as a piece of paper on the floor. Blindfold one student and appoint another as guide. Have the guide give directions to the blindfolded student to get him/her through the course. It's often useful for the guide to follow along closely with the blindfolded student as he/she negotiates the course. This activity is particularly good for developing trust among students, precision in directions, and careful listening skills.

9.6 Hide and Seek

This activity is a version of the children's game "Hide and Seek." Before class, hide something in the classroom. Students need to find the object by asking yes/no questions that pinpoint the location of the hidden item. When the students ask a question, you respond "hot" if the answer to the question points to a location that is very close to where the object is hidden, "warm" if relatively close, and "cold" if far away from the hidden object. Students keep asking questions until the object is found. This activity is also excellent for practicing question formation.

9.7 Adèle's House

Before class, prepare a dialogue in which the participants discuss the layout of a room belonging to an imaginary person named Adèle. If you have a tape recorder, record the dialogue. If not, you can read it to your class. Give the students a bare-bones layout of a room and tell them that they'll "furnish" it after they listen to a discussion of the layout. Read the dialogue or play the tape and have the students fix up the room.

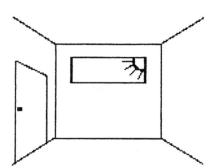

Variation: Instead of Adèle's room, you can do the same activity with a building plan, a city map, a supermarket or supermarket shelf, a library, a shopping center, a tool box, a factory, or a workshop, etc.

9.8 Legos

Bring to class a set of children's blocks or Legos (multi-colored plastic building blocks). Make sure you have enough blocks for all of your students to have several of their own.

Pair the students up and have them sit back to back. Have one student in each pair create a design or pattern with his/her blocks. Limit the time to one or two minutes so that the partners don't get restless while they wait. Have the "designer" get his/her partner to recreate the same design or pattern by giving verbal instructions. When the students are done, have them compare their designs. Go over the differences in the patterns with the students to show them how to be more accurate in giving their instructions.

9.9 Fractured Narrations

Before class, find a picture or pictures with enough prepositional phrases for a narration. Let's say you've found a picture with the following: The sun is shining, but there are a few white, puffy clouds in the sky. A bird is in its nest. A chipmunk is arranging nuts in a tunnel, etc. Prepare a narration based on the picture that contains factual errors. (It's a beautiful day today. See? The sun is peeking out from behind the tree. A bird is next to its nest. A frisky chipmunk is taking nuts out of the tunnel, etc.) Note: Don't change every preposition; it'll be far more challenging if some of the prepositional phrases are left correct. Tell the students that they're going to hear a narration that contains errors and that they'll be asked to write down as many of the errors as they can. Present the narration to the class several times so they can find all the errors. Go back and check to see that they've caught them all.

10

Genitives

"Mice's and men's best-laid plans?"
"The best-laid plans of mice and men?"

We're about to investigate one of the most deceptive topics of English grammar. The reason it's so deceptive is that what appears to be quite straightforward and relatively uncomplicated on the surface (after all, aren't we just talking about *-'s/-s'* and *of?*) is really somewhat perplexing when you get below the surface. As with other topics covered in this book, we're going to focus our attention on those points that tend to be troublesome to understand and explain. Although many ELT grammar books refer to *-'s/-s'* and *of* as "possessives," we prefer to use the broader term "genitives," which includes any and all of their uses, some of which do not indicate possession. We're sure you'll understand why we don't want to limit ourselves to the term "possessives" as you read on.

The *-S* Genitive

To begin with, let's examine the most typical uses of what we refer to as the **-s genitive** because it's found as an *-'s/-s'* on the end of a noun. Take a look at the dialogue on the following page and note how the *-s* genitive is used.

A: **Phyllis'** daughter just joined a **girls'** football team.

B: Really? Was it the **school's** idea to create a football team for girls?

A: I think so. Anyway, she was great in **yesterday's** game. One funny thing, though. The team insists on having their mascot at every game. It's the cutest little white dog.

B: Ah, that's nice.

A: Yeah. They say the **dog's** presence brings them luck.

As already mentioned, most ELT grammar books refer to -*'s*/-*s'* as the possessive ending. Remember that -*'s* is attached to singular nouns *(clerk's)* and irregular plural nouns that do not end in -*s (children's)*, but only the apostrophe is added onto singular nouns ending in -*s (boss')* and regular plural nouns *(boys')*. Though often the case, it's not the only reason that -*'s*/-*s'* is used. In the dialogue you've just read, which examples of the -*s* genitive would you say clearly demonstrate possession or belonging? Write your observation on the following line:

_____

The answer is that there are just two times when the -*s* genitive clearly shows possession or belonging in our dialogue, and that's with the name "Phyllis" and in talking about the dog. We can definitely say that Phyllis has a daughter, so she's *Phyllis' daughter*, and that the dog has presence, so it's *the dog's presence*. This way of thinking about the -*s* genitive leads us to the first use of the -*'s*/-*s'*: we tend to use the -*s* genitive as a marker of possession or belonging on words that represent people. We tend to use it the same way for animals *(a dog's bark; an alligator's stealth; a canary's song)*. In fact, we can make a general observation that **we use the -*s* genitive for possession or belonging on words that represent living things (people and animals)**.

What, now, are we going to do with the rest of the cases of the -*s* genitive in our dialogue? For instance, how can we explain the -*s'* in the phrase *a girls' football team*? It's not that the team is a possession of the girls or that it belongs to the girls; similarly, we can't say that "the idea" is a possession of the school. We can say, however, that the presence does belong to the dog. Is there a simple way to paraphrase all of these phrases to see them in another light? If you were going to paraphrase them, what common way could you come up with? Write down your idea on this line:

_____

We've used paraphrasing before to find the essence of a grammatical construction, and we can use it in this situation, too. Another way to say each of these phrases is "The girls have a football team." / "The school had an idea." / "The dog has presence." The verb **have is a common element in these sentences,** and that's an easy way to explain this genitive to your students. In fact, many teachers traditionally use *have* in a paraphrase to teach their students the meaning of -*s* genitive phrases as well as when they teach possessive adjectives (*my, your, his,* etc.). You should just keep in mind that *have* doesn't always mean the same thing, like possession; it's got lots of interpretations depending on context.

☀ *Troubleshooter* ☀

At times there's confusion over how to write the -*s* genitive when a name ends in the letter *s*. We can make the following observations to help you and your students on this point:

☞ In the rules of such countries as Great Britain, the -'*s* is added to a name even if it ends in -*s*:

Phyllis ⟶ Phyllis's

☞ In the rules of such countries as the United States, only the apostrophe is added to a name that ends in -*s*:

Phyllis ⟶ Phyllis'

Keep in mind that there's no difference in pronunciation whether the genitive is written one way or the other.

Getting back to our dialogue, we still have to account for the -'*s* on the end of *yesterday*. First of all, let's take a look at some similar words and phrases and see if the -*s* genitive can be added to them as well. How about choices like *today/this week/ Monday/next month*? Yes, the -'*s* works nicely with these, too: *today's newspaper/this week's stock reports/Monday's weather forecast/next month's tournament*. What observation can you make about these words and phrases?

If you've written that we can use the -*s* genitive with words and phrases that denote **periods of time**, you've got it right.

Let's move on by comparing the following two phrases. Decide if they're grammatical or not and check the boxes appropriately:

the school's idea   ☐ grammatical   ☐ ungrammatical
the school's wall   ☐ grammatical   ☐ ungrammatical

We already know that "the school's idea" is grammatical, but what about "the school's wall"? The answer is that it's ungrammatical. Why is there a difference? We're not going to answer this question just yet, but we'll get back to it very soon.

✹ *Troubleshooter* ✹

💡 Be prepared for an inevitable occurrence: Your students may tend to drop the -*s* genitive when you're not drilling them on it and produce phrases such as *my mother house* and *the teacher pen*. Don't get too exasperated over this—and don't stop correcting them either!

💡 Another problem you'll have to deal with concerns the pronunciation of the -*s* genitive. Interestingly enough, the rules are identical for pronouncing the regular plural -*s* on nouns.

☞ If the noun ends in a voiceless sound, pronounce the -*s* genitive as /s/:

Jeff's /ǰɛfs/   Scott's /skats/

☞ If the noun ends in a voiced sound, pronounce the -*s* genitive as /z/:

Brenda's /brɛn-dəz/   Ann's /ænz/

☞ If the noun ends in /s/, /š/, /z/, /ž/, /č/, or /ǰ/, pronounce the -*s* genitive as /ɪz/ or /əz/:

Bess' /bɛs-ɪz/   fish's /fɪš-ɪz/   Georges' /žorž-ɪz/   Mitch's /mɪč-ɪz/

☞ In some dialects of English, the /ɪz/ sound for the possessive marker is dropped on nouns that end in /z/. In other dialects, however, it's kept:

Charles' /čarlz/ or /čarlz-ɪz/

Let's observe some other ways we use the -*s* genitive when possession is *not* the meaning by taking a look at another dialogue:

A: Let's have some coffee.

B: Okay. Oh! Don't use the large, white mug. That's **Mom's** mug.

A: All right. So what's happening with that law suit between the paper mill and us over dumping pollutants into the bay?

B: I'm happy to say the **committee's** trip to the capital was a success, and they've persuaded the government to step in.

A: That's great! Who's on our side in the government?

> B: Tess Hyman. I really like her. She's a **politician's** politician.
>
> A: Terrific! You know, I bet we used at least a hundred **dollars'** worth of stamps mailing out all of those flyers.
>
> B: I guess so. Well, with Tess behind us, getting anti-pollution regulations enforced should be **child's** play.
>
> A: I hope so. Wouldn't it be wonderful to be able to swim to your **heart's** content in that water again and not worry about pollution?

Note the words in bold print. In order to zero in on the uses of the *-s* genitive in this dialogue, we'll take each item that appears above separately and add some other examples to it. Perhaps that will help you figure out how to categorize each kind of *-s* genitive we've used. When you think you've got a category for each set of phrases, identify it on the line we've provided for you.

1. Mom's coffee mug / Dad's easy chair / John's side of the bed
   (Note: think of a category other than possession or belonging)

   _____

2. the committee's trip / the enemy's retreat / Tahani's promotion

   _____

3. a politician's politician / a man's man / a poet's poet

   _____

4. 100 dollars' worth / 500 pesos' worth / 6,000 liras' worth

   _____

5. child's play / everyone's dream / men's clothing / lovers' lane

   _____

6. to your heart's content / at journey's end / at death's door

   _____

Granted, this is one of the most difficult tasks we've asked you to do, but even if you've only come up with two or three of the categories, you're doing fine. Here's the way we see these categorizations of the *-s* genitive. You might have used different wording, but if the concepts are the same, that's all that counts:

1. a preferred thing:
- that's the coffee mug that Mom is partial to; all the other coffee mugs may belong to her, too, but that one is her favorite mug and she doesn't like others using it
- that's the easy chair that Dad likes the most
- that's the side of the bed that John always sleeps on

2. actions that the head noun has done or received:
- the committee took that trip (they're the "doers")
- the enemy retreated (they're the "doers")
- Tahani got that promotion (she's the "receiver")

3. the best; the epitome:
- a politician that other politicians would like to emulate
- a man who other men can admire for his manly qualities
- a poet who is held in esteem by other poets

4. an amount of money equal to (used with " . . . worth of . . .")

5. things that seem appropriate (paraphrased with "for"):
- play that is appropriate for a child
- a dream for everyone
- clothing for men
- a place that seems appropriate for lovers to meet at

6. pat phrases (formulaic phrases):
- tend to be idiomatic and disregard rules for using -'s/-s'

Now we'll go back to answer that question we gave you about why it's grammatical to say "the school's idea," but it isn't to say "the school's wall." **The -s genitive is normally not used with non-living things. However, when one noun has two different meanings (i.e., a living and a non-living thing), we use the -s genitive for the living thing.** There's a definite difference in the meaning of "school" in the previous two phrases. In the phrase "the school's idea," we're really talking about the administration, in other words, the *people* who run the school; therefore, it's proper to use -'s. In the phrase "the school's wall," we're not talking about the administration but the actual physical structure, which is a non-living thing, so we don't normally use the -'s in that case. Instead, we'd say "a wall *of* the school" (and we'll discuss the word *of* in the next part of this chapter). An alternative way of communicating this would be to create a compound form and say "a school wall."

One exception to using *of* instead of -'s for non-living things can be found in newspaper headlines. You could see a headline like this one splashed across the front page of your daily newspaper: *School's Wall Collapses! No One Hurt!* This convention in "newspaper talk" may simply have come about in order to save space, but whatever its reason for being, it doesn't seem to be the norm in standard spoken English.

When *school* represents a living thing, i.e., "people," it's being used as a collective noun. Can you think of any other collective nouns, this time representing groups of people or geographical areas, that we can add the -'s/-s' to? Here are a few examples: our *club's* next meeting/*New York's* skyscrapers/their *class'* tenth reunion/*Honduras'* coastline.

Other collective nouns represent animals, and we can use -'s on such words as *herd*, *pride*, and *pack*: the *herd's* migration patterns/the *pride's* adult females/a *wolf pack's* territory.

Here are other examples of things that can take the -'s/-s'. They're things that we perceive as performing actions: our *ship's* first mate/the *plane's* departure/an *ICBM's* range/the *earth's* orbit/*Uranus'* position in the solar system.

So are we done with the -s genitive? Not quite; we still have two important areas to talk about, and one of them can be seen in this next dialogue:

A: What are you doing tomorrow?

B: Well, first I'm going to the ⬚ doctor's ⬚ and then I'm meeting my sister for lunch at ⬚ Murphy's ⬚. I've got nothing special planned after lunch, though.

A: Well, that's not far from ⬚ St. Jerome's ⬚. How about meeting me there in the afternoon to help me with my daughter's wedding arrangements?

B: Sure, I'd love to. My son's wedding there a year ago was just beautiful, and I'm sure your ⬚ daughter's ⬚ will be, too.

Unlike all the other forms of the -s genitive that we've looked at up to now, this time we have the form standing on its own without any accompanying nouns. Take a look back at the words we've boxed in and guess which nouns you could add after them through the help of context:

the doctor's _____

Murphy's _____

St. Jerome's _____

your daughter's _____

We're sure you've filled in the blanks with **office (surgery), Restaurant (Pub/ Tavern), Church,** and **wedding.** This wasn't such a hard task because the context of the dialogue helped you figure out what these words with -'s stood for. **We can use the -s genitive on its own when it's clear what it refers to.**

Now we're coming to the last point we should discuss about the *-s* genitive in this section of the chapter. Look at the following phrases and decide if they mean the same thing or different things.

> Gilbert and Sullivan's works
> Gilbert's and Sullivan's works
> ☐ same   ☐ different

Even though these phrases may seem the same at a quick glance, they're really quite different in meaning. Try to figure out what the difference is and write your thoughts on the following lines:

_____

_____

When we have two or more names and all the people involved are connected to the head noun (in this case, "works"), **only the final name, the one closest to the head noun, gets the *-'s/-s'*** ("Gilbert and Sullivan's works," meaning the works that Gilbert and Sullivan created together). However, **if the head noun is distinct for each person mentioned, each name gets *-'s/-s'*** ("Gilbert's [works] and Sullivan's works"—in other words, works that they didn't create as a team).

Another example of this phenomenon is "Athena and Aristoteli's children" as compared to "Athena's and Aristoteli's children." How would you interpret the difference in meaning between the two phrases?

_____

_____

In the **first example**, Athena and Aristoteli **had children together**; in the **second example, Athena has some children, and Aristoteli has some children, but they didn't have them together.**

Group Genitives

Another phenomenon that occurs with the *-s* genitive is called the group genitive. What happens is that the end of a compound noun or a phrase describing the head noun receives the suffixed *-'s/-s'*; in other words, the whole phrase is treated as a single unit. What follows are four examples of typical group genitives:

> a judge advocate's caseload/the notary public's office
> my sister-in-law's boss/a man-about-town's wardrobe

These next three group genitives are rather unusual but possible. They're likely to be found in colloquial speech rather than formal writing and can be a lot of fun. We'll be discussing a more formalized way of dealing with such awkward phrases later on:

> the guy who works in the mailroom's wife
> the neighbor whose wife won two Caribbean cruises' house
> the woman who I spoke to's son

The -S Genitive in a Nutshell

used for people and animals:

- **possession/belonging:**
  Myrlande's skirt/the parakeet's feathers
- **paraphrasing with *have*:**
  Yuri's fever (Yuri has a fever.)
  the dog's fleas (The dog has fleas.)
- **a preferred thing:**
  Iris' place at the dinner table
  my dog's spot for burying things
- **head noun does/receives action:**
  Bill's resignation/the lion's kill (doers)
  the thief's arrest/the zebra's capture (receivers)
- **showing esteem:**
  a surgeon's surgeon/a teacher's teacher
- **appropriateness (can be paraphrased with for):**
  soldiers' uniforms (uniforms for soldiers)
  a tiger's habitat (the habitat for a tiger)
- **collective nouns (groups of people or animals):**
  the committees' members/the flock's dominant ram

used with words representing periods of time:
this month's gas bill/tomorrow's weather/a day's wages

amount of money equal to (always with *worth of*)**:**
thirty euros' worth of gasoline/100 rubles' worth of cheese

on words representing periods of time with *worth of*:
three weeks' worth of work done in five days

sometimes for nonliving things that are perceived as performing actions:
these cars' special features/the train's dining car/the sun's rays

formulaic phrases (pat phrases):
a hair's breadth/a stone's throw/at arm's length
a doctor's appointment/a dentist's appointment

on its own when the reference is clear:
The family reunion is going to be at my cousin's.
He works at Harrod's.

 when two or more names share the head noun:
Bill and Ted's Excellent Adventure

 group genitives:
The Out-of-Towners' Guide to Auckland
the man who got shot in the leg's medical bills

The Of-Genitive

A: Magda, did you know the brother **of** that boy you're dating has been arrested?

B: Anton's brother? Arrested?

A: He's been charged with stealing the car **of** that nice old couple who live right next door to his parents.

B: The Nagys' car? I don't believe it!

A: Believe it! I never did like him. He's nothing like Anton.

The dialogue you've just read offers us a convenient transition from the *-s* genitive to the *of*-genitive. According to what we stated in the first part of this chapter, the *-s* genitive should be the proper form when we focus on living things, but we can clearly see the *of*-genitive used for some of the people mentioned in our dialogue. Why is that? In fact, not only have we used both forms of the genitive in this dialogue, but we've even used them at different times for the same people. Isn't that strange! Or is it? After you take another look at the way *-'s/-s'* and *of* are used in this dialogue, can you come up with an explanation to defend both uses? If you can, write your ideas on the following lines:

_____

_____

Although the *-s* genitive is the more typical form we use for possession or belonging when living things are involved, **we tend to use the *of*-genitive if we're using an adjectival clause to describe the head noun**: "the brother of that boy *you're dating*"/"the car of that nice old couple *who live right next door to his parents.*" True, in colloquial speech we might hear group genitives used in these two cases: "that boy you're dating's brother"/"that nice old couple who live right next door to his parents' car." Even though all group genitives are slightly bizarre, this first one seems more plausible than the second one simply because it's shorter and easier to deal with. Using the *of*-genitive in these cases certainly saves us a lot of trouble. Let's take a look at one more dialogue that demonstrates the *of*-genitive in this way:

A: Remember that song "Scarborough Fair"?

B: Yeah, sure. In fact, I remember it was on an album that was a birthday gift to me from the parents **of** a high school friend I tutored in algebra.

A: So what ever happened to your friend?

B: I hear he married the daughter **of** some math genius who's always winning awards!

Now that we've discussed how *of* can be used in place of *-'s/-s'* under certain circumstances, we should restate the most typical use for the *of*-genitive, which we mentioned a few pages back when discussing those phrases "the school's idea" and "a wall of the school." Whereas the *-s* genitive seems to be used primarily with living things, **the *of*-genitive seems to be used primarily with non-living things (both concrete and abstract)**. Here are some examples for you to look at. Note that you probably wouldn't interchange them with the *-s* genitive:

> the color of that <u>shirt</u>/the cost of a <u>computer</u> (concrete things)
> the taste of <u>lamb</u>/the price of <u>fish</u> (food items ‑non‑living things)
> a line of <u>defense</u>/a standard of <u>conduct</u> (abstract things)

𝕸 *Troubleshooter* 𝕸

Genitive forms aren't used the same way in every language. A case in point is how the *of*-genitive is used in some languages where we use the preposition *in*:

> Spanish: El desierto más grande | *del* | mundo. *(del = of the)*
> English: The largest desert | *in* | the world.

A possible explanation for this is that English focuses on *location* rather than possession in such sentences.
Expect some of your students to demonstrate this bit of language interference.

A·ɔ· Partitive Genitives

A very common use for the *of*-genitive deals with a category that we can place under the umbrella of **partitives**, concrete and abstract words that represent a part of the whole. Take a look at the following dialogue which demonstrates this use:

> A: Have you seen that new **pair of gloves** I just bought?
> B: Weren't they on the **top of the dresser?**
> A: I thought so, but they're not there now!
> B: I have a **piece of advice** for you. Don't leave things lying around.
> A: And here I am ready to go to the store and I was going to wear them. Where can they be?
> B: What do we need at the store?
> A: Oh, let's see . . . a **can of coffee,** half a **kilo of butter,** two **loaves of bread,** and some other things as well.
> B: Coffee? There's a can of coffee on the kitchen counter.
> A: What you see is a coffee can, but it's empty. Well, gloves or no gloves, I'm on my way.

Just as we've done before, let's list the various highlighted phrases that appear in this dialogue and see if we can identify categories for the partitive genitives they represent. Where there aren't many examples, we've given you some more to look at. Write your categories on the blank lines.

1. a pair of gloves/a pair of scissors/a stack of dishes/a set of knives

_____

2. the top of the dresser/the back of the chair/the leg of the table

_____

3. a piece of advice/a time of plenty/a heap of trouble

_____

4. a can of coffee/half a kilo of butter/two loaves of bread

_____

So what would you call these categories under the umbrella heading of partitives? As we see it, the first category is simple—it's just anything that comes in **pairs or sets**. The next category deals with **parts of things**; the third category deals with **abstracts** that can't be counted but which we feel the need to think of as if they could be. Finally, our fourth category deals with **measures** and, although these three examples all have to do with food, the category isn't limited to food alone: *a pound of nails/a ball of twine/a ream of paper.*

By the way, did you notice that curious twist on words at the end of the last dialogue? Person B says that she saw a can of coffee sitting on the kitchen counter, but Person A explains that what she saw was a coffee can—an empty one at that. What's going on here? How would you explain the difference between a coffee can and a can of coffee? Here are a few more examples just to help you out. When you've got an idea, write it down on the lines below:

a cup of tea/a teacup
a jar of mayonnaise/a mayonnaise jar
a barrel of oil/an oil barrel

_____

_____

We bet that you've been able to explain the difference in the phrases we've just given you. When describing the specific uses for these containers, we make compound nouns: *a coffee can/a tea cup/a mayonnaise jar/an oil barrel.* But when we speak about what's inside the containers (amounts, in these cases), we use the partitive genitive: *a can of coffee/a cup of tea/a jar of mayonnaise/a barrel of oil.*

A·;· **Appositives**

Finally, we have one more use for the *of*-genitive that can seem a bit perplexing. Look at the next dialogue and see if you can figure out what the reason for this use is:

A: Why are you so excited today?

B: Because the **President of Fulania** is going to be the guest speaker at our graduation exercises.

A: That's terrific! I hear he's a **jewel of a speaker**.

B: That's what I've heard, too. It's amazing to think that he comes from such a humble background.

A: Oh, really?

B: Yes. He comes from the **little village of Abadoo** in the desert part of the country, but he spent quite a few years in the **city of Leicester**, you know, in England.

A: Do you know what his speech is going to be on?

B: Uh-huh. "The **Art of Active Listening**," whatever that is.

What role do you think the *of*-genitive is playing in all these phrases? Here's a little hint: All of them except one deal with literal usage and the other one is idiomatic. After you've given this some thought, write your conclusions on the following lines:

_____

_____

In all of the phrases we've highlighted (except for "a jewel of a speaker"), there's one basic purpose for using the *of*-genitive and that is **to explain more about the preceding noun**. All these phrases answer the question *which?* or *what?* The president of what? Fulania. Which little village? Abadoo. What city? Leicester. Which art? Active listening. This quirky use for the *of-genitive* is called the **appositive use**.

As for the other phrase, "a jewel of a speaker," this is an idiomatic use of the appositive construction meaning *a very good speaker*. Other examples of this kind of usage are *a beast of a night, a prince of a man, a nightmare of a flight*.

🍳 *The Of-Genitive in a Nutshell*

🥜 **used to focus on some aspect of most non-living things (concrete and abstract):**
the texture of the snow/the roll of the waves
the heart of the matter/the depth of his anguish

🥜 **with head nouns that are followed by adjectival clauses:**
the son of the lady *I introduced you to at the party*

🥜 **used as a partitive for concrete and abstract things:**
 • **pairs or sets:** a pair of glasses/a set of rollers
 • **parts of things:** the limbs of a tree/the pages of a book
 • **abstracts:** a bit of pleasure/a moment of silence
 • **measures:** 4 liters of gasoline/10 yards of cloth

🥜 **used as an appositive to explain or describe the preceding noun:**
the Book of Kells/the Cliffs of Dover

🔺 *Troubleshooter* 🔺

It's a good idea to keep in mind that there are several languages that don't have genitives such as we have in English. In those languages, the genitive is expressed simply by the syntax of the phrase, that is, where the words are placed. Let's look at some disparate languages and see how they do fine without a true genitive form. To demonstrate our point, we'll use the phrase *the boy's book.*

☞ Haitian Creole:	liv	ptigason-an	
	the book	the boy	
☞ Arabic:	kitab	alwalad	
	book	the boy	
☞ Amharic:	yɛliʲu	madzhaf	
	the boy	book	
☞ Cantonese:	nam-haɪji	dɛk	sɪ
	boy	the	book

If you find your students having a lot of trouble with the English genitive forms, it might be because their languages simply don't have the equivalents of our -'s / -s' or of.

❧ **The Double Genitive**

We've covered the -*s* genitive and the *of*-genitive separately, but there are occasions when the two are used together—that's why we call this structure the double genitive. It's really quite an odd-looking form, especially to students, but one that's quite commonly used. Let's take a look at a couple of these:

friends of the priests'/a son of the teacher's

To the student, this construction may be very confusing. Most likely, the student would say that it's the -*'s*/-*s'* on the end of each phrase that makes it so odd. Isn't it enough to say *friends of the priests* or *a son of the teacher* and leave it at that? It might be, except for the fact that we normally use the -*s* genitive for living things. No, something else is going on here. The student might be more comfortable with the construction *the priests' friends* and *the teacher's son* (assuming he or she has already learned this basic genitive form), but are these accurate paraphrases of our original phrases? What's your opinion?

_____

_____

The answer is that **the paraphrases** we've come up with ***don't* accurately reflect the meaning of our original phrases**. The reason is that they inadvertently mislead us. Saying *the priests' friends* leads us to believe that the priests have only a certain number of friends or that specific friends who we've already mentioned are being cited; likewise, saying *the teacher's son* makes us think that the teacher has only one son or, once again, he's the son we've already mentioned—and that's not the case. The truth is that these people are just some friends out of several that the priests have *(friends of the priests')* and the other person is just one of at least two sons that the teacher has *(a son of the teacher's)*. There's nothing intrinsically wrong with saying *the priests' friends* and *the teacher's son* as long as it's true that the priests do only have these friends and the teacher only one son, or that we've already mentioned these people. If, however, that isn't the case, we have to find another way to express our ideas, and this is where the double genitive helps out.

Let's focus for a moment on the indefinite articles (zero article or *a/an*) that are used in the double genitive construction. What if a student of yours says, "They're the friends of the priests'"? Is this acceptable? Think about what you'd say to your student and write it on the following lines:

_____

_____

It turns out that **you can't say a sentence like the one the student created because *the* indicates exclusivity**. The whole purpose of this odd construction is to communicate that these people are just *some* of their friends, so if your student uses *the*, he defeats this purpose. Of course, there's an easy way to circumvent this whole problem and that's by paraphrasing once again. Instead of saying *friends of the priests'*, we can say *some of the priests' friends*, and instead of saying *a son of the teacher's*, we can say *one of the teacher's sons*.

Getting back to that student for a moment, let's say he wasn't finished after he said, "They're the friends of the priests' . . ." but wanted to say something about these people. Could saying *the* end up being grammatical after all? See if you can figure this out:

It so happens that **your student can definitely make the phrase perfectly grammatical** by adding adjectival information that will then give exclusivity to those people. For example, he could say "They're the friends of the priests' *who won that trip to Tahiti*." If there's this kind of exclusivity, it's all right to use *the*. Note also that the clause *who won that trip to Tahiti* must go with *friends* because *priests'* —as a genitive form—cannot be the *who*.

There's one more thing to be said about the double genitive. It's quite common to use possessive pronouns (*mine, yours, his,* etc.) as the second element in this construction. Here are two examples:

friends of mine/a neighbor of theirs

This use of possessive pronouns goes hand in hand with the use of the -*'s*/-*s'* in the double genitive that we've just finished discussing. On a final note, there's one aspect of this form which is rarely taught. Here are four examples of it. Try to identify what's going on:

This nose of mine is quite aristocratic.
That cat of theirs is lovable, isn't she?
That parrot of yours woke me up again this morning!
Those kids of hers always manage to get into mischief.

If you've written that this **double genitive plus the addition of the demonstratives *this, that, these,* or *those* shows some sort of extra emotion or feeling**, you've hit on it exactly. Among other things, this special phrase can communicate **affection or disdain, approval or disapproval**.

-'S/-S' vs. *Of*: The Gray Areas

We've finally arrived at the last topic concerning the genitives. It's a problematic topic that perhaps deals more with style than grammar. Read the following items and choose the genitive form that seems *more appropriate to each situation* and check it off. (Here's a tip: Go by your first impressions; don't think about them too much!)

1. "My lords and ladies, ladies and gentlemen, it is my distinct honor to present to you His Royal Highness, Juan Carlos de Borbón,

    ☐ *Spain's King.*"   ☐ *the King of Spain.*"

2. "Our next story on the *Evening News* has to do with

    ☐ *Spain's plans* for the upcoming summer Olympics."
    ☐ *the plans of Spain* for the upcoming summer Olympics."

3. A: Are you taking any literature courses next semester?
   B: Yes. I'm going to take a course called

    ☐ *"Hemingway's Novels."*   ☐ *"The Novels of Hemingway."*

4. "Welcome to my class, ladies and gentlemen. I'm glad that you've signed up for this course, and I hope you enjoy the subject as much as I do.

    ☐ *Hemingway's novels* have greatly contributed to international literature."
    ☐ *The novels of Hemingway* have greatly contributed to international literature."

5. "Good evening. My name's Ruth and I'll be your server this evening. Besides the seafood listed on our menu,

    ☐ *the catch of the day* is sea bass. Just let me know when you're ready to order."
    ☐ *the day's catch* is sea bass. Just let me know when you're ready to order."

6. A: Hi, Joe! How did the fishing go today?
   B: Not bad at all, Frank. How about you?
   A: We did just fine, I'm glad to say. So what are you planning to do with

    ☐ *the catch of the day?*   ☐ *the day's catch?*

   B: We'll be selling it to some of those restaurants along the beach.

Style in language can be a difficult thing to pin down. There really are no hard-and-fast rules that cover every given situation concerning style and which option *(-'s/-s'* or *of)* to choose, but there are some conclusions we can draw from observing how a great many native speakers handle phrases like the six items you've just dealt with. We'll wait to give you our conclusions a little later; right now, let's go over the items.

First of all, here's what the majority of native speakers would choose:

> **1. . . . Juan Carlos de Borbón, the King of Spain.**
> **2. . . . Spain's plans for the upcoming summer Olympics.**
> **3. . . . a course called "The Novels of Hemingway."**
> **4. Hemingway's novels have greatly contributed . . .**
> **5. . . . the catch of the day is sea bass.**
> **6. So what are you planning to do with the day's catch?**

Compare your choices to these. Then see if you can figure out what seems to be the underlying factor that accounts for the choices that were favored. When you've come up with an idea, write it down on the following lines:

_____

_____

The answer may lie in what we refer to as **formulaic phrases**, that is, certain traditional usages in a language that may or may not go along with the usual conventions. Sometimes it's quite easy for us to decide why one of these formulaic phrases is used in a given situation, but sometimes it's not so clear. We probably all agreed that saying "the King *of Spain*" in Item 1 *sounded* more appropriate in that situation than saying *"Spain's King"* even though *Spain's plans* seems perfectly appropriate when the newscaster says it as he refers to that country's plans for the summer Olympic games. Pretending a little, we can imagine hearing Item 1 during the formal presentation of a visiting monarch to the Court of St. James in London.

As we've said, there are no hard-and-fast rules on this subject, but there does seem to be a tendency we can discern. **It appears that the formulaic phrases that employ the *of*-genitive tend to sound more formal to us than the *-s* genitive and give the phrase an air of importance or dramatic effect.** This "feel" that native speakers have seems to govern which genitive they choose, but we want to stress that there are probably exceptions to our observation.

Now let's talk about Items 2 through 6. Because university course titles are usually presented in formal catalogues, most people would choose "The Novels *of* Hemingway" even though entitling the course "Hemingway's Novels" works just as well, grammatically speaking. Conversely, most people would feel it's appropriate for a professor to use the *-s* genitive in his introductory remarks to the class (Hemingway's novels), perhaps because there's no need for him to *sound* more formal or dramatic in his opening comments.

People are of the opinion that by saying "the catch of the day," our server seems to give the phrase that extra dramatic or important air which she might want to impart to her customers. The fisherman, on the other hand, is just making small talk with another fisherman, so people feel he has no need to give the phrase any special effect ("the day's catch").

There's one more troublesome issue we'd like to address concerning the gray areas of the genitives. In many scholarly, traditional works on English grammar, mention is made that the *-s* genitive is used with "higher" animals and the *of*-genitive with "lower" animals. We find these rules to be questionable; after all, where is the line to be drawn between what is a "higher" animal and what is a "lower" animal? Is it wrong to say "my turtle's food" or "a mosquito's wings?" Or is it that those two creatures are too "low" on the scale for the *-s* genitive? Many—if not most— native speakers would not flinch either way if they heard someone say "a mosquito's wings" or "the wings of a mosquito." Likewise, would they cringe if they heard someone say "the song of a canary" instead of "a canary's song?" We doubt it. We think it best to leave well enough alone and simply say that there are certain gray areas concerning *-'s/-s'* and *of* where both forms are probably more acceptable than not, and the use of one or the other may best be left up to the individual.

Teaching Tips

10.1 Simon Says

Even though possessive adjectives aren't covered in this book, we wanted to include this very energetic activity here. Most students are first introduced to genitives as possessive adjectives *(my, your, his, her, its, our*, and *their)*. It's fun to practice these forms with the game "Simon Says." The object of "Simon Says" is to find out who the best listener in class is. The best listener is the student who makes no mistakes carrying out what the teacher tells him/her to do. To play the game, the teacher asks all the students to stand up and follow his/her directions *exactly*. This doesn't sound like such a hard thing to do, and indeed it wouldn't be but for the fact that you yourself don't have to do what you've ordered the students to do. You might say, "Put a finger on the end of your nose" as you put your finger on the end of your nose. You might just as well put your finger on your chin. But any student who's put a finger on his/her chin is out of the game and has to sit down. Hearing one thing and doing another is reason for expulsion. Any directions that you give should have a genitive form in them. (Touch the leg of your chair.) The game continues until there's only one student left standing.

10.2 Descriptions: "This Is My . . . "

Give each student a fairly uncomplicated picture, one that doesn't have too many details in it. Divide the class into groups of approximately ten. One by one, each student shows his/her picture to all the members of the group and briefly says what it contains ("There's a green sofa in my picture." / "There are two kids in mine." / "There's a beautiful queen in my picture." etc.). After all the pictures have been described, ask the students to write down as much information as they can remember about each of their group's pictures. Model example sentences, highlighting the various genitive forms. ("Charlie's sofa is green. One of the legs of the sofa is broken." / "The children in Hugo's picture have red hair. I think the tips of their shoes are dirty." / "Jean-Claude's picture had a queen in it. I think she's the Queen of Sheba.")

10.3 Family Resemblances

People in the same family often resemble one another. Have the students use genitives to describe themselves and their family members. "I have my mother's disposition and my father's eyes. I've also got my grandmother's figure" and so on.

10.4 Modified Clozes

Students whose languages don't have as wide a variety of genitive forms as English does often have a difficult time trying to decide which English form to use. To help them get a better feel for the *-s* and *of*-genitives, create a group of sentences or a modified cloze activity before class (see *Appendix 2, Cloze Activities*). Be sure that the cloze contains a variety of the different genitive forms. Here's a brief sample:

_____ (books/$0 million)

Last month, the English-speaking world was stunned to learn that two old-looking texts discovered in _____ (basement/castle/one/Queen Elizabeth/trunk) were actually written by William Shakespeare and Geoffrey Chaucer. _____ (Shakespeare and Chaucer/works) were in almost perfect condition even though they'd been in the trunk for _____ (hundreds/years). The texts, a play and _____ (Bible/copy) were immediately sold, earning a _____ (king/ransom).

10.5 What's the Difference?

Before class, find or create pairs of pictures that are similar but not identical in details (like pictures from catalogues). Have two students work together and give them one of the pairs of pictures. Get them to discover the differences in their pictures by asking questions about the various items. To get the specific information that the students need, tell them to use a variety of genitives in their questions and answers. Here are some typical questions and answers: "Is there a flower on the front of the sweater?" / "No, there's nothing on the front of the sweater." "Is there anything over the back of the chair?" / "No, but there's a sweater on the seat of the chair." "What was in the dog's mouth?" / "There was nothing in the dog's mouth."

10.6 Non-restrictive Clauses

Before class, write a group of sentences with non-restrictive relative clauses using *whose* before class. (Example: The most popular Civil War film is *Gone With the Wind,* whose heroine lives on a plantation called Tara.) Have the students rewrite the sentences using appropriate genitive forms. Note: This activity can also be done in the reverse; give the students sentences with genitives and have them create the non-restrictive relative clauses. Here are some examples of the types of sentences you would write and answers your students might come up with. "The most popular Civil War film is *Gone With the Wind,* whose heroine lives on a plantation called Tara." (" ... film is *GWTW. GWTW's* heroine lives on a plantation called Tara.") "Air conditioning and helicopters were invented by Leonardo DaVinci, whose later years were spent in France." (" ... by Leonardo DaVinci. DaVinci's later years were spent in France.") "The long cold spell devastated the economy in Florida, whose revenue is based on tourism and agricultural products." (" ... economy in Florida. Florida's revenue/The revenue of Florida is based on tourism and agricultural products.")

11

Compound Nouns and Adjectives

"It was a one-eyed, one-horned, flying purple people eater."

A: You know, I just bought a rubber baby buggy bumper.

B: A what?

A: A rubber baby buggy bumper.

B: What on earth is that?

A: Well, the baby buggy that I put my baby in when I go out for a walk used to have a metal bumper on it.

B: Yeah, so?

A: Well, this new bumper's made of rubber to cushion any shocks if I bump the baby buggy into something.

B: Oh, now I get it! It's a bumper made of rubber that protects your baby in the buggy from hard knocks.

A: Exactly! It's a rubber baby buggy bumper!

B: Of course.

The humorous dialogue you've just read deals with an interesting and yet perplexing phenomenon of English for teachers, namely, making compound forms. In this chapter, we're going to deal first with compound nouns and then look at compound adjectives. We dealt briefly with one type of compound noun in the section of Chapter 6 entitled *When Nouns Are Adjectives*, so some of the introductory material in this chapter should sound familiar.

Before we get going, we want to let you know that this chapter is going to be handled differently from what you've seen up to now. The subject of compounding can be treated in two ways, and we can describe those ways best by drawing the following analogy. Picture a large body of water. There's the surface area, which is relatively uncomplicated. The water is clear, a good deal of light can penetrate it, and that makes it easy to see your way round. This is where people go snorkeling. Then there's the deep water. Less light can penetrate these depths. There are rocky outcroppings to avoid and a good deal of muck on the bottom. These elements make the going somewhat hazardous and make seeing difficult. This is where people go scuba diving. You can enjoy certain things while snorkeling, but a real feeling for what can be found in the waters can only be experienced through scuba diving.

So it is with compounding. The introductory sections of the two major parts of this chapter will be like snorkeling. They'll offer you a basic investigation into the material that will prove immediately useful in the classroom. Then will come a deeper look, like scuba diving, which will offer you more detailed exposure to the material if you'd like to dive a little more. At first glance, you may wonder why we've included such complex information. To anticipate your reaction, we want to explain the reasons for approaching the topic in this way. Simply put, if you've got a clearer picture of the rules and combinations that English has for creating compound nouns and adjectives, you'll be able to help your students in these two main ways.

First, you'll be able to show them how they can understand compound forms when they come across them for the first time; if they understand how they're constructed, they'll understand their meanings more easily. Second, if they understand how these forms are put together, that is, which combinations are and are not possible, they'll be able to create their own compound forms whenever the situation arises—and situations will arise. Even if they create compound forms that a listener has never heard before, he/she will instantly understand what they're talking about if they put the elements together the right way.

Here's one example to demonstrate how this process works. Let's say that we've just told you we have a bathroom telephone in our house. More than likely you've had no trouble understanding what we said. Had we said that we have "a telephone bathroom," you'd be looking at us with a very confused expression on your face. The reason it works when we say "a bathroom telephone," even if you've never heard that phrase before, is that all of us understand the basic rule we've used to construct this compound form, and so it has meaning.

⚡ Compound Nouns

To begin with, let's see if we can come up with a simple definition of what a compound noun is. In our dialogue, the speakers talked about a baby buggy. "Baby buggy" is a good example of a compound noun. The part of the baby buggy discussed was a buggy bumper, another good example of a compound noun. What, then, would you say a compound noun is? See if you can write a simple recipe for making a compound noun on the line that follows:

_____

You've probably come up with something like this: **Take two nouns, put them together, and you've got a compound noun.** Okay, that's certainly the basic idea, but rarely are things that simple in language. One observation we'd like to reiterate from Chapter 6 is that language is so marvelous that it allows us to select words that really have no necessary connection with each other, put them together, and create a brand new word or concept.

Getting back to the issue at hand, we should first ask ourselves which noun do we place first and which one second? Is it possible to say *bumper rubber* instead of *rubber bumper?* And if it is possible, do they mean the same thing? Well, the answer to the first question is *yes*, we can say *bumper rubber*, but the answer to the second question is *no*, they don't mean the same thing. Let's see why.

To start, we have to understand the order that the nouns are placed in within the phrase. **The last noun is the <u>head noun</u>**, the noun being described. Therefore, **the noun before the head noun is a <u>descriptive element</u>**, one that tells us some detail about the head noun. With this information, let's see if you can interpret what it means when we say *rubber bumper* or *bumper rubber*.

A rubber bumper is _____.

Bumper rubber is _____.

The interpretation of *a rubber bumper* **is a bumper that's made of rubber**, and in this case, we're using *rubber* as an adjective. This phrase is *not* a compound noun, but simply a head noun with another noun being used adjectivally (see Chapter 6). It's important to understand that it's still a bumper, whether it be a rubber bumper or a metal bumper or even a plastic bumper—it's still a bumper. Because we haven't created a new entity, but have only described what the bumper is made of, we know it's not a compound noun.

The interpretation of *bumper rubber*, on the other hand, **is that it's some sort of rubber specially formulated to be made into bumpers**—a totally different thing. In this case, the word *bumper* is not just being used as an adjective; rather, together with the head noun, *rubber*, it represents a totally new entity, a specific material *(bumper rubber* as compared to, say, *tire rubber)*, and is indeed a compound noun.

Another example of this linguistic juggling act is *housework* vs. *workhouse*. *Housework*, of course, is all of the cleaning and washing, etc., that goes on in and around the house. A *workhouse*, however, is something totally different. It was a place like a prison during the 19th century (made familiar to us by Charles Dickens) where debtors were forced to stay and work. What a difference word order can make!

What else is important for our recipe? Here are a few more compound nouns. See if you can describe the head noun in each case by paraphrasing. We've done the first one as an example.

1. A knife sharpener is <u>a tool or appliance that is used to sharpen knives</u>.

2. Candlelight is _____.

3. A toy store is _____.

4. A coin slot is _____.

If you've followed our example, you've probably written that *candlelight* **is the light from candles, a** *toy store* **is a store where toys are sold, and a** *coin slot* **is a slit in a hard surface where metal money can be inserted** (like part of a vending machine). What slight but important change do you notice in the descriptive nouns as they appear in the compound form compared to their appearance in your paraphrases? Write your observation on the following line:

_____

The observation is that **the descriptive nouns usually appear only in the <u>singular</u> when used to make compound nouns** even if they refer to more than one thing. So, even though it's the light coming from candles, it's called *candlelight*. There are exceptions to this rule, though, such as *the appropriations committee, a sports car,* and *the arms race.* These exceptions arise when words that usually appear only in the plural become the descriptive elements. The majority of descriptive elements in a compound noun, however, do appear in their singular form.

We'd like to ask you a question from an earlier chapter now. Do you remember a reason that the descriptive noun should stay in the singular form even when it represents a plural? If you recall the reason, state it here:

_____

We can answer this question about why descriptive nouns normally stay singular with a rule about adjectives that we covered in Chapter 6. We know that **adjectives aren't pluralized in English, and since these descriptive nouns work just like adjectives, they follow that same basic rule.** That's probably why (by analogy with another common rule in English) the descriptive nouns aren't usually found in the plural.

There's one more ingredient needed in our recipe for making compound nouns. We're only going to treat it briefly here because we'll be dealing with it in detail in our first chapter on autosegmental features, Chapter 15. It has to do with stress. In short, **the stress** (some people call it **the accent**) **falls on the descriptive element in a compound noun,** *not* on the head noun: a KNIFE sharpener; CANdlelight; a TOY store; a COIN slot.

A Deeper Look

We've now covered the basic recipe for a compound noun, but we're not done yet. So far, we've looked into a compound noun that's formed from two nouns, but there are other combinations that we can use to make compound nouns—nine others, actually, for a total of ten.

Let's do some sleuthing. Below are compound nouns that represent all the combinations we can make. Look them over and figure out what those ten combinations are. (You know that the first one is **noun + noun.**) Write down the combinations on the blanks directly above the list. You'll notice short blanks after each word, but don't worry about them for now. To give you some help, we'll tell you that you're going to find combinations with **gerunds** (*-ing* forms), **particles** (similar to prepositions; you'll read more about them later), **adjectives**, **verbs**, and the word *self*.

1. ____noun + noun____   6. _____

2. _____   7. _____

3. _____   8. _____

4. _____   9. _____

5. _____   10. _____

railroad __n + n__	ice skating _____	sleeping bag _____
self-esteem _____	writer-for-hire _____	Bigfoot _____
washing machine _____	passerby _____	girlfriend _____
sundown _____	insight _____	throughway _____
put-down _____	self-defense _____	downpour _____
skin diving _____	blackmail _____	runner-up _____
upswing _____	cleaning fluid _____	maid-of-honor _____
funny bone _____	pin-up _____	duck hunting _____
by-law _____	lighthouse _____	breakthrough _____
mother-in-law _____	overkill _____	self-control _____

Now that you've decided what the other nine combinations are, go back and label them in abbreviated forms in the short blanks that we've provided after each compound noun. We've already done the first one for you.

☆ **Troubleshooter** ☆

💡 Students may ask you why some forms are written as one word (compound nouns), but others as two words (noun adjuncts).

The only help we can offer is that the tendency is to write commonly used, easily recognizable words as one word, but there's no rule to explain this phenomenon of the written language.

💡 Another question that often comes up deals with hyphenation. Again, there's no set rule for this, but here are some observations that may help:

☞ Compounds formed with a noun + particle tend to be hyphenated (sun-up, time-out, runner-up)

☞ Compounds formed with a verb + particle* tend to be written the same way (make-up, sit-in)

☞ Compounds beginning with *self* are always hyphenated (self-respect, self-evaluation)

*Note that *down* as a particle seems to be an exception (sundown, breakdown, touchdown)

Here are the ten combinations that you'll find represented in our list. Understanding which elements can go together and how they go together will help your students figure out new vocabulary items they're bound to come across and will also give them the skills necessary to build their own compound nouns when the case arises.

noun + noun	*railroad / lighthouse / girlfriend*
noun + gerund	*skin diving / ice skating / duck hunting*
noun + ★particle	*sundown / passerby / runner-up*
noun + phrase	*mother-in-law / writer-for-hire / maid-of-honor*
gerund + noun	*washing machine / cleaning fluid / sleeping bag*
adjective + noun	*funny bone / blackmail / Bigfoot*
***self-* + noun**	*self-esteem / self-defense / self-control*
★particle + noun	*by-law / insight / throughway*
verb + particle	*put-down / pin-up / breakthrough*
particle + verb	*upswing / overkill / downpour*

★Don't worry if you wrote "preposition" instead of "particle" for words like *up, down, by, in, through,* and *over*. There's a slight difference between a preposition and a particle.

A preposition must always have an object either mentioned or implied *(up the stairs/by the door/in the house)*, but a particle has no object following it *(Look up!/Come in!/pass by)*. Although there are some prepositions that can't be used as particles and vice versa, most of the time the two words are interchangeable.

One last word we'd like to say about compound nouns is that the ten combinations we've gone over in this chapter don't account for every compound noun in English. There are other possibilities—we might call them **fringe combinations**—which don't seem to follow any commonly used pattern. Examples of these are *newlyweds, comeuppance, wherewithal,* and *do-gooder.*

ᴬᵛ᷉ **Compound Adjectives**

A: Darn it! It's time to get my garden ready for planting.

B: You don't seem too thrilled with the idea.

A: I'm not. It's a **backbreaking** job.

B: Maybe that's because you use **old-fashioned** methods.

A: What do you mean, old-fashioned methods?

B: You still use those **twenty-year-old** handtools of yours and nothing else, right?

A: Right. So what?

B: Go out and buy some **up-to-date** equipment like a **gas-powered** tiller and a **state-of-the-art** mulcher. They'll save you a lot of toil. And they'll save your back, too.

A: Hmmm. That's a **work-saving** idea. Thanks!

The most typical kind of compound adjective, and the kind that teachers need to deal with quite early on, is the **hyphenated form**. In the dialogue you've just read, all but one of the examples are hyphenated compound adjectives. Happily for us teachers, most of these adjective forms are not so wordy. Let's take a look at some common ones by doing another paraphrasing activity. Complete the following sentences by rewording what their initial parts tell you. We've done the first one as an example.

1. A note that's worth five liras is _____ a five-lira note _____.

2. A snake that's six feet long is _____.

3. Watermelons that weigh five kilos are _____.

4. A wall that's two meters thick is _____.

5. Children who are six years old are _____.

Reworking the descriptions of these head nouns *(note, snake, watermelons, wall, children)* is really quite straightforward. The paraphrases you should have are **a six-foot-long snake/five-kilo watermelons/a two-meter-thick wall/six-year-old children.**

What's the one major internal change you had to make in order to create these hyphenated compound adjectives? Write your answer on the following line:

_____

The one major internal change was that you had to **make the plural items singular** in each case: *feet* became *foot*, *kilos* became *kilo*, *meters* became *meter*, and *years* became *year*. So why is there a need for this change? By now you should have that answer down pat! Write it on the following line:

_____

Even though these phrases contain plural elements when they appear after the subjects they are describing, **once they've been turned into the components of compound adjectives, they're rarely pluralized in English.** It's as simple as that!

Let's take a moment to discuss how we can explain to students about when and why we tend to hyphenate compound adjectives. It seems to be the case that the vast majority of compound adjectives are indeed hyphenated, most assuredly ones that contain numbers *(a three-year-old filly/a 100-acre farm/a 1,000-rupee check)*. What's very important for students to understand is that there is a reason for this convention in the written language. In short, it's to show that even though we may be using two, three, four, or even more descriptive words before the head noun, **these words are being linked together as if they were one word representing one idea. The hyphens act as the links; they're a visual aid on the written page to let the reader know that these descriptive phrases are to be treated as whole units.**

As we mentioned earlier, what we've gone over so far is the basic compound adjective form that's most commonly taught in classes. It's a bit tricky for students to know when to hyphenate the appropriate phrase, make any plural element singular, and then front the whole thing before the head noun. In many languages, genitive or possessive forms are used to do what we accomplish in English with compound adjectives. In

Spanish, for example, it would be typical to say "a stamp of thirty cents" *(una estampilla de treinta centavos)* instead of "a thirty-cent stamp," so you can see how much adjusting your students may have to do when they learn this English form. As an example of how bizarre their phrases could be if they didn't use the English form, think about how your students might try to say "my mother tongue" by following the rules of their language. They'd probably end up saying *the tongue of my mother!*

A Deeper Look

Like the ten combinations we found for compound nouns, compound adjectives (besides the hyphenated form we've already covered) have many combinations—eleven, to be precise. Four of these are combinations containing **nouns**, three contain **adjectives**, two have **adverbs**, and two have **particles**. Look at the list of compound adjectives at the bottom of the page and repeat the procedures you used for the identical kind of exercise that dealt with compound nouns. We've used "dove-tailed" as an example; it's composed of *noun + noun + -ed*. You'll find these combinations also include **present participles** (another *-ing* form) and **past participles** at the end.

1. __noun + noun + ed__   7. _____

2. _____   8. _____

3. _____   9. _____

4. _____   10. _____

5. _____   11. _____

6. _____

dove-tailed **n + n + ed**	low-flying _____	hard-hitting _____
light-hearted _____	well-preserved _____	moonstruck _____
outstanding _____	fast-growing _____	ingrown _____
flea-ridden _____	foul-smelling _____	down-trodden _____
good-looking _____	bow-legged _____	duty-free _____
french-fried _____	nerve-racking _____	overbearing _____
narrow-minded _____	far-fetched _____	long-held _____
short-lived _____	ill-conceived _____	carsick _____
easy-going _____	uplifting _____	pig-headed _____
fuel-injected _____	backbreaking _____	short-sighted _____
outspoken _____	airtight _____	thought-provoking _____

Now that you've identified these ten other combinations for compound adjectives, and now that you've gone back and labeled each one with an abbreviation to identify it, here are the eleven combinations you should have found:

noun + noun + -ed	*dove-tailed / pig-headed / bow-legged*
noun + present participle	*nerve-racking / backbreaking / thought-provoking*
noun + past participle	*flea-ridden / fuel-injected / moonstruck*
noun + adjective	*duty-free / carsick / airtight*
adjective + noun + -ed	*light-hearted / short-sighted / narrow-minded*
adjective + present participle	*good-looking / foul-smelling / easy-going*
adjective + past participle	*long-held / french-fried / short-lived*
adverb + present participle	*low-flying / fast-growing / hard-hitting*
adverb + past participle	*far-fetched / ill-conceived / well-preserved*
particle + present participle	*outstanding / overbearing / uplifting*
particle + past participle	*outspoken / ingrown / downtrodden*

Have you noticed anything interesting about the hyphenation of compound adjectives? We certainly have! If you need to, take another look at all of the examples in italics and then note your observation on the following line:

_____

What's so interesting is that **every form of compound adjective except for two that we've cited most often uses hyphenation, but the ones beginning with a particle don't.** Why don't compound adjectives that begin with a particle hyphenate? Your guess is as good as ours! It just seems that compound adjectives formed with particles and present or past participles are written as single, unhyphenated words.

Something else we'd like to say about compound adjectives is that the eleven combinations we've gone over in this chapter don't account for every compound adjective in English. There are other possibilities, just as there are the "fringe combinations" with compound nouns which don't follow any commonly used pattern. Examples of these compound adjectives are *brand-new, would-be, catch-all,* and *stir-fry.*

Once again, we'd like to emphasize the reason for presenting you with what some might consider an overwhelming amount of information that may make your head spin. Understanding the possible combinations for the formation of compound adjectives can only go to help your students recognize the meanings of new words they come across or give them the tools to make their own compound forms. Of course, what's most important is that they master the basic ideas of compounding (especially concerning hyphenated forms) and develop the skill to use these constructions at will. If they learn the other possible combinations of compound adjectives listed above, you can consider that a bonus.

There's one last category for us to examine. The adjectives in this group are **hyphenated pat phrases** which have become standard vocabulary items and should be learned as such. Here are some examples:

devil-may-care	holier-than-thou
do-it-yourself	middle-of-the-road
down-and-out	run-of-the-mill
fly-by-night	up-and-coming

✳ Troubleshooter ✳

One area of compounding that's often overlooked deals with adverbial forms. These tend to be pat phrases that students should learn just as they are. Here's a short list of some typical ones with example sentences showing how they're used adverbially:

aboveboard:	All of the company policies are *aboveboard*.
back to front:	You're wearing that sweater *back to front*.
inside out:	He wears his socks *inside out* at times.
side by side:	The cat and dog slept *side by side*.
top to bottom:	I read the report *top to bottom*.
upside down:	The children hung *upside down* on the monkey bars in the playground.

Make it a point to incorporate adverbial compound forms like these in your lessons on compounding.

Teaching Tips

11.1 Disappearing Dialogues

"Disappearing dialogues" are excellent for practicing any written or oral grammar point. Before class, prepare a 4-to-6-line dialogue that contains several examples of the grammar point you want to deal with—in this case, compounds. Prepare an overhead transparency of the dialogue or write it on the board. Give the various roles in your dialogue to different groups in your class. Model the dialogue for your students and have them repeat after you. Go through the dialogue two or three times to get them comfortable with it and then begin your "disappearing act" by placing pieces of paper on the overhead or erasing small bits of the dialogue. Cue the "actors" to start the dialogue again, repeating it completely, even those parts of it that are now obscured or erased. Go through the dialogue several times more, each time covering more and more until it's completely gone; by that time, students will have no doubt learned their parts by heart.

11.2 Rearranging Compound Nouns

Because students often have trouble with the interpretation and actual construction (what part goes where) of compounds, one effective way to get your students more comfortable with them is to take them apart and have the class reconstruct them. Before class, decide which words you want to use and put them on an overhead transparency, a handout, or the board. Put the first element of each compound in Column A and the second element in Column B. Make sure that you mix up the elements. Have the students reconnect the compounds and provide a definition.

A	B
1. bird	a. pool
2. off	b. bath
3. show	c. up
4. foul	d. shoot
5. swimming	e. down

11.3 "I See . . . "

Pictures from your Picture File can be used to stimulate compound recognition and formation. Select a picture with a lot of detail in it. Either divide the class into small groups or keep them together. Have your students find as many compound nouns and adjectives as they can.

11.4 Password

Password is a game based on the American television quiz show of the same name. The object is to get your team/partner to guess a word before another team/partner guesses it. Before class, write up a list containing a wide variety of compounds that the students will work with. In class, divide the students into groups of at least four. Two students become "Team A" and the other two, "Team B." (*Password* is especially good for large classes because it's quite easy to have several games going on at the same time if you walk around the class and referee.) One person on each team becomes the "giver" and gets one of the pre-selected vocabulary items (e.g., mother-in-law). The other person becomes the "guesser."

Flip a coin to see which team goes first; in this case, let's say it's Team A. Giver A gives his/her partner a one-word clue *(relative)*. The givers have to be very careful with their clues. If the clue contains any part of the targeted word, they lose their turn (Giver A says, for example, *mother* as his/her clue). Guesser A has one chance to come up with the word. If he/she guesses wrong, it's Team B's chance to try. Giver B gives his/her partner a different one-word clue for the same word *(spouse)*. If Guesser B gives a wrong guess, play returns to Team A.

Continue like this for five or six clues. (You don't want to frustrate the givers or guessers by beating a word to death, and any more than six clues is likely to be beating it to death.) If Guesser B gives the correct word, that round of play is over and Team B gets a point. Givers and guessers change roles and start with a new word. The first clue for the new word is given by the team that won the previous point. The game continues until all the words have been played or time is called. To play *Password* with larger teams, rotate guessers each time a new clue is given.

11.5 What Is This?

Find real objects or just pictures of objects that you think are unusual or unknown to your students. Divide the class into small groups and have them decide what the items are. Students then write up ads for their items making sure that they use several compounds in their descriptions. (Suggest appropriate compounds if your students need help.)

11.6 Cinquains

A *cinquain* is a five-line poem that's excellent for practicing compounds. (*Cinquain* comes from the French word for "five"—*cinq*). Here's one way to compose a cinquain. On Line 1, state the topic in one word. On Line 2, describe the topic in two words (an adjective and noun or two adjectives/nouns). On Line 3, list actions that describe the topic in three words (three verbs, three gerunds, or even a three-word sentence). Line 4 is for a description of the topic in four words. Line 5 restates the topic in five words. Don't forget to have your students give their cinquains a title! Feel free to adapt your cinquains to the needs of your particular class as there's no one way or best way to create them. Show your students a couple of examples of cinquains and divide the class into small groups. Have the groups compose their own cinquains, making sure that they include at least one compound adjective and one compound noun in their poems.

Title:	*Poetry*
Topic:	Poems
Adjectives:	Uplifting, thought-provoking
Action:	Don't always rhyme
Description:	Truth about humanity
Restatement:	They provide insight into life.

12

Modal Auxiliaries in the Past

"There's no point thinking about what might have been."

As we made clear in Chapter 8, modal auxiliaries are a very complex part of the English language. The complexities that teachers and students have to deal with stem from the amazing array of meanings and nuances that modals convey. In Chapter 8 we focused on the uses of modals in the present and future; now it's time to deal with them in the past. In Chapter 16 we'll be investigating the transformations that modals go through when they're changed from the present into the past via indirect speech. For example, when "He says he *may*" is changed to the past, we end up with "He said he *might*." Such changes are basically straightforward and mechanical and are made without causing major alterations in meaning.

There's a need, however, to have another chapter in order to deal with some not-so-simple combinations in form—and some not-so-obvious changes in meaning—that modals undergo when they're put into the past and indirect speech isn't involved. You'll see our point as soon as you've finished looking at our first dialogue.

Can/Could/Could Have

Let's begin our investigation of modals in the past, which include what some refer to as **modal perfects**, by seeing what happens to *can* and its other forms:

A: Did you hear what Lucia did? I **couldn't believe** my ears when Izanil told me.

B: What? I didn't hear anything. Tell me.

A: She turned down a one-year scholarship to the Sorbonne.

B: She what? But why? What an incredible opportunity!

A: I know. She **can't have been** in her right mind.

B: You mean she **could have had**[1] a scholarship to the Sorbonne for a whole year?

A: Uh-huh.

B: Who knows . . . she **could have had**[2] a very good reason for turning it down. I'd just like to know why things like that never happen to me!

A: Well, I think she **could have discussed** it with us first before saying no. After all, aren't we her best friends?

What we're confronted with in this dialogue is the fact that we have five different uses of *can*, all of which represent something in the past. How should we interpret them? Keeping in mind the context surrounding each form, think about what these phrases mean and write down your interpretations on the following lines:

I couldn't believe my ears . . . _____

_____

She can't have been in her right mind . . . _____

_____

. . . she could have had[1] . . . " _____

_____

. . . she could have had[2] . . . " _____

_____

. . . she could have discussed it with us . . . _____

_____

Now let's see how your interpretations compare to ours:

I couldn't believe my ears ... Even though what Speaker A is saying technically means that she *wasn't able to believe what she heard,* it's being used in this context idiomatically to mean *she found it hard, if not impossible, to believe what she heard.* Whether it's idiomatic or not, however, *couldn't* does represent the past of *can't* in its meaning of **inability**. It follows, then, that the affirmative *could,* being the past of *can,* means **ability**. It seems straightforward and uncomplicated, wouldn't you say? Well, let's go on with this idea and take a look at the following. Read these two mini-dialogues and decide if the word in bold makes sense or doesn't make sense to use:

Dialogue 1

A. **Could** she get to the interview on time yesterday?
☐ makes sense to use   ☐ doesn't make sense to use   ☐ not sure

B. Yes, she **could**. Traffic was lighter than she'd expected.
☐ makes sense to use   ☐ doesn't make sense to use   ☐ not sure

Dialogue 2

A. Guess what! I **could** buy that car yesterday!
☐ makes sense to use   ☐ doesn't make sense to use   ☐ not sure

B. You **could**? That's great!
☐ makes sense to use   ☐ doesn't make sense to use   ☐ not sure

In **Dialogue 1, both** speakers' sentences **make sense to use,** but in **Dialogue 2, neither** speakers' sentences **make sense to use**. So why does *could* make sense in the first dialogue but not in the second? Can you think of a reason for this odd situation? If you've got an idea, write it down on the following lines:

_____

_____

The reason that *could* doesn't make sense to use in Dialogue 2 is that **we don't use the affirmative *could* in statements or questions when we talk about an action that's been <u>accomplished</u>**. Saying "I could buy that car yesteday" means the person had the money, credit line, or whatever available to buy the car, but it doesn't clearly state that the person actually bought the car. Instead of saying, "I *could buy* that car yesterday," people would just say "I *bought* that car yesterday."

The reason that *could* makes sense to use in Dialogue 1 is that **it's all right to use it in a question and its reply**, **affirmative or negative, as long as we're talking about former ability**.

Here's another example of using *could* in this way:

When I was a young girl, I <u>could</u> dance all night long.

She can't have been in her right mind . . . Speaker A is saying that she doesn't believe Lucia was in her right mind when she made that decision; in other words, "it's impossible that she was in her right mind" or "I'm sure she wasn't in her right mind." Obviously, this is quite a strong statement, one which leaves no room for any other opinions. We should also mention that the use of ***can't have* + past participle** tends to be more British than American, even though you'll hear it used occasionally in American speech.

Just as we did above with *couldn't*, let's see if this sentence will work for us in the affirmative:

She can have been in her right mind . . .

Well, what do you think? Do you consider this sentence acceptable or unacceptable?

☐ acceptable   ☐ unacceptable

This sentence is **unacceptable**. We don't use ***can have* + past participle** when we're sure about what occurred in the past. There's another modal that we use for this idea and we'll get to it in just a moment.

Before moving on to our next phrase, let's investigate if there are other ways we can express this idea of disbelief. Think about it and see if you can fill in the following line with two other phrases containing modals that basically mean the same idea as "She can't have been in her right mind":

_____

We do have other phrases that will serve the same basic purpose:

She <u>couldn't</u> have been in her right mind . . .
and
She <u>mustn't</u> have been in her right mind . . .

So what's the difference, if any, in using *can't*, *couldn't*, and *mustn't* in this idea? If you've got some thoughts on the matter, write them down here:

_____

It turns out that there's really no big difference among the three phrases concerning the strength or force of the ideas. Some speakers feel that using *can't* or *mustn't* tends to seem stronger while others don't. Using *couldn't*, on the other hand, tends to be less forceful to some and more forceful to others. When it comes right down to it, **they all basically convey the same idea.**

. . . she could have had[1] a scholarship . . . Speaker B's communicating that Lucia had the chance to accept a scholarship, *but didn't*. That little underlined addition is the most important part of the idea to keep in mind, that Lucia *didn't accept* the scholarship even though it was possible for her to do so.

So how does this phrase work in the negative? Are we going to have the same problem with it that we had with the previous two? Let's see:

> . . . she couldn't have had a scholarship . . .

Here we go again. Let's see what your answer is this time:

☐ acceptable   ☐ unacceptable

Well, we've finally found a negative version that's **acceptable**! But what about its meaning? Is there some sort of radical change in meaning, or has it basically stayed the same, only gone negative? What do you say?

☐ same   ☐ different   ☐ not sure

Believe it or not, the answer is that **it's the same** and yet **it's different**! What's the same is that "it was possible for her to have a scholarship," becomes "**it wasn't possible/it was impossible for her to have a scholarship**"; that's the same basic concept with the negative added. What's different, however, is that we don't have that addition tagged on to the end as we had above for *could have* (she had the opportunity, *but didn't take it*). Unlike *could have*, the meaning of *couldn't have* has no hidden extras.

. . . she could have had[2] a very good reason . . . Compared to the context of the phrase *could have had* that we've just worked on, this *could have had* has a very different meaning. In this context Speaker B means "**it's possible she had a very good reason**" for not accepting the scholarship.

And do we have additional ways to express the same idea with other modals? Let's see if you can come up with any on the following line:

_____

Even though it may frustrate you, we're going to hold off giving you our answers until we get to the next section of the chapter. Be patient with us and everything will come together nicely! In the meantime, let's look at the fifth and last phrase from our dialogue that still needs interpreting.

. . . she could have discussed it with us first . . . This phrase is somewhat confusing because it carries two ideas wrapped into one. As we've already seen, the basic idea is that "she had the chance to discuss it with us, <u>but she didn't</u>." The most important idea that Speaker A is saying, however, is that **"it was wrong of her not to discuss it with us first."** In other words, **there's a gentle form of reproach or criticism contained within the phrase which can only be seen through the context**.

 "Can"/"Could"/"Could Have" in a Nutshell

 couldn't
= past of *can't* **meaning "wasn't/weren't able to":**
I couldn't come to your party because I was sick.

Note 1: used in the affirmative when representing *ability* **in the past:**
Years ago, my horse could run like the wind.

Note 2: not used in the affirmative when the focus is on
an accomplished act:
*I could do it. (preferred version: I *did* it.)

Note 3: *be able to* **can be <u>assumed</u> to stand for an accomplished act even though this isn't strictly its meaning:**
They were able to get the shipment out by 5:00 p.m.

 can't have + past participle
= disbelief:
She can't have driven so many kilometers in one day if she stayed within the speed limit.
= impossibility (a strong statement not used in the affirmative):
He's a paraplegic. He can't have gotten out of the wheelchair without assistance.

 could have + past participle
= opportunity existed, but wasn't taken or didn't occur:
I know she had nothing better to do that evening. She could have gone with us to the movies.
= mild reproach for something not done:
He found out about the coming lay-offs long before they happened, and I thought he was my friend. He could have warned me that I was going to be laid off. Some friend!

 couldn't have + past participle
= disbelief (perhaps weaker or more tactful than *can't have***):**
She's such a nice person. She couldn't have been so thoughtless.
= impossibility:
You couldn't have been there if you were with me at the time!

𝒜𝒿 **May Have/Might Have**

For various uses in the past, *may* and *might* can be just as complicated and confusing as *can*. You'll see in Chapter 16, by the way, that *might* is used as the past of *may* in indirect speech:

> I was told that he <u>might</u> join us, but I bet he won't.

However, that's not what we plan to show you in this chapter.

Unlike *could*, **might can never stand on its own <u>as a past form</u> without indirect speech** being involved (*He might go with us. / She said he might go with us). So what happens to *may* and *might* in the past when indirect speech isn't involved? Take a look at our next dialogue to see them in action:

A: Where's Gianni? He always joins us for lunch on Mondays.

B: He **may have gone** to the hospital to see his father. You know, his father's been there for a couple of days.

A: Nothing serious, I hope.

B: Not really. He should be out of there in another day or so.

A: Well, he **might have said something**[1]. Here I've gone and ordered his usual lunch for him. I hope I can find our waitress to cancel it before they make it or I'll be stuck with two checks!

B: He **might have said something**[2] to your assistant. I think I heard her talking to him on the phone this morning.

Just as we did with our first dialogue, let's see if you can come up with your own interpretations for the phrases we've marked in bold depending on their context, and then we'll compare our interpretations to yours:

He may have gone to the hospital . . . _____

_____

. . . he might have said something[1]. _____

_____

He might have said something[2] . . . _____

_____

Let's get right to our interpretations and see how closely yours match ours:

He may have gone to the hospital . . . Speaker B's idea is that **"it's possible that Gianni went to the hospital."**

Now see if you can come up with two other phrases using different modals that carry the same meaning. Think about it and write your two alternate phrases on the following line:

_____

The phrases we're thinking of are

He <u>might</u> have gone to the hospital . . .

and

He <u>could</u> have gone to the hospital . . .

There are native speakers who tend to think that *may have gone* is a more confident guess than *might have gone*, but you really don't have to make such fine distinctions for your students. And if you remember our discussion about *could have*, we said that there was another meaning for *could have* when found in another context—and here it is. In our previous dialogue about Lucia and that one-year scholarship, the phrase *she could have accepted it* had that additional meaning in the context, notably that she didn't accept it. In the context of this dialogue, however, "He could have gone to the hospital" simply means what was possible in the past (the speaker's guessing about what happened), and nothing more.

Now that you've seen how *may, might,* and *could* can be interchangeable when the meaning is possibility in the past, we can give you our answers for those two phrases we held off discussing back on page 228. "She <u>could</u> have had a very good reason . . ." can also be expressed by saying:

. . . she <u>may</u> have had a very good reason . . .

or

. . . she <u>might</u> have had a very good reason . . .

It's worth mentioning that when *may/might have* is used in the negative (*may/might not have*), there's no change in meaning other than the obvious negation of the idea.

. . . he might have said something[1] This phrase is quite a different matter from the use of *might have* that we've already investigated. In the context of our dialogue, this phrase doesn't deal with a past possibility at all. It actually is Speaker A's **gentle or polite way of reproaching** his friend, Gianni, for not having let them know that he wouldn't be joining them for lunch. Can you think of another *gentle* way of stating this idea with a different modal? If you can, write it down on the following line:

The other way this idea can be expressed is

. . . he <u>could</u> have said something.

You'll recall that in the previous chapter we spoke about how *could* is used at times to soften meaning. What you've just seen is an example of that. We'll get to yet another way of expressing reproach—although in a stronger tone—later on in the chapter.

Before we move on to the next use of *might have*, we should consider what happens to our phrase " . . . he might have said something" when it's put in the negative. What do *you* think?

We hope you realize that you were just given a trick question! Oddly enough, the answer is that you can't use *might have* in the negative when it represents a **reproach**. When we use *might have* to reproach somebody, it's always in the affirmative. Now let's see what the last phrase means.

He might have said something[2] **. . .** In the context of our dialogue, Speaker B is saying that "It's possible Gianni said something" to Person A's assistant. Notice how these two identical phrases have such different meanings *in context!*

But what are two other ways this idea can be expressed with two different modals? Write the phrases down on the following line:

The two phrases we're sure you wrote are

He <u>may</u> have said something . . .
and
He <u>could</u> have said something . . .

Remember that if "He could have said something . . ." is put into a different context, it can mean that gentle or polite form of criticism that we found in the sentence "He might have said something . . . " However, keep in mind that *may have* can't be used in this way no matter what the context is.

"May have"/"Might have" in a Nutshell

 may have + past participle
= possibility (a bit more confident):
I'm not sure, but she may have been married once before.

 might have + past participle
= possibility (a bit less confident):
She might have had children by her first husband, but I really don't think so.
= mild reproach for something not done:
I can't believe they left without me. They might have waited a little longer, you know. I was only five minutes late.

Should Have/Ought to Have

A: I'm sorry, honey. I just wanted to surprise you for your birthday.

B: Well, you've certainly done that!

A: I guess I **should have bought** you a birthday cake.

B: Did you follow the recipe carefully?

A: Well, not really. I thought I'd improvise a little. Maybe I **shouldn't have been** so daring, huh?

B: And I didn't even really want a cake. I **ought to have told** you that I wanted to start developing healthier eating habits on my birthday.

A: Nothing's gone right today! I wanted the kids here before you got home so we'd all be here to surprise you. They **should have been** here thirty minutes ago; it's only a fifteen-minute ride.

B: Don't worry. They'll be here soon. You know, you really **oughtn't to have gone** to so much trouble, but I think you're a sweetie for trying so hard to surprise me—and you did!

A: Happy birthday, Love.

After all the hard work you've done with *can't have* and *could have* and *may have* and *might have*, you'll be pleased to learn that this next section, which deals with *should have* and *ought to have*, will be easier to deal with. The reason is that the meanings of these two modal forms in the past are pretty clear—just as they are in the present/ future. So let's get right to work interpreting the phrases in bold from our dialogue:

. . . I should have bought you a birthday cake. _____

_____

. . . I shouldn't have been so daring . . . _____

_____

I ought to have told you . . . _____

_____

They should have been here thirty minutes ago . . . _____

_____

You oughtn't to have gone to so much trouble . . . _____

_____

Now let's compare your interpretations to ours:

. . . I should have bought you a birthday cake. Speaker A is saying that he didn't buy his wife a birthday cake, and he realizes that that was a mistake. In short, he's saying **"I made a mistake by trying to bake you a birthday cake instead of buying you one."** As you can see, the meaning of *should* in the past is not so obvious and usually ends up being somewhat of a challenge to get across to students. It can be a troublesome form because it's used in the affirmative to refer to something that *didn't* happen in the past: Speaker A didn't buy a cake, but rather baked a cake, and now realizes that it was a mistake to do that.

. . . I shouldn't have been so daring . . . Speaker A is now saying that he was too daring when he improvised on the cake recipe and he regrets it. In short, he's saying **"I made a mistake by being so daring."** Once again, the meaning of *should* in the past can be troublesome. This time it's used in the negative to refer to something that *did* happen in the past: Speaker A was too daring in experimenting with that recipe and now realizes that it was a mistake.

I ought to have told you . . . Speaker B is saying that she didn't tell her husband her plans to get into healthier eating habits, and she realizes that it was a mistake not to tell him ahead of time. What she means is **"I made a mistake by not telling you."** Once more, our affirmative phrase refers to something that *didn't* happen in the past. Note that we can use *should have* in this sentence just as easily as *ought to have*.

They should have been here thirty minutes ago . . . Speaker A is now using the meaning of *should* that many students tend to forget, namely, **"I expected them to be here thirty minutes ago (but they haven't arrived yet)."** This meaning of expectation can also work in the negative, that is, when you didn't expect something to happen even though it did:

> We hardly studied for that exam. By all rights, we shouldn't have passed it.

There's one other modal perfect form that can express this idea of expectation. If you think you know which one we're thinking of, write it down on the following line:

That other modal perfect we're thinking of as a possibility for expectation is **ought to have**, and if we had used it in that line from our dialogue, we would have had this sentence:

> They <u>ought to have</u> been home thirty minutes ago.

You . . . oughtn't to have gone to so much trouble, . . . Speaker B is using *oughtn't to have* in a very kind, gentle way. True enough, she's saying "**You made a mistake by going to so much trouble,**" but the statement comes across softly; what she really means is that "**It wasn't necessary for you to go to so much trouble.**" Note once again that we can use *shouldn't have gone* just as easily as *oughtn't to have gone* in this sentence.

By the way, some native speakers have a tendency to drop the word *to* when using this modal perfect in the negative, resulting in *ought not have* or the more typically heard *oughtn't have* ("You oughtn't have gone to so much trouble."). One last note to mention is that Americans tend to use *should* much more than *ought to* in all of these forms, present/future or past. This preference for *should* is especially noticeable in the negatives.

 ## *"Should have"/"Ought to have" in a Nutshell*

 should have/ought to have + past participle
= reproach for something <u>not done</u>:
You should have called the police when that happened.
You ought to have called the police when that happened.
= expectation:
They should have been here by now.
They ought to have been here by now.

 shouldn't have/oughtn't (to) have + past participle
= reproach for something <u>done</u>:
Look at all these leftovers! She shouldn't have cooked so much food just for the three of us.
Look at all these leftovers! She oughtn't (to) have cooked so much food for just the three of us.

= expectation:

One dose of the vaccine should have been enough.

He shouldn't have needed another one.

One dose of the vaccine ought to have been enough.

He oughtn't (to) have needed another one.

A: Must Have/Had To

Even though it isn't strictly a modal auxiliary, we're going to explore the semi-auxiliary *have to* at the same time that we look at *must* in the past. The reason for this pairing of the two will become apparent to you as you read our next dialogue:

A: Did you hear the news about Mark and Marci?

B: No, what?

A: I **had to sit** down when I heard it. The doctor told them that Marci was going to have quadruplets.

B: What! Oh no! What **must** they **have felt** at hearing that?

A: They were probably in shock. I know *I* would have been! But guess what?

B: There's more?

A: It turns out the doctor was wrong.

B: I don't believe it! The doctor **didn't have to put** them through all of that. They **mustn't have been** too pleased with him.

A: They were furious—and yet relieved at the same time.

B: I bet. So, how did it turn out?

A: Well, Marci's not having quadruplets after all—she's having triplets instead!

Let's investigate *must have* and *have to* in the past by keeping the same format that we've been using all along. So here are the items in bold that are waiting for your interpretation:

I had to sit down . . . _____

_____

What must they have felt . . . _____

_____

The doctor didn't have to put them through all of that _____

_____

They mustn't have been too pleased with him _____

_____

We've got a lot of ground to cover, so let's get right to it:

I had to sit down . . . Speaker A is saying **"It was necessary for me to sit down."**

What must they have felt . . . Speaker B is guessing about what Mark and Marci's emotions were at that time. She's really saying, **"I wonder what they felt . . . "** This use of *must* deals with asking for a logical conclusion or conjecture.

The doctor didn't have to put them through all of that . . . Speaker B is saying that **"It wasn't necessary for the doctor to put them through all of that,"** and the idea is a form of criticism in this context. Used in a different context, *didn't have to* simply means *it wasn't necessary*.

They mustn't have been too pleased with him . . . Now Speaker B states that **"I'm sure they weren't too pleased with him"** *(the doctor),* which once again is making a conclusion.

You may not realize it, but something's missing. There's a very important use of *must* which we can use for a present or future idea, but not for a past idea. Can you figure out which meaning is missing from the uses in the past? Here's some help. See if you can transfer this sentence into the past:

> You mustn't park here between 7 and 9 a.m.

Well? Could you do it? We hope you couldn't! You'll have to pardon us, but this was another trick question. We just wanted you to discover for yourself that you can't put *mustn't* in the past for this meaning. And, of course, we're sure you understand now that the meaning we're talking about is **prohibition**.

So how then can we say this idea in the past? The only way to do it is by paraphrasing the idea. Let's see if you can come up with sentences that do communicate the same idea for the past. By the way, we've come up with four!

_____

_____

_____

_____

Here are the four paraphrases that we've thought of:

> You <u>couldn't</u> park there between 7 and 9 a.m.
> They <u>didn't let</u> you park there between 7 and 9 a.m.
> You <u>weren't allowed</u> to park there between 7 and 9 a.m.
> You <u>weren't permitted</u> to park there between 7 and 9 a.m.

Of course there are other variations, but these are the principal ways you'd transfer our original sentence into the past since *mustn't* has this time defect when it comes to this meaning.

⚡ *Troubleshooter* ⚡

💡 Students have a great deal of difficulty knowing which words in a phrase or sentence should receive the main stress, an area of grammar often overlooked by their teachers.

When dealing with modals in the past (modal perfects), this problem needs addressing. Here are some guidelines on how modal perfects are pronounced:

☞ The first auxiliary receives the stress, so *have* is unstressed
(e.g., *He COULD have gone.*).

☞ The *h* in *have* tends to be dropped.

☞ The vowel /æ/ reduces to schwa /ə/ or practically disappears altogether, so that we end up with *He COULD've gone* in our flow of speech.

💡 Because of these reductions, students don't seem to hear the auxiliary *have* at all when they listen to native speakers. Make sure you explain these pronunciation variations and practice them with your students.

💡 We'll be investigating much more about these reduced sounds, like that *h* in *have*, when we get to Chapter 15.

"Must have"/"Had to" in a Nutshell

had to
= necessity (past of *must*):
Before they could leave the airport, they had to clear customs.

***must have* + past participle**
= logical conclusion/certainty:
When Carlitos saw that snake slithering toward him, he must have been petrified.
= conclusion/conjecture:
I can't imagine how they must have felt when they heard the dreadful news.

A Word About *Would*

In Chapter 8 we discussed the unusual use of stressed *would* when it refers to a certain characteristic of somebody or something in a reproachful way. If you recall, we explained that it can be an immediate response to something that has just occurred:

> A: Well, everything's ready, isn't it? Let's tell everyone they can start eating now.
>
> B: Uh-oh.
>
> A: What is it?
>
> B: I don't see the dessert. Wasn't your brother supposed to bring it?
>
> A: Yes, he was. He **WOULD** forget to do that. You can never count on him to remember anything!

Now we can expand upon this use to include any time in the past:

> A: I don't know why, but I was thinking about those neighbors we used to have who drove us crazy with their stereo.
>
> B: Oh, yes, I remember them only too well. They **WOULD** always play their music too loud. Well, I, for one, am not sorry that they moved away!

A⁓⁓ Would Rather Have/Would Sooner Have

We've finally reached the last modal forms to look at in the past. Here's our final dialogue for the chapter which will show you how they're used. Write their interpretations below.

A: Well, did you enjoy the concert?

B: Not at all. I'**d rather have stayed** home.

A: But I thought you liked chamber music.

B: Let me put it this way: I'**d sooner have watched** the grass grow!

A: Oh!

I'd rather have stayed home _____.

_____

I'd sooner have watched the grass grow _____.

_____

And now to the final comparison between your interpretations and ours:

I'd rather have stayed home . . . Speaker B is saying that, **"If she had been
given the choice, staying home was preferable to going to that concert."**

I'd sooner have watched the grass grow . . . Speaker B reiterates her preference
at the same time that she makes a sarcastic remark about doing something extremely
boring. She's saying that **"If she had had the choice, she would have watched
the grass grow; watching the grass grow is likely to be more exciting than
attending that concert."**

In both cases, of course, the unspoken, but understood, second part of either idea
is "I *would rather/sooner have . . . than . . .*" Well, let's see if you can finish off these sentences by adding that unspoken, but understood, second part which comes after the
word *than*:

I'd rather have stayed home than . . .
or
I'd sooner have watched the grass grow than . . .

And the answer is **. . . than to have gone . . . / . . . than have gone . . . / . . . than gone to that concert!**

Teaching Tips

12.1 Miming Modals

Before class, create a list of activities for students to mime (swallow a fly; lose a check-book or wallet; look for a lost shoe; walk on a tightrope, etc.). Have your students try to figure out the activities that volunteers have chosen to mime by using past modals in their guesses ("He shouldn't have opened his mouth!" / "She must have dropped the checkbook/wallet when she got out of the car." / "Her dog must have buried it!" / "I wouldn't have had the nerve to do that!")

12.2 Cause and Effect

Select pictures from your Picture File that have a potential cause-and-effect relation-ship. Have students brainstorm sentences about the pictures using past modal forms. For example, if you have a picture of a man with a broken leg, some sentences that your students might come up with are, "He shouldn't have gone bungee jumping." / "He might have gotten that broken leg skiing." / "He couldn't have seen that ba-nana peel." Note: This tip can be used for conditional practice (see Chapter 20). "If that bungee cord hadn't been so long, he wouldn't have hit the ground and broken his leg." / "He wouldn't have slipped, fallen down, and broken his leg if he'd seen that banana peel," etc.

Variation: Find a picture that's big enough for the entire class to view and that has a variety of details and action in it. Display it so that students, who have been divided into small groups, can use modals to brainstorm sentences about the picture. Let them work for five to ten minutes and then have them put their pencils down. Be firm about this time limit. Have each group present their "brainstorms." Give one point for each sentence that uses a modal correctly and a second point for each sentence that no other group has come up with. The group with the most points is declared the "winner."

12.3 This Is What Might Have Been!

Come up with the names of locally or internationally known famous and infamous people from the past or present. List them on the board. Divide the class into small groups and let them create as many sentences as they can think of about these peo-ple using past modal forms. This is what you might hear: "He must have been a bet-ter general than Napoleon." / "Marie Antoinette shouldn't have said, 'Let them eat cake!'" / "Lyndon Johnson might not have become president if Kennedy hadn't been assassinated." Note: This tip can also be used for conditional practice.

12.4 *Plan a Field Trip*

Plan a field trip with your students . . . and then take it. When you get back into the classroom, review how it went, using modals in your observations.

12.5 *Graphs and Charts*

Create or find a graph or chart like the following one that contains enough information to stimulate a discussion about it. Let the students think of comments about the graph or chart using modals. You might hear, "It must have been a hot summer; their electric bills were much higher this year than they were last year." / "They can't have had much money left over at the end of the month." Note: This activity can also be used to practice conditionals: "I would have moved to a city with lower rents if I'd had to use that much of my salary to pay my rent." Feel free to use the following example of a pie chart in your classes if you wish.

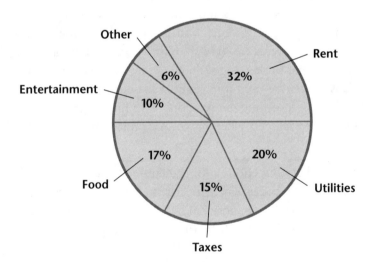

12.6 *Did You Hear What I Heard?*

Think of a controversial or lively topic for your students to discuss. Divide the class into an even number of small groups. Pair two groups together; one of the groups will discuss the topic, the other will listen and take notes. The listeners should write down comments about what they've heard that bother them, could be restated, were incorrect, well-stated, etc. Encourage the use of past modal forms where appropriate.

13

Passives and Causatives

"What's done is done 'cause I got it done."

The Passive Voice

> auxiliary BE + PAST PARTICIPLE of verb
>
> I **am** expect**ed**.
>
> You **were** promot**ed**.
>
> She **has been told**.

Over the past several years, few areas of grammar have been discussed and de-bated more than the passive voice even though the heart of the matter is con-cerned with style rather than grammaticality. It's said that the passive voice is being overused and that it's simply a clever way to restate the active voice. The truth of the matter is—as far we see it—that passive forms aren't overdone and have prac-tical uses that aren't simply restatements of active forms. Without doubt, the passive voice has a life, a flavor, and an importance of its own and should be taught as an es-sential grammatical form.

By the way, in case you haven't noticed, the opening paragraph is just chock full of passive voice constructions! Can you identify them? Let's see if you can pick them out of the first paragraph and copy them onto the following lines:

_____   _____

_____   _____

_____   _____

These are the passive voice constructions you can find in the first paragraph:

have been discussed	**is concerned with**
is said	**is being overused**
aren't overdone	**should be taught**

In each of these phrases, you can easily identify the auxiliary *be* (*been/is/is/ is being/aren't/be*) and the past participles of the targeted verbs (*discussed/concerned/said/ overused/overdone/taught*). Seeing how we've used the passive voice in our first paragraph should answer the question as to whether we feel it's overused. Our answer is obviously *no*.

So what exactly is the passive voice? Read this opening dialogue, check out the parts in bold, and see if you can figure out why this verb form exists:

A: Have those novelty items from China arrived yet?

B: Yes. In fact, they **were delivered** from the port just this morning. What do you want us to do with them?

A: Well, they really **should be taken** over to the Hanson Street warehouse, don't you think?

B: Okay. I'll get on it right after I finish up these reports.

A: Those reports **were supposed to be finished** and **sent** on to our main office a couple of days ago, right?

B: Well . . . yes, but I **was called** out of town and didn't get back until two days ago, remember?

A: Oh, yeah. I forgot. Well, let's get them out as soon as we can.

Any theory? Here's a little hint: There are subjects in sentences that actively do something, but there are other subjects that don't actively do anything. If you think you can explain why the passive voice has been used after certain subjects in our dialogue, write down your thoughts on this line:

_____

In order to understand why the passive voice is needed, we have to examine the subjects in the phrases. In every case in the dialogue where we have a passive construction, **the subject isn't active**, that is, **it isn't doing the action of the verb; someone's doing something to it, but it isn't doing the action itself.** Those Chinese novelty items didn't deliver themselves; someone from the company or the port delivered them, but the delivering person is not related to the topic of the conversation. Likewise, the novelty items can't take themselves over to the warehouse; someone has to take them over there. In every sentence with a phrase in bold in our dialogue, the subject isn't the "doer." Knowing this much about passives, let's create a basic rule: **If the subject of our idea isn't the doer of the action—in other words, isn't active—the verb that follows is likely to be in the passive voice.**

There are other reasons that we use the passive voice, but we'll get to those later on.

⚡ *Troubleshooter* ⚡

💡 Even though every language has some form or other of the passive voice, not every language uses it the same way. English and Hawaiian tend to use the passive voice more frequently than many other languages do.

💡 What appears as a passive voice construction in English may not be a passive form in other languages even though they communicate the same idea:

☞ In French it's common to use the impersonal pronoun *on* with the active verb where the passive voice would be used in English:

On parle français ici.
French is spoken here.

The closest English equivalent to this would be *One speaks French here.*

☞ In Russian it's often the case that the reflexive form of the verb is used where a passive voice is found in English:

/kak nazıváyɛtsa ɛta úlitsa/
What's this street called?
(literally: "How does this street call itself?")

Now let's see if it's really true that when the subject isn't the doer, the verb should be in the passive voice. Look at this next dialogue and pay special attention to the phrases in bold:

A: Well, Anita, today you're going to learn how to make bread.

B: Great. What's first?

A: Okay. You see that **I've already mixed together the flour, salt, and water,** right?

B: Uh-huh.

A: Now **we add the yeast that I dissolved** in some warm water. Next we mix it all up.

B: Okay. I get it.

A: Now we put the dough in a warm, dark place.

B: Why do we do that, Mommy?

A: Because **the dough has to rise.** The yeast, the warmth, and the darkness will help this process to happen.

B: What do you mean, rise?

A: **The dough will grow** and **double** in size.

B: Wow! That means we can have two loaves instead of one!

According to our rule, if the subject isn't the doer, the verb that follows is likely to be in the passive voice, and we know that we form the passive by using the auxiliary *be* plus the past participle of the targeted verb. Even though all the sentences in our dialogue look fine as they are, let's see if we can transform them into the passive voice. We'll need to go through two steps:

1. Make the object our new subject and throw out the old subject.

2. Change the targeted verb by placing the auxiliary *be* in front of it (being careful to keep the same tense or aspect as in the active form) and by using the past participle of the verb.

Here's a visual to show you what we mean:

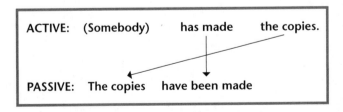

On the line below each phrase we've adapted from the dialogue, check to see whether you can write these phrases in the passive voice.

1. I've mixed together the flour, salt, and water . . .

_____.

2. We add the yeast that I dissolved . . .

_____.

3. We put the dough in a warm, dark place . . .

_____.

4. . . . the dough has to rise . . .

_____.

5. . . . the dough will grow and grow . . .

_____.

6. . . . the dough will double in size . . .

_____.

Any problems? We certainly hope so! The reason you should have had some trouble is because **Numbers 4**, **5**, and **6 can't be transformed into passive voice phrases**. Before we get into these three, however, let's see if your other phrases match ours:

1. The flour, salt, and water have been mixed together
2. The yeast that I dissolved/that was dissolved is added
3. The dough is put . . .

And now to those other three phrases. Why can't they be transformed into passive voice constructions? For three reasons: First, the subjects are the doers, and that should really be the end of it. But there are two more important reasons we'd like to bring to your attention. If you notice, there are no objects in Numbers 4, 5, and 6 to make into new subjects, and that's our second reason. Now on to our third.

To figure out what that third reason is, let's do some more linguistic sleuthing. Look at these two phrases and decide which one is grammatical and which one isn't:

1a. The sun rose.	☐ grammatical	☐ ungrammatical
1b. The sun raised.	☐ grammatical	☐ ungrammatical

And what about the next two?

2a. He rose his hand.	☐ grammatical	☐ ungrammatical
2b. He raised his hand.	☐ grammatical	☐ ungrammatical

Rose is **grammatical** in **1a**, but **ungrammatical** in **2a**. *Raised* is **ungrammatical** in **1b**, but **grammatical** in **2b**.

What could be happening to cause such a turnabout? What does *raise* need to make its phrase grammatical that *rise* doesn't need? Write down your answer on this line:

Perhaps you've noticed that there's no object in "The sun rose," which is the grammatical phrase, but there *is* an object in "He rose his hand," and that's ungrammatical. The same holds true with the other two phrases: "The sun raised" has no object, so it's ungrammatical, but "He raised his hand" has an object, so it *is* grammatical. So what can we interpret all this to mean? What connection is there between these verbs and the objects?

It all comes down to this simple observation: If we use the verb *raise,* there must be an object in the phrase; if we use the verb *rise,* there can be no object. This is because there are three kinds of verbs in English:

- transitive verbs, which have objects,
- intransitive verbs, which have no objects, and
- a group of interesting verbs that can either have or not have objects, in other words, which can be transitive or intransitive.

Raise is a good example of a transitive verb ("He raised <u>his hand</u>"); *rise* is a good example of an intransitive verb ("The sun rose"), and a verb like *weigh* is a good example of the other group of verbs that can be either transitive or intransitive:

> The butcher <u>weighed</u> the turkey. (transitive)
> The turkey <u>weighed</u> 10 kilos. (intransitive)

Getting back to Numbers 4, 5, and 6 on page 247, we can say that they can't be turned into passive voice constructions because they contain verbs that are acting as intransitive verbs. *Rise* is one of those verbs. What are the other two in those phrases?

The other two words acting as intransitive verbs in our dialogue are *grow* and *double.* But are these verbs always intransitive? The answer is *no.* In other sentences, both of these verbs can have direct objects, which will make them transitive verbs ("I grow <u>prize-winning flowers</u>." / "By investing wisely, we doubled <u>our income</u> in just two years."). The important point here, however, is that they're intransitive in this dialogue and therefore can't be transformed into passive voice constructions. **No verb that is intransitive**

can be made into a passive voice construction. So now you have all three reasons that Numbers 4, 5, and 6 couldn't be made into passive voice constructions.

When the Doer is Unveiled

Up to this point, we've mentioned that the passive voice is used when the subject in a transitive sentence isn't the "doer." But what if we choose to mention who or what the doer is? How can we do that? It's really quite simple; all we need to do is add the preposition *by* after the passive phrase and then fill in the doer:

> Thousands of houses were destroyed <u>by the hurricane</u>.
> Everyone knows that the earth is warmed <u>by the sun</u>.
> The suspect is being interrogated <u>by two detectives</u>.

That was simple enough, wasn't it? Well, maybe there's a bit more to it than that. There's another preposition that's often found in passive constructions, and we're going to find it in our next dialogue. In addition, there's an odd construction that looks like an active phrase in the simple past but really isn't, and we're going to find that in our dialogue, too. Both of these are items rarely covered in classes even though we think it's clear that they should be. Take a look to see what we're talking about:

A: I can't get over how childish some students in this school can be.

B: I'll say. Who would have thought there'd be a food fight in the cafeteria? I still can't believe it **was started by** friends of yours.

A: And I can't believe that the assistant principal **was hit** in the face **with** all those pats of butter.

B: I only know that I was totally embarrassed when I saw the headline in the school paper today.

A: Oh? I haven't seen it. What does it say?

B: Nothing much, just "Assistant Principal **Buttered**! Two Students **Suspended**."

As we mentioned, we've got two interesting items in this dialogue and we'll examine them separately. The first one concerns the choice of preposition that follows our passive constructions. The first phrase in bold has the preposition *by* following it to introduce the doer, in this case, "friends of yours," and this is the typical preposition taught to students. But what about the next passive construction? In this phrase we don't have the word *by* introducing the doer, but rather the word *with*. Before we ask you that ever-familiar question as to why this is so, look at the examples on the following page and think about the difference that the prepositions create.

The instruments were sterilized <u>by the nurse</u>.
The instruments were sterilized <u>with steam</u>.

Think you've figured out how to interpret each sentence? If you have, write your thoughts on the lines that follow:

_____

_____

In our first sentence, the nurse is obviously the active doer, and **the preposition** ***by* introduces the active doer**. So what role does *the steam* play if we use it with that alternate preposition? **Using *with* introduces what we can call the *instru-ment*,** in other words, what the doer used to accomplish the action. Here are a few more examples of each:

Showing the active doer:	She was bitten <u>by a squirrel</u>.
	The violinist was accompanied <u>by a pianist</u>.
	The car was checked out <u>by my mechanic</u>.
Showing the instrument:	He was knighted <u>with a sword</u>.
	The newlyweds were showered <u>with rice</u>.
	They were honored <u>with the Nobel Prize</u>.

Simple and clear cut, right? Well, before we get too comfortable, compare the next two sentences with the ones you've just seen:

The windshield of his car was smashed <u>by a brick</u>.
The windshield of his car was smashed <u>with a brick</u>.

Maybe it's not so simple after all. Most native speakers would say that both of these sentences sound all right, but they certainly wouldn't accept this interchange of *by* and *with* in those other sentences we've just seen. Would you?

She was bitten <u>with a squirrel</u>.
The car was checked out <u>with my mechanic</u>.
He was knighted <u>by a sword</u>.
The newlyweds were showered <u>by rice</u>.

So what's going on? If these four sentences are clearly strange, why don't we feel the same way over those two sentences about the car windshield? Before you answer this question, let's just look at another example where *by* and *with* seem to work equally well:

Wilting plants can be revived <u>by warm water</u>.
Wilting plants can be revived <u>with warm water</u>.

Can you find a reason to explain why these pairs of sentences sound equally good, but those others don't? When you think you've hit on something, write your ideas down on these lines:

_____

_____

This is a very tricky feature of the passive voice, as we're sure you've discovered for yourself. The answer to our last question is that **we can use either *by* or *with* when the person or thing mentioned can act either as the doer or the instrument**. In basic terms, it's all a matter of focus. Let's go back to our sentences about the car windshield. We can look upon the brick as the thing that actually smashed the windshield and say:

> The windshield of his car was smashed <u>by</u> a brick.

In this case, the brick might have fallen from the rooftop. On the other hand, we can say that the brick was the instrument used by someone to break into the car or attack it. In that case, we can also say:

> The windshield of his car was smashed <u>with</u> a brick.

Perhaps in this expanded version, this last sentence will be clearer:

> The windshield was smashed (<u>by an irate pedestrian</u>) <u>with</u> a brick.

The same explanation holds true for the other pair of sentences where both *by* and *with* seem to work. When we say "Wilting plants can be revived <u>by</u> warm water," we're focusing on the fact that the warm water itself can actually revive those plants and is therefore the doer. When we say "Wilting plants can be revived <u>with</u> warm water," we're focusing on what can be used by someone to accomplish this result. It's amazing how troublesome two little words can be! And it is also amazing how much information they carry.

Reduced Passives

Now that we've explored *by* and *with,* let's get to that other item we found in the last dialogue. One of the speakers mentioned that the headline in the school paper read "Assistant Principal Buttered! Two Students Suspended." Many students get confused when they read headlines like this one because they think it means that the assistant principal buttered something and that two students suspended somebody! Why do you think they come up with such odd interpretations?

_____

The reason is that **they're assuming the verbs *butter* and *suspend* are being used in their active sense rather than their passive sense**, and the fact that direct objects are lacking totally escapes the students anyway. What they need to be shown is that it's a time-honored gimmick in newspaper headlines to save space by omitting determiners and auxiliaries. As far as the passive voice is concerned, the auxiliary *be* is omitted to save space. When the students are shown that the phrases are really "The Assistant Principal <u>Was</u> 'Buttered!' Two Students <u>Were</u> Suspended," they should remember that these omissions occur the next time they see such headlines.

Another occasion when we find reduced passive forms can be seen in the following dialogue:

A: Hello, Professor Ozawa.
   How's your visit to the States?

B: Fine, but I don't understand
   American holidays very well.

A: Oh? Tell me about it.

B: Well, the holiday just
   celebrated[1] **called**[2]
   "Halloween"—it's very odd.
   I saw children and adults
   frightened[3] by one another,
   but they seemed to enjoy it. I found a pumpkin **lit**[4] with a candle
   inside **placed**[5] near the front door of my apartment building.
   And there was this grotesque face **carved**[6] on it!

A: Well, you see, Professor . . .

B: But nothing was as strange as the apples. Nothing.

A: The apples?

B: Yes, the apples. When I went to a Halloween party, I could not
   believe how the host was serving the fruit. There were the apples,
   put[7] in a large tub of water. And I saw the guests **forced**[8] to take
   them out of the water with their teeth!

A: Now, Professor, give me a chance to explain. You see . . .

You know that we're dealing with reduced passive forms, so what words do you think have been eliminated from the parts that appear in bold in our dialogue?

1._____   5._____

2._____   6._____

3._____   7._____

4._____   8._____

With a little bit of reconstruction work, we're sure you've realized that *which, that,* or *who* has been eliminated from all the parts in bold together with various forms of the auxiliary *be.* Here are the answers we have that should match yours. (Keep in mind that in *informal* English *which* and *that* are interchangeable, as are *who* and *that*):

1. **that has [just] been/was**
2. **that is**
3. **who were (being)**
4. **that was**
5. **that had been**
6. **that had been**
7. **that had been**
8. **who were being**

And now to the reasons. There's a simple rule that we can use for all of the bold parts in our dialogue: **When you have a relative clause that begins with *who* or *that* and contains a passive voice form, the relative pronoun and the auxiliary *be* can be eliminated.** That's how we go from " ... this holiday <u>that is</u> called 'Halloween' ... " to " ... this holiday called 'Halloween' ... " Here are a few more examples to show you this rule in action:

Turkey (that is) <u>roasted</u> slowly comes out succulent.
Plants (that are) <u>cared for</u> well will flourish.
They adopted that child (who had been) <u>orphaned</u> during the war.

Finally, we want to mention that other occurrences of a reduced passive construction can be seen typically on signs. Sometimes, in fact, not only is the auxiliary *be* eliminated, but even the subject can be eliminated when the sign clearly shows who or what is intended:

Why Bother with the Passive Voice?

Why should we bother using the passive voice at all? Why not make things simpler and just stick to the active voice? Let's take one more look at the sentences we used to show how *by* introduced the active doer in our passive constructions and compare them to the same ideas in the active voice:

Thousands of houses were destroyed by the hurricane.
Everyone knows that the earth is warmed by the sun.
The suspect is being interrogated by two detectives.

The hurricane destroyed thousand of houses.
Everyone knows that the sun warms the earth.
Two detectives are interrogating the suspect.

Any ideas? See if you can think of a reason that, at times, we might prefer the three passive voice sentences over their active counterparts and write your thoughts on these lines:

_____

_____

What it all comes down to once again is a matter of focus. Are we focusing on the hurricane or on the houses? Are we discussing the sun or the earth? Is our main interest on the detectives or the suspect? When we answer these questions, we also answer whether or not to use the passive voice. **If we want the focus to be on the doer, we use the active voice; if we want the focus to be on the receiver, we use the passive voice.**

Two other good reasons for using the passive voice can be found in the next dialogue, so let's examine it:

A: Did you hear that **it was announced** we can expect an increase in taxes again?

B: Not again! **Haven't taxes been raised** enough over the past few years?

A: I know. It's getting ridiculous. Well, **I've been told** that my company may just move out of the country and go to one where they won't have to pay so much corporate tax.

B: Really? Well, I can't say I'm surprised.

Why do you think that both Speaker A and Speaker B have used the passive voice in talking about possible future tax hikes? They could just as easily have chosen to use the active voice, but they didn't. Concentrate on only the first two phrases in bold and see if you can figure out why they've chosen the passive voice:

_____

_____

One reason that both speakers have chosen the passive voice is that **the doers are understood**, which is a very clever way **to avoid redundancy** in the conversation. When Speaker A says " . . . it was announced . . . " we understand immediately from the context that she means *by the government or the media;* when Speaker B says "Haven't taxes been raised enough . . . " it's clear she means *by the government.*

But what about the last statement in bold when Speaker A says " . . . I've been told . . . "? Why has she chosen to go with the passive voice in this instance?

The reason is that **she doesn't want to divulge her source**. Many people use the passive voice to avoid giving away their source of information or to be tactful so as not to point an accusatory finger directly at someone. Here's an example that demonstrates tact:

> A: I hear you had some bad luck with the EireCo merger.
> B: Well, because the contracts weren't delivered on time, the deal
>   fell through.
> A: Tough luck, Cormac.

Perhaps Person A knew exactly who was responsible for those contracts not reaching their destination on time, but Cormac wasn't going to be the one to point that finger or rub it in. Just imagine if the conversation had gone something like this:

> A: I hear you had some bad luck with the EireCo merger.
> B: Well, because Hayes didn't deliver the contracts on time, the deal
>   fell through.
> A: Tough luck, Cormac. Never did think much of that Hayes fellow.

Whew! Quite a different "flavor" in the conversation! In this case, at any rate, there may very well be something cultural in the use of the passive voice.

🦋 *Troubleshooter* 🦋

One of the toughest ideas to get across to students when they learn the passive voice is the difference between a sentence in the timeless form and one in the real present:

The suspect <u>is</u> interrogated.

The suspect <u>is being</u> interrogated.

Almost without exception, your students will tend to think that the first sentence above is in the present and never consider the second example.

Stress to them that, except for stative verbs, *am/are/is being + past participle* is the *real* present in the passive voice.

Interestingly enough, many of the verbs that can be used as a way to avoid divulging the source of information or to be tactful belong to a group of verbs called "reporting verbs," which we'll be covering in Chapter 16. Besides *announce*, which we've already seen, here are some of the more typical ones you'll find that go a long way to accomplish these ends: *admit, declare, explain, mention, point out, report, say, state,* and *suggest*.

A Word About "Get"

To begin our discussion about *get*, let's first consider how it's used with adjectival forms. What's the difference between *get married* and *be married*? Write down your thoughts here:

_____

Get means "become" when it's followed by an adjective and *become* means that there's a change in a condition or state of being; in other words, something that existed previously is now being changed. **The verb *be*, on the other hand, deals only with the state of being at a certain time and has no reference to what conditions were like before.**

Examples: Antonio got angry with Sara when she embarrassed him.
(= the moment when his mood changed)

Antonio was angry with Sara for a couple of days.
(= the period of time that his anger lasted)

Let's see if you can explain the difference between these next two sentences. Write your interpretations on the lines that follow:

I <u>got</u> sick after eating greasy food.
I <u>was</u> sick for a whole day after eating greasy food.

_____

_____

Using *get* in our first sentence shows us a change that took place in the speaker's condition. He obviously felt fine before eating that greasy food, but his condition changed and he became sick later on. (Remember that when preceding an adjective, *get* is synonymous with "become.")

As you recall, the verb *be* **deals only with the state of being at a certain time and has no reference to what conditions were like before**. It's true that we can also say "I was sick after eating greasy food," but most native speakers would tend to perceive a difference because *be* is ambiguous in this context: Is the speaker talking about his immediate reaction to the food after eating it or is he talking about a longer condition or being unwell, possibly as a result of having eaten it or possibly just coincidentally? Using *get* eliminates the potential for this kind of ambiguity.

Now let's consider how *get* is used in passive voice phrases. Some speakers consider *get* more informal than *be* with passive constructions, but we feel that the point is debatable. Moreover, there are certain nuances we can create by using *get* that are simply not communicated with *be,* which tends to be a more *neutral* verb. It's a very tricky area, this difference between *be* and *get,* and one that's often a matter of personal preference or interpretation.

See if you find any difference between the sentences in each of the following pairs. If you do, try to put into words what that difference is on the lines that we've provided:

1. She was transferred. / She got transferred.
   ☐ a difference   ☐ no difference

_____

2. He was arrested. / He got arrested.
   ☐ a difference   ☐ no difference

_____

3. She was chosen. / She got chosen.
   ☐ a difference   ☐ no difference

_____

4. Were you observed? / Did you get observed?
   ☐ a difference   ☐ no difference

_____

We told you this matter would be tricky! We ourselves doubt that there's just one interpretation for any differences between *be* and *get* in sentences such as the ones we've given you. However, we'll give you an interpretation that many native speakers do make.

Some people feel that there may be a sort of psychological involvement with *get* as it appears in the first three examples that isn't felt with *be.* They tend to feel that *be* simply has no special nuance to it and that it just seems to report what happened. **Get may help to create a stronger sense of the subjects having helped cause the outcomes.** Using *get* in the sentences leads some people to think that the subjects may have played an active role in the outcomes; they themselves did something. In other words, they weren't just totally *passive.*

Example 4 is perhaps the most interesting of our pairs of sentences. Some people report that **using** *get* **in this idea connotes that the subject was scheduled for some sort of visit/evaluation** (perhaps by a supervisor at work), whereas using *be* could be interpreted simply to mean "Did anybody see/evaluate you?"

We want to stress once again that these are interpretations that many native speakers have come up with, but they certainly aren't the only ones. Some people may find no appreciable difference between *be* and *get* in our pairs of sentences, and others may say they'd never say this one or that one in their idiolects.

Of course, nuances like these aren't easy to communicate to students, and there's a good chance that these fine points won't even come up in your classes. We feel, all the same, that it's good for you to be aware that they do exist because an observant student of yours may ask you one day what *get* means in a passive construction!

Passive Oddities

The passive voice can lead us into some really strange areas which drive teachers slightly mad when trying to explain certain specific items and drive students slightly mad when trying to understand them. Let's examine three of these in the next dialogue:

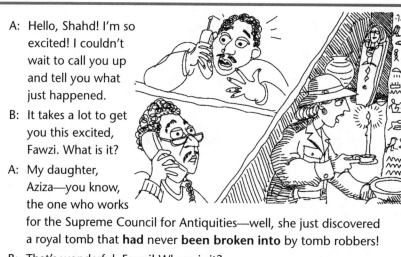

A: Hello, Shahd! I'm so excited! I couldn't wait to call you up and tell you what just happened.

B: It takes a lot to get you this excited, Fawzi. What is it?

A: My daughter, Aziza—you know, the one who works for the Supreme Council for Antiquities—well, she just discovered a royal tomb that **had** never **been broken into** by tomb robbers!

B: That's wonderful, Fawzi! Where is it?

A: It's near Tell-el-Amarna. And guess what! I have permission to visit the site while the tomb contents **are** still **being emptied out!**

B: I guess Aziza **will be given** some sort of award for having made such a discovery.

A: I doubt that an award **will be given** to her. It seems that awards for such things **have been done away with** in order to create more team spirit in the Supreme Council.

The first oddity that we can see in bold is something quite peculiar to English and very troublesome for students. How did we ever arrive at such an odd-looking construction as *had been broken into?* The first thing our students probably wonder is "broken into *what?*" They find it most unusual to end a phrase with a preposition in this way (see Chapter 9), especially in a passive construction. How would you explain this construction to your students? Think about it and write your ideas on the following line:

To help us deal with the construction under question, first we should look at the active verb form, which in this case is *break into.* This is what some call a two-word verb and others call a phrasal verb. Still others call it an idiomatic verb (see Chapter 17 for more about two-word verbs). Actually, all three names work perfectly well. The important thing to notice about *break into* is that it must be treated as a whole unit and not looked upon as two separate words. We can see that this is important since the word "break" has a different meaning without that preposition-like particle *into.* Moreover, we can find a one-word synonym for this two-word verb—"plunder" or "loot."

Now, if we understand that *break into* must be treated as a single unit, we can see how it will appear in the passive construction. Just as we can say "be plundered/looted," we can also say **be broken into**. This is how we arrive at a sentence like "*The tomb hadn't been broken into.*" Stress to your students that they should **always consider two-word verbs as single units, not as individual parts**.

The next encounter we have with a two-word verb in our dialogue works the same way. We can think of *remove* as a one-word synonym for *empty out,* and go from "They're removing the tomb contents" to "The tomb contents are being removed." It works no differently for *empty out:*

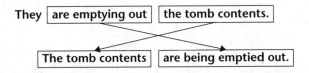

Going along with this method of changing a two-word verb from active to passive, we might as well mention the three-word verb (also known as a phrasal-prepositional verb or idiomatic verb) that we have in our dialogue. "They <u>have done away with</u> awards for such things" becomes "Awards for such things <u>have been done away with</u>." Other verbs in this group are ones like *check up on, look in on,* and *put up with.*

The last oddity we find in the dialogue has to do with the verb *give.* Following are two short sentences we've derived from the longer ones in the dialogue. Let's take a look at what's happening:

She will be given an award.

An award will be given to her.

What strikes students as so strange about a pair of sentences like this one is that the same verb is being used to create both ideas. If "<u>She</u> will be given . . . ," how can we say "<u>An award</u> will be given . . . "? How can the two different things *be given*?

Let's see if you can figure out a way to explain this phenomenon. We'll give you a couple of hints: If you collapse the two sentences into one sentence in the active voice, you'll be on the right track and you should end up with an active verb and two objects.

The active sentence is _____ .

Now that you've arrived at the active sentence, how can you account for being able to use *give* to make both passive sentences? Any ideas?

_____

The fact is that we're dealing with something unusual about the verb *give*, and that unusual quality is that it has both a direct object (an award) and an indirect object (her). What we've got here is called a **ditransitive verb**, that is, a verb that has two objects, both a direct and an indirect object. **When we have ditransitive verbs** like *give*, **we can form two passive voice constructions, one for each of the objects**.

If our active voice sentence is

They will give her an award.

or

They will give an award to her.

we can say

She will be given an award.

and

An award will be given to her.

Other common ditransitive verbs are *bring, deliver, do, mail, owe, read, send, tell,* and *write*.

Let's move on to another oddity; let's look at the next dialogue and see what's in store for us. Focus your attention on how each of the three verbs in bold is used in the active and passive voice and what that does to its meaning:

A: Aziza, your father told me all about your wonderful find. We're all very proud of you.

B: Thank you, Uncle Shahd.

A: I understand the tomb **is located** near Tell-el-Amarna.

B: That's right.
I **located** the tomb not far from the southern limits of the ancient capital.

A: Tell me, Aziza, does the tomb **contain** lots of gold and precious stones?

B: Well, yes. And it's interesting that almost all of the jewelry **is contained** in just two rooms. But there's a lot of wealth in those two rooms!

A: You know, I've always wondered why Pharaoh Akhenaton wanted to build his capital in such an arid, dusty part of the country.

B: Oh, no, Uncle Shahd. It wasn't so dry and inhospitable 3,500 years ago. Papyrus always **grew** around there, and wheat and barley **were grown** there for hundreds of years.

Find anything odd about the meaning of each verb when it appears in the active voice and when it appears in the passive voice? Let's come up with synonyms or interpretations for some of the words in bold. First, you give it your best effort, and then we'll give it ours:

The tomb is located . . .

_____

I located the tomb . . .

_____

Does the tomb contain . . .

_____

. . . the jewelry is contained . . .

_____

Papyrus always grew . . .

_____

. . . wheat and barley were grown . . .

_____

The remarkable thing about these verbs is that they undergo an amazing change in meaning when they switch from the active to the passive voice. Let's see how our interpretations compare to yours:

The tomb is located	=	**the tomb is/lies**
I located the tomb	=	**I found/discovered the tomb**
Does the tomb contain	=	**Does the tomb have**
the jewelry is contained	=	**the jewelry is held/kept**
Papyrus always grew	=	**Papyrus always lived/flourished**
wheat and barley were grown	=	**wheat and barley were cultivated/farmed**

There are a number of verbs that go through this same change or metamorphosis when they're used in the active or in the passive voice. Among them are _fly/be flown, turn/be turned, work/be worked,_ and _leave/be left._ A most amazing phenomenon indeed!

One more oddity involves the following verbs. If you think in terms of active and passive voice and about the steps we use to transform an active sentence into a passive one, what strange thing do you notice about sentences like the following?

> We have a new DVD player.
> He lacks initiative.
> That car costs £10,000.

I notice that _____ .

What you should notice is that you can't transform those three sentences into the passive voice. The verbs in question (_have, lack,_ and _cost_) belong to the group we call **stative verbs** (see Chapter 3), and they don't have passive counterparts even though they appear to be transitive by having objects. Most stative verbs don't have this oddness about them, but the ones that do are quite common. They include _ache, belong, contain, equal, fit, hold (= contain), hurt (= be painful), matter, mean, mind (= object), resemble, seem, sound_ (intransitive use), _suit,_ and _tend._

And since we've mentioned some verbs that have no passive voice counterparts, let's give equal time to some verbs that have no active voice counterparts. "What?" you say. "Can there be such verbs?" Well, there certainly can be—in fact, there are.

> A: I know if we just persevere, we'll find King Solomon's mines.
> B: But the ancient map says the treasure should **be situated** right here. Do you see any sign of a fabulous treasure?
> A: I'm sure the mines **are located** right in this area—maybe right under our very feet. The problem is, it**'s rumored** that only those who truly believe in the legend will find the treasure!

If we take the three verbs in bold and mechanically transform them into active voice forms, we get:

> . . . someone should situate the treasure right here.
> . . . someone locates the mines in this area . . .
> . . . someone rumors that only those who believe in the legend . . .

The problem we have with the first two lines is that they're misleading. Nobody is situating or locating anything anywhere. As we've already discovered with the verb *locate*, in the passive voice the idea is that something *is* or something *lies* someplace, and people finding it have nothing to do with the idea.

As for our third example, it's not even grammatical because, believe it or not, there's no such verb—transitive or intransitive—as *to rumor*. It turns out that the phrase *it's rumored* is very idiomatic, very strange, and very specialized, to say the least. Talk about oddities! And two more extremely common examples of such oddities are *be born* and *report*:

> In a hospital, babies are born in the delivery room.
> The oldest person on record is reported to have been 124 when she died.

These verbs are a passive form, what is left of the active verb *to bear (a child)* and *to report*. Like *to call someone a name* or *to be named,* the passive form is much more common than the active form.

But we're not through yet! Take a look at the following dialogue:

A: Wish I could go to lunch already. I'm starving!

B: Well, here's a banana.

A: Thanks.

B: Why are you having such a problem with it? Bananas **peel** with no trouble at all.

A: I don't know why. Okay, I finally got the skin off!

B: I love bananas. They **eat** easily.

A: Well, let's get back to the work we're doing on my car. This owner's manual is driving me nuts. It **reads** like a mystery novel!

B: By the way, how much is your car worth now?

A: It **sells** for around $23,000.

See anything very odd indeed about the verbs in bold? What do you think?

What's so very strange about those verbs is that they're in the active voice, yet their subjects can't do those actions. Bananas don't peel themselves or eat anything, a book can't read, nor can a car sell anything. And yet these verbs are used in this way all the time in normal, conversational English. They belong to a small group of verbs that some linguists refer to as **pseudo-passives**. They look active in form, but they're passive in meaning. They're just another quirk of English grammar.

Other verbs that can work the same way are:

iron:	Those blouses <u>iron</u> easily.
measure:	The bedroom <u>measures</u> 8' x 12'.
test:	She <u>tested</u> negative for HIV.
wash:	Unlike most sweaters, this one <u>washes</u> well.

Before we leave the passive voice, there's just one last oddity that we'd like to bring to your attention, and here it is:

All of us assume that we will colonize the moon one day.

The way this sentence stands now, the subject is *all of us*. But if we want to change the focus of the sentence and put it on the assumption, in other words, make the assumption our subject, we can transform this into a passive voice sentence. What should the sentence end up being if we do this? You try it out first:

We know that we have to take the current object and transform it into our new subject. So what's the object of our verb *assume*? It's actually everything after the verb. Note that an object doesn't necessarily mean just one or two words; it can end up being a whole phrase or clause. To see how incredibly varied objects can really be, see the first *Troubleshooter* in Chapter 14. At any rate, this is how your transformed sentence should have come out:

That we will colonize the moon one day is assumed by all of us.

We can change our focus even more if we want to by concentrating our attention on the moon rather than on ourselves. If we make this change, how will our new sentence look? (Here's a hint: You should still begin your sentence with "That . . ."):

If we want to make the moon our focus in that part of the sentence, we're going to have to make it our new subject in the clause, so our revised sentence should be:

That the moon will be colonized one day is assumed by all of us.

Fine, you say. We've now done our little juggling act and created some passive voice counterparts for our original active voice sentence. All three of these sentences are perfectly usable even though our second and third versions do seem awkward. But why are they awkward? It's because English has this interesting "balancing act" between the subject of a sentence and everything that follows the head verb. In English we prefer to keep the subject relatively short and simple but don't mind building up whatever comes after the head verb:

All of us assume <u>that the moon will be colonized one day</u>.

So when we load up the subject instead of what comes on the other side of the head verb, we find it awkward and uncomfortable:

<u>That the moon will be colonized one day</u> is assumed by all of us.

We can pick and choose among all of these versions of the same idea depending on where we want to place the focus.

Just when you might think we're done with this topic, we've got a surprise for you. There's one more version of our idea that we can come up with. It's perhaps the oddest version of them all, especially for students. Let's see if you can produce it before we give it away. (Here's another hint: You should begin the sentence with "It . . . "):

The only reason we have to begin our last version with *it* is because English requires us to begin with some sort of subject, even if it's what we call the **empty subject**, that is, one that really has no major significance except that it helps us conform to the rules of grammar. Actually, you'll see how *it* is redundant in our new version:

It's assumed by all of us that the moon will be colonized one day.

Does your version match ours? We hope so! And can you see why *it* is really redundant? Just imagine two people having this slightly odd chat:

> A: Yes, it's definitely assumed.
> B: What's assumed?
> A: That the moon will be colonized one day.
> B: Well, why didn't you say that in the first place?

This last version of ours is the most difficult for students to grasp and master on their own, even though native speakers don't think it particularly awkward, at least in very formal English. Consider the *it* subject to be a fill-in. When there is no real subject (just a verb), we often plug *it* in as subject:

It's raining.   It's snowing.   It's a shame.   It's funny.

The Passive Voice in a Nutshell

used when the subject isn't the doer:
I'm being helped, thank you.

used to avoid redundancy when doer is understood:
Don't you think midterm exams have been scheduled early this term?

used to avoid giving away a source of information:
I'm told you don't like it here.

used to be tactful:
My goodness! The bathroom floor still hasn't been washed.

used only with transitive verbs:
The pies were baked in the oven.

Bake **is transitive here:** [They] baked the pies in the oven.
Bake **is intransitive here; no passive voice possible:**
She bakes well. The pies baked in the oven. They just sat in there on the rack and baked.

* *by* **is used to introduce the doer:**
  These pies were baked by our son.

* *with* **is used to introduce the instrument:**
  Those items were purchased with a credit card.

* **reduced passive voice is used in headlines (to shorten the number of words used):**
  More Investigations Demanded on Environmental Issues

* **reduced passive voice is used in relative clauses:**
  Houses painted with a primer and two coats of paint hold up better against weathering.

* **commonly used on signs:**
  Copies Made Here

* **passive voice meaning can differ from active voice:**
  She left at about 4:15. (= departed)
  He was left penniless. (= ended up)

* **pseudo-passives:**
  Merchandise sells for much more at retail prices than at wholesale prices.

ꙮ Causatives

We'll now take a look at a small but important group of verbs that do just what their name says: **they cause something to happen—usually**. Causative verbs like *order* and *want* are very clear in meaning to students, but two others are quite difficult for them to understand. Let's see how these two verbs work in our next dialogue:

> A: Didn't you **have** your house **painted** recently?
>
> B: Yes, after a lot of grief. Would you believe I went through three painters before I **got** it **done**?
>
> A: Three? That's incredible! Why three?
>
> B: Well, the first one hurt his back and the second one **had** his truck **stolen**. I was a nervous wreck thinking that something would happen to the third one, too.
>
> A: So how did the job turn out?

> B: Oh, just great! First I **had** the walls **pressure-cleaned** and then I
> **had** them **covered** with one coat of primer and two coats of
> paint. The house looks sensational.
>
> A: Well, I've got to **get** my house **painted** too, so let me have your
> painter's name and phone number, okay?

You can see that the two verbs we're dealing with in this dialogue are *have* and *get*. A question like the opener in our dialogue usually confuses students because they can't understand what *have* is doing in the sentence. It's obviously not possession and it certainly isn't the present perfect auxiliary, so what is it? How would you define the verb *have* as it appears here? Before you answer this question, we should look at the grammatical pattern and context that the verb is in. In fact, we might as well look at the pattern that *get* is in, too, since it's the same one. On the line below, write down what you see as the grammatical pattern:

What we're talking about is this structure:

have/get + **direct object + past participle of verb**

That's how we come up with sentences like "I had my house painted." / "I had the walls covered." / "We got the job done."

As an aside, we'd like to mention that there are two other patterns we have for the causatives that are used in the active sense rather than the passive sense described in this chapter:

have/get + **direct object + base verb**
have/get + **direct object + *-ing* verb**

They're used with direct objects that are animate and can do things:

I had the painter <u>apply</u> two coats of paint.
He got me <u>thinking</u> that he really didn't know his job.

We'll be coming back to these uses of *have* and *get* and other causatives in Chapter 14.

Now we can try to define *have* and *get* when they appear with this special pattern. Let's focus on *have* for the moment. How would you define the verb in this context for your students?

Have is really quite interesting in that it's actually **a combination of two ideas**: to ask/tell someone to do something and that something is done. It's a more exact idea than simply saying:

I asked him to paint my house.

In the sentence you've just read, we know what the request was, but we can only assume that the work was carried out. Now read this sentence:

I had my house painted.

In this sentence, we know that not only was the request made, but the work was also completed. It's a very efficient verb, this *have*. Even if we put the sentence in the future and say "I'm going to have my house painted," we still have a strong sense that the job will be done.

But why do we need the past participle in this pattern? Why not use the base verb or the simple past for that matter if the sentence is in the past? If you've got an answer, write it down on the following line:

_____

_____

What we're looking at is another example of **a reduced passive voice**—which is why this causative pattern is included in this chapter. We could interpret our causative sentence to mean that "I told someone to paint the house, and it was <u>painted</u>:"

I had the house <u>painted</u>.

In one other use of *have* in our dialogue, the meaning is the same:

I had the walls <u>pressure-cleaned</u> . . .

Before we move on to *get,* there's still one use of *have* as a causative that's very different from what we've already discussed. Let's go back to the sentence in the dialogue which says " . . . the second one had his truck stolen." This is where things may get very troublesome. What on earth does *have* mean in this context? If we go with the meaning we've already discovered for this causative, what interpretation can you give to the sentence?

_____

_____

According to the strict definition of *have* in a causative pattern, the sentence must mean that **the painter arranged for his truck to be stolen, and it was**! Even though this is highly unlikely in this particular context, keep in mind that it *is* a plausible interpretation. For the context of our dialogue, though, there's got to be some other meaning for this sentence—but what is it? Think about it for a moment and see if you can figure it out. Then write your interpretation on the following lines:

_____

_____

This is a tough one. To begin with, it will help if we think about the meaning of *have* in a sentence like *I had car trouble last week*. We certainly don't mean possession in this sentence, so what does *have* stand for? In Chapter 3 we discussed the various uses of stative verbs and changes in their meanings depending on how they're used. In the sentence about the car trouble, *have* really means "this was my experience last week." **Have can mean what is happening to someone**. Another example of this use can be seen in a sentence like "I'm having a party next week at my house."

Now, if we keep this use of *have* in mind, how can we interpret " . . . the second one had his truck stolen . . . "?

_____

The answer is that it means **his truck being stolen/that his truck was stolen is what happened to him**. This is an unusual use of *have,* and one that really challenges teachers to explain and students to understand and use properly.

Now we have to consider *get,* which isn't as easy an undertaking as you might think. Let's take another look at the first sentence containing *get*:

I went through three painters before I got it done.

Why did the speaker choose to use *get* instead of *have*? What difference, if any, is there in meaning between *have* and *get*? Here's another chance for you to show your linguistic prowess, so write your idea on the following line:

_____

If you remember during our discussion of *be* and *get* in the passive voice on page 257, we said that *be* seems to have a more *neutral* usage than *get* does. There are certain nuances we communicate with *get* that don't seem to come across with *be,* and their interpretations can differ depending on the context. This difference is reflected in the use of *have* and *get* as causatives. There are times when both verbs can be used the same way, but there are other times when native speakers feel that *get* communicates something more than *have* does. In the example sentence we've just seen, the speaker probably used *get* instead of *have* because what should have been a simple project turned into a difficult situation. **Get can carry with it a sense of extra effort or a stronger implication than** *have*, and because the speaker had to put more into accomplishing his goal (using three painters) than he might have otherwise had to do, he chose to use *get* to communicate this idea.

Let's try a little experiment now. Look at the following sentences and decide whether you'd prefer to complete them with *have* or *get* or, if you don't feel there's any marked difference with either one:

1. After long and hard negotiations, she _____ the contracts signed.
       ☐ had   ☐ got   ☐ either one

2. I just _____ my poodle clipped. Doesn't she look beautiful?
       ☐ had   ☐ got   ☐ either one

3. We're thinking about _____ a room added on to our house.
       ☐ having   ☐ getting   ☐ either one

4. A: How many times have I mentioned that this door still doesn't close right?
   B: _____ it fixed!
       ☐ Have   ☐ Get   ☐ either one

5. Because of her political clout, she _____ herself appointed to the Council.
       ☐ had   ☐ got   ☐ either one

6. It's really late. _____ the baby dressed so we can leave.
       ☐ Have   ☐ Get   ☐ either one

7. How dare you say such things! I won't _____ my wife spoken to like that!
       ☐ have   ☐ get   ☐ either one

Interesting little exercise, isn't it? For the most part, there really are no right or wrong answers, just tendencies that native speakers have as to which verb they'd use or whether either verb will do. Here's what many people checked off for their answers. Let's see how close your answers are to theirs:

1. got   2. either one   3. having   4. Get   5. got   6. Get   7. have

There are two closing comments we'd like to make. The first concerns numbers 4 and 6, which are commands (imperatives). There seems to be a tendency to use *get* in a causative sentence when giving an order. This may be because *get* has a stronger feeling about it than *have* does. The other comment is about Number 7. The fact is that *have* can take on a different meaning when combined with certain direct objects and past participles. In Number 7, *have* really means "permit," "allow," or "let."

Teaching Tips

13.1 Writing Definitions

Before class, prepare different lists of ten to fifteen common or proper nouns. Distribute the lists to small groups of students, who'll prepare short definitions for these nouns. Have them write their definitions on separate pieces of paper without including the nouns being described. Be sure that they use passives in their definitions. Here's a sample of what you might give the students: "Television sets," "Eggs," and "the Bahamas." And here are some definitions that they might come up with: "machines that are created to be modern-day baby sitters," "food which is forbidden to people who have high cholesterol," and "the first islands that were discovered by Europeans in 1492." When all the nouns are defined, distribute only the definitions to different groups of students and ask them to figure out what their classmates have defined.

Variation: Prepare a list of sentence beginnings similar to the ones below. Divide the class into small groups and have them complete the sentences. Encourage the use of passives in the completions. "I know a person who . . . " / "I dislike things which . . . " / "I've never been to a place that . . . " / "Teachers who . . . " / "Books that . . . " etc.

13.2 Transactions, Events, Activities

Give the students a list of establishments where transactions, events, and activities take place (a restaurant, hotel, gym, laboratory, gas/petrol station, store, etc.). Have your students come up with as many examples of what happens there as they can think of by using passives. (This can be done as a contest and/or individually or in groups.) If this activity is done as a game, give each student or group a point for every passive example they come up with. Give them a bonus point for every passive example that no one else has thought up. Here are some examples they might create: "Food is served there." / "Customers are waited on there." / "The guest rooms are cleaned by housekeepers." / "The guests are greeted by the front desk clerks."

13.3 Describing Processes and Procedures

Have students describe a procedure or process that they know about, being aware of where passives might be appropriate. Some procedures that they might describe are: how to test the pH of a liquid, how to reupholster a chair, how to make cheese, etc. Let the students share their knowledge with the entire class.

13.4 Newspaper Headlines

Cut out a variety of newspaper headlines containing reduced active and passive forms. Have students work in small groups to reconstruct the complete headlines.

13.5 *Before and After Scenes*

Find or make pairs of pictures that show "before" and "after" scenes. Have the students use passives to describe the changes that they note. ("A beautiful skyscraper is being erected on the corner. When that's done, the roads around the construction site will be resurfaced," etc.)

Variation: Prepare a map of a run-down inner city. Include various landmarks (polluted river, abandoned buildings, empty lots, etc.). Have small groups of students clean up the city, sharing their revitalization plans with the entire class. They should discuss what has/hasn't been done, what will/won't be done in the near future, what could/couldn't be done right away, etc.

13.6 *Maps*

Use the map of a country that has the country's products on it (oil, corn, rice, cattle, etc.). Have the students describe the various products shown by making up appropriate sentences: "Corn and wheat are grown in the Midwest." / "Dairy products are produced in Wisconsin." / "Petroleum is produced in Venezuela and emeralds are mined in Colombia."

Variations:

1. Cut whatever map you've used into states, provinces, etc. and have the students piece it back together, all the while describing what information is provided.

2. Replace the map just described with one the students have invented or one you've found of their own country, state, province, etc. Describe the products using appropriate passives.

13.7 *Keeping Abreast of the News*

If you teach in an English-speaking country, here's a good activity for your students. After they're able to recognize the various passive forms, reduced or otherwise, have them keep abreast of the news by posting passive forms that they find in the news on bulletin boards you've put up around the room. Label the various boards: "Local News," "National News," and "International News." The kinds of news that get posted might be items like these:

Local News	National News	International News
New School Board Elected Tuesday	President's Spouse to Be Awarded Franklin Prize by TangeloCorp	Peace Declared in . . .

13.8 Conducting Surveys

This tip is also meant for teachers who have classes in English-speaking countries or in countries where there's a sufficient number of English speakers. If you have students who can do some of their classwork outside the classroom, this is a golden opportunity to get outside and talk to people and practice passives at the same time. Divide your class into groups of four or five and have them create surveys on subjects that are important to them or topical at the moment. Tell them that they'll actually conduct the surveys (surveying at least twenty-five people) and will give a formal report on their findings. To reinforce the activity, have them write up their findings.

13.9 Creating Ads

Bring in newspaper ads. Distribute the ads to small groups of students. Ask them to go through the ads to prepare a list of any passives they've found. Write up the phrases from the various groups on a sheet for an overhead projector or on the board and ask the students to create an ad for a product of their choice, real or imagined. Have them use the passive phrases they've seen in the newspaper ads.

13.10 Reconstructing Headlines

This activity gives your students practice using their knowledge of the world rather than the knowledge of material you've previously discussed in class to solve a problem. Before class, cut out as many newspaper headlines as you need so that when your class does this activity, each small group will have their own headline or two to work with. Put the articles they came from aside for the moment. Number each article and then number each word of the headline with the same number that you've given to its article. Cut up each headline into separate words, attaching each of the words to a *separate* small piece of paper. If you can't put the individual words on separate slips of paper, blacken out the backsides of the headlines so that the students don't get confused as to what exactly they're supposed to be looking at. Mix up the words belonging to one headline and then hold the words together with a paper clip. Divide the class into groups and give them one or two of the headlines that have been clipped together. Tell the students to reconstruct each headline, and when they've done so, to brainstorm what they think the article that goes with it is about. Now give each group the article that its headline belongs to. Tell them to have someone read the article aloud to the group so they can compare the real article to what they guessed the article was about.

13.11 Flow Charts and Far-reaching Consequences

Create a situation that has far-reaching consequences (a 72-hour blackout in a large city; an epidemic; people being able to live up to 150 years of age, etc.). Divide the class into small groups and have them create a flow chart of the consequences that might occur during or after the event. Here's an example of what we mean:

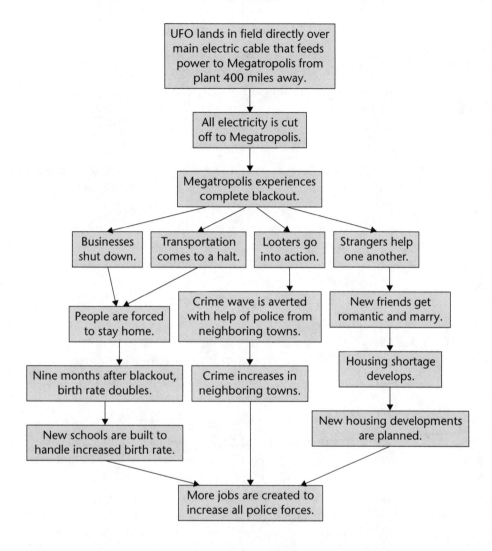

Put up the charts around class and have a discussion about their similarities and differences. Focus the students' attention on places where the passive can/should be used.

13.12 *Writing Campaign Speeches*

Divide the class into groups of three or four and have them write a campaign speech for someone running for office or someone who wishes to be principal or headmaster of a school, director of a company, etc. Encourage the use of passives in the speeches ("If I'm elected, taxes will be reduced."). Have the groups present their speeches to the entire class and then hold an election; students will vote for the candidate that presented the most convincing speech. After the winner is announced, ask the students to discuss why they voted for the candidates they did.

13.13 Animal Escapes Zoo!

Divide the class into small groups. Have them create a news report about an animal that has escaped from the zoo. They'll need to brainstorm details of the event so that the report will have plenty of relevant details and facts. All members of the group will "participate" in the news report.

13.14 Interviews

Divide the class into groups of three to four. Have the groups think of people they'd like to interview. After five minutes, bring the class back together and list on the board four or five of the better, more interesting, more unusual interview choices. Put the groups back together and let them choose the person they'd like to interview from this list on the board. Ask them to write down questions that a reporter from a local newspaper, radio station, TV station, or online magazine might ask this person. Encourage the use of passives.

13.15 Writing a Critique

Let your students become art critics for a day. Find pictures in your Picture File (see Appendix 1) that have pieces of art in them (sculptures, paintings, wall hangings, etc.). In small groups, students will write critiques of the artwork using passives where appropriate. Let students share their works of art and critiques with their classmates.

13.16 Matching Headlines and Articles

Before class, cut a newspaper up into several articles and number each article. Remove the headlines from the articles you've chosen. Think up less obvious headlines for the articles, making sure to use passive and causative verb forms. To make the activity more challenging, create more headlines than you have articles. In class, write these new headlines on the board and place the numbered articles on your desk. Let each student or group of students take an article and match it to one of your new headlines. Once the headlines and articles have been properly reconnected, ask the students to read the article that they have, letting them know that they'll eventually be asked to explain what they've read to the whole class or a smaller group of students.

13.17 Creating a New Game

Divide the class into groups and have them invent an entirely new game: the rules, the equipment needed, the name of the game, etc. Make sure students are aware how rules can use passive and causative forms ("Two dice are needed." / "The fastest runner is declared winner." / "Get the students divided into three teams." / "Have one student from each team chosen as captain," etc.). When everything has been worked out, tell the groups that they're going to "act out" their games for their classmates. The "action" is to be done *silently*. The rest of the class, working in groups or individually, writes down the rules as they perceive them. Have them compare the rules they've perceived with the rules as they were originally written.

13.18 Creating a New Product

Have the students work in groups of two or three to create a product and its logo, slogans, advertising copy, etc. They'll write up their advertising layout for the product and present the finished ad for the entire class to see. The students will then vote for the most effective ad, which will be given "The EngAd" award ("English in Advertising"). Encourage the use of passives and causatives.

13.19 Let's Demonstrate

Have your students plan a street demonstration. They need to prepare all the details of the demonstration: what they're demonstrating against, how angry they are, where the demonstration will take place, etc., making sure that they incorporate passives and causatives where appropriate. Students will also prepare the picket signs, banners, and slogans for the demonstration. Stage the demonstration, but be careful. If noise is a problem, take the groups outside or to the school cafeteria, etc. If demonstrations are too touchy a subject, substitute the demonstration with a meeting in which consumers air a complaint against a certain company.

14

Direct Object Companions

"The Queen of Hearts' men painted all the white roses red."

We're about to examine what we've dubbed **direct object companions**, troublesome grammatical gems which are really quite commonplace. They're troublesome because some of them don't seem to have obvious explanations, while others don't seem to conform to some of the basic rules of English.

The first thing we should do in this chapter is explain what we mean by direct object companions as far as teachers are concerned. We see them as **phrases placed right after the direct objects which have special descriptive connections to those direct objects**, and they're classified into seven distinct types:

noun phrases	***-ing* verb phrases**
adjective phrases	**past participle phrases**
base verb phrases	**prepositional phrases**
infinitive verb phrases	

Besides the fact that they all share the important characteristic of describing the direct objects they follow, they also share a certain pattern which we'll soon discover.

It's important for you to understand from the start that what we've labeled direct object companions (we'll call them DOCs for short from now on) come from quite diverse backgrounds and have quite different uses and meanings, which is probably why they aren't put together under one label in other grammar books as we're doing here. We're presenting these forms in this way because it makes sense, from a teacher's standpoint, to see all of these varied types under one umbrella, direct object companions. And because they all share the same pattern, it makes more sense for students, too. As you're going through this chapter, remember that all the DOCs are quite diverse and that you would probably not teach them together as a unit.

In this chapter we'll be investigating the first six types we mentioned earlier; the seventh, prepositional phrase DOCs, really needs no special investigating, although you'll see numerous examples of them anyway as we go on.

To start things off, then, we really should first consider what we mean when we say a "direct object":

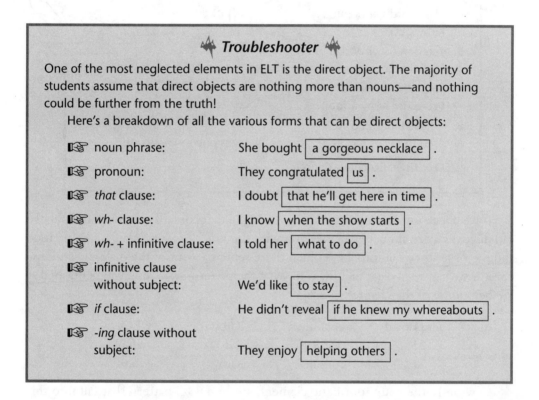

≪ *Troubleshooter* ≫

One of the most neglected elements in ELT is the direct object. The majority of students assume that direct objects are nothing more than nouns—and nothing could be further from the truth!

Here's a breakdown of all the various forms that can be direct objects:

☞ noun phrase: She bought │ a gorgeous necklace │ .

☞ pronoun: They congratulated │ us │ .

☞ *that* clause: I doubt │ that he'll get here in time │ .

☞ *wh-* clause: I know │ when the show starts │ .

☞ *wh-* + infinitive clause: I told her │ what to do │ .

☞ infinitive clause
  without subject: We'd like │ to stay │ .

☞ *if* clause: He didn't reveal │ if he knew my whereabouts │ .

☞ *-ing* clause without
  subject: They enjoy │ helping others │ .

✍ **Noun Phrases**

Let's get started by looking at our first DOC:

A: Have you heard the news?

B: What news?

A: The Board's appointed Kirby **CEO***.

B: You don't say! Well, I call that **a coup**!

A: You must be joking! I consider Kirby **a fool**!

B: What's that thing we used to say as children? Oh, yes. "It takes one to know one."

*CEO = Chief Executive Officer

If we check out the sentences in our dialogue that contain the nouns in bold, we can discover a certain pattern emerging with the kinds of words that are being used and the order they fall into. Let's pluck those sentences out of the dialogue and discover if we can see a clear picture as to what the pattern is, the one we mentioned at the beginning of the chapter:

The Board	's appointed	Kirby	CEO.
I	call	it	a coup!
I	consider	Kirby	a fool!

Obviously, there are four basic elements in the DOC pattern that fall into this special order. How would you write out what the order is?

_____

The basic order that's emerged is the way all sentences with noun phrase DOCs are formed and the four elements are immovable. So what is our word order?

<u>subject</u>	+	<u>verb</u>	+	<u>direct object</u>	+	<u>noun phrase</u>
The Board		has appointed		Kirby		CEO.
I		call		it		a coup!
I		consider		Kirby		a fool!

This is a good time to mention that the basic pattern is the same for every kind of DOC: **subject + verb + direct object + DOC**. In addition, we want to point out that the noun and adjective phrase DOCs are also called **object complements**. One thing these object complements do is that both of them "rename" the object. What we mean is that we can imagine an equal sign or the verb *be* between the object and the DOC. Here's an example for each object complement:

> The Board's appointed Kirby CEO. → Kirby = CEO/Kirby is CEO.
> We painted the house peach. → The house is peach.

Just to digress for a moment and probe a little deeper, we might find it worth pointing out that there are two ways of interpreting the nature of noun phrase DOCs depending on what the whole statement tells us. Let's look at the following two sentences and see if we can find any noticeable difference in the relationship between the noun phrase DOCs and their verbs:

> 1. They appointed Kirby CEO.
> 2. I consider Kirby a fool!

In Sentence 1 the speaker is describing the result of what the Board did and how Kirby (the direct object) was affected. The verb being used is one that's brought about change, so the nature of this kind of noun phrase DOC is that it deals with **a resulting condition**. Here are some more examples of sentences with verbs that can bring about some form of change and noun phrase DOCs that show a resulting condition:

> We <u>named</u> the kitten <u>Kukui</u>.
> They <u>elected</u> her <u>president</u>.
> Circumstances <u>made</u> him a <u>hero</u>.

Other verbs commonly found in conjunction with noun phrase DOCs that show resulting conditions include

designate:	Hasn't the boss designated Robin head secretary yet?
nominate:	They're going to nominate Sharif Secretary General.
select:	The Dean selected Zoltan department chair.

In Sentence 2, on the other hand, the speaker is describing his perception or opinion of Kirby. The kind of verb being used doesn't bring about change, so this kind of noun phrase DOC deals with **a pre-existing condition** (in this case, of Kirby's). Here are two more examples of sentences that demonstrate pre-existing conditions:

> They <u>think</u> me <u>a coward</u>.
> Hollie <u>calls</u> her boat "<u>The Wave Dancer</u>."

Here are other verbs that are used for pre-existing conditions:

consider: They consider her a genius.
find: We found him a boor.
imagine: I imagined myself king of Atlantis.
prove: She proved the story a hoax.

Verbs with Prepositions and Noun Phrase DOCs

One last area concerning noun phrase DOCs has to do with a small group of verbs that go hand in hand with a preposition, usually *as*. Sometimes the preposition is optional, but sometimes it isn't. Remember, though, that there is still that "renaming" of the object (object = *be* DOC). Here's an example of each type:

They chose Edison Park (as) the site for their picnic.
She mistook me for her son's teacher.

Other verbs with the optional use of the preposition include these:

appoint: The President appointed her (as) Ambassador to Fulania.
consider: They consider her (as) the hospital's top surgeon.
elect: We elected him (as) club treasurer.
make: They're going to make the spare bedroom (into) a nursery.

Other verbs with the mandatory use of the preposition include the verbs in this list:

accept: Believe it or not, our pet pig accepted a stray kitten as her own baby!
change: The wicked witch changed the prince into a frog.
define: Psychiatrists define his behavior as schizophrenic.
intend: They only intend the cottage as a summer home.
mistake: When Columbus reached the New World, he mistook it for India.
regard: I regard her as my best friend.
see: We see AIDS as the worst epidemic of the 20th and 21st centuries.
take: She took her miraculous recovery as a sign from heaven.
Do you take me for a fool?
treat: Cinderella's step-sisters treated her as a maid.
turn: Maeve's kiss turned the frog back into a prince.
use: Prehistoric people used flint as knife blades.

And as for two-word verbs (phrasal verbs) that have the mandatory use of the preposition, we can cite these three:

count on: I can't count on them as good financial advisors.
put on: We want to put on this show as a charity event.
settle on: They settled on that site as their homestead.

✌ᵕᵕ **Adjective Phrases**

Let's get right to it by looking at how adjective phrase DOCs work in our next dialogue. Remember that they're object complements, too, just as nouns were:

A: Didn't your home use to be white?

B: That's right, but we painted the house **peach** last month. Why do you ask?

A: Well, I thought I'd drop by yesterday and say hello. Only trouble was I got confused because I was looking for a white house.

B: That's a shame. We'd still love you to come over.

A: So why peach?

B: Well, we consider the color **tropical**, and this is the Riviera after all. My wife wanted the house **hot pink**, but that color makes me **really sick**, so I couldn't agree to that.

A: I find peach **pretty** for houses. Good choice!

B: Thanks!

As we've pointed out a few times, perhaps the most awkward situation that can happen to a teacher occurs when a student asks a question that puts the unwary instructor on the spot because he or she is at a loss to give a quick response. The questions that follow, which relate to our dialogue, will give you a taste of how that feels:

Question 1: Aren't *peach, tropical, hot pink, sick,* and *pretty* just adjectives in these sentences?

☐ yes   ☐ no

If you've answered **yes**, that leads us to . . .

Question 2: Don't we always teach beginning students that we put adjectives before the nouns they describe (for example, *the big box* and not *the box big*)?

☐ yes   ☐ no

If you've answered **yes** again, that leads us to . . .

Question 3: Then why is it that the speakers in our dialogue have gone against that basic rule by placing the adjectives *after* the nouns they describe?

If we check out the sentences in our dialogue that contain adjectives in bold, we can see the same pattern emerges as we found with noun phrase DOCs. Let's go back to the dialogue and plug those sentences into our pattern to see how it develops:

subject	+	verb	+	direct object	+	adjective phrase
We		painted		the house		peach.
We		consider		the color		tropical.
My wife		wanted		the house		hot pink.
Pink		makes		me		really sick.
I		find		peach		pretty.

Just as before, all of these sentences conform nicely to our pattern. As we mentioned previously, the four basic elements in the DOC pattern are immovable, but additional words can be placed between some of these elements (for example, we can use a frequency adverb between *I* and *find* and place an intensifier like *very* before *pretty* to end up with this sentence:

I <u>always</u> find the color peach <u>very</u> pretty for houses.

We should also mention that the adjective phrase DOC can appear in the comparative form:

I find peach *prett<u>ier</u>* than pink.

and the superlative form:

Of all the students in our class, the teacher considers Ed the *bright<u>est</u>*.

Is there any other similarity we can notice about adjective and noun phrase DOC sentences besides the fact that they share the same pattern? Do adjective phrase DOCs have pre-existing and resulting conditions?

☐ yes   ☐ no

The answer to our question is **yes**. Just as with noun phrase direct object companions, there are really two conditions for the adjective phrase DOCs, depending on what the whole statement tells us. Let's examine the following two sentences to find the noticeable difference in the relationship between the verbs and the adjective phrase DOCs:

1. We painted the house peach.
2. We consider the color tropical.

In **Sentence 1** the speaker is describing the result of what he and his wife did and how the house (the direct object) was affected. The verb being used is one that's brought about change, so the adjective phrase DOC has **a resulting condition**. Here are some more examples of sentences with verbs that can bring about some form of change and adjective phrase DOCs with resulting conditions:

We <u>made</u> the baby <u>happy</u>.
My next-door neighbor <u>got</u> me <u>upset</u>.
He <u>licked</u> the spoon <u>clean</u>.
The auctioneer <u>declared</u> the bidding <u>open</u>.
She <u>sliced</u> the bread <u>thin</u>.

Here are verbs other than those we've used that are commonly found in conjunction with adjective phrase DOCs that have resulting conditions:

pull: He pulled the rope tight.
push: I pushed the door open.
put/set: He put/set me straight.
wipe: She didn't wipe the table clean.

And then there's the idiomatic use of *drive*: That perfume drives him wild/crazy!

In **Sentence 2** ("We consider the color tropical.") the speaker is describing his perception or opinion of that color. The kind of verb being used doesn't bring about change, so the nature of this kind of adjective phrase DOC is that it's **a pre-existing condition** (in this case, of the color). Here are some more examples of sentences that demonstrate pre-existing conditions:

I <u>found</u> her <u>charming</u>.
He <u>drank</u> the tea <u>cold</u>.
They <u>left</u> the door <u>open</u>.
Did you <u>buy</u> the fish <u>fresh</u>?

There are other verbs that can produce sentences with adjective phrase DOCs that show pre-existing conditions:

call: I call him impulsive.
declare: They're about to declare themselves bankrupt.
find: We found it really hard to do.
hold: She isn't holding the camera steady.
imagine: I'd imagined her older than she was.
keep: Did she keep the food warm?
prove: They proved me wrong—again!
think: Do you think my opinion outrageous?

And then there's the idiomatic use of these two verbs:

hold: I hold you responsible.
run: New babies run their parents ragged.

A Word About "It"

An odd thing can happen with the pronoun *it* in the adjective phrase DOC pattern. Take a look at what we mean:

> A: Well, Smithers, have you decided on whether or not you'll be joining our expedition?
>
> B: I've given the subject a great deal of thought, and I think **it** ludicrous **to put together yet another expedition in search of the Yeti.**
>
> A: I'm sorry to hear you say that. I find **it** disappointing **that you've taken such a conservative position.** We believe **it** very possible **that the Yeti**, that strange hairy half-man, half-ape creature, **does in fact exist in the Himalayas.** There certainly have been enough sightings over the years.
>
> B: Well, Pinkerton, I'm sorry to disappoint you, but I consider **it** foolish **to invest more time and money on such an absurd enterprise.**

Why on earth do we have the word *it* in the direct object position within all of these sentences containing adjective phrase DOCs? And what exactly does *it* mean in these sentences? See if you can answer these questions on the following lines:

_____

_____

You can look at the word *it* in these sentences as being either **anticipatory** or **redundant**. *It* is basically a device we use to introduce the following part of the sentence that explains what *it* means. In other words, *it* actually means the same thing as the part of the sentence it anticipates. That's why many call this *it* the "anticipatory *it*."

For example, in our first sentence,

> I think <u>it</u> ludicrous to put together yet another expedition . . .

the word *it* really means

> to put together yet another expedition . . .

The same is true in the next sentence that contains *it*:

> I find <u>it</u> disappointing that you've taken such a . . . position.

What does *it* stand for in this sentence?

The answer is that *it* stands for **that you've taken such a conservative position**.

Notice that there are two kinds of explanatory sections, one that begins with *an infinitive* and one that begins with *that*. Both are quite commonly used in this type of adjective phrase DOC sentence. And it's worth mentioning that a certain verb is dropped in this construction, which gives the sentence a much more formal sound when it's dropped. Can you think of which verb it is?

The answer is that it's some form of the verb *be:*

. . . and I think it <u>is</u> ludicrous to put together yet another expedition . . .

We can say that with certain verbs that exhibit the adjective phrase DOC pattern, it's not unusual to find the "anticipatory *it*" placed in the direct object position with an explanatory part following. We should also mention that, in some cases, this same phenomenon of the "anticipatory *it*" plus DOC can occur with nouns as well:

> I consider <u>it</u> a crime <u>that you're going to waste that food</u>.
> We think <u>it</u> a mistake <u>to get married at such a young age</u>.

Later on in this chapter we'll be looking at how whole sentences can be used as DOCs with just a couple of grammatical changes.

An Adjective DOC Puzzler

Just when you think you're getting comfortable with direct object companions, we're going to ask you to contend with a peculiar phenomenon that sometimes occurs with adjective DOCs. This is another example of when your students could get very confused considering what they've already been taught about adjective word order. You'll see what we mean when you read this next dialogue:

> A: Oh, Martha! Loving you is the greatest joy of my life!
> B: Oh, George! Loving you is the greatest joy of my life, too!
> A: Oh, Martha! We have so much in common.
> B: Oh, George, I know! Our tastes are definitely compatible.
> A: I like steak **rare**, and so do you.
> B: And I like coffee **black**, and you do, too.
> A: I only eat oysters **raw**, and so do you.
> B: And I only enjoy yogurt **plain**, and you do, too.
> A: Oh, Martha!
> B: Oh, George!

We can see that the sentences with words in bold fit our pattern just as the other DOCs did:

subject	+	verb	+	direct object	+	adjective
I		like		steak		rare.
I		like		coffee		black.
I		eat		oysters		raw.
I		enjoy		yogurt		plain.

But so what? Can't we say "I like rare steak" or "I eat raw oysters?" Aren't these two sentences with the adjectives in the *right* place okay?

    ☐ Yes, they are.   ☐ No, they aren't.   ☐ Perhaps.

Of course, the answer to our question is **Yes, they are**.

And don't those sentences with the normal adjective placement mean the same thing as the sentences in our dialogue?

    ☐ Yes, they do.   ☐ No, they don't.   ☐ Perhaps.

The answer to this second question is **Perhaps**. So what exactly is going on? The answer lies in the fact that we're not just dealing with ordinary adjective phrase DOCs, but with a very special kind indeed.

What's the difference in meaning between using adjectives like rare, black, raw, and plain in their regular positions before the nouns and making them into adjective DOCs by placing them after the nouns? We can find the answer if we examine the meaning of both kinds of sentences. The truth of the matter is that in the sentences found in our dialogue, we're dealing with some verbs that create a special meaning if we use the adjective DOC pattern.

Take a closer look at these two sentences to see what we mean:

> 1. I like black coffee.   2. I like coffee black.

We can sum up the difference between them very simply: **it's a matter of focus**. In **Sentence 1** we're focusing on **an entire item** and not on any particular condition of that item; it's not just coffee and it's not just something black—it's black coffee. But in **Sentence 2** our focus has changed. We're really saying we like coffee, but when it's black (that is, without cream or sugar). Now we're focusing on **a <u>condition</u> of the item** rather than on the whole item.

By the way, notice how the verb *to be* has been dropped from these sentences with object complements:

> I like steak (to be) rare.
> I like coffee (to be) black.

To get back to our point, compare these next two sentences:

> 1. I like raw oysters.   2. I like oysters raw.

Which statement would you say is focusing on a certain condition rather than on the item as a whole?

> ☐ Sentence 1   ☐ Sentence 2

If you've checked **Sentence 2**, you're getting the idea. In Sentence 1 the speaker says that he likes a particular type of seafood dish, "raw oysters," and there's really nothing else under discussion. In Sentence 2, however, the speaker's saying that he likes oysters, and then he quickly adds how he likes them, " . . . (when they're) raw." We're sure you see now that there's a definite change in focus even though in many cases we admit it can be a minor one.

Another way to look at these special adjective DOC sentences is to realize that they usually answer the questions "How do you like _____ ?" or "How do you prefer _____ ?" or "How do you want _____ ?" For example:

> A: How do you like your steak?
> B: I like it medium rare.

It's important to remember that this minor but real difference in focus is found in this adjective DOC pattern only with certain verbs. Besides the ones we've used in our examples, we can include other verbs in this list:

dislike: Many people dislike their drinks cold.
have: They always have their tea sweet.
keep: Keep this ring safe for me.
like: When they work outdoors, they like the weather cool.
love: Patti loves her men tall, dark, and handsome.
need: The surgeon needs her instruments ready at all times.
prefer: When I go swimming, I prefer the water calm.
serve: They serve this potato soup cold.
take: We normally take our coffee black.
want: She wants her vegetables crisp.

ᐧᣞᐧ Infinitive Verb Phrase DOCs

Here we are at our third type of direct object companion. It may surprise you to find infinitive verb phrases in a chapter on DOCs. Nevertheless, they are a type of DOC, so let's get right to them. This short dialogue will show you how the infinitive verb phrase DOC works:

A: Did Marcel get everything we need from Jean Louis to make more signs for our yard sale?
B: Yes, he did.
A: Good. By the way, do you know where he is now?
B: I think he's downstairs. Would you like **me to get him**?
A: Yes, please. I **want him to do something** important for me.

As with the other DOCs we've explored so far, we have the same basic pattern for the infinitive verb phrase DOC:

	subject	+	verb	+	direct object	+	infinitive verb phrase
Would	you		like		me		to get him?
	I		want		him		to do something.

The fact is that there's a group of verbs that prompt this particular pattern. It's interesting to note that certain causative verbs (see Chapter 13) are included in this group, as you'll see.

Besides the verbs we've already used in our examples, there are other verbs that prompt this pattern with the infinitive verb phrase DOC. (Note that the verbs with a star can trigger an alternative behavior, which you saw earlier with noun phrase DOCs.) The verbs with the infinitive phrase DOC include

allow:	She allowed him to leave.
★ **appoint:**	The committee appointed them to lead the expedition.
★ **believe:**	They believe him to be a spy.
★ **cause:**	What caused them to get so upset?
compel:	A strong feeling of guilt compelled him to confess.
condemn:	The court condemned him to serve thirty years.
★ **consider:**	Don't you consider it to be a victory for our side?
★ **expect:**	We expect her to arrive here shortly.
★ **feel:**	They feel his attitude to be too pessimistic.
★ **find:**	Haven't you found Mr. Greenbaum to be quirky?
force:	She'll force us to resign.
★ **get:**	Did you get her to agree?
★ **hate:**	We hate Grandpa to sit all alone in the park every day.
help:	Can you help me to tie this package?
★ **imagine:**	They'd imagined her to be shorter than she was.
intend:	We intend him to fulfill his obligations.
know:	I know him to be a man of his word.
★ **like:**	She likes her curry to be spicier than most people do.
mean:	I meant this chapter to have only twenty pages.
★ **need:**	We need them to be here by 5 o'clock.
permit:	They won't permit us to stay past noon.
★ **report:**	She reported the town to be under quarantine.
★ **suppose:**	We supposed the place to be more tranquil.
★ **want:**	I want you to be home early tonight.
★ **would like:**	We would like dinner to be ready by 7.

As we said, the verbs with an asterisk have an alternative; they can drop the infinitive part of the DOC and then be left with a noun, an adjective, a prepositional phrase, or an adverb, which will then become the DOC. Take a look at what we mean and keep in mind that *to be* can be placed in the blank before the underlined words. There's one exception you should find:

The committee appointed them _____ the leaders.

They believe him _____ a spy.

The arthritis causes him _____ great pain.

Don't you consider it _____ <u>a victory</u> for our side?

They had imagined her _____ <u>a boor</u>.

Have you figured out which sentence above contains our exception? It's "The arthritis causes him great pain." The infinitive verb which has been dropped in this instance could be *to have, to suffer, to experience,* or *to feel*.

As we said, you can also end up with an adjective phrase DOC when the infinitive phrase DOC *to be* is dropped:

They don't believe him _____ <u>sincere</u>.

Don't you consider our side _____ <u>victorious</u>?

She felt them _____ <u>untrustworthy</u>.

We find this strategy _____ <u>risky</u>.

They'd imagined her _____ <u>shorter</u> than she was.

He needs these copies _____ <u>darker</u>.

We'd supposed the place more _____ <u>pristine</u>.

The doctor wants you _____ <u>thinner</u>.

You can also drop *to be* and be left with a prepositional phrase DOC (and here are the examples we said you'd see when we started this chapter off):

Should we consider him _____ <u>at risk</u>?

They expect us _____ <u>on time</u>.

We felt her _____ <u>in terrible danger</u>.

I didn't find them _____ <u>in financial straits</u>.

She got him _____ <u>in trouble</u>.

Don't you hate syrup _____ <u>on ice cream</u>?

We imagined her _____ <u>in silks and gold</u>.

She doesn't like nuts _____ <u>in candy bars</u>.

She reported the town _____ <u>under attack</u>.

Mom wants the kids _____ <u>in bed</u> now!

She would like dinner _____ <u>by seven</u>.

Continuing right along, we find that there are some verbs that permit you to drop *to be*, leaving you with an adverb in the DOC position:

The director expects all of us _____ <u>there</u> at noon.

The pharmacist says he needs you _____ <u>here</u> right away.

The 6 o'clock news reported Godzilla _____ <u>downtown</u>.

My parents really want me _____ <u>home</u> early tonight.

There's one more element that can become the new DOC when the verb to be is dropped. It's the past participle, but we'll talk about that at length later in the chapter. Until we get to it, here are two examples:

She expects the copies _____ <u>made</u> by noon.

They found him _____ <u>unaffected</u> by the news.

One extra note: the verb *help* is very strange because it can have an infinitive verb phrase DOC, as already shown in our list ("Can you help me to tie this package?"), or it can have a base verb DOC without any change in meaning ("Can you help me tie this package?"). Just as with the past participle phrase DOCs, you'll be exploring base verb phrase DOCs in this chapter. In fact, the base verb phrase DOCs are coming up right away.

-ing Verb and Base Verb Phrases

We've now arrived at the fourth and fifth types of direct object companions, and it will make matters more interesting to examine them in the same section. Our next dialogue is a continuation of the conversation about Kirby becoming CEO on page 280; it will show you just how these two DOCs work, so let's take a look:

B: And just how did you happen to learn of this marvelous news?

A: I overheard Northrop **dictating** a memo to his secretary. He must have been preparing the official announcement of this ghastly news about Kirby.

B: Did you actually hear him **proclaim** that Kirby had definitely been selected?

A: Yes, unfortunately.

B: Then tomorrow we can be prepared to hear grown men and women **wailing** and see them **pulling** their hair out. It should be great fun to watch them **react** to Northrop's memo. I love to watch people **carry on**!

A: Well don't be so overjoyed, my friend. I recently heard Kirby say that he thought your department could stand some new blood in charge of it.

B: Really? Hmm. Well, early retirement does have its bright side.

We can see that there are two types of DOCs in this dialogue, the base verb phrase (and, by the way, the base verb is also known as the "bare infinitive") and the -*ing* verb phrase (and the -*ing* is also known as the present participle). Naturally, the question we have to ask right off is, what do these two DOCs represent? By discovering the answer, we'll understand how to use them.

-ing Verb Phrases

For the moment, let's deal only with -*ing* DOCs. In order to make it easier to work on them, we'll let you in on one important fact: **The sentences containing -*ing* and base verb phrase DOCs are really either combined forms of two smaller sentences or they're reduced forms from longer, single sentences.** In fact, we can come up with at least three reconstructed versions for most of these DOC sentences. In just a moment we'll give you examples of what we mean.

First off, let's take another look at the sentences that contain the -*ing* DOC. Here's the same pattern that we've seen with the other DOCs:

subject	+	verb	+	direct object	+	-ing verb phrase
I		overheard		Northrop		dictating a memo.
We		'll hear		grown men and women		wailing.
We		'll see		them		pulling their hair out.

Now let's see if you can reconstruct one pair of shorter sentences and one or two versions of longer, single sentences for each of the following "finished products." Here's an example to show you what to do:

> I saw some geese flying south for the winter. =
> I saw some geese. They were flying south for the winter.
> I saw some geese that were flying south for the winter.
> I saw some geese as they were flying south for the winter.

Now you try it:

1. I overheard Northrop dictating a memo. =

_____

_____

_____

2. We'll hear grown men and women wailing. =

_____

_____

_____

3. We'll see them pulling their hair out. =

_____

_____

Let's compare your versions to ours. We can reconstruct **Sentence 1** in the following ways:

> **a. I overheard Northrop. He <u>was dictating</u> a memo.**
> **b. I overheard Northrop, who <u>was dictating</u> a memo.**
> **c. I overheard Northrop while/as/when he <u>was dictating</u> a memo.**

For **Sentence 2** we've come up with these other versions:

a. We'll hear grown men and women. They<u>'ll be wailing</u>.
b. We'll hear grown men and women who<u>'ll be wailing</u>.
c. We'll hear grown men and women while/as/when they<u>'re wailing</u>.

And finally, for **Sentence 3** we have these alternatives:

a. We'll see them. They<u>'ll be pulling</u> their hair out.
b. We'll see them while/as/when they<u>'re pulling</u> their hair out.

So what do we get from having done all of this reconstruction work? We can now clearly see what verb form the *-ing* verb phrase DOC represents. What does it stand for?

You can see that we keep finding the **progressive form of the verb** in these reconstructed sentences with the *-ing* verb phrase DOC. This can be the past progressive ("He <u>was</u> dicta<u>ting</u> a memo.") or future progressive ("They<u>'ll be</u> pull<u>ing</u> their hair out.") depending on the time frame and context of the sentence. There are also times when we use the *-ing* DOC to **emphasize an action that went, goes, or will go on and on** ("We'll hear them <u>complaining</u> about the Board's decision for weeks.").

Well, if we can use the past and future progressive, we certainly should be able to use the present progressive as well, and here's an example of that:

A: I can't believe you're eavesdropping on the people in the next apartment! Well . . . what do you hear?
B: I can hear him **yelling** at her about some bills or something.
A: Well, I hate it!
B: What? His yelling at her?
A: No, your eavesdropping!

How should we reconstruct the sentence "I can hear him yelling at her . . . " in two smaller sentences and then in one longer, single version?

What you come up with is probably something like these:

     a. I can hear him. He<u>'s yelling</u> at her . . .
     b. I can hear him as he<u>'s yelling</u> at her . . .

As you can see, the present progressive is what's produced the *-ing* verb phrase DOC in this case.

We're about to list other verbs that are commonly used with the *-ing* DOC, but first we'd like to mention the fact that some of these verbs require the *-ing* verb phrase DOC while others use it optionally. For example, a speaker may choose to say something like this:

I heard him play his violin last night.

or

I heard him playing his violin last night.

Unless you want to be a stickler, there's really very little difference in this instance between those two sentences. This is an important point to keep in mind. As you can see from our two examples, **those verbs that use the *–ing* verb phrase DOC may opt for the base verb phrase DOC in certain cases.** To help you out, we're going to list the following verbs in two categories, one with verbs that require the *-ing* DOC and one with verbs that use it optionally:

Verbs that Require the -ing DOC

catch:	The teacher <u>caught</u> her daydreaming again.
discover:	He <u>discovered</u> a new tributary flowing into the Amazon River.
find:	Have you <u>found</u> many flies buzzing around?
keep:	They <u>kept</u> me waiting for almost an hour!
leave:	I <u>left</u> her napping when I went to work.
perceive:	It's almost impossible to <u>perceive</u> plants growing.
smell:	I definitely <u>smell</u> something burning.
spot:	They <u>spotted</u> an owl feeding her young.
start:	She can <u>start</u> the car running by popping the clutch.
stop:	How did you ever <u>stop</u> them fighting?

Verbs with the Optional -ing DOC

feel:	I <u>felt</u> someone staring/stare at me.
get:	She <u>got</u> the car running/to run by popping the clutch.
hear:	We've <u>heard</u> him singing/sing in the shower.
notice:	I <u>noticed</u> you wearing/wear new clothes every day this week.
observe:	They <u>observed</u> the comet chunks smashing/smash into Jupiter.
overhear:	Did you <u>overhear</u> him dictating/dictate a memo?
see:	I <u>see</u> her leaving/leave home at the same time every morning.
watch:	I love to <u>watch</u> waves pounding/pound against the shore.

It's interesting to note that all of the verbs in this second category of having the optional -*ing* DOC are verbs of perception except for *get* (see *Causatives and Direct Object Companions* further on in this chapter).

An Odd Direct Object Alternative

In all of the examples just cited, we clearly see the direct objects in their proper position within the DOC pattern we revealed at the very beginning of this chapter. But as our next dialogue will show, things can change:

> A: Why did you ever get Nagib those drums for his birthday? **I can't stand him practicing** day after day after day! There's no peace in this house anymore!
>
> B: I didn't know **you couldn't stand his practicing. I rather like his beating** out those rhythms.
>
> A: You can't mean it! How **can you** possibly **like him beating** away incessantly on that blasted contraption!
>
> B: Well, if it really bothers you that much, I'll tell him to go practice outside in the backyard.
>
> A: What? And have all the neighbors complaining? Just **forget my saying** anything about it. I'll just put cotton in my ears!
>
> B: Fine. As far as I'm concerned, **I've already forgotten you saying** a word about it!

As we're sure you've noticed, we have three pairs of phrases in bold in our dialogue with the same verb appearing in each pair. But what strange occurrence do you see when you compare the components of each pair? On the following line, indicate what you think this oddity is:

Something very odd indeed has happened to the direct object in one of the phrases of each pair. What's happened is that **the direct object pronoun has been replaced by a possessive adjective, or vice versa**:

. . . stand him practicing . . .	→	. . . stand his practicing . . .
. . . like his beating . . .	→	. . . like him beating . . .
. . . forget my saying . . .	→	. . . forget you saying . . .

By the way, these changes don't just happen with direct object pronouns, but with proper nouns and all animate nouns as well:

I hate $\left\{\begin{array}{l}\text{Nagib}\\\text{Nagib's}\end{array}\right\}$ banging away on his drums.

We dislike arguing over $\left\{\begin{array}{l}\text{our son}\\\text{our son's}\end{array}\right\}$ practicing on his drums.

At face value, this bouncing back and forth between direct objects and possessive forms certainly seems like a strange change all right, but it really isn't so strange once you understand what's going on. There's a small group of verbs that give the speaker the option of using either the direct object or the possessive form before an *-ing* phrase because of a change in focus.

Let's go back to our first pair of phrases and take a closer look. Although some consider this difference a minor shift in focus, it seems that saying "I can't stand <u>him</u> practicing day after day" focuses the speaker's fury on Nagib. On the other hand, saying "I didn't know you couldn't stand <u>his</u> practicing . . ." seems to focus more on Nagib's activity rather than on Nagib himself. And there's the key to understanding why it isn't so odd to use the possessive form in place of the direct object. After all, the speaker's discussing Nagib's activity, in other words, <u>his</u> activity, that is, <u>his</u> beating the drums, and not Nagib himself.

Before we move on to another topic, we'd like to take you back for a moment to the dialogue that accompanied the section dealing with that "anticipatory it" in the direct object position with the explanatory phrase following the adjective DOC. As the proverb goes, "There's more than one way to skin a cat," and so it is at times with grammar, too. Here are the sentences we focused on in that previous section for you to look over again:

> I think <u>it</u> ludicrous to put together yet another expedition . . .
> I find <u>it</u> disappointing that you've taken such a . . . position . . .

As far as the first sentence is concerned, instead of saying "I think it ludicrous to put together . . .", which doesn't spell out just who exactly would do this "putting together," we can clarify things by saying "I think it ludicrous *for us* to put together . . ." Aha! "For us to put together . . ." shows whose activity this activity would be, so we can opt for the possessive adjective to accomplish the same thing: We can use a possessive adjective (in this case, *our*) and change the explanatory phrase into an *-ing* phrase:

> I think <u>(our) putting</u> together yet another expedition . . . ludicrous.

And as for the second sentence, we know that *you* is the subject of the explanatory phrase, so we can change that to the possessive adjective *your*, convert the explanatory phrase to an *-ing* phrase, and end up with

> I find <u>your taking</u> such a . . . position disappointing.

We can't use this alternative for the direct object in every phrase that has an *-ing* DOC, but some typical verbs other than the ones we've already shown you that will allow this switch are in this list:

adore:	She adores her son/son's playing accordion.
afford:	We can't afford Mary/Mary's taking ballet classes.
can't stand:	Yussef can't stand Nagib/Nagib's playing his drums.
despise:	Mina despises her neighbors/neighbors' partying all night.
dislike:	Yussef dislikes Nagib/Nagib's practicing on the drums.
distrust:	They distrust their nasty neighbor/neighbor's being so nice.
enjoy:	Why don't you enjoy our daughter/our daughter's singing?
hate:	Do you hate him/his fawning over you all the time?
love:	They love their mother/mother's going back to school.
mind:	Do you mind me/my sitting here?
regret:	She regretted him/his leaving so soon.
remember:	They don't remember us/our inviting them to the party.
resent:	Pauline resents you/your blaming everything on Arthur.
risk:	Michelle can't risk Grant/Grant's finding out the truth.
stop:	I've tried to stop him/his eating all those rich foods.

Have you noticed any interesting connection that most of these verbs have? It seems that the majority of them share the common theme of being verbs of "like" or "dislike." The only exceptions are *afford*, *remember*, *risk*, and *stop*.

Another Option to the
-ing Verb Phrase Direct Object Companion

Since we're on the subject of options, there's one more we'd like to mention. A quick glance at the following two sentences will show you what that option is:

I really don't mind Nagib playing his drums in the afternoon,

but I really don't like him $\left\{ \begin{array}{l} \text{playing} \\ \text{to play} \end{array} \right\}$ in the evening.

So what's the difference between these two sentences? Write your observation on the following line:

_____

We can substitute the *-ing* verb phrase DOC in this sentence with an infinitive verb phrase DOC. We have to point out, however, that this substitution can occur only when a very small group of "like"/"dislike" verbs is used, but we think them worth mentioning because they're such commonly used verbs. They include the verbs on this list:

dislike: She dislikes her son coming/to come home so late.
hate: I hate Grandpa being/to be left alone all day.
like: She likes me making/to make dinner once in a while.
love: Don't you love the rain tapping/to tap on your windows at night?
prefer: I'd prefer them arriving/to arrive a little earlier.

Base Verb Phrases

Now we'll move on to the other sentences from the dialogue on page 294 which contain base verb phrase DOCs. As we can confirm once again, the pattern that the base verb phrase DOCs appear in is identical to the pattern for all the other DOCs:

	subject	+	verb	+	direct object	+	base verb phrase
Did	you		hear		him		proclaim that . . .
	I		'll enjoy		watching them		react to Northrop's memo.
	I		love		to watch people		carry on!
	I		heard		Kirby		say that . . .

Let's examine base verb phrase DOCs by repeating the activity we did for the *-ing* verb phrase DOCs. This time, reconstruct two shorter sentences and one longer sentence that reflect the ideas in the following examples:

1. Did you hear him proclaim that Kirby had been selected? =

_____

_____

2. It should be fun to watch them react to Northrop's memo. =

_____

_____

3. I love to watch people carry on! =

_____

_____

4. I heard Kirby say your department needs some new blood. =

_____

_____

Let's get right to our reconstructions and see how closely yours resemble ours. For **Sentence 1** we've come up with these two:

a. Did you hear him? <u>Did</u> he <u>proclaim</u> that Kirby had been selected?
b. Did you hear him when/as he <u>proclaimed</u> that Kirby had been selected?

For **Sentence 2** we have these:

a. It should be fun to watch them. They <u>will react</u> to Northrop's memo.
b. It should be fun to watch them when/as they <u>react</u> to Northrop's memo.

For **Sentence 3** we've got these revisions:

a. I love to watch people. They <u>carry on</u>!
b. I love to watch people when/as they <u>carry on</u>!

And finally, for **Sentence 4** we can substitute either of these:

a. I heard Kirby. He <u>said</u> your department needs some new blood.
b. I heard Kirby when/as he <u>said</u> your department needs some new blood.

Things are more complicated with the base verb phrase DOC than they were with the *-ing* verb phrase DOC. Instead of one common quality found in the reconstructed *-ing* DOC verbs (forms of the progressive aspect), we find one surface form (the base verb) representing three underlying verb forms (past, future, and timeless) exhibiting one commonality, non-progressive aspect. We know this by looking at the time of the first verb in the sentence. Here's a diagram to show you what we mean:

```
We went to watch the birds  ┐
We'll go to watch the birds  ├  feed their young.
We go to watch the birds    ┘
```

Getting back to all of those sentences we've just looked over, we'll deal first with Sentences 1 and 4. What verb form does the base verb direct object companion represent in these two sentences?

_____

The answer is that the base verb phrase DOC can represent **the simple past**.

But now we have to deal with Sentence 2. Obviously the base verb DOC doesn't represent the simple past in that sentence, so what does it mean? If you have any hunches, write them down on this line:

_____

First of all, let's think about what our **verb phrases** are: **they will react** and **when/as they react**. Of course, our first verb phrase is the simple future, and we can interpret it in this case to mean a future prediction (see Chapter 5). The second verb phrase also signifies the simple future, but we know that when words such as *when* precede the verb (once again, see Chapter 5), we don't show the future form in the verb; nevertheless, it's still the simple future.

Before we come up with the definitive answer as to what the base verb phrase DOC represents in Sentence 2, we have to ask you this question: What big difference do you perceive between an *-ing* DOC and the base verb DOC that we find in Sentence 1 ("Did you hear him <u>proclaim</u> that Kirby had been selected?") and Sentence 4 ("I heard Kirby <u>say</u> your department needs some new blood") now that we understand what their underlying reconstructed forms are? Check the boxes for the answers you agree with:

> The *-ing* DOC represents that the speaker
>
> ☐ made it clear he witnessed the completion of the action.
>
> ☐ made it clear he witnessed an action in progress.
>
> The base verb DOC represents that the speaker
>
> ☐ made it clear he witnessed the completion of the action.
>
> ☐ made it clear he witnessed an action in progress.

The answer to our first statement is that the *-ing* DOC represents that the speaker **made it clear he witnessed an action in progress**. We can figure this out because the *-ing* DOC represents the progressive verb form, so the action was *in progress* at the moment that the speaker was referring to.

The answer to our second statement is that the **base verb DOC** represents that the speaker **made it clear he witnessed the completion of the action**. We can figure this out because the base verb DOC represents the simple past, which is always used for finished actions, so the speaker knows that the action *was finished* during the time he was referring to.

Now, getting back to Sentence 2 with the use of the future ("It should be fun to watch them *react* to Northrop's memo"), do you figure that this use of the base verb DOC means the speaker thinks he will or will not witness the completed action?

> ☐ will   ☐ will not

If you've checked off that the speaker thinks he **will** witness the completed action, you're doing just great! There's nothing inherent in the simple future that represents an unfinished or continuing action; on the contrary, it normally means that the action will be a thing done. So, even though the reconstructed forms of the DOC verb for Sentence 2 look quite different from those in Sentences 1 and 4, the base verb DOC really does represent the same fundamental idea of a finished action after all.

Finally, we have Sentence 3 ("I love to watch people carry on!"). What verb form do you think is represented in this case?

It's the simple present or, as we prefer to think of it, **the timeless form** (see Chapter 3). In fact, the whole statement is timeless. The speaker is simply making a general observation about what he loves to do, and time really doesn't enter into it at all.

There's one more point to make about Sentence 3 before we move on. It would be perfectly grammatical for the speaker to say "I love to watch people <u>carrying on</u>" instead of *carry on*. Both sentences are general observations, so what nuance can you find between the two? Write any thoughts you have on the line that follows:

If you recall our discussion about the *-ing* DOC representing an ongoing action, the difference between using the *-ing* DOC and the base verb DOC in this sentence is that **the *-ing* DOC means** the speaker loves to **watch the process as it's happening**, whereas **the base verb DOC signifies that** the speaker loves seeing **the whole action happen from start to finish**.

Here is a list of the other verbs that are commonly used in conjunction with the base verb phrase:

feel: I felt something bite me.
notice: She noticed him take something out of her purse.
observe: We observed the eagle catch its prey in one swoop.
overhear: The manager overheard us complain about the food.
spot: Did you ever spot a little bitty toad catch a big, fat horse fly?

Before we leave these revelations about the *-ing* and the base verb phrase direct object companions, let's have a little fun with the two following pairs of sentences. In the first pair, one of the sentences is grammatical, but the other one isn't. You decide which is which.

1. I saw two cars crashing.   ☐ grammatical   ☐ ungrammatical
2. I saw two cars crash.   ☐ grammatical   ☐ ungrammatical

Now let's see if you can defend why you believe each sentence to be grammatical or ungrammatical. Write down your thoughts on these lines:

\
_____

\
_____

\
\

Because it means that the speaker didn't witness the end of the action since the -*ing* DOC represents the progressive verb form, **Sentence 1** is **ungrammatical**. The problem with the sentence is that when two cars crash, the action is so short, it's highly unlikely—if not impossible—that the speaker didn't witness the event from beginning to end. That's why **Sentence 2** is **grammatical** because it uses the base verb DOC to represent the simple past to show that the speaker witnessed the completed action.

Now let's just have a little more fun by doing the same thing with this second pair of sentences, except in this case, decide which sentence means that the DOC action happened repeatedly and which sentence means that it happened only once:

    1. I heard her sneezing.   ☐ once   ☐ repeatedly

    2. I heard her sneeze.   ☐ once   ☐ repeatedly

Can you defend why you believe she sneezed only once or repeatedly in each sentence? Write down your thoughts on these lines:

\
_____

\
_____

\
\

It turns out that she sneezed **repeatedly** in **Sentence 1**, but she sneezed only **once** in **Sentence 2**, and the reasons are as follows:

In the first sentence, we have the -*ing* DOC, which represents an action *in progress*. Since an individual sneeze is of such short duration, it stands to reason that we're dealing with a series of sneezes in order for it to be in progress, not just one; therefore, the action happened repeatedly.

In the second sentence, we have the base verb DOC, which represents a *completed action*. Since we're talking about a sneeze—and it's very possible to sneeze just one time—we tend to think that she only sneezed once. Amazing how a little grammar can change things!

We don't want to beat a dead horse, but there's just one more group of sentences we'd like you to consider, so take a look at these and check off the corresponding box you agree with for each:

1. They saw a man standing in a field.
    ☐ plausible   ☐ implausible

2. They saw one lone tree standing in a field.
    ☐ plausible   ☐ implausible

3. They saw a man stand in a field.
    ☐ plausible   ☐ implausible

4. They saw one lone tree stand in a field.
    ☐ plausible   ☐ implausible

Isn't it interesting! **Sentences 1, 2, and 3** are **plausible**, but **4** is **implausible**. Why do you think that is? Here's your chance to solve yet another minor mystery of the language:

_____

_____

The reason that Sentence 4 is implausible while the other three are plausible goes along with everything we've said about the *-ing* and the base verb phrase DOCs. **Sentence 1 means that they saw a man who was already standing**, or upright, in a field, and **the same holds true in Sentence 2 for that one lone tree. Sentence 3**, on the other hand, **means that they saw a man stand**, or stand up, in a field because the base verb DOC means they witnessed a completed action—and there's the catch. **We've never** (and we're sure you've never) **seen a tree do this sort of action**. That's why **Sentence 4 is implausible**.

It's important to remember, however, that the interpretations we've just made only hold up because we've been having fun with actions of very short duration or actions that can only apply to animate direct objects, not trees. As we mentioned previously, there are other occasions when the speaker has a perfectly grammatical choice of using the *-ing* or base verb phrase DOC almost at random without any major change in meaning or grammaticality. As you'll recall, the examples we cited on page 297 were "I heard him <u>playing</u> his violin last night" and "I heard him <u>play</u> his violin last night."

Past Participle Phrases

At long last, here we are at the sixth and final type of direct object companion we need to investigate. One interesting point to mention from the outset is that we can find pre-existing as well as resulting conditions with past participle phrase DOCs just as we did with nouns and adjectives.

So without further comment, let's see how they appear in context:

> A: I'm so excited I could burst!
>
> B: Why? What's happening?
>
> A: It's my wife. I'm going to see her **honored** as Teacher of the Year!
>
> B: I didn't know she'd even been nominated.
>
> A: Let me tell you, it's been a long, difficult process, and I witnessed practically everything. I saw her **interviewed** and **re-interviewed**, I saw her **tested** and **re-tested** on her subject area, and I saw her background **checked** and **re-checked**.
>
> B: But I'm sure it was all worth it. Congratulate her for me!

Before we get into the thick of things, let's just quickly see how the DOC pattern works with past participles, too:

subject	+	verb	+	direct object	+	past participle phrase
I		'm going to see		her		honored . . .
I		saw		her		interviewed . . .
I		saw		her		tested . . .
I		saw		her background		checked . . .

Well, it's certainly obvious that the past participle verb phrase DOC fits our pattern like a glove. And speaking of obvious, the obvious question we want to ask you is why you think these DOCs are past participles. Why should that form of the verb be used in these instances? Any idea? Write it down on the following line if you think of a reason:

The answer to our question is that the past participle is used for this type of DOC because **it represents the remnants of a phrase that contains the passive voice**. To prove our point, let's see if we can expand on the first sentence in our dialogue with the past participle DOC:

I'm going to see her <u>when she's being honored</u> as Teacher of the Year.

Now that we have a reconstruction of what the expanded sentence can look like, we see how this phrase has been reduced with only the past participle remaining. In fact, the sentence has actually been reduced twice. The first reduction is the elimination of " . . . when she's . . . ," so that we have

I'm going to see her being <u>honored</u> as Teacher of the Year.

From there we can reduce it even further by eliminating the auxiliary *be* from the passive voice construction:

I'm going to see her <u>honored</u> as Teacher of the Year.

Yet there's another way of looking at the totally expanded sentence before it's reduced. The sentence might also be, "I'm going to see her when she <u>is honored</u> as Teacher of the Year." This sentence also neatly reduces by first eliminating " . . . when she . . . " and then eliminating *is*.

Now we have the "finished product," so to speak. Of course, the part or parts that are eliminated to reduce the sentence to only the past participle phrase as a DOC can vary quite a bit. Look at the following sentences and see if you can reconstruct the parts that have been eliminated to arrive at the reduced finished products:

I saw a koala _____ cuddled in a little girl's arms.

I found the boat _____ tied up to the dock.

Among the variations that you could come up with for the first sentence are:

. . . when/as/while it was (being) . . . ; . . . that/which was (being) . . .

And for the second sentence we have:

. . . which/that had been . . . ; . . . which/that was . . .

Besides the verbs that we've used in our examples of past participle phrase DOCs, we can also include

feel:	She felt her mouth numbed by the dentist's injections.
hear:	I heard the march played by two bands.
like:	Oddly enough, Samantha likes her toast burned/burnt.
need:	The doctor needs these instruments sterilized.

> **want:** They want their bathroom remodeled.
>
> **watch:** Have you ever watched hatchlings fed by their mother?

Once again, there's a commonality shared by most of these verbs. It's the fact that they are verbs of perception.

⚕ Causatives and Direct Object Companions

It's worth making further observations about a few of the causative verbs we included in our discussions earlier in this chapter because of their interesting relationship to certain DOCs. This next dialogue will show you what we mean:

A: Hi, Krystyna! Ooh, you look disgusted.

B: I'm trying to figure out why my car stalls almost every time I stop at a red light. It's infuriating!

A: I'll give you a hand if you'd like.

B: Great! Do me a favor. Get behind the wheel and start the engine for me, okay?

A: Sure thing. But what are you trying to do?

B: Well, I first want to **get** it **started**, then **keep** it **idling** for a few minutes, and see if it stalls again.

A: Okay. Ready when you are.

B: Fine. **Start** it **going**. That's it. Good. Now **let** it **run** for awhile. I'm sure we'll **have** it **working** fine in no time at all.

You'll recall that we covered quite a lot about causative verbs back in Chapter 13. We can see another example of the forms we covered in that chapter in the first phrase in bold from this dialogue, "get it started." Now, however, we're up against something else with the remaining phrases in bold. We can see two other kinds of DOCs being used, the *-ing* verb phrase DOC, which represents an action in progress, and the base verb phrase DOC, which stands for a completed action.

The question is, why should we use the *-ing* DOC after the verbs *keep, start,* and *have,* but we use the base verb DOC after the verb *let*? (By the way, even though *let* isn't strictly a causative verb, it functions the same way in a sentence with a DOC, and that's why it's being included here.) Is there a reason for the choice of DOC, or is it just a random, arbitrary decision in the language?

We certainly know by now that we can create reconstructions of most sentences with DOCs by making either two shorter sentences or one longer one before anything is reduced, so before you try to answer our last two questions, see if you can make one reconstruction of each phrase, and do it in any way you find convenient:

1. I want to keep it *idling.* =

2. Start it *going.* =

3. Now let it *run* for awhile. =

4. We'll have it *working* fine. =

Some possible reconstructions we've come up with are as follows. See how closely yours come to ours:

> **1. I want to keep it in a state in which it's idling.**
> **2. Start it so that it's going.**
> **3. Now let it alone. It will run for awhile.**
> **4. We'll have it in a condition in which it's working fine.**

If we look at the reconstructions in this way, we can see why the choice of DOC after these causative verbs isn't random or arbitrary at all. In Sentence 1 the idea of *keep* is to maintain an action, so it makes sense that *idle* should appear in the progressive verb form to show an action in progress. Once this form has been reduced, it becomes the *-ing* DOC.

In Sentence 2 the idea of *start* similarly means that something is to begin its operation, so it makes sense once again to have *go* in the progressive form. And in Sentence 4 the same idea holds true for *have*, since the meaning is that the car *will be working* fine—again, the progressive aspect. And as before, when these forms are reduced, they become the *-ing* DOC.

But why should the base verb DOC be used after *let* in Sentence 3? The answer is that *let* means to allow something to happen, and it covers from the beginning to the end of that something. Since the whole duration of the action is implied, it makes sense to use the base verb DOC to represent the idea of a complete action. Here are the other verbs that work in this way:

> **help:**   She's helping me plan the party.
> **make:**   He made his son apologize.
> **have:**   I had them redo their work.

Before we end this chapter, let's take a closer look at one of our causatives. Even though it's going to be somewhat of a repetition from Chapter 13, we think causatives worth reviewing. As you look at our final dialogue for this chapter, notice that the causative in question, *have*, can carry three different DOCs depending on the action cited or the nature of its direct objects:

A: Did I tell you how much I like the new paint job on your house?

B: Why, thanks a lot. You just wouldn't believe the aggravation I had with the painter!

B: What happened?

A: To begin with, he didn't think it necessary to pressure-clean the sides before putting on the primer. He **had** me **pulling** my hair out over that. So I stayed home from work and **had** him **pressure-clean** the sides while I watched to make sure he'd do it.

A: You don't say!

B: Oh, yes. When I need repairs or maintenance around my house, I **have** it **done** right!

You've noticed that the *-ing* verb phrase DOC has been used with the causative *have* ("He had me <u>pulling</u> my hair out over that."). We now know that the *-ing* DOC represents the past progressive verb form in this case ("I was pulling my hair out.") to show the action caught in progress at that moment.

Next, we see that the base verb phrase DOC has been used with *have* ("I had him <u>pressure-clean</u> the sides"). As we know by now, the reason for this DOC is to communicate that the action was completed, that the speaker witnessed the action from beginning to end.

But now we have to wonder why the past participle verb phrase DOC has been used in the last sentence of the dialogue after the same causative ("I have it <u>done</u> right!"). Let's focus our attention on just the base verb and the past participle phrase DOCs. Why isn't the base verb phrase DOC being used in talking about doing a job right? What difference do you see between these two sentences in our dialogue that can account for this change in DOC?

The answer lies in our understanding of whether the direct object is **the doer, in which case we use an active voice form** (base verb or *-ing* form), **or isn't the doer, in which case we use a passive voice form** (past participle). In the sentence "I had him pressure-clean the sides," *him* means the painter, and obviously the painter was the doer:

(I had him.) <u>He</u> pressure-clean<u>ed</u> the sides.

That's why we need the base verb DOC which represents a form of the active voice. On the other hand, in the sentence "I have it done right," *it* represents the job, and the job is obviously not the doer, so we have the need for the past participle DOC to represent the reduced passive voice form:

(I have it.) It is done right.

Here is another example of have with these two kinds of DOCs:

I had the tailor <u>alter</u> my suit pants.
I had my suit pants <u>altered</u>.

 ### Direct Object Companions in a Nutshell

noun phrase:	The voters elected her Prime Minister.
adjective phrase:	He keeps his life simple.
base verb phrase:	Do they like to watch planes take off?
infinitive verb phrase:	She asked her neighbor to rake his leaves.
***-ing* verb phrase:**	I felt the horsefly biting me on the arm.
past participle phrase:	You didn't send that letter registered, did you?
prepositional phrase:	We left the house in shambles.
causative verbs:	We had the vet spay our cat. We got our cat spayed. The comedian had the audience roaring with laughter.

Teaching Tips

14.1 I've Got a Problem . . .

No tip in this book could ever be used with just one grammatical point, and this one is no exception. This one gives you a chance to recycle a second grammar point, gerunds (*-ing* nouns). Have students write down five to six things that bother them, make them crazy, nervous, sad, happy, etc. Here are some typical answers: "My daughter leaves her clothes all over her room." / "My husband never thanks me for fixing his meals." / "My children fight all the time." / "My teacher always asks me the hardest questions." Once they've written down their gripes or worries, collect and redistribute them to different students. Have the students walk around the room to find out who wrote the papers that they have. Once all the students have matched papers and authors, let them choose one or two of the most interesting statements to share with the class. Make sure that they use *make*, *drive*, and *get* in all their answers. ("Her son's leaving clothes all over his room gets Shelley very upset." / "Never being thanked for fixing her husband's meals makes Vianney sad." / "Hearing his children fight all the time drives Robin mad," etc.)

14.2 Nationalities

Before class, cut sheets of paper up into strips. Have enough strips for each student to have six or eight (whatever the number you give them, make sure they get an even number of strips). On half their strips of paper, have the students write one nationality per strip. Then tell them to write down a characteristic of each nationality they've chosen—one per strip—making sure they use an appropriate DOC (e.g., "Americans" / "The Japanese" / "The Irish" / "Russians" on four strips, and "like their drinks cold." / "cook their rice sticky." / "don't like the weather too warm. / "have borscht hot or cold" on the other four strips). When they've finished, collect all the strips, mix them up well, and redistribute them to the students. If they get one of their own, give them another. Let the students walk around the room to find out who has a match to whatever strips they have. If you want to ensure that the right nationalities get matched to their characteristics, thus eliminating mismatches when all is said and done, have students compare handwriting to verify a proper match before claiming one.

14.3 Free Help!

There are few people who would refuse to take all the free household help they could get if offered it. Divide the class into pairs or small groups and ask them to imagine that they now have this help. Their job is to prepare lists of chores for their help to do. What would they *expect/want/ask/order/get/permit/allow/compel* these people to do? Share ideas once the groups have brainstormed their lists with their classmates.

14.4 *Imagine*

Divide the class into small groups. Tell them they're going to go camping, hiking, snorkeling, wandering about a big city, etc. Have them imagine what they *might/won't see, hear, smell, watch, catch, notice, discover, observe, spot,* etc. while they're out. Have the students share their answers with their classmates after they've discussed them.

14.5 *I Can't Stand . . .*

Verbs of "liking" and "disliking" are commonly used, and when they are, a DOC is likely to be used, too. Here's a chance to release pent up frustrations and practice DOCs at the same time. All of us have pet peeves, things that we don't like. In small groups, have students write down things they can't stand. When they've produced their lists, ask them to share their pet peeves with their classmates, making sure that they use "can't stand" in all their answers. Are there any trends? Unusual answers? Discuss them.

Variation: Your students have practiced making complaints. Now repeat the activity and have them use a wide variety of "like" and "dislike" verbs (*adore, despise, enjoy, hate, like, love, regret, resent,* etc.). Make sure that they match a verb with an appropriate situation; it would be ludicrous for them to match *despise* with "see butterflies in my backyard!"

14.6 *Pantomimes*

Divide the class into groups of four to five. Ask each group to prepare a one- or two-minute pantomime. Make sure all members of each group are included in the pantomime and that there's a lot of action in it. Have one group present its pantomime while the rest of the students jot down notes about what's happening. After a pantomime is presented, have each group review their notes and create a master list of what they saw. Then lead a discussion of what actually happened. Each action that a group has correctly noted earns them a point; each action that no other group has mentioned gets them two points. Each use of a DOC or causative verb and a DOC gets three points. Tally up the scores and the "best describers" win.

14.7 *Commands and Permissions*

Before class, prepare various commands and permissions; write each on an individual slip of paper. Make sure that you create enough so that each student has a couple of slips. Here are some typical commands and permissions: "Sit on the floor." / "Hum a tune." / "Escort me to the back of the room." / "It's okay to chew gum in class." / "You can put away your books," etc. Let each student do what one of his/her slips says to do—without directly saying what's going on. Ask other students to explain what they see and make sure they use *have, let,* or *make* in their comments.

14.8 Fix It Up

Before class, think up things that need some sort of fixing: a broken air conditioner, a floor that's sticky, a skirt that's too long, a table that's scratched, etc. Based on these things, make up a list that might look like this: "Have it fixed." / "Have it mopped." / "Get it shortened." / "Get it refinished." Make copies of these sentences or write them on the board. Tell students that they need to figure out what needs fixing or doing. Have them write down their ideas. When all the groups have finished creating their own version of "a broken appliance" / "a dirty floor" / "a skirt that's too long" / "a scratched table," let the various groups share their ideas.

15

Autosegmental Features, Part 1

"His name's Castro, but he's not one of theee Castros."

In the subtitle above, you must have noticed the two extra "e's" in the word *the*. Why on earth would anyone add two extra letters like that? What are we trying to tell you?

To answer these questions, we're going to put you to work right away. Why do you think we added extra "e's" to the word *the*?

English has some amazing features, and the subtitle for this chapter has definitely targeted one of them. By adding two extra "e's," we're letting you know **we want you to pronounce the definite article** /ði/ even though the standard pronunciation before a noun beginning with a consonant sound is /ðə/ (see Chapter 2).

We could have accomplished this just by writing one extra "e" instead of two (*thee*), so why did we choose to add a third "e" (*theee*)?

We did this to let you know that even though it isn't routinely done, **we want you to stress the definite article** in the sentence. (Note that we'll be using two ways to show the main stress on words: CAPITAL LETTERS or /fə - nɛ - tɪk træn- skrɪp - šən/ with an accent mark (´) over the the stressed syllables. Also note that a colon represents an elongated vowel sound.) So the sentence has gone from

... but he's not one of /ðə/ Castros.

to

... but he's not one of /ði/ CAStros.

to

... but he's not one of /ði:/ Castros.

It's all well and good that you've figured out what we had in mind for the definite article in that sentence, but why did we go through this bother, and why did we think you would understand what we were getting at?

Before we get to the answer, we'd like to make a very serious suggestion. The best way to understand and get a feel for what we're going to be talking about in this chapter and in Chapter 18 is to say each example you come upon OUT LOUD. Trust us; saying the examples out loud to yourself will make these two chapters much more meaningful and understandable. One word of caution: We don't recommend you work on these chapters with people around!

So, why did we think you would understand our variation on stress and pronunciation for *the?* The reason is that it's become a convention to write t–h–e as *"theee"* when this word is emphasized. As all native English speakers know, these changes in t–h–e signify that the writer or speaker is discussing some well known subject. "The CAStros" could refer to any family bearing that name, whereas "THEEE Castros" refers to that internationally known family from Cuba.

Even though we've demonstrated the change in meaning by using two devices (stress and pronunciation), the same effect can really be accomplished simply by the stress falling on the definite article with no change in pronunciation. The pronunciation change is secondary in importance with stress being the primary device used to attain this extra communication. When this effect is achieved, we've come upon a feature of English that makes this language unique, the phenomenon of **autosegmental features**, also known as **suprasegmental features** or **prosody**. In short, **autosegmental features are changes in stress or intonation** (the rising or falling of the voice) **which dramatically influence the meaning of single words, phrases, or whole sentences**.

This is the first of two chapters in which we'll have some fun exploring this rarely discussed subject, which many consider quite troublesome since there don't seem to be many rules to go by. Because there are so many interesting points to investigate, it will be easier to divide the information into this chapter and Chapter 18.

We'll start off investigating stress in this chapter by seeing how it affects single words, then noun phrases, and finally verb phrases, all of which can have dramatic changes in meaning depending on where the stress is placed. In Chapter 18 we'll see how whole sentences are affected by stress and intonation.

The point of this chapter and Chapter 18 isn't just to show you the mechanics and some major rules for autosegmental features, but also to let you have some fun exploring this tricky area of the language and sensitizing yourself to it.

So, without further ado, let's take a look at how single words are affected by autosegmental changes.

A͟ᵕᵒ Stress and Single Words

Let's take the plunge right into the world of autosegmental features by looking at the first dialogue for this chapter.

We're going to let you do a little exploring on your own now. In our dialogue, except for the words *contrary* and *content*, all of the words in bold are followed by a superscript[1] or a superscript[2]. (We'll get to *contrary* and *content* later.) Under the corresponding heading below, write each of these words and put the syllables that you think should be stressed in capital letters. We've done the first one to get you started.

A: How's your **rebel**[1] doing?

B: My "**rebel**"? Oh, you mean my teenage son. Well, he's still a very **contrary** person, and he still **rebels**[2] against parental authority, of course, but **contrary** to what you may think, he's no different from many others.

A: Has he **progressed**[2] at all at school?

B: Yes, as a matter of fact. He's shown a great deal of **progress**[1]. He's **produced**[2] some excellent grades lately.

A: Well, I'm really glad to hear it. Oh, look at the time! I've got to get to the supermarket before it closes. Ben, the manager of the **produce**[1] section, is saving some fresh asparagus for me.

B: Hmm. Not **content** with canned asparagus anymore? And what's this Ben's **object**[1] in being so nice to you?

A: I **object**[2] to the tone I hear you using! And there's no **content** to your implication. He's just a very nice man, I'll have you know.

Words Followed by [1]

_____REBel_____

_____

_____

_____

Words Followed by [2]

_____

_____

_____

_____

If we jump from Column 1 over to Column 2 on each line, this is what we end up with:

REBel	**reBEL**
PROgress	**proGRESSED**
PROduce	**proDUCED**
OBject	**objECT**

We hope you've arrived at the same answers that we have. But what can we make out of all of this information? Look over these pairs of words and see if you can come up with one observable pattern emerging. When you think you've hit upon something, write your conclusion on the following line:

The observation that you can make from all these words is that when the same word is used for both the noun and the verb, **the nouns have the stress on the first syllable and the verbs have the stress on the final syllable**:

REBel (n.)	re**BEL** (v.)
PROgress (n.)	pro**GRESS** (v.)
PROduce (n.)	pro**DUCE** (v.)
OBject (n.)	ob**JECT** (v.)

Not surprisingly, when such a basic stress change occurs, important phonological changes can take place with the vowels. Just look at the sound changes that happen with the four pairs of words we've spotlighted:

	Nouns	Verbs
rebel:	/rέ- bəl/	/ri - bέl/ or /rɪ - bέl/
progress:	/prá- grɛs/ or /pró- grɛs/	/prə - grɛ́s/
produce:	/pró- dus/	/prə - dús/
object:	/ab´- jɛkt/	/əb - jɛ́kt/

Who says English is easy! Let's remember that such phonological changes are very challenging for teachers to teach and students to learn.

The most we can say, at any rate, is that with words that fall into this pattern, there's a *tendency* for the stress to go to the initial syllable for nouns and to the final syllable for verbs. Keep in mind, though, that that isn't always the case. It's easy to cite examples that don't follow this observation. Words like *alarm*, *control*, and *display* have the stress on the final syllable for both the noun and verb, and words like *balance, fashion*, and *preview* have the stress on the first syllable. Here's what we mean:

> The aLARM clock is set for 5:45 a.m. (n.)
> The slightest noise aLARMS our dog. (v.)
> The movie stars attended the PREview. (n.)
> The director PREviewed the editor's work. (v.)

As far as tendencies go, another one we can mention is that many stressed long vowel sounds, such as the /i/, the /a/, and the /o/ in the nouns we've targeted, tend to "reduce" to a schwa sound, /ə/, when the stress is changed. You can see that happening with *rebel, progress, produce,* and *object.*

So far, we've investigated four of the six pairs of words from our dialogue, but we've got two more to deal with, *contrary* and *content.* Something quite different is going on in these cases. Let's repeat the phrases that these words are in. Add an accent mark over the syllable in each word that you feel should receive the stress:

> 1a. . . . he's still a very CONTRARY person . . .
> 1b. . . . but CONTRARY to what you may think . . .
> 2a. Not CONTENT with canned asparagus anymore?
> 2b. . . . there's no CONTENT to your implication.

Contrary is an adjective when the stress is on the middle syllable, but it's an adverb when the stress is on the first syllable. The adjective *conTRAry* (/kən - tré - ri/) is used exclusively to describe a person who invariably goes against what everybody else says or wants:

> I say "yes"; she says "no." I say "good"; she says "bad."
> And then she has the nerve to say that *I'm* conTRAry!

The adverb *CONtrary* (/kán - tre - ri/) simply means "opposite" or "against":

> CONtrary to popular belief, the stock market isn't all that risky.

A͞3· LEGATVM PERPLEXVM ROMANVM—
or, A Confusing Legacy from Rome

As far as the word c–o–n–t–e–n–t goes, something really unusual happens when you change the stress on it (and we'll see that the same holds true for o–b–j–e–c–t). If you say *CONtent* (/kán - tɛnt/) or the plural form, *CONtents*, you've got a noun, and you're talking about what's inside something or some important ideas (in a speech, for example). However, when you change the stress and say *conTENT* (/kən - tɛnt/), you've got an adjective, and you mean "satisfied." Not only did the part of speech change, but the meaning has changed, too!

Is it possible that we're not dealing with autosegmental features anymore, but with some other phenomenon? No, we're still in the remarkable realm of autosegmental features. Both forms of the word c–o–n–t–e–n–t come from the same Latin past participle, *contentus,* which comes from the verb *continere,* meaning "to contain," so it's not English that's caused this phenomenon, but Latin. Somewhere in the evolution of that language, the past participle, *contained,* took on an additional idiomatic use that meant "happy" or "satisfied." So in Latin, *contentus* could mean *contained, the content(s),* or *happy/satisfied.* If you want to blame anyone for this confusing development which we've inherited in English, blame the Romans, not the English!

And as we've mentioned, the same holds true for o–b–j–e–c–t. If the stress is on the first syllable, *OBject* (/áb - jĕkt/), you've got a noun which means, among other things, something perceptible by the senses or the focus of some sort of attention. If you put the stress on the final syllable, *obJECT* (/əb - jĕkt/), you've got a verb which means to *oppose* or *disapprove.* Both variations come from the Latin past participle, *objectus,* which comes from the verb *obicere,* meaning "to throw something in the way." Somehow down the centuries the past participle developed an extra idiomatic meaning which has held on in the Romance languages, and even in English.

Before moving on, here are two more of these really strange single words which, on the surface, have little obvious connection in meaning when their stress is changed:

DIgest (n.) /dáɪ - jĕst/	diGEST (v.) /daɪ - jĕst/ or /dɪ - jĕst/
MInute (n.) /mí - nɪt/	miNUTE (adj.) /maɪ - nút/ or /maɪ - nyút/

⟨⟩ More Examples of Stress Changes and Parts of Speech

Unlike what we've just discussed, for the most part, when a single word can have two different stresses, the part of speech may change, but its basic concept doesn't. A *REBel* is a person who *reBELS;* you show *PROgress* when you *proGRESS;* and *PROduce* is what a farmer has *proDUCED* on his farm.

Here's a brief list of some common single words in which the stress changes when the part of speech changes, but the basic meaning doesn't. Keep in mind, though, that some of these words, especially the verbs, do have common secondary meanings as well:

Nouns		**Verbs**	
Ally	/ǽ - laɪ/	aLLY	/ə - láɪ/
CONduct	/kán - dəkt/	conDUCT	/kən - dəkt/
CONflict	/kán - flɪkt/	conFLICT	/kən - flíkt/
CONtract	/kán - trækt/	conTRACT	/kən - trǽkt/
CONtrast	/kán - træst/	conTRAST	/kən - trǽst/

Nouns		**Verbs**	
CRItic	/krí - tɪk/	criTIQUE	/krɪ - tík/
DIScard	/dís - kard/	disCARD	/dɪs - kárd/
DIScharge	/dís - čarǰ/	disCHARGE	/dɪs - čárǰ/
IMprint	/ím - prɪnt/	imPRINT	/ɪm - prínt/
INsult	/ín - səlt/	inSULT	/ɪn - sált/
PERfume	/pə́r - fyum/	perFUME	/pər - fyúm/
PERmit	/pə́r - mɪt/	perMIT	/pər - mít/
PERvert	/pə́r - vərt/	perVERT	/pər - və́rt/
REcall	/rí - kɔl/	reCALL	/ri - kɔ́l/
REcord	/rέ - kərd/	reCORD	/ri - kɔ́rd/
RElapse	/rí - læps/	reLAPSE	/ri - lǽps/
REmake	/rí - mek/	reMAKE	/ri - mέk/
REplay	/rí - ple/	rePLAY	/ri - plέ/
REwrite	/rí - raɪt/	reWRITE	/ri - ráɪt/
UPset	/ə́p - sɛt/	upSET	/əp - sέt/

We should point out that, even though it's more common to find words which can be either nouns or verbs depending on the stress, some single words can be adjectives or verbs, again depending on the stress. Examples:

ABsent (adj.)	/ǽb - sɪnt/	abSENT (v.)	/æb - sέnt/
PERfect (adj.)	/pə́r - fɪkt/	perFECT (v.)	/pər - fέkt/

There's one other phenomenon—not common, thank goodness—which we thought we'd give you two examples of for the fun of it. Here's what we'd like you to do. First, read each of the two following adjectives out loud. Then rewrite each word on the line under it, appropriately showing where the stress should fall by capitalizing the syllable you've stressed:

compact   upset

_____   _____

After saying these two adjectives out loud, you should realize that most native speakers put the stress on the final syllable in c–o–m–p–a–c–t (although some do place the stress on the first syllable), and everyone puts the stress on the final syllable of u–p–s–e–t. In that case, you should have written "**comPACT**" or "**COMpact**" and "**upSET.**"

Now let's repeat this little exercise, but this time you'll be saying two phrases out loud instead of two single adjectives. Once again, rewrite each adjective on the line under the phrase it's in, showing where the stress should be by capitalizing the appropriate syllable:

a compact car   an upset stomach

_____   _____

Uh–oh! If you've pronounced these two phrases the way native English speakers do, you've made an interesting change in the stress. The stress should have switched to the first syllable in each adjective (there's no option now for c–o–m–p–a–c–t) so that you'd end up saying "**COMpact**" (*a* **COM**pact **CAR**) and "**UPset**" (*an* **UP**set **STO**mach). Yes, the mysteries of English just keep getting "curiouser and curiouser"!

We needn't go into lengthy linguistic explanations as to why this loss of option and shift of stress have occurred; suffice it to say that you will come upon exceptions like these two, and you can simply accept them for what they are, exceptions. It just seems that **with certain adjectives** like the two we've cited, **if they come before the nouns they describe** *(an* **UP**set **STO**mach), **the stress is placed on the first syllable, whereas if they follow verbs like** *be* **or** *get (My* **STO**mach *is up***SET**), **the stress is on the final syllable**. This odd occurrence seems to happen with a very small number of pat phrases, so don't overly concern yourself with it. And, by the way, another example is an item commonly associated with music and computers, *a* **COM**pact *DISC*!

Stress and Noun Phrases

Okay, it's time for more fun, which will get under way when you read our next dialogue. First of all, here's a note about stress as you'll find it throughout the rest of this chapter. Even though it's true that a multi-syllable word or a noun phrase containing an adjective and a noun will have what's commonly referred to as primary and secondary stress, for the purposes of the two chapters on autosegmental features, we're going to use capitalized words in bold to show both the primary and secondary stress. In reality they're so close in the spoken language as far as ELT is concerned that we need not go too deeply into the subject.

One other point you should remember is that the spoken language had existed long, long before the written language came into being. Keeping that in mind, in spite of the fact that a word can be written as one word (backbone) or two (car keys), **all of the examples we'll have comparing such forms will be written as two or three separate words with only stress playing the key role in determining meaning**. We don't want visual clues to give anything away!

Remember: **stress the words that are capitalized.** In fact, as we've already suggested, read this next dialogue aloud to make sure you hear the stress clearly:

A: Hello?

B: Hello, Yoshi. This is Dr. Killian.

A: Oh, hello, Dr. Killian. I'm glad you've called. How are you?

B: Just great. Say, Yoshi, what are you up to?

A: Oh, I'm just fooling around in the **DARK ROOM**.

B: Excuse me?

A: I'm trying to develop some photographs.

B: Oh! You're in your **DARK** room.

A: I have some great pictures here of my July 4th trip to Washington, D.C. I've got a good picture of myself eating a **HOT DOG** standing in front of the **WHITE HOUSE** and watching a parade with Revolutionary War soldiers and some **RED COATS**.

B: All I can say, Yoshi, is that if your photos really show what you've just described to me, the tabloids would pay a fortune for them!

So why does Dr. Killian make that quip? Obviously it's because Yoshi doesn't realize what he's said. The question is, do *you?* Let's see if you can figure out which is which. Match the noun phrases below with their corresponding pictures, and then write the letter of each picture on the blank line under its matching phrase:

1   2   3   4

___   ___   ___   ___

A. a DARK ROOM / B. a DARK room   C. a HOT DOG / D. a HOT dog

Here's how we match up these noun phrases with the pictures. Compare ours to yours and see how we all did:

A DARK ROOM is a room that has very little or no light in it, so **2** is **A**, but a DARK room is a room where photographs are developed, so **1** is **B**.

A HOT DOG is a live dog that feels hot, so **4** is **C**, but a HOT dog is a kind of sausage, usually eaten in a bun, so **3** is **D**.

Now let's look at two more pairs of noun phrases differentiated by the stress they receive:

1	2	3	4

E. the WHITE HOUSE / F. the WHITE house   G. a RED COAT / F. a RED coat

Let's see how you did with these:

The WHITE HOUSE is a specific house that's painted white, so **2** is **E**, but the President of the United States lives in the WHITE House, so **1** is **F**.

A RED COAT is just a coat that's dyed red, so **3** is **G**, but a RED coat was an 18th century British soldier, so **4** is **H**!

Isn't it amazing what a little change in stress can do! We already had a taste of this phenomenon where stress can change meaning at the beginning of the chapter when we came upon words like *content* and *object*, but then we were exploring single words. Here, we're working with noun phrases in the form of compound nouns (see Chapter 11) and adjectives + nouns (see Chapter 6).

If you were going to sum up how you can differentiate between an adjective + noun and a compound noun for your students, what would you tell them? Can you discern a pattern emerging from all of the examples we've had? Write down your thoughts on the following line:

_____

The pattern that we see emerging is that **if you have an adjective + noun, put the stress more or less equally on both elements (a HOT DOG), but if you have a compound noun, put the stress on the first element only (a HOT dog).**
To make this point even sharper, let's stick with the dog and see more examples of our stress pattern at work. First, we'll simply describe a dog:

a BIG DOG   a NICE DOG

an OLD DOG   a STRAY DOG

In all of the previous examples, the stress is placed just about equally on both the adjectives and the nouns. But now let's distinguish different kinds of dogs by their breeds or specially assigned tasks:

> a SHEEP dog
> a WATCH dog
> a GUARD dog
> a HOUND dog

Now the stress has changed and been placed only on the first element in each of these noun phrases. This is certainly a convenient way to distinguish adjective + noun combinations from compound nouns.

Changing meaning by changing stress is a unique feature of English, but one that rarely gets touched on in classes. There's really no reason, however, that this subject shouldn't be covered gradually, even at the beginning level. Students can be made to understand through pictures, etc., that a "HOT DOG" is not the same thing as a "HOT dog." Lengthy explanations aren't necessary; what you might want to do is model the phrases enough times, have the students parrot them accurately, and then devise some discrimination exercises to reinforce this area of autosegmental features.

There are lots of examples to contrast adjective + noun phrases with compound nouns. Let's take a look at a few more. Look at the pictures that follow. Under them is a pair of phrases, one adjective + noun and one compound noun. Match the letter of each phrase with its corresponding picture by writing the appropriate letter on the blank line under each picture:

A. the BIG TOP / B. the BIG top   C. CHEAP skates / D. CHEAP SKATES

Okay! Let's get right to it and see how well you've matched things up:

The BIG TOP can be a specific, large spinning toy, so **1** is **A**, but the BIG top is another name for the large circus tent, so **2** is **B**.

CHEAP SKATES are skates that are inexpensive or poorly made, so **3** is **D**, but CHEAP skates are stingy people, so **4** is **C**.

5	6	7	8

E. the BIG house / F. the BIG HOUSE   G. a HIGH BROW / H. a HIGH brow

And here are the match-ups for these next two pairs:

The BIG HOUSE is a large house, so **5** is **F**. The BIG house is a slang term used by gangsters et al. to mean "prison," so **6** is **E**.

A HIGH brow is someone who has superior learning or culture, so **7** is **H**, but a HIGH BROW means a large area of forehead commonly seen on someone (usually a man) with a receding hair line, so **8** is **G**.

And now for our last two pairs of noun phrases:

9	10	11	12

I. NEW YEARS / J. NEW Year's   K. a LONG hair / L. a LONG HAIR

Let's see how they match up:

NEW Year's (short for New Year's Eve or Day) is a holiday, so **9** is **J**, but NEW YEARS means future 12-month calendar cycles, for want of a better definition, so **10** is **I**.

A LONG hair is a person who's deeply involved in the arts, especially classical music, so **11** is **K**, but a LONG HAIR is a hair which happens to be long, so **12** is **L**.

One other area we should examine deals with a noun + the *-s genitive* (see Chapter 10) and its accompanying head noun. Look at these examples, and this time see if you can write simple definitions for them. By the way, we've deliberately omitted the apostrophes:

1a. a CALFS LIVer = _____

1b. CALFS liver = _____

2a. a BRIDES maid = _____

2b. a BRIDES MAID = _____

It seems that changing stress on phrases such as these will change meaning just as we've seen happen with compound nouns compared to adjectives + nouns. Here are our versions to compare to your definitions. We bet they're very close if not exactly the same:

1a. a CALFS LIVer = an internal organ of a calf
1b. CALFS liver = a food
2a. a BRIDES maid = a female friend or relative who attends the bride at a wedding
2b. a BRIDES MAID = a female servant in the employ of the bride

Write down your observation of the stress pattern you see from our examples when there's an element with the *-s genitive*:

_____

It turns out that the pattern is just the same as it is when dealing with a compound noun or adjective + noun: **if the possessive word plus its head noun form a new word, just as a compound noun does,** (calf's liver/bridesmaid), **the first element receives the stress. If we're simply dealing with a head noun and explaining who or what it belongs to** (a calf's liver/a bride's maid), **the possessive noun shares more or less equal stress with the head noun,** just as the adjective does.

Here are some more examples without apostrophes. Let's see if you can define them all now that you've got a handle on how influential stress is:

1a. the CARpenters tools = _____

1b. the CARpenters TOOLS = _____

2a. the MENS club = _____

2b. the MENS CLUB = _____

From observing where the stress falls, we know that 1a and 2a form new terms just as compound nouns do. For the same reason, we know that 1b and 2b are simply possessive nouns + head nouns. And now to our definitions with the apostrophes added:

1a. = the tools used by carpenters (carpenters' tools)
1b. = the tools owned by one or more carpenters (carpenters' or a carpenter's tools)
2a. = a club for men only (men's club)
2b. = a club which certain men are members of (the men's club)

Before we move on to explore other ways that stress influences meaning, here's a little activity for you to try out to see if you've got a good idea of the stress tendencies we've just outlined. We've given you some phrases with the stressed parts capitalized just as we've done before in this chapter. You figure out each phrase and write it out as it should "normally" appear on the first line provided. Next, fill in the parentheses that follow with the part of speech it is. And finally, write a short, simple definition. We've done the first one to get you started:

PINK eye: _____pinkeye_____ (noun) _____conjunctivitis_____

PINK EYE: _____ (   ) _____

BLACK BALL: _____ (   ) _____

BLACK ball: _____ (   ) _____

FROGS LEGS: _____ (   ) _____

FROGS legs: _____ (   ) _____

BLUE print: _____ (   ) _____

BLUE PRINT: _____ (   ) _____

And here's a pair that's more fun if you see the two parts first in phonetic transcription. Here's a tip: in one of the phrases, /do/ is an informal term for *money*.

/wín dó/: _____ (   ) _____

/wín do/: _____ (   ) _____

It can be a lot of fun to see how meaning can change depending on where stress falls. Here are the rest of our answers to the exercise you've just done:

PINK EYE:	pink eye (adj. + n.)	an eye that appears pink
BLACK BALL:	black ball (adj. + n.)	a ball that's black
BLACK ball:	blackball (v.)	ostracize
FROGS LEGS:	frogs' legs (poss. n. + head n.)	the legs of frogs
FROGS legs:	frogs' legs (poss. n. + head n.)	a food
BLUE print:	blueprint (n.)	an architect's drawn plan

BLUE PRINT:	blue print (adj. + n.)	a print that's colored blue
/wín dó/:	win dough (v. + n.)	win money
/wín do/:	window (n.)	panes of glass in a wall

And now for the *pièce de résistance!* The most fun you can have in getting sensitized to how stress can change meaning when dealing with noun phrases is to scrutinize examples like the ones you're about to see, or even better, think up some of your own. We'll supply you with the elements that each phrase contains; then we'll give you a simple definition as your clue. *You* construct the example and show the proper stress for whichever meaning you're working on by using accent marks or capitalizing the stressed parts. Have fun!

timer   old   cheap

1a. This is an inexpensive device purchased many years ago that was used to time food while it was cooking.

It's _____.

1b. This is a stingy senior citizen.

He's _____.

gun   hand   second

2a. This is a small gun that was bought used.

It's _____.

2b. This is not the first gun, it's the second gun.

It's _____.

guests   house   crazy

3a. These are psychotic people who are staying with friends.

They're _____.

3b. These are people who are visiting a mental hospital.

They're _____.

Definitely an amusing activity for more sensitization to stress! At any rate, let's get right to our answers so you can compare them to yours:

1a = a CHEAP, OLD TIMer	1b = a CHEAP old-TIMer
2a = a SECond-hand GUN	2b = a SECond HANDgun
3a = CRAzy HOUSE guests	3b = CRAzy house GUESTS

A⅗· Stress and Verb Phrases

In a way, we've already introduced this section of the chapter by giving you the following pair of phonetic transcriptions (/wín do/ and /wín dó/). Here's how both could appear in one sentence:

> At the racetrack, I stepped up to the WINdow
> and placed a bet because I love to WIN DOUGH.

Here are some more examples of the same language phenomenon at work:

> 1a. She's making the DOG RUN.
> 1b. She's making the DOG run.
>
> 2a. Have you ever seen a HORSE fly?
> 2b. Have you ever seen a HORSE FLY?

You'll notice that there are two blank lines coming up for each item that we've just given you. On the first line for each item, see if you can identify the phrases we're focusing on. Are they compound nouns or direct objects + base verb DOCs? On the second line, paraphrase what each one means:

1a. _____

_____

1b. _____

_____

2a. _____

_____

2b. _____

_____

Here's what you should have come up with:

1a. direct object + base verb DOC
She's forcing the dog to run.

1b. compound noun
She's making the dog's exercise area.

2a. compound noun
Have you ever seen this insect species?

2b. direct object + base verb DOC
Have you ever seen a horse up in the air?

We hope you think these are as much fun as we do. But fun aside, is there any sort of stress pattern that you can discern that could explain what's going on? When you've figured it out, write your thoughts on the following line:

_____

We already know that we can tell if something's a compound noun when the first element receives the main stress for the whole phrase (DOG run/HORSE fly). What's new is that this is the first time in the chapter that we're dealing with a direct object and its DOC. From our observations, we can tell that, unlike what happens with the compound nouns, **the direct object and its DOC receive more or less the same amount of stress**.

Let's try another pair. Look at the capitalized parts to get the right stress and see if you can decipher what they mean by the change you observe in the stress:

> 1. I like to watch my CAT FISH.
> 2. I like to watch my CAT fish.

1. _____

2. _____

Sentence 1, which has **a direct object and its DOC** with more or less equal stress on both elements, means that **the person likes to watch the cat as it fishes** (at a pond, for example). **Sentence 2** contains a direct object, which turns out to be **a compound noun** with stress only on the first element. The sentence means **the person likes to watch the catfish** (a species of fish) perhaps while it's slithering about up and down the side of a fish tank. A remarkable difference, to say the least!

Because sentences like the two we've just examined are so much fun, let's look at some more examples. Observe where the stress is in the following pairs of sentences and write your interpretations on the lines provided. Then we'll give you ours to compare. Note that we're giving these to you in phonetic transcription so that spacing and spelling won't tip you off!

> 3. I was /hóm sɪk/.
> 4. I was /hóm sík/.

3. _____

4. _____

> 5. She wrote /tu mɛ́ ni/ people.
> 6. She wrote /tú mɛ ni/ people.

5. _____

6. _____

       7. You've /gát mi/.
       8. You've /gát mí/.

7. _____

8. _____

And now to our interpretations. **Sentence 3** means **"I missed my family and friends, etc.,"** while **Sentence 4** means **"I was sick at home."** **Sentence 5** means **"She wrote (letters) to a large number of people,"** but **Sentence 6** means **"She wrote (letters) to more people than she had to."** Finally, **Sentence 7** means **"You've caught me"** or **"You've found me out,"** while **Sentence 8** means **"I have no idea."**

And then there's something like the next pair which also demonstrates how important stress can be in English. You decide where the stress should be put by writing in an accent mark over the stressed part or parts:

/aɪ yərn/ = a metal   versus   /aɪ yərn/ = I really want

If we want to communicate that we're talking about that common metal, the stress will be on the **first syllable**, so we have /áɪ - yərn/. But if we want to communicate that we really want something, we put almost **equal stress on the subject and verb** and get /áɪ yə́rn/.

Another interesting area for us to observe is to see how stress works with modal auxiliaries. We're going to reiterate some points from a *Troubleshooter* in Chapter 8. To start things off, though, let's look at this short dialogue:

A: Hello, Helene? This is Bossie Owambawa.

B: Hi, Bossie.

A: Listen, Helene. I **/kæn go/** with you to Nairobi this weekend.

B: Oh, that's too bad.

A: Huh? But I thought you wanted me to go with you.

B: I do. Didn't you just say you couldn't ?

A: No, I said I could!

B: Oh? I'm all confused.

Why is Helene confused? It's simple: Bossie added an extra stress that created a miscommunication. Can you explain what happened? Try to work it out on the line that follows:

_____

The basic pattern regarding stress and modal auxiliaries is that **all modals are unstressed when they accompany a verb, are affirmative, and don't carry any extra meaning** (such as emphasis):

> He may GO with us on the trip.
> She can SPEAK three languages.

When the modals are negative, however, they receive more or less equal stress with their verbs:

> He MAY not GO with us on the trip.
> She CAN'T SPEAK three languages.

And this is the reason that Helene got so confused. **Bossie stressed both the modal and its verb, so it sounded like a negative to Helene.**

With the modal *can*, we even have an important change in pronunciation between the affirmative and negative that truly affects communication:

- Unstressed can is really pronounced /kɪn/. In fact, there's practically no vowel sound at all.

- Stressed *can't*, on the other hand, has a strongly pronounced vowel, which in certain varieties of British English is /a/, /kant/, and in American English it's /æ/, /kænt/.

- In addition, the final *t* in *can't* is unreleased /t̥/. In fact, all final *t*'s have a tendency to be unreleased in American as well as other varieties of English. For all intents and purposes, the unreleased *t* makes that consonant practically inaudible. These two phenomena, the added stress, and the unreleased /t̥/ result in a modal that sounds negative simply because it's got the stress on it and the strongly pronounced vowel: /kænt̥/ in American English, or /kant̥/ in some varieties of British English.

The use of stress with *will* and *would* in verb phrases (see Chapter 8) is also very interesting. We learned in that chapter that these modals can represent an action characteristic of the person the speaker is talking about. Here's a sample of what we mean:

A: You remembered to water all the house plants before we started this vacation, didn't you?

B: Uh-oh, I forgot to.

A: Great! You **WOULD** forget to do that. It's just like you!

B: Okay, so I forgot. You don't have to be so nasty about it.

A: Do you realize how much money we spent on those plants? Now they'll probably all die.

B: You **WILL** go on about money. Money, money, money! It's the money you're concerned about, not the plants!

Notice how Person A stresses *would* in her little tirade? If the modal weren't stressed, we'd lose the meaning; in fact, the sentence wouldn't make any sense at all. This example shows you how important this stress can be. What Person A is really communicating is that she knows Person B did something typical, the kind of thing he's done many other times in the past.

Person B, though, has a chance to respond with a short tirade of his own. By stressing *will*, he says he knows how typical this kind of reaction is for his wife. Notice again that if the modal weren't stressed, the sentence would completely lose meaning.

The difference between the two modals when used this way is that **stressed *will* expresses a general observation about someone's characteristic behavior, and stressed *would* expresses the same ideas but only about something in the past**.

Sensitizing your students to the kinds of changes in communication that are brought on by this addition of stress on certain modals will go a long way to stopping any misunderstandings that can easily arise.

Teaching Tips

15.1 Jazz Chants

Use poetry to practice the stress, intonation, and rhythmic patterns of the language. *Jazz Chants* and limericks (page 126) are especially good for this practice.

15.2 Phone Messages

Because telephone answering machines and voice mail are so common today, this activity gives students a chance to practice the messages that these machines record. Before class, think up pairs of phrases that feature an autosegmental contrast (CONtrast vs. conTRAST, EXport vs. exPORT, COMpound vs. comPOUND, etc.) and write them on individual slips of paper.

The different stress patterns of certain pairs of numbers (in particular 13/30, 14/40, 15/50, 16/60, 17/70, 18/80, 19/90) also provide numerous occasions for miscommunication to occur—thirTEEN vs. THIRty as, for instance, in telephone numbers (641-1330). Include one of these troublesome numbers on each slip you've prepared. Create enough slips so that each group of students will have one.

Divide the class into pairs or groups of three. Let them brainstorm an appropriate message for an answering machine, making sure that they incorporate their autosegmental pairs into the message. In addition, students should be made aware that there are cultural conventions which, when broken, cause misunderstanding (e.g., how to say telephone numbers, dates, prices, etc.). If you have a tape recorder, let them record the messages. If not, they can say the messages aloud for their classmates. Have one of the groups "leave their message."

To test the effectiveness of the messages, have all the other students who are listening to them fill out a form like the message form that follows. To check that appropriate autosegmental forms were said and heard, have the message takers check their messages against what was said. If an error has occurred and the message leavers made it, have them repeat their message, providing correction where necessary. If the message takers made the mistake, go over the error with them.

WHILE YOU WERE OUT

TO: _____   TIME: _____

FROM: _____   DATE: _____

NUMBER: _____

MESSAGE: _____

_____

_____

_____

_____

_____

_____

TAKEN BY: _____

15.3 A Pronunciation Game

This activity★ takes quite a while to prepare, but once it's done, it's well worth the effort. Prepare a game board similar to the one here.

75		73		71
	74		72	70
62	64	66	68	
61	63	65	67	69
59	57	55	53 **F R E E**	
60	58	56	54	52
44	46	48	50	
43	45	47	49	51
41	39	38	36	
42	40	**F R E E**	37	35
27	29	31	33	
26	28	30	32	34
24 **F R E E**	22	20	18	
25	23	21	19	17
9	11	13	15	
8	10	12	14	16
6	4	2		
7	5	3	1	

For your convenience, you may copy the one here and enlarge it.

Here are the rules of this game. The objective is to be the first one to cross the finish line. Create twenty-five to thirty short phrases or sentences containing autosegmental contrasts. Write one of these phrases or sentences in various boxes throughout the game board. Note that there are seventy-five boxes on our board, so you'll end up with quite a few blank boxes. You'll then have an empty box or two followed by

★ Rinvolucri, Mario. 1985. *Grammar Games*. New York: Cambridge University Press.

a box or two containing the autosegmental contrasts you created earlier. Make "bonus boxes" for added interest (spread around three or four "FREE" boxes in the middle of the board). Your students will play the game in groups of four to six, so make as many copies of the game board as is necessary for the number of groups you have. You'll also need to have a die for each group playing and as many different buttons or coins as you have students. Note: Any coin can be used for two different players— one can be "heads" and the other "tails." These coins and buttons will serve as the "game pieces" to be moved. Give each group playing the game a board, a die, and as many coins or buttons as there are players. Have the students roll the die to see which one of them goes first. The game begins!

Each student takes a turn rolling the die and moving his/her game piece ahead that many spaces. If he/she lands on an empty space, one with no writing in it, the player just stays there and the next person rolls. If the player lands on a space with a phrase in it, he/she must recite the phrase correctly or be forced to go back three spaces. The members of the group are the referees as to what's correct and what's not, but you'll want to wander around the classroom so you can be the arbitrator if called upon. If a player lands on a space already occupied, he/she moves back to the nearest space behind. And if a player lands on the "FREE" box, he/she gets to roll a second time. The game continues until one player crosses the finish line.

There are several ways a player can cross the finish line. He/She can roll the die and go across the line because the number rolled is large enough to get across. A more challenging way is to require that a player land on Box 75 exactly. This can occur in two ways. (1) A player can cross the finish line by rolling the die and moving only when rolling a number which will land the player on Box 75 exactly. (2) The player can roll the die and move forward as many spaces as the die allows and then back as many spaces as necessary to complete the number rolled. For example, if a player is in Box 73 and rolls a "five," he/she moves forward two spaces and back three, ending up in Box 72. To stay in Box 72, the player must "win" the box according to the rules stated above. Whatever the case, you decide what rule you want your students to use for crossing the finish line before the game begins and make sure you tell them the rules.

15.4 Gossip

The pronunciation of dates is difficult not only for English language learning students, but also for English speakers who hear these students pronounce them. This very simple tip gives students the opportunity to practice this troublesome feature of the language. Tell the students to arrange themselves in a line from oldest student to youngest (or vice versa). After they've arranged themselves, have the first person in the line call out his/her birthday using proper autosegmental forms. This activity is particularly good at the beginning of the course as it gives students an opportunity to learn more about their classmates. In addition, you can learn when your students' birthdays are and celebrate them when the time comes!

16

Indirect Speech

"He said that she said that I said that . . ."

One of the reasons that language teaching has always proven to be such a stimulating—and at times vexing—discipline is the never-ending array of points of contention among grammarians. One area of English teaching that has been traditionally troublesome deals with indirect speech, that is, **communicating what you or someone else has said or thought or is going to say or think**. In many cases, indirect speech is also known as **reported speech**, but we'll only use the term "indirect speech" in this chapter.

A certain degree of controversy exists over what's considered acceptable and unacceptable in this problematic area of English grammar. In this chapter we'll be exploring the more traditional forms that are commonly taught in ELT grammar books. We'll also be dealing with the conversational forms that seem to go against the rules, but which most people now consider to be just as acceptable. In addition, we'll be exploring certain grammatical patterns that aren't traditionally placed in the unit on indirect speech in most ELT grammar books even though they're definitely part of this topic. And later in this book (Chapter 22), we'll be discussing some changes that we've observed occurring with indirect speech.

Besides being troublesome for grammarians, indirect speech creates numerous headaches for teachers and their students. If you're wondering what makes this area of English such a problem, it's because changing direct into indirect speech, or vice versa, requires quite a number of transformations, and it's the complications resulting from these transformations that create all the hassles.

There's one final note we'd like to make before starting our investigation into
how we go from

"Where can I buy a copy of this book?" he asked.

to

He asked me where he could buy a copy of that book.

Verbs like *say* and *ask*, which are commonly used in indirect speech, are referred to
as **reporting verbs,** and in Appendix 4 you'll have a chance to take a deeper look at
reporting verbs and what grammatical patterns go with them.

Ay Lexical Transformations

Let's take a look at this dialogue to discover four transformations involved in going
from direct to indirect speech:

> Hans: The lawn's a mess!
>   Jost should help me
>   rake the leaves up.
>
> Jost: What's Dad saying?
>
> Anna: **He says you should
>   help him** rake all the
>   leaves up because
>   the lawn's a mess.
>   (Minutes pass.)
>
> Hans: Well, is Jost going
>   to help me or not?
>
> Anna: Jost, are you going to help your father out?
>
> Jost: Sure, in a minute. I want to hear the end of this CD I got for my new
>   CD player. It's almost finished.
>
> Anna: Hans, **he says he wants to hear** the end of that CD he just got for his
>   new CD player. He'll be right out.

If we examine what the speakers say in this dialogue, we can find four transformations that have taken place. First, let's compare what Hans originally says to Anna and
what Anna says when she relays the message to their son, Jost. Underline any changes
that you see between the two statements:

Hans: Jost (He) should help me rake all the leaves up.

Anna: . . . you should help him rake all the leaves up . . .

The first transformation we can see is that there's been a change in the pronouns.
If you underlined **Jost (He), you, me,** and **him,** you're doing just fine. When Hans

communicated his feelings, he said "**Jost (He)** should help **me** . . . " When Anna relayed that message, however, she had to change the two pronouns when talking directly to Jost about his father: " . . . **you** should help **him** . . . " Although many teachers new to ELT find this transformation to be very elemental and logical, seasoned teachers know how confusing this sort of transformation can be for students.

It follows, then, that if the pronoun subjects are changed, the possessive adjectives like *my* and *your* and possessive pronouns like *mine* and *yours* will change, too. You'll see this change when you compare the following two phrases. Underline any change you notice:

> Jost: . . . this CD I just got for my new CD player.
> Anna: . . . that CD he just got for his new CD player.

You should have underlined **my** and **his** for this change. This is the second transformation we've noted for indirect speech.

The next transformation ties in with the first, when the subject changes. In this case we're dealing with verbs, which will change, too. In our first pair of example sentences, since the verb *help* is preceded by a modal auxiliary in the preceding phrases (*should*), there's no obvious change in the verb form between " . . . he should help . . . " and " . . . you should help." This change, our third transformation, is obvious in our next pair of phrases when " . . . I want . . . changes to . . . he wants . . . "

The fourth transformation takes place when we compare what Jost said and what Anna said. Underline any *new* difference you see between these two statements:

> Jost: . . . I want to hear the end of this CD . . .
> Anna: . . . he wants to hear the end of that CD . . .

This is a perfect time for us to discuss an interesting phenomenon of language called **deixis**, which deals with the nearness or remoteness of something to the speaker. To explain it simply, deixis has to do with our perception of what is "near" or "far" from us. At times, it can be literal, as when I say *this book* for a book that I have in my hand or *that book* for a book sitting on a table across the room. At other times, we can apply this concept of "near" and "far" to abstract things.

To continue with this point, we normally say "That's too bad" because we're talking about a situation which we can separate ourselves from and *that* refers to the situation. Moreover, *That's too bad* has become a formulaic or pat sentence which we don't have other ways to express except to substitute *That's* with *It's*.

Another interesting way deixis can be noticed is in the response "That's true." When someone has made a statement that you agree with, you say "That's true" because the other person said it, not you. In recent years, however, many people have started saying "This is true," and even though it isn't the standard response, people are probably using *this* instead of *that* to show even greater agreement with what the other person has said by bringing it *closer*.

Getting back to identifying that fourth transformation in the conversation between Jost and Anna, if you underlined **this** and **that**, you're doing great. Because Jost was listening to a CD in his portable CD player, he referred to it as *this* CD; when Anna relayed what her son was saying to Hans, she said *that* CD because she was distanced from the CD. The change of *this* to *that* is another typical, but tricky, transformation that occurs with indirect speech. Such a transformation brought on by deixis is not confined only to *this/that* and *these/those*; we also find it common with words or phrases that deal with time, but we'll get to those transformations later on.

To recap what we've already discovered about indirect speech, we can state that **changes will occur with pronouns, with possessive adjectives and possessive pronouns, with verbs, and with words that deal with relative distance such as *this/these*.**

⚡︎ A Note About *Say*

One note we'd like to make before going on has to do with the verb *say*. When Anna relays what Hans has said about Jost and what Jost has replied, she uses the simple present *(he says)* instead of the simple past *(he said)* even though both speakers were finished talking before Anna relayed their messages. What do you think accounts for this use of the simple present which might not seem the appropriate form at first glance? Write down any thoughts you have on the following line:

_____

It's so customary for native speakers to use the simple present when reporting what someone has just said that the reason for this use tends to get obscured. The answer is that it's similar to the use of the simple present called the **narrative style** (see Chapter 3). Even though it isn't truly the narrative style, Anna has chosen the simple present because she's relaying what someone has just said; in other words, she's doing so *immediately* after the other person has spoken. This immediate reporting is also evident when sportscasters use the simple present as the narrative style to bring the listeners as close as possible to the event that's happening:

He gets the ball! He kicks it past the goalie! He scores!

⚡︎ A Note About *Tell*

An interesting thing happens with the verb *tell* in one special use of indirect speech. Look over these two sentences and check the boxes for the statements you agree with:

    1. They told me that you're doing a fine job.
      ☐ The speaker has heard this once.
      ☐ The speaker has heard this more than once.

    2. They tell me that you're doing a fine job.
      ☐ The speaker has heard this once.
      ☐ The speaker has heard this more than once.

With the use of the **simple past** for the verb *tell* in **Sentence 1**, most native speakers would say that the speaker has heard this **only once**, but with the use of the **simple present** for that verb in **Sentence 2**, we have quite a different situation. In this case it can signify that what the speaker has heard has been said **more than once**, which neatly reflects that typical use of the simple present for events that happen repeatedly.

Backshifting

Let's move on now to other important transformations that are usually necessary for indirect speech. Read the following dialogue and note changes that occur from what the original statements are to what they become when reiterated. To help you out, we've copied the original sentences on the first, third, and fifth lines that follow the dialogue. You write the reiterated phrases on the second, fourth, and sixth lines and underline any changes you notice:

Anna: Jost, your father's still waiting for you to help him.

Jost   I'm going to help him in just a minute.

Anna: You said you were going to help him in just a minute ten minutes ago!

Jost: Okay! This CD's almost over.

Anna: You said that CD was almost over ten minutes ago, too! Do you remember what I told you just the other day?

Jost: Of course I do. You said, "If you want your allowance, young man, you'll have to earn it."

Anna: That's right. I told you if you wanted your allowance, you'd have to earn it. So take off those headphones and go earn it!

1a. I'm going to help him in just a minute.

1b. You said you _____.

2a. This CD's almost over.

2b. You said _____.

3a. If you want your allowance, you'll have to earn it.

3b. I told you _____.

We've now entered into the area of verbs and auxiliaries. Here are the three phrases written in indirect speech:

1b. You said you <u>were</u> going to help him in just a minute . . .
2b. You said that tape <u>was</u> almost over ten minutes ago, too!
3b. I told you if you want<u>ed</u> your allowance, you'<u>d</u> have to earn it.

The new change we notice in the indirect forms of these sentences involves the tenses in the original statements:

I'm → you **were**

this CD's → that CD **was**

you **want** → you wanted / you'll → you'd

This phenomenon happens quite often. When reporting verbs are in the past, the verbs from the original statement are usually affected. Most grammarians call this **backshifting**. A general, traditional rule of thumb that we can use is that **if the reporting verb is in the past, most auxiliaries and all verbs that follow will take "one step" back into the past as well. If they're already in the past, they'll go back further into the past—to past perfect.**

Let's see if we can apply this traditional rule. What follows are phrases in indirect speech that can be put into the past. Rewrite the phrases in the past on the lines we've provided. We've done the first one for you as an example:

1. He says he is   He said he was
2. She admits she was   _____
3. I swear I'm going to   _____
4. We promise we will   _____
5. He denies he's been   _____
6. You claim you can   _____
7. They think they may   _____
8. He says he shall   _____
9. We admit we have to   _____
10. I tell you I must.   _____

Here are the phrases as they appear with the traditional transformations when the reporting verbs are in the past:

2. She admitted she**'d been**
3. I swore I **was** going to
4. We promised we **would**
5. He denied he**'d been**
6. You claimed you **could**

7. They thought they **might**
8. He said he **should**
9. We admitted we **had to**
10. I told you I **had to**.

There are two observations we should make at this point. The first one is that Number 2 and Number 5 have become the same; both now have the verb in the past perfect. **When the simple past (was) moves "a step back" into the past, it goes into the past perfect; when the present perfect (has been) moves into the past, it also goes into the past perfect.** The second observation we can make is that *must* **has become** *had to* for this past transformation, but only when it means "necessity."

At this point, let's take a look at some more phrases we'll change from the present to the past. See what you can do with these:

1. He admits he could   <u>He admitted he could</u>

2. He admits he could have   _____

3. She says she would   _____

4. She says she would have   _____

5. I swear I should   _____

6. I swear I should have   _____

7. We think we ought to   _____

8. We think we ought to have   _____

9. They claim they might   _____

10. They claim they might have   _____

11. I tell you you'd better   _____

12. I'm sure it must be old.   _____

We're sure you've noted that the only change you can make in each phrase is with the reporting verb by putting it into the past (***admitted, said, swore***, etc.). So, one last observation about these auxiliaries and backshifting is that **they don't change when**

they're put into indirect speech. The reason is that they're past forms historically, so no changes are needed.

So that you'll have a clear picture of how the traditional rules for backshifting work, here's a chart that shows just what happens when a direct statement is converted into indirect speech:

TENSE TRANSFORMATIONS			
Direct Speech	→	Indirect Speech	Examples
simple present	→	simple past	"I **live** here." → She said she **lived** there.
present progressive	→	past progressive	"I**'m** feeling fine." → He said he **was** feeling fine.
present perfect	→	past perfect	"We**'ve** been busy." → They said they**'d** been busy.
present perfect progressive	→	past perfect progressive	"She**'s** been working late." → I told you she**'d** been working late.
simple past	→	past perfect	"I **tried** to call you." → He said he**'d** tried to call me.
past progressive	→	past perfect progressive	"He **was** working too hard." → I told you he**'d been** working too hard.
past perfect	→	no transformation	"We hadn't thought of that." → I admitted we hadn't thought of that.
past perfect progressive	→	no transformation	"He'd been telling the truth." → I told you he'd been telling the truth.

And what about the auxiliaries? They, too, have formal rules to change them from direct to indirect speech. Here are two charts that show you those transformations. The first one deals with modal auxiliaries and the expression *had better* when they represent present or future time:

PRESENT/FUTURE AUXILIARIES			
Direct Speech	→	Indirect Speech	Examples
will	→	would	"I **will** ('**ll**) do it." → He said he **would** (he'**d**) do it.

(Present/Future Auxiliary chart continued on the next page)

PRESENT/FUTURE AUXILIARIES, *continued*		
Direct Speech → **Indirect Speech**		**Examples**
would	→ no change	"I **wouldn't** do it." → You said you **wouldn't** do it.
can	→ could	"I **can** do it." → She said she **could** do it.
could	→ no change	"We **couldn't** do it." → They said they **couldn't** do it.
may	→ might	"I **may** do it." → I said I **might** do it.
might	→ no change	"I **might** not do it." → He said he **might** not do it.
should	→ no change	"I **should** do it." → He said he **should** do it.
ought to	→ no change	"I **ought to** do it." → She said she **ought to** do it.
must	→ had to	"I **must** do it." → She said she **had to** do it.
had better	→ no change	"I **had** ('d) better do it." → He said he **had** ('d) better do it.

The second chart deals with the modal perfects, which you'll recall are the modal auxiliaries in the past:

MODAL PERFECTS		
Direct Speech → **Indirect Speech**		**Examples**
would have	→ no change	"I **wouldn't have** done it." → He said he **wouldn't have** done it.
could have	→ no change	"I **could have** done it." → She thinks she **could have** done it.
may have	→ no change	"I **may have** done it." → I think I **may have** done it.
might have	→ no change	"I **might have** done it." → They think I **might have** done it.

(Modal Perfects chart continued on the next page)

MODAL PERFECTS, *continued*		
Direct Speech →	**Indirect Speech**	**Examples**
should have →	no change	"I **should have** done it." → You think I **should have** done it.
ought to have →	no change	I **ought to have** done it." → He says I **ought to have** done it.
must have →	no change	"I **must have** done it." → You told me you **must have** done it.

Now we have to pose another question: Can *is* remain unchanged in the phrase "He told me he is ... " or is it necessary to change it to "He told me he was ...?" Before answering this question, let's examine some phrases that don't adhere to the traditional transformations. Decide if they're acceptable or unacceptable and check the appropriate box:

1. He told me he is ...　　　☐ acceptable　☐ unacceptable
2. I said she's been ...　　　☐ acceptable　☐ unacceptable
3. They admitted they'll be ...　☐ acceptable　☐ unacceptable
4. She wrote she's going to ...　☐ acceptable　☐ unacceptable
5. You denied you were ...　　☐ acceptable　☐ unacceptable
6. He realized he must ...　　☐ acceptable　☐ unacceptable

Most native speakers would say that **all six phrases are acceptable**. Well, if these six are acceptable, what does that say about all those transformations we previously made, and what does it say about those two charts which list the indirect speech transformations?

Time is a relative concept; what a short span of time is for you can seem like an eternity to someone else. This holds true for what we call the **time continuum**. As we write these words on this page, it's the present for us; when you read these words, it will be our future but your present. The same can be demonstrated for the past: The time that we're working on this page is your past but our present. In short, time really is a constantly moving, relative dimension, and this fact of perception can impact heavily on how we create a sentence in indirect speech.

Let's take another look at the phrase "He said he'd been" and discuss some other forms we can come up with. "He <u>said</u> he'<u>d</u> <u>been</u>" clearly shows us two different time periods in the past, the simple past (said) and the past perfect (had been), so at the time he said this, he was referring to something at a time further in his past. "He <u>said</u> he <u>was</u>" is another possibility, though. When he made this statement, he was talking about the same period of time he was in or possibly about some general observation. Both phrases, however, do refer only to some concept of the past.

What about if the period discussed is *not* in the past even though the statement was made in the past? That's when we get an indirect sentence like "He <u>said</u> he <u>is</u>." **This use of the present shows us that the situation is still true for both the person who made the statement and for the listener or reader. It can also be used for universal truths or facts that are timeless** (see Chapter 3):

> Isaac Newton show<u>ed</u> compelling evidence that gravity <u>is</u> a real force.

True, this statement can also be kept completely in the past so that we can say "Isaac Newton show<u>ed</u> compelling evidence that gravity <u>was</u> a real force," but it's perfectly acceptable to use the simple present in the part of the sentence about gravity since this is a universal, timeless fact.

And what about the future? As we've already demonstrated to you, one person's future will eventually end up being another person's past: "She <u>said</u> she <u>would</u> be" signifies that her future falls into what we now consider the past, but "She <u>said</u> she <u>will</u> be" shows that it's just as much our future as it is hers.

The best way to make these ideas clearer is to add some extra context to our phrases, so let's see how they seem to you with that extra context:

1. Last week, Vitus <u>said</u> he<u>'d been</u> in the hospital for six months last year.
2. At the time he was hospitalized, the doctors <u>said</u> he <u>was</u> in need of surgery on both legs.
3. During our talk last week, Vitus <u>said</u> he<u>'s</u> still in physical therapy.
4. When Vitus started his physical rehabilitation program, he <u>said</u> he<u>'d be</u> a difficult client for his therapist.
5. During our conversation the other day, Vitus <u>said</u> he<u>'ll be</u> in need of a rehab program for a long time to come.

In the most rigid approach at transforming these statements into indirect speech, Number 3 becomes " ...Vitus <u>said</u> he <u>was</u> still in physical therapy" and Number 5 becomes " ...Vitus <u>said</u> he<u>'d be</u> in need of a rehab program for a long time to come." These are traditional, clear-cut transformations, and no one can seriously dispute the fact that they're perfectly grammatical. The point is, however, that a great number of native speakers feel more comfortable with Numbers 3 and 5 as they appear above—so much so that we have to accept them as viable alternatives as long as the time reference is clear and hasn't been compromised. The reason that so many people feel more comfortable with Numbers 3 and 5 brought into the present and the future respectively is that the sentences relate better to <u>our</u> time showing that we're sharing the same time continuum with Vitus.

But what about the following two sentences?

1. Cleopatra said she loves Marc Antony.   ☐ acceptable   ☐ unacceptable
2. Cleopatra admitted she always will.   ☐ acceptable   ☐ unacceptable

The answer to these two sentences is that they're both **unacceptable**, and we're sure you agree. But why is it so easy in these two cases to say firmly that they're unacceptable when we had alternatives for the sentences we covered about Vitus? Think of an answer to this question and write your thoughts on the following line:

_____

The reason these two sentences are unacceptable is that the subject of both sentences is a long-dead historical figure, and this totally eliminates any chance of something about Cleopatra being in *our* present or *our* future. Vitus, on the other hand, being someone who's still very much alive, is a person whose past can be our past, whose present can be our present, and whose future can be our future. Because of this important difference between Cleopatra and Vitus, we have more alternatives when creating indirect statements about Vitus than we do about Cleopatra.

Before leaving this topic, let's take a quick look back at the phrase "We realiz<u>e</u>d we <u>must</u>" and give it some more context just as we did to those other phrases about Vitus. After you read our expanded sentence, check off the boxes that voice your opinions:

When I told him how unhappy we were with his procrastinating, he realiz<u>e</u>d he <u>must</u> complete the stock analysis reports by the end of the month or suffer the consequences.

1. *Must* refers mainly to that situation in the past.
   agree ☐   disagree ☐   don't know ☐
2. *Must* refers to a general observation in this sentence.
   agree ☐   disagree ☐   don't know ☐
3. I tend to think that those reports are one of his ongoing duties.
   agree ☐   disagree ☐   don't know ☐

The answer to **Sentence 1** is that *must* can't refer only to the past, so the box to check is **disagree**. *Must* can, in fact, refer to a timeless idea and a general observation just as the simple present can, so the box to check for **Sentence 2** is **agree**.

As for the last statement, because *must* reflects the simple present, which can mean routine or repeated activity, we tend to feel that those stock analysis reports are an ongoing responsibility of his, so for **Sentence 3** we'd check **agree**.

We know that we can also say "He realiz<u>ed</u> he <u>had to</u>," so our sentence can read:

When I told him how unhappy we were with his procrastinating, he realiz<u>ed</u> he <u>had to</u> complete the stock analysis reports by the end of the month or suffer the consequences.

What, then, is the difference? See if you can figure out a different interpretation for this sentence and check off the boxes that follow just as you did before:

1. *Had to* refers mainly to that situation in the past.

   agree ☐   disagree ☐   don't know ☐

2. *Had to* refers to a general observation in this sentence.

   agree ☐   disagree ☐   don't know ☐

3. I tend to think that those reports are one of his ongoing duties.

   agree ☐   disagree ☐   don't know ☐

Because *had to* is in the past, we can assume that it refers mainly to that specific situation at that specific time, so we'd check **agree** for **Sentence 1**. In the strictest sense of backshifting for indirect speech, we can say it's possible that *had to* refers to a general observation, but most native speakers would tend to feel it doesn't since it *is* in the past. For that reason, we'd check **disagree** for **Sentence 2**. Finally, because *had to* is in the past, we tend to think that those reports were a one-time responsibility, or at least not an ongoing one, so we'd check **disagree** for **Sentence 3**.

The point that we want to stress is that, although there are definite rules for backshifting, they tend to be adhered to much more in formal spoken and written English than in conversational English. There are many exceptions to those rules (if you want to think of them as exceptions), and they can easily be defended depending on where the person making the indirect statement is on the time continuum in relation to the person that he/she is referring to.

⁓ Troubleshooter ⁓

It's safe to say that most—if not all—languages have forms of indirect speech. The problem for teachers, however, is that it's not customary in many languages to use indirect speech as much as we do in English. Direct reporting of what has been said is quite common in many other languages and presented to the listener almost like lines from a script. This does occur in English, too:

A: So he says, "I don't feel like going."
B: And what did you say to that?
A: Stay home and sulk if you want to!

If you find your students having trouble with all the transformations common to indirect speech (changes in pronouns, determiners, tenses, etc.), it may simply be that they're not used to this style of recounting what someone said.

⁓ Time and Space

If you remember, near the start of this chapter we touched on the phenomenon known as deixis and showed how it influenced the transformation we made from *this* to *that*. Now let's get back to some other ways that deixis affects indirect speech. Look at the following sentences written in direct speech. You'll notice that we've rewritten them into indirect speech and underlined the part of each sentence that needs to be changed. We've inserted blanks where one word or more than one word should go to complete the transitions, and we're going to leave it to you to decide what should go in those blanks. Write your answers on the lines:

1. "I've lived <u>here</u> for five years," Dot told me.

   When I visited Dot at her home the other day, she told me that she'd lived _____ for five years.

2. While I was visiting Angie, she said, "It's 4:30 <u>now</u>, so it's time for me to go to work."

   Angie told me it was 4:30 _____ and time for her to go to work.

3. At the end of our chess match last Thursday, Jules said, "I'll meet you <u>tomorrow</u> at 7:30 for a rematch."

   Jules told me he'd meet me _____ at 7:30 for a rematch.

4. "The mail wasn't delivered <u>yesterday</u>," Ian said the other day.

   The other day, Ian said that the mail hadn't been delivered _____ _____.

5. Sanjay said yesterday, "We tried that new Vietnamese restaurant <u>last night</u>."

   Yesterday Sanjay told us that he and his wife, Gita, had tried that new Vietnamese restaurant _____.

6. "If you <u>come</u> to my office, I'll have the report ready for you," David said when I asked him about it last week.

   Last week, David said if I _____ to his office, he'd have the report ready for me.

7 . "Blossom, did you <u>take</u> the desserts and coffees to table 12?"

   "Yes, I did."

   "That's odd. The customers at table 12 told me you'd forgotten to _____·_____ _____ the desserts with their coffees."

   Without any delay, let's get to the answers:

1. here/there	**5. the night before**
2. then	**the previous night**
3. the next/following day	**6. went/came**
4. the day before	**7. bring**
the previous day	

   The only answer we need to comment on is Number 1. Why can we leave *here* unchanged or change it to *there?* Can you think of two different things that *here* can refer to in the original quote which would make you decide to leave *here* alone or change it to *there?*

   _____

   When Dot said, "I've lived <u>here</u> for five years," we don't really know without more context whether she means "in this house/apartment" or if she means "in this city/ town/country." If Dot means her home, we should change *here* to *there* because we're somewhere else now. However, if she means "this city/town/country" and we're in one of those places, we can leave *here* unchanged since the reference is the same for us as it was for her at the time she made the statement.

   The seven examples you've just worked on give you a good idea of how complicated these transformations are for students. Not only do we have the seven changes we've focused on for this exercise, but we also have the typical changes with the pronouns, possessives, verbs, and auxiliaries that we've already discussed—and we're not done yet!

Infinitives

Let's look at the following dialogue to continue our exploration of indirect speech:

> **Her:** We have to make more banners for the Independence Day parade.
>
> **Me:** Okay. Do we have enough cardboard, wood, and marking pens to make them?
>
> **Her:** No, as a matter of fact, but Jeremy has all that stuff. **Stop off at his place after work and pick it all up.**
>
> **Me:** Fine.
>
> **Her:** Oh, and **could you make sure that he and all of his friends know what time we're supposed to meet at City Hall?**
>
> **Me:** Sure.
>
> **Her:** By the way, **don't forget to bring the snacks and drinks for all us hungry banner makers.**

Did you notice a difference as to who the speakers are in this dialogue? No Person A and no Person B this time! Let's pretend that one of the speakers is you and the other one is a friend of yours. You'll also notice that certain phrases have been written in bold because we're going to focus our attention on them.

Let's also pretend that you're being questioned about this conversation you had with your friend. Based on what was said during the conversation, answer the following questions that the questioner (Q) is about to put to you.

By the way, don't use *that* or *if* when you begin filling in the blanks for your second and third replies:

Q: At the start of the conversation, what did your friend tell you?

Me: She told me that _____

_____.

Q: So what did she say when she realized you didn't have the materials to make more banners?

Me: She told me _____

_____.

Q: What else?

Me: She asked me _____

_____ .

Q: Is that it?

Me: Before I left, she advised me _____

_____ .

Here's what we'd put in those blanks. Compare our completions to yours:

- She told me that **we had to make more banners for the Independence Day parade.**
- She told me **to stop off** **at Jeremy's place after work to pick up the stuff we'd need to make the signs.**
- She asked me **to make sure** **that Jeremy and all of his friends knew what time we were supposed to meet at City Hall.**
- . . . she advised me **not to forget** **the snacks and drinks.**

We're sure that your completions match ours pretty closely. The most important parts are the ones in bold, and we hope that yours match these exactly. The first one reflects the kind of transformation we've already discussed concerning the backshifting of the semi-modal *have to*, which just as easily could have been *must* in the direct speech sentence. There's a marked difference, however, in the grammar we've used for the other three completions.

In these three cases, we've used infinitive forms (*to stop off/to make sure/not to forget*) after *tell*, *ask*, and *advise*, and this infinitive use has led us into a different way of creating indirect speech. There are some reporting verbs which can cause the use of a special grammatical pattern that goes as follows:

	reporting verb	+	**indirect object**	+	**infinitive verb**
She	told		me		to stop off
She	asked		me		to make sure
She	advised		me		*not to forget

⚡ *Troubleshooter* ⚡

Notice we have an asterisk before *not to forget*. This is to call your attention to the fact that most students get confused over how to create the negative infinitive form. It's very common for students to create forms such as *to don't say*.

Make sure you point out that the negative word *not* is placed before the infinitive to produce *not to* + verb.

By the way, we'd like you to note that imperative forms quite often take on the pattern with the infinitive verb when they're transformed into indirect speech. In the last dialogue, the person you were talking to used three imperative forms:

<u>Stop</u> off at his place and <u>pick</u> it all <u>up</u>.
. . . <u>don't forget</u> to bring the snacks and drinks . . .

When we put these ideas into indirect speech, we used the infinitive verbs:

She told me <u>to stop</u> off and <u>(to) pick</u> it all <u>up</u>.
She advised me <u>not to forget</u> to bring the snacks and drinks.

Even though we've now seen that some verbs can trigger a pattern with an infinitive verb, there's another pattern that we can use after such verbs to create indirect speech statements. Can you think of an alternative way to communicate the following ideas?

1. She's convinced me to see a doctor.

   She's convinced me (that) _____.

2. They told us not to report the accident.

   They said (that) _____.

The other way that we can create indirect speech phrases after verbs like *convince, tell,* and *say* is by using the modal auxiliaries **should** or **ought to** so that we end up with the following indirect statements:

   1. She's convinced me (that) <u>I ought to/should see a doctor.</u>
   2. They said (that) <u>we shouldn't/ought not to report the accident.</u>

Before leaving this section on infinitives, we want to mention some verbs that give us a choice in the following pattern; they can be directly followed by an infinitive verb with or without sticking in an indirect object:

   She asked (me) to be excused.

The kids are begging (us) to go to the circus.
I've promised (them) to help you, haven't I?

Direct to Indirect Questions

For the last major area that we need to investigate in indirect speech, let's look at the following dialogue. As you read it, think about what new changes, additions, and transformations you can pick out, and then see if you can supply the information we ask you for after you've read the dialogue:

A: Good morning, Jason. You're late again, aren't you?

B: Good morning, Wendy—and yes, I am. You haven't seen the boss yet this morning, have you?

A: As a matter of fact, just a little while ago he asked me **if I'd seen you this morning.**

B: Oh, great! He warned me about being late again. Well, why did he ask you that?

A: I think he wanted to know **whether you had the tax files in order.**

B: Oh, no! I forgot all about them!

A: He even asked me **where you keep them**, but I didn't know.

B: Why do I get the feeling that I should start looking through the want ads in today's paper?

A: Hmm. You don't have to ask me **why you get the feeling.** I think we both know!

You'll notice that we put some key phrases in the dialogue in bold print. Here's what we'd like you to do:

> a. Reconstruct each phrase in bold print as you think it would appear exactly as the person asked it.
>
> b. List any lexical addition or deletion you find.
>
> c. List any new transformation you find in each phrase (something that we haven't discussed already).

We've done all of Number 1 for you to show you what we mean.

1. a. _____ "Have you seen . . . / "Did you see Jason this morning?"_____

b. _____ *If* has been added

c. Question word order (have [you] seen) inverted to statement word order ([I] had seen)

2. a. _____

   b. _____

   c. _____

3. a. _____

   b. _____

   c. _____

4. a. _____

   b. _____

   c. _____

If you've found this activity challenging, you'll develop a lot more compassion for your students who have to tackle all of these additions and transformations in their new language! Well, here are the answers as we see them.

2. a. "Does he have the tax files in order?"
   b. *Whether* has been added and question word *Does* has been dropped
   c. question word order has been changed into statement word order
3. a. "Where does he keep them?"
   b. question word *Does* has been dropped
   c. question word order has been changed into statement word order
4. a. "Why do I get the feeling . . . ?"
   b. question word *do* has been dropped
   c. question word order has been changed into statement word order

The first two questions (Have you seen Jason this morning? / Does he have the tax files in order?) belong to a certain type of question. Do you remember what we call it?

☐ yes/no question   ☐ *wh-* question

The next two questions (Where does he keep them? / Why do I get the feeling . . . ?) belong to another type of question. Can you identify what type of question these are?

☐ yes/no question   ☐ *wh-* question

Those **first two** belong to the category we call **yes/no questions** because the response they typically prompt begins with either *yes* or *no*. The **other two** are the type we call ***wh-* questions** because all of them (with the exception of *how*) start off with words that begin with the letters *wh-* (*who[m], what, where, when, why, which,* and *whose*). These are also known as **information questions** because they elicit information rather than a simple "yes" or "no."

What we now need to consider is what difference and what similarity exist between the way the yes/no questions are transformed into indirect speech and the way the *wh-* questions are transformed. What major difference and similarity do you see? Let's take a second look at two items from our dialogue to work this problem out:

Yes/No Question: The boss said, "Have you seen Jason today?"
                   The boss asked me if I'd seen you today.

Wh- Question: The boss said, "Where does he keep the tax files?"
                   The boss asked me where you keep the tax files.

Think about what difference and similarity you see between the indirect sentences based on these two question types and then write your observations on the following lines:

Difference: _____

_____

Similarity: _____

_____

Let's first discuss the major difference between transforming the two types of questions into indirect speech. When we deal with a yes/no question, we have to add either ***if, whether***, or ***whether or not*** before the transformed question phrase. We can even add ***whether*** before the question phrase and place ***or not*** at the end of the sentence:

"Have you seen Jason this morning?"
The boss asked me <u>if</u> I'd seen you this morning.
The boss asked me <u>whether</u> I'd seen you this morning.
The boss asked me <u>whether or not</u> I'd seen you this morning.
The boss asked me <u>whether</u> I'd seen you this morning <u>or not</u>.

And likewise:

"Does he have the tax files in order?"
The boss asked me <u>if</u> you had the tax files in order.
The boss asked me <u>whether</u> you had the tax files in order.

The boss asked me <u>whether or not</u> you had the tax files in order.
The boss asked me <u>whether</u> you had the tax files in order <u>or not</u>.

The addition of one of these choices <u>isn't</u> made when we transform *wh-* questions into indirect speech. This is because the phrases *if, whether*, and *whether or not* show us that the questioner really has no idea what the answer will be; it could just as easily be *no* as *yes*. In other words, there's a fifty-fifty chance as to what the initial reply will be and the phrases we've added reflect that situation. This doesn't hold true for *wh-* questions, which seek information of a different nature.

By the way, the most common reporting verbs that can cause the addition of *if, whether, whether or not,* or *whether . . . or not* are **ask** and **wonder**.

Now what about the transformational similarity between the two types of questions when they end up in indirect speech? What we see is that both question forms are normally changed into statement forms by dropping the auxiliary *do/does/did* when it's used to form a question or by changing the word order from a question to a statement:

Have you seen . . . ?	→	. . . I had seen . . .
Does he have . . . ?	→	. . . you had . . .
Where does he keep . . . ?	→	. . . where you keep . . .
Why do I get the feeling . . . ?	→	. . . why you get the feeling . . .

So why do we tend to make this complex change from question to statement form? It's really quite understandable: **The speaker is <u>telling</u> you what she or someone else said, not asking you, so keeping question auxiliary words or question word order would just not be appropriate.**

Exclamations

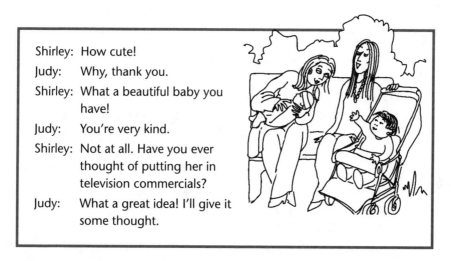

Shirley: How cute!
Judy: Why, thank you.
Shirley: What a beautiful baby you have!
Judy: You're very kind.
Shirley: Not at all. Have you ever thought of putting her in television commercials?
Judy: What a great idea! I'll give it some thought.

In this dialogue, we've got three sentences that are considered exclamations. We've repeated them below so that you can work with them. Think about how you'd explain what these two people have said by using indirect speech. Then write your versions on the lines we've provided. Notice that we've given you two lines for each direct exclamation—see if you can come up with two versions. We've started you off on Number 1:

1. How cute!

   Shirley told Judy _____

   Shirley said (that) _____

2. What a beautiful baby you have!

   _____

   _____

3. What a great idea!

   _____

   _____

Here are the versions we've come up with. Compare yours to ours, and let's see how close we all are:

   1. **Shirley told Judy how cute her baby is/was.**
      Shirley said (that) Judy's baby is/was cute.
   2. **Shirley said (that) Judy has/-'s got/had a beautiful baby.**
      Shirley told Judy what a beautiful baby she has/-'s got/had.
   3. **Judy told Shirley (that) it/that was a great idea.**
      Judy said what a great idea it/that was.

Just to make sure we've got this nailed down, how would you interpret this next exclamation in indirect speech? Again, think of two possible ways to talk about this emergency situation:

_____

_____

We can interpret this exclamation two ways: **He shouted that there was a fire. / He yelled that the place was on fire.**

 Indirect Speech in a Nutshell:

Changes occur with the following elements:

pronouns:
"I'll see you later, guys."
Fouad says (that) he'll see us later.

possessive adjectives and pronouns:
"It's my book, not yours!"
Kim says (that) it's her book, not mine.

verbs (tenses):
"He isn't coming in."
She told us (that) he wasn't coming in.

deixis:
"This child of mine is a genius!"
He says (that) that child of his is a genius.
"We'll see you here later."
They said (that) they'd see us there later.

auxiliaries:
"My company can't finish the project on schedule."
She admitted (that) her company couldn't finish the project on schedule.

time words and time phrases:
"I'll see you tomorrow evening."
He said (that) he'd see us the following evening.

the use of the infinitive verb (including imperatives):
"Please fax the contracts to St. Petersburg."
The boss told me to fax the contracts to St. Petersburg.

additions (*if/whether/whether or not/whether . . . or not*):
"Are you planning to visit her soon?"
He asked us if we were planning to visit her soon.
He asked us whether we were planning to visit her soon.
He asked us whether or not we were planning to visit her soon.
He asked us whether we were planning to visit her soon or not.

deletion of *do/does/did* in questions:
"Why does he hold down two jobs?"
She wonders why he holds down two jobs.

word order changes (from question to statement order):
"Have they handed in their reports?"
He's asking if they've handed in their reports.

exclamations:

"Quick! <u>Help</u> me, Jodi!"

He shouted to Jodi that he needed help. / He shouted for Jodi to help him.

Well, we've finally made it through all the complications of indirect speech. Before bringing this chapter to a close, though, we'd like to make one last note about reporting verbs and the grammatical patterns that follow them.

Believe it or not, there are fourteen patterns that can follow these verbs, and because this can be overwhelming, we're going to present this deeper look in Appendix 4. Use that section as a reference whenever the need arises.

Teaching Tips

16.1 Transforming Sample Sentences

The most common way to practice the changes that take place when direct speech is transformed into indirect speech is to give students sentences to "transform." Make sure you include a wide variety of verb forms, pronouns, and adverbs that necessitate changes in the sentences you give your students.

16.2 "Don't Do What I Say . . ."

Find things that are good for providing directions (recipes, road maps, road signs, obstacle courses, etc.). Ask the students to prepare directions and then have individual students give directions to you. Follow some of the directions, but *don't* follow all of them. When students call your attention to your mistakes, they should use indirect speech. For example, "No, Mamata said that you were to turn right, not left." / "Didn't Iris tell you to put in two teaspoons of sugar, not one?" etc.

16.3 Telephone

This is the traditional "Telephone Game." It requires basically no preparation and needs only quiet in the classroom. Before class, prepare a short message containing an example of direct speech. One student whispers this sentence to the student to the right using appropriate indirect speech. Let your students know that they're permitted to hear the details only *once,* and only then, through whispers. That student whispers what she "thinks" she's heard to the person next to her. *He* whispers what he thinks he's heard to the person on his right. *She* whispers the sentence . . . This continues until all the students have passed the message on. At the end of the telephone conversation chain, the final student reports out loud what's been passed on to him. Because it's rare to have the message reach the end of the class unadulterated, the person who started the conversation can tell the class what he initially said. Backtrack on the chain to find out where and how the message has gone astray.

16.4 *Giving Directions and Instructions*

Prepare several barebones instructions before class (how to repair a dripping faucet, how to steam mussels, how to get to a particular place, etc.). Give one of your students one of the instruction sheets and have her go out of the class, staying right by the door. She'll explain the instructions she has to a second student who's been chosen to stand just inside the door and relay the information his classmate has given. The classmates left inside will write down the instructions as they've been relayed. Make sure that the student relaying the instructions uses a wide variety of indirect speech. Repeat the activity several times so more than just a couple of students get a chance to explain their instructions.

16.5 *Interviews*

Have each student write a note to a classmate next to, behind, or in front of him or her. Questions and personal comments work very well ("Where do you live?" / "Who's your favorite actor?" / "You speak English very well," etc.) Let the students pass the messages to their classmates and have them respond in any appropriate manner to the questions or comments. Ask several volunteers to tell the class what messages or questions they've received. ("Paolo asked me where I lived." / "Nana asked me who my favorite actor is." / "I'm glad that Telly said that I spoke English very well," etc.) Collect the comments, check them, and return them during the next class. Read aloud any interesting ones that you've come across.

16.6 *Relating Stories*

Divide the students into groups of three: a "storyteller," a "secretary," and a "reporter." The storyteller's job is to relate an interesting experience to the secretary and the reporter. The secretary listens carefully and takes notes. When the storyteller is finished relating the experience, the secretary repeats it. Notes can be used to help remember the specifics. The reporter corrects any faulty details and adds omissions. Rotate roles twice and repeat the activity. This way, each student will be storyteller, secretary, and reporter.

16.7 *Discussing Comic Strips*

Collect a wide variety of comic strips. Divide the class into small groups. Make sure that you've got enough strips for each group of students to have a couple of them and that the strips contain a wide variety of speech patterns (statements, questions, commands, etc.). Hand out the comic strips and tell the students to recount what the characters are saying. Then write up a summary of their strips using indirect speech. Let the students share their summaries with their classmates.

16.8 What Does This Picture Say?

Select several pictures from your Picture File, ones with people or animals in them. Ask your students to tell you what's being said, asked, discussed, reported, denied, etc. by those in the pictures. This is what you might hear: "The cow told the farmer that the grass was a little dry for her taste." / "The farmer explained that the grass was dry because it hadn't rained in a long time." / "Her calf said that she preferred clover," etc.

16.9 Back-to-Back . . . What Did You Say?

Select a picture from your Picture File for every two or three students, making sure the pictures don't have too many or too few details. Separate the students into groups of two or three and ask them to sit back-to-back. Give one of the students a picture. The student who has the picture is the "art expert," the other(s), the "artist(s)." The job of the art expert is to describe the picture to the artists, who'll reconstruct the picture as faithfully as possible without being able to see it. The art expert isn't permitted to show the picture to the artists until their drawings are complete. Stress that accuracy is the goal of the drawing, not quality. Encourage the use of indirect speech as the artists ask for clarification and the experts restate their directions.

16.10 Eavesdropping

Divide the class into an even number of groups of two or three so that two groups ("talkers" and "eavesdroppers") can work together. The talkers have a conversation about anything they want; let them talk for two or three minutes. The eavesdroppers listen intently to the talkers. When all the groups of talkers have finished, rearrange the groups, making sure that you've paired different pairs of talkers and eavesdroppers. Ask the eavesdroppers to tell the members of this new group of talkers what they overheard. Switch talkers and eavesdroppers and repeat the activity a couple of times, letting each group be talkers and eavesdroppers at least once. Wander around the class to provide assistance with accurate eavesdropping.

16.11 Interpreting Letters

Divide the class into groups of two or three and ask them to write a love letter, letter of complaint, business letter, etc. to an imaginary person or company. Have them include as many details as possible in their letters. Have each group exchange its completed letter with another group of students and ask one of the members of each group to "interpret" their letter aloud . . . in indirect speech. Let the groups exchange letters several times so each member of the group has a chance to "interpret" at least one letter.

16.12 Application Forms

Bring in enough application forms for all the members of your class to have one of their own. Distribute them to your students and have them fill them out *except for the blank where their names go!* Collect the forms and redistribute them. Have the students go around the room trying to find out who completed the form they've been given. Encourage the use of indirect speech as the students circulate around the room. Don't let students show the application forms to their classmates; they need to ask questions to find out who wrote the application. For example: "Who claims to be 43 years old?" / "Who says that he lives on Beacon Street?" etc. At the end of the activity, collect all the application forms so that they can be used for *Tip 16.16*.

16.13 Who Said That?

Have students brainstorm quotes that are famous or quotes that have been made by people around them. They can even be ones linked to people they know of. Here are some examples:

> "Let them eat cake!"—Marie Antoinette
>
> "I have a dream."—Martin Luther King
>
> "Ask not what your country can do for you, but what you can do for your country."—John F. Kennedy
>
> "I came, I saw, I conquered."—Julius Caesar
>
> "I think; therefore, I am."—Descartes
>
> "That's one small step for man, one giant step for mankind."—Neil Armstrong
>
> "Workers of the world, unite!"—Karl Marx
>
> "Grandma, what big teeth you have!"—Little Red Riding Hood
>
> "Drink your milk!"—your mother

Put the quotes on the board (you or your students can do it) or write them out on small slips of paper, but don't identify who said them. Assign several quotes to small groups of students and have them write questions about the quotes: "Can you remember who said he thought, therefore, he was?" etc. Have students from the various groups ask their classmates to answer their questions and reconstruct their group's quotes.

16.14 Enrolling in a New School

Divide the class into two groups, "school principals"/"head masters" and the "parents of a potential student" at the principal's/head master's school. If your class is too large for the two halves to work together comfortably, divide the groups further into smaller groups of principals and parents. Tell the parents that you understand they're thinking about enrolling their child in this school and that they need to get information about the teachers, curriculum, students, etc. in order to decide if this is the right school for their child. How do they get this information? They need to think up questions to ask the principal. Typical questions can be: "We need to know when school begins and gets out." / "How much do books cost?" / "What immunizations does our child need?" etc.

While the parents are thinking up questions, the principals will brainstorm information that they should give to all potential parents. Principals might say: "We should tell them what class their child will be in, how much the tuition is, what field trips we're planning," etc. Give the parents ten to fifteen minutes to come up with their questions and the principals the same amount of time to come up with their information. Then pair two or three parents and two or three principals together. Have them ask and answer the questions, writing down the information they get. Be sure students use appropriate indirect speech for clarifications when needed. Bring the class back together and discuss the questions and information that they've heard. Let them decide who they think the best parents and the best principals are.

Variation: Have your students brainstorm situations in which someone needs to know something. ("What does a doctor need to know about his/her patients?" / "What should drivers know before they get a driver's license?" / "What do immigrants need to know about moving to another country?" etc.) After a number of situations have been thought up, ask students to brainstorm responses to the topics raised. Encourage the use of indirect questions and statements.

16.15 Relaying Instructions

Before class create situations in which one person relays instructions or information to another (a woman is under the sink trying to fix a leak; her husband is on the phone relaying directions from a plumber / a man is trying to change a baby's diaper (nappy); his friend is on the phone to his wife, who's giving instructions / a child is trying to figure out the rules to a game; a friend is talking to someone outside who knows how to play the game / a nurse in a hospital is interviewing someone who's brought an amnesia victim into the hospital / a witness at a trial is giving testimony; the judge can't hear, so the court stenographer repeats what the witness is saying, etc.). Make copies of the situations and distribute them to your students, who are divided into groups of three. Have them prepare role plays for the situations.

16.16 Amnesia

Use the application forms that your students previously completed (see *Tip 16.12*) and hand them out, making sure that you don't give a form to its real owner. Pair up the students; one student will be an amnesia victim, the other, someone who knows the victim. The amnesia victims ask their partners questions to help them reconstruct their pasts. The partners respond with information from the application forms that they have.

16.17 Repeating Dialogues

For those of you who are acquainted with the listening section of the TOEFL, prepare enough TOEFL-like dialogues before class so that each group of students (who are divided into groups of three) have at least one dialogue. The students will memorize their dialogues and present them to the entire class. Have students from other groups repeat the information they've heard, using indirect speech.

16.18 Making Up Stories

Before class, select four or five topics (names of various people, objects, places, times, idiomatic expressions, etc.) and write several examples of each topic on separate slips of paper. You'll want to have the same number of examples of each topic as you'll eventually have groups of students working on the activity. Make piles of all related slips. When it's time to do the activity, divide the class into groups of four or five. Give each group one slip from each of the piles you've created. Ask the students to make up a story and accompanying narration based on and including all the information on their slips. One or two students can be secretaries (or rotate the job so that all the students have a chance to write). The secretary's job is to write down the story that the group is creating. One by one, the different groups will act out their stories while a member of their group reads it. As one group is acting out its story, a second group is taking notes on it; then this group acts out its story while a third group takes notes, etc. For homework, the students write a report on one of the stories they saw from the notes they took.

16.19 Campaign Speeches

It's election time. Divide the class into groups of two or three and have them create campaign speeches for someone running for senator, minister, president, etc. Be sure the candidates make lots of campaign promises. When the speeches are complete, have the students of each group divide their speech into halves or thirds (depending on the size of the groups) and tell them that they're going to give their half or third of the speech in front of another group. Tell the students who'll be listening to the speeches that they need to take notes. After all the groups have given their speeches and notes have been reviewed and refined, have an election. In addition, tell the students to write up a news report of the speech for homework.

17

Two- and Three-Word Verbs

"Read it over, think about it, and get back to me."

Two-Word Verbs

One of the characteristic features of Germanic languages—and English is one of them—is the existence of and great dependence on what are commonly referred to as two-word verbs, phrasal verbs, or idiomatic verbs. **What is a two-word verb? It's a verb that has a very special relationship with a following preposition-like word. (We'll call it just a preposition because that's what it looks like.)** We have to tell you, though, that things won't begin and end with two-word verbs in this chapter. In the first part of the chapter we'll be exploring two-word verbs, but later on we'll be venturing into the realm of three-word verbs.

An Overview

Let's talk a little about the nature of two-word verbs. The first thing to note is that two-word verbs share all of the common features we find in one-word verbs:

They can take tense:

> She <u>listens to</u> that radio program every Friday night.
> They <u>thought of</u> an unusual name for the baby.

They can take aspect:

> I'<u>m planning on</u> throwing a party. Want to come?
> We <u>haven't looked at</u> these old photos in many years.

They can be transitive and/or intransitive:

> He <u>gave up</u> the cause.
> He <u>gave up</u>.

Without doubt, it would be almost impossible to hold down a normal-sounding conversation in English without these words that are so typical of the language. Take a look at our first dialogue and see what we mean:

(Knock! Knock! Knock!)

A: Enter.

B: Hi, Griselda! It's five o'clock, time to dress yourself in your hat and coat and remove yourself from the office. A group of us are contemplating descending to "The Blue Dragon," removing some food from the premises, returning to Maria's, then having dinner together. What do you say? Want to join us?

A: I really don't have the desire to because I'm trying to recover from this terrible cold I've had for days. Oh, and could you please extinguish that cigarette? It'll cause another one of my famous coughing spells to happen.

Odd, you say? It certainly is! Yet even though there's nothing inherently wrong with the dialogue, it just doesn't sound "natural." Let's see how this dialogue appears if said in "normal-sounding," conversational English:

(Knock*!* Knock*!* Knock*!*)

A: **Come in.**

B: Hi, Griselda! It's five o'clock, time to **put on** your hat and coat and **take off**. A group of us are **thinking about going down** to "The Blue Dragon," **picking up** some food to **take out, going back** to Maria's, and having dinner together. What do you say? Want to join us?

A: I really don't **feel like** it because I'm trying to **get over** this terrible cold I've had for days. Oh, and could you please **put out** that cigarette*?* It'll **bring on** another one of my famous coughing spells.

That's more like it, you say? It certainly is! This second version is definitely the way almost all—if not all—native speakers would carry on this conversation, except for the verb *take out* which, in some dialects of English, is *take away*.

But what's happened? Why is it possible for us to come up with two versions of the same conversation, both containing perfectly acceptable vocabulary, yet one is looked upon as being "odd" and the other is considered "normal"? This isn't something you could easily do in other languages.

The reason lies in the historical development of English vocabulary, and for more insights into that, you might want to take a course in the history of the English language if you haven't already done so. We will mention, though, that English is really comprised of two major "camps" of vocabulary, the Anglo-Saxon (Old English) and Norman French (Latin-derived although Scandinavian-influenced).

Although we are grossly oversimplifying, the key to it all is that the Norman French greatly influenced the language. Beginning in the eleventh century, Norman French was the language of the new English royalty, nobility, government officials, clerics, and academicians (when they weren't speaking Medieval Latin). Because of that, a good deal of the vocabulary which started coming into English at that time is even now associated with so-called high society or so-called intellectuals. In fact, many native English speakers even have a somewhat derisive name for a lot of the words that came into English through Norman French; they call them "two-dollar words" or "five-dollar words" or something along those lines. Because of all this, much of the vocabulary English inherited from Norman French is still the lexicon that's either preferred in print and in formal situations—or at least it sounds more formal to native speakers.

Vocabulary that's come down to us from Anglo-Saxon, which was the common language of the peasants and what had previously been the native ruling class, is still considered more "down to earth" and the language of the ordinary man and woman. This differentiation between the two vocabularies is so noticeable that, if Norman French-derived words are used in place of a great many commonly used Anglo-Saxon words in an informal conversation among friends, you can be sure that the person not using the Norman French words will take unwanted notice of the lexical choices the other speaker's making and may even make a joke about it.

Suffice it to say that two-word verbs have many difficult areas, and we've only just begun to touch on them.

"I'm Stuck on You": Necessary Partnerships

Two-word verbs only mean what they mean because of the combination of verb plus preposition. Some grammarians make a difference between a verb plus a preposition ("Look at it.") and a verb plus a particle ("Look it up."). We aren't going to make that distinction here and split hairs over it since this differentiation won't be relevant to what we're about to discuss. We'll just use the term "preposition" throughout this chapter.

A great example is the verb *look*. If you simply shout "Look!" the listeners will immediately be confused. Where are they supposed to direct their vision? In another case, if you simply say "Look, Mary . . . " it's just a way for you to stall for time as you collect your thoughts or as a way of telling Mary that you're serious about what you're about to say and she should pay attention.

⚜ *Troubleshooter* ⚜

If you have students whose native language is a member of the Romance languages, which come from Latin, you should understand that they won't have the attitude about "formal" vocabulary that native English speakers do. These students are more likely to use the words on the left (Latin) than the words on the right (Anglo-Saxon):

extinguish	put out
distribute	hand out
surrender	give in
vomit	throw up

There's nothing wrong with the words on the left except they're not the common choices in many types of everyday situations. Moreover, this problem isn't only true with two-word verbs, but with English vocabulary in general.

A rule of thumb: If there's a choice between an Anglo-Saxon derivative and a Latin derivative and meaning doesn't change between the two, students should go for the Anglo-Saxon word until they've spoken English for a long time and have learned the fine points that exist between quasi-synonymous Anglo-Saxon and Latin-derived words like the following:

☞ *Student:* I have to go to the airport to *receive* a friend.
Native Speaker: I have to go to the airport to *meet* a friend.

And yet we can still say *Her Majesty will receive the ambassador at two o'clock.* And we still have *reception* lines! Be careful of these tricky words like *recevoir/recibir/receive*, which are called "false or deceptive cognates*."

☞ *Student:* It's so hot in here, I'm incinerating!
Native Speaker: It's so hot in here, I'm burning up!

*If you teach English to Spanish speakers exclusively, you'll find the following intermediate-to-advanced supplemental student workbook very useful in helping your students avoid the pitfalls of deceptive cognates: *Men Can Get Embarrassed, Too! Confusing English Vocabulary for Spanish Speakers* by Richard Firsten, published by Alta Book Center Publishers, Burlingame, California, USA.

But what about when we say *look into* or *look over*? We now have two totally distinct verbs with totally distinct meanings. This happens to be another rough part of dealing with two-word verbs. *Look into* means *investigate* and *look over* means *check, examine,* or *observe.* In two-word verbs like those we've cited, there's such a close relationship between the two elements that, if viewed as individual elements, the meaning they create together disintegrates. But more on this point later.

🜲 *Troubleshooter* 🜲

Native speakers don't normally think of two-word verbs as separate elements; rather, they view them just like the cliché, *two peas in a pod.*

Students, on the other hand, focus their attention on the verb element and disregard the accompanying particle in most instances.

Here are two tips to make learning two-word verbs easier on your students:

☞ Emphasize the fact that they should view each two-word verb as a *single item* and learn it that way.

☞ Don't present your students with a list with one verb and a slew of particles. Don't give them a "killer" like *get* and confront them with *get around, get away, get by, get behind, get in, get over, get through, get up,* etc.

Let your students learn two-word verbs as they come up naturally in conversations, readings, or compositions.

Literal vs. Figurative Meaning

While we're on the subject of discussing what two-word verbs are and what they mean, let's discuss the fact that a combination like *look up* has two meanings. One of these meanings is literal:

A: Marie! Hey, Marie!

B: Where are you?

A: **Look up**! Up here in the tree!

B: Oh! There you are!

But then we also have a figurative, or idiomatic, meaning:

A: Where are you off to?

B: The library.

A: How come?

B: I've got to **look up** some stuff in the encyclopedia.

The problem here is that *look up* isn't a two-word verb in both of these dialogues. In our first dialogue with the literal meaning, we're really dealing with the verb *look* on its own and the directional adverb *up*. In our second dialogue, though, *look up* is a single unit with the idiomatic meaning "to gather information." **Be careful not to confuse a verb followed by an adverbial preposition and a real two-word verb!** This topic will come up again a little later, at which time we'll delve into some helpful hints on the subject about distinguishing when a verb just has an accompanying adverb or when it's really a two-word verb.

As for real two-word verbs, all of them don't have both a literal and a figurative meaning, but a great many of them do. The literal meanings stem from the literal use of the preposition, so *put <u>on</u>* can really mean "to put something on your body" *(clothing, make-up, cologne)*. This verb has its figurative meaning, too: "put (someone) on" can mean "to fool" or "play a joke on someone by telling the person something untrue."

Before we leave this area of literal and figurative meanings, we'd like to mention one special figurative use that four prepositions share when they're combined with certain verbs. Check out the two-word verbs in bold in our next dialogue. What's the one meaning you can come up with for the prepositions *down, off, out,* and *up*?

A: Oh, no! All the lights have **gone out**!

B: This is ridiculous! Ours is the only house in the dark.

A: Ouch! Darn it! I stubbed my toe on the couch.

B: Walk slowly. It's easy to get **mixed up** about where things are in the dark.

A: It's funny how, when you don't pay your electric bill, they'll **cut off** your electricity in a flash.

B: So, you didn't pay the bill on time again!

A: It's at moments like this that I feel like **burning down** their plant!

So what do you think our four prepositions mean when combined with those verbs and used in this context?

Down, off, out, and *up* all mean _____.

The basic idea that these four prepositions share in our dialogue is **completely** or **something completed**. By the way, it turns out that *up* is the one that occurs most often in two-word verbs with this use.

To show you how these four prepositions work to give their accompanying verbs this extra meaning of "completely," we have some more examples:

add up	mix up	throw off
burn out/up/off	pack up	total up
clean up/out/off	rinse off/out	tough out
curl up	sell out/off	wear out/off/down
eat up	speak up/out	work off
ice up	size up	block up/off/out
lace up	straighten up	chop up/off/down
mess up	tear down/up/off/out	cool down/off
open up	toss out/off	dust off
rev up	trim down/off	hack up/off/down
save up	wash up/off/down	knot up
slow down/up	wipe off/up/out/down	match up
single out	beat up	nail up
stock up	chew up/off	plug up
take on/up/away/over/out	cloud up	shut up/down/off/out
tie up/down/off	dry off	stir up
trade off	grow up	stitch up
warm up	knock off	sweep up/out/off
wind up/down	mark up	tidy up
air out	mop up	round up
cheer up	pay off	touch up
clog up	roll up/down	use up
drink up	sew up	weed out
fill up/out	stamp out	wrap up
jazz up	slice up/off	zip up
lock up	sum up	

. . . and the list goes on and on!

To Separate or Not to Separate—That Is the Question!

We're now coming to the trickiest part of dealing with two-word verbs, but before we begin, we should mention that we'll only be dealing with transitive two-word verbs, those that require a direct object ("Pick it up, Billy."), since intransitive two-word verbs ("Listen up, Billy.") can't have direct objects and are therefore irrelevant to this discussion.

In our next dialogue, you'll see just how confusing the way two-word verbs are used can be for English language students—and their teachers:

A: Nikos! Come here this instant!

B: What is it, Mom?

A: **Look at** your room! Just **look at** it!

B: Aw, gee, Mom.

A: It's a pig sty! How can you be my son?

B: I'll **clean up** my room. I will.

A: You'll **clean** it **up**? When? A human life span is just so long! I'm going to **call up** your father in Athens and tell him not to bring you any gifts when he comes home next weekend!

B: Oh, no, Mom! Don't **call** him **up**! Don't do that!

A: Well then, **put away** all those clothes and games and books. That's right, **put** them **away**!

B: Okay, okay!

A: You know, I was **looking for** your yellow sweater to sew on a button that had fallen off and I couldn't find it under all of this mess! I **looked for** it everywhere, but it was hidden! From now on, **listen to** your mother. **Listen to** me when I tell you to do something!

The important thing for us to observe in this dialogue is that some of the two-word verbs in bold have been kept together whenever they appear, but others are together in one spot and split apart in another. Let's make a preliminary list of those that we find kept together throughout and another list of those which have been split apart:

Always Kept Together	Sometimes Split Apart
_____	_____
_____	_____
_____	_____

Here's the list that we've come up with:

Always Kept Together	Sometimes Split Apart
look at	clean up
look for	call up
listen to	put away

When you examine these verbs, the two questions that must come to mind are, why can we separate *clean up, call up,* and *put away* but not the others, and when is it okay to separate the ones that can be separated?

When we examine the prepositions we've seen linked to the verbs *look* and *listen*, we find that they belong to a group which has restrictions on it. These prepositions are **about, across, against, ahead (of), at, by, behind, for, from, into, of, through, to, upon,** **and with(out)**. Let's call them **Group A**. With Group A prepositions, we can make any number of two-word verbs. For example:

come across	look for	look upon
deal with	look into	mean by
look at	look to	think of

Notice how we've used *look* as much as possible? We've done this simply to make a point about how important the prepositions are for the new meanings that are created when they're linked up even with the same verb. Nevertheless, as we strongly recommended in the last "Troubleshooter," they shouldn't be taught together in this way.

Getting back to the topic at hand, what can we say about the other prepositions that are linked to verbs in our dialogue? It happens that they belong to another group which includes **up/down, in/out, on/off,** and **aside/away/back/over**. Let's call them **Group B**. Just as with Group A, we can make any number of two-word verbs with Group B prepositions:

put away	put in	put out
put back	put off	put over
put down	put on	put up

There's an interesting observation we can make about these ten prepositions. Look back at them as they've been presented to you and see if you can figure out what our observation is. We'll give you a hint by saying that it's got to do with the relationship each one in a set has to the other one it's paired with. When you've got an idea, write it down on the following line:

_____

The observation we have in mind has to do with the fact that these ten prepositions are **opposites**. The first three pairs of them should be obvious, but even the grouping of those last four fall into this category as we can see when we contrast such two-word verbs as *go away/come back* and *turn over/turn back*. This fact may be very useful to your students as they try to get a handle on these verbs.

So why all of this need to know which prepositions belong to Group A and which belong to Group B? The answer lies in the fact that **all two-word verbs made with** the Group A prepositions cannot be separated, but the great majority of those that belong to Group B can be separated. That's why we saw some verbs (*look at*, *look for*, and *listen to*) always kept together in our dialogue, but others (*clean up*, *call up*, and *put away*) kept together or separated:

Inseparable Group A Prepositions:
"<u>Look at</u> your room! Just <u>look at</u> it!'"
"I was <u>looking for</u> your yellow sweater.
"I <u>looked for</u> it everywhere."
"<u>Listen to</u> your mother. <u>Listen to</u> me when I tell you
   to do something.'"

Optionally Separable Group B Prepositions:
"I'll <u>clean up</u> my room." "You'll <u>clean</u> it <u>up</u>?"
"I'm going to <u>call up</u> your father." "Don't <u>call</u> him <u>up</u>!"
"<u>Put away</u> all those clothes and toys.
   That's right, <u>put</u> them <u>away</u>!"

Focusing on these two-word verbs which have Group B prepositions, can you see when the prepositions have been separated from the verbs? First consider what's happened to the direct objects and from your observations, come up with a rule you can give your students:

With two-word verbs containing Group B prepositions, we must separate the verb from its preposition when

_____.

When we look over the separable two-word verbs that contain Group B prepositions, we see that **they've been split apart** because **when the direct object is a pronoun, it gets placed between the two elements**. That's why when Nikos' mother changed *room* to *it*, the verb *clean up* had to be split apart and *it*, the pronoun, was placed between the two elements:

And so it goes with the rest of the two-word verbs that have Group B prepositions.

But there's one more little trick that two-word verbs with Group B prepositions can do. Let's go back to those verbs from our dialogue and see if we can split them apart without transforming the direct objects into pronouns:

I'll clean up my room. ————————————————————————

I'll call up your father. ————————————————————————

Put away those clothes. ————————————————————————

We can make the same maneuver with these two-word verbs even when the direct objects aren't changed into pronouns, so we end up with sentences like these:

I'll clean <u>my room</u> up.
I'll call <u>your father</u> up.
Put <u>those clothes</u> away.

Remember that this separation with a noun phrase as direct object is optional, whereas when a pronoun is used, the separation is a *must!*

We now have all the information we need to make some general rules for two-word verbs with **Group B** prepositions:

- **We can leave the verb together with its preposition.**
- **We can choose to separate the verb from its preposition and place the direct object in between the two elements when the direct object is a noun phrase.**
- **We have to separate the two elements and place the direct object in between when it's a pronoun.**

But when we say that we can *choose* to separate the verb and Group B preposition when the direct object isn't a pronoun, how do we know when we've made the right choice? When should we leave the two elements together and when should we separate them? It would be nice to have guidelines to help us out.

Well, the only rule of thumb that we can offer you is that **when the direct object tends to be lengthy, most native speakers find it awkward to separate the verb and its Group B preposition**:

Please look over <u>those files I left on your desk</u>. (comfortable)
Please look <u>those files I left on your desk</u> over. (awkward)

Other than that, it's really up to the speaker to decide on how to handle the verb and preposition.

One final point is worth noting. For the most part, the more idiomatic a two-word verb is, the greater the likelihood there is that the two elements (the verb and the preposition) will be separated when the direct object is a pronoun. (You'll be seeing a notable exception to this observation quite soon, though.)

By idiomatic, we mean that, as separate entities, the verb and the preposition don't give us any hint as to what their meaning will be when they're used together. For example, when we examine the two elements in *give up* (meaning *to stop using* or *doing*), we have *give*, and we have *up*, but when they're separate entities, we have no notion as to what they can mean when put together.

As for this tendency of idiomatic two-word verbs to separate the verb and preposition when the pronoun is introduced, let's see how two examples work like this. We can see that the two-word verb *look at* isn't idiomatic at all; it means exactly what it says. In this case, the verb and preposition stay together and we say "<u>Look at</u> the bird's nest." / "<u>Look at</u> it." But when we have a highly idiomatic two-word verb such as "turn down" (meaning *to reject*), the verb and preposition must separate when the pronoun is used: "I <u>turned down</u> his offer." / "I <u>turned</u> it <u>down</u>."

At any rate, take our advice and don't fret over it. Did we just say "don't fret over it" instead of saying "don't fret it over"? Wait a minute! Isn't *over* in our list of Group B prepositions and isn't *it* a pronoun? Doesn't that mean we have to separate the verb from the preposition and stick the pronoun in between? What's going on now?

Verbs with Allied Prepositional Phrases

Before you start fretting over what we realized about *fret over it,* we can give you a simple explanation. The point is that *fret* is *not* a two-word verb. Actually, *fret* is a one-word verb that can have an allied prepositional phrase. As we mentioned earlier in this chapter, don't get confused between two-word verbs and one-word verbs that have allied prepositional phrases!

So how do we know the difference between a real two-word verb and a one-word verb with one of those allied phrases? Sometimes it's easy to tell the difference, but sometimes it isn't. Let's go back to *fret* for a moment to see how easy it can be to spot the difference.

In the following example, *fret* is intransitive:

> She was fretting all day.

But let's say we want to mention what she was concerned about. We can do that, but we have to use either *over* or *about* to accomplish it:

> She was fretting <u>over her upcoming job evaluation</u>.

We've now created an allied prepositional phrase.

As you can see, *over* is simply a preposition in this context that we use before the noun phrase, so we don't have to deal with the intricacies of two-word verbs. If we want to change the object of the preposition (*her upcoming job evaluation*) into the pronoun (*it*), we keep the verb and preposition in their original positions and say:

> She was fretting <u>over it</u>.

But as we've said, it isn't always easy to know whether we're dealing with a two-word verb or not, and here's a case in point. Even though ELT grammar books normally show *look at* as a two-word verb, no one's come up with the definitive proof of this one way or the other:

Is it   He | looked at | me   ?

Or is it   He looked | at me | ?

Hmm ... Not so simple, right? This is exactly how most grammarians feel about it, too! The point is that there are cases that show some sort of overlapping, and these cases are not worth troubling over since nothing has really been settled in the debate over whether or not they're two-word verbs. Therefore, because we don't think you have to bother about getting too deep into this topic, your students don't have to bother with the problem either.

Verbs with Allied Adverbial Phrases

This situation is different from what we've just discussed about prepositional phrases. Now we're going to investigate how to distinguish real two-word verbs from one-word verbs with allied **adverbial** phrases. In this case, we really can see a big difference, and we have easy guidelines to help us make the distinction.

Below are some examples of verbs with allied adverbial phrases. There are two things we'd like you to do while you read these examples. First, notice how the prepositions are inside the brackets (to highlight the fact that they're part of the adverbial phrases). Second, think about which *wh-* words you would use to create questions that have the *bracketed* parts as their answers:

The teacher called. / The teacher called | on her cell phone | .

He ran. / He ran | up the stairs | .

The report went. / The report went | into his personnel file | .

The reason we asked you to notice that the prepositions are inside the boxed-in parts of these sentences is to show you that they aren't prepositions that go with the verbs. On the contrary, their relationship to the verbs is just a momentary alliance that can be changed easily enough. Instead of saying "The teacher called <u>on</u> her portable phone," we might want to say "The teacher called <u>from</u> the top of the stairs." What we want to stress is that there is no intrinsic, locked-in relationship between the verb and the preposition that's part of an adverbial phrase.

And as far as which *wh-* words can be used to create questions for each of those bracketed parts, which ones would you come up with?

_____ and _____

The ones we'd use to create questions are **how** and **where**:

> Q: <u>How</u> did the teacher call?
> A: On her cell phone.
>
> Q: <u>Where</u> did he run?
> A: Up the stairs.
>
> Q: <u>Where</u> did the report go?
> A: Into his personnel file.

This examination of evidence leads us to a tip that can help you figure out if you're dealing with a verb that just happens to be followed by an adverbial phrase or a real two-word verb. **If *where, when, why*, or *how* can be used to ask a question about the phrase that follows the verb, the verb is <u>not</u> a two-word verb.**

Just to make sure that you get the point, here are examples for the other two *wh*-words we've cited:

> **She called <u>in time</u> to stop us from leaving without her.**
> *<u>When</u> did she call?*
>
> **He was punished <u>for telling a lie</u>.**
> *<u>Why</u> was he punished?*

So what you've just looked at is not *call in* or *punish for*. You're simply looking at *call*, which happens to be followed by the preposition *in*, and *punish*, which is followed by the preposition *for*. These are *not* two-word verbs. However, what about this gem?

> She called in in time, so we didn't leave without her.

Now we've got a double-whammy! We've got the two-word verb, *call in*, plus an adverbial phrase, *in time*. Just imagine how your students' eyes would be popping out while looking at this sentence!

But now what about real two-word verbs? We're about to give you three more examples of them. (Note that we're using the three identical "openers" that we've used previously just to show you the contrast.) We're going to ask you to do the same things you did before for those three sentences. First, note that in these examples, the prepositions are together with the verbs inside the boxes. Second, think about which one-word verbs you can use as substitutes for the boxed-in parts.

> **The teacher called. / The teacher** `called on` **a student to recite.**
>
> **He ran. / He** `ran up` **a big bill at the hotel.**
>
> **The report went. / The report** `went into` **his financial dealings.**

The boxed-in parts, our two-word verbs, should be looked at as whole units. As far as our request goes, which one-word verbs would you use as synonyms for the boxed-in parts?

_____ , _____ , and _____

The verbs are *selected/chose*, *charged*, and *investigated*. And now we have the second part of our tip for you on how to make sure you're dealing with a one-word verb with an adverbial phrase or a two-word verb: **If you can think of a one-word verb as a synonym for it, you're likely to have a two-word verb**.

Another Two-Word Verb Headache

Up to this point in the chapter, we've told you which prepositions we've labeled as Group A and which ones we've labeled as Group B, but the sad truth of the matter is that there are times when a few prepositions cross over that fine line that could distinguish them so neatly. Sometimes Group B prepositions end up taking on Group A characteristics as our next dialogue will demonstrate. That's why we didn't say earlier that *every* Group B two-word verb can be separated:

> A: I can't **get over it**.
> B: What?
> A: Tanya. She's always been so shy.
> B: What happened?
> A: She told Robert to go jump off a bridge! Can you believe it?
> B: Tanya said that? I wonder what **came over her**?

Well, there you have it, an example of a so-called Group B preposition (*over*) suddenly acting like a Group A preposition. Is there an easy explanation for it? Not really; it just happens sometimes with certain two-word verbs with idiomatic meanings in which the prepositions behave like Group A prepositions. So accept the fact that there are some two-word verbs that the students will have to learn to use in special ways that differ from the norm. Here's a little hint about all of these: Group B prepositions can become A's, but A's can never become B's!

And speaking of idiomatic meanings, here are some examples of where the meaning of the phrase changes when the position of the preposition and the object changes:

I know there's a lot of noise outside, but we can talk over it.
("talk over it" meaning "talk as loud or louder than the noise")

I know we don't agree on the issue, so let's talk it over.
("talk it over" meaning "discuss the issue")

Your investigation is going very well. <u>Keep on</u> it.
("Keep on it" meaning "continue the investigation.")

If you're feeling cold, don't take your sweater off. <u>Keep</u> it <u>on</u>.
("Keep it on" meaning "Don't remove the sweater.")

Happily, most two-word verbs don't create this kind of nightmare for English language teachers and their students, but it's important to be aware that they do exist.

A Word About the Passive Voice

Let's look at this next dialogue to see how two-word verbs and the passive voice work together:

A: Where's Pete? I haven't seen him for quite a long time.

B: Yeah, I know. He's **been laid up** for a couple of weeks with a bad back. It's really a shame.

A: His back again? Gosh, that back of his **has been looked at** by more doctors than I can count!

B: Well, now it's **been seen to** by yet another big shot doctor from the medical school.

A: I sure hope his back's **being looked after** by someone who knows what he's doing. He's just got to feel better soon. After all, his fields have got to **be plowed up** in just a few weeks to get ready for spring planting.

The main thing to remember about transitive two-word verbs that can be transformed into passive voice constructions is that **the prepositions always stay together with the verbs**.

Three-Word Verbs

As if things weren't complicated enough, we now have to consider three-word verbs! Yes, they really do exist, and this next dialogue will show you what we mean:

A: I can't **keep up with** you. You just work too fast for me.

B: Don't worry. With a little more practice, you'll **catch up to** me. Say, why don't we take a break?

A: Good idea! I'd love some coffee.

B: So, how do you like working here?

A: It's been okay. And I really appreciate the way you've never **looked down on** me just because I'm new here and don't know all the procedures yet.

B: That's okay. I think it's important to **get along with** all my co-workers if I can, experienced or not. And besides, you're **picking up on** all the procedures here very fast.

A: Gee, I hope so. Gosh! Look at the time! I've got to **look in on** my daughter in the day-care center. I'll see you later.

We hope that you can put up with this chapter for a little longer. (Oops! We've just used another three-word verb, *put up with*.) These complicated lexical items can be quite problematic for English language learners for obvious reasons.

One nice point we can mention about three-word verbs is that, except for a very few idiomatic expressions, **their direct objects always come after them whether they're nouns, noun phrases, or pronouns**, so there's no worry about separating the verbs from their prepositions. There's one catch, however, that deals with those idiomatic expressions, but we'll get to it in a moment. The first three examples in bold from our dialogue will show you what we mean about those direct objects, though:

I can't <u>keep up with</u> you.
You'll <u>catch up to</u> me.
You've never <u>looked down on</u> me.

And now, here are a few of those idiomatic exceptions. In these cases, there are really two objects, the direct object and the object of the preposition. **The strange thing about these exceptions is that the direct object**, whether it's a noun, noun phrase, or pronoun, **must be placed in between the verb and its preposition**, and then the object of the preposition follows all of that:

I'd like to take <u>Mr. Butcher</u> up on <u>his offer</u>.
Sorry I can't take you to the circus, son. I'll make <u>it</u> up to <u>you</u>.
Let me try to put <u>it</u> across to <u>her</u> in a less subtle way.

There's one last thing that needs to be mentioned about three-word verbs. Some of them are transitive *(put up with)*, in which case they must have a direct object, but sometimes they can be intransitive *(back down [from])*, in which case there can be no direct object. Here are examples of transitive three-word verbs:

She didn't keep up <u>with</u> her workload.
The district attorney backed down <u>from</u> prosecuting them.

In the two cases we've given as examples, *her workload* and *prosecuting them* are the direct objects of these three-word verbs. When the direct objects are mentioned, the verb and its two accompanying prepositions must be used.

However, these three-word verbs can also be used intransitively:

She didn't keep up.
The district attorney backed down.

If they can be used as intransitive verbs, three-word verbs drop the second preposition and actually become two-word verbs!

Remember to teach three-word verbs just as we've suggested you teach two-word verbs, as whole units, not as individual components. And make sure that your students understand that the allied prepositions just have to be memorized along with the verb forms—that's the only way to learn them. So, as an example, it's not *put*, and it's not *put up*, it's *put up with*, and the students will just have to put up with learning them in this way!

A Bounty of Nouns and Adjectives

To finish off this chapter, we'd like to mention the fact that English is a richer language not only because of its two- and three-word verbs, but also because of the enormous number of interesting nouns and adjectives that spring up from them (see Chapter 11).

Some nouns are formed with the preposition attached to the front of the word (**preposition + verb**). By the way, notice that only Group B prepositions can be fronted like this:

Δan intake   an outbreak   an overlook
an onlooker   Δout-takes   an upsurge

Most nouns, however, keep the same order as the two-word verbs they come from (**verb + preposition**):

Δa dropout   Δpush-ups   a pushover
a breakthrough Δfallout   Δa put-down

Adjectives, too, can be combinations either of preposition + verb or verb + preposition:

an <u>overthrown</u> dictator	<u>ongoing</u> problems	<u>incoming</u> flights
△<u>take-out/take-away</u> food	<u>pick-up</u> sticks	a <u>made-up</u> story

What's interesting to note is that a good number of nouns and adjectives coming from two-word verbs (like the ones with the triangle in front of them) are relatively recent developments in the history of the language, and that's a marvelous way to see how language keeps growing and changing. New terms are generated all the time, often from older two-word verbs, to keep up with the changing times and with newly-developed technology.

Teaching Tips

17.1 Modified Cloze Activity

Find a text that contains a variety of one-, two-, and three-word verbs in it. Create a cloze exercise (see *Appendix 2*) based on the chosen text. The verbs you take out and replace with blanks will depend on the type of verbs you're removing. For example, if the original text contains a one-word verb and you want your students to practice a two- or a three-word verb, put two or three blanks in that spot. If the text contains a two-word verb and you want them to practice a one- or a three-word verb, put one or three blanks in that spot. Make enough copies of the cloze (one for each student or pair of students), or write the text on the board, and have the students complete it, filling in the blanks with *one* and *only one* word per blank.

Variation: Make up a modified cloze activity based on a short story, poem, recipe, etc. that's complete when two- and three-word verbs are used to fill in the blanks.

17.2 Oral Matching

Prepare an oral matching activity based on two- and three-word verbs.

17.3 Rearrangements

Before class, find two or three sentences with not many more than twenty-five words total in them. It's useful if the sentences are related, but it isn't absolutely necessary (He took off his coat and scarf and said to himself, "I'll never get over her even if I end up a hundred." He broke down and wept.). Be sure your sentences contain two two- or three-word verbs. On the board, write each word of the sentences perpendicularly instead of horizontally in three to four columns, leaving plenty of space between the columns. What you'll then have looks like the following:

He	himself	end
took	I'll	up
off	never	a
his	get	hundred
coat	over	he
and	her	broke
scarf	even	down
and	if	and
said	I	wept
to		

Divide the class into small groups and have them create a story with the vocabulary you've provided. However, now they'll work horizontally (the way English normally works!), putting their ideas in the blank areas between the columns, using the vocabulary words in the places that they find them. Let them know that they can also use words in two different columns together. Remind them to use two- and three-word verbs wherever they can. If the students need more space between the columns, they can have it. This is what you might see:

Janusz wasn't a happy person. Things had been pretty bad at the office lately, but he felt like his luck had finally changed. But sitting in the dark was getting him depressed again, so he got up and turned on the lights. He needed to go over all the events of the past month one more time, so . . . <u>he</u> sat down and thought about <u>himself</u> and all that had taken place. "I just knew this was going to <u>end</u> badly if Piro <u>took</u> over the company . . . " etc.

17.4 Want Ads and Advertising

Bring in want ads or the advertising sections of newspapers. Have enough so that all your students have some to work with. Pair up your students and have them go through the ads/advertising and circle examples of any two- and three-word verbs they find. Have one pair read their ads to a second pair, making sure that they don't give away what product they're talking about. The second pair will guess what's being sold or what the product is.

Variation: On the board, write examples of the verbs that the students found in this tip. Pair the same students again and let them create new want ads/advertising making sure that they use several two- and three-word verbs.

17.5 Creating Stories

For homework have the students think up no more than four sentences that have two- and three-word verbs in them. The next day, divide the class into groups of two or three and have them show their group the sentences they created. Make sure that *all* the students understand the meanings of the verbs their groupmates have selected.

Wander around the room to help out if needed. After they've discussed all the sentences thoroughly, have them select three to five sentences from among those they've been discussing and then tell them to create a short story which incorporates the chosen sentences.

Variation: Have individual groups mime the sentences they worked with in this tip and let their classmates guess what's happening.

17.6 Designing International Signs

Divide the class into pairs or groups of three. Tell the students that they've been asked to participate in an international design competition to create new signs for various public or private places. The winners of the competition will have the honor of seeing their signs displayed in the most prominent art gallery the country has—your classroom! There's one requirement for those who participate in the contest: they must draw signs that are based on two- and three-word verbs . . . and they *cannot* use any words in their signs, just as international signs don't contain any words. Encourage them to be literal or figurative in their interpretations; let their imaginations run wild. Here are some ideas we had; "translations" follow this tip.

1.
2.
3.
4.

5.

1. Pick up your room.
2. Get out of the garden, rabbit!
3. Lay off the salt!
4. Turn in your homework by 3 PM.
5. Do not turn on the lights!

Have the class vote for which groups have the most imaginative signs and place ribbons or stars on them. Then put up all the signs your students have created.

17.7 Mystery Bags

Bring several bags to class, enough for groups of three to five students to have a bag of their own. Make sure the bags you bring in can't be seen through. Ask the students to put something of their own into the bag (coins, nail file, lipstick, lighter, etc.) and exchange bags with another group. Have the students create a story around *all* the contents of the bag, making sure they use two- and three–word verbs.

17.8 Pictures and Two-/Three-Word Verbs

Before class, find a picture of one or two people; choose a picture that is simple, without too many details. Attach it to the top corner of a large sheet of blank paper. Divide the class into groups of six to eight students. If possible, have a copy of the picture for each group; if not, you can display it in front of the class. Your students' task is to create a paragraph about the people in the picture by using two- and three-word verbs. Choose one student to give a name to the people; that student also begins the process of describing the picture: "These are my cousins, Eudora and Zelda Fedora."

If each group has a copy of the picture, let the members write their story on the actual sheet with the picture on it. If they don't have individual copies, have them write their paragraphs on separate pieces of paper. If students need help thinking up phrasal verbs, you can help by putting some on the board.

18

Autosegmental Features, Part 2

"It's not always what you say, but how you say it."

Here we are, back among the autosegmental features that can be so perplexing yet so interesting because of the unexpected richness that they add to English. Back in Chapter 15 we investigated how stress influences the meaning of single words and phrases, and now we're about to explore how stress can also alter the meaning of whole sentences. In addition, we'll be taking a close look at the marvelous ways that intonation influences English. And remember that suggestion we gave you in Chapter 15, that all the items you find in this chapter will be more meaningful if you sound them out loud. So speak up!

Stress and Whole Sentences

As we said at the beginning of this chapter, stress can have an amazing influence on whole sentences in English. It's interesting to note that not all types of words take stress however. You'll find stress carried by nouns and verbs for the most part unless special meaning or emphasis is being given to some other element, such as an article or preposition.

Let's look at three sentences right away in which the primary stress is different for each one and see how stress affects meaning. Give the capitalized words the primary stress.

1. WE baked the fish.
2. We BAKED the fish.
3. We baked the FISH.

If you heard someone say each of those sentences, stressing the highlighted word in each one, what would you infer? What information is there between the lines? Write your thoughts on these lines:

In Sentence 1 _____.

In Sentence 2 _____.

In Sentence 3 _____.

The way we see it, in **Sentence 1** the speaker is stressing *we* and **telling the listener that it wasn't somebody else who baked the fish**, but the speaker and another person.

In **Sentence 2** the speaker is stressing *baked*, meaning that **they baked the fish and didn't fry or poach it**.

Finally, in **Sentence 3** the speaker is stressing the fact that **they baked the fish and not, perhaps, some bread or cookies**.

It's interesting to note that in all three cases the speaker could be using stress to rebut or refute what someone has just said and that the element in question or in doubt is the element that is stressed. **In whole sentences, stress is typically used in rebuttal. It's also used when repeating part of a sentence** that the listener has misunderstood or not heard clearly the first time:

> A: I had a lot of fun today practicing my Polish
>   with the supervisor's wife.
> B: Oh. I didn't know your supervisor's Polish.
> A: My supervisor ISN'T Polish; his WIFE is.

There's another phenomenon of stress in whole sentences that we'd like to show you now. Take a look at the following sentences. In each one, decide which word should get the primary stress and underline it or draw an accent mark over the appropriate vowel. (We'll continue capitalizing the stressed words or parts of words to show the stressed elements):

> 1. There's where I told you to sit.
> 2. There's something under the table.

Hmm. Notice any difference in where the stress should go? In **Sentence 1**, the word **there** should get the stress, but in **Sentence 2**, the *some-* in *something* gets the primary stress, not *there*. Any observation you can make about this?

_____

_____

When the word *there* **is used to show where something is located** (our first sentence), **the main stress falls on it. When the expression** *there* **+** *be* **is used meaning "something exists"** (our second sentence), *there* **never receives the main stress.**

Now note the difference between the next two examples by underlining the stressed part in each one or adding accent marks over those parts:

1. There's a good dog in that house.
2. There's a good dog!

Sentence 1 should be marked: "**There's a <u>good dog</u> in that house**." But **Sentence 2** should be marked: "**<u>There's</u> a good dog**." In the **first sentence**, we're again using the expression that simply means **something exists** in that house, in this case, a good dog, so *there* doesn't receive the stress. In the **second sentence**, though, this idiomatic expression with the stress on *There's* really means that the speaker is **directly praising the dog**.

One other area concerning whole sentences in which stress plays a very important role has to do with pat phrases. In these cases, if the primary stress is changed, the sentences either fall apart or leave the listener saying "Huh?"

Here are some test cases to show you what we mean. We've deliberately misplaced the primary stress in each example to show you how bizarre the sentences can become to the ears of native listeners and how the sentences have even lost meaning. Make sure you say them out loud so you'll see just how bizarre they've become:

1. A: THAT'S the scariest movie I've ever seen.
    B: I'll SAY!
2. A: Boy, IS it hot today!
    B: YOU can say that again!
3. A: Hi. HOW are you?
    B: Fine, THANKS. How ARE you?

Now rewrite the sentences above, showing where the stress ought to go:

1A: _____.

1B: _____.

2A: _____.

2B: _____.

3A: _____.

3B: _____.

Here are the exact same mini-dialogues repeated with the correct primary stress in each sentence:

1. A: That's the scariest movie I've EVER SEEN.
   B: I'LL say!

2. A: BOY, is it HOT today!
   B: You can say THAT again!

3. A: HI. How ARE you?
   B: FINE, thanks. How are YOU?

The last test case is one of our favorites because of the reactions you get from people when the stress is kept on *are* instead of shifting over to *you* in Person B's response. Try it some time on an unsuspecting victim and just watch what happens!

The first statement in mini-dialogue 1 is a real gem as far as showing how stress can influence the meaning "between the lines." In our version, we've had Speaker A stress *ever* because the idea is *throughout my entire life.* But there are other extra meanings that could be focused on instead of the time frame if we choose to change the primary stress.

Now take a look at the following two versions of the same sentence. They show the primary stress on different parts. On the line that follows each version, write down what you would interpret the stress to mean. Have fun with this! (Note that we've underlined *I* in the second sentence to show that it receives the stress.)

That's THE /ði/ SCAriest MOvie I've ever seen!

_____

That's the scariest movie I've ever seen!

_____

In our first repetition, now with the primary stress more or less equally on "THE SCAriest MOvie," the speaker is saying **"of all the movies I've ever seen, that one was by far the scariest."** The stress on these elements in the sentence plus the exaggerated pronunciation of the definite article (/ði/, not /ðə/), is about the strongest way we can show the superlative idea.

In our second repetition with the primary stress put only on *I*, the speaker is saying **"I don't know about the rest of you, but as far as I'm concerned . . . "** In other words, the speaker is focusing here on comparing him-/herself to the others who have just seen that movie. It's wonderful, and yet very complex, how a change like this small shift in stress, in which one particular part of the sentence receives the primary stress, can change both focus and meaning.

Before we leave this fascinating and often overlooked area of stress and whole sentences, let's have some more fun. First of all, look at the three pairs of phrases that follow. They're actually real headlines taken from newspapers. See if you can figure out the difference in meaning between the two phrases in each pair by focusing on where the stress falls. One headline is straightforward; the other, we think you'll find, is very funny:

> 1. Juvenile Court to Try SHOOTing Defendant
> 2. Juvenile Court to Try SHOOTing DeFENdant

Headline Number 1 means

_____.

Headline Number 2 means

_____.

> 3. Hospital Sued By SEVen Foot DOCtors
> 4. Hospital Sued By SEVen FOOT Doctors

Headline Number 3 means

_____.

Headline Number 4 means

_____.

> 5. Squad Helps DOG BITE VICtim
> 6. Squad Helps DOG Bite Victim

Headline Number 5 means

_____.

Headline Number 6 means

_____.

And what about these two sentences? They're not headlines, but . . .

> 7. Isn't it funny how LITtle kids like ONions?
> 8. Isn't it funny how LITtle KIDS like ONions?

Number 7 means it's odd that

_____.

Number 8 means it's odd that

_____.

The only way to enjoy these three pairs fully is to say them out loud to make sure you're putting the stress on the right spots. And here's how they should be interpreted according to where the stress falls:

Number 1 = The court is going to try a person accused of shooting someone.

Number 2 = The court is going to try to shoot the defendant.

Number 3 = The hospital is being sued by doctors who are seven feet tall.

Number 4 = The hospital is being sued by seven podiatrists.

Number 5 = The squad helped a dog to bite its victim.

Number 6 = The squad helped a person who'd been bitten by a dog.

Number 7 = It's odd that children hardly like onions at all.

Number 8 = It's odd that young children like onions.

And finally for this section of the chapter, following you will find two pairs of sentences written for you in phonetic transcription. Carefully note where the stress lies in each one. (For the sake of this exercise, we're going to use accent marks over the stressed syllables even though accent marks aren't usually used when writing in phonetic transcription.) When you've said each sentence out loud a few times, write out the "normal-looking" sentence on the blank line below it. We think a grin will come across your face when you've figured these out:

1. /aɪ kʊd - əv slɛpt fɔ́r déz/.

_____

2. /aɪ kʊd - əv slɛpt fɔr déz/.

_____

3. /du yə hæv tú wɔ́ - tər lɪ - liz/ ?

_____

4. /du yə hǽv tu wɔ́ - tər lí - liz/ ?

_____

We know you may not think this fair, but we're going to go against tradition and not give you the answers here to check against your own. We've placed the answers at the end of the chapter so you won't be so easily tempted to peek at what the sentences should be in their traditionally written form! Of course, if you can't wait till then, you can always turn to page 413 of this chapter and see what's what. That's up to you!

✦ *Troubleshooter* ✦

One interesting exception to the pattern we've been exploring is when an object is a pronoun. A very common problem that students have is learning that object pronouns, whether direct or indirect, don't normally receive the stress in their phrases unless some extra communication is involved:

☞ Pronouns as direct objects: She LIKES him / I CAUGHT them / You LOVE her.
☞ Pronouns as indirect objects: He MADE it for us. / I THREW it to you.

Students almost invariably stress the object pronoun and then throw off the whole rhythm and melody that the English phrase should have.

Make sure to spend time working on this with your students. Use techniques such as choral repetition and chants to get your students used to the parts of a sentence that do and don't get stressed.

An Aside About Pronunciation and Object Pronouns

We're about to digress for a moment because there's something very interesting that concerns pronunciation in the first three examples of the *Troubleshooter* you've just seen. We feel it's worth bringing to your attention and it's got something to do with the object pronouns in the top three sentences (She LIKES him. / I CAUGHT them. / You LOVE her.). Can you figure out what typically happens to the pronunciation of those object pronouns? Think about it and then write down your thoughts on the following line:

_____

The interesting point that we'd like you to become aware of is the fact that **in many varieties of English, the initial consonant sound in the words *him, them,* and *her* may be dropped so that we end up saying *'im, 'em,* and *'er.*** Actually, *'im* is pronounced /ɪm/, *'em* is pronounced /əm/, and *'er* is pronounced /ər/. This is another one of those points that are seldom if ever taught in classes. Say those three examples from the *Troubleshooter* out loud at your normal rate of speech and you may find yourself doing just what we've pointed out if you're a native speaker.

The question we need to answer is, does this phenomenon happen all the time when we say these object pronouns or is it perhaps that this reduction happens only some of the time? Take another look at our last *Troubleshooter* to see if you can figure out the answer to this question. Then come up with your own examples of short sentences that contain these object pronouns. Write your observations on the lines that follow:

_____

_____

The answer is that **we almost always drop the initial consonant sound from these object pronouns in typical spoken English**. It doesn't matter whether they're preceded by a verb or a preposition—we almost always drop that initial consonant sound. Here are some more examples for you to say out loud:

> I saw-ɪm in the bookstore.
> They got it from-ər the other day.
> We went with-əm to dinner.

One variation is that in some dialects the object pronoun *them* can quite often be reduced to / ðm / with the vowel dropping out instead of the initial consonant sound dropping out, so we end up with:

> I'll write th-m a note.
> instead of
> I'll write 'em a note.

Many students don't even hear these object pronouns when they listen to native speakers who are making this pronunciation change in a stream of speech. Perhaps that might explain in part why students so often leave out object pronouns when they speak or even write.

As an aside, we think it appropriate to mention here that this phenomenon of dropping that initial *h* also happens to the subject pronoun, *he* (/i/), and the two possessive adjectives, *his* (/ɪz/) and *her* (/ər/). Here's what we mean:

> A: I need to see what's-'er-name.
>   Do you know where she is?
> B: Do you by any chance mean Sally?
> A: Yeah, Sally. Her son just got a job
>   here, but 'e forgot to give me 'is
>   Social Security number.

One interesting note before we move on is the fact that the initial *h* in *her* does not get dropped if it begins a sentence ("Her son just got a job . . ."). The same holds true, of course, for *he* and *his* as well.

◢◥ *Some* and *Any* **Revisited**

Before we conclude our discussion about stress, we should take another look at *some* and *any*, which you'll remember we first saw back in Chapter 7. To start this off, let's review a dialogue that you first saw there:

> A: Didn't you go to the movies last night?
>
> B: Uh-huh. We saw the new Mel Gibson movie.
>
> A: Was it **any** good?
>
> B: I liked it a lot, but Nadia wasn't feeling well, so I don't think she enjoyed it very much—and that's unusual because if she can have her choice of **any** kind of film, it'll always be one with Mel Gibson in it!
>
> A: I'm sorry to hear she didn't feel well. Is she **any** better today?
>
> B: Yeah, lots. She even went to work.

Following are the three contexts in which *any* appears in our dialogue. To refresh your memory about what we started to do in Chapter 7, say the following lines out loud a few times as naturally as you can and see if you recall the difference as to which word receives the primary stress. When you've recalled the difference, write an accent mark over the word that has the primary stress or the words that seem to share the primary stress:

1. Was it any good?

2. Is she any better today?

3. . . . if she can have her choice of any kind of film . . .

Any easier to do it this time around? The trick really is to say the lines as naturally as possible, that is, by sort of "eavesdropping" on yourself. Let's see if the words you've chosen are the same as ours:

1. Was it any góod?
2. Is she any bétter today?
3. . . . if she can have her choice of ány kind of film . . .

We can see that the primary stress is on the adjective in Numbers 1 and 2, but it's moved to the word *any* in Number 3. This is what happens when ***any*** means "**it doesn't matter which one.**"

But does this phenomenon only occur in this case? Let's look at this next dialogue to find out:

> A: I hear you're think-
> ing about living in
> Bangladesh for a
> few years. **Any**[1]
> truth to that?
>
> B: Yes, I've been
> thinking about it
> for awhile now.
>
> A: But aren't you
> afraid of the
> typhoons they get
> there? I remember reading about one that killed hundreds of people.
>
> B: Well, it wasn't just **any**[2] old typhoon, you know. It was one of the
> worst.
>
> A: I remember that people were desperate for **any**[3] help they could get
> to rebuild their lives.
>
> B: They certainly were. But you see how they bounced back? Those
> Bangladeshis are tough people!

As you can see, *any* has been used three times in this dialogue. In two of the three occurrences, *any* should receive the primary stress for that part of the sentence. Can you figure out which two occurrences have the primary stress? Look at each phrase we've copied for you from the dialogue. Next, decide whether you feel *any* does or doesn't receive the main stress in that phrase by checking the appropriate box. Finally, see if you can interpret just what *any* means in each case:

1. Any truth to that?

   ☐ receives main stress   ☐ doesn't receive main stress

   Any means: ————————————————————

2. . . . it wasn't just any old typhoon . . .

   ☐ receives main stress   ☐ doesn't receive main stress

   Any means: ————————————————————

3. . . . people were desperate for any help they could get . . .

   ☐ receives main stress   ☐ doesn't receive main stress

   Any means: ————————————————————

This is how we see it:

1. *Any* **truth to that?**
   (Doesn't receive main stress; the stress is on *truth*.
   Any **means: even a little**

2. **. . . it wasn't just** *any* **old typhoon . . .**
   (Receives main stress.)
   Any **means: ordinary, typical, usual, run-of-the-mill**

3. **. . . people were desperate for** *any* **help they could get . . .**
   (Receives main stress.)
   Any **means: as much or as little**
   (for countable nouns: as many or as few)

Of course the question now arises, if stress can be a factor in determining the meaning of *any*, can it work the same way for *some*? Why don't we look at this next dialogue to see if that's so:

> A: Hi, Hemant. Were there any messages for me while I was out?
>
> B: Come to think of it, two people came by looking for you, but I didn't know where you'd gone.
>
> A: Oh, I should have told you that **some** friends might stop by.
>
> B: Sorry I couldn't tell them where you were. By the way, that's **some** gorgeous car I saw you drive off in.
>
> A: Oh, you like it? Lata and I just couldn't resist buying it.
>
> B: **Some** of us in the office would love to go for a spin in it.
>
> A: **Some** day we'll do just that!

We want to warn you right off that this next part is full of subtleties. As you see, there are four occurrences of *some* in this dialogue. Here are a few hints to help you figure out what's going on:

- in one occurrence, *some* receives equal stress with the phrase that accompanies it;
- in two occurrences, *some* receives stress, but its accompanying phrase doesn't;
- in one other occurrence, *some* doesn't receive any stress at all.

Let's see if you can figure out which is which. Write down the phrases that begin with *some* under the appropriate heading below:

Equal Stress with Its Accompanying Phrase:

Receives More Stress than Its Accompanying Phrase:

_____

_____

Doesn't Receive Primary Stress:

_____

A very tricky assignment indeed! Let's see if you've come up with the same phrases that we have for these headings:

Equal Stress with Its Accompanying Phrase: SOME GORGEOUS CAR
Receives More Stress than   SOME of us
   Its Accompanying Phrase: SOME day
Doesn't Receive Primary Stress: some FRIENDS

As we can clearly see now, stress can play a role in how we use *some* as well as how we use *any*. But what can *some* mean when it receives equal stress with its accompanying phrase, when the stress goes to the following phrase, or when it receives the primary stress?

We've repeated our phrases for you to work on. After you've considered the various meanings, write your interpretations for *some* on the accompanying lines:

SOME GORGEOUS CAR:

_____

SOME day:

_____

some FRIENDS:

_____

Once again, let's discover whether your interpretations come close to or actually match ours:

^Δ **SOME GORGEOUS CAR** = a very/quite a gorgeous car
^{ΔΔ} **SOME of us**   = a few/an unspecified number of us
^{ΔΔΔ} **SOME day**   = an unspecified/vague day in the future
   some FRIENDS   = a few/an unspecified number of friends

Notice the single triangle before "some gorgeous car"? The reason for it is that we want to ask you if you can think of a word we could substitute for *some* in this idea. Here's a hint: it's an article.

———————————————

And the answer is ... **one**! In Chapter 2 we discuss how the indefinite article can be used idiomatically as an intensifier just as *some* is here.

In addition, did you notice the two triangles before *some of us*? It's because we want to ask you if you can figure out at least one of the two reasons that *some* is stressed in this phrase but not in the last one (*some* friends) even though it has the same meaning. This is a tough one, but let's see what you can come up with:

———————————————

The first reason that *some* receives the stress in the phrase *some of us* is that **some is a pronoun in this case, not a determiner (*some* friends), and we show that it's a pronoun by stressing it**.

The second reason that *some* receives the stress in this case is that, in normal speech, **prepositional phrases with object pronouns (of us) are very rarely stressed**. About the only time you'll ever hear the stress put on the object pronoun is when somebody is emphasizing the word in a kind of comparison:

It wasn't some of THEM who got awards; it was some of US!

And finally, we're sure you noticed the three triangles before the phrase *some day*. In this phrase, *some* receives the stress, too, unlike in the phrase *some friends*. Why does it receive the stress in this case? It doesn't contain any prepositional phrase, so there must be another reason. Can you figure out what that reason is?

———————————————

It's not the unspecified number that prompts us to stress *some* in the phrase we're investigating; **it's the idea of vagueness**. Whenever we want to create a phrase like this which refers to something vague rather than an unspecified number, we stress *some* in the phrase:

SOMEbody/SOMEtime/SOMEwhere/
SOMEthing and also SOMEday (or some day)

A͡ɔ̈ Intonation

English is called an intonation language. That means that English uses **intonation, the rising or falling of the voice (also known as pitch) and the raising or lowering of volume** to change meaning or to change syntax as, for example, when a statement becomes a question.

On several occasions in the first part of this chapter, we qualified our observations concerning various stress patterns by showing you what these patterns appeared to be, barring any extra communication or meaning desired by the speaker. That extra communication or meaning really comes into play, though, when we start exploring intonation.

It's such a challenging job to teach intonation that many teachers view it as something that's basically unteachable. Quite a few believe that students don't *learn* intonation, they *acquire* it through long exposure to it. Students who have sensitive ears and the gift of mimicry (and the "Musical Intelligence") will become somewhat adept at using English intonation, but those who aren't sensitive to the phonology of the target language and who have a great deal of difficulty with pronunciation probably won't become adept at developing correct English intonation patterns.

This isn't to say that teachers should avoid presenting certain common intonation patterns that their students ought to at least recognize even if they don't actively produce them. That kind of recognition is indeed very important to students. So what we plan to do in this section of the chapter is to explore some common, but challenging, intonation patterns and look into that extra communication which we've hinted at so often.

Is It a Question or Exclamation?!

We know that there are times when certain items in English can overlap in appearance even though their meanings may be quite different. A case in point is how a given verb form, such as the simple present, can have such varied meanings (see Chapter 3).

Well, here's one that rarely gets enough attention in classes, and it's another example of how intonation can be so all-important for meaning in English. This dialogue will show you what we're talking about:

A: **Am I excited!**

B: Oh? What's up?

A: I've just won a one-week trip for two to London! All expenses paid!

B: Wow! **Are you lucky!**

A: I'll say! **Am I lucky** or what? I loved it the first time I was there a few years back.

B: Unbelievable! Is London interesting for tourists?

A: You've got to be kidding. Boy,
is London interesting!

B: But what about the London-
ers? Were they nice?

A: Gosh, **were they nice**! Everybody was so friendly and helpful. And perfect strangers
called me "love." **Were they
ever friendly**!

What do you see happening in this dialogue? There's some kind of overlapping going on, so let's see if you can identify what it is:

It shouldn't be too hard to see that **the same phrase can be used both as a yes/no question and as an exclamation. It all depends on what intonation the speaker uses**. In Chapter 1 we accounted for all sorts of interesting sentences that appear in question word order but aren't questions at all. The sentences we have in this dialogue, on the other hand, are perfect examples of when a sentence can be used both ways, and there are lots of examples:

Are you ever mistaken?	Are you ever mistaken!
Was he in trouble?	Was he in trouble!
Do they have the wrong idea?	Do they have the wrong idea!
Did they enjoy themselves?	Did they enjoy themselves!
Can she play the harp?	Can she play the harp!
Will she be a great singer?	Will she be a great singer!
Is he going to regret it?	Is he going to regret it!
Have we ever goofed?	Have we ever goofed!

Isn't it incredible what a change in intonation can accomplish? If rising pitch is used at the end of each sentence, the speaker has created a yes/no question. But if falling pitch is used, the speaker has created an exclamation.

One additional observation we should make about all of these exclamations (apart from the fact that they all retain the question word order) is that the speaker usually puts some sort of extra-added "punch" or exaggerated emphasis on key words just to make sure the listener understands that what's being said is indeed an exclamation:

Are YOU EVer misTAKen!
Was HE in TROUble!

And what about that word *ever* when it appears in the questions on the left and in the exclamations on the right? Do you think the word has the same interpretation in both the questions and the exclamations or is there a change in meaning?

☐ a change in meaning   ☐ no change in meaning

Surprisingly, **there's quite a big change in meaning** from the question to the exclamation. Now that you know there is, how would you interpret the meaning of *ever* in each case? Write down your thoughts on these lines:

In the question, *ever* means _____.

In the exclamation, *ever* means _____.

It's fascinating how one little word can be used in such different ways depending on what kind of sentence it's found in. **In questions, *ever* means *at any time in someone's life*. In exclamations, *ever* means nothing in particular; it's really an intensifier adding a little extra "punch" to the idea, nothing more.**

Tag Questions, Right?

One of the most misunderstood intonation patterns that teachers and students need to deal with is found in tag questions. First off, we'd like to point out how we plan to represent changes in intonation on these pages—not an easy task at all. When we change pitch, it seems as if our voices "go up" or "go down," and tag questions lend themselves beautifully to demonstrate this change in intonation. We'll show a rising pitch by literally making the affected words go up higher (superscript) than the rest of the words in the phrase or sentence, and we'll represent a falling pitch by making the affected words go down (subscript). Take a look at the following statement with its tag question to see what we mean:

He GOT the proMOtion, DIDn't he?

Obviously we're showing you a tag question with rising pitch. The first part of our example is the basic statement, and the statement will be spoken the same way whether the tag question is added on or not. Notice the two parts of the statement that receive the main stress, the verb (*got*) and the direct object (*promotion*). Keep in mind that, as far as the tag question goes, **the first part of the tag will always receive the main stress**.

Now let's look at the same statement and tag question, only the tag this time appears quite different:

He GOT the proMOtion, DIDn't he?

If we compare this second statement and its tag with our first example, we can see that the statements are exactly the same in both versions and the words used in the tag questions are identical, too. The difference is that our second example has a falling pitch. The question we need to ask is, why can we use two opposite "directions" for the pitch in our tag questions? If you can explain this phenomenon, write your idea down on the following lines:

_____

_____

It turns out that the speaker determines whether to use a rising or falling pitch in the tag question depending upon what is or isn't anticipated about the answer to the question. **When it's not known if the answer will be "yes" or "no," a rising intonation is used, but when a specific "yes" or "no" is anticipated, a falling pitch is normally used.**

In our two examples, the speaker of the first sentence used a rising pitch and really didn't know whether the person being discussed had gotten the promotion or not. On the other hand, the speaker of the second sentence used a falling pitch, anticipating that the person under discussion had, in fact, gotten the promotion. So why did the second speaker even bother to ask the question if he thought he already knew the answer? It's that **the second speaker was looking for confirmation of an already-formed conclusion**. This is the most typical reason for using tag questions with falling pitch. Some people liken this kind of tag question to the rhetorical question.

Echo Tag Questions

Our next dialogue contains these wonderful little additions known as echo tag questions. The reason they're called "echo" tags is that they *echo* or repeat part of what the other speaker has just said. After you've read the dialogue, we'll discuss why we consider them so interesting and why intonation plays such an important part in their use:

> A: Guess what! Pavel's getting married!
>
> B: **Is he?**
>
> A: Yes. He says he loves the girl very much.
>
> B: **Does he?**
>
> A: Uh-huh. They'll be spending their honeymoon in Yalta.
>
> B: **Will they?**
>
> A: Mm-hmm. And he gave her a gorgeous engagement ring.
>
> B: **Did he?**
>
> A: Oh, it's just beautiful! I've seen it.
>
> B: **Have you?**
>
> A: Too bad they can't take more than one week for the honeymoon.
>
> B: **They can't?**
>
> A: No, it's just too expensive. Well, it's nice to see that you're as excited about this as I am.

Every item in bold is an echo tag question. The thing that writers must find frustrating about them is that the simple punctuation of using a question mark doesn't really tell the reader how the speaker who's making the echo tags feels.

Let's try a little experiment to make clear what we mean. If you haven't already done so, read the dialogue out loud now and use a *rising* pitch for every echo tag. Then write down on the line we've provided anything that comes to mind concerning how you think the speaker feels about this whole situation:

_____

An echo tag with rising pitch reveals many things about the speaker's feelings and reactions to what's being said. In this case, with rising pitch, we would say that the speaker is possibly **surprised**, **interested**, **excited**, **wants to know more**, etc.

Now let's repeat this exercise, only this time, use a *falling* pitch for all the echo tags *except the last one*. Then write down how you think the speaker feels on the following line:

_____

What a difference! With this dramatic change in intonation we get an entirely different picture of how the speaker feels about the situation. We'd say that the speaker is possibly **skeptical**, **annoyed**, **pessimistic**, **sarcastic**, **uninterested**, etc.

Now let's think for a moment about how echo tags are put together. One way they can be constructed is by first repeating the verb *be* or the first auxiliary and following it with a pronoun that substitutes for the subject, so we have ***be*/first auxiliary + subject pronoun** ("Is he?" / "Will they?"). The other way is to use the simple present or simple past of the auxiliary **do + subject pronoun** ("Does he?").

But what about "They can't?"? Why do you think it's all right for Speaker B to use the construction **subject pronoun + first auxiliary**?

_____

The reason is simply that **some echo tag questions can be created with the construction subject pronoun + first auxiliary**, too. Try it out and you'll see that every one in our dialogue can be rearranged to have subject pronoun + first auxiliary.

But we have one more area to investigate. If you can choose subject pronoun + *be*/first auxiliary or *be*/first auxiliary + subject pronoun, does this mean that the constructions are always interchangeable? Let's examine one of our echo tags to find out:

A: Guess what! Pavel's getting married!

B: Is ^he?   He ^is?
   Is _he?   He _is?

So what do you think?

☐ Yes, they are.   ☐ No, they aren't.   ☐ Only sometimes.

The answer is **Only sometimes**. The reason has to do with the speaker's mood and what's being communicated "between the lines." **If the speaker's mood is "up" and positive** (using rising pitch), **either construction can be used. However, if the speaker is "down" or annoyed or sarcastic** (using falling pitch), **only the construction <u>*be*/first auxiliary + subject pronoun</u> can be used**. So **the echo tag question *He is?* with <u>falling</u> pitch isn't possible**.

Intonation and Punctuation

It's important to remember that the spoken language had existed a long, long time before the written language came into being. When writing did make its mark on the language, so to speak, the aspect we call punctuation was influenced in many ways by the intonation of the spoken language.

It's fascinating to see how a simple stream of words can be transformed into either a statement, a question, or an order simply by the intonation that's used and the punctuation marks that were invented over the centuries to reflect the intonation. Take a look at our next dialogue to see this wonderful facility of language in action:

A: I know my wife hasn't been with the company for long, but she's shown herself to be a hard worker. **She's getting a raise.**

B: **She's getting a raise?**

A: **She's getting a raise!**

B: Okay, boss. Sure thing, boss.

What more needs to be said? The period shows us that a statement has been made with its basically straight-line intonation:

She's GETTing a RAISE.

The question mark identifies a question with its rising pitch at the end:

She's GETTing a RAISE?

And the exclamation mark tells us that volume has been increased and key words have been "punched":

She's GETTing a RAISE!

We even have one more use of punctuation that some people feel is somehow more satisfying because it lets the reader know that there's more than one thing going on with the speaker. In this case, not only is the speaker repeating information just received to verify what's been said, but also registering surprise or shock:

She's GETTing a RAISE?!

More Effects of Intonation

To end this section on intonation, and this chapter for that matter, we think it will be fun to see some other marvelous ways that intonation can influence meaning. The best way is simply to present you with some choice examples and let you have fun figuring out what's going on.

First of all, look at the following two sentences. You'll note a vertical bar that we've inserted between two words in Sentence 2. This bar represents the minuscule pause that native speakers "feel" the presence of in a stream of speech. In linguistics, this phenomenon is known as "juncture," and in many instances, the written language accounts for this tiny pause by inserting a comma:

1. I don't know TIna LouISE.
2. I don't know ᵀⁱna ❙ LouISE.

After you say these sentences out loud, how would you interpret them judging from the stress you observe, the change in pitch, and the pause bar in Sentence 2?

Sentence 1:

_____

Sentence 2:

_____

Let's see how close your interpretations are to ours. The way we see it, **Sentence 1** means that **the speaker's stating the fact that he/she doesn't know this person named Tina Louise** (as opposed to someone else who does).

Sentence 2 means **the speaker's talking to someone named Louise and says that he/she doesn't know Tina**. Quite a difference!

Let's get to another pair of these sentences. This time, though, we've had to put a part of each sentence in phonetics so we don't give too much away. And once again, to make matters simple, we're going to use accent marks over the stressed syllables.

On the blank line for each sentence that follows, copy the sentence and recreate the part in phonetics as it appears in "normal" writing:

1. Where's the /fón bɪl/?

2. Where's the / fón ▌ bíl/ ?

Sentence 1:

_____

Sentence 2:

_____

Sentence 1 is "Where's the phone bill?" Obviously this means that the speaker's looking for the telephone bill and is asking someone if he/she knows where it is.

Sentence 2 is "Where's the phone, Bill?" The speaker's talking to someone named Bill and asking him if he knows where the telephone is. Notice how high the pitch has gone for *phone* because this is a question, not a statement. Also, note that even though the pitch has come down on "Bill," it hasn't come back down to the level that the question began on.

Want to try your hand at a couple more? This time, however, we're going to give you both sentences entirely in phonetic transcription. And here's a hint: In this variety of English, final "r's" are dropped. After you've said them out loud a few times, write each one out on the blank line as it usually appears in written form.

1. /yu hæv ə gʊd ᵃɪ ▌ dí - ə/

2. /yu hæv ə gʊd aɪ- dí - ə/

Sentence 1:

_____

Sentence 2:

_____

If we write out **Sentence 1** as it usually looks, we come up with **"You have a good eye, dear."** In other words, the speaker is complimenting someone by saying that the person has good taste in art or decorating, or that he/she can easily spot things that are being looked for.

If we write out **Sentence 2**, we end up with **"You have a good idea,"** which needs no further explanation. Of course we mentioned that the speaker drops the final "r" from a word, or at least "flattens" it. The fun will only work with this pair of sentences if you drop those "r's."

How about just one more pair? We're sure you're getting good at sorting these out!

1. /hi kwɪt yú - zɪŋ hɪp - nó - sɪs/
2. /hi kwɪ́t ┃ yu - zɪŋ hɪp - nó - sɪs/

Sentence 1:

_____

Sentence 2:

_____

When **Sentence 1** is written out normally, it's **"He quit using hypnosis."** This, of course, means that he stopped using hypnosis.

Written out normally, **Sentence 2** looks like this: **"He quit, using hypnosis."** That little pause, which the comma represents, changes the meaning totally. In this case, he stopped doing something (e.g., smoking, overeating, etc.) by using hypnosis!

The Answers for Page 396

1. I could have slept four days.
2. I could have slept for days.
3. Do you have two water lilies?
4. Do you have to water lilies?

Teaching Tips

18.1 "Drawing" Music

Bring in a recording of a piece of instrumental music. Make sure the tempo of the music isn't too fast. Have large sheets of paper for the students to draw several lines similar to those that composers use when writing music (see the sample that follows). In pairs or small groups, tell the students to plot out the music on the staff as you play short bits of the music. Tell them that they don't have to know *how* to write music;

they just have to provide an impressionistic version of what they "hear." When they've composed their "music," let them write lyrics that fit the music they've "composed."

18.2 Tag Questions

Write up fifteen to twenty sentences that contain tag questions. Also prepare an answer sheet (or write one on the board) similar to the following:

1. Certain ———   Uncertain ———
2. Certain ———   Uncertain ———

In class, say the sentences for the students twice; tell them that they'll indicate whether the information you're communicating expresses certainty or uncertainty. When you say the sentences, add rising intonation for uncertainty and falling intonation for certainty. The students will check off the appropriate word.

18.3 Poetry*

Here's a great activity for practicing stress and rhythm. Divide the class into small groups. Have them choose one of the following topics (or any other that you may come up with). Ask the students to list as many examples of the topic as they can. Here are some suggested topics: fruits/vegetables, famous people, colors, languages, cities/countries, or merchandise in a certain store. Once they have a list of at least twenty examples of the topic, have them create a poem using some or all of the items in their lists. Make sure that they pay attention to rhythm and intonation as they construct their poems. Below is an example of an especially nice rhythmic poem ... one you just might use with poems that your student create:

Me
(If you weren't you, who would you like to be?)
Paul McCartney   Gustav Mahler
Alfred Jarry   John Coltrane
Charles Mingus   Claude Debussy
Wordsworth   Monet   Bach and Blake

Charlie Parker   Pierre Bonnard
Leonardo   Bessie Smith
Fidel Castro   Jackson Pollack
Gaudi Milton Munch and Berg

Béla Bartok   Henri Rousseau
Rauschenberg and Jasper Johns

Lukas Cranach   Shostakovich
Kropotkin Ringo George and John . . .

Guillaume Apollinaire
Cannonball Adderly
René Magritte
Hieronymous Bosch . . .
and last of all
me.

⋆Maley, A. and A. Duff. 1985. *Drama Techniques in Language Learning.* New York: Oxford University Press, pp. 210–11.

18.4 Storytelling

Before class, write up ten to twelve comprehension questions (*wh-* questions and yes/ no questions). These questions can be based on either an actual reading passage your students have never seen before or they can be created out of thin air. In this activity, make sure that some of your questions focus on autosegmental features. But whatever the case, the questions should look and sound like they've been based on a *single story.* The questions should also be open-ended enough so that when they are answered, they allow for your students' creativity and imagination.

Divide the class into groups of three to four and provide them with a copy of the questions. Tell them to answer the questions *without* having any text to refer to; this creates a barebones "storyline." Once this "storyline" has been created, have the groups exchange papers and write up a complete, fleshed-out story using their answers to the questions and anything else that seems necessary. Then have them read their stories aloud to the class. When all the groups have read their stories, discuss the differences they've come up with. If you've based your questions on a real reading passage, read it to your students. If not, let them know that their stories are the "real stories."

19

Subjunctives, Hopes, and Wishes

"When you wish upon a star . . . "

One of the things that makes us human is our amazing ability to imagine, to ponder what might be or might have been, and to suppose how things could be different. All of this stems from another ability that we possess, being able to distinguish what's real from what's unreal and to dabble in both realms. Language reflects these abilities of ours in some very interesting ways, and this chapter will explore the fascinating but complicated ways that English deals with these abilities.

The Indicative and Subjunctive Moods

To start us off on our investigation, we should first discuss the difference between these two moods. When we speak in grammatical terms, the word "mood" doesn't refer to how you're feeling, but rather to a perception of something being real or unreal, a fact or a supposition. The first mood that everyone learns when tackling a foreign language is called the **indicative mood**. It's the mood we use for **real events, past, present, or future**. When we say "We plant flower beds around the house every spring" or "We're going to plant beds of chrysanthemums and marigolds," we're using the indicative mood and dealing with factual events.

It's a different story, however, when we get into the realm of what's contrary to fact or just a supposition. Then we enter the **subjunctive mood**, which says to us that we have **an idea that's hypothetical or deals with the imagination** (meaning that whatever we're talking about never happened, isn't happening, nor may ever happen). **The subjunctive mood conveys an idea based on a thought rather than a fact or an idea contrary to the reality of the situation being discussed.**

You already know all about verbs in the indicative mood because the indicative mood is found in all the verb forms we've already covered in this text. As for putting verbs in the subjunctive mood, we'll be dealing with that in detail a little further on.

As far as time and the subjunctive are concerned, the four basic areas reckoned with are **the past, the timeless area (also called general time), the (real) present, and the future**.

Nothing can be more maddening for teachers than to go from one grammar source to another and find a morass of terms and definitions for various forms of the subjunctive. Many grammarians call the form used for the present the "past subjunctive" and the form for the past the "past perfect subjunctive." Others say that conditional sentences (which we'll get to in Chapter 20) don't contain the subjunctive, but rather use the past for the present and the past perfect for the past. The reason they inadvertently make all of this terminology so complex is that they're focusing on the actual verb form being used rather than its function or meaning. We consider this focus on form a great mistake. Now you know why this matter can get so confusing.

We're going to stick to a simple premise to make the whole thing easier and more logical; if an idea refers to the present, we'll call the verb form the present subjunctive, and if it refers to the past, we'll call it the past subjunctive.

It's time now for us to show you some examples of the subjunctive at work. These sentences will deal with imaginary ideas, ones that are contrary to the reality of the situations that set them up. To lead into the use of the subjunctive, we're going to use the verb *wish*, a verb with a special relationship to the subjunctive.

Look these examples over carefully, identify the time of each sentence in bold, and from your own observations, write corresponding rules you can tell your students about how to form the subjunctive:

1a. They're broke again. **They wish (that) they <u>were</u> rich. In fact, they wish I <u>were/was</u> rich and (that) everybody <u>were/was</u> rich!**
  Note: We can use an optional *that* after *wish* when it's used with the subjunctive.

1b. He hates being plain-looking and shy. **He wishes he <u>looked</u> like a Greek god and <u>could</u> be more outgoing. He wishes he <u>didn't have to</u> be like that.**

1c. She's gardening in the hot sun. **She wishes she <u>were/was lying</u> in her hammock with a cold drink in her hand instead.**

2a. I didn't pay the rent on time and had to pay a late fee. **I wish I <u>had paid</u> the rent on time.**

2b. Their little girl got upset when she heard them arguing. **They wish they <u>hadn't been arguing</u> while she was home.**

2c. It's too bad she couldn't wait for us. **We wish she <u>could have waited</u>.**

3a. Andy won't go to college. **We wish he <u>would reconsider</u>.**

3b. Andy's going to take a job at his uncle's service station. **We wish he <u>weren't/wasn't going to</u> do that.**

Rule 1a: _____

_____

Rule 1b: _____

_____

Rule 1c: _____

_____

Rule 2a: _____

_____

Rule 2b: _____

_____

Rule 2c: _____

_____

Rule 3a: _____

_____

Rule 3b: _____

_____

Here are the rules:

Rule 1a: To form the present or timeless subjunctive of the verb *be*, borrow the simple past form *were* and use it for all persons, or you may elect to use *was* for first and third person singular.

> Note: In some varieties of English, it is considered more
> educated or formal to use *were* exclusively.

Rule 1b: To form the present for stative verbs, the timeless subjunctive for all other verbs, and the modal auxiliaries *can* and *must*, use the past form. Use *had to* for *must*.

> They wish they <u>didn't need</u> a larger house.
> They wish they <u>lived</u> in a larger house.
> They wish they <u>could</u> buy a larger house.
> They wish they <u>didn't have to</u> move.

Rule 1c: To form the real present (present progressive) subjunctive, use the auxiliary *be* in the present subjunctive (*were/was*) plus the main verb with *-ing*.

> I wish I <u>were/was</u> making more money.

Rule 2a: To form the simple past subjunctive for all verbs, including *be*, use the past perfect form.

> She wishes she <u>hadn't been</u> sick last night.
> She wishes she <u>had gone</u> to the party last night.

Rule 2b: To form the past progressive subjunctive for all verbs, use the past perfect progressive form.

> We wish we <u>had been paying</u> attention to the map.

Rule 2c: To form the past subjunctive of the modal auxiliary *could*, use the perfect modal form.

> She wishes she <u>could have gone</u> to the party.

Rule 3a: To form the simple future subjunctive for all verbs, use the modal auxiliary *would* + the base verb.

> We wish you <u>would</u> come with us tomorrow.

Rule 3b: To form the subjunctive of the future expression *be going to*, use the present subjunctive of *be* (*were/was*) plus *going to*.

> I wish I <u>were/was going to</u> go on vacation soon.

Without any doubt, the subjunctive is a very curious form in English since there are no distinct verb forms that are exclusively set aside for it as there are in many other languages. There's one general rule that we'd like you to observe in action. Take a careful look at the following comparisons between reality (the indicative mood) and unreality (the subjunctive mood). Can you make a parallel between what's going on here and indirect speech?

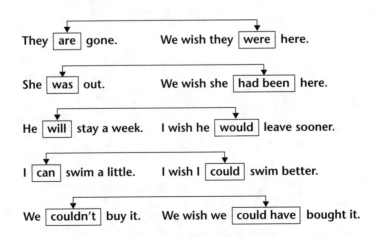

Do you see anything interesting happening when you focus on the boxed-in words? On the following line, write down what you think is going on. Think about indirect speech, if that will help you.

_____

What's going on is that we have another form of the phenomenon called **backshifting**. Notice how each form in the indicative mood is moved one step back in time, so to speak, when we go into the subjunctive mood—just like the action we found with backshifting of the verb forms in indirect speech. This little observation may go a long way in helping you teach the subjunctive forms to your students.

Hope vs. Wish

Here we have two verbs that conveniently allow us to explore the differences between the indicative and the subjunctive moods. *Hope* and *wish* concern themselves with diametrically opposed concepts, and our first dialogue will give you a clear indication of how opposed these two verbs are.

Before we get to the dialogue, though, we'd like to point out something. Don't confuse *wish* as we're using it in this chapter with its other meanings. *Wish* can equal what the subject would like for him-/herself:

> She wishes to leave now.

or it can mean what we want for someone else:

> We wish him all the best of luck.

As for the meaning we'll be focusing on in this chapter, that will become clear to you as soon as you read our first dialogue, so let's get to it:

A: Well, **I** hope everybody**'s** here by noon.

B: Yeah.

A: What's the matter? You seem depressed.

B: It's just that **I wish** we **didn't need** to do things like this.

A: But we've just got to make people understand how important it is to donate blood. Anyway, with the media attention this rally will get, **I hope** we**'ll convince** lots of people to help the blood banks out.

> B: I **hope** you're right. By the way, did you tell Maria to bring lots of orange juice? The donors are going to need it.
>
> A: Yes, I did. I just **hope** she **remembered** to get it. In fact, I **wish** I **had brought** some for us to have right now.

Let's review some facts about the situation in this dialogue. Answer the following questions by checking off the boxes you agree with:

1. Is it probable that the others will arrive by noon? ☐ yes ☐ no
2. Is there a chance people will be convinced? ☐ yes ☐ no
3. Is it possible that Speaker A's expectations can come true? ☐ yes ☐ no
4. Is it possible that Maria remembered to get the orange juice? ☐ yes ☐ no
5. Do the persons in this dialogue feel there's a possibility that such rallies are unnecessary? ☐ yes ☐ no
6. Is there a possibility that Person A brought some orange juice? ☐ yes ☐ no

Questions 1–4 are **yes**; questions **5** and **6** are **no**.

Okay. Now that you've compared your answers to ours, let's put together all the sentences in our dialogue that use *hope,* and then those that use *wish.* Note that the numbers before the grouped sentences that follow correspond to the questions and answers we've just seen:

> 1. I hope everybody's here by noon.
> 2. I hope we'll convince people.
> 3. I hope you're right.
> 4. I hope she remembered to get lots of orange juice.
> 5. I wish we didn't need such rallies.
> 6. I wish I had brought some orange juice for us.

What we should ask ourselves right off is why the persons in this dialogue chose to use the verb *hope* in the first four ideas. For one thing, we can see that the verbs that follow are in the indicative mood (*is/will convince/are/remembered*). For another, we need to consider the situations that led to those four hopes (the corresponding questions and answers we've seen) to help us figure out why they used *hope.*

Then we have to consider why they chose to use the verb *wish* in the last two ideas. To begin with, we can see that the verbs that follow in those two sentences are in the subjunctive mood, present and past respectively (*didn't need/had brought*). What we'll also need to do is look back at those last two corresponding questions and answers to see what the situations were that led to them using *wish*.

Now that we've done this big lead-in, we're going to ask you to do a bit of detective work. By reviewing the question-and-answer section and the corresponding grouped sentences, and knowing what you know now about the indicative and subjunctive moods, can you choose the two common elements found in the first four sentences that aren't found in the last two? And what two elements can be found in those last two sentences that aren't found in the first four? If you choose the right ones, you'll understand why the persons in the dialogue used *hope* in some of the sentences and *wish* in the others.

1. In the first four sentences, a possibility exists.   ☐ I agree   ☐ I disagree
2. In the first four sentences, the outcome is known.   ☐ I agree   ☐ I disagree
3. In the last two, the speakers talk about reality.   ☐ I agree   ☐ I disagree
4. In the last two, they're unhappy with the situations.   ☐ I agree   ☐ I disagree

Without delay, then, let's see if you're thinking the same way we are: **Numbers 1 and 4 are I agree**; numbers **2** and **3** are **I disagree**.

So the two common elements we find in the first four sentences with *hope* are **possibility** and **ignorance of the outcome**. In all four cases, the situations mentioned can come true even though our rally-goers don't know the outcomes yet. Since there's no reason to believe their ideas haven't taken place, aren't taking place, or may not take place, they use *hope*. To sum it all up, **we use *hope* when there's a real possibility that something happened, is happening, or is going to happen. The key to this use, though, is the fact that we <u>don't know</u> the outcome**.

Now what about the last two sentences? The two common elements we find in both ideas that use *wish* are that **they're contrary to the reality of the situations** and **the speakers are unhappy about the events they're speaking of**. The truth is that they feel they really do need to have such rallies in order to get people to donate blood, and the other reality is that Person A didn't bring any orange juice for them to have. In addition, they show unhappiness over the reality of the situations. So **we use *wish* to communicate imaginary ideas when we know the outcome but are unhappy with it. It's a way for us to say that we know what already happened, is happening, or is going to happen, but it would be nice to have things otherwise.**

Now let's go back for a moment to the way we show futurity with *hope*. You may have noticed that Speaker A used both the simple present and the simple future form with the verbs that follow *hope*, yet they both represent the future:

> I hope everybody's here by noon.
> I hope we<u>'ll</u> convince people . . .

Is there any difference between using the simple present or the simple future after *hope*? What do you think?

☐ yes   ☐ no

Before we give you our answer, let's see if we can interchange the two forms without causing any havoc to meaning:

> I hope everybody's here by noon.
> I hope everybody will be here by noon.
>
> I hope we'll convince people . . .
> I hope we convince people . . .

Well, do you find any noticeable difference in meaning? We certainly don't, so the answer to the question above is **no**. In fact, in Chapter 5 we talk about how the simple present can be used for the future, so this use shouldn't seem at all strange to you. To sum it up, **when the verb *hope* is in the present, we can use the simple present as well as these other forms for the following verb to connote futurity**:

> We hope you <u>come</u> to our party.
> We hope you're <u>coming</u> to our party.
> We hope you're going to <u>come</u> to our party.
> We hope you<u>'ll come</u> to our party.

But we haven't exhausted the forms that a verb can have after *hope* when *hope* is in the present, and here are the rest:

the present perfect:	She hopes you <u>haven't caught</u> her cold.
the present perfect progressive:	We hope she<u>'s been taking</u> her medicine.
the simple past:	I hope she <u>didn't kiss</u> you at the party.
the past progressive:	We hope she <u>wasn't handling</u> the food.
the infinitive verb:	She hopes <u>to be</u> over her cold in a couple of days.

Notice that in each of the previous situations, the subject doesn't know the outcome yet—that's why *hope* works.

And now what about *wish*? We've already shown how we use the present subjunctive and the past subjunctive after this verb, and now it's time to see how it works in the future:

Dialogue 1

> A. You know how much Fred and Fran hate cigarette smoke.
>   I **hope** you **won't light up** while we're in their home.
>
> B. Please! Do we have to go over this again?

Dialogue 2

> C. You know how much Frank and Freida hate cigarette smoke.
>   I **wish** you **wouldn't light up** while we're in their home.
>
> D. Please! Do we have to go over this again?

Both of these mini-dialogues concern the future. In Dialogue 1 Person A is communicating a hope for the future about her husband's behavior, and in Dialogue 2, Person C is making a wish for the future about her husband's behavior. Notice that **we use *would* as the form for the future subjunctive with verbs that follow *wish*, but we can use *were/was going to* as well**.

Now we need to ask you the same question as before: Do you discern any difference in meaning between what Person A says and what Person C says? After all, each idea shows the speaker's desire for the future, right? So what do you think? Is there a difference or not?

☐ yes   ☐ no

Even though both speakers are clearly showing their desires for their husbands' future behavior, the answer is **yes**, there's a very important difference between what Person A says and what Person C says. That difference isn't so much in the messages themselves as it is in each speaker's feelings about the situation. By responding to the following statements, you should get at the heart of their feelings when they made those comments to their husbands:

1. Person A is optimistic that her request will be honored.

   ☐ I agree   ☐ I disagree

2. Person C is optimistic that her request will be honored.

   ☐ I agree   ☐ I disagree

The choice of using *hope* or *wish* when discussing an issue in the future can make a world of difference. By using *hope*, Person A is demonstrating optimism that her husband won't smoke while in their friends' home, so for **Sentence 1** we would check **agree**. And, by the way, we should note that this sentence is actually a <u>**tactfully**</u> **expressed command**.

Conversely, by using *wish*, Person C is expressing a basic pessimism about her husband's refraining from smoking in their friends' home, so for **Sentence 2** we would check **disagree**. We should also note here that this sentence, compared to what Person A said, is a <u>**weakly**</u> and <u>**pessimistically**</u> **expressed command**.

To sum it all up, Person A believes there's at least a fifty-fifty chance that her husband won't smoke in their friends' home, but Person C thinks her husband will smoke there even though she'd rather he didn't. Oops! We've just used another phrase that can trigger the subjunctive, *would rather*, and we'll get to this one in just a moment.

 "Hope" in a Nutshell

 hope **= feel a possibility that something happened, is happening, or will happen. In other words, the outcome of the event is still unknown.**

Verbs after *hope* can take the following forms:
- **simple present:** I hope this meeting doesn't take too long.
- **present progressive:** We hope she's feeling better.
- **simple past:** He hopes they made up.
- **past progressive:** We hope you weren't waiting too long.
- **present perfect:** We hope he's made his flight.
- **present perfect progressive:** I hope you've been listening.
- *be going to:* She hopes he isn't going to disappoint her again.
- **simple future:** Let's hope everything will be all right.

modal auxiliaries (other than *will*) and semi-modals that follow *hope*:
- *can* **(present/timeless):**
  I just hired that woman to be my secretary. I hope she can spell well.
- *can* **(future):**
  It'll be a great party. We hope you can make it.
- *have to/have got to:*
  I hate it when my neighbor gets away with things. I hope he has to/has got to pay a big fine for burning those old truck tires of his in his backyard.
- *hope* **+ present/future = a tactfully expressed command:**
  I hope you('ll) remember to pick up some coffee on your way home from work this evening.

"Wish" in a Nutshell

 wish = feel a desire for something that is contrary to fact; show unhappiness over a situation

Verbs after *wish* take the following forms:

- **present subjunctive:**

  He wishes I were/was neater.

  I wish you knew him better.

- **past subjunctive:**

  I'm sure they wish we hadn't come yesterday.

- **future subjunctive:**

  She wishes I were/was coming along tomorrow.

  She wishes I were/was going to come along.

  She wishes I would come along.

modal and semi-modal auxiliaries (besides *would*) that follow *wish*:

- ***could* (present and timeless subjunctives):**

  It's too bad he's working now. We wish he could be here.

  I envy the freedom that birds have. I wish I could fly like them.

- ***could have* (past subjunctive):**

  I know they weren't able to save up enough money for that new car, but I wish they could have bought it.

- ***have to* (present and timeless subjunctives):**

  I wish I didn't have to work so hard to make a living.

  (past subjunctive):

  She has to pay someone to type everything for her. She wishes she had had to take typing in high school so she could do all the typing herself now.

  (future subjunctive):

  I was told to report there by 6:00 a.m. next Saturday. I wish I didn't have to get up so early next Saturday morning!

 wish + *would/wouldn't* = a weakly expressed command:

I wish you wouldn't use the phone so much.

Phrases Which Force the Present and Timeless Subjunctives

> A: Sasha, have you looked at a clock lately? **It's time we got going**.
>
> B: What's the rush? Masha's plane won't arrive for another half an hour. **It's not as if we were** late.
>
> A: Well, you know I don't want your sister to get off the plane without anybody there to greet her. **Suppose it were you** arriving. Wouldn't you want somebody there to greet you as you **got** off the plane?
>
> B: **If only you weren't** so obsessive about being on time!
>
> A: That's just the way I am. And besides, **I'd sooner we had to** wait for her than vice versa. Now let's get a move on!
>
> B: Okay! Okay!

As you can see, this dialogue is chock full of phrases that require us to use the subjunctive mood with the verbs that follow. Let's interpret the phrases in bold to see other ways we can express these ideas. Write sentences that paraphrase their meanings on the lines we've supplied:

It's time we got going.

_____

It's not as if we were late.

_____

Suppose it were you arriving.

_____

If only you weren't so obsessive . . .

_____

I'd sooner we had to wait for her . . .

_____

There isn't just one correct way to interpret each phrase, but here are some paraphrases that we've come up with. Compare yours to ours and see how closely they coincide:

"It's time we got going" means *we have to leave now or we'll be late.*

There's a certain urgency in the idea. Does this interpretation surprise you? If it does, compare this phrase:

"It's time (for us) to get going."

Any difference in meaning between the two phrases? Write your interpretation of this second phrase on the following line:

_____

The second phrase means **this is the scheduled time that we're supposed to leave.** It doesn't contain the urgency that the subjunctive verb form does. Now let's look at the rest of our phrases:

"It's not as if we were late" means **We're not late.** (contrary to fact)

"Suppose it were you arriving" means **Let's pretend that you're the one who's arriving.** (imaginary)

"If only you weren't so obsessive . . . " means **It's too bad that you're so obsessive . . . / I'd like you to be less obsessive . . .** (contrary to fact)

"I'd sooner we had to wait for her . . . " means **It would be preferable for us to wait for her . . .** (imaginary)

These phrases belong to a select group of expressions that require the use of the subjunctive with the verbs that follow them. Here's a list of some of the most commonly used ones. For some of them, we've added notes you may find interesting; for others, we've posed some questions:

as though/as if:
> He's acting *as though* he <u>were</u> president of the company.
> Someone should remind him that he's only an assistant to the janitor!

It's not as though/It's not as if:
> Stop crying so much. *It's not as if* she <u>were dying</u>.
> The doctor says she's going to make a full recovery.

If only:
> 1. *If only* we <u>were</u> more aggressive in our efforts!
> 2. *If only* we <u>knew</u> why he did that.

3. *If only* we <u>had started</u> with these rallies years ago.

4. *If only* we <u>could have convinced</u> people more easily.

An interesting observation about *if only* is that the word *only* can be detached and moved around. Take a look at these examples. What three rules can you make out from our four sentences?

1. If we were <u>only</u> more aggressive in our efforts!

2. If we <u>only</u> knew why he did that.

3. If we had <u>only</u> started with these rallies years ago.

4. If we could <u>only</u> have convinced people more easily.

So what rules can you come up with based on what you see?

1. _____

2. _____

3. _____

There really are specific rules for where we can move *only* (see Chapter 1):

Rule 1: Place *only* **after *be*** (Sentence 1).

Rule 2: Place it **between the subject and a simple verb form** (Sentence 2).

Rule 3: Place it **after the <u>first</u> auxiliary** (Sentences 3 and 4).

We can also place *only* as the first word in the *if*-clause, but we'll get into this word order in detail when we hit Chapter 20.

By the way, you might find it interesting to note that *only* functions just as an adverb of frequency would as far as word order goes.

(Just) imagine: *Just imagine* you **had been given** a one-year scholarship to the Sorbonne last semester. I wonder what you'd be doing right now.

It's time/It's about time/It's high time: An unusual note about these phrases is that they can be used with the past indicative or the present subjunctive, but it isn't always so easy to distinguish one from the other. Look at these two mini-dialogues and see if you can figure out which one contains the present subjunctive and which one uses the past indicative:

Dialogue 1

A: Have you heard? After relying on her husband for years to drive her everywhere, Reiko went to driving school and got her license.

B: Really? Well, it's about time she **learned** how to drive!

☐ present subjunctive   ☐ past indicative

Dialogue 2

A: Karl, now that I'm working full time, you've just got to help me around the house. It's time you **learned** to do the laundry and even cook some meals.

B: Okay, I'm willing to give it a try.

☐ present subjunctive   ☐ past indicative

Dialogue 1 contains the **past indicative**, and **Dialogue 2** uses the **present subjunctive**. Now that you've identified these forms, the questions that must be faced are, why does Speaker B use the past indicative in the first dialogue, and why does Speaker A use the present subjunctive in the second? If you think back to what we said at the beginning of this chapter about the difference between the indicative and subjunctive moods, you should figure out the answers.

Speaker B uses the past indicative in the first dialogue because _____

_____ .

Speaker A uses the present subjunctive in the second dialogue because _____

_____ .

When **Speaker B** uses *it's about time* with **the past indicative**, she's making an observation about **an actual fact** that she's just found out. And, if you recall from the start of this chapter, we said that the indicative mood is used for real facts.

On the other hand, when **Speaker A** uses *it's time* with **the present subjunctive**, she's saying that this is the appropriate time for something to happen or that it's even overdue, but it's **still not an accomplished act**. And, if you recall once again what we said at the start of this chapter, the subjunctive mood is used when discussing thoughts rather than actual facts.

(Just) suppose: *Just suppose* everybody **practiced** strict conservation. Can you imagine how much better off the world would be?

would rather/would sooner: What's worth noting about these two phrases is that sometimes the base verb form is used after these expressions, but sometimes the subjunctive form is used. Compare what the speakers say in the following mini-dialogue and write down what you observe that makes Speaker A use the base verb form and Speaker B use the subjunctive:

> A: You know, I'd rather **use** paper bags than plastic ones. At least they're biodegradable.
> B: I'd rather **we used** paper, too.

Have you figured it all out? Well, here's the solution to the mystery. **When the subject of the expressions** *would rather* **or** *would sooner* **is the same as the subject that goes with the following verb, we only use the base verb form and don't need to repeat the subject:**

$$\boxed{\text{I}}\ \text{would rather} + \boxed{\text{I}}\ \text{use} = \boxed{\text{I}}\ \text{would rather}\ \boxed{\text{use}}$$

However, **when the subject of the following verb is different from the subject of the expressions** *would rather* **or** *would sooner*, **we use the subjunctive form and need to state both subjects:**

$$\boxed{\text{I}}\ \text{would rather} + \boxed{\text{we}}\ \text{use} = \boxed{\text{I}}\ \text{would rather}\ \boxed{\text{we}}\ \boxed{\text{used}}$$

would that: Although we're listing *would that*, it by no means is a commonly used expression. It's actually an archaic form that you'll only find in very old writings or affected speech, and it means basically the same thing as **if only**. We thought we'd list it here in case you or your students ever come across it:

> *Would that* we <u>were</u> young again!
> *Would that* I <u>could</u>!

A The Mandative Subjunctive

The word "mandative" obviously comes from the word *mandate,* which means *command* or *instruct,* and that basically sums up how the mandative subjunctive is used— to command or instruct. As to why this form is considered a subjunctive form, wait until you've seen our first dialogue and then you'll understand the reason.

The odd feature you'll notice is that **we use nothing more than the base verb form for the mandative subjunctive no matter if our idea's in the present, past, or future.** The reason this odd feature doesn't become a problem concerning how to interpret the time is that **the verb that precedes the mandative subjunctive carries the time.**

Here's a dialogue showing the mandative subjunctive at work:

A: I'm really glad that the city government has finally passed a law about recycling.

B: So am I. But it'll be very important that everybody **participate** or it may not make a difference.

A: True. Did you see the guidelines they printed in the paper telling people how to recycle?

B: Uh-huh. They suggested that we **separate** paper products from metal ones, and they said it was necessary that all cans and bottles **be** rinsed out.

A: So when is all of that stuff going to be picked up?

B: The law requires that recycled material **not be** picked up on the same day as regular garbage and trash. So each municipality has to come up with another day each week for that stuff.

Notice how the base verb form is used in each case to form the mandative subjunctive? The question is, what triggers it? Can you pick out the part of each of Speaker B's sentences that caused her to use the mandative subjunctive? When you've zeroed in on them, copy them over on the following lines:

_____

_____

The key to when we need the mandative subjunctive lies with the phrases that trigger it. In our dialogue, they are these sentence starters:

    It'll be important (that) . . .   **It's necessary (that)** . . .
    They suggested (that) . . .   **The law requires (that)** . . .

There are three things we'd like you to notice. First of all, within these phrases we have a future form, a past form, and a timeless form, yet the mandative is in the base verb form throughout. Next, we have *that* after each phrase, but it's optional. And finally, because the mandative subjunctive is comprised only of the base verb form, the only way to make it negative is to put *not* in front of it (" . . . not be picked up . . . ").

A question that may have entered your mind is why there's a need for a subjunctive form after phrases like the four we've already seen. As we've recently reiterated, one reason for the **subjunctive** is that it can deal with **a thought rather than a fact**, and that's exactly why we use the mandative subjunctive in these cases. When Person B said " . . . it'll be very important that everybody participate, . . . " it was not a fact but a thought. If we were to say "everybody's participating" we're talking about a fact, but in our dialogue this isn't true yet.

Along the same lines, if we were to say "everybody participates," it could be interpreted as something traditional or usual, and "everybody will participate" can mean a future prediction or some such interpretation for the future. None of these forms is satisfactory for our current purpose since fact, prediction, and the like aren't parts of our speaker's idea, and we don't want to be locked into any specific time anyway. The mandative subjunctive cleverly avoids any ambiguity with these other verb forms.

So what other phrases trigger the mandative subjunctive? Here are some common ones. The three main types of phrases are verb phrases, noun phrases (derived from many of these verbs), and adjective phrases. Here are the verb phrases—and remember that *that* is optional:

    advise that   ask that
    command that   demand that
    forbid that   insist that

move that	order that
propose that	recommend that
request that	require that
suggest that	urge that

And here are the noun phrases derived from many of these verbs. With noun phrases *that* is not an option; it must be used.

The advice that	The order that
The command that	The recommendation that
The demand that	The request that
The prohibition that	The requirement that
The move that	The suggestion that

Now let's look at a few examples of how these noun phrases force the mandative subjunctive:

The advice that she <u>not quit</u> her job fell on deaf ears.

The order that the prisoner <u>be</u> released was carried out.

The suggestion that he <u>seek</u> medical attention made sense.

And now to the adjective phrases. Here, the word *that* is optional again.

It's advisable that	It's necessary that
It's essential that	It's traditional that
It's imperative that	It's urgent that
It's important that	It's vital that

By the way, in informal speech the adjective phrases we've listed can also be followed by a verb in the simple present indicative:

It's essential he <u>takes</u> this medicine regularly.

Even though this use of the simple present indicative goes against the reason for the existence of the mandative subjunctive, it nevertheless must be recognized as an alternate form for the simple reason that so many native speakers use it this way. This is a good example of what you'll be exploring later on in Chapter 22 when we deal with some changes that English has already experienced, is experiencing right now, and will continue to experience in the future.

There's one last point we should make before moving on. If you take a second look at the sentences in our dialogue on page 432, can you think of other ways to communicate the same ideas without using the mandative form? Think about how you'd paraphrase those sentences and write your paraphrases on the lines that follow:

1. It'll be very important that everybody participate. =

   It'll be very important _____.

2. They suggested that we separate paper products from metal ones. =

They suggested _____.

3. They said it was necessary that all cans and bottles be rinsed out. =

They said it was necessary _____.

4. The law requires that recycled material not be picked up on the same days as regular garbage and trash. =

The law requires _____.

Once again there's undoubtedly more than one way to paraphrase each of these sentences, but here are our entries to compare to your own:

1. **It'll be very important for everybody to participate.**
   It'll be very important that everybody should participate.

2. **They suggested that we should separate paper products from metal ones.**

3. **They said it was necessary for all cans and bottles to be rinsed out.**
   They said it was necessary for us to rinse out all cans and bottles.

4. **The law requires that recycled material must not/cannot/should not be picked up on the same days as regular garbage and trash.**

Have you noticed that *should* pops up in half of the sentences we created? ***Should*** **is quite commonly used as an alternative to the mandative subjunctive**, maybe because some native speakers consider the mandative subjunctive very formal, archaic, or even somewhat harsh. Using the word *should* seems to soften the impact for them.

⩗ A Modern Language Oddity: The Formulaic Subjunctive

As we've often mentioned, there are those tense, awful "moments of truth" all teachers face at one time or another when they come across a grammatical form that leaves them absolutely at a loss to explain. Well, here we go again! Reading this next dialogue should simulate one of those dreadful experiences for you, and what we're going to ask you to do after you've read it will give you an additional idea of how that "moment of truth" might feel:

A: Did you hear about that latest nuclear power plant accident?

B: Yes, I did. **God help us** if things like that continue!

A: **Heaven forbid!** **Suffice it to say** the earth won't be here too long if they can't be more careful with those places.

B: I don't know about that. **Come what may**, I think the earth will still be here—but life on earth won't be!

A: At least not as we know it. I get shivers just thinking about my great-grandchildren, "the mutants"!

You might be thinking you'd like to avoid those phrases in bold because you know what's coming next. Well, in case you're dying to know what we'd like you to do now, it's really quite simple. Just find one or more ways to paraphrase each of the phrases in bold. Let's see what you can come up with:

God help us… _____

_____

Heaven forbid! _____

_____

Suffice it to say… _____

_____

Come what may… _____

_____

Now that you've written down your paraphrases, it's our turn to write down ours, so here's what we've come up with:

God help us . . . We hope God will help us . . . / Only God can help us . . .
Heaven forbid! I certainly hope not! / I pray that doesn't happen!

Suffice it to say . . . It's enough to say . . . / What it comes down to is . . . / To sum it all up . . .

Come what may . . . Whatever happens . . . / Whatever the outcome . . .

What we're dealing with is a group of pat expressions that native speakers use without even thinking about the grammar involved. Students should memorize these expressions *as is* and only care about what they mean and when it's appropriate to use them. The name which some grammarians call the subjunctive that appears in all of these pat phrases is the **formulaic subjunctive**. As the name implies, this subjunctive is part of a *formula,* which is just another way to say a pat phrase. So you need scratch your head no more. If your students come across one or more of these little gems, or if you decide they should be taught to your advanced students, you don't have to worry about going into deep, lengthy explanations over them. They're relics of a very old use of the English subjunctive, and that's all there is to it!

Here are some other phrases that include the formulaic subjunctive:

Be that as it may . . .   Long live . . .
Far be it from me to . . .   Lord have mercy!
(God) bless you . . .   So be it.
(God) damn/darn it!   Till death do us part.

In some of the phrases we've just cited, a more modern-sounding rendering can be given by the addition of the modal auxiliary *may*:

May God help us.   May ——— live long.
May God bless you.   May the Lord have mercy!

Teaching Tips

There's only one *Teaching Tip* for this chapter because wishes, hopes, and conditionals just seem to be made to go together. When people wish and hope ("I wish I knew how to do this." / "I hope it stops raining soon"), they frequently explain why ("If I knew how to do this, I wouldn't have to call you every fifteen minutes for help." / "If it ever stops raining, I can hang out my laundry"). We recommend that you jump ahead to Chapter 20 and pick out those tips where wishing and hoping are targeted. Now here's the one tip for this chapter.

I Wish You'd Sit Next to Me!

This very simple activity is particularly good for students to learn their classmates' names and how to pronounce them accurately. Divide the students into groups of eight or nine. Have each group make a circle and add one extra chair to the circle. Let the student who has the empty chair on his or her right ask a classmate to move into the empty chair by saying "I wish X would sit next to me." X moves to the chair and the student who now has the empty chair on his or her right does the same.

20

Conditional Sentences

"If music be the food of love, play on."

In the previous chapter, we dealt with that wonderful human ability to create real or unreal ideas and to conjecture about how things might be. In this chapter we're going to continue that process of using our minds via language to create real and hypothetical situations. We'll be seeing a good deal of the grammar we covered in Chapter 19, but it will be used in new ways as we continue exploring the realms of reality and unreality in English through the constructions we call conditional sentences.

The reason that this type of sentence is called a "conditional" sentence is that something takes place on condition that something else happens first. It's really a case of cause and effect, so one event takes place depending on whether or not the other event takes place. The following sentence is a typical example:

If he proposes, she'll marry him.

The sentence above is typical of a conditional sentence because her marrying him is dependent on his proposing to her—that's the condition. The second event will only occur if the first one takes place.

Now that we've established what a conditional sentence is, we've got a lot of exploring to do into how it's constructed and what variations it has. What we need to do to keep this exploration understandable is to pick the sentence apart much like a dissection and study the elements that go to make up the whole—and that's just what we're about to do.

Before we get started, though, we'd like to mention that we're going to deal with the topic of conditional sentences the same way we've dealt with some other topics in this text. First, we'll be investigating the basic grammatical forms that all teachers should understand and teach to their students at the appropriate level. Then we'll be offering you the option of taking a deeper look, should you care to, so you can delve into more intricate and subtle areas of the subject.

✍️ Real Conditional Sentences: Timeless, Present, and Future Forms

The first thing to consider is the fact that **there are always two parts to any conditional sentence**. One of these parts commonly starts with *if*, so we'll call it the *if* **clause**. The other part happens only when the event in the *if* clause occurs, so we'll call it the **conditional clause**. Remember that there must always be these two parts, although at times the conditional clause doesn't have to be stated if it's understood from the context, and vice versa.

Real Timeless Conditional Sentences

A: So how was your Mexican vacation?

B: Just the greatest! We had a marvelous time.

A: Did you get to see a bullfight?

B: We certainly did.

A: Okay, tell me something. Is it true that **if a bull sees red, it gets all upset**?

B: No, that's just an old myth. In fact, **if you show a bull something red, it doesn't make the least bit of difference.**

A: Just as I thought! I knew that was a lot of nonsense.

B: Of course it is. Actually, **if you let a bull see something mauve, that's when he gets mad!**

As we can see in our dialogue, real timeless conditional sentences deal with what the speaker perceives as being universal truths. Just as the simple present can reflect this idea of something that always is and therefore has no temporal boundaries (Chapter 3), it can be used in *both* clauses of a conditional sentence to demonstrate the same concept. Here are some other examples of this type of conditional sentence:

You <u>get</u> pink paint if you <u>mix</u> red paint with white.

If the monsoons <u>don't come</u> to Asia, droughts <u>occur</u>.

The same holds true when *can* or the present perfect is used:

> A: Your son <u>can</u> be very cranky if he <u>doesn't get</u> a nap.
> B: But if he <u>has</u> his nap, he's as sweet as sugar.
>
> A: Your son <u>gets</u> very cranky if he <u>hasn't had</u> a nap.
> B: But if he's <u>had</u> his nap, he's as sweet as sugar.

When we want to express a real, timeless idea, remember that we can use the simple present in both clauses. We can also choose to use *can* or the present perfect in one of those clauses. You'll see a little further on how this use of *can* or the present perfect isn't always the case if we're dealing with a real conditional sentence in the present.

Real Present Conditional Sentences

Just as its name says, this type of real conditional sentence deals with the present, but it can do so in two ways. In the next dialogue, you'll see one of these ways:

> A: Oh, boy! The boss is going to have your head for coming in so late again.
> B: **If he's** angry, **it doesn't matter** one bit.
> A: Doesn't matter? You know how easily he fires people.
> B: **If he isn't** happy with me, I really **don't care.**
> A: Don't care? Brother! You act as if you've won the lottery or something!
> B: Well, guess what?
> A: You didn't! You didn't! You did?

In this type of real present conditional sentence, the *if* clauses contain the present (*he's/he isn't*), and the conditional clauses do, too (*doesn't matter/don't care*).

One other important point to notice about the *if* clauses in the dialogue you've just seen is that each one is really acting as a rhetorical device by restating what's already known.

Now let's see the other way we can form a real present conditional sentence:

A: Wait up, Rodrigo! Where are you heading?

B: To the train station to pick up my Uncle Pancho.

A: Well, **if you're going** down there, **I'll come** along, okay?

B: Sure. But what for?

A: I want to pick up a job application.

B: Gosh, I should have been there to pick him up an hour ago.

A: Uh-oh. **If he's been waiting** there all this time, **he won't be** in such a good mood.

B: Tell me about it! Uncle Pancho's got a real temper. And **if he's tried** to call my house, **he'll be** even more upset because our phone's not working.

A: You know what? Don't introduce me to your uncle when we get there. I'll meet him some other time!

In this other way of making a real present conditional sentence, the *if* clause contains a verb which is in some other form of the present than we've just seen. In the case of our dialogue, the **present progressive**, **present perfect**, and **present perfect progressive** have now been used.

So what about the conditional clauses in this second type of real present conditional sentence? They invariably use some form of the future although it's very typical to find the modal auxiliary *will* being used. The reason the conditional clause must be in some form of the future is for the simple reason that whatever is being mentioned in this clause can't happen until the event in the *if* clause takes place, so the conditional clause gets pushed into the future.

By the way, there's one present verb form that's conspicuously missing from our dialogue. We'll be discussing it momentarily.

Real Future Conditional Sentences

A: You know what, Rodrigo? Instead of my going with you to the train station, do you think you could pick up an application form for me?

B: No problem, Jaime. I'm on my way there anyway. **If you need one, I'll pick one up for you.**

> A: You're a real pal, Rodrigo. And **if you ever want me to do you a favor, I'll be very happy to oblige.**
> B: Well, there *is* something.
> A: Just name it!
> B: **If you get the job you're going to apply for, will you treat me to dinner?**
> A: Need you ask? It's as good as done!

Now that you've read this dialogue, let's consider the verbs in the *if* clauses of the real future conditional sentences we've just seen. Remember we said that there was one present verb form conspicuously missing from our real present conditional sentences? Well, here it is. You can't help but notice that even though this section is supposed to be dealing with the future, all three *if* clauses contain verbs in **the simple present**. Well, we've got to confess something to you. We've been very sneaky. We stuck in one verb that really does refer to the present and not the future at all. Which one is it?

1. If you | need | an application form . . .

2. If you ever | want | me to do you a favor . . .

3. If you | get | the job you're going to apply for . . .

☐ Sentence 1   ☐ Sentence 2   ☐ Sentence 3

The truth of the matter is that **Sentence 1** really refers to the present, and we know that because of context, but because *need* is one of those special stative verbs (see page 33), we don't use the progressive form.

So what about the other two verbs, which are also in the simple present in those *if* clauses? What they really refer to is the future, but **in a real future conditional sentence, we don't normally show an obvious future form in the *if* clause; we use the simple present instead.** There are a couple of exceptions to this rule, but we'll deal with them later on when we take a deeper look.

So if the simple present can mean the future, can it mean other things, too? Maybe it can, but we need to keep in mind that context is everything. Only through context can we really understand the time in many of the *if* clauses. To prove this point, let's try an experiment. Following are three sentences, each one beginning with the same three words. Read each sentence, decide whether the type of conditional sentence is time-less, present, or future. Then write the appropriate identifications in the blank spaces we've provided:

1. _____ <u>If you see</u> holes like this in wood, it means termites are present.

2. _____ <u>If you see</u> Heinz that far away, your eyes are better than mine.

3. _____ <u>If you see</u> Birgit, give her my regards.

Isn't it amazing how the same three words can be used for such different aspects of time! Of course, it's the conditional clause in each sentence that gives you the necessary context and information to figure out the time of the *if* clause. It turns out that **Number 1** is **timeless, Number 2** is **present,** and **Number 3** is **future**.

To be sure, we're playing around here with a stative verb, *see,* which means that the real present isn't so obvious as it would be with an active verb, but these are among the troublesome points that both teachers and students have a hard time dealing with.

Getting back to real future conditional sentences, we should mention that there are also many modal auxiliaries that can be found in the *if* clause and that carry a future meaning:

can:	If I <u>can</u> have a few more minutes, I'll be done with this job.
may/might:	If I <u>may/might</u> have a word, there's something that's been bothering me.
should:	If you <u>should</u> need some extra money, I'll be glad to help you out. (We'll be dealing with *should* in more detail later on when we take a deeper look.)
must/have to:	If she <u>must/has to</u> give up her vacation this year, she won't be at all happy about it.

Now let's take another look at the conditional clause. The only thing worth mentioning again is that this is the place where we commonly find the obvious future form of the verb. And, as we've also mentioned before, although it's more typical to find *will* as the agent of the future in a real future conditional clause, native speakers also use *be going to*—but that's not all.

Just as we've found modal auxiliaries in the *if* clause, we can also find just about all the modals (*can, may, might, should, ought to,* and *must*) and the semi-auxiliary *have to* in the conditional clause as well. (In our next dialogue, you'll come across lots of examples.) Right now, let's look at a sentence that contains the modal *may*:

If you don't ask her soon, you <u>may</u> not get a chance to.

Here are other examples of conditional clauses that contain modals:

> If he doesn't propose soon . . .
>> . . . she <u>might/could</u> lose interest in him.
>> . . . he <u>should/ought to</u> get his head examined!
>> . . . he <u>must</u> be some kind of fool.

When you really think about it, even though we no longer have *will* or *be going to* in these conditional clauses, they still express a future idea. Except for *must* (which is being used here for a logical conclusion), the other modals we've added (*might, could, should, ought to*) all have a future reference. And, as far as our use of *must* for a logical conclusion is concerned, we still understand that the whole idea is in the future because **the future can be implied in the *if* clause even though its verb form isn't obvious**.

There's one more point we'd like to make concerning the use of modals. We can create the following real future conditional sentence:

> If you don't propose to Fiona soon, you <u>won't</u> get a chance to.

But we can also use *may*:

> If you don't propose to Fiona soon, you <u>may not</u> get a chance to.

Is there any difference between the two modals? Of course there is! We know that *may* means **possibility**, but in contrast to *may*, what does *will* tell us in this context?

Using *will* means that the speaker is **very sure** of the result, and that's an important difference in the communication.

⚡ *Troubleshooter* ⚡

Students don't usually understand how important the difference is between *will* and *may* in real conditional sentences.

Get them to see that if they use *will*, it means they're expressing a certainty, whereas if they use *may*, *might*, or *could*, they're only saying that there's a chance this will be the outcome.

These other modals give the speaker a "margin of safety" that *will* doesn't. Just check out these two sentences to see which one makes the speaker seem a little foolish:

☞ If you get the flu again, you *may* catch pneumonia.
☞ If you get the flu again, you *will* catch pneumonia.

Before moving on, let's take another look at that last sentence—the reasonable one—in the *Troubleshooter*. There's another interesting way this idea can be constructed. Just take a look:

> Get the flu again and you may catch pneumonia.

Are we still dealing with a conditional sentence? Of course we are, but it's gone through a bit of a metamorphosis. On the following line, account for the changes that have taken place:

_____

What's happened is that *If you* **has been dropped and the conjunction** *and* **has replaced the comma.** A sentence like this can be very confusing for students, who tend to interpret the first part of the sentence as an imperative form as if you were ordering somebody to get the flu again! There's one more point to be made about this type of conditional construction, which has to do with the subject of the idea. Can you figure out what this important point is?

_____

What's necessary to keep in mind is that **you can only make this conditional sentence construction for the second person, singular or plural (you).** It doesn't work with any other subject. So, practice this construction with your students and they'll become better English speakers!

Now we've dissected the basic parts that go into making a conditional sentence, in this case, a real conditional sentence. One more thing to mention is the fact that the two clauses that make up this construction can be reversed without affecting meaning. Even though we don't usually get into punctuation, we think it interesting and important to note that when the *if* clause starts off a conditional sentence, we generally add a comma after it, but not the other way round:

And speaking of the order of the words or phrases in a conditional sentence, we're going to digress for a moment to mention that there's one strange occurrence when a word inversion takes place within this type of sentence. Here's an example in the typical word order for a conditional sentence:

> We'll cancel the field and track event <u>only if it rains</u>.

Everything looks normal, right? Well, let's say we want to begin our idea with the underlined part that now appears at the end. How should we continue the sentence then?

Only if it rains _____.

You know we gave you a hint by saying that there was some sort of word inversion to deal with, so have you figured it out? The rest of our sentence should be **. . . will we cancel the field and track event**. It's not that this form is totally new for you; we dealt with similar inversions back in Chapter 1. The rule basically is that **we reverse the order of the subject and the first auxiliary in the conditional clause if we begin a conditional sentence with the phrase** *Only if . . . .* Here are other examples for you to look at:

> Only if it had rained <u>would we</u> have canceled the picnic.
> Only if you admit your mistake <u>are you</u> going to feel better.
> Only if he takes his medicine <u>can he</u> expect a full recovery.
> Only if she'd gotten the raise <u>could she</u> have afforded to move.

And do you remember that we said we generally place a comma after the *if* clause when that clause starts off a conditional sentence? Well, as you can see from all of the examples you've just read, that comma isn't used when the conditional sentence starts off with *Only if . . . .*

But we're not through yet! What if the verb in the conditional clause is in the simple present/timeless form? If that happens, we don't have any auxiliary to reverse position with the subject. So what do we do? We've got to have something that can be reversed with the subject if we want to keep our rule intact. Any idea what the solution is? Here's a sentence for you to work with:

> If you water house plants prudently, <u>they grow</u> well indoors.

Let's take this idea and rework it by starting off with our phrase of the moment. Can you finish it? Try it and see what you come up with:

Only if you water house plants prudently _____.

It's really astounding how the language comes up with ways to keep rules intact. In this case, since the original idea doesn't include an auxiliary, we need something else, so the language turns in this case to the word that fills in for the auxiliary when there isn't any, namely, *do*. So the way we'd complete our mystery sentence is by saying **. . . *do they grow* well indoors**!

Of course, the same holds true when the simple past is used:

> If she ate the right foods, <u>she felt</u> good.
> Only if she ate the right foods <u>did she feel</u> good.

There's one difference in the construction of the sentences that start off with *Only if . . .* and have the verb inversion with *do*. The difference is that you can't reverse the order of the clauses in these sentences. They must always begin with the *only if* clause! (These two sentences are acceptable: "She felt good only if she ate the right foods." or "Only if she ate the right foods did she feel good." However, this one is not: "Did she feel good only if she ate the right foods.")

We've now explored the different types of real conditional sentences in detail. If all the material is clear to you, and if this much is what your students learn to handle well, that will be just fine. If, however, you'd like to explore further into the intricacies of real conditional sentences, the next section, entitled *A Deeper Look,* should interest you.

A Deeper Look

To delve deeper into this subject, let's begin by taking a second look at the *if* clause in the real future conditional sentence. If you recall, we said that we normally use the simple present in that clause, but we added that there were a couple of exceptions to the rule. That's what we'll focus on here to start things off. One good reason to focus on these exceptions is that they rarely appear in student grammar books—and they definitely should.

Check out the following dialogue and see if you can figure out why the speakers haven't adhered to our basic rule of using the simple present in the *if* clause:

A: Good afternoon. DeMarco, Taylor, and Gross. May I help you?

B: Yes, please. May I speak to Mr. DeMarco?

A: Certainly. Your name, please?

B: Tell him Ms. Pizarro is calling.

A: **If you'll hold** the line, I'll put you through. One moment.

C: Hello, Ms. Pizarro! How are you?

B: Just fine, thank you. I'm calling to see if we can set up a date to finalize those contracts.

C: Of course. Let's see . . . **If it will fit in** with your schedule, can we do it the morning of the 18th?

B: Yes, that'll be fine. Shall we say at ten?

C: Perfect.

Hmm . . . Very curious, wouldn't you say? Just off the top of your head, do you have any idea why the phrases in bold seem okay, and do you detect any difference at all between each of our phrases in bold and counterparts in the simple present? If you do, write your thoughts on the following line:

Before we let you know if you're on the right track, let's compare the first phrase in bold from our dialogue with its counterpart and discover if there's any difference between them:

If you<u>'ll hold</u> the line, I'll put you through.
If you <u>hold</u> the line, I'll put you through.

Now check the boxes that work for you:

1. The two phrases mean the same thing: ☐ agree   ☐ disagree
2. There's no difference in register: ☐ agree   ☐ disagree

Very tricky, isn't it? It so happens that there really isn't any important difference in the meaning of the two phrases as used in our dialogue, so for **Number 1** we'd check **agree**. As far as register (formality) is concerned, many native speakers do detect a slight difference with "If you'll hold the line" being more formal. So for **Number 2** we'd check **disagree**.

The reason that "If you'll hold the line" sounds more formal to many speakers is that it shows a little bit of deference to the other person. Believe it or not, in this phrase *will* **represents a desire or wish to do something**, harking back to the original meaning of this modal auxiliary when it was still a verb in Old English, so we can paraphrase this by saying "If you wish to hold the line" or "If you want to hold the line." By showing that there's an interest in the desire of Speaker B to do so, Speaker A is demonstrating a sort of deference to the person, making the phrase more formal sounding, a little more polite.

"If you hold the line" seems to many speakers to be a straightforward phrase that contains none of this deference. Realizing this difference makes it more understandable when you hear people use this typical response to the following inquiry:

> A: Shall I make some coffee for our guests?
> B: Yes, if you <u>will</u>.

In this response, Person B could just as easily say *if you'd like to, if you care to, if you want to,* and so forth. The important thing to keep in mind is that this *if* clause with *will* doesn't focus on the time at all; it focuses on the <u>will</u>ingness of the other person to do something.

By the way, there's an alternate word we can use instead of *will* in Person B's response. Can you think of it? Write down the word you think can replace *will* on the following line:

The optional word we can use in place of *will* is **would**. And what do you think the difference is between using *will* and using *would* in this way in the *if* clause?

☐ *would* is more deferential   ☐ *would* is less deferential

Interestingly enough, many native speakers feel that *would* is **more deferential** than *will* in a response like *If you would.*

In other cases, *would* can show less optimism than *will* on the speaker's part as far as some other person agreeing to do something. Just compare these two mini-dialogues:

Dialogue 1

> A. If you'**ll** listen to reason, I'm sure we
>   can find a solution to this problem.
> B. Fine. I'm willing to hear you out.

Dialogue 2

> C. If you'**d** listen to reason, I'm sure we
>   could find a solution to this problem.
> D. Fine. Go ahead. I'm listening.

We'd never say that there's a major difference between what Person A says in Dialogue 1 and what Person C says in Dialogue 2, but there *is* a slight change. In Dialogue 1 Person A probably feels that Person B will be a little more open-minded to any suggestions. In Dialogue 2, however, it sounds like Person C is a bit more exasperated because he doesn't really think Person D will be open to suggestions.

Of course, emotion and body language can greatly influence how Persons A and C feel as they make their pitches, but as far as language is concerned, there is this slight difference between *will* and *would*.

One last point is that it's important to state again that *will* and *would,* as they appear in these *if* clauses, don't deal with time but with somebody's willingness to do something.

Now what about that other phrase in bold from the dialogue on page 448? Let's take another look at this phrase together with its counterpart and check off the boxes as we did before:

If it <u>will fit in</u> with your schedule . . .
If it <u>fits in</u> with your schedule . . .

1. The two phrases mean the same thing: ☐ agree ☐ disagree
2. There's no difference in register: ☐ agree ☐ disagree
3. There's no difference in the time focus: ☐ agree ☐ disagree

Well, do the two phrases basically mean the same thing? We'd have to say they do, so for **Number 1**, we'd check **agree**. Now then, is there a difference in register? This time we have to say that most people don't discern any significant difference in formality because it has nothing to do with willingness, so for **Number 2**, we also have to check **agree**. And is there any difference in the time focus? There really is because "If it will fit in" focuses exclusively on some time in the future, whereas "If it fits in" can deal with either right now, general time, or the future, depending on context. So for **Number 3**, we have to check **disagree**.

Now let's move on to something else. Our next dialogue is quite a lengthy one, but we've got a reason for that. There are going to be two phrases in the following conditional sentences that replace the word *if* in the *if* clauses. Let's see if you can pick them out:

A: Haven't you and Fiona been going together long enough? Are you guys ever going to get married?

B: I want to marry her—you know I do, but I never seem to find the right moment to propose. Don't worry, I'll ask her soon.

A: If you don't ask her soon, you may not get a chance to.

B: Why do you say that?

A: Haven't you seen the way Sean looks at her? If he sees that nothing's happening between you, he'll get ideas in his head—if you know what I mean.

B: Don't say that! Do you really think so? Okay! I'll propose to her at the company dance tomorrow night if she seems receptive.

A: Terrific! And I'll be the best man at your wedding—provided Fiona accepts.

B: Don't say things like that! I know she'll accept . . .

A: . . . assuming she still loves you.

B: Well, yes, sure. I don't have a second to lose. Forget tomorrow night! I've got to find Fiona now! Fiona, where are you?

So, what are the two new "*if*-meaning" phrases that you haven't seen in the example sentences we've already dealt with? Write them down on the following line:

——————————————— and ———————————————

The new phrases that we haven't come across yet can be found in the following sentences from our dialogue:

And I'll be best man at your wedding—provided Fiona accepts.
. . . assuming she still loves you.

We've substituted *if* with *provided* and *assuming*, and these are our new phrases. So *if* isn't the only word we can use to introduce what we've dubbed the "*if* clause." This fact should be kept in mind when teaching this topic.

Besides the two phrases we see in our dialogue, namely *provided (that)* and *assuming (that),* there are other substitutes with the meaning of *if:*

as long as:	We can all get on well <u>as long as</u> we respect one another.
in case:	<u>In case</u> I get there first, I'll hold a seat for you.
in the event (that):	<u>In the event</u> it rains, we'll have the party indoors.
on condition (that):	We'll drop the law suit <u>on condition</u> that he apologize.
providing (that):	He'll be hired <u>providing</u> his credentials check out.
so long as:	You'll feel fine <u>so long as</u> you take your medicine.
unless:	(see the next *Troubleshooter*)
whether or not:	They'll get married <u>whether or not</u> we approve.

There's one more item that we can use in place of *if* in a conditional sentence, and it's the word **otherwise**. But it's not that simple. Check out the following example:

They'll have to put up $25,000; <u>otherwise</u>, the deal's off.

How can you paraphrase this sentence if you begin with *If?* Try writing a sentence down on the following line:

It's really interesting how we've got to change things around to come up with an accurate paraphrase for our sentence with *otherwise.* The one we've come up with is: **If they don't put up $25,000, the deal's off.** We're sure your paraphrase is basically the same as ours. As you can see, unlike the way all those phrases can easily substitute for *if, otherwise* has to be understood in a very different way and used accordingly.

One extra thing worth taking note of is where the word *otherwise* is placed. If you look back at our last sentence with it, you'll see that it's the only conditional word attached to the conditional clause ("the deal's off") rather than the *if* clause ("They'll have to put up $25,000").

As we've already said, the important point for teachers to remember is that ***if* is not the only word that can introduce the *if* clause**, nor is *if* the only word that teachers should teach.

A·:· Real Conditional Sentences and the Imperative

A form that tends to get overlooked in student grammar books is the use of the imperative, or command form of the verb, in real conditional sentences. The imperative, however, can be used in two different ways in this type of sentence. One of these ways is quite straightforward and uncomplicated. In this case, the imperative appears in the conditional clause. This next dialogue will show you a couple of examples.

A: You're going to the supermarket now, right?

B: Uh-huh.

A: Good. Do me a favor. If you see tomatoes on sale, **pick** me **up** about five pounds. I'm going to make a big pot of spaghetti sauce.

B: Sure thing. Oh, and can you do me a favor in return?

A: Okay. What is it?

B: If my mother calls while I'm out, **tell** her I'll stop by her house on the way home from the supermarket.

༈ *Troubleshooter* ༈

If there's one word that gives teachers and their students a lot of grief, it's *unless*. One reason for this problem is that *unless* contains a hidden, negative idea, and when something's not obvious, it becomes troublesome.

Another reason is that there are times when this little word is interchangeable with *if . . . not*, but there are other times when it isn't.

The thing to keep in mind is that *unless* really means *except on the condition that . . .* If you can't use this lengthy phrase in your idea, you can't use *unless* in the sentence, but you *can* use *if . . . not*.

☞ *if . . . not* and *unless* are interchangeable when we create a real conditional sentence:
She won't join us tonight *if* she *doesn't* feel better.
(She won't join us tonight except on the condition that she feels better.)
She won't join us tonight *unless* she feels better.

☞ *Unless* won't work, however, in a sentence like this:
He loses his temper so easily, it'll be amazing *if* he *doesn't* have a stroke one day.

Why won't it? It's because we can't use our long phrase in this idea and still make any sense:

He loses his temper so easily, it'll be amazing *except on the condition that* he has a stroke one day.

The other way the imperative can be used in real conditional sentences is more complicated because the conditional aspect of the idea may not be so obvious to students. Take a look at what we mean:

> A: Gee, Grandpa, I really like going fishing with you.
>
> B: And I like going fishing with you, too, Naoko! Now, **catch us some big, fat fish, and we'll take them home** for everyone to eat tonight.
>
> A: Okay, Grandpa. Oh! Look at my line! Look how it's pulling, Grandpa!
>
> B: All right, Naoko. That means you've got a really nice fish on your hook. **Reel it in quickly or the fish may get away.**
>
> A: Like this? Wow! Look at how big it is, Grandpa!
>
> B: You did a fine job, Naoko. Yes, there'll be fish for dinner tonight!

This time, the imperative is found at the beginning of each sentence in bold. Notice that the first part of each sentence (" . . . catch us some big, fat fish" / "Reel it in quickly . . . ") is connected either by *and* or by *or* to the second part (" . . . we'll bring them home . . . " / " . . . the fish may get away").

So why are we including these sentences in a chapter on conditionals? It's because hidden within each one there really is a more typical-looking conditional sentence. In fact, the first parts of these sentences aren't really imperatives at all; they're reduced *if* clauses. Can you create these more typical real conditional sentences that can begin with the usual *if* clause? Here are a couple of lines for you to write your paraphrases on:

_____

_____

If we want to paraphrase the sentences in bold from our dialogue with more typical-looking conditional sentences, we end up with these sentences:

> **If you catch us some big, fat fish, we'll take them home for everyone to eat tonight.**
> **If you don't reel it in quickly, the fish may get away.**

One final note worth mentioning here is that we can use the word *otherwise* after an imperative in the *if* clause to explain what will happen if the listener doesn't carry out the imperative:

Reel it in quickly; <u>otherwise</u>, the fish may get away.

There's nothing else that needs to be said about the use of imperatives in conditional ideas except that they're very commonly used and shouldn't be overlooked by teachers.

Some Nuances with Real Conditional Sentences

A: Miss Khan, are you on your way over to New Accounts?

B: Yes, Mr. Buzurg.

A: Good. **If you happen to see** Jamshid, please ask him if he's all set with his presentation for Bokhara Textiles.

B: You've forgotten, sir. Jamshid's on a skiing trip, but he'll be back tomorrow.

A: Oh, that's right. Well, **should you pass** by his desk, leave him a message to call me first thing when he gets in.

Just like an artist who uses various shades of the same color to give depth, richness, and texture to a specific area of a painting, English uses its own form of shading to accomplish the same thing. Throughout this book we've come across this wonderful ability that language has time and time again, and here we have yet another example of it.

Mr. Buzurg could simply choose to say "If you see Jamshid . . ." and " . . . if you pass by his desk . . . ," but he doesn't. Instead, he uses other devices in these two real conditional sentences: **happen to** and **should**.

Happen to is a phrase that's just placed in between the subject and its verb:

If you see
↑
| happen to | If you happen to see

Should, on the other hand, is somewhat more complicated. Actually, Mr. Buzurg jumped a step between saying " . . . if you pass by . . ." and ". . . should you pass by . . ."

The first step is that *should* can be placed in between the subject and its verb just as we do with *happen to*:

Now we get to the step that Mr. Buzurg took. He eliminated *if,* moved *should* into that spot, and created this new type of *if* clause:

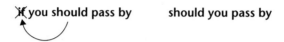

The question is, why bother? Do you perceive a difference between using or not using these phrases?

☐ yes   ☐ no

Well, we've got to admit that we do, so we'd check **yes**. But what is that difference? If you have an idea, write it down on the following line:

_____

The reason that a speaker might choose to use one of these phrases—or even a combination of them—in place of the basic *if* clause is that the speaker's dealing with what he/she feels is the **likelihood** of the event actually taking place.

Let's try a little experiment. You're about to find a list of various ways we can create the *if* clause. On a scale of 1 to 4 (1 = most likely to occur, 4 = least likely to occur), write the number which you feel will correspond to the degree of likelihood that the event will take place—in the speaker's opinion, that is. And by the way, two of these numbers should be used twice:

_____ If he wins first prize, . . .

_____ If he should win first prize, . . .

_____ Should he win first prize, . . .

_____ If he happens to win first prize, . . .

_____ If he should happen to win first prize, . . .

_____ Should he happen to win first prize, . . .

Quite confusing, right? It's not that there's a hard-and-fast rule about how these clauses should be ordered according to their degree of likelihood, but there is a tendency among native speakers to give them the following order:

__1__	**If he wins first prize, . . .**
__2__	**If he should win first prize, . . .**
__2__	**Should he win first prize, . . .**
__3__	**If he happens to win first prize, . . .**
__4__	**If he should happen to win first prize, . . .**
__4__	**Should he happen to win first prize, . . .**

We'd like to point one more thing out to you about a phrase like "Should he win first prize." Where do you think the word *not* ought to go if we choose to turn this phrase into a negative idea? Place *not* where you think it should go:

Should   he   win   first   prize, . . .

The word ***not*** is placed **between the subject and the verb** in this kind of inverted phrase, so we end up with **"Should he not win first prize . . ."** What's important to keep in mind is that *not* doesn't travel with the auxiliary when the auxiliary is fronted to mean *if* in this type of inversion. If it does travel with the auxiliary, we have a completely different idea:

Shouldn't he win first prize . . .

Of course, this form is a simple yes/no question that means "Doesn't he deserve to win first prize?" Quite a difference!

And if that's not enough, there's yet another phrase we can stick in to lower the degree of likelihood even more, and that happens to be the phrase *by (any) chance*:

If <u>by chance</u> he wins the prize, . . .
If he <u>by any chance</u> wins the prize, . . .
Should he <u>by any chance</u> win the prize, . . .
If he wins the prize <u>by any chance</u>, . . .

When Real Conditional Sentences Aren't So "Iffy"

There's another important point to mention that can occur with real conditional sentences that has to do with the word *if.* Another word we can use as a substitute for *if* in real conditional sentences is **when**, but it isn't all that simple as there are several factors that determine whether or not we can make this substitution.

We'd like you to look over the following sentences that we've lifted either from examples or dialogue boxes you've already seen to determine for yourself whether there's any change in meaning when we substitute *if* with *when*. First, decide whether there's a change in meaning in each sentence. Then, if you think there is a change, describe that change on the following blank line:

1a. If/When you see holes like this in wood, it means termites are present.

1b. You get pink paint if/when you mix red paint with white.

☐ a change in meaning   ☐ no change in meaning

_____

2a. If/When you see Birgit, give her my regards.

2b. I'll look up your aunt if/when I get to Jakarta.

☐ a change in meaning   ☐ no change in meaning

_____

3a. We'll cancel the field and track event only if/when it rains.

3b. If/When you see tomatoes on sale, pick me up a few pounds.

☐ a change in meaning   ☐ no change in meaning

_____

4a. If/When he isn't happy with me, I really don't care.

4b. If/When he's angry, it doesn't matter one bit.

☐ a change in meaning   ☐ no change in meaning

_____

And now to our answers. The sentences in **Number 1** demonstrate **no change in meaning** between using *if* or *when*. We can say, then, that **these two words are totally interchangeable when we state general concepts or universal truths**.

The sentences in **Number 2** show **a change in meaning**. In Sentence 2a, *if* tells us that the speaker isn't certain that the meeting will take place between the listener and Birgit. *When*, on the other hand, tells us that there's no doubt in the speaker's mind that the listener's going to see her. Sentence 2b works exactly the same way. Using *if* in this sentence tells us that the speaker isn't definite about stopping in Jakarta. Using *when* shows that the speaker is certain about going there. So, to sum up, ***if* implies a lack of certainty** in these situations while ***when* does imply certainty**.

The sentences in **Number 3** also demonstrate **a change in meaning**. In Sentence 3a, *if* tells us that the speaker's probably talking about a specific upcoming track and field event, but *when* makes it sound as if the speaker's talking hypothetically about any time that rain may occur during a field and track event. Sentence 3b works the same way. *If* implies an immediate possibility that the speaker's roommate will find tomatoes on sale since she's going to the supermarket right now. *When* really means "whenever," and the speaker's posing a hypothetical situation (*whenever* or *any time* you see tomatoes on sale). In fact, because the roommate's going to the supermarket right now, we can't use *when* in this situation (see the dialogue box, page 453). In short, **if is used when discussing some immediate upcoming event** while **when deals with hypothetical situations**.

The last two sentences work like those in Number 3, so they also show **a change in meaning** even though there's a difference in focus. With *if* in both **4a** and **4b**, the ideas are actually rhetorical. Person A has made it clear that the boss is unhappy with Person B, so Person B's restating an already known fact is just a rhetorical device used to reiterate what's already common knowledge, and it deals with the immediate situation. *When*, as we've already seen, really means *whenever*, so the sentences with this word don't deal with the present situation as it exists in the dialogue box on page 440. With *when* the sentences deal with a hypothetical situation.

But we're not done yet! Here are some more sentences that we've already come across in this chapter. You decide if they work just as well with *when* as they do with *if*. If, by chance, you determine that they don't, see if you can figure out why they don't, and write your thoughts down on the blank lines that follow:

> When you see Heinz that far away, your eyes are better than mine.
> When you don't propose to Fiona soon, you may not get a chance to.
> When you'll hold the line, I'll put you through.
> When you get the job you're going to apply for, will you treat me to dinner?
> When you're going downtown, I'll come along, okay?
>
> ☐ they work fine ☐ they don't work fine

_____

_____

One quick read-through of the preceding sentences should make it clear that these examples **don't work fine** using *when* in place of *if*. Although there are a few picky points that we could get involved in, we can just sum up the reason they don't work by saying that *when* contradicts the situations each of these sentences is part of. In each case, *when* really stands for *whenever*, and that's not the intent of these ideas. They're dealing with immediate situations, not hypothetical or general ones, so *when* just simply doesn't work.

So, to put it all in a nutshell, we can say that **when is a perfectly fine substitute for *if* in real conditional sentences that deal with factual observations, universal truths, or the speaker's certainty about future situations**.

ÆÖ Unreal Conditional Sentences: Timeless, Present, and Future Forms

In meaning, the big difference between real and unreal conditional sentences is that the real ones represent something that happens ("If it rains, puddles form"), is *happening* ("If you're feeling so sick, I'll take you to the doctor's"), or will happen ("If she gets here early, I'll show her the photos"). In contrast, unreal conditional sentences deal with impossible situations because we can't alter the past, the present, or the future. We can find a good analogy by comparing real and unreal conditional sentences to the major difference between *hope* and *wish*. Just as we found important differences in the verb forms which follow *hope* and *wish*, we find the same grammar differences between real and unreal conditional sentences.

Unreal Timeless Conditional Sentences

Although this isn't the most common type of unreal conditional sentence, it's worth looking at a few examples. So let's examine the following dialogue to see how it's used:

> A: I'm worried about that hole in the ozone layer. Aren't you?
>
> B: Of course I am. A lot of people don't realize how serious this is. If there **were** no ozone layer around the earth, the planet **wouldn't be** protected from lots of harmful radiation coming from the sun.
>
> A: That's right. And a lot more people **would get** skin cancer and cataracts if the ozone layer **didn't filter out** those harmful rays.
>
> B: Well, I just hope scientists find a way to stop the hole from getting bigger!

Just as with real conditional sentences, exploring the unreal types is like exploring cause and effect relationships. The *if* clause is the cause; the conditional clause is the effect. The dialogue you've just read is a good example of this relationship.

As for the actual construction of these unreal timeless conditional sentences, we can see that the *if* clause contains the subjunctive verb form (reflecting the simple present for timeless ideas) and the conditional clause uses the modal auxiliary *would* with the verb. (The conditional clause can use *could* just as well: "If we had wings, we could fly.") You should note that we find the same basic construction in unreal present conditional sentences as well.

Unreal Present Conditional Sentences

Let's see how close this type of unreal conditional sentence is to the timeless versions we've just explored:

A: How are you feeling now?

B: The same.

A: That's too bad. If you **were feel-ing** better, I**'d suggest** that we go to the movies this afternoon.

B: Oh? What's playing?

A: *Godzilla vs. Dracula.*

B: Well, I **wouldn't go** to see that film even if I **felt** fine!

We can see that there's an extremely close parallel between the sentences in this dialogue and the one that demonstrated the timeless kind of unreal conditional sentence. In the *if* clauses we have the present subjunctive reflecting imaginary ideas about the realities of the situation:

> If you <u>were</u> feeling better . . .   (but he <u>isn't</u> feeling better)
> . . . even if I <u>felt</u> fine!   (but he <u>doesn't feel</u> fine)

Before leaving the *if* clause, we should mention that there are some other words we can use in the present subjunctive; these are the modals **can** for ability or possibility (which becomes **could**) and **must** for necessity (which becomes **had to**):

> If you <u>could</u> live anywhere, where would it be?
> If I <u>had to</u> choose a place to live, it would be right here!

Now what about the conditional clauses? Notice that the verb is in what we commonly call the **conditional** form. Normally, the unreal timeless, present, or future conditional is expressed by the modal auxiliary **would** in American varieties of English for all persons:

> If I were you, I <u>would</u> watch what I say.

But in British and Australian varieties, **should** can be used instead for first person singular and plural:

> If I were you, I <u>should</u> watch what I say.

Besides *would* and *should* in the unreal conditional clause, we can find other modals such as **could** (for *can*) and **might** (for *may*). In addition, *must* can be expressed as **would have to**. It's no wonder that this type of sentence is sometimes referred to as the *subjunctive-conditional*, giving deference to both parts of the sentence. Here are two more examples to show you unreal conditionals that weren't covered in our dialogue:

> If I didn't take so many vitamins, I <u>might</u> get sick more often.
>
> He <u>would have to</u> get another job if his wife didn't work.

⚡ *Troubleshooter* ⚡

Look at the following sentence:

> If Alain was here, I didn't see him.

A sentence like this can confuse native speakers and our students alike. The part that's so confusing is the use of *was*. Is it a subjunctive form or what?

Well, the answer is that it isn't the subjunctive at all. Actually, it's just the simple past in what we can term a rhetorical *if* clause that just echoes what someone else has said:

> A: Did you know that Alain was here today?
> B: If Alain was here, I didn't see him.

A Deeper Look

Nuances with Unreal Present and Future Conditionals

A: Gee, Mr. Buzurg, it's too bad about Jamshid breaking his leg on that skiing trip.

B: Yes, it's a real shame, Miss Khan.

A: If he **were to get back** to the office really soon, could he still give that presentation to Bokhara Textiles?

B: It's too late. Mustafa's already given them the presentation, and they've decided to sign with us.

A: So Mustafa's going to get that nice bonus instead of Jamshid.

B: I'm afraid so. **Were he** here right now, however, I'd tell Jamshid not to worry. Another big account will come along soon enough.

Once again we find the speakers using shadings in meaning. The shadings to be found in these two phrases aren't of paramount importance for students, so teachers need not focus too much on them when they teach unreal conditional sentences. This doesn't mean, however, that your more advanced students shouldn't be able to recognize what the phrases mean when they hear them or see them in writing—and, of course, it would be wonderful if they learned to use them in writing and in speaking as well.

In our dialogue, Miss Khan could have said *If he got back* . . . instead of "If he were to get back . . . ," and Mr. Buzurg could have said "If he were here . . . " instead of "Were he here . . . ," but they didn't. The question is, do we have the same phenomenon taking place in these two instances that we saw previously on pages 456 and 457?

First let's talk about *were to.* Do you perceive a difference between saying "If he got back . . . " and "If he were to get back . . . ?"

☐ yes ☐ no

If you do perceive a difference, how can you explain what that difference is? Work it out and write it down on the following line if you've got an idea:

We have to say that we do indeed feel **there's a difference** between the two phrases. We also have to say that the difference does seem to mirror what we found on pages 456 and 457, namely, **the degree of likelihood as perceived by the speaker** that the event mentioned can actually take place. Many native speakers would say that even though both sentences are in the unreal conditional form, saying **"If he got back . . . " seems to be more likely to occur** in the speaker's mind than "If he were to get back . . . " does. When inserted within the *if* clause, this phrase can also sound **more polite** or **deferential**. Compare the thinking of Speaker A in these three mini-dialogues to see what we mean:

Dialogue 1

> A. If I **ask** you to let my great aunt Sophie come live with us, what **will** you say?
>
> B. What do you think I'll say?

Dialogue 2

> A. If I **asked** you to let my great aunt Sophie come live with us, what **would** you say?
>
> B. What do you think I'd say?

Dialogue 3

A. If I **were to ask** you to let my great aunt Sophie come live with us, what **might** you say?

B. Hmm. That might depend on how long you're thinking of.

Can you see the difference in effect that one form may have from the others? One interpretation is that Speaker A is showing relative optimism in Dialogue 1, but the optimism turns to slight pessimism in Dialogue 2 and a great deal of pessimism in Dialogue 3. It's interesting to note that in the most deferential request (Dialogue 3), Speaker A chose to use *might* instead of *would*. If you remember, in Chapter 8 we discuss this use of *might* for ultra-polite requests, and *might* does seem more appropriate than *would* in this deferential approach.

Before leaving the phrase "**If he were** to get back . . . ," we should talk about the alternate form we have: "**Were he** to get back . . ." How is this form created? Look at the two phrases closely. Do you see any connection between how this first phrase "evolves" into the other and what happened to *should* on those previous pages? We're sure you do see a connection. In fact, the same phenomenon is taking place here. So, how would you explain the way we end up with "Were he to get back . . . ?"

_____

_____

Once more we have to go through two steps to reach our target word order. The basic clause is "If he were to get back . . ." Step 1 is to eliminate the word *if*:

If̶ he were to get back...

Step 2 is to move *were* to where *if* used to be:

I̶f̶ he were to get back...

he were to get back...

So we go from *he were* to *were he*. Now we need to ask you if you feel any difference between saying "If he were to get back . . ." and "Were he to get back . . ."

☐ yes   ☐ no

If you do perceive a difference, what is it? Write down your thoughts on the following line:

_____

Again, we have to say that we feel **there is a difference** between the two phrases, albeit a minor one. The difference has to do with the level of **register**. Many native speakers tend to feel that saying **"Were he to get back . . . "** is more formal sounding** than saying "If he were to get back . . . " And that's about the size of it.

Now let's talk about Mr. Buzurg saying *"Were he* here right now . . . " By this time you should be an expert on how to form this construction. So, how would you explain the way we end up with "Were he here right now . . . "?

_____

_____

Once more we have to go through those two steps to reach our target word order. The basic clause is "If he were here right now . . . " **Step 1 is to eliminate the word *if*; Step 2 is to move *were* into the spot where *if* used to be.** Making this change means we go from *he were* to *were he*.

And once more, we have to say that **there's another minor difference** between the two phrases in their **register**. Many native speakers tend to feel that saying **"Were he here right now . . . " is more formal sounding** than saying "If he were here right now . . . "

Before leaving these oddities of unreal present and future conditional sentences, we should take a look at that alternative form of *be* in the present subjunctive that many people use in these sentences, namely, *was*. We've already mentioned that many people say things like "If she <u>was</u> here . . . " instead of "If she <u>were</u> here . . . " and that the big difference is that, to many native speakers, the former sounds less educated and/or less formal than the latter. The question is, are *was* and *were* interchangeable in the two phrases we've been discussing, namely, "If he were to get back . . . " and "Were he to get back . . . ?" What do *you* think?

☐ yes   ☐ no   ☐ yes and no

In case you haven't already done it, let's try out both forms of the verb in the two phrases and see what we get:

If he <u>were</u> to get back to the office really soon, . . .
If he <u>was</u> to get back to the office really soon, . . .

Well, even though it might hurt the ears of some native speakers to hear *was* used instead of *were* in this clause, we have to say that it is indeed a possible alternative simply because so many native speakers use it. Now let's see if the same thing happens with the other phrase:

> <u>Were</u> he here right now, . . .
> <u>Was</u> he here right now, . . .

Oops! Sorry. It won't work this time. The answer to our opening question is **yes and no**. Any guesses as to why *was* just doesn't work in the second construction, but it does work in the first one we tried out?

There are three reasons. One has to do with **register** again, that level of formality that can at times be so important in language. The first phrase we tried out was not created to make the idea more formal sounding, so it's irrelevant whether we use *were* or *was*. The next phrase, however, is a construction specifically used for more formal-sounding language, and since *was* is considered less formal to begin with by so many native speakers, it would be a totally inappropriate choice to use in this formal construction; in fact, it would actually defeat the purpose. That's the first reason you'll never hear a native speaker say "Was he here right now, . . ."!

The second reason is that "Was he here right now, . . ." sounds like a yes/no question.

The third reason is that in the sentence "If he *were* here right now, . . ." there are two clues to the "*if*-ness" of the meaning (the words *if* and *were*). Removing the *if* shifts the meaning of *if* onto the word *were* to give the *if*-meaning, which *was* cannot carry. Thus the sentences must read "*Were* he here right now, . . ."

A *Because Of* Goes Subjunctive

One of those vocabulary oddities that students learn is the difference in usage between *because* and *because of*. Students are taught that the word *because* is followed by a verb phrase:

> We go to Carlo's for dinner because <u>he makes great lasagna</u>.

They're also taught that *because of* must be followed by a noun phrase:

> We go to Carlo's for dinner because of <u>his great lasagna</u>.

But what do we do if we want to discuss going to Carlo's house and having his lasagna in an unreal conditional idea? Take a look and see for yourself:

A: Well, Carlo did it again! Nobody can make lasagna like he can. His lasagna is out of this world!

B: True. I'm stuffed. And everything else we've ever eaten over here has been equally good.

A: Yeah, I guess that's true. But **if it weren't for** his lasagna, he wouldn't be a finalist in the annual faculty cooking contest at school.

B: I know it. Ah, what a cook!

There you have it! The phrase *if it weren't for* is what we need to use in an unreal timeless or present conditional sentence to replace *because of* in order to show the only cause or reason for something else happening. In other words, any time an idea is imaginary and needs to show the cause or reason for something happening, *because of* can't be used to accomplish this purpose. By the way, if you want to come up with the converse of the sentence that Speaker A said with the phrase "If it weren't for . . . " in an indicative (real) idea, what will it be? Let's see what you can come up with:

_____

Although there are multiple variations that we can come up with, here are two that come to mind for us:

Because of his lasagna, Carlo's a finalist in the annual faculty cooking contest at school.

It's only because of his lasagna that Carlo is a finalist in the annual faculty cooking contest at school.

Before we move on to a new topic, we have two more little challenges for you. As you well know by now, in our exploration of conditional sentences, we've come upon a few examples where we can change register by doing some fancy changes to a phrase such as eliminating a certain word and inverting the positions of other words. Well, what can you think of to make the phrase "If it weren't for" more formal sounding? Check back a bit in this part of the chapter if you need to, and as your next little challenge, let's see what you can create:

We can change <u>if it weren't for</u> to _____.

The answer is that we can change "If it weren't for" into the very formal-sounding phrase *were it not for* by going through the following steps:

1. **Eliminate *if.***
2. **Take the negative verb out of its contracted form.**
3. **Move *were* to where *if* used to be.**

And that's how you do it. Very formal sounding indeed!

Now, for your last little challenge, can you think of a reduced version of "If it were not for?" We'll even give you a hint: two out of the five words in the expression have to be eliminated—but which two are they?

The two words to eliminate are _____ and _____,

so, the reduced form is _____.

Well, it so happens that the two words you need to eliminate are *it* and *were*, so the answer to our last challenge is that the reduced form of "If it weren't for" is *if not for*, and it's used exactly like its longer counterpart:

<u>If not for</u> his lasagna, Carlo wouldn't be a finalist
in the annual faculty cooking contest.

Here's one final note about unreal conditional sentences in the present or timeless form. Go all the way back to the first page of this chapter, page 438, and take another look at the quote given at the top of the page. Notice anything peculiar about the timeless subjunctive verb in the *if* clause? How would you explain that form of the verb?

It so happens that using the base verb here as the timeless subjunctive form ("If music <u>be</u> the food of love, play on!") is another example of the **archaic, or formulaic subjunctive** that still lingers on in modern English in certain pat phrases and the like (see Chapter 19).

Unreal Conditional Sentences: The Past

Just as we dealt with two parts that make up each unreal conditional sentence in the timeless, present, and future forms, we'll be doing the same thing with this type of sentence in the past. With that little reminder, let's look at our next dialogue concentrating on the phrases in bold:

A: Good morning, Alessandra. What are you smiling about?

B: I just stopped a mother duck and her babies from getting killed.

A: How'd you do that?

B: She was trying to lead them across a busy road, but couldn't. So I stood out there, stopped the cars, and she led them across!

A: Aren't you the little heroine!

B: That's right! If I **hadn't been** there, the ducks **might have died.**

A: Oh, I'm sure she **would have managed** to get them across.

B: No way! If she **had tried** to lead the babies across on her own, a car **would have hit** them.

A: Okay, okay. You're the office heroine for the day, all right?

B: Right!

Now that you've looked over the phrases in bold, we're going to give you a few questions to answer that will help you make some observations about the grammar in our dialogue:

1. What mood is used in the *if* clauses? _____

2. What's used to make this verb form? _____

3. What's the time of the modals in the conditional clauses? _____

4. What's used to make these modal forms? _____

After everything we've covered concerning the subjunctive and conditional forms, you probably haven't had much trouble filling in the blanks. Here are our answers. Let's see how closely yours match ours:

1. the subjunctive mood   **3. the past**
2. the past perfect   **4. the modal perfect form**

Of course, we have to keep remembering that these ideas are in the realm of imagination. In one of the two sentences that follow, though, the speaker is quite sure of her statement, while in the other she's playing it safe by not being so definite. Figure out which is which:

> 1. If I hadn't been there, the ducks might have died.
>   □ She's definite.   □ She's not definite.
>
> 2. If she'd tried to lead the babies across on her own,
>   a car would have hit them.
>   □ She's definite.   □ She's not definite.

You know by now that it's the modal in the conditional clause which gives us the information that we need to check the correct boxes. By using *might* in **Sentence 1**, the speaker is saying that **she's not definite**, so she's playing it safe. On the other hand, by using *would* in **Sentence 2**, the speaker is saying that **she's definite** about the final hypothetical outcome.

By the way, what other modal perfect phrase could Speaker B use instead of *might have* to convey that same idea?

The other modal perfect phrase that would work equally well is ***could have***. And before we leave this topic, there's one other modal that we can use, the past form of *must*, *had had to:*

> I would have died for her if I'd had to!

↝ Mixing and Matching Unreal Conditional Clauses

Up to this point in our exploration of unreal conditional sentences, we've been doing something that some might call artificial; we've been presenting sentences that are all neatly in the past, present, future, and timeless form. But, of course, language doesn't work like that all the time. Look at our next dialogue and you'll see what we mean:

A: Come on, Dad! Let's ride our bikes together. What do you say?

B: I know it's Saturday, Debbie, but I'm too tired. You go ahead.

A: Aw, gee, Dad. Come on! We'll have a great time!

B: Working two jobs isn't easy, Debbie. Some other time, okay?

A: But if you **hadn't worked** till late last night, you **wouldn't be** so tired now.

B: And if I **didn't work** those two jobs, I **wouldn't have had** the money to buy your bicycle!

C: Don't go making Debbie feel guilty that you got her a bike, John. You **wouldn't need** two jobs if you **hadn't started** feeling envious of your brother Ned's good fortune!

As far as time is concerned when it comes to unreal conditional sentences, what do we see going on in this dialogue? In the order that the three sentences with phrases in bold appear, what do *you* see? Write down the time contained in each phrase on the following lines:

_____ + _____

_____ + _____

_____ + _____

We find the following: **the past + the present / general time + the past / the present + the past**. So obviously, we can mix and match time clauses in unreal conditional sentences and don't have any rigid system to adhere to. A point to get across to your students is that past actions can have past consequences, but past actions can also have present consequences. Moreover, because we're dealing with the realm of imagination anyway, there's no reason that we can't mix any times together if we feel like doing so!

A Deeper Look

Those Nuances and Unreal Past Conditional Sentences

It's time for you to do some more linguistic sleuthing. Remember those phrases we covered earlier in this chapter that create various shadings within conditional sentences such as "if you happen to" and "if they should?" Well, here they are again! What we'd like you to do is think about each one in the following list and decide if it can be used in an unreal *past* conditional sentence the way it can be used in a real present or future conditional sentence. You'll have to do some detective work on each one before you check the boxes you agree with. To solve this little linguistic mystery, think up an unreal past conditional sentence and transfer each of our phrases into the past to see if it works before you check off any boxes.

Remember, the question is, can each of these phrases be used in an unreal past conditional sentence?

1. If _____ happen to . . .	☐ it can	☐ it can't
2. If _____ should . . .	☐ it can	☐ it can't
3. Should _____ . . .	☐ it can	☐ it can't
4. If _____ by (any) chance . . .	☐ it can	☐ it can't
5. If _____ were to . . .	☐ it can	☐ it can't
6. Were _____ to . . .	☐ it can	☐ it can't

What this task required was some careful thought by creating examples in the past and seeing if our phrases could be plugged into them. Without further ado, here are our answers for you to compare to yours:

1. If you happen to: **it can** If you had happened to see her, you would not have believed the color she'd dyed her hair!
Note: Keep in mind that this phrase is the only one in this group that can be used in the negative as well: "She could have gotten into a lot of trouble if you hadn't happened to warn her in time."

2. If you should: **it can't** "If you should have seen her . . . "? (No way!)

3. Should you: **it can't** "Should you have seen her . . . "? (Forget it!)

4. If you by any chance: **it can** If you by any chance had seen her . . .

5. If you were to: **it can't** "If you had been to see her . . . "? (Impossible here because the meaning changes!)

6. Were you to: **it can**   "Had you been to see her . . . "

We don't think so since the meaning changes here, too!

And what about the expression "If it weren't for," its formal counterpart "were it not for," and the reduced form "if not for?" Can these be used in an unreal past conditional sentence?

☐ they can   ☐ they can't

The answer is that they certainly **can**:

<u>If it hadn't been for</u> wanton killing, the dodo wouldn't have become extinct.
<u>Had it not been for</u> wanton killing, the dodo wouldn't have become extinct.
<u>If not for</u> wanton killing, the dodo wouldn't have become extinct.

꜀ꜝ Phrases that Create Hypothetical Situations

In conversational English, we have two phrases that replace *if* for setting up hypothetical situations which may be real or unreal and which may refer to the present, the future, or the past. Let's see if you can pick them out:

A: Well, I'm off to Australia for a three-week vacation!

B: That's wonderful! So, have you made all your reservations for hotels?

A: Nope, I'll just "wing it," as they say.

B: No reservations? What if you get to Sydney and there aren't any hotel rooms vacant? What will you do then?

A: There's always something available.

B: Say there isn't. What will you do, sleep in the streets?

A: You worry too much. Besides, that's the way I always travel. I did the same thing last year in North Africa.

B: Well, you were just lucky. What if there hadn't been any rooms vacant? Would you have slept on the desert sands?

So what are those two useful phrases that replace *if*? Write them down on the following lines:

_____ and _____

The two phrases in this dialogue that do such a neat job of replacing *if* and setting up hypothetical situations are **what if** and **say**, and they're completely interchangeable because they mean exactly the same thing.

What's interesting to note about them is that, just like conditional sentences, they can refer to real situations:

> What if/Say you get to Sydney and there aren't any hotel rooms vacant . . .

or they can refer to unreal situations:

> What if there hadn't been any rooms vacant?
> Say there hadn't been any rooms vacant.

The main reason we mention these two phrases here is that they're another example of things not usually covered in student grammar books, and they should be since they're such useful conversational devices.

Teaching Tips

20.1 "If I Had a Hammer"

Teach your students the folk song "If I Had a Hammer."

20.2 I Wish You'd Sit Next to Me!

Before class think up groups of three to four similar items. Divide the students into small groups and have them discuss which item in the list they prefer and why, making sure that they use "*if*" in their discussions.

Here are some examples of the items that you can use with your students and the statements that they might make:

- snake, bee, kangaroo
- tomato, carrot, lettuce
- morning, afternoon, evening
- summer, winter, spring, fall
- running, canoeing, skating, bowling
- beaches, mountains, forests, plains
- etc.

- If I were a bee, I'd be able to make honey.
- If I had some better tomatoes, I'd make us some spaghetti sauce.
- I'd be in bed right now if it were nighttime.
- I could go skiing if it were winter.

20.3 Proverbs

Bring in or have students bring in proverbs that are imperative forms ("Look before you leap." / "Don't count your chickens before they hatch." / "Never a borrower nor a lender be," etc.). Let your students explain the reasons for these proverbs by using *if* ("If you don't look, you may/could hurt yourself." / "If you count on something before it happens, you may be in for a big disappointment." / "You won't be upset that your friend hasn't returned the money you lent him if you make it a policy not to lend money in the first place.")

20.4 The Alphabet Game

This is another version of *The Alphabet Game* (see page 25). One student starts off the game by saying: "I want to go to _____ this summer. If I go to _____ on vacation, I'll take _____ with me," or "I'm not a genius, but if I were, I could _____." The next student repeats the information the first student has said and adds something of his or her own ("If I go to _____ on vacation, I'll take _____ and _____ with me"). Every student repeats what's been said before and adds his or her own piece of information to the conditional sentence heard up to that point. The sentence gets longer and longer and harder and harder to repeat, but it's good for developing your students' memories. To show them that this isn't an impossible thing to do and that you've been paying attention to them, you be the last one, repeating everything that's been said by all your students!

20.5 Hopes and Wishes for the Future

Ask your students to brainstorm their wishes and hopes for the future (the winner of a specific election, people living to be 150 years old, world peace, all telephones equipped with TV screens, etc.). Put their ideas on the board. Then have them create reasons for their wishes and hopes ("If X wins the election, he'll vote for universal medical coverage." / "If people lived to be 150, they'd be alive in two centuries." / "We wouldn't have to spend so much on military hardware if there were world peace," etc.).

20.6 My Dream House

Divide the class into small groups and ask them to draw the floor plan of their dream house. After the plans have been made, let the "architects" exchange plans with another group, who now become "prospective home owners." The home owners now discuss the designs using wishes and hopes to make the home more "theirs." Of course, reasons must be provided for why the changes are to be made. Remind the students to use conditionals for their reasons ("We hope the downstairs bathroom has a door that leads out to the pool. If it does, we'll be able to enter the house right after swimming").

20.7 I Wish I Were . . .

Bring in pictures of all sorts of animals or a list of famous people. Have the students make wishes about the animals ("I wish I were a kangaroo") and people ("I wish I were a multi-millionaire"). Then have them explain their wishes ("If I were a kangaroo, I could carry all my books in my pouch." / "If I were a multi-millionaire, I would be able to help poor people").

20.8 Fairy Tales

Fairy tales always have plenty of problem situations in them. Use them as a basis for brainstorming wishes, hopes, and lots of conditional sentences.

20.9 I Regret: I Wish I Hadn't . . .

Have students brainstorm regrets they have and regrets they've heard others state. You can even add your own. Write them on the board and then have them expound on the regrets by using conditionals.

20.10 Advice Letters

Have your students write and respond to advice letters by using wishes, hopes, and conditionals.

20.11 Superstitions

This tip gives students the opportunity to work with and learn traditional sayings that come from superstitions. These traditional sayings are often formed with *if* clauses ("If you step on a crack, you'll break your mother's back." / "If your palm itches, you're going to inherit money." / "If you find a penny in the street, you're going to have good luck." / "If your nose itches, you're going to kiss a fool," etc.). Divide the class into small groups and have them come up with several examples of these sayings. Have the students share their sayings with the entire class.

Variation: Have your students make up new superstitions containing *if* clauses, or let them bring in ones from their own cultures.

20.12 Tic Tac Toe

Create a "Tic Tac Toe" game (British "Naughts and Crosses") or game of Concentration based on wishes and conditionals (see *Appendix 3*).

21

ELT "Waifs"

"We're poor little lambs who have lost our way . . . "

I t's time to begin winding down. You've gotten through twenty intensive chapters; now, however, it's time to start unwinding. This chapter and Chapter 22 will help you do just that.

We have to make a little confession: Most of what you're going to see in this chapter isn't found in most traditional ELT texts. We're not going to be delving into yet another area that always seems to present problems for teachers and their students. Instead, we're going to deal with what we consider to be *ELT waifs,* that is, words or phrases or phenomena of the language that rarely if ever get included in student grammar books or even in whole-language or competency-based student series, but—in our opinion— should be. There are quite a few of these neglected aspects of the English language, and we think you'll find it enlightening to be made aware of these seldom-taught items.

Ellipsis

As in keeping with the traditional way we've presented most material, we'll start your discovery—or rediscovery—of these ELT waifs by asking you to look at the first dialogue for this chapter:

> A: Hi, Bruce. Eaten yet?
>
> B: No, Gerry. You?
>
> A: Me, neither. Want to go out for pizza?
>
> B: Don't feel like it. How about ordering in?
>
> A: Fine with me.
>
> B: Good. Coming over here, then?
>
> A: Sure. Be over in a jiffy.
>
> B: Mind picking up some sodas on the way over?
>
> A: No problem.
>
> B: Looking forward to that first slice with pepperoni.
>
> A: Me, too. See you soon.
>
> B: Bye!

A very typical, normal-sounding dialogue, wouldn't you say? There's nothing unusual at all about the way Bruce and Gerry have been talking—or is there? Can you figure out what's "different" about the way this dialogue goes compared to what you normally find in student books? When you've discovered the "difference," write down your idea on the following line:

———————————————————————————————————————

The phenomenon that's taken place throughout our first dialogue is that **the beginning words have been dropped from almost every sentence**. This is one manifestation of a linguistic phenomenon known as **ellipsis** (or you might know the term "truncation"). Let's have some fun reconstructing the parts that both speakers have dropped:

A: Hi, Bruce. _____ eaten yet?

B: No, Gerry. _____ you?

A: Me, neither. _____ want to go out for pizza?

B: _____ don't feel like it. How about ordering in?

A: _____ fine with me.

B: _____ coming over here, then?

A: Sure. _____ be over in a jiffy.

B: ——————— mind picking up some sodas on the way over?

A: ————— no problem.

B: ————— looking forward to that first slice with pepperoni.

A: Me, too. ————— see you soon.

B: ————— bye!

Now that wasn't tough at all, we bet. Without any delay, let's get right to what we'd use to fill in those blanks so you can see how closely your fill-ins come to ours:

Have you ...	**That's (It's)** ...	**It's (That's)** ...
Have ...	**Are you** ...	**I'm** ...
Do you ...	**I'll** ...	**I'll** ...
I ...	**Would you (Do you)** ...	**Good-**

Quite an assortment of phrases, wouldn't you say? It seems that this kind of ellipsis **usually happens with one or more words that open a sentence and that often have weak stress**. At times, **words in the middle of a sentence can get dropped, too**. If you reread all the sentences that show this kind of ellipsis in our dialogue, you'll realize just how unstressed the dropped parts are. You can also see that all of our examples, save the last one, delete the subject, auxiliary and/or verb.

Now why is it that there doesn't seem to be any confusion on the part of the listener or the reader as to what the missing parts are? It's simply because either the grammar itself or the context of the situation will keep things clear.

Here are a few more examples for you to have fun with. In addition, we're going to throw in a couple of items in which the beginning syllable of a word is dropped instead of a whole word, and you might even find a word dropped from the middle of a sentence or two. Write your fill-ins on the blank lines provided:

1. Anything else?   ————————————

2. I did it 'cause I got bored.   ————————————

3. I didn't know he was sick.   ————————————

4. I'll be home tonight.   ————————————

5. We'll meet you 'bout ten o'clock.   ————————————

6. Anybody know the right answer?   ————————————

7. Nice woman, that Ethel.   ————————————

8. He's been gone about two hours.   ————————————

For these extra items we've given you, here are the answers we'd supply for the blanks:

1. Is there ...   **4. at**
   Will there be ...   **5. a–**
   Would you like ...   **6. Does** ...
   Do you want ...   **7. She's a** ...
2. be–   **8.** ... **for** ...
3. ... **that** ...

We'd like to take a detour for a moment and discuss that little troublesome word *home* in Number 4. This seemingly innocent word can be much more difficult to teach than you might think because of when you can and can't drop its accompanying preposition, that bane of all teachers, *at*, which we're sure you remember from Chapter 9. Compare the following sentences that we've placed into three categories:

Category 1   **Category 2**
I'm going home.   I feel at home.
I've often flown home.   I worked at home.
I drove home.   I'll see you at home.
I'll see you home.   I'll be calling you at home.
I can't take you home.   I've seldom called on them at home.
I'd never walked home before.   Please make yourself at home.
He ran home to his mother.   She lives at home with her parents.

Category 3
I'm (at) home.
I sat (at) home.
I remained (at) home.
I'm staying (at) home.

In Category 1 you never use *at*; in Category 2 you have to use *at*; in Category 3 *at* is optional. Can you come up with any rules why *home* works these three different ways? Think about the kinds of verbs in each category and then write any thoughts you have on the subject on the following lines:

Category 1: ―――――――――――――――――――――――――――――――

Category 2: ―――――――――――――――――――――――――――――――

Category 3: ―――――――――――――――――――――――――――――――

This is how we see it, so compare your ideas to ours. In the rules this is what we've found:

Category 1: Don't use *at* + *home* after verbs that imply movement.
Category 2: Use *at* + *home* after verbs that imply stationary location.
Category 3: *At* is optional after certain verbs that imply "remaining."

And what's most interesting is to compare the fourth sentence in Category 1 ("I'll see you home") to the third sentence in Category 2 ("I'll see you at home"). In the Category 2 sentence, *see* really means "meet," but in the Category 1 sentence, *see* has an idiomatic meaning that equals the same idea as "escort" or "accompany," a verb implying movement. Only the preposition *at* makes the difference clear in this case!

Now getting back to that last group of eight sentences with ellipsis, you can see that this sort of thing is a common phenomenon in the spoken language. So when would this type of ellipsis be taught if you were planning a curriculum? It would probably be best to teach most of it at an advanced level. The reasoning behind this suggestion is that students ought to master these words and structures as they are in their entirety. After that's been accomplished, you can feel more secure in showing them the shorter versions used in the spoken, informal language. That doesn't mean, however, that certain items can't be introduced at the beginning level, such as "Bye!" or "See you later."

Relaxed Pronunciation

Along similar lines, there's a phenomenon in pronunciation that's involved with ellipsis. We've dubbed it **comic book English** when attempts are made to reproduce in writing how the words sound when spoken. Even though quite a few spellings have actually become standardized in comic books, we must admit that some of the spellings you're about to see are our own inventions to mimic the spoken word.

Take a look at our next dialogue to get a sample of what we mean. By the way, *Ahm = I'm.* We've written it this way to capture how it's typically pronounced in an informal situation.

A: Whatcha doin'?

B: Did'n'cha see?

A: Nope. Couldja do it one more time?

B: Okay, but wouldja pay attention this time?

A: Ahm gonna look at nothin' else!

B: Awright then. Here goes . . .

A: Geez! That's terrific!

B: Wanna try it? All you gotta do is hold this in your left hand and do that with your right.

A: Gotcha!

Before we do anything else, let's have you rewrite this dialogue in "standard" form:

A: _____

B: _____

A: _____

B: _____

A: _____

B: _____

A: _____

B: _____

_____

A: _____

If we rewrite the dialogue, this is what we come up with, and we've put the affected parts in bold:

> **A:** What **are you doing?**
> **B:** **Didn't you** see?
> **A:** No(pe). **Could you** do it one more time?
> **B:** Okay, but **would you** pay attention this time?
> **A:** **I'm going to** look at **nothing** else!
> **B:** **All right** then. Here goes . . .
> **A:** **Jesus!** That's terrific!
> **B:** **Do you want to** try it? All you**'ve got to** do is hold
>   this in your left hand and do that with your right.
> **A:** **I've got you!**

As you can see, this dialogue really demonstrates a combination of what we term "relaxed" pronunciation and ellipsis. There's really no point in trying to list the weighty phonological rules that account for these pronunciation variations. Let's just say that we feel you should teach them **in chunks**, that is, *would you* comes out sounding like *wouldja* /wʊ - ǰə/, *want to* ends up as *wanna* /wa - nə/, *going to* becomes *gonna* /gə - nə/ or /gɔ - nə/, *what did you* becomes *whad-ja* /wə - ǰə/, and *what are you* is *whatcha* /wə - čə/, etc.

In addition, remember that *I'm* has reduced to *Ahm*, /am/, which, by the way, is typical of Southern U.S. pronunciation whether in formal or informal situations.

Then there's the matter of the final /g/ in the *-ing* suffix being dropped, so that /- ɪŋ/ becomes /- ɪn/. This is a common pronunciation, and yet hardly gets a mention in classes.

One note we'd like to add concerns the exclamation "Geez!" Some expressions such as "geez" have developed because of certain taboos placed on names or expressions that have religious meaning. Because many people feel that using the name "Jesus" or saying "God" in any sort of exclamation is a form of blasphemy at worst, or impolite and low class at best, expressions like *geez* have become popular. Other forms for this particular avoidance are *jeepers, golly, gee-whiz, gee*, and even *sheesh!*

We certainly haven't accounted for all the possibilities here in this type of ellipsis or in relaxed pronunciations, but that's not the point of what we're doing. We mainly want to make you aware of the fact that these two phenomena do exist and are a vital, integral part of spoken English. For that reason, there should be a unit in any enlightened, dynamic grammar course to cover these aspects of the spoken language, and they should most certainly be taught to advanced students.

✏ Intensifiers

Now let's move on to some other neglected "waifs" of the language that rarely—if ever—get included in lessons. Check out our next dialogue to see which ones we're going to spotlight now:

> A: Hi, neighbor! You're ready to do some cooking I see.
> B: Just waiting for the coals to be ready.
> A: But, ooh, you don't look too happy. What's up?
> B: You see that big house over there at the corner?
> A: Uh-huh.
> B: Well, the owner just sold it.
> A: He did that **rather** fast, didn't he? So why are you glum?
> B: Well, my cousin was trying to buy it, but the guy was asking **way** too much for it—at least *we* thought he was.
> A: Exactly how much over the true market value do you think he was going?
> B: About $25,000.
> A: **That** much, huh? It really was **far** more than what was a reasonable price. So the people who bought it paid a lot more than they should have.
> B: Right. It's a shame. My cousin and his wife really wanted that **very** house. It's really **quite** beautiful.
> A: I think you can put the chicken on the barbecue grill now. The coals look **good and** hot.

Can you think of one or more words you can substitute for the ones that we have in bold? (Notice we've put "way" and "far" together.) Let's see what you come up with:

too	= _____
over	= _____
rather	= _____
way/far	= _____
that	= _____
very	= _____
quite	= _____
good and	= _____

The way we loosely interpret the items in bold, we can substitute them with:

too	=	**very**	"You don't look <u>very</u> happy."
over	=	★	
rather	=	**surprisingly/**	"He did that <u>surprisingly</u> fast."
		really	"He did that <u>really</u> fast."
way/far	=	**much**	". . . the guy was asking <u>much</u> too much for it . . ."
that	=	**so**	"<u>So</u> much, huh?"
very	=	**exact**	"My cousin and his wife wanted that <u>exact</u> house."
quite	=	**really very**	"And the house is <u>really very</u> beautiful."
good and =		**★★really/very**	"The coals look <u>really</u> hot."

So why are these words or phrases called **intensifiers**? It's because they "intensify" or strengthen the meaning of the words they precede in one way or another.

Before we get to our mystery word, *over*, we'd like to say a few more things about *very, way, quite,* and *that.*

"Very"

Very is always an intensifier, and even beginning students learn to use it with adjectives *(very good)* and adverbs *(very well)*. It's also used with the quantifiers *many* and *much,* es-

---

★Don't concern yourself with the mystery we've intentionally added regarding "over." We'll get to that momentarily.

★★And, by the way, we should point out that another phrase which means the same thing as *good and* is **nice and**, so Person A could just as easily have said "The coals look <u>nice and</u> hot."

pecially in negative contexts (*not very many/not very much*), and with *few* and *little* (*very few tests/very little patience*).

It's important to remember that this useful word is an intensifier that does more than what we've just explained. What about *very* paired up with a noun?

A dishwasher is the <u>very thing</u> you need to make life easier.

It's not such a rare occurrence in English to hear *very* used this way with a noun. It isn't an intensifier, but it means "exact." Our paraphrase of the example you've just seen is "A dishwasher is the exact thing you need to make life easier."

Here are some other examples of pairing up *very* with nouns:

You're the <u>very person</u> I've been looking for!
This is the <u>very spot</u> where the treasure's buried.

Before moving on, we'd like to mention two expressions. The first one is **one's very own + noun phrase**. This phrase can be taught as a pat expression without much additional thought given to it. In fact, you can't really paraphrase this expression; *very* is simply used to intensify *own*—and it's redundant at that!

The vegetables you're eating came from <u>my very own garden</u>!

The other expression is **very much the + noun phrase**, which means "really a ... " Just check out the following example to see what we mean:

Her grades at college have always been excellent. She's <u>very much the scholar</u>.

"Way" and "Far"

Way and *far* are sometimes used interchangeably and colloquially as an intensifier with *too, too many*, and *too much* (*way/far too big; way/far too many tests; way/far too much money*) although some people would say that *far* sounds more formal than *way*. They also do an effective job with the comparative forms *more, fewer*, and *less* (*way/far more interesting; way/far fewer mistakes; way/far less time*).

Way is also used (more commonly than *far*) with prepositional phrases that include *up, down, over, under, ahead, behind, back, in*, and *out* (*way up there/way down yonder/way over in the next town/way under age*, etc.).

In addition, *way* can be used with adjectives that begin with the prefixes *over-* and *under-* (*way overpriced/way underweight*).

"Quite"

As we've mentioned with *very, quite* is usually taught to students with an accompanying adjective (*quite good*) or adverb (*quite well*), but we can do quite a lot more with *quite*!

To begin with, *quite* **can be followed by the indefinite article + a noun phrase that doesn't contain an adjective**. In this case, it means *something* or *somebody worth noting:*

> She's quite a scholar.

Or we can use *quite* **+ a noun phrase that contains an adjective** to mean *really* or *very:*

> And she's quite a famous author now.

Finally, we can use *quite* **+ the definite article and a noun phrase** (usually without an adjective) to mean *definitely a* or *for sure:*

> Yes, she's quite the scholar.

And can you think of another expression we've recently had that means the same thing as *quite a . . .* or *quite the . . .*? Of course! It's *very much a/the . . .*

> Yes, she's very much the scholar.

"That"

As an intensifier, we 've seen that *that* really means the same thing as *so* (*that* expensive = *so* expensive). Notice that it's used only as in reference to something already said:

> It weighed 400 lbs. I never thought it would be <u>that</u> heavy!

But it's not alone in this usage. We also have *this* working the same way:

> A: Well, dear, did you buy the patio furniture that was on sale?
> B: I certainly did!
> A: Fine. By the way, how much was it?
> B: Here's the bill. It was only $1,249.95. It was a steal!
> A: You mean you got robbed! If I had known it was **this** expensive, I'd have said to forget it!

Just as with *that*, we can substitute *this* with *so* for this usage as an intensifier. The question, of course, is when do we use *this* as an alternative to *so*, and when do we use *that*? Any idea on the subject? Here's a line for you to jot it down if you've got one:

There's nothing better in teaching techniques than to be able to recycle material previously covered so that your students get to practice it again, but perhaps in a new way. That's exactly what's happening here. Knowing when to use *this* or *that* means knowing about the phenomenon explored at various times in this book, **deixis**. Choosing to use *this* or *that* is all a matter of how close to the situation the speaker feels. Accordingly, we use *this* for something we feel proximity to, e.g., something we're actually holding in our hands at the moment ("Look at this vase. Have you ever seen a vase this gorgeous?"). Conversely, we use *that* for something we feel somewhat removed from. Since Person A in the last dialogue was holding the bill for the patio furniture in her hand, she used *this* in her response to hearing and seeing the price.

Using *this* and *that* in place of *so* is very common, especially in spoken English. They definitely have to be counted among our ELT waifs and should be taught to intermediate or advanced students.

"Over"

And now for our mystery item! As you may have already realized while writing your substitutions for the intensifiers, this little item can be difficult to interpret. Some native speakers don't really think it means anything in particular—and it doesn't, at least not when it accompanies adverbs of place (*here/there/at my cousin's/in Azerbaijan*, etc.).

However, there's another use for this mysterious intensifier which needs mentioning here. **We use *over* in all sorts of phrases, but especially with verbs of movement:** *come over, go over, drive over, walk over, take* something *over*, and *run over* are examples we can point to.

It can be hard to know when it is or isn't appropriate to use this intensifier. For example, you can just as easily say *Come here* as you can say *Come over here*. Nobody would say there's any big difference between those two sentences. And, of course, there's an idiomatic use of *come over* meaning *come to my house*:

> A: What time are you coming over tonight?
> B: Oh, around 8:30, I guess.

But it isn't all that simple. We've shown how the word can be used, but we still haven't defined what *over* means when it's used as an intensifier. Let's investigate the word some more. First, compare the following two sentences and check the boxes you agree with:

1a. She went over to the cabinet and opened the door.

    ☐ sounds "complete"   ☐ doesn't sound "complete"   ☐ can't decide

1b. She went to the cabinet and opened the door.

    ☐ sounds "complete"   ☐ doesn't sound "complete"   ☐ can't decide

Most native speakers tend to think that **both sentences sound complete**; it's simply that 1a seems to sound a little "better"! Whatever the reason might be, the important thing for us to recognize is that it doesn't seem to matter whether *over* is included or not in sentences like the ones you've just seen because there isn't any real change in the obvious or underlying meaning.

But we're not stopping there. Now compare these two:

2a. He walked to the grocery store for some cheese.
2b. He walked over to the grocery store for some cheese.

☐ sound the same   ☐ sound different   ☐ can't decide

Uh-oh! Things have changed now. Many native speakers would agree that there is a **difference** between the two sentences. But what is it? Let's see if you can figure out what difference there may be:

Sentence 2a: _____

Sentence 2b: _____

It's incredible how one little preposition can add such nuance to a sentence! This is how we might interpret the two sentences: **2a** simply deals with the verb *walk*, and the only interpretation we can put on it aside from the obvious is that **the speaker is possibly focusing on the fact the he <u>walked</u> to the store rather than <u>drove</u>.** It seems to us that if the speaker hadn't had anything like this in mind, he/she might have opted for a verb like *go* and said "He <u>went</u> to the grocery store for some cheese."

Our other sentence is a different matter. **2b** doesn't seem to focus on the act of walking at all; instead, the focus seems to be on a new element, the proximity of the store to wherever our cheese buyer had been. **By saying "he walked <u>over</u> to the grocery store," it seems that the speaker is implying the store is relatively close by**.

If you aren't completely sold on this explanation, compare these next two sentences concerning a beautiful island off the southeast coast of Spain and check the boxes you agree with:

3a. We're flying to Majorca.
3b. We're flying over to Majorca.

☐ In 3a they live near Majorca.

☐ In 3a they don't live near Majorca.

☐ In 3a we don't know how far they are from Majorca.

□ In 3b they live near Majorca.

□ In 3b they don't live near Majorca.

□ In 3b we don't know how far they are from Majorca.

Many native speakers would have no trouble distinguishing distance in these two sentences. **In 3a we don't know how far they live from Majorca,** but **in 3b we do know that they live near Majorca**!

More ELT Waifs

Moving right along, here's another dialogue to ponder over. The conversation between Sylvia and Mark is quite a long one, but it contains lots of items that also fall into that woeful category we've called ELT waifs:

A: It's absolutely incredible!

B: What is, Sylvia?

A: How many people believe in UFO's these days. There must be something to it.

B: Oh, not you, too!

A: But, Mark, there have been sightings **galore**!

B: And there's **a great deal of** exaggerating, too.

A: I **kind of** believe those reports. I'll tell you something, but **kindly** refrain from laughing at me, all right?

B: Okay. So tell me.

A: I think I saw a UFO myself. It looked like an upside-down saucer and there was a red**dish** light all around it. And there was a strange humming sound coming from it.

B: **Sort of** a free sound and light show, eh?

A: Very funny. Anyway, size**wise** it must have been as big as a house.

B: And when did this all happen, pray tell?

A: The night I had that really high fever . . . you remember.

B: Oh, you mean the night your temperature soared to 104° **or so**? Now I get it. You were hallucinating!

Well, maybe Sylvia didn't see any UFO's after all, but we certainly see quite a few ELT waifs in bold. Let's continue defining or paraphrasing them just as we did earlier:

galore	=	_____
a great deal of	=	_____
kind of	=	_____
kindly	=	_____
-ish	=	_____
sort of	=	_____
-wise	=	_____
or so	=	_____

There are lots of ways we can define or paraphrase the ELT waifs we've found in the previous dialogue, so we'll list our substitutions and you compare them to your own. It's not the exact words that matter, just the essence:

galore = very many
a great deal of = very much/a lot of/*lots of
kind of = more or less

(★We'd like to point out that even the phrase *lots of* is very rarely taught as an alternate form for *a lot of!*)

kindly = please
-ish = similar to/something like/around
sort of = similar to/like; more or less
-wise = concerning/as far as/in regards to
or so = more or less

Now that was all pretty straightforward, right? We agree, except that there are some interesting points to mention about a few of these particular ELT waifs. Let's see if you can answer the following questions from what you've observed in the dialogue or from what you already know:

1. Judging from our dialogue, what's the word order rule for *galore*?

_____

2. What's different between *galore* and *a great deal of?*

_____

3. Since *kindly* means the same thing as *please,* can we interchange the two phrases whenever we want? (If your answer is *no,* explain why not.)

_____

_____

4. We've figured out what *-ish* means. The question is, what kinds of words can it be added to?

_____

5. From what you see in the dialogue, what's the word order rule for *kind of?*

_____

6. In our dialogue, *kind of* is used in one type of environment and *sort of* is used in another.

   What observation can you make about what types of words can be used in conjunction with *kind of* and *sort of?*

_____

_____

7. *Kind of* and *sort of* mean *more or less* and *or so* does, too. Does that mean we can interchange the first two expressions with *or so* anytime we want? (If your answer is *no,* explain why not.)

_____

_____

And now the answers:

1. **The word** *galore* (which some consider to be informal) **always follows the noun it modifies.** This is because of its etymology. *Galore* comes from Irish (*go leor*) meaning "to sufficiency"; this expression follows the noun it modifies.

2. *Galore* **can be used to modify either a countable noun** (UFO's galore) **or a non-count noun** (money galore). *A great deal of*, on the other hand, can only be used with non-count nouns (" . . . a great deal of money").

3. Although it's true that *kindly* means *please,* **we can't interchange them whenever we feel like it.** *Please* can be put in three places in a sentence: before the verb, after modal auxiliary + subject in a question, or at the end of

the sentence: "Please open the door." / "Would you please open the door?" / "Open the door, please." And we can also use please in a short answer: "Would you like some more coffee?" "Yes, please."

Kindly, on the other hand, sounds more formal, but can't appear in final position the way *please* can: "Kindly open the door." / "Would you kindly open the door?" And it's never used in short answers. The one exception is that some speakers in the American South can be heard to say "Thank you kindly," which really means "Thank you very much."

4. **The suffix *-ish* is normally added to nouns** (*childish/foolish*), **but it can also appear with adjectives**, especially colors (*pinkish/brownish*), and, in very informal usage, with practically any adjectives (*cold-ish/new-ish*) or with adverbs (*late-ish/early-ish*). **It's even used in some time expressions to mean "around"**: "I'll see you eight-ish." (Notice that the preposition *at* is dropped in the time expression when this suffix is added to the hour. Also note that in spelling, this use of *-ish* includes a hyphen.)

5. *Kind of*, if used to modify a verb phrase, **can come between the subject and the verb** ("I kind of believe . . .") **or between the first auxiliary and the verb** ("I've kind of been doing not much of anything").

6. As we've already seen, ***kind of* can be used in a verb phrase, and *sort of* works the same way**. In addition, **we can use these two phrases before adjectives or adverbs** to modify them (*kind of pretty/sort of quietly*).

7. Even though *kind of, sort of,* and *or so* all mean *more or less,* **or so is used exclusively with measurements or time** (*three liters or so/at 8 o'clock or so*). Because of this rule, another way to paraphrase *or so* is to say *approximately.*

And here's a word to the wise about the suffix *-wise*. First of all, it looks like the adjective *wise,* but that's as far as its connection with *wise* goes. The suffix comes from the Old English word *wise* /wi - zə/, meaning "manner." We should mention the fact that many conservative speakers continue to frown on the use of this suffix as a substitute for phrases like *as far as* or *concerning* or *like a . . .* except in so-called standard words such as *clockwise* and *lengthwise.* In response to this, we'd just like to mention that there's a long-standing tradition of using this suffix on all sorts of words (*weatherwise/businesswise,* etc.)—even inventing new combinations. How about *ELT-wise*?!

For that reason, we feel that the suffix should be given its due since so many native speakers use it regularly. It's not our place to judge any expression that becomes so popularly used; if it works and enough native speakers use it and accept it, that's good enough! (We'll be discussing more on this topic in our last chapter.)

Now let's continue our investigation into ELT waifs by looking at another dialogue:

A: I'd like to thank both of you very much for participating in our discussion on the need for more understanding and tolerance in this ever- shrinking world of ours. I think your responses to the audience's questions were very insightful. Well, good night.

B: Good night! Good night! **Am I thirsty**! You'd think someone would have had the sense to put some water and glasses on the dais for us! Would that be asking too much?

C: All you had to do was ask for some, **Judge**. You could have done that, but you didn't. I'll tell you this, though: the air conditioning could have been colder.

B: Why, that's ridiculous, **Professor**. I was freezing!

C: **You were freezing**? You must be getting very old or very sick! Not only was it hotter than Hades in here, but it was horribly stuffy **as well**. I could hardly breathe!

B: Don't you talk to *me* that way, **Professor** Smythe! And **how come** you're always contradicting me, **by the way**?

C: I'm not on trial here, **Judge**! And don't tell me that I always contradict you. I only do it when you're wrong—which is most of the time, **come to think of it**!

B: Why you...

A: Well, **Your Honor, Professor**. Before I leave the hall, I just wanted to thank you once again for showing us how to become more tolerant and understanding human beings. Good night again.

Although you may be asking yourself if the words or phrases in bold are really ELT waifs, let us assure you that they certainly are. Every type of item highlighted in our dialogue receives less attention than it should, and that's why they've been included among our waifs.

There's no real need to approach these items as we've done with previous ones since meaning is not an issue here. What we'll do is review each one as it appears in the dialogue and discuss it.

"Am I thirsty!"

Although this form of exclamation was discussed in Chapter 1 and again recently in Chapter 18, those were neither the places nor times to discuss this construction as an ELT waif. The sentence we have in our dialogue is a fine example of an exclamatory construction. The point is that this kind of exclamation isn't included regularly even though it's such a common way to make exclamations in English. Moreover, it's especially effective because of that dramatic element the extra "punch" on key words seems to create.

Judge/Professor

Now we're getting into a real sore point with us, the use of titles. It's hard to find satisfactory explanations about the typical titles used in English, nor is it easy to find creative exercises that demonstrate how culturally bound their uses are. Here's a typical example that will bring home our point:

A: Good morning, José.

B: Good morning, Teacher.

A: José, my name's not "teacher." Please call me Ms. Quinn.

B: Okay, Teacher.

For someone coming from another culture, it might be hard to figure out why the teacher bothered to mention this custom to poor, unsuspecting José, who thinks he's being polite. Because of cultural interference and the fact that most native English speakers aren't aware how other languages deal with titles, in our eyes, José seems "unpolished" at best, rude at worst. In many cultures there's nothing wrong with using a person's job as his/her title, so if you're a teacher, you're *maestro, ya mu'alimi, Madame le Professeur, ravi, Herr Professor, Hodjam, sungzenim,* and on and on and on! Well, that's fine for other cultures (like the Hispanic, the Arabic, the French, the Israeli/Hebrew, the German, the Turkish, and the Korean cited here), but in polite Anglo-American culture, you're not supposed to call your teacher "Teacher"!

There certainly aren't many jobs that can be turned into acceptable titles in English. Can you think of a few yourself? Write some of them down on the following lines:

_____   _____

_____   _____

_____   _____

_____   _____

We're sure you didn't have too much trouble coming up with jobs that can double as people's titles even though there really aren't many in English. Here's our list of examples for you to compare. Among others, we've thought of these few: **Doctor** (medical doctors, dentists, Ph.D.'s), **Nurse**, **Professor**, **Dean**, **Judge**, **Senator**, **Governor**, **Councilman/Councilwoman**, **Prime Minister**, **Father** (Catholic and Orthodox priests), **Rabbi**, **Officer** (of the police), and many military titles such as **Lieutenant**, **General**, and **Admiral**.

And here's an interesting side note: Ever wonder why Americans think nothing of saying "Mr./Madam President," or "Mr./Madam Speaker" (the head of the House of Representatives in the U.S. Congress), or "Mr./Madam Mayor"? After all, they'd never feel comfortable with "Mr./Madam Boss," "Mr./Ms. Magistrate," or the like. Well, we'd guess it's the influence of the French concerning some terms we borrowed from them a little over 900 years ago. In French it's quite common to say such phrases as "Monsieur le Président," or "Madame le Docteur." By analogy, we came up with a few of our own like the three cited above.

At any rate, students should be made aware early on of such culturally bound titles and of when it's appropriate to call a person by his/her job and when it isn't.

"You were freezing?"

In Chapter 18 we dealt with echo tag questions and how the intonation pattern that's used with them will affect their meaning and show us something about how the speaker feels at that moment concerning the situation. Now we're dealing with what are called **echo questions** (without the "tag").

There are many types of echo questions. In our dialogue we come across the type that's a complete repetition of what the other person has just said:

> A: I was freezing.
> B: You were freezing?

The question we have for you is, why does Person B use this echo question? Think about it and write down any thought you have on the following line:

_____

There can be any of a number of reasons that Person B would choose to make an echo question. He might be saying it to show **surprise** or **disbelief**. He might even use it simply for **clarification** to make sure he hasn't misunderstood what the other person said. And there may be other reasons as well.

The three possible interpretations of the echo question in question that we've given you are amazingly controlled by the intonation that the speaker uses. To bring this point home, let's play a little guessing game. Here's our echo question visualized for you with three different intonations. Look them over and decide which inter-pretation we've made (surprise, disbelief, or clarification) goes with which version:

1. You were **|** freezing?   _____

2. You were freezing?   _____

3. You were freezing?   _____

Just as we said earlier, English is definitely an intonation language. Teachers can never stress enough (no pun intended) how dependent communication can be upon the intonation used by the speaker. So how do we match our three interpretations with the intonation patterns visualized above? **Number 1** demonstrates repeating the sentence for **clarification, Number 2** shows **disbelief,** and **Number 3** indi-cates **surprise**!

By the way, this type of echo question can also be abbreviated by using just the key word or words:

A: I was freezing.
B: Freezing?

But there's another typical kind of echo question, and Person B could have cho-sen to go that route if he'd wanted to:

A: I was freezing.
B: You were what?

In this kind of echo question, the speaker chooses an appropriate *wh-* question word to end the echo question with. In this case, since Person A used a verb, Person B had to go with *what.* Let's look at a few more examples to show how other *wh-*words are applied:

A: I'm seeing Shoshana.   A: I went to Pergola.   A: See you at 6.
B: You're seeing <u>who</u>?   B: You went <u>where</u>?   B: See me <u>when</u>?

Need we say how common this kind of question making is? And yet echo ques-tions are rarely taught. They have indeed become ELT waifs!

"As Well"

Not much need be said about this expression except that it's another way to say *also, too,* or *in addition* and comes at the end of a phrase or sentence. It's quite a common ex-pression, but it hardly ever appears in active vocabulary lists for students to learn.

"How Come?"

It's true that this expression (which means *why?*) is mentioned from time to time in student books, but we thought we'd give it some attention in this chapter because it's not just a matter of what it means. The point we want to make is that there should be enough practice with it so that the students understand the construction of the question that *How come* begins. What's the odd thing about a question that starts off with "How come . . . "?

The answer is that **the question isn't constructed like a question at all. It's actually in the form of a statement**:

How come <u>he speaks Finnish</u>? He's not from Finland.
How come <u>she doesn't like ice cream</u>? It's so good!

An expression as strange sounding as this one, which makes a question without using the normal construction for a question, deserves attention even though many consider *How come* informal English. It is commonly used in speech, so students should know about it. *How Come* is a condensed version of the phrase "**How** did it **come** to pass . . . ?" or "**How** did it **come** to be that . . . ?" So if a student requests an explanation of its derivation, this is it.

"By the Way"/"Come to Think of It"

The final items in bold from our dialogue represent pat phrases that we think have also become ELT waifs. Not nearly enough time is devoted to introducing students to these and many other gems that make conversation flow smoothly. It seems that many teachers like avoiding them because they're often quite difficult to explain and even more difficult to demonstrate clearly so that students really understand when it's appropriate to use them.

The two we chose for our dialogue aren't even the tip of the iceberg. It's up to you to make yourself more aware of expressions like these, create a list of the high frequency ones and figure out when the best times will be to teach them.

In the last appendix, Appendix 8, you'll find a list of some of the more commonly used expressions that help conversation flow so much more easily. It's not at all a complete list—we don't think there could be such a thing—but it will give you an idea of the kinds of expressions we feel have become ELT waifs. In this list you'll find introductory phrases, combining phrases, retorts, rejoinders, and exclamations, among others, so refer to it often.

Negative Questions

"Woe is me!" goes out the cry of many a teacher who fights the constant battle of getting students to form questions correctly in English. Talk about troublesome!

One question form that really confuses students is the negative question because it can be used for so many different purposes. This next dialogue of ours will point them out:

A: **Aren't I supposed** to take the kids for their yearly physicals?

B: Wait a minute. They went for physicals not too long ago.

A: No, that was for their vaccination boosters. **Don't you remember?**

B: Hmm, I guess so.

A: Honey, can you take the kids there for me?

B: But that's something we agreed would be *your* job!

A: **Can't you** ever **do** me a favor without making me feel so guilty? I accidentally scheduled our club's charity bazaar for then.

B: I don't understand what the big deal is. **Can't you reschedule** the kids' physicals?

A: I could, but the doctor's going out of town for a few weeks. **Won't you do** me this favor? Please?

B: Oh, all right! But this isn't the first time you've done something like this. Please be more careful in the future.

A: I will, I will. **Aren't you** the nicest husband in the world!

Each one of the negative questions highlighted in our dialogue serves a different purpose for the speaker who's uttered it. Let's see your linguistic sleuthing back in action as you figure out *what the underlying purpose is* for each negative question. Think about the situation and the context for each question to help you solve the mystery. We've done the first one for you to get you started:

Aren't I supposed . . . _____The speaker expects the answer to be "yes"_____

Don't you remember? _____

_____

Can't you ever do me a favor . . . _____

_____

Can't you reschedule . . . _____

_____

Won't you do me this favor? _____

_____

Aren't you the nicest . . . _____

Not so simple, is it? At any rate, here are our interpretations of the underlying purposes for the rest of the negative questions from our dialogue:

Don't you remember?   She also expects his answer to be *yes*.
Can't you ever **do** me a favor . . .   She's scolding him.
Can't you reschedule . . .   He's showing disbelief and annoyance.
Won't you do me this favor?   She's trying to persuade him.
Aren't you the nicest . . .   She's using a question form as an exclamation.
                                         Moreover, it softens up the person or the situation.

As we can see, there are lots of underlying reasons for people to use negative questions! Before leaving this topic, we'd like to go back for a moment to our first negative question, "Aren't I supposed to take the kids for their yearly physicals?" Isn't this a strange situation, using *aren't* for 1st person singular? *We* think so, and we know that students certainly do! Any ideas as to why this is?

_____

In order to understand this strange phenomenon, we first have to look at the negative question without contractions. In that case, the question would be:

Am I not supposed to take the kids for their yearly physicals?

The problem is that **when this construction is used, it seems to signal impatience, annoyance, even anger—and certainly sarcasm.** If this is the case, we can't use it regularly just as a plain negative question, now can we? For that reason, and by some quirk of the language, the contraction *aren't* was elected to substitute for *am I not* because the contraction doesn't exist in standard English, so that's how we end up with *Aren't I . . . ?* instead of *Amn't I . . . ?* Make a note that we can never use *are* in the affirmative with 1st person singular, statement or question!

And while we're on the subject, what about all the other possible negative questions without contractions? Well, let's review the ones from our dialogue and see how they would look in the full non-contracted form:

Am I not supposed to take the kids . . . ?

Do you not remember?

<u>Can you not</u> ever <u>do me a favor</u> . . . ?

Can you not reschedule . . . ?

<u>Will you not do</u> me a favor?

<u>Are you not</u> the nicest husband in the world!

As they might say in comic book English, "Yuck!" Not only do they all sound horribly sarcastic and nasty, but they also sound like something out of the eighteenth century at best! In other words, they sound archaic and very unpleasant. Without doubt, that's why you rarely hear negative questions without contractions. Case closed!

22

Where English Is Going

"A journey of a thousand miles begins with one step."

It's been quite a journey, but we've now reached the final chapter. We've investigated many different areas of English and arrived at answers to explain the amazing ways that the language works. The language that you've seen in this book reflects a remarkable history that goes back into the remote past when words were only spoken and writing was very rare indeed.

English has changed over the centuries (let's say from the year 1000 to the present) more than any other language known to humankind. And these changes have taken place in all of its components: its phonology, morphology, syntax, grammar, and lexicon. As an example of what we're talking about, take a look at the following. It's the first line from *The Lord's Prayer*, presented here in four versions to show you how the language has changed over the centuries. (By the way, that strange-looking letter you'll find in the Old English version is pronounced like our *th* as in the word *thorn*.)

Old English/Anglo-Saxon (up to ca. 1100)
Fæder ūre þū þe eart on heofonum, sī þīn nama gehālgod.

Middle English (1100–1500)
Oure fadir that art in heuenes, halewid bē thī nāme.

Early Modern English (1500–1700)
Our father which art in heauen, hallowed be thy name.

Current Standard English
Our Father, who are in Heaven, may Your name be holy.

Quite amazing, isn't it? You can clearly see the profound changes that have occurred over the centuries to individual words and to the structure of the phrases. So, if English has changed so dramatically in the past, who's to say it won't continue evolving in the future? Undoubtedly it will.

That's the purpose of this final chapter, to see if we can gain any insights into where English may be heading in the future. We've caught a glimpse of what changes it's gone through in the past and have learned to understand a great deal more about its present stage of development. So let's speculate about what might happen in the future to areas of this most flexible of languages. We think you'll find what you come upon quite interesting.

The process of change is ongoing and relentless—in all of life, not just in language—so it's time for us to consider what changes may be in store for the language down the road. Of course, these are only going to be our personal predictions, some based on what's happened to the language so far and some on what's already happening to it nowadays. But who knows? Maybe somebody will dust this book off with its pages all yellowed and cracking a couple of hundred years from now, look at the predictions we're about to make and say, "They weren't so outrageous after all!"

To keep this chapter simple and not so wordy, we're just going to list a few changes that may become "correct" English at some point in the future. We're zeroing in on certain items because we've already noticed changes going on with them and think you may have, too. At any rate, think about each one and decide whether you agree or disagree. At least you can't say we're wrong about anything—none of us will be around to tell . . . not in this lifetime!

✦ Nouns

1. Some irregular plural nouns may lose their sense of plurality and be considered singular. Such words as *data, criteria, phenomena,* and *media* fall into this category:

   Your data isn't complete.

2. Other nouns with irregular plurals, especially low frequency nouns, may develop regular plural endings, so it's conceivable that *oxen* will become *oxes,* and *shrimp* will become *shrimps*:

   How many shrimps do you have in your shrimp cocktail?

✦ Other Vocabulary Changes

1. There will be hundreds and hundreds of new words generated by the continuing evolution in technology. Most of these new words will be verbs and nouns. Words that have already become common in the very recent past are *to hack, to email, to download, voice-mail, CD, DVDs,* and *spam.*

2. Some words will either disappear or become rarer and rarer in everyday speech. *Fewer* may be replaced almost exclusively by *less*:

> This bread has less calories than that kind.

As might be replaced the same way by *like*:

> She did it just like she should.

In addition, *lay* will replace *lie*:

> I think I'll lay down for a while.
> I saw it laying on your desk.

3. *There's* may be used for both singular and plural subjects in the present, and *there was* will follow suit for the past if this happens:

> There's lots of reasons for saying this.

By analogy, *here's* might be used for both singular and plural subjects, too:

> Here's the books you ordered.

The question word *Where's* might be used for both singular and plural subjects, too:

> Where's the bargains you said this store has?

4. The phrase *a whole nother* may become commonplace and accepted in which the initial syllable of <u>*another*</u> has gotten detached from the rest of the word and been fronted:

> She had <u>a</u> whole nother life when she lived overseas.

5. Saying dates using cardinal rather than ordinal numbers will become accepted and either remain as an alternative way of saying a date or actually replace the older, traditional way:

> <u>April one</u> instead of <u>April first</u>

Writing dates may also be under change. The way most native speakers learn to write a date is month + number for the day, year (April 1, 2006). You can also see the date written as a number for the day + month + year (1 April 2006). This variation will become more and more commonly seen in the future.

6. *They* may be considered proper usage to agree with the words *everyone, everybody, someone, somebody, anyone, anybody, no one,* and *nobody* even though the verb directly following will still remain in the 3rd person singular if the simple present or the word *was* is used:

> No one knows if they're to be here by 3:00 p.m. or not.
> Somebody called, but they didn't leave a name.

It follows, then, that if this usage does become standard, *their* will be used for the possessive forms.

> Everybody was here with their spouses and children.
> Did anyone leave their umbrella at my house?

7. Reflexive pronouns will probably become acceptable variations in place of personal pronouns:

> Everybody went to the party except for Ellen and myself.
> "How are you today?" "Fine, thanks. And yourself?"

𝒜𝒷 *-ly* Adverbs

In some ways, *-ly* adverbs are becoming the dinosaurs of Modern English, that is, they're becoming rarer and rarer in speech. We should add, though, that this change isn't happening in every occurrence. What leads us to believe they'll disappear in certain situations is that we've noticed more and more examples of the loss of *-ly* adverbs over the past twenty years or so. Here are some of them:

> real interesting
> fresh baked bread
> You can breathe easy now.
> He can do it quicker than me.

Another adverb that should be on the "endangered species list" is *well*:

> "How's it going?" "Good."

𝒜𝒷 Verbs

1. That third person singular -s/-es in the simple present may finally fall off and then future teachers won't have to pull the hair out of their heads anymore because their students keep forgetting to use it!

2. By the same token, *doesn't* may disappear as the negative form in the simple present to be replaced completely by *don't*. We've witnessed this loss happening in certain dialects of English, and we've been hearing it happening for decades in song lyrics, especially in rock-and-roll, hard rock, and country-and-western music.

3. *Do, does,* and *did* may fall out of use in question making for the simple present and simple past respectively. If that happens, the statement form will be used with rising intonation for the yes/no questions:

You speak Tibetan?

4. More irregular verbs may become regular, especially lower frequency verbs:

   She shaked his hand with a firm grip.

5. Split infinitives will become correct:

   I'll show you how to quickly get this job done.

6. Double negatives might come full circle and be fine again (as they were in Old English):

   I didn't ask for no trouble.

   After all, this use is commonly heard everywhere that English is spoken.

7. The mandative subjunctive could disappear altogether to be replaced by *should* or *ought to* + verb:

   I suggest that she see a doctor. → I suggest that she should see a doctor.

8. Complicated subject–verb agreement which confuses native speakers today may change as far as what's considered "correct" usage:

   Either you or she are going to have to do it.

9. It will become acceptable to use two conditional phrases in a present or past unreal conditional sentence as an alternative to using the present subjunctive in the if-clause and the conditional in the other clause:

   If she would just study harder, she'd get better grades.
   If he would have asked me, I would have helped.

   In fact, this is commonly heard nowadays in many—if not all—areas of the English-speaking world.

◈ Other Predictions

In general, much to the chagrin of many teachers, there may be a loosening of the reins that control what is and what isn't acceptable usage. People may become less concerned with whether or not the correct form is being used and more concerned with the clarity of communication. A continuing upsurge in technological as opposed to literary writing may be responsible for this trend. In addition, videos, CDs, DVDs, the Web, and television (or whatever other audio-visual forms of communication come along in the future) could result in less reading of books, magazines, and newspapers. This tendency to get away from these types of printed matter may help to desensitize people as to how the written word looks or how a message should sound. A very good case in point is the way standard rules of English grammar and spelling are very often broken in email messages.

Among other areas of language that may be affected by the media and movies, vocabulary and certain grammatical constructions may become more universally standardized, or at least people anywhere will understand area-specific words or phrases because of the exposure they'll get. We see this happening already because of television and movies: "I'll put another shrimp on the *barbie*," says an Australian to the television viewer if he'll come down under for a visit; "Don't get your *knickers* in a twist!" shouts the husband to his angry wife in a British film showing in an American movie house; "*Tell me about it*," comments an American as she agrees with something her friend's just said on Irish television.

As we've already mentioned, we even see grammatical constructions changing because of influences from one form of English or another beginning to dominate "World Englishes." Examples that readily come to mind are the way *will* may be replacing *shall* in British English just as it has in other varieties such as North American English, and the way the North American negative verb form *don't/doesn't/didn't have* is now more and more being used in Britain alongside the older, more traditional negative forms *haven't/hasn't/hadn't*:

> I haven't the time to do it. / I don't have the time to do it.

One other grammatical construction that may very well change doesn't have to do with influences from other forms of English, but rather from a change in syntax when the verb *be* is employed in *wh-* questions. In indirect speech, the traditional position for *be* is at the end of the phrase:

> He told us where the bakery is.

The reason for this position for *be* is because of the basic rule used in indirect speech when a hidden *wh-* question is being "reproduced," so to speak: Since the question ([Where] is the bakery?) is now becoming part of a statement, regular subject + verb word order is to be followed ([where] the bakery is).

It seems that it's becoming more and more common to keep *be* in the same position it held in the original question, so we end up with

> He told us where is/where's the bakery.

Other examples:

> I'll point out which man is Mr. Kelly.
> I can't remember when is his appointment.
> They aren't sure who's the new dean.

Of course, what's most important to keep in mind after looking over all of our predictions is that we shouldn't ever lose sight of the fact that language keeps evolving, sometimes slowly, sometimes quickly, but relentlessly—and the purists can't do anything to stop it from happening.

In ending this final chapter, we'd like to leave you with a quote that we've always liked. Who originally said it, we don't know, but it must have been someone very wise. We hope you enjoy it as much as we do:

> *Language is the hallmark of an educated person.*
> *To say a thing efficiently is the province of the scientist.*
> *To say a thing beautifully is the province of the poet.*
> *Be both.*

Appendix 1

Picture Files

The single most useful teaching aid you can have is a Picture File, which doesn't cost much to make. All you need is magazines, some glue or tape, sturdy paper or other backing material, and a pair of scissors.

To put your file together, choose magazines that have lots of pictures and cut out anything you find of interest. Don't overlook simple ones because even the simplest may have various teaching points to focus on. Use large pictures in front of the entire class; use large or small ones for individual or small group work. Trim the edges and glue the pictures onto sturdy backing sheets. (Construction paper or tag board is excellent for this purpose.) On the back of each mounted picture, list a variety of teaching points that picture can be used for.

Let's take a look at a picture and we'll show you what teaching points we can use it for.

Vocabulary Items

Outdoors:

tree, flowers, grass, bushes, sign, sidewalk, walkway

Parts of houses:

roof, porch, stairs, chimneys, shingles, windows, siding, basement

Idioms:

You shouldn't count your chickens before they're hatched.

Grammar Points

Present Progressive:

They're walking, strolling, looking, thinking; He's pointing, wearing, holding; She's hoping, planning, imagining.

Countable and Uncountable Nouns:

grass, bushes, money, sign

Active and Passive Voice:

The house was built in 1902.

They built the house in one year.

The man wonders if they can afford a down payment on that house.

The house is being sold by a well-known realty company.

Past Tense:

Who was the first family to live there?

The family decided to look for a new house.

Simple Present:

Big houses are a lot to take care of.

Victorian houses tend to be very large.

Present Perfect:

The house has been for sale for a long time.

Present Perfect Progressive:

My parents have been looking for a new house for a long time.

Wish vs. Hope:

They wish the house didn't cost so much.

She hopes that the owners will accept their bid.

Modals:

You must save if you want to buy a house.

Prepositions:

in the yard, on the sidewalk, next to his wife, in front of them, with their parents, on the front porch, for a down payment, at home

Pronunciation

/aɪ/ vs. /au/ vs. /ɔɪ/
/aɪ/: sign, high
/au/: house, brown
/ɔɪ/: point, boy

/s/, /z/, vs. /ɪz/:
/s/: steps, roofs, plants, payments
/z/: trees, windows, stairs, signs
/ɪz/: bushes, porches, prices, houses

See how much you can do with one picture? But don't overlook simple pictures on plain backgrounds. They can be productive, too.

Once you have a stack of pictures ready to go, number them. Then make a master list of the teaching points you've found in the pictures. Next to each point, list the numbers of all the pictures that fit that teaching point. In other words, your master list will tell you what topics (grammar, vocabulary, pronunciation, etc.) your files contain and what pictures can be used to demonstrate these points. This way, when you teach a particular lesson, you can go to your master list and quickly pull out the pictures you need. Any time you add to your file, you can easily update your master list.

Here's an additional comment about writing the teaching points your pictures represent on the back of the pictures. When you hold up a picture and the teaching point appears on the back for you to see, you don't have to crane your neck to look at what it is you're holding up. The students see the picture; you see the teaching point!

Why do all of this work to create a Picture File? A teacher-made Picture File suits you, your needs, your students, and the subjects you're teaching. Commercial sets of pictures could never give you this personalized touch at a price that most teachers can afford. Moreover, if a picture goes out of date, is lost, or is destroyed, replacing it doesn't require that you buy a new set; just find another magazine and there you have your replacement.

Appendix 2

More Strategies and Activities that Work

This book has dealt with some of the most difficult features of the basics of English grammar. A point we'd like to stress from the outset is that this book, even though it is a grammar book, was not written with the intention of telling you that you should teach grammar as a separate entity in your classes. On the contrary, we feel that grammar should be an integrated part of your lessons. Teachers can plan that they will teach the present progressive or articles or whatever this week and break the topic down into individual lesson plans. In doing so, however, teachers shouldn't overlook an essential point, namely that **language should always be taught in meaningful context**. You can handle the present progressive or modal auxiliaries or whatever is being taught very effectively within the context of meaningful situations that your students can relate to—and that's the key element: **situations or topics that your students can relate to**. We've usually been able to get to know the kinds of students we've had in any given class after only a short time, and if you can do this kind of assessment too, you should be able to determine where their interests lie as a group and what subjects "turn them on."

Even if you teach the grammar component in an intensive English program which separates the four basic language skills into different classes (grammar, reading, writing, conversation), you can still teach each grammar point in the context of something cultural, scientific, or topical. Use introductory dialogues like the ones found abundantly in this book. Create exercises that deal with the grammar points in sentences related to the topic. Plan activities such as the ones featured in the *Teaching Tips* that relate to the topic. By planning your teaching in this way, you'll be doing your students a tremendous service:

- They'll experience the grammar realistically and meaningfully,
- they won't feel burdened by grammar drill after grammar drill, and
- they'll learn something important for their growth and development besides language.

On the following pages you'll find samples of various types of exercises that have proven very effective in reinforcing specific points of grammar or in developing more holistic practice for the students. As you know, there's really nothing very new under the sun. The exercises selected for this appendix aren't revolutionary; rather, they're solid, reliable, adaptable exercises that you can create with very little effort once you've mastered their styles.

You may notice that the exercises that follow progress in a certain direction, and the reason for this sequence bears explanation. Over the years, we've found that the best language teaching methodology and most practical approach to teaching and reinforcing specific grammar points are accomplished through the use of **mechanical, meaningful/manipulative**, and **communicative** exercises as championed by Christina Bratt Paulston and Mary Newton Bruder, two eminent leaders in the field of ELT to whom all of us owe a debt of gratitude. These concepts deal with a "weaning process" in which teachers gradually turn over control of the language to their students. This is how they work:

Mechanical: The teacher has complete control of the responses and knows exactly what the correct ones should be as there are very few correct responses to each item. The students have few choices to make. They plug in some words or carry out a transformation, but they don't even have to understand all the vocabulary in order to do the exercises correctly.

Example 1: *Make this sentence negative:*
He **likes** to study the environment. → _____
He **doesn't like** to study the environment.

Example 2: T: What's this?
S: It's a gift/birthday gift/present . . .

Meaningful/Manipulative: The teacher gives up some control of the responses, but knows that there's a limited number of correct ones and can anticipate what they'll be. The students now have a few choices to make, which may change the meaning of their responses to some degree, thereby allowing them to show some individuality. The students assume partial responsibility for the utterances they produce.

Example 1: *Fill in the blank:*
The ozone layer _____ disappear.
's going to/isn't going to/will (won't)/might (not)/may (not)

Example 2:   Take a look at this picture and describe what's happening.

(The student is given a picture and now selects what part[s] of the picture he or she wants to talk about. Of course, the student can also choose not to talk about a part of the picture. He/She is indeed manipulating the language.)

Communicative: The teacher relinquishes all control of the responses and can't always anticipate what they'll be. The students are now in complete control of their responses and can be as individual as they wish. They now assume full responsibility for the utterances they produce.

Example 1:   T: *Isn't the Internet a wonderful thing?*
S_1: I know it.
S_2: I especially like email.
S_3: I don't have a computer yet.
S_4: They're still too expensive for a lot of people.
T: But they keep getting cheaper and cheaper

Example 2:   T: *I had a great weekend. How about you?*
S_1: It wasn't so good. I had to work.
S_2: It was fine. I went to a great party.

A.≈ Slot Substitutions

This type of exercise is to be used for *oral* practice. In these exercises, the teacher does the following:

1. models the basic structure
2. has the class repeat the model
3. calls out the first substitution(s)
4. calls on a student to insert the substitution(s)
5. calls out the second substitution(s), etc.

Why use slot substitutions? Actually, there are lots of good reasons, but we want to stress right from the outset that they are of *limited* use and should never be relied on for any length of time in making lesson plans.

The first reason to use slot substitution drills is that they help sensitize the students to English word order. (You have to know where words can be inserted in order to give correct responses.) Second, they're wonderful for listening comprehension. (If you don't hear it right, you can't repeat it right.) Third, students learn inductively what elements of language belong to one class, and therefore, they learn, for example, how modals work in sentences. Fourth, they sensitize the students to changes that many kinds of words must make to conform to the new versions of the sentences. Here's what we mean:

T: He**'s** going to the dentist tomorrow.

Ss: He's going to the dentist tomorrow.

T: *they*

S: **They're** going to the dentist tomorrow.

T: *yesterday*

S: They **went** to the dentist **yesterday**.

(**T** = teacher; **Ss** = students; **S$_1$** = student 1)

Single Slot Substitution

T: I'll probably stay home this evening.

Ss: I'll probably stay home this evening.

T: *go to a movie*

S$_1$: I'll probably go to a movie this evening.

T: *write some letters*

S$_2$: I'll probably write some letters this evening.

T: *watch TV*

S$_3$: I'll probably watch TV this evening.

Double Slot Substitution

T: She bought a hat last week.

Ss: She bought a hat last week.

T: *you/dress*

S$_1$: You bought a dress last week.

T: *I/jacket*

S$_2$: I bought a jacket last week.

T: *the neighbors/car*

S$_3$: The neighbors bought a car last week.

Multiple Slot Substitution★

T: Her blouse has flowers on the front.

Ss: Her blouse has flowers on the front.

T: *his shirt/buttons/cuffs*

S$_1$: His shirt has buttons on the cuffs.

T: *my jacket/a dragon/back*

S$_2$: My jacket has a dragon on the back.

T: *their shoes/taps/heels*

S$_3$: Their shoes have taps on the heels.

★Go cautiously with the multiple slot substitutions. After all, there are three pieces of information for the students to remember in each item, and lower level students will probably find these too tough. If you think your students can handle it, write the three items to be substituted in large print on a card and show the students what items they are to substitute:

Teacher says: Her blouse has flowers on the front.

Students say: Her blouse has flowers on the front.

Teacher says: *his shirt/buttons/cuffs*
         (while showing a larger version of the card to the right)

his shirt – buttons – cuffs

Moving Slot Substitution

T: He's going to a movie tonight.
Ss: He's going to a movie tonight.
T: *show*
S_1: He's going to a show tonight.
T: *last night*
S_2: He went to a show last night.
T: *they*
S_3: They went to a show last night.

Now you've seen a wide variety of slot substitutions and how they're put to work. We have to stress, however, that these exercises are only to be used as introductory activities. The teacher should always be vigilant that students be moved as quickly as possible to manipulative and communicative activities so they can take control of the language as soon as they feel comfortable doing so.

A Cloze Procedures

Another type of exercise that should become a staple kind of classroom language learning activity for all language teachers is called the *cloze procedure*. It can play a very important role in the language classroom. Actually, there are two main types of cloze with many variations, the pure cloze and the modified cloze. This is how you create them:

Pure Cloze: Take any passage that's as close to 350 words in length as you can get. Leave the first and last sentences intact. Beginning with the second sentence, take out every 5th to 9th word and replace it with a blank. Make all of your blanks equal in length. Only a single word is acceptable for each blank and keep in mind that a contraction is a single word, too! If the blank falls where there's a date, number, proper noun, or otherwise unreconstructible word, then the next word should be replaced by the blank instead. The words that are omitted should be words that your students already know.

Note: It's a more difficult exercise if every 5th word is omitted than if every 9th word is omitted. You'll probably prefer to eliminate every 7th or 9th word, at least at the beginning.

As far as correcting the cloze exercises that the students have completed, there are two lines of thought on the subject. Some people insist that only the exact word that was eliminated should be accepted as the correct answer. Others, however, argue that any word that completes the idea appropriately should be accepted.

Just in case you'd like to know, here's the current thinking on the two methods of correction just mentioned. Accepting any appropriate word while correcting a cloze seems, at least on the surface, the only fair way to go. Why shouldn't teachers accept any answer that works? Why should students be penalized for not being able to read the mind of the person who wrote the text? Here's why:

1. Accepting any appropriate word makes it much harder to correct because the teacher needs to keep in mind the entire context while trying to focus on each answer; it's also harder to correct when there are very large groups doing the activity.

2. Correcting in this way takes a lot more time.

3. Using this method is only slightly more statistically reliable, so you be the judge.

The most important use of pure cloze procedures is to test your students' overall mastery of the language (whole language). A blank may replace any kind of word; generally, it's the overall competence and comprehension that your students have which will allow them to figure out what possible item can go in each blank.

Modified Cloze: Write your own sentences or passages in which you plan to focus on any given discrete point. The length of the sentences or the whole passage depends on your knowledge of what your students can handle. If you're dealing with prepositions or articles or the like, eliminate whatever words are being targeted and keep the blanks equal in length throughout. If you're dealing with verbs, draw in each blank and write the verb to be used in parentheses before or after the blank. The students will quickly learn that they're to use the verbs in parentheses to fill in the blanks.

As for correcting this kind of cloze, you should apply the rule of thumb that any appropriate words or forms of verbs that work to complete the sentences are acceptable.

Some Tips About Cloze Procedures

1. Avoid "spoonfeeding" your students. For example, don't tell them in the parentheses to use a negative form of a verb; let them figure that out through the context. (Of course, make sure that the context is clear.)

2. Focus on one discrete point at a time in a *modified* cloze procedure. In other words, don't eliminate prepositions in the same exercise in which you eliminate verbs. Keep your focus

3. Always treat phrasal verbs (two-word verbs or three-word verbs) as single entities so that your students will view them in this way. For example, don't put the verb *look* in parentheses and its allied preposition-like particle outside the parentheses like this:

_____ (look) at

_____ (look) for

It's always better for the students to understand phrasal verbs as whole items and learn them in that way:

———————————— (look at)

———————————— (watch out for)

4. Tell your students to read everything at least twice before filling in any of the blanks. Such surveying should be used for all reading as it is important for students to learn to assess what they are going to read and to get an idea of the context. If they don't do this survey assessment first, they'll probably make avoidable mistakes.

That's all we have to say about these exercises. Following are some examples of cloze procedures. We hope that you find them to be useful, clear examples of the kinds of exercises you can easily create for your classes. By the way, if you'd like to, feel free to copy them out of this book and use them in class to get you started.

A Pure Cloze Procedure

Fill in the blanks with appropriate words to complete the sentences.

Yuri had been in the United States for just three months. Now he was having mixed emotions ———————————— whether it had been a good ———————————— for him to leave Russia after ————————————. He was sitting in the school ————————————, having his lunch, and looking at ———————————— faces of all the other students. ———————————— were laughing, clowning around, and having ———————————— great time, but Yuri wasn't. He ———————————— understand English well enough to get ———————————— jokes, and he always had the —————————————even though he knew it was —————————————that the students were talking about ————————————. It wasn't supposed to be like ————————————. What had happened to all the ———————————— and enthusiasm he had felt about ———————————— to America? Why was he beginning to feel ———————————— towards all the other students? He ———————————— know the answers to those questions, ———————————— that things didn't look very good.

Yuri glanced up at the clock ———————————— the wall and knew that the ———————————— was going to ring any minute, ———————————— he didn't feel like going to ———————————— next class. It was social studies, ———————————— Yuri's inadequate knowledge of English made ———————————— difficult for him to follow the ———————————— or keep up with the rest ———————————— the class. He was seriously thinking _____ cutting class and just hanging out _____ the park near his home.

No, _____ had always been a good student _____ in Kiev, and he didn't want _____ get in trouble for cutting classes.

_____ a deep, sad sigh, Yuri got _____ off his chair, collected the pieces _____ aluminum foil that his mom had _____ to wrap his sandwich and apple _____ , closed his lunch box slowly, _____ started heading toward the trash barrel _____ always sat near the cafeteria exit. _____ stopping to throw away his garbage, Yuri _____ the wrappers up in the air _____ some legendary American basketball star about _____ make an incredible trick shot, and _____ up hitting his classmate, Anna, right _____ the head with the messy wrappers.

_____ expected a scene: she was going _____ yell at him and call him _____ , but she didn't. She just started laughing, and for the first time since his arrival in this country, Yuri felt a part of something.

Modified Cloze Procedures

The first of these exercises is for practice discrimination between the simple past and present perfect. It's in the form of a letter.

Example 1: Fill in the blanks with the verbs in parentheses. If no verb appears in parentheses, think of one that will fit.

Dear Pam,

It _____ (be) a long time since I _____ (write) you. I _____ (have) any time to write you last month because I _____ (be) extremely busy. The school year _____ (just/end), and during the last three weeks of the semester, I _____ (have) a chance to do anything except correct papers, hand in final grades, and sleep. Besides all that, over the past week and a half, I _____ (write) twenty-two letters of recommendation for various students and _____ (interview) three candidates for the position as my new secretary. In my last letter I _____ (tell) you that I _____ (need) a new secretary, _____?

So, Pam, how ———————— (your life / be) since we last
———————— (correspond)? ———————— (you / make) any plans for
your vacation yet? The last time you ———————— (write) me, you
———————— (say) that you ———————— (want) to get away for a
month or so during the summer. ———————— (you / decide) where to go?
I ———————— (decide) to stay home this summer and tend the flowers in my
back yard!

Write me soon, and let me know all about your summer plans.

Love,
Artie

Example 2: This second example is for practice with prepositions. The sentences have been numbered for ease of identification during review. Fill in the blanks with appropriate prepositions. Some of the prepositions are parts of two-word verbs.

Cooking with Carmen

1. Carmen decided to make a chef's salad ———————— dinner.
2. She took all the vegetables she had ———————— ———————— her refrigerator and put them ———————— the kitchen counter.
3. She got ———————— a large salad bowl, a cutting board, and a sharp knife.
4. First, she washed some lettuce ———————— the kitchen faucet and drained it thoroughly to get all the excess water ————————.
5. Then, she got a clove of garlic ———————— the basket she had hanging ———————— one corner of the kitchen, took ———————— the skin that covered it, and rubbed the garlic clove all ———————— the inside of the salad bowl.
6. Next, she tore the lettuce leaves ———————— little pieces and put them all ———————— the bottom of the salad bowl because she wanted the lettuce ———————— all the other vegetables.
7. She cut tomatoes ———————— wedges, cucumbers and scallions ———————— slices, and some zucchini and American cheese ———————— long, thin pieces, and placed all these items ———————— the lettuce ———————— the bottom of the bowl.
8. After that, she threw ———————— lots of pieces of cooked turkey and ham and slices of hard boiled eggs and added some sliced radishes and mushrooms ———————— the bowl as well.

9. Finally, she shook her salad dressing and poured it all _____ everything. Carmen knew she had created a work of art!

Example 3: This is a dialogue for overall verb practice good for recycling. Fill in the blanks with the words in parentheses. If there are blanks without words after them, think of what you can write in those blanks.

Bob: Hello.

Ann: Hello, Bob? This _____ Ann.

Bob: Oh, hi, Ann! Long time, no see. What _____ (happen)?

Ann: What _____ (you / do) next Saturday night?

Bob: Nothing special. Why?

Ann: I _____ (think about) _____ (have) a party at my place, and I _____ (wonder) if you _____ (like) _____ (come).

Bob: I _____ (love) to. Who else _____ (come)?

Ann: Well, I _____ (call) anybody else yet. You _____ the first one.

Bob: The first one? I _____ (flatter)! _____ there anything I _____ (bring)? Some drinks or food or something?

Ann: No, thanks. I _____ (already / take care of) all that. By the way, _____ (you / like) _____ (bring) a date?

Bob: Sure.

Ann: _____ (you / still / see) that girl I _____ (meet) at your house a couple of months ago?

Bob: No, we _____ (stop) _____ (see) each other three weeks ago.

Ann: Oh, I _____ sorry _____ (hear) that. She _____ (seem) very nice.

Bob: Yeah, well, that _____ the way it _____ (go).

Ann: Okay then. I _____ (see) you Saturday night around 8:30.

Bob: Great! See you then! Bye.

A̶ʓ̇ Incomplete Dialogues

Exercises like the ones that follow work best when students pair up and put into practice an old proverb, "two heads are better than one." These exercises really get the students thinking. The students should first read the *entire* dialogue at least twice before attempting to fill in the missing parts. Stress this helpful hint: **The line that follows the blank area they're about to work on probably contains information that will help them figure out what may work logically in the blank.**

Why incomplete dialogues? There are some compelling reasons that make them such effective exercises. They serve as marvelous activities for reading comprehension, for sensitivity to language components, for reasoning, and for critical thinking. Students can stretch their language ability and help their classmates learn, too. Incomplete dialogues also allow the students the special freedom found in manipulative and communicative activities. Here are the two major areas in which the skills just noted come into play through the use of incomplete dialogues:

1. Reading Comprehension: The students are forced to read thoroughly and find clues within the dialogue to identify where the situation takes place and enhance understanding of what's going on. Attention to punctuation is also very important as meaning can change depending on what punctuation has been used and where it's been placed. Here's an example:

A: Acme Plumbing. Jim _____ . _____?

B: Yes, please. _____ .

A: I'm afraid that job's been taken.

Let's see just how much there is for the students to deal with in the excerpt above which was taken from a longer exercise. To begin with, the readers have to determine what the situation is (Are the speakers face to face? Are they on the phone?) Because of the way Person A (Jim) starts the conversation, the readers should deduce that the speakers are on the phone.

Now, from what is referred to in reading pedagogy as "knowledge of the world," the readers must decide what Jim could possibly say in the short blank following his name. Thinking back to similar situations they've experienced on the phone when calling a company, the readers should understand that Jim is saying something to identify himself ("Jim speaking" or "Jim here" or "Jim talking" or maybe his last name).

Next we have a long blank ending in a question mark. The readers must see the question mark (and it's surprising how many students fail to note punctuation as a clue at first glance), realize there must be a question in that blank, and determine what would be appropriate for Jim to ask at that moment. From their "knowledge of the world," the readers should be able to figure out that Jim is probably saying something like "May

I help you?" or "What can I do for you?" But wait a minute! The following line begins with Person B saying "Yes, please." That means we have to eliminate "What can
I do for you?" as a possible question for Jim to ask because "Yes, please" wouldn't be an
appropriate response to "What can I do for you?" We must conclude that Jim has said
"May I help you?" and then Person B's response works just fine.

Finally, how can we figure out what Person B says next? We need to look at Jim's
reply; that's where we'll get the hint we need to fill in the next blank. Jim says, "I'm
afraid that job's been taken." His answer gives us quite a bit of information to work
with. If he mentions "that job," Person B must have asked about a specific job, so we
know that we've got to think of a specific job to mention in the blank. In addition,
Jim says he's afraid that job's been taken, and this information leads us to the conclusion that Person B was attempting to apply for that job—otherwise, Jim would
have no reason to make that statement. So we have these two pieces of information:
Person B wants to apply for a job and it's for a specific job he/she knows about, not
just any job. (Everything we've been discussing, especially in this paragraph, demonstrates clearly how important critical thinking can be to reading and language learning in general as well as the principles of deixis.)

So what can we put in that final blank? Possibilities are "I'm calling about the
ad I saw in the paper for a plumber's assistant." or "I'd like to know if you're still looking for a bookkeeper." or "A friend of mine told me he saw your ad for a secretary."

Notice how the situation we've been working with is deliberately left quite open;
that's to allow the students to come up with different ideas.

While the students are paired up and working on one of these dialogues, walk
around the room and offer assistance when the students seem stuck. When they're finished and you've checked over their work, have the best of the lot presented to the
class in the final versions. The students will find it interesting to compare what they've
come up with to what their classmates have created.

2. Sensitivity to Language Components: The readers must search out clues within
the dialogue that can establish the correct tense or aspect of verbs, and those words that
students typically rush over, like prepositions, take on an importance which the students
don't often realize they have. Just look at the following examples:

> A: Who are you sending that fax _____?
> B: Our main office.
>
> A: Who are you sending that fax _____?
> B: My boss. She said to get it out right away.

The students are invited into becoming more sensitive to language by having to
figure out which prepositions will work in these blanks in order to elicit the responses
provided. This is another use of critical thinking.

The following examples of incomplete dialogues get progressively more difficult. You decide which difficulty level is most appropriate for your students.

Work with a classmate and complete the following conversations.

Example 1

A: I just dropped my glove. Would you mind _____?

B: Why don't you _____?

A: Can't you see that _____?

B: Oh, I didn't notice. All right. Here you are.

Example 2

A: That's not your jacket; it's my jacket. _____!

B: Aw, can't I _____ for this evening?

A: No, you can't. You should have _____ first.

Example 3

Tom: Hi, Pat! _____?

Pat: Oh, everything's fine, thanks. _____?

Tom: She's fine, too.

Pat: _____?

Tom: To that little restaurant across the street for lunch.

Pat: _____?

Tom: Sure! I'd love to have some company.

Example 4

Ken: _____?

Hal: Really? When?

Ken: _____.

Hal: Well, that's wonderful! Let me be the first to congratulate you!

Ken: _____.

Example 5

Sam: _____?

Ben: To the grocery. I need to get some dog food and paper towels.

Sam: You don't look so good. _____?

Ben: Not really.

Sam: What's the matter?

Ben: _____.

Sam: That's awful! _____?

Ben: Just two days ago.

Sam: _____?

Ben: Actually, there is something you could do. _____

_____?

Sam: Sure, no problem. I can't guarantee anything, but I'll see what I can do.

Ben: _____.

Sam: Don't mention it. And cheer up. Everything'll be all right.

Ben: _____.

Sam: Well, see you later.

Ben: _____.

Sam: You don't need to say that again. What are friends for?

Appendix 3

Games

Appendix 2 offers you straightforward, serious, time-honored activities that you can use to teach or reinforce any grammar point you choose to focus on; Appendix 3 offers you ways to have fun dealing with grammar as a change of pace. We hope you find these activities as enjoyable and as effective as we have over the years. The time and effort it might require to create the materials for each game will be well worth the while, and from then on, you'll always have the materials available to you whenever you feel it time to "lighten up" your classes. Enjoy these changes of pace!

Tic Tac Toe (British "Naughts & Crosses")

Tic Tac Toe is a good game for a practice or wrap-up session and can be played by students at any proficiency level. The object of the game is for one team to be the first to get three X's or three O's in a row horizontally, vertically, or diagonally. Here's how you play it.

Before class, select nine pictures from your Picture File on one teaching point and prepare them for play. For example, if you're practicing the simple past, you may want the class to practice two points, the simple past and *wh-* question formation. But how can you get the students to use what you may have in mind for them (both regular and irregular verbs and a variety of *wh-* question words)? Look at a picture you have chosen from your file. Think of *wh-* words and verbs that can be used to make questions about that picture. Cut a sheet of paper into small slips. On each slip, write down one *wh-* word and one verb that the group can use to make an appropriate question. Now, using paper clips, attach these slips onto the front of the picture anywhere that won't obscure the scene.

To begin the game, lay the nine pictures face down on the floor in three rows of three. Cut a piece of paper into eight smaller pieces, writing an "X" on four of them and an "O" on the other four. Divide the class into teams (the X's and the O's) and have the X's start. The X's choose one of the pictures, turning it over and leaving it on the floor for the whole class to study. The team members have to perform what is asked of them on the pictures. The team looks at their chosen picture and prepares a group response. Give students enough time to work out a response that's acceptable to the entire group. A single spokesperson gives his/her team's question and answer in order to win the square.

You should rotate spokespersons so that as many students as possible have a chance to speak and be accountable for their grammar and pronunciation. If you have a large class, you can double the number of spokespersons by having one student give the question and a second, the answer. You should let the spokesperson have two chances to give the group's responses; this way he/she can correct the responses if necessary and you're sure to hear what's said.

If the question and answer are correct, the team puts an "X" on the picture, which is now out of play. If the responses are wrong, the picture is turned back over and it's the "O" team's turn to play. They can choose the picture that's just been turned back over or they can choose another one. Remember—both teams have the opportunity to study and discuss the picture that was chosen. Thus both teams have the opportunity to discuss the teaching point even if only one team is actually playing that picture. This rule may seem to give one group an unfair advantage, the second team having all that additional time to formulate correct responses, not to mention the chance of hearing an incorrect response, but it doesn't always prove to be the case. Frequently, the second team makes mistakes on the same picture, even with that extra time to study it. Part of the object of any language-learning activity is to give as many students as much opportunity to practice the language as possible.

The game continues until one team wins three pictures in a row or a tie occurs.

Concentration

Concentration is a matching game that does take a good amount of time to prepare initially, but once you make the playing cards, you can use them again and again. The object is for students to match as many pairs of cards as possible. Here's one way to cut this task down to size: Have your students make your cards. Not only will that cut down on your work, but it will also give your students practice on the language points your game is focusing on.

To prepare the playing cards, find thick paper (index cards, tag board, cut up file folders, etc.) that can't be seen through when placed face down on a table. Cut the cards into a size that can be seen by all the students playing the game. We recommend that you use cards that are approximately 2½" or 8 cm. square. You'll want between twenty to twenty-five pairs of cards per teaching point. If you have fewer, the game's not very challenging; if you have more, it's too hard (see the "Note" that follows).

The Concentration game we describe here is a review of irregular verbs in the simple past and past participle forms. Choose twenty irregular verbs you want your students to review; put one past tense form on each card. Put the corresponding past participles on the other twenty cards. Now you have forty verb cards:

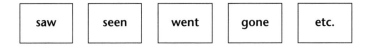

If you have a large class, you'll want to make additional sets of cards. We recommend that you have no more than four to five students per set of cards, otherwise, one round takes too long and the students get restless waiting for their turn to come up again. Now you're ready to play.

Shuffle the cards well and lay them face down in neat rows on the students' desks or on the floor. It's important that the cards be in some sort of order because the students need to remember where they've seen each verb once it's been turned over. One student starts by turning over two cards and leaving them face up for everyone to see. If the cards match, the student gets to keep the pair, earning 1 point. The same student can keep on selecting pairs of cards until he/she makes a mistake. If the two cards don't match, the student must return them to the exact position they were in to begin with. This exact placement will help the other students remember where the cards are when it's their turn to play. Students keep on playing until all cards have been matched; the one with the most points/pairs wins the game.

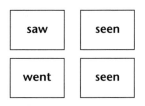

Note: Sometimes students aren't quite sure whether the two cards they've chosen make a match, so it's important for you to walk around the room and monitor the game and give advice when needed. Circulate to keep everything going smoothly, especially if you have more than one game going on. It's possible—we've done it with ten games going on at once!

A: The Clothesline

The Clothesline can be used to introduce, practice, or review grammar. Regardless of how you use it, what you need to begin with is a clothesline, a way to hang it, and some large pieces of scrap paper.

For our example, we'll show how you can introduce yes/no questions. Before class you'll need to prepare the vocabulary words you'll be working with. Each word will be written on a separate piece of paper, so don't choose words that are too long or paper that's too small. The back of scrap paper or used paper is perfect for this activity because only one side needs to be blank for writing on.

Your vocabulary for this lesson will include subject pronouns, the verb *be*, and adjectives. You'll also want to have the appropriate punctuation marks on hand. Write each word on the bottom half of a piece of paper and fold it in half.

ǝɥ	ʎǝɥʇ	sı	ǝɹɐ	ploͻ	llɐʇ	¿	·ͻʇǝ
he	they	is	are	cold	tall	?	etc.

Stack all the pronouns together, all the verbs together, and all the adjectives together. Attach the clothesline, hang up the vocabulary in separate stacks, and you're ready to teach yes/no questions.

Stand behind the clothesline and ask the students to repeat the sentence they see after you've said it. Some teachers attach the clothesline to the board, but the disadvantage is that you might block the view of the clothesline for some students, even if you're off to the side. And, if you're in front of the line, your arms can get in the way when you're changing the words. If at all possible, you should stand behind the clothesline.

Ask the students to repeat the sentence they see after you.

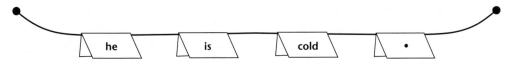

Begin showing students how English makes yes/no questions by rearranging the subject and verb papers. Don't forget to adjust your punctuation!

Continue these rearrangements and substitutions until the students are comfortable with the changes.

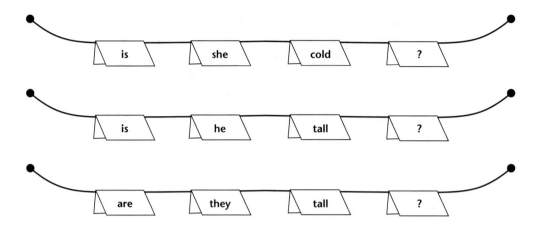

Note: You can make this a "substitution drill" by pulling off the vocabulary words that you previously stacked up on top of each other one by one.

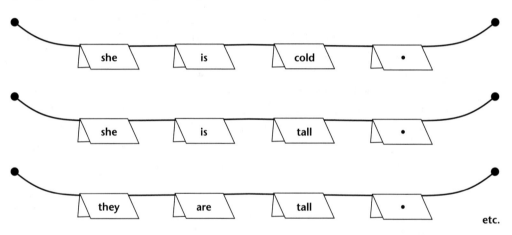

etc.

Later, you can test their comprehension of the new grammar by taking all the vocabulary and punctuation marks off the clothesline and distributing them to the students. Ask one student to go up to the clothesline and hang up his/her word. Then ask the other students to add their words one by one, making any changes in word order that are required and making sure that each addition makes sense. (It's like a living, moving slot substitution drill!) Be sure to have plenty of slips of paper with punctuation marks on them so the students will be invited to make both statements and questions.

A note Oral Matching

Use this activity for review. Before class begins, you'll need to prepare questions and statements and their logical responses; they can be complete sentences or partial sentences. Put the separate sentences or parts of sentences on individual slips of paper and mark each one with an "A" or a "B" (A = beginning phrase; B = finishing phrase). Make enough pairs for each student to have at least two slips. This example will focus on two-word verbs.

> A: Where do I get the No. 25 bus?

> B: You can pick it up at the corner.

> A: You look like you need a ride, Ben.

> B: I sure do. Can you drop me off downtown?

> A: Mister, this is where you get off the bus!

> B: At this stop? Thanks!

Make sure to remember that "A" slips and "B" slips can be either questions or statements. A closer look at our examples will show you what we mean. We suggest that you keep a master list of your dialogues so you can monitor the students' responses more easily or prompt them when they get confused or make mistakes.

Hand out the slips and have a student with an "A" slip read it aloud. The other students need to listen carefully, but only the one who has the matching "B" slip responds. (A challenging variation is to have the students memorize the information on their slips so they can recite their parts of the dialogues by heart.) Continue until all the matches have been made.

Scramblers

A "Scrambler" is a take-off of a Jumble©, a scrambling activity that's fairly easy to prepare. Here's how you do it. Let's say that you've been working with your students on question forms. Choose a target word or phrase related to question forms that will be the final answer to the puzzle; since we're working on question forms, let's use the word QUESTIONABLE as our target word. Come up with a sentence, phrase, or clue that uses your target word. You might want to use an illustration to help your students solve the puzzle (see what follows). Next, think of four or five words which together contain the letters needed to spell out QUESTIONABLE. These words can be, but don't have to be, related to the topic. The game becomes much more challenging, though, if the words are *not* related to a single topic.

Scramble the letters of each of the four or five words. Next to each scrambled word, write a blank space corresponding to each letter. In your mind's eye, picture where each letter falls on the blanks when the word has been unscrambled. Then underline only those blanks that have the letters needed to spell out the target word.

Now put the activity on the board or on a handout. What the students need to do follows the two sample Scramblers. The first Scrambler is on the topic of "questions" and the second, "holidays."

Do You Have Any Questions?

E A L T I O S   __ __ __ __ __ __ __

E R R E U I Q   __ __ __ __ __ __ __

C I R O N A G   __ __ __ __ __ __ __

E H A B E T N   __ __ __ __ __ __ __

What the 5 W's Produce . . .

Who? What?
Where? When?
Why?

" __ __ __ __ __ __ __ __ __ __ __ __ responses"

Scrambler

A C H I M R S S T

__ __ __ __ __ __ __ __ __

A A D E E I L N N S T V Y

__ __ __ __ __ __ __ __ __ __ , __ __ __ __ __

A E E N R S W Y

__ __ __ __ __ __ , __

A A B D L O R Y

__ __ __ __ __ __ __ __

     Why we are doing this . . .

It's __ __ __ __ __ __ __ __ __ __ __ !

Now it's the students' turn to work. First, tell them what the topic of the Scrambler is. Next, have them unscramble each word and put one letter in each one of the blanks. When they have unscrambled all the words and filled in all the blanks, tell them to write the underlined letters out in a line and unscramble them to find out what the target word or phrase is.

Appendix 4

A Deeper Look at Reporting Verbs

In Chapter 16, we promised further exploration of the intricacies of indirect speech. This appendix will afford you the chance to take a deeper look at all the patterns that can follow reporting verbs.

We're going to help you examine these fourteen patterns in the following way: First, you'll find a numbered list of all the patterns. Then you'll find the reporting verbs with examples of each pattern that can follow them. To make things easier, the corresponding number of each pattern in the list below is in front of a sentence that exemplifies it.

The Patterns (rp = reporting verb)

1. rp (+ optional *that* . . .)
2. rp + *to* + *indirect object* (+ optional *that* . . .)
3. rp + *indirect object* (+ optional *that* . . .)
4. rp + <u>*wh-* clause</u> or <u>*wh-* phrase</u>
5. rp + *to* + *indirect object* + <u>*wh-* clause</u>
6. rp + *indirect object* + <u>*wh-* clause</u> or <u>*wh-* phrase</u>
7. rp + <u>infinitive verb</u>
8. rp + *indirect object* + <u>infinitive verb</u>
9. rp + *to* + *indirect object* + <u>infinitive verb</u>
10. rp + <u>*if/whether*</u>
11. rp + *indirect object* + <u>*if/whether*</u>
12. rp + <u>gerund</u> (verb + *-ing*)
13. rp + *to* + *indirect object* + <u>gerund</u> [verb + *-ing*]
14. rp + *direct object* + <u>infinitive verb</u> DOC

ADD

1. At the end of her talk, she **added (that)** used batteries thrown into landfills could also contaminate ground water.
4. When she was telling you about safe ways to dispose of pollutants, did she **add where** you could take used motor oil and used batteries for proper disposal?

ADMIT

1. I **admitted (that)** I didn't like her cooking.
2. I **admitted *to her* (that)** I didn't like her cooking.
4. I **admitted why** I preferred to eat out.
5. I **admitted *to her* why** I preferred to eat out.
12. I **admitted taking** the money without permission.

ADVISE

1. Her memo **advised (that)** it would be a long meeting.
3. She **advised *us* (that)** the meeting would go on for a long time.
6. She **advised *us* how** we should dress for the meeting. / **how** to dress for the meeting.
8. She **advised *us* to be** prepared for a long meeting.

AGREE

1. We **agreed (that)** it would be wise to meet with them.
4. We **agreed where** to meet / **where** we should meet.
7. We **agreed to meet** with them and discuss the matter.

ALLEGE

1. He **alleges (that)** our drinking water supplies are still being contaminated.

ALLOW

8. The doctor only **allowed *him* to have** two cups of coffee a day.

ANNOUNCE

1. They **announced (that)** they were planning to get married.
2. They **announced *to everyone at the party* (that)** they were planning to get married.
4. They **announced when** and **where** the wedding would take place.
5. They **announced *to everyone at the party* when** and **where** the wedding would take place.

ARGUE

1. We **argued (that)** there were more economical ways to recycle things.
7. The defense attorney **argued to dismiss** the case.

ASK

1. They **asked (that)** they be allowed to leave early.
4. I **asked** <u>where</u> they were going.
6. I **asked** *them* <u>where</u> they were going.
7. They **asked** <u>to be allowed</u> to leave early.
8. They **asked** *me* <u>to allow</u> them to leave early.
10. They **asked** <u>whether</u> they could leave early.
11. They **asked** *me* <u>if</u> they could leave early.

ASSERT

1. He **asserted (that)** he'd never met the man.
2. He **asserted** *to us* **(that)** he'd never met the man.
4. She **asserted** <u>where</u> their meeting had taken place.
5. She **asserted** *to us* <u>where</u> their meeting had taken place.

ASSURE

3. I **assure** *you* **(that)** you've got nothing to lose.

BEG

1. She **begged (that)** the court hear her appeal.
7. She **begged** <u>to be heard</u> in court.
8. She **begged** *the court* <u>to hear</u> her appeal.

BOAST

1. They **boasted (that)** their car was the best.
2. They **boasted** *to us* **(that)** their car was the best.

BRAG

1. They **bragged (that)** their car was the best.
2. The **bragged** *to us* **(that)** their car was the best.

CLAIM

1. You **claimed (that)** you spoke four languages, didn't you?
2. You **claimed** *to me* **(that)** you spoke four languages, didn't you?
7. You **claimed** <u>to speak</u> four languages, didn't you?

COMMAND

1. The general **commanded (that)** his troops cease fire.
6. The general **commanded** *his troops* <u>where</u> to retreat.
8. The general **commanded** *his troops* <u>to cease</u> fire.

COMPLAIN
1. We **complained (that)** the food had been served cold.
2. We **complained** *to the waiter* **(that)** the food was cold.

CONFESS
1. She **confessed (that)** she'd always wanted that job.
2. She **confessed** *to us* **(that)** she'd always wanted that job.
4. She **confessed** <u>why</u> she'd lied on her résumé.
5. She **confessed** *to us* <u>why</u> she'd lied on her résumé.

CONVINCE
3. You **convinced** *them* **(that)** it wasn't their fault.
6. You **convinced** *them* <u>why</u> they weren't to blame.
8. You **convinced** *them* <u>not to blame</u> themselves.

DECLARE
1. He **declared (that)** the race should begin.
2. He **declared** *to the cheering crowd* **(that)** the race should begin.
4. He **declared** <u>who</u> the winner was.
5. He **declared** *to the cheering crowd* <u>who</u> the winner was.

DEMAND
1. I **demanded (that)** they permit me to see the judge.
7. I **demanded** <u>to see</u> the judge.

DENY
1. Don't **deny (that)** you took the money!
2. Didn't you **deny** *to them* **(that)** you had taken the money?
4. Don't **deny** <u>what</u> you've done.
5. Don't **deny** *to us or yourself* <u>what</u> you've done.
12. Don't **deny** <u>taking</u> the money!
13. Don't **deny** *to us* <u>taking</u> the money!

DIRECT
6. We **directed** *them* <u>where</u> to go.
8. We **directed** *them* <u>to follow</u> the detour signs.

DISAGREE
1. He **disagreed (that)** she was a better tennis player.

EXPLAIN

1. They **explained (that)** we'd find the map in the desk.
2. They **explained** *to us* **(that)** we'd find the map in the desk.
4. They **explained** <u>where</u> we'd find the map.
5. They **explained** *to us* <u>where</u> we'd find the map.

FORBID

8. They **forbade** *her* <u>to see</u> the young man again.

HINT

1. He kept **hinting (that)** he wanted to quit his job.
2. He kept **hinting** *to his wife* **(that)** he wanted to quit his job.
4. He **hinted** <u>what career change</u> he wanted to make.
5. He **hinted** *to his wife* <u>what career change</u> he wanted to make.

INFORM

3. The landlord **informed** *us* **(that)** the rent would be going up.
6. The landlord also **informed** *us* <u>how much</u> the new rent would be.
8. The landlord **informed** *us* <u>to pay</u> the rent by the 7th of each month.
11. My daughter always **informs** *me* <u>if</u> she's going to be late.

INSIST

1. Even though people thought him strange, Columbus **insisted (that)** the world was round.

INSTRUCT

1. She **instructed (that)** her collection of antique dolls should be donated to the local museum.
1. She **instructed (that)** her antique doll collection be donated to the local museum.
6. She **instructed** *her children* <u>where</u> to donate her antique dolls.
8. She **instructed** *her children* <u>to donate</u> her antique dolls to the local museum.

MAINTAIN

1. Even after his conviction, he **maintained (that)** he was innocent.

NOTIFY

3. We **notified** *her* **(that)** all of her wishes had been carried out.
6. The bank **notified** *her* <u>when</u> to pick up her loan money.
8. The bank **notified** *her* <u>to pick up</u> her loan money by Friday.
11. Please **notify** *me* <u>if</u> it comes in early.

ORDER

1. The captain **ordered (that)** his men lay down their weapons.
1. The captain **ordered (that)** his men should lay down their weapons.
4. The captain **ordered <u>what</u>** his men should do.
6. The captain **ordered** *his men* <u>when</u> to begin their surrender.
8. The captain **ordered** *his men* <u>to lay down</u> their weapons.

PERMIT

8. They **permitted** *us* <u>to take</u> one bag each onto the plane.
12. They **permitted** <u>taking</u> one bag onto the plane.

PERSUADE

3. He **persuaded** *us* **(that)** we should postpone our trip.
6. He **persuaded** *us* <u>where</u> we should go on our vacation.
8. He **persuaded** *us* <u>to postpone</u> the trip.

PRAY

1. They **prayed (that)** their daughter would get home safe and sound.
2. They **prayed** *to God* **(that)** their daughter would get home safe and sound.
7. They **prayed** <u>to be guided</u> by divine intervention.
9. They **prayed** *to God* <u>to be guided</u> by divine intervention.

PREDICT

1. She **predicted (that)** there would never be another world war.
2. She **predicted** *to us* **(that)** there would be no more war.
4. She **predicted** <u>which</u> countries would bring about world peace.
5. She **predicted** *to us* <u>which countries</u> would initiate world peace.
12. She correctly **predicted** <u>his winning</u> the primary.

PROCLAIM

1. They **proclaimed (that)** UFO's weren't imaginary.
2. They **proclaimed** *to us* **(that)** UFO's weren't imaginary.
4. He **proclaimed** <u>which</u> government he was loyal to.
5. He **proclaimed** *to the consul* <u>which</u> government he was loyal to.
7. He **proclaimed** <u>to be</u> loyal to the government of Fulania.

PROMISE

1. I **promised (that)** I would be more attentive, didn't I?
3. I **promised** *you* **(that)** I would be more attentive, didn't I?
4. I **promised** <u>how</u> I'd be different in the future.
6. I **promised** *you* <u>how</u> I'd be different in the future.
7. I **promised** <u>to be</u> more attentive, didn't I?
8. I **promised** *you* <u>to be</u> more attentive, didn't I?

PROPOSE
1. He **proposed** (**that**) we should accept the budget as presented.
1. He **proposed** (**that**) we accept the budget as presented.
2. He **proposed** *to us* (**that**) we should accept the budget as it was.
4. He **proposed** <u>what</u> we should do.
5. He **proposed** *to us* <u>what</u> we should do.
7. He **proposed** <u>to be</u> more careful in the future.
12. He **proposed** <u>accepting</u> the budget as presented.

RECOMMEND
1. I **recommended** (**that**) she should see an accountant.
1. I **recommended** (**that**) she see an accountant.
2. I **recommended** *to her husband* (**that**) she see/should see an accountant.
4. I **recommended** <u>what</u> she should do.
5. I **recommended** *to her husband* <u>what</u> she should do.
14. I **recommended** <u>him to be</u> the next Ambassador to Luxembourg.
12. I **recommended** <u>seeing</u> an accountant.

REGRET
1. They **regretted** (**that**) they had to miss our party.
4. They **regretted** <u>what</u> they had to do instead of going to the party.
12. They **regretted** <u>having</u> to miss our party.

RELATE
1. We **related** (**that**) the treasure was buried nearby.
2. We **related** *to them* (**that**) the treasure was buried nearby.
4. We **related** <u>where</u> the treasure might be found.
5. We **related** *to them* <u>where</u> the treasure might be found.

REMARK
1. He **remarked** (**that**) it was getting late.
2. He **remarked** *to her* (**that**) it was getting late.
5. He **remarked** *to me* <u>why</u> he thought the idea was such a good one.

REMIND
3. She **reminded** *him* (**that**) their friends were coming over.
6. She **reminded** *him* <u>who</u> was coming over.
8. She **reminded** *him* <u>to pick up</u> some ice cream after work.

REPLY

1. He **replied (that)** he wouldn't forget the ice cream.
2. He **replied** *to her* **(that)** he wouldn't forget the ice cream.
4. He **replied** <u>why</u> he had forgotten to meet us.
5. He **replied** *to me* <u>why</u> he had forgotten to meet us.

REPORT

1. They **reported (that)** all the lights in the town were out.
2. They **reported** *to us* **(that)** all the lights in the town were out.
4. They **reported** <u>what</u> had happened.
5. They **reported** *to us* <u>where</u> the lights were out.
12. They **reported** <u>seeing</u> the lights go out all over town.
13. They **reported** *to us* <u>seeing</u> the lights go out all over town.

REQUEST

1. You **requested (that)** we should sell your car for you, right?
1. You **requested (that)** we sell your car for you, right?
4. You **requested** <u>what</u> you wanted us to do with your car, right?
7. We **requested** <u>to be given</u> a ten percent commission.

SAY

1. They **said (that)** the rainforests had to be saved.
2. They **said** *to us* **(that)** the rainforests had to be saved.
4. They **said** <u>what</u> we have to do to save the rainforests.
5. They **said** *to us* <u>what</u> we have to do to save the rainforests.
7. They **said** <u>to save</u> the rainforests before it's too late.
9. They said *to us* <u>to push</u> for more conservation efforts.

STATE

1. They **stated (that)** racism was universally unacceptable.
2. They **stated** *to us* **(that)** racism was universally unacceptable.
4. They **stated** <u>what</u> was universally unacceptable.
5. They **stated** *to us* <u>what</u> was universally unacceptable.

SUGGEST

1. I **suggested (that)** he should get a second opinion.
1. I **suggested (that)** he get a second opinion.
2. I **suggested** *to him* **(that)** he get/should get a second opinion.
4. I **suggested** <u>what</u> he should do.
5. I **suggested** *to him* <u>what</u> he should do / <u>what</u> to do.
9. I **suggested** *to him* <u>to get</u> a second opinion.
12. I **suggested** <u>getting</u> a second opinion.
13. I **suggested** *to him* <u>getting</u> a second opinion.

SWEAR

1. He **swore (that)** he'd always be loyal.
2. He **swore** *to his commander* **(that)** he'd always be loyal.
4. He **swore** <u>what</u> he would do.
5. He **swore** *to his commander* <u>what</u> he would do.
7. He **swore** <u>to remain</u> loyal at all costs.
9. He **swore** *to his commander* <u>to remain</u> loyal at all costs.

TEACH

1. You **taught (that)** it was wrong to waste water.
3. You **taught** *us* **(that)** it was wrong to waste water.
4. You **taught** <u>why</u> we should use water responsibly.
6. You **taught** *us* <u>why</u> we should use water responsibly.
8. You **taught** *us* <u>to conserve</u> water.

TELL

3. I **told** *you* **(that)** it would be an interesting speech.
6. I **told** *you* <u>what</u> the speech would be about.
8. I **told** *you* <u>to come</u> listen to his speech.
11. I'**ll tell** *you* <u>whether</u> I can come to the meeting.

THREATEN

1. They **threatened (that)** they'd reveal her plans.
3. They **threatened** *her* **(that)** they'd reveal her plans.
4. They **threatened** <u>what</u> they'd do.
7. They **threatened** <u>to reveal</u> her plans.

URGE

8. We **urged** *him* <u>to get</u> some medical attention.

WARN

1. He **warned (that)** we'd better take him seriously.
3. He **warned** *us* **(that)** we'd better take him seriously.
6. He **warned** *us* <u>how long</u> he would wait.
8. He **warned** *us* <u>to take</u> him seriously.

WONDER

4. He **wondered** <u>why</u> I hadn't brought along more money with me.
10. I **wondered** <u>if</u> I had enough money for the airfare.

Appendix 5

Troubleshooting Pronunciation

You may find this appendix a real eye opener. What we'd like to do is point out some glaring areas of mispronunciation that generally aren't corrected enough. Just as the "Troubleshooters" throughout this book deal with areas not often covered in other books, this appendix on pronunciation will do likewise.

To begin with, let's define what we mean when we say "So-and-so has a *foreign* accent." In a nutshell, we mean that the person in question uses sounds that are either nonexistent in English phonology or uses sounds that English does have—but in the wrong place. In other words, we mean that this person imposes the phonology of his/her language onto English. That's how we recognize that the person isn't a native speaker.

Nobody expects a non-native speaker to have native-like pronunciation, so that's not the goal an English language teacher—or any foreign language teachers—should have. What we really want to have as our goal is to reduce the non-English sounds as much as possible so that they don't interfere with communication or draw unnecessary attention to themselves. The points that we mention in this appendix, if applied conscientiously and diligently, will help non-native speakers reduce the non-native sounds. The rest of this appendix deals with the points we want to get you thinking about.

The Letter "O"

English language learners whose first languages use the Roman alphabet see the letter "o" and immediately go for the pronunciation of that letter as it is in their native languages. This assumption leads to the strangest pronunciations of the most high-frequency English words.

The truth of the matter is that, in a vast number of English words, the letter "o" is pronounced /a/ or /ɔ/, but not /o/, and which of these two sounds is employed depends on what regional variation or dialect the speaker uses.

(As a side note, we'd like to add that even the so-called "long vowel" in English is not pronounced as it is in other languages. Many other languages have what is called a *pure* "o." It's pronounced much like the English long vowel, but the lips, rounded as the sound is made, stay relatively open and somewhat loose. In the English version of this sound, the lips continue to close more and more tightly after you begin to say the sound, so that in essence, the English sound is really a combination of /o/ + /u/. In fact, in the International Phonetic Alphabet, the English sound is shown as /oʷ/ or /oᵘ/ to account for these combined sounds.)

Getting back to the sound in question, we should look at some examples of common words in which the "o" is pronounced either /a/ or /ɔ/ depending on the dialect. (Where there's more than one "o," we've underlined the one we're focusing on):

Bob	cop	knock	Robert
bother	d<u>o</u>ctor	Mom	stop
bottle	dollar	not	Thomas
college	got	Pop	Tom
comedy	hot	rob	tom<u>o</u>rrow

The point is, whether you pronounce these words and so many others like them with the sound of /a/ or /ɔ/, the sound we're focusing on is definitely not pronounced /o/ in English. Don't let your students get away with always pronouncing the letter "o" as /o/. Catch them on it every time you hear it mispronounced and break a bad habit before it gets firmly entrenched.

⚒ The "D" in *Dry*; The "T" in *Try*

Although it isn't the case in every dialect of English, at least it <u>is</u> the case that in some dialects the /d/ in *dry* and the /t/ in *try* are not pronounced as they are in other environments. To begin with, the fact is that in these English dialects, this /d/ is pronounced more like /ǰ/ than /d/ when it precedes /u/ in some words like *educate*.

The reason is that, at one point, the word was pronounced /ed - yu - ket/. In speaking quickly, this combination of /d/ + /yu/ became palatalized and changed to the one sound /ǰ/. Another example is *gradual* /græ - ǰu - əl/.

The same phenomenon happened with the /t/ in a word like *ritual*, where /rɪt - yu - əl/ became /rɪ - ču - əl/.

For some speakers this mutation even happens when /d/ or /t/ precede /r/. So /d/ mutates to a sound close to /ǰ/: *drop* /ǰrap/, and /t/ mutates to a sound closer to /č/: *troup* /črup/.

Here's a short list of words which have these typical sound changes for "d" and "t" in some dialects of English. Note that there are certain words in bold; that's because these words really seem to grate on the ears of native English speakers when mispronounced, so concentrate on them. By the way, if a word contains more than one "d" or "t," the one that goes through this sound change is underlined:

"d" → /ǰ/		"t" → /č/	
address	drizzle	**adventure**	**situate**
adrift	drop	**architecture**	**situation**
arduous	drown	attract	**spatula**
cauldron	drug	attraction	**structure**
draft (draught)	drunk	contract	**torture**
draw	**educate**	contribute	traffic
drawer	**education**	contribution	train
dread	**gradual**	**dentures**	tree
dream	**graduate**	**factual**	trial
drill	**graduation**	**mutual**	true
drink	**schedule**	**punctuate**	truth
drip	squadron	**punctuation**	**virtual**
drive	withdraw	**ritual**	**virtue**

⌁ The *Flapped D*

Since we're on the subject of the letter "t," we'd like to mention another sound that's often neglected in teaching pronunciation—at least in teaching North American pronunciation. The sound is called a "flapped d" /D/ because, even though it appears as a "t" or "tt" in writing within a word, it's pronounced like a "d," only made a little faster and perhaps more loosely with the tip of the tongue than a regular "d." The tip of the tongue literally *flaps* quickly against the roof of the mouth on the alveolar ridge behind the top front teeth where a regular "d" sound is made. In North American English the basic rule is that **/t/ mutates to /D/ when it's found between a stressed and an unstressed vowel or when it follows /r/.**

Here are some words that have this change from /t/ to /D/. Once again, we've underlined the "t" or "tt" that goes through the sound change if there are other "t's" in a word:

attitude	batter	bitter	butter
cattle	data	eatery	fatter
fritter	glitter	go-getter	heater
hotter	jittery	item	kettle
later	latter	little	Marty
matted	matter	nutty	otter
party	Patti	pretty	quitter

rattle	static	tatter	tattle
utter	★victuals	wetter	whetted

★In case you're wondering about this word, remember it's pronounced /vɪ - Dəlz/ with the "c" becoming silent and the "ua" reducing to schwa (like "vittles")!

⅍ Juncture

Moving right along, here's yet another tidbit in pronunciation that's often neglected. In linguistics, "juncture" means the joining point of two sounds, and what we'd like to focus on is when the last consonant sound of one word and the first consonant sound of the next word are the same or closely related. When that's the case, the two words are basically joined as they're pronounced so that for all intents and purposes they sound like one word.

As an example, take the combination of *bus stop*. Most English language learners will try to pronounce these words as completely separate units, but native speakers will join them together to produce:

bus stop /bə́s:tap/

The one thing to keep in mind is that **the /s/ is held a fraction longer than it would normally be held,** and this is shown in phonetics by the addition of a colon to indicate the lengthened sound. In other words, the tip of the tongue is kept in the position for /s/ just a fraction of a second longer so that we account for the double /s:/ sound. This holding onto the sound a bit longer is typical of how this kind of juncture is pronounced. Here's a list of more phrases and sentences to show you all kinds of possibilities:

a grab bag	He'll confess soon.
red dots	fair reasons
rough friends	★the first state
Don't bug Grandpa.	a sweet taste
sick kids	a bath thermometer
small lamps	Bathe the baby!
tame monkeys	Save vampires!
tan natives	pinkish shrimp
ripe pineapples	She loves zebras.

★This example of juncture is interesting because it works a little differently. The /st/ in *first* combines with the /st/ in *state*, so the result is that people say "the /fərs:tet/." This combined form can make for fun and pun when you contrast it with "the fur state" or "the first ate" or even "the first date!"

There are two exceptions to our rule. The first is when we're dealing with the sound /č/. We never have a lengthening of the sound when one word ends with this consonant sound and the next word begins with it: *a rich child/not much chance*. In other words, there is no juncture.

The other exception works the same way with the sound of /ǰ/: *orange juice*.

But we're not finished with juncture yet. So far, we've discussed the primary way this phenomenon happens, but that isn't the only way. Another way it takes place is when the final consonant sound of one word is closely related to the first consonant sound of the next word. One clear example is the juxtaposition of a voiced sound and its voiceless counterpart:

> They're trying to bri<u>be P</u>auline.

or a voiceless sound plus its voiced counterpart:

> Do you think you could hel<u>p B</u>ob?

The trick is that, instead of merging both sounds into one longer one, the voiced and voiceless sounds still maintain their independence, so to speak, but **the first of the two sounds is held (not released) a bit longer and then it "slides" into the second sound**.

Here are some more examples of this kind of juncture:

re<u>d t</u>omatoes	bi<u>g k</u>ids
a cu<u>te d</u>oll	slee<u>k g</u>azelles
a rou<u>gh v</u>ersion	hi<u>s s</u>on
I cra<u>ve f</u>rench fries.	the Pari<u>s z</u>oo

∿ The Most Common Vowel Sound in English

If you ever want a good trivia question to ask people at a party, here it is: What's the most common vowel sound in the English language? Answer? The schwa! Yes, believe it or not, the /ə/ is the vowel sound most commonly found in English words. It pops up where non-native speakers would least expect it to be, and here's a list of words to demonstrate our point. Every underlined vowel or combination of letters is pronounced /ə/ by the majority of native English speakers:

<u>A</u>meric<u>a</u>	h<u>u</u>ngry	<u>o</u>pposed	<u>u</u>nb<u>e</u>liev<u>a</u>ble /əl/
b<u>a</u>nan<u>a</u>	ic<u>i</u>cl<u>e</u> /əl/	p<u>a</u>ternity	val<u>e</u>dict<u>o</u>ry
C<u>o</u>lombia	j<u>u</u>nk	quadr<u>a</u>nt	w<u>o</u>ndr<u>ou</u>s
d<u>e</u>vel<u>o</u>p	kang<u>a</u>roo	R<u>o</u>bert<u>a</u>	xyl<u>o</u>phone
el<u>e</u>ph<u>a</u>nt	l<u>a</u>ment<u>a</u>bl<u>e</u> /əl/	sel<u>e</u>ction	y<u>ou</u>ng
fr<u>o</u>m	min<u>i</u>m<u>a</u>l	tr<u>ou</u>bles<u>o</u>me	zebr<u>a</u>
g<u>i</u>raffe	nati<u>o</u>n<u>a</u>l		

So when you teach pronunciation, stress this observation and sensitize your students to be aware of how prevalent the sound /ə/ is in English.

A̴̕ The Final *-ate*!

One more area that never seems to get enough attention involves words that end with the three letters *-ate*. Understanding how to pronounce this final syllable correctly isn't hard at all, so English language teachers should take the time to teach the rules and make sure to correct students when they mispronounce the syllable. There doesn't seem to be a lot of trouble when the word is a verb; you simply pronounce the *-ate* /et/ with the silent "e" making the previous vowel long. Students have usually already learned this rule of pronunciation. It's when the word is a noun or adjective that the trouble really sets in. English language learners invariably pronounce all words that end in *-ate* as if they were verbs.

Here's how the rules go (even though there are a few exceptions):

- **If the *-ate* is at the end of a verb, pronounce it /et/.**
- **If the *-ate* is at the end of a noun or adjective, pronounce it /ət/ or /ɪt/.**

Here are some words that show these changes in pronunciation:

aggregate (v., n., adj.)	graduate (v., n., adj.)
alternate (v., n., adj.)	initiate (v., n.)
appropriate (v., adj.)	intimate (v., n., adj.)
associate (v., n., adj.)	laminate (v., n.)
delegate (v., n.)	moderate (v., adj.)
deviate (v., n.)	postulate (v., n.)
elaborate (v., adj.)	separate (v., adj.)

Some more examples of adjectives that end in *-ate* with the pronunciation of /ɪt/ or /ət/ are *collegiate, delicate, intricate, obstinate, passionate,* and *surrogate*.

We should point out that there are a few exceptions in which the *-ate* is pronounced /et/ even though the word is a noun. These include *diplomate, magnate, magistrate, potentate,* and *reprobate*.

Tip #1: *Voiced and Voiceless Sounds*

On page 51 in Chapter 4, we give the rules for pronouncing the *-ed* regular past tense and show which sounds are voiced and which are voiceless. We should mention here that the same rule applies for pronouncing the regular plural *-s/-es* as well.

What we'd like to do here is give you a tip that will help your students really understand why some sounds are called voiced and others voiceless. Have the students place the curved edge of one hand (running from the thumb to the index finger) up against their throats. While they keep their hands in that position, tell them to say the vowel sound /i/ and to hold it. While they're making the sound, ask them if they feel a vibration on their hands. If they're doing it right, they will. Explain to them that all vowel sounds are voiced and that they will always feel a vibration when making a vowel sound.

Now have them do the same thing with a voiced consonant sound like /z/. Again they should feel vibration on their hands. Now switch to the related voiceless consonant sound /s/. This time, they should feel no vibration on their hands. Let them keep practicing with voiced and voiceless consonant sounds, comparing when they do and don't feel vibrations. We suggest these pairs:

$$/v/ \sim /f/ \qquad /z/ \sim /s/ \qquad /g/ \sim /k/ \qquad /ð/ \sim /\theta/$$

After a while, they'll get the hang of it and start to understand more clearly which sounds are voiced and which aren't.

We'd like to mention something about teaching the pronunciation of the four pairs you've just seen. We'll focus on the /v/ and the /f/ for this demonstration, but it works the same way for the other pairs as well.

If you have students who speak a language like Spanish, which doesn't differentiate much between /b/ and /v/, here's a tip to help them learn how to say /v/ in English. Make them aware of how they pronounce /f/; the top front teeth are placed over the lower lip. Tell them to say /f/ and hold the sound while they concentrate on where their top front teeth are and on the fact that they're blowing air out of their mouths but not using their voices. While they're making the sound of /f/, tell them to start vibrating their vocal chords. As soon as they do this, they'll make a perfect /v/ sound because the only difference between /f/ and /v/ is whether or not it's voiced or voiceless. This holds true in the reverse, as for example in Arabic, where the students' voices have to be "turned off" to make the sound /p/ instead of the voiced /b/.

Tip #2: Pronouncing "th" (/ð/ and /θ/)

Yes, we know that these are just about the most difficult sounds for English language students to master. Here's one method that has worked wonders for many of our students who have had trouble pronouncing "th":

Have your students get small hand mirrors. Give them three lists of words, the first with the "th" in initial position on each word, the second with the "th" in medial position, and the last list with the "th" in final position (e.g., *thumb/method/bath* and *then/weather/bathe*). Tell them to practice saying each word as they look at their mouths in their hand mirrors. Tell them they should see their tongues projecting out past their teeth and that their lips should be slightly apart. If they can't see their tongues projecting out past their teeth, they're not saying the sound right.

This is a good method for them to practice producing the sounds correctly without the teacher having to be present. It will also stop them from "faking" the sounds by substituting them with /t/, /d/, /f/, /v/, /s/, or even /z/!

Tip #3: A Picture Says a Thousand Words

Another way to help your students produce English sounds more accurately is by showing them clear, uncluttered pictures or diagrams of a mouth so they can see precisely what's going on inside when a certain sound is made. Here's an example of what we mean—and you don't have to be a Picasso or Rembrandt to create decent pictures!

th

/θ/   /ð/

Clear enough? For the purposes of the classroom, it should do just fine. And here's one more example:

tip of tongue

top front of teeth ⟶

/ð/   /θ/

Tip #4: Spelling Unfamiliar Names Over the Phone

It's always been a difficult thing to spell people's last names, especially in countries which have immigrants from all over the world. Many names are familiar to most English speakers, but many others aren't, so spelling them correctly can be a problem.

The time when this spelling is most difficult is while talking on the phone. The reason? There are pairs of consonants that sound very similar when pronounced over the phone, so it's easy to mistake one for the other. Traditionally, native English speakers have used a little device to avoid mistakes when writing down these similar sounds. The examples we're going to give you are the typical words people use to make sure the listener understands which letter is being said, but any common words will do. The important point is that your English language learners should start developing the habit of using these words or words like them when spelling difficult names over the phone. So, here they are:

"b" as in "boy"	"d" as in "dog"
"f" as in "Frank"	"m" as in "Mary"
"n" as in "Nancy"	"p" as in "Peter"
"s" as in "Sam"	"t" as in "Thomas"
"v" as in "Victor"	"z" as in "zebra"

The sounds above are the ones that can easily be confused over the phone. For example, there are:

/b/ ~ /p/   /d/ ~ /t/   /f/ ~ /s/   /m/ ~ /n/

Appendix 6

It All Adds Up: 1 + 1 = 2

The English spelling system is one of the more troublesome aspects of this language. Just ask any English student; or for that matter, ask any native English speaker! For now, let's focus in on the problem of whether to double or not double the final consonant when the past and progressive endings, -*ed* and -*ing*, are added. Write a rule (including examples, exceptions, and explanations if there's a need) that correctly predicts this phenomenon of the doubling or lack of doubling of the final consonant (i.e., swi<u>mm</u>ing vs. tal<u>k</u>ing).

Do your rules account for all of the following forms?

begin**n**ing	ironing	prefe**rr**ed	remembered
forbi**dd**ing	raiding	ru**bb**ed	combed
permi**tt**ing	editing	handica**pp**ed	reaped
ski**mm**ing	disarming	be**gg**ed	longed

And what about . . . ?

pani**c**	plow	box	trave**l**

You haven't given up, have you? We didn't think so, so here are our observations about the double consonants that may prove helpful to you and your students. If you

---

can add and know how to pronounce the word, you can't go wrong! The adding part is easy; the stress part is a bit trickier. And, of course, this rule only works well if you know how the word is pronounced. So here it is. (v. = vowel; c. = consonant)

$$1 + 1 = 2; \quad 1 + 2 \neq 2; \quad 2 + 1 \neq 2$$

1 stressed vowel + 1 consonant = 2 consonants

$$1 \text{ v.} + 1 \text{ c.} \quad = \quad 2 \text{ c.}$$

$$\text{occ} + \textbf{ú} + \textbf{r} \quad = \quad \text{occú } \textbf{rr} \text{ ed}$$
$$1 \text{ v.} + 1 \text{ c.} \quad = \quad 2 \text{ c.}$$

$$\textbf{ó} + \text{p}\quad \textbf{e} + \textbf{n} \quad \neq \quad \text{ópe } \textbf{nn} \text{ ed}$$
$$1 \text{ unstressed v.} + 1 \text{ c.} \quad \neq \quad 2 \text{ c.}$$

1 vowel + 2 consonants ≠ 2 consonants

$$\text{j} + \textbf{u} + \textbf{mp} \quad \neq \quad \text{jum pp ing}$$
$$1 \text{ v.} + 2 \text{ c.} \quad \neq \quad 2 \text{ c.}$$

2 vowels + 1 consonant ≠ 2 consonants

$$\text{f} + \textbf{ai} + \text{l} \quad \neq \quad \text{fai } \textbf{ll} \text{ ed}$$
$$2 \text{ v.} + 1 \text{ c.} \quad \neq \quad 2 \text{ c.}$$

Note: Knowing the rules for adding *-ed* and *-ing* to verbs is particularly useful because the same rules are also applicable when you add the endings *-er* and *-est* to adjectives when creating comparative and superlative forms and *-er* to verbs when creating nouns.

begi**nn**er	cli**pp**er	ho**tt**er	mea**n**er	slee**k**est
bi**gg**er	faste**n**er	kin**d**est	re**dd**est	wa**sh**er

Appendix 7

More Fun with Autosegmental Features: A Stress-Caused Metamorphosis

Noun	vs.	**Verb**	**Noun**	vs.	**Verb**
ADdress		adDRESS	EXport		exPORT
ATtribute		atTRIbute	EXtract		exTRACT
COMbine		comBINE	IMpact		imPACT
COMEon		comeON	IMport		imPORT
COMmune		comMUNE	IMprint		imPRINT
COMpound		comPOUND	INcrease		inCREASE
COMpress		comPRESS	INsert		inSERT
CONduct		conDUCT	INsult		inSULT
CONsole		conSOLE	INtrigue		inTRIGUE
CONsort		conSORT	INvite(slang)		inVITE
CONstruct		conSTRUCT	PERfect		perFECT
CONtest		conTEST	PERmit		perMIT
CONtrast		conTRAST	PREsent		preSENT
CONvict		conVICT	PROceeds		proCEEDS
DEfect		deFECT	PROgress		proGRESS
DIgest		diGEST	PROject		proJECT
EXcise		exCISE	PROtest		proTEST
EXploit		exPLOIT	REcess		reCESS

Variable Noun	vs.	**Verb**	**Adjective**	vs.	**Noun**
DEtail / deTAIL		DEtail	inVALid		INvalid

Adjective	vs.	**Verb**	**Prep.**	vs.	**Phrase**
CONverse		conVERSE	INto		in TWO
PERfect		perFECT			

Phrases

Adj. + Noun	**Comp. Noun**	**Adj. + Noun**	**Comp. Adj.**
BLACK BIRD	BLACKbird	FIRST rate	FIRST RATE
BLUE BIRD	BLUEbird	SECOND class	SECOND CLASS
RED NECK	REDneck		

Adj. + Noun	vs.	**Comp. Verb**	**Noun**	vs.	**Adj./Adv.**
WHITE WASH		WHITE wash	INstep		in STEP

Adjective	vs.	**Adverb**	**Noun**	vs.	**Phrase**
OUTside		outSIDE	INtern		in TURN

Various

FORty / for TEA

Now THERE'S a good girl. / Now there's a GOOD GIRL . . . yonder.

GOING to EAT, John. / Going to eat JOHN.

Appendix 8

Rejoinders, Exclamations, Etc.

Back in Chapter 21 we discussed the phrases that add so much to the flow of conversation. Following is a list of some of the more frequently used phrases that only touches the tip of the iceberg. Teach these marvelous items that spice up English conversation to your students when you deem it appropriate to do so.

Here are some general rules to go by:

- When a phrase in our list begins with a capitalized word, it indicates that it's usually found as an introductory phrase.
- If the first word of a phrase begins with a small letter, it means that the phrase may either be an introductory phrase or found elsewhere in the sentence.
- If a phrase has the subject "I" or the object "me" in it, any personal pronoun or a person's name can be substituted in that spot except where otherwise noted.
- If a phrase contains the general pronoun "you," no other pronoun can be substituted.
- Three dots found after a phrase mean that the sentence continues in this spot.

After all is said and done . . .	all in all
And how!	as a matter of fact
as far as I'm concerned	As I was saying . . .
at first glance	believe it or not
By the way . . .	Can you beat that?!
Come on!	come to think of it
(The) Fact is . . .	Far be it from me to . . .
For one thing . . .	(and) for another . . .

For what it's worth . . .
Get it?
How about that!
I'll say! (only with "I")
interestingly enough
In the second place . . .
It's just that . . .
it's not that so much that . . .
Leave it to me to . . .
No kidding!
Only time will tell.
On second thought . . .
Over my dead body!
Say what you will . . .
sooner or later
Speaking of which . . .
Tell me about it! (only with "me")
to put it plainly
(The) Trouble is . . .
Try as I may . . .
whatever the case may be
What I'm trying to say is . . .
when you come right down to it
Why bother . . . ?
You bet!
You can say that again!
You never know.

from the very start
God willing
if it comes to that
In case . . .
In the first place . . .
it's all a matter of . . .
It's more that . . .
Know what I mean?
No fooling!
once (= when)
On one hand . . .
On the other hand . . .
Putting personal feelings aside . . .
See what I mean?
So then . . .
Stick to the point!
to put it mildly
to tell the truth
(The) Truth of the matter is . . .
(So) What else is new?
What I mean is that . . .
(what) it (all) boils down to (is . . .)
whether I like it or not
Wouldn't you know it!
You bet your life . . .
You don't say.
You're kidding!

Index

a vs *an*: see "articles, indefinite"
a vs *one*: see "articles, indefinite"
above: 159–160, 162, 166–167, 170
adjectives: 90–110, 214
  compound forms: 217–221
    adjective + noun + ed: 219–220
    adjective + past participle: 219–220
    adjective + present participle: 219–220
    adverb + past participle: 219–220
    adverb + present participle: 219–220
    fringe combinations: 220
    hyphenated pat phrases: 221
    hyphenation: 217–218
    idiomatic expressions: 106
    noun + adjective: 219–220
    noun + noun + ed: 219–220
    noun + past participle: 219–220
    noun + present participle: 219–220
    particle + past participle: 219–220
    particle + present participle: 219–220
  ordering: 96–104
    age: 99–100, 103
    brand name: 98–99
    cardinal numbers: 101, 103
    color: 98–99, 103
    condition: 99–100, 103
    determiner: 98–103
    location: 102–103

    material: 97–99, 103
    measurement: 99–100, 103
    opinion: 97–99, 103
    ordinal numbers: 101, 103
    origin: 97–99, 103
    pattern: 99, 103
    possessive adjectives: 100, 103
    power: 96–99, 103
    purpose: 96–99
    season: 99–101, 103
    shape: 101–103
    temperature: 101–103
    time: 101, 103
  punctuation: 106–107
  verbal adjectives: 90–95
    -ed forms: 91–95
      pronunciation: 93
    -ing forms: 91–95
adverbial prepositions: see "two-word
  verbs"
adverbs:
  compound forms/pat phrases: 221
  frequency: 5–7
    inversion with fronted negative
      adverbs: 6
    position: 5–6
  inversion with other fronted negative
    adverbs: 7

after: 80, 160, 164, 168, 171
aged: 93
already: 45
always: 5
Amharic: 203
an: see "articles, indefinite"
an vs *a*: see "articles, indefinite"
Anglo-Saxon: 371–372, 501
any: 111–127 also see "*some* and *any*" and
    "autosegmental features (whole
    sentences)"
    compound pronouns: 119–121, 122–124
    in negative statements: 113
    in questions: 114–118
    just a little: 116–117
    Nutshell: 125–126
plural of indefinite article: 112
stress: 118
Arabic: 11, 105, 203
archaic subjunctive: see "subjunctives,
    hopes, and wishes"
around: 160–161, 164–165, 169, 171
articles: 11–25, 98, 100
    definite article: 11, 17–23
        pronunciation: 17–18
        with geographical terms: 22–23
        with means of transport: 21
        with proper nouns: 20–21
        with works of art: 21
    indefinite article: 11–17, 112
        a vs *an*: 12–13
        a vs *one*: 13–15
        "fast food English": 16–17
        one (idiomatic use): 14
        pronunciation: 11
        with double genitives: 204–205
        with pat phrases: 15–16
        with proper nouns: 21
    zero article: 15–16, 112
as soon as: 80
as well: 493, 496
at: 69, 171–178
attorney general: 105–106
**autosegmental features (single words,
    noun and verb phrases)**: 140, 316–338
    compound nouns vs nouns + adjectives:
        324–327
    definite article: 316–317
    noun phrases: 323–330, 555

pat phrases: 323
-s genitive: 327–329
single words: 318–323, 554–555
verb phrases: 331–333, 555
    compound nouns vs direct object
        DOC's: 331–332
    with modal auxiliaries: 333–335
**autosegmental features (whole sen-
    tences)**: 391–415
any: 399–401
intonation: 404–413
    exclamations: 404–406
    falling pitch: 405–407, 409
    rising pitch: 405–408
intonation and punctuation: 410–413
juncture: 411–413
pronunciation and object pronouns:
    397–398
rebuttal: 392
repeating when misunderstood: 392
some: 401–403
stress: 391–397
there / there + be: 392–393
away from: 159–160, 163, 167, 170, 179

backshifting: 420, also see "indirect
    speech"
be: 6, 29, 33
    in passive voice: 244, 253
    vs *get*: see "passive voice"
be able to: 154, 179
be about to: see "futures"
be due: see "futures"
be going to: see "futures"
be supposed to: 179
be to: see "futures"
be unable to: 154
be used to: 179
be used to vs **used to**: 65
before: 80, 160, 163–164, 168, 170
below: 159, 162–163, 167, 170
blessed: 93
bowlegged: 93
British English: 132, 227, 334, 371, 506
Bruder, Mary Newton: 513
by: 160–161, 164, 168, 171–172, 176–177,
    249–251
by the time: 80
by the way: 493, 497

Cambridge University Test of English: 62
can: 128, 130–136, 138, 179
   ability: 131
   advice/suggestion: 135–136
   autosegmental feature: 334
   capability: 133
   hypothetical possibility: 131, 133–135
   Nutshell: 138
   permission: 132–133
   pronunciation: 132
   request: 138
cannot / can't: 130–133, 138
   disbelief: 131
impossibility: 131
   Nutshell: 138
   prohibition: 132–133
   pronunciation: 132
cannot have / can't have + **past participle**:
disbelief: 225–227
impossibility: 225–227
Nutshell: 229
cardinal numbers: see "adjectives, ordering"
causatives: 267–277
   have vs *get*: 267–271
   with base verb: 268
   with *–ing* verb: 268
   with past participle: 267–268
Chinese/Cantonese: 11, 203
cloze procedures: 516–521
   modified cloze: 517, 519–521
   pure cloze: 516–517, 518–519
Cockney English: 13
collective nouns: see "nouns, collective"
colloquial speech: see "style"
come to think of it: 493, 497
comic book English: see "pronunciation, relaxed"
commands: see "imperatives"
communicative exercises: 513–514
complex verbs: see "verbs, complex"
compound adjectives: see "adjectives, compound forms"
compound adverbs: see "adverbs, compound forms"
compound nouns: see "nouns, compound forms"
conditionals: 438–476
   conditional clause: 439–440
      containing the effect: 460

word inversion with auxiliaries: 446–447
word inversion with simple present/timeless tense: 446–447
if clause: 439–441
   containing the cause: 460
   replacements for *if*: 450–452
phrases for hypothetical situations: 473–474
reversing clauses: 445
   real conditional sentences: 438–460
      future: 441–452
         certainty: 444
         formality/register: 448–449
         if clause with *will*: 447–450
         if clause with *would*: 449–450
         if vs *when*: 457–460
         imperatives: 452–455
         likelihood of happening: 455–457
         possibility: 444
         second person reduced form: 445
      present: 440–441
         rhetorical device: 440
      rhetorical *if* clause: 462
      timeless: 439–440
   unreal conditional sentences: 460–474
      because of: 466–468
      certainty: 470
      conditional clause with *could/would*: 460
      formality/register: 463, 465–466, 468
      if clause with the subjunctive: 460
      likelihood of happening: 462–464
      mixing time: 470–473
      past: 468–470
      possibility: 470
      present: 461–466
      timeless: 460
      word inversion: 464–465
consonants, when to double: 552–553
could: 128–139
   ability, former: 226
   advice/suggestions: 135–136
   Nutshell: 138–139
   permission: 137–138
   polite request: 136–137
   real possibility: 133–135, 137–138

could have + **past participle**: 225, 228–229
  mild reproach for something not done:
    229, 232
  missed opportunity: 225, 228
  Nutshell: 229
  possibility: 228, 232
could not / couldn't: 129, 139
  disbelief: 139
  impossibility: 131
  inability, former: 226
  Nutshell: 229
could not have / couldn't have + **past participle**: 227–228
  disbelief: 227
  impossibility: 228
  Nutshell: 229
court martial: 105–106
critical thinking: 522–523
crooked: 93

dare: 153
definite articles: see *articles, definite*
deixis: 486–487, 523, also see "indirect
  speech"
demonstratives: 98
determiners: see "adjectives, ordering"
dialogues, incomplete: 522–525
direction: 3, 5
direct object companions (DOC's):
  278–315
  adjective phrase DOC's: 283–290
    focus: 287–289
    idiomatic use: 286
    pre–existing conditions: 285
    resulting conditions: 285
  anticipatory *it*: 286–287, 299
  base verb phrase DOC's: 301–306
    completed action/from start to finish:
      303–304
    one-time action: 304–306
    simple future: 303
    simple present/timeless form: 304
  causatives + base verb, -ing, and past participle DOC's: 309–312
  infinitive verb phrase DOC's: 290–293
  -ing verb phrase DOC's: 293–298
    action happening repeatedly:
      304–306
    action in progress: 303

  direct object pronouns vs possessive
    adjectives: 298–300
  -ing verb phrase DOC vs infinitive
    verb phrase DOC: 300–301
  optional vs required *–ing* DOC:
    297
  noun phrase DOC's: 280–282
  Nutshell: 312
  object complements: 281
  past participle phrase DOC's: 307–309
  verbs with prepositions and noun phrase
    DOC's: 282
direct objects: 3–5, 19, 278–279, 378–379,
  385
ditransitive verbs: 258, 260
do as auxiliary: 32
  reproachful characteristic behavior:
    140–141
"doer": see "passive voice"
don't have to: 150
don't have to vs *mustn't*: 150–151
down: 178

echo questions: 495–496
ellipsis: 477–481
emphasis:
  word order: 6–8
  one: 15
exclamations: 8, 184, 494, 556–557, also
  see "indirect speech" and "autosegmental
  features (whole sentences)"
fast food English: 16–17
for: 42–45
forget-me-nots: 106
formality: see "style"
formulaic phrases: see "pat phrases"
formulaic subjunctive: see "subjunctives,
  hopes, and wishes"
French: 20, 39, 105, 245, 494–495
from: 159–160, 163, 167, 170
future perfect: 77–78
  Nutshell: 85
future perfect progressive: 78
  Nutshell: 85
future progressive: 78–81
  Nutshell: 86
futures: 71–89
  be about to: 77, 179
    Nutshell: 85–86

be due: 82
   Nutshell: 86
be going to: 73–77, 179
   Nutshell: 85
   pronunciation: 73–74
be to: 83–84, 179
   Nutshell: 86
be sure: 84
   Nutshell: 86
make sure: 84
   Nutshell: 86
present progressive: 72, 74–77
   Nutshell: 85
shall: 76
simple present: 72–73
   Nutshell: 85
will: 74–77, 79–81, 441–450
   conditionals: 441–446
   Nutshell: 85
   predictions: 74
   promises: 75
   pure/simple future: 74, 79–80
   requests: 75
   simple vs progressive forms: 81
   tendencies: 75
   threats: 75

galore: 489–491
games: 526–533
   "Clothesline, The": 528–530
   "Concentration": 527–528
   "Oral Matching": 530–531
   "Scramblers": 531–533
   "Tic Tac Toe" ("Naughts and Crosses"):
      526–527
genitives: 189–210
   choice between -s or of: 206–208
   formulaic phrases: 206–207
   of-genitive: 198–203
      appositives: 202
      double genitives: 204–206
         choice of articles: 204–205
         with demonstratives: 205–206
         with possessive pronouns: 205
      formulaic phrases: 206–207
      Nutshell: 203
      partitives: 200–201
         abstractions: 200–201
         measurements: 200–201

      pairs/sets: 200–201
         parts of things: 200–201
      with abstract nouns: 199
      with adjective clauses: 198–199
      with concrete nouns: 199
      with non-living things: 199
   -s genitive: 189–199
      amounts of money/worth: 193–194
      appropriateness: 193–194
      epitome: 193–194
      esteem: 193–194
      formulaic phrases: 193–194,
         206–207
      group genitives: 196–197, 199
      head noun as "doer" or "receiver":
         193–194
      Nutshell: 197–198
      paraphrase with *for*: 193–194
      paraphrase with *have*: 191
      possession/belonging: 190
      preferred things: 193–194
      pronunciation: 192
      spelling: 191
      with living/non-living things:
         194–195
      with loss of head noun: 195
      with periods of time: 191
      with two nouns: 196
   style: 206–208
German: 494
get vs be: see "passive voice"
get vs have: see "causatives"
great deal of, a: 489–491

had best: 128
had better: 128
had to: 236–237
   Nutshell: 239
Haitian Creole: 203
have: 33–35, 191
   have vs get: see "causatives"
have got to: 179
have to: 153–154, 179, 355
Hawaiian: 245
Hebrew: 11, 494
home: 480–481
hope: see "subjunctives, hopes, and wishes"
how come: 493, 497
how: 5, 7, 10

idiolect: 148
if **clause**: 279, also see "conditionals"
imperatives: 4
in: 42–44, 159–161, 166, 170, 172–173,
    175–177, 179–180
indefinite articles: see "articles:
    indefinite"
indicative mood: see "subjunctives, hopes,
    and wishes"
indirect objects: 4
indirect speech: 339–368
    backshifting: 343–351
    charts: 346–348
    deixis: 341–342, 352
    exclamations: 360–362
    infinitives: 354–357
    lexical transformations: 340–342
    narrative style: see "style"
    Nutshell: 362–363
    questions: 357–360
    reporting verbs: 340, 344, 355, 534–542
    say: 342
    tell: 342–343
    time and space: 352–353
    time continuum: 348–351
infinitives: see "direct object companions"
    and "indirect speech"
informality: see "style"
instrument in passive voice: 250
intensifiers: 483–489
into: 159–161, 166, 170, 179–180
intonation: 496, also see "autosegmental
    features (whole sentences)"
intransitive verbs: 247–249, 369, 380,
    386
involuntary actions: see "stative verbs"
Irish: 491
-ish: 489–492
Israeli: 494

jagged: 93
Japanese: 20
juncture: 546–547, also see "autosegmental
    features (whole sentences)
just as: 80

kind of: 489–492
kindly: 489–492
Korean: 494

lately: 44–45
Latin: 11, 181, 183, 371–372
learned: 93
listening comprehension: 514
Lord's Prayer, The: 501

man-of-war: 106
may: 128, 143–146
    may as well: 145
    Nutshell: 146
    permission: 143–144
    real possibility: 143–144
    rhetorical device: 144
    wish (very formal): 448
may have **+ past participle**: 230–233
    possibility: 231–232
meaningful/manipulative exercises:
    513–514
mechanical exercises: 513
*Men Can Get Embarrassed, Too!: Confusing
    English Vocabulary for Spanish Speakers,*
    by Richard Firsten. Alta Book Center
    Publishers, Burlingame, CA: 372
Middle English: 501
might: 128, 143–146
    might as well: 145
    Nutshell: 146
    permission: 143–144
    possibility: 143–144
    request (very formal): 146
    rhetorical device: 144
    suggestion: 145
might have **+ past participle**: 230–233
    mild reproach: 231–232
    possibility: 231–232
modal auxiliaries in the past: 224–242,
    also see "can't have + past participle,"
    "could," "could have + past participle,"
    "may have + past participle," "might have
    + past participle," "must have + past par-
    ticiple," "ought to have + past participle,"
    "should have + past participle," "would
    have + past participle"
**modal auxiliaries in the present or
    future**: 128–157, also see "can," "could,"
    "may," "might," "must," "ought to," "shall,"
    "should," "will," "would"
modal perfects: 224, also see "modal auxil-
    iaries in the past"

mother-in-law: 106
must: 128, 149, 150–153, 154, 345
  conclusion: 150–151
  conjecture: 151–152
  Nutshell: 153
  requirement/necessity: 150–151
  vs *should/ought to*: 149
must not / mustn't:
  Nutshell: 153
  prohibition: 150–151
  vs *don't have to*: 151–152
must have + past participle:
  236–239
  conclusion/conjecture: 236–237
  logical conclusion/certainty: 236–237
  Nutshell: 239
must not have / mustn't have + past participle: 227, 236–239
  disbelief: 227
  logical conclusion: 236–237

naked: 93
near (to): 160, 164, 168, 171
need: 33, 155
negative questions: 498–500
ne'er-do-well: 106
next to: 160, 164, 168, 171
no- in compounds: 122–124
Norman French: 371
notary public: 105
nouns:
  collective: 193–195
  compound forms: 212–217
    descriptive element: 213–215
      singular vs plural: 214
    fringe combinations: 217
    hyphenation: 216
    noun adjuncts: 216
    noun + noun: 213–215
    stress: 215
    with adjectives: 215–216
    with gerunds: 215–216
    with particles: 215–216
    with phrases: 215–216
    with *self-*: 215–216
    with verbs: 215–216
  head: 96, 213, 218
now: 27

object complements: see "direct object companions"
object of a preposition: 180, 380
of: 23, also see "genitives"
off: 159–161, 165, 178–179
off of: 159–161, 165
Old English: see "Anglo-Saxon"
on: 159–161, 165, 169, 172–173, 177–179
one: see "articles, indefinite"
  idiomatic usage: 15
  one vs *a*: 13–15
onto: 159–161, 165, 169
or so: 489–492
ordinal numbers: see "adjectives, ordering"
ought to: 128, 147–150, 356
  advice/opinions: 147
  and *should* vs *must*: 149
  expectation: 147
  Nutshell: 150
ought to have + past participle: 233–236
  Nutshell: 235
  reproach for something not done: 233–234
ought not to have / oughtn't (to) have + past participle: 233–236
  Nutshell: 236
  reproach for something done: 233–235
out: 162, 166, 170, 179
out of: 159–161, 166, 170, 179–180
outside: 179
over: 159–160, 162, 166, 170, 178

particles: 216–217, 220, 371
passé composé: 39
passerby: 106
passive voice: 91, 243–266
  avoiding redundancy: 254
  be vs *get*: 256–258
  being tactful: 255
  "doer": 250, 254
  focus: 254
  Nutshell: 266–267
  oddities: 258–266
    changes in meaning from active to passive: 261–262
    lengthy subject phrases: 264–266
    no active voice counterparts: 263
    pseudo-passives: 264

three-word verbs: 258–259
two-word verbs: 258–259, 384
past participle phrase DOC: 307–309
reduced passives: 251–253, 269
past: 160–161, 164, 168, 171
past continuous: 56, also see "past progressive"
past participle of verbs: 91
in passive voice: 243–244
with causatives: 268–269
past perfect: 60–62, 345
Nutshell: 62
timeline: 62
vs past perfect progressive: 63
with simple past: 61–62
past perfect progressive: 63
Nutshell: 63
timeline: 63
vs past perfect: 63
past progressive: 31, 53–59, 79
actions in progress: 53–54, 56
interrupted actions: 56–57
longer action: 57–58
Nutshell: 59
repeated action vs simple past: 56–57
timelines: 59
with actions of different duration: 57–58
with *while* and *when*: 59–60
past, simple, see "simple past"
pat phrases: 15–16, 193–194, 207, 435–437
Paulston, Christina Bratt: 513
peaked: 93
periphrastic modals: 128, also see "semi-auxiliaries"
phrasal verbs: see "two-word verbs"
phrasal-prepositional verbs: see "three-word verbs"
picture files: 509–511
possessive adjectives: 191, also see "adjectives: ordering"
possessive determiners: 98
possessives: see "genitives"
post-posed prepositions: see "prepositions, post-posed"
predictions for future changes: 501–507
clarity vs correct form: 505–506
grammatical items: 504–505, 507
lexical items: 502–504, 506
-ly adverbs: 504

pre-posed prepositions: see "prepositions, pre-posed"
prepositions: 158–188, also see individual prepositions, "two-word verbs," "three-word verbs"
dropping the preposition: 4
figurative meanings: 169–171
followed by a verb: 179
idiomatic meanings: see "figurative meanings"
literal (physical) meanings: 159–169
post-posed: 180–184
pre-posed: 183–184
simple vs complex forms: 158
vs particles: 216–217
prepositional phrases, fronted: 8
prescriptive grammar: 16, 148
present continuous: 27, also see "present progressive"
present participle of verbs: 91
present perfect: 37–45, 51, 63, 345
bridge from past to present: 37
completed actions: 54
door to the future: 38–39
events from past affecting present: 39–40
Nutshell: 40
recent events: 39–40
timelines: 40
uninterrupted actions from past: 37
vs simple past: 37
present perfect progressive: 41–42, 63
Nutshell: 42
timeline: 42
present progressive: 26–29, 31–32, 41, 79
future usage: see "futures"
in passive voice: 255
narratives: see "style"
Nutshell: 29–30
real present: 26–27, 29
temporary situations: 27–29, 35–36
timeline: 29
when to teach: 32
with *always*: 36
with *be* in a temporary state: 36
pronunciation, relaxed: 481–483
pronunciation bugaboos: 543–551
"d" in *dry*; "t" in *try*: 544–545
final *-ate*: 548
flapped "d": 545–546

juncture: 546–547
letter "o": 543–544
schwa: 547–548
spelling over the telephone: 550–551
"th": 549
voiced and voiceless sounds: 549
pronunciation of object pronouns:
  see "autosegmental features (whole
  sentences)"
prosody: see "autosegmental features (single
  words)"
punctuation: 522

questions, negative: 498–500

ragged: 93
reading comprehension: 522–523
register: see "style" formal/informal
rejoinders: 556–557
relative clauses: 253
relative pronouns: 253
reported speech: see "indirect speech"
reporting verbs: see "indirect speech"
  Appendix 4
  Romance languages: 321, 372
round: see "around"
rugged: 93
runner-up: 106
Russian: 11, 20

-'s /-s': see "genitives"
say: see "indirect speech"
semi-auxiliaries: 128, 153–155, 179, see
  also "be able to," "be unable to," "dare,"
  "had best," "had better," "have got to,"
  "have to," "need," "used to," "would
  rather," "would sooner"
shall: 128
should: 128, 147–150, 154, 356
  advice/opinions: 147
  and *ought to* vs *must*: 149
  expectation: 147
  Nutshell: 150
  substitute for *if*: 149
should have + **past participle**: 233–236
  expectation: 233–235
  Nutshell: 235–236
  reproach for something not done:
    233–234

should not have / shouldn't have + **past
  participle**: 233–234, 236
  Nutshell: 235–236
  reproach for something done: 233–234
simple past: 31, 50–52, 54–57, 59, 61, 66,
  345
  finished action: 51
  just + simple past: 40
  Nutshell: 52
  one time action: 52
  pronunciation: 51
  shorter action: 57–58
  timeline: 52
  vs present perfect: 37
simple present: 30–36, 41
  fact: 30
  future form: 72
  generalizations: 30
  habitual actions: 30
  long-term/permanent actions: 30,
    35–36
  narratives: see "style"
  Nutshell: 36
  timeless: 30
    in passive voice: 255
  truths: 30
  with *always*: 36
since: 42
slot substitutions: 514–516
  double: 515
  moving: 516
  multiple: 515
  single: 515
so far: 45
some and *any*: 111–127, also see "*some*,"
  "*any*," and "autosegmental features (whole
  sentences)"
some: compound pronouns: 119
  derisive use: 121
  in affirmative statements: 111–112
  in questions: 114–116
  more or less: 112
  Nutshell: 124–125
  part of: 115
  plural of indefinite article: 112
  pronoun: 116
  with countable and uncountable nouns:
    116
sort of: 489–492

Spanish: 14, 20, 199, 219, 372, 494
spoonful: 106
stative verbs: 32–36, 41
  no passive voice counterparts: 262
  voluntary vs involuntary verbs: 33–34
stick-in-the-mud: 106
stress: 479, also see "autosegmental features" (both sections)
style:
  formal/informal: 11–12, 20, 59, 448–449, 465–466, 492
  narrative: 29–31, 342
subjects: 2–5, 18, 245
subjunctives, hopes, and **wishes**: 416–437
  forming the subjunctive: 417–419
  formulaic/archaic subjunctive (pat phrases): 435–437, 468
  hope vs *wish*: 420–425
  indicative mood: 416–417, 419, 430
  mandative subjunctive: 432–435
    phrases that trigger the mandative subjunctive: 433–435
  Nutshell (*hope*): 425
  Nutshell (*wish*): 426
  phrases that trigger the subjunctive: 427–432
  subjunctive mood: 416–417
  wish: 417–419
  wish vs *hope*: 420–425
suprasegmental features: see "autosegmental features (single words)"
syntax: 1–10

Teaching Tips:
  Adjectives: 107–110
  Articles: 24–25
  Autosegmental Features (single words, noun and verb phrases): 335–338
  Autosegmental Features (whole sentences): 413–415
  Compound Nouns and Adjectives: 221–223
  Conditional Sentences: 474–476
  Direct Object Companions: 313–315
  Futures, The: 86–89
  General Information: 8–9
  Genitives: 208–210
  Indirect Speech: 363–368
  Modal Auxiliaries in the Past: 241–242

Modal Auxiliaries in the Present or Future: 155–157
Passives and Causatives: 272–277
Pasts, The: 67–70
Prepositions: 184–188
Presents, The: 45–49
Some and *Any*: 126–127
Subjunctives, Hopes, and Wishes: 437
Two- and Three-Word Verbs: 387–390
Word Order: 9–10
tell: see "indirect speech"
that (in relative clauses): 182
there / there + be: see "autosegmental features (whole sentences)"
three-word verbs (phrasal-prepositional verbs): 178, 258–259, 384–386, 517–518
  direct objects: 385
  generating nouns and adjectives: 386–387
  intransitive verbs: 386
  prepositions: 385
  transitive verbs: 386
through: 160–161, 164, 168, 171
time phrases: 3, 5
titles: 494–495
to: 159–160, 163, 167, 170, 173–174, 180, 183
TOEFL: 62
toward(s): 159–160, 163, 167, 170
transitive verbs: 247–248, 369, 375, 386
truncation: see "ellipsis"
Turkish: 158, 494
two-word verbs (phrasal verbs): 178, 369–384, 517–518
  adverbial prepositions: 374
  and direct objects: 378–379
  figurative meanings: 373–374
  generating nouns and adjectives: 386–387
  idiomatic verbs: 369, 379–380
  literal meanings: 373–374
  prepositions: 374–375, 379, 377, 379–382
  to separate or not: 375–380
  with allied adverbial phrases: 381–383
  with allied prepositional phrases: 380–381
  with passive voice: 384

under: 159–160, 162, 167, 170, 178
unless: 453
until: 80